D0604579

Academic
Learning
Series

Microsoft®
Windows® 2000
Network Infrastructure
Administration Second Edition

Microsoft®

PUBLISHED BY
Microsoft Press
A Division of Microsoft Corporation
One Microsoft Way
Redmond, Washington 98052-6399

Library of Congress Cataloging-in-Publication Data
MCSA/MCSE Self-Paced Training Kit. Microsoft Windows 2000 Network Infrastructure
Administration / Microsoft Corporation.--2nd ed.
        p. cm.
    Includes index.
    Title of 1st ed.: MCSE Training Kit. Microsoft Windows 2000 Network Infrastructure Administration
    ISBN 0-7356-1772-4
    ISBN 0-7356-1870-4 (Academic Learning Series)
    1. Electronic data processing personnel--Certification.   2. Microsoft
software--Examinations--Study guides.   3. Computer networks--Examinations--Study
guides.   I. Title: Microsoft Windows 2000 network infrastructure administration.   II.
Microsoft Corporation.   III. MCSE training kit. Microsoft Windows 2000 network
infrastructure administration

    QA76.3 .M32658   2002
    005.4'4769--dc21   2002141581

Printed and bound in the United States of America.

1 2 3 4 5 6 7 8 9   QWT   8 7 6 5 4 3

Distributed in Canada by H.B. Fenn and Company Ltd.

A CIP catalogue record for this book is available from the British Library.

Microsoft Press books are available through booksellers and distributors worldwide. For further information about international editions, contact your local Microsoft Corporation office or contact Microsoft Press International directly at fax (425) 936-7329. Visit our Web site at www.microsoft.com/mspress. Send comments to *tkinput@microsoft.com.*

Active Directory, BackOffice, Microsoft, Microsoft Press, MS-DOS, Visual Basic, Windows, and Windows NT are either registered trademarks or trademarks of Microsoft Corporation in the United States and/or other countries. Other product and company names mentioned herein may be the trademarks of their respective owners.

The example companies, organizations, products, domain names, e-mail addresses, logos, people, places, and events depicted herein are fictitious. No association with any real company, organization, product, domain name, e-mail address, logo, person, place, or event is intended or should be inferred.

For Microsoft Press
Acquisitions Editor: Kathy Harding
Project Editor: Karen Szall
Author: Craig Zacker

SubAssy Part No. X09-15269
Body Part No. X09-34823

For nSight, Inc.
Project Editor: Kristen Ford
Desktop Publishers: Mary Beth McDaniel and
    Donald Cowan
Technical Editor: Kurt Dillard
Copy Editor: Joseph Gustaitis
Indexer: Jack Lewis

Contents

About This Book .... **xv**

Features of This Book xv

About the CD-ROMs xvi

Before You Begin xvi

    Prerequisites xvii

    Reference Materials xvii

    Conventions Used xvii

    Chapter and Appendix Overview xix

    Where to Find Specific Skills xxi

    Getting Started xxiv

    Setup Instructions xxvi

The Microsoft Certified Professional Program xxxiii

    Microsoft Certification Benefits xxxiv

    Requirements for Becoming a Microsoft Certified Professional xxxvi

    Technical Training for Computer Professionals xxxvii

Technical Support xxxviii

Chapter 1   Introducing Microsoft Windows 2000 Networking **3**

About This Chapter 3

Before You Begin 3

Lesson 1: The OSI Reference Model 4

    Introducing the OSI Reference Model 4

    Using the OSI Model in the Real World 15

    Lesson Review 16

    Lesson Summary 17

Lesson 2: Installing and Binding Windows 2000 Network Components 18

    Introducing the Windows 2000 Networking Components 18

    Installing Windows 2000 Networking Components 22

    Binding Windows 2000 Networking Components 23

    Exercise 1: Installing and Binding Protocols 24

    Lesson Review 25

    Lesson Summary 26

Chapter 2   Introducing TCP/IP **27**
About This Chapter 27
Before You Begin 27
Lesson 1: TCP/IP Overview 28
TCP/IP Standards 28
TCP/IP Architecture 29
TCP/IP Protocols 31
Exercise 1: Examining ARP Traffic with Network Monitor 42
Exercise 2: TCP/IP Protocols 45
Lesson Review 45
Lesson Summary 46
Lesson 2: IP Addressing and Subnetting 47
IP Address Structure 47
Subnet Masks 49
Subnetting 52
Exercise 1: Subnetting a Class B Address 60
Lesson Review 60
Lesson Summary 62
Lesson 3: Understanding TCP and UDP 63
TCP 63
UDP 73
Exercise 1: TCP Header Fields 74
Exercise 2: TCP and UDP Functions 75
Lesson Review 75
Lesson Summary 77

Chapter 3   Implementing TCP/IP **79**
About This Chapter 79
Before You Begin 79
Lesson 1: Installing and Configuring TCP/IP 80
Configuring TCP/IP 83
Configuring Basic TCP/IP Properties 83
Configuring Advanced TCP/IP Properties 86
Exercise 1: TCP/IP Configuration Requirements 90
Lesson Review 91
Lesson Summary 92

Lesson 2: Using the Windows 2000 TCP/IP Tools . . . . 9.

Ping 93

Tracert.exe 95

Pathping.exe 97

Ipconfig.exe 99

Arp.exe 100

Netstat.exe 101

Nbtstat.exe 103

Nslookup.exe 104

Telnet.exe 105

Ftp.exe 106

Exercise 1: TCP/IP Utilities 106

Lesson Review 107

Lesson Summary 107

Chapter 4   NetWare Networking with Windows 2000 . . . . **109**

About This Chapter 109

Before You Begin 109

Lesson 1: Introducing IPX and NWLink 110

Introducing IPX 110

IPX Protocols 111

Windows 2000 and NetWare Compatibility 118

Exercise 1: IPX Properties 119

Lesson Review 120

Lesson Summary 120

Lesson 2: Using the Windows 2000 NetWare Clients 121

Installing Client Service for NetWare 121

Configuring NWLink 124

Configuring Client Service for NetWare 126

Using Gateway Service for NetWare 127

Exercise 1: Installing and Configuring NWLink 132

Lesson Review 134

Lesson Summary 135

Chapter 5   Implementing the Dynamic Host Configuration Protocol 137
    About This Chapter 137
    Before You Begin 137
    Lesson 1: Introducing DHCP 138
        Understanding the Origins of DHCP 138
        DHCP Messaging 141
        Understanding DHCP Communications 146
        Exercise 1: DHCP Message Types 150
        Lesson Review 150
        Lesson Summary 151
    Lesson 2: Using the DHCP Server 152
        Implementing DHCP 152
        Installing Windows 2000 DHCP Server 153
        Authorizing a DHCP Server 154
        Creating a Scope 156
        Activating a Scope 160
        Creating a Superscope 161
        Configuring DHCP Options 161
        Deploying DHCP Options with User Classes 164
        Creating a Reservation 167
        Exercise 1: Examining DHCP Traffic 169
        Exercise 2: Configuring Scopes 174
        Lesson Review 174
        Lesson Summary 175
    Lesson 3: Administering DHCP 176
        Monitoring DHCP Activity 176
        Controlling Conflict Detection 179
        Compacting the DHCP Database 180
        Using DHCP Relay Agents 180
        Integrating DHCP with DNS 182
        Lesson Review 185
        Lesson Summary 186
    Lesson 4: Troubleshooting DHCP 187
        Preventing DHCP Problems 187
        Troubleshooting DHCP Clients 188
        Troubleshooting DHCP Servers 190
        Lesson Review 192
        Lesson Summary 192

Chapter 6   Routing IP **193**

   About This Chapter 193

   Before You Begin 193

   Lesson 1: Understanding IP Routing 194

      Routing Principles 194

      Routing Tables 197

      Routing Hardware 203

      Routing Software 205

      Exercise 1: Routing Tables 205

      Lesson Review 205

      Lesson Summary 206

   Lesson 2: Routing with RRAS 207

      Configuring RRAS 207

      Manually Configuring RRAS 210

      Implementing Demand-Dial Routing 210

      Configuring Demand-Dial Interfaces 214

      Creating Static Routes 217

      Exercise 1: Configuring RRAS 221

      Lesson Review 222

      Lesson Summary 223

   Lesson 3: Using Dynamic Routing Protocols 224

      Dynamic Routing Protocols 224

      Understanding RIP 226

      Installing RIP 228

      Understanding OSPF 231

      Installing OSPF 232

      Exercise 1: Configuring RRAS 233

      Exercise 2: Static and Dynamic Routing 234

      Lesson Review 234

      Lesson Summary 236

Chapter 7   Understanding the Domain Name System **237**

   About This Chapter 237

   Before You Begin 237

   Lesson 1: IP Host Naming and DNS 238

      Using Host Tables 238

      Designing the DNS 240

Introducing the Domain Name Space 241

Understanding Domain Name Servers 247

Understanding Resolvers 249

Exercise 1: Understanding DNS Terminology 249

Lesson Review 250

Lesson Summary 250

Lesson 2: Resolving Host Names with DNS 251

DNS Messaging 251

Resolving a Name 255

Name Server Caching 257

Performing Reverse Name Lookups 258

Exercise 1: Understanding DNS Communications 260

Lesson Review 261

Lesson Summary 262

Lesson 3: Planning a DNS Implementation 263

DNS Considerations 263

Exercise 1: Implementing DNS 264

Lesson Review 270

Lesson Summary 271

Chapter 8   Using the Windows 2000 DNS Server 273

About This Chapter 273

Before You Begin 273

Lesson 1: Installing and Configuring Windows 2000 DNS 274

Installing DNS Server 274

Implementing a Caching-Only Server 277

Exercise 1: Testing a Simple Query on a DNS Server 278

Lesson Review 279

Lesson Summary 279

Lesson 2: Working with Zones 280

Creating a Zone 280

Creating Active Directory–Integrated Zones 285

Delegating Zones 286

Configuring Dynamic Updates 289

Exercise 1: Configuring Zones 290

Lesson Review 292

Lesson Summary 293

Lesson 3: Working with Resource Records 294
Understanding Resource Record Types 294
Viewing Resource Records 297
Creating Resource Records 298
Exercise 1: Adding Resource Records 300
Lesson Review 302
Lesson Summary 302
Lesson 4: Configuring Zone Transfers 303
Zone Replication and Zone Transfers 303
Zone Transfer Security 306
DNS Notification 307
Lesson Review 308
Lesson Summary 309
Lesson 5: Monitoring and Troubleshooting DNS 310
Monitoring DNS Servers 310
DNS Troubleshooting Scenarios 313
Lesson Review 316
Lesson Summary 316

Chapter 9   Implementing Windows Internet Name Service 317
About This Chapter 317
Before You Begin 317
Lesson 1: Introducing NetBIOS 318
NetBIOS Naming 318
Registering and Resolving Names 321
NetBIOS Name Caching 322
Using Lmhosts 323
Using Broadcast Transmissions 327
Using NetBIOS Name Servers 330
Understanding NetBIOS Node Types 330
Exercise 1: NetBIOS Name Resolution Concepts 333
Lesson Review 333
Lesson Summary 334
Lesson 2: WINS Name Registration and Resolution 335
Understanding WINS Messaging 335
Understanding the NetBT Message Formats 339
Lesson Review 344
Lesson Summary 344

Lesson 3: Implementing WINS 345
    Installing a WINS Server 345
    Configuring a Windows 2000 WINS Client 347
    Supporting Non-WINS Clients 348
    Maintaining the WINS Database 350
    Exercise 1: Installing and Configuring WINS 352
    Lesson Review 354
    Lesson Summary 355
Lesson 4: Configuring WINS Replication 356
    Replication Overview 356
    Configuring a WINS Server as a Push or Pull Partner 356
    Planning How Many WINS Servers to Use 359
    Initiating Database Replication 359
    WINS Automatic Replication Partners 360
    Configuring WINS Database Replication 360
    Lesson Review 362
    Lesson Summary 362

Chapter 10   Securing Network Protocols **363**
    About This Chapter 363
    Before You Begin 363
Lesson 1: Using Packet Filters 364
    Understanding Packet Filtering 364
    Configuring Packet Filters in the TCP/IP Client 367
    Configuring Packet Filters in RRAS 371
    Lesson Review 375
    Lesson Summary 376
Lesson 2: Using IPsec 377
    Securing IP Communications 377
    IPsec Standards 382
    IPsec Protocols 382
    Transport Mode and Tunnel Mode 386
    L2TP Tunneling 388
    Exercise 1: Understanding IPsec Terminology 388
    Lesson Review 389
    Lesson Summary 389

Lesson 3: Deploying IPsec 390
IPsec Components 390
Deploying IPsec 392
Running IPsec Policy Management 392
Creating a New Policy 393
Creating Policies in Active Directory 396
Configuring IPsec Policies 396
Configuring IPsec for Tunnel Mode 406
Exercise 1: Using IPsec 406
Lesson Review 408
Lesson Summary 408

Chapter 11   **Using the Remote Access Service** **409**
About This Chapter 409
Before You Begin 409
Lesson 1: Introducing the Remote Access Service 410
Overview of Remote Access 410
Remote Access Security 413
Installing a Remote Access Server 416
Exercise 1: RAS Authentication Protocols 420
Lesson Review 420
Lesson Summary 421
Lesson 2: Configuring a Remote Access Server 422
Configuring RAS Server Properties 422
Allowing Inbound Connections 427
Using Multilink 428
Using RRAS with DHCP 430
Exercise 1: Configuring a RAS Server 430
Lesson Review 431
Lesson Summary 432
Lesson 3: Managing Remote Access Security 433
Configuring Authentication 433
Controlling User Access 437
Exercise 1: Creating a Remote Access Policy 447
Lesson Review 448
Lesson Summary 450

Lesson 4: Virtual Private Networking 451

    Implementing a VPN 451

    Integrating a VPN in a Routed Environment 457

    Integrating VPN Servers with the Internet 457

    Managing Virtual Private Networking 458

    Exercise 1: Creating a VPN Connection 459

    Lesson Review 462

    Lesson Summary 462

Chapter 12   Using Network Address Translation 463

    About This Chapter 463

    Before You Begin 463

Lesson 1: Introducing NAT 464

    Routing to the Internet 464

    Understanding NAT 465

    Exercise 1: Understanding NAT Communications 470

    Lesson Review 471

    Lesson Summary 471

Lesson 2: Installing and Configuring NAT 472

    Implementing NAT 472

    Installing NAT with RRAS 472

    Configuring RRAS to Use NAT 478

    Configuring NAT Interface Properties 482

    Configuring NAT Properties 486

    Exercise 1: Configuring a NAT Installation 489

    Lesson Review 490

    Lesson Summary 491

Lesson 3: Installing Internet Connection Sharing 492

    Differentiating ICS and NAT 492

    Installing ICS 493

    Configuring ICS 494

    Lesson Review 497

    Lesson Summary 498

Chapter 13   Implementing Certificate Services **499**

About This Chapter 499

Before You Begin 499

Lesson 1: Introducing Certificates 500

Understanding Encryption Keys 500

Understanding Certificates 502

Exercise 1: Understanding Certificates and Encryption 507

Lesson Review 507

Lesson Summary 508

Lesson 2: Installing and Configuring Microsoft Certificate Services 509

Preparing to Install MCS 509

Protecting a CA 510

Installing Certificate Services 510

Configuring a CA 514

Backing Up and Restoring a CA 519

Exercise 1: Installing a Stand-Alone CA 522

Lesson Review 523

Lesson Summary 524

Lesson 3: Managing Certificates 525

Certificate Enrollment 525

Creating the Certificates Console 527

Using the Certificates Console 529

Revoking Certificates 534

Removing EFS Recovery Keys 535

Exercise 1: Requesting a Certificate Using the CA Web Interface 536

Lesson Review 537

Lesson Summary 538

Chapter 14   Monitoring Network Activity **539**

About This Chapter 539

Before You Begin 539

Lesson 1: Monitoring Windows 2000 Activity 540

Using Event Viewer 540

Using the Performance Console 544

Using the Shared Folders Snap-in 552

Exercise 1: Monitoring System Performance Parameters 559

Lesson Review 560

Lesson Summary 560

Lesson 2: Monitoring Network Services 561
    Monitoring DHCP Activity 561
    Monitoring WINS Activity 565
    Monitoring DNS Activity 567
    Monitoring RRAS Activity 568
    Monitoring IPsec Activity 572
    Lesson Review 573
    Lesson Summary 573
Lesson 3: Using Network Monitor 574
    Overview of Network Monitor 574
    Capturing Frame Data 576
    Using Capture Filters 577
    Displaying Captured Data 579
    Using Display Filters 580
    Network Monitor Performance Issues 581
    Exercise 1: Capturing Frames with Network Monitor 582
    Lesson Review 582
    Lesson Summary 583

Appendix   Questions and Answers **585**

Glossary **647**

Index **687**

About This Book

Welcome to *MCSA/MCSE Training Kit—Microsoft Windows 2000 Network Infrastructure Administration*. This book was developed for information technology (IT) professionals who need to design, plan, implement, and support a Microsoft Windows 2000 network infrastructure or who plan to take the related Microsoft Certified Professional (MCP) exam 70-216, *Implementing and Administering a Microsoft Windows 2000 Network Infrastructure*.

Features of This Book

This book contains the following sections, which are designed to help you improve your real-world skills and prepare for exam 70-216:

- Each chapter opens with a "Before You Begin" section that prepares you for completing the chapter.
- The chapters are then divided into lessons. Whenever possible, lessons contain exercises that give you an opportunity to use the skills being presented or explore the part of the application being described.

▶ Within the exercises, step-by-step procedures are identified with a bullet symbol like the one to the left of this paragraph.

- At the end of each lesson is the "Review" section that you can use to test what you have learned.
- The review is followed by the "Summary" section, which identifies the key concepts from the lesson.
- The Appendix, Questions and Answers, contains all the questions asked in the book and the corresponding answers.
- The Glossary lists and defines the terms associated with your study of implementing and administering a Windows 2000 network infrastructure.

Read the "Before You Begin" section of this introduction before you start the lessons.

About the CD-ROMs

This book includes a Supplemental Course Materials CD-ROM. This CD-ROM includes an electronic version (eBook) of the training kit. The second CD-ROM contains a 120-day evaluation edition of Windows 2000 Server.

For more information about the contents of the CD-ROM, see the section titled "Getting Started" later in this introduction and review the Readme.txt file included in the root directory of the CD-ROM.

Before You Begin

This book will teach you how to plan your network infrastructure around features supported by the Windows 2000 operating system. Issues such as network protocol and services are introduced and compared based on the requirements of your organization. This includes using the Internetwork Packet Exchange/Sequenced Packet Exchange (IPX/SPX)–compatible protocol to integrate with Novell NetWare. The primary focus of network protocols throughout this book is Transmission Control Protocol/Internet Protocol (TCP/IP) because it is the Internet-standard protocol and is the best choice for enterprise networks. You will learn how to utilize, manage, and configure the TCP/IP protocol and use features such as Network Basic Input/Output System (NetBIOS), Windows Internet Name Service (WINS), Dynamic Host Configuration Protocol (DHCP), and Domain Name System (DNS). You will also learn how to configure, manage, and troubleshoot routing and remote access, including setting up virtual private networks (VPNs).

Note   For more information about becoming a Microsoft Certified Systems Engineer or a Microsoft Certified Systems Administrator, see the section entitled "The Microsoft Certified Professional Program" later in this introduction.

Each chapter is divided into lessons. Most lessons include hands-on procedures that allow you to practice or demonstrate a particular concept or skill. Each lesson ends with a set of review questions to test your knowledge of the lesson material and a short summary of the major points covered in the lesson.

The "Getting Started" section of this introduction provides important setup instructions that describe the hardware and software requirements to complete the procedures in this course. It also provides information about the networking configuration necessary to complete some of the hands-on procedures. Read through this section thoroughly before you start the lessons.

Prerequisites

This course requires students to meet the following prerequisites:

- Knowledge of the fundamentals of current networking technology is required.
- Knowledge and experience administering Microsoft Windows NT 4.0 networks is recommended.
- Successful completion of the *MCSE Training Kit—Microsoft Windows 2000 Server* is recommended.

Reference Materials

You might find the following reference materials useful:

- *Microsoft Windows 2000 Server Resource Kit*
- Windows 2000 Server Help
- Windows 2000 white papers and case studies, available online at *http://www.microsoft.com/windows2000/server/default.asp*

Conventions Used

The following conventions are used throughout this training kit.

Notes

Several types of Notes appear throughout the lessons.

- Notes marked **Tip** contain explanations of possible results or alternative methods for performing tasks.
- Notes marked **Important** contain information that is essential to completing a task.
- Notes marked **Note** contain supplemental information.
- Notes marked **Caution** contain warnings about possible loss of data.

Notational Conventions

- Characters or commands that you type appear in **bold** type.
- *Italic* in syntax statements indicates placeholders for variable information. *Italic* is also used for book titles and URLs.
- Names of files and folders appear in initial capital letters, except when you are to type them directly. Unless otherwise indicated, you can use lowercase letters when you type a file name in a dialog box or at a command prompt.

- File name extensions, when they appear without a file name, are in lowercase letters.

- Acronyms appear in all uppercase letters.

- Monospace type represents code samples, examples of screen text, or entries that you might type at a command prompt or in initialization files.

- Square brackets [ ] are used in syntax statements to enclose optional items. For example, [*filename*] in command syntax indicates that you can choose to type a file name with the command. Type only the information within the brackets, not the brackets themselves.

- Braces { } are used in syntax statements to enclose required items. Type only the information within the braces, not the braces themselves.

- Icons represent specific sections in the book as follows:

Icon	Represents
	A hands-on practice. You should perform the procedure to give yourself an opportunity to use the skills being presented in the lesson.
	Lesson review questions. These questions at the end of each lesson allow you to test what you have learned in the lessons. You will find the answers to the review questions in Questions and Answers appendix at the end of the book.

Keyboard Conventions

- A plus sign (+) between two key names means that you must press those keys at the same time. For example, "Press ALT+TAB" means that you hold down ALT while you press TAB.

- A comma (,) between two or more key names means that you must press each of the keys consecutively, not together. For example, "Press ALT, F, X" means that you press and release each key in sequence. "Press ALT+W, L" means that you first press ALT and W at the same time, and then release them and press L.

- You can choose menu commands with the keyboard. Press the ALT key to activate the menu bar, and then sequentially press the keys that correspond to the highlighted or underlined letter of the menu name and the command name. For some commands, you can also press a key combination listed in the menu.

- You can select or clear check boxes or option buttons in dialog boxes with the keyboard. Press the ALT key, and then press the key that corresponds to the underlined letter of the option name. Or you can press TAB until the option is highlighted, and then press the spacebar to select or clear the check box or option button.

- You can cancel the display of a dialog box by pressing the ESC key.

Chapter and Appendix Overview

This training kit combines notes, hands-on procedures, and review questions to teach you how to design, implement, administer, configure, and troubleshoot a Windows 2000–based network. It is designed to be completed from beginning to end, but you can choose a customized track and complete only the sections that interest you. (See the next section, "Where to Find Specific Skills," for more information.) If you choose the customized track option, see the "Before You Begin" section in each chapter. Any hands-on procedures that require preliminary work from preceding chapters refer to the appropriate chapters.

This book is divided into the following sections and chapters:

- The "About This Book" section contains a self-paced training overview and introduces the components of this training kit. Read this section thoroughly to get the greatest educational value from this self-paced training and to plan which lessons you will complete.

- Chapter 1, "Introducing Microsoft Windows 2000 Networking," describes the structure of the Open Systems Interconnection (OSI) reference model and how network operating systems use a protocol stack to communicate with each other. This chapter also introduces the interface that you use to install and bind protocols in Windows 2000.

- Chapter 2, "Introducing TCP/IP," describes the functions of the various protocols in the TCP/IP suite and the structures of the protocol headers. You also learn about IP addressing and how to create subnets on your network.

- Chapter 3, "Implementing TCP/IP," describes the process of installing and configuring the TCP/IP protocols on a Windows 2000 computer, as well as the functions and use of the TCP/IP tools included with the operating system.

- Chapter 4, "NetWare Networking with Windows 2000," introduces the IPX protocol suite, developed by Novell for use with its NetWare network operating system, and describes how to install the IPX protocols and the NetWare clients included with Windows 2000.

- Chapter 5, "Implementing the Dynamic Host Configuration Protocol," covers the DHCP service that enables a computer running Windows 2000 Server to dynamically assign IP addresses and other TCP/IP configuration parameters to the client computers on your network, whether they are running Windows or not.

- Chapter 6, "Routing IP," describes how you can use a computer running Windows 2000 Server as a multiprotocol router by implementing the Routing and Remote Access Service. This chapter also covers the process of installing routing protocols, such as RIP and OSPF.

- Chapter 7, Understanding the Domain Name System," introduces the concept of host and domain names and the origins of DNS. This chapter also covers how DNS clients and servers work together to resolve names into IP addresses.

- Chapter 8, "Using the Windows 2000 DNS Server," describes how to install and configure the DNS Server included with Windows 2000. You learn how to create zones and resource records and configure name servers to perform zone transfers.

- Chapter 9, "Implementing Windows Internet Name Service," describes the use of NetBIOS names in the Windows operating systems and the various name registration and resolution mechanisms included in Windows 2000. You also learn how to use WINS on a computer running Windows 2000 Server to support client computers running earlier versions of Windows.

- Chapter 10, "Securing Network Protocols," introduces the concept of packet filtering and explains how Windows 2000 implements it in the TCP/IP client and in RRAS. You also learn how to use the IP security (IPsec) extensions to encrypt data as it is transmitted over the network.

- Chapter 11, "Using the Remote Access Service," covers another function of the Windows 2000 Routing and Remote Access Service, which enables users at remote locations to dial in to a Windows 2000 server and connect to its network. This chapter also introduces the concept of virtual private networking, in which a client connects to a remote network using the Internet as its medium.

- Chapter 12, "Using Network Address Translation," examines a firewall technique integrated into RRAS that enables you to assign unregistered IP addresses to your client computers and still let them access the Internet using a Network Address Translation (NAT) server as an intermediary.

- Chapter 13, "Implementing Certificate Services," describes the use of certificates in the Windows 2000 public key infrastructure and how to implement Microsoft Certificate Services, the certificate authority included with Windows 2000 Server.

- Chapter 14, "Monitoring Network Activity," describes how to keep tabs on the activities of the various protocols and services introduced in the previous chapters as well as how to capture and analyze network traffic using the Network Monitor application provided with Windows 2000 Server.

- The Appendix, "Questions and Answers," lists all the review questions, showing the page number for each question and the suggested answer.

- The glossary provides definitions for many of the terms and concepts presented in this training kit.

Where to Find Specific Skills

The following tables provide a list of the skills measured on certification exam 70-216, *Implementing and Administering a Microsoft Windows 2000 Network Infrastructure*. The tables identify both the skills and where in this book you will find the lesson relating to each skill.

Note Exam skills are subject to change without prior notice and at the sole discretion of Microsoft.

Installing, Configuring, Managing, Monitoring, and Troubleshooting DNS in a Windows 2000 Network Infrastructure

Skill Being Measured	Location in Book
Install, configure, and troubleshoot DNS	
Install the DNS Server service	Chapter 8, Lesson 1
Configure a root name server	Chapter 8, Lesson 1
Configure zones	Chapter 8, Lesson 2
Configure a caching-only server	Chapter 8, Lesson 1
Configure a DNS client	Chapter 3, Lesson 1
Configure zones for dynamic updates	Chapter 8, Lesson 2
Test the DNS Server service	Chapter 8, Lesson 1
Implement a delegated zone for DNS	Chapter 8, Lesson 2
Manually create DNS resource records	Chapter 8, Lesson 3
Manage and monitor DNS	Chapter 8, Lesson 5; Chapter 14, Lesson 2

Installing, Configuring, Managing, Monitoring, and Troubleshooting DHCP in a Windows 2000 Network Infrastructure

Skill Being Measured	Location in Book
Install, configure, and troubleshoot DHCP	
Install the DHCP Server service	Chapter 5, Lesson 2
Create and manage DHCP scopes, superscopes, and multicast scopes	Chapter 5, Lesson 2
Configure DHCP for DNS integration	Chapter 5, Lesson 3
Authorize a DHCP server in Active Directory service	Chapter 5, Lesson 2
Manage and monitor DHCP	Chapter 14, Lesson 2

Configuring, Managing, Monitoring, and Troubleshooting Remote Access in a Windows 2000 Network Infrastructure

Skill Being Measured	Location in Book
Configure and troubleshoot remote access	
Configure inbound connections	Chapter 11, Lesson 2
Create a remote access policy	Chapter 11, Lesson 3
Configure a remote access profile	Chapter 11, Lesson 3
Configure a VPN	Chapter 11, Lesson 4
Configure multilink connections	Chapter 11, Lesson 2
Configure Routing and Remote Access for DHCP integration	Chapter 11, Lesson 2
Manage and monitor remote access	Chapter 14, Lesson 2
Configure remote access security	
Configure authentication protocols	Chapter 11, Lesson 3
Configure encryption protocols	Chapter 11, Lessons 1 and 3
Create a remote access policy	Chapter 11, Lesson 2

Installing, Configuring, Managing, Monitoring, and Troubleshooting Network Protocols in a Windows 2000 Network Infrastructure

Skill Being Measured	Location in Book
Install, configure, and troubleshoot network protocols	
Install and configure TCP/IP	Chapter 3, Lesson 1
Install the NWLink protocol	Chapter 4, Lesson 2
Configure network bindings	Chapter 1, Lesson 2
Configure TCP/IP packet filters	Chapter 10, Lesson 1
Configure and troubleshoot network protocol security	Chapter 3, Lesson 2
Manage and monitor network traffic	Chapter 14, Lesson 3
Configure and troubleshoot IPsec	
Enable IPsec	Chapter 10, Lesson 3
Configure IPsec for transport mode	Chapter 10, Lesson 3
Configure IPsec for tunnel mode	Chapter 10, Lesson 3
Customize IPsec policies and rules	Chapter 10, Lesson 3
Manage and monitor IPsec	Chapter 14, Lesson 2

Installing, Configuring, Managing, Monitoring, and Troubleshooting WINS in a Windows 2000 Network Infrastructure

Skill Being Measured	Location in Book
Install, configure, and troubleshoot WINS	Chapter 9, Lessons 3 and 4
Configure WINS replication	Chapter 9, Lesson 4
Configure NetBIOS name resolution	Chapter 3, Lesson 1
Manage and monitor WINS	Chapter 14, Lesson 2

Installing, Configuring, Managing, Monitoring, and Troubleshooting IP Routing in a Windows 2000 Network Infrastructure

Skill Being Measured	Location in Book
Install, configure, and troubleshoot IP routing protocols	
Update a Windows 2000–based routing table by means of static routes	Chapter 6, Lesson 2
Implement demand-dial routing	Chapter 6, Lesson 2
Manage and monitor IP routing	
Manage and monitor border routing	Chapter 6, Lesson 2; Chapter 14, Lesson 2
Manage and monitor internal routing	Chapter 6, Lesson 3; Chapter 14, Lesson 2
Manage and monitor IP routing protocols	Chapter 6, Lesson 3; Chapter 14, Lesson 2

Installing, Configuring, and Troubleshooting Network Address Translation (NAT)

Skill Being Measured	Location in Book
Install Internet Connection Sharing	Chapter 12, Lesson 3
Install NAT	Chapter 12, Lesson 2
Configure NAT properties	Chapter 12, Lesson 2
Configure NAT interfaces	Chapter 12, Lesson 2

Installing, Configuring, Managing, Monitoring, and Troubleshooting Certificate Services

Skill Being Measured	Location in Book
Install and configure Certificate Authority (CA)	Chapter 13, Lesson 2
Issue and revoke certificates	Chapter 13, Lesson 3
Remove the Encrypting File System (EFS) recovery keys	Chapter 13, Lesson 3

Getting Started

This training kit contains hands-on procedures to help you learn about implementing and administering a Windows 2000 network infrastructure. To complete these procedures, you must have one computer running Windows 2000 Server or Windows 2000 Advanced Server.

A few exercises require two computers to meet the lesson objectives. If you have only one computer, read through the steps and familiarize yourself with the procedure as best you can.

For the exercises that require networked computers, you need to make sure the computers can communicate with each other. The first computer will be configured as a domain controller.

It is recommended that you set up the server on its own network so you do not inhibit your production network or affect other users in your existing domain. However, it is possible to use your existing network with your server.

Caution   If your computers are part of a larger network, you *must* verify with your network administrator that the computer names, domain name, and other information used in setting up Windows 2000 do not conflict with network operations. If they conflict, ask your network administrator to provide alternative values and use those values throughout all the exercises in this book.

Several exercises require you to make changes to your servers. This might cause undesirable results if you are connected to a larger network. Check with your network administrator before attempting these exercises.

Hardware Requirements

All hardware should be on the Microsoft Windows 2000 Hardware Compatibility List (HCL). The latest version of the HCL can be downloaded from the hardware compatibility Web page at *http://www.microsoft.com/hcl/default.asp.* Each computer must have the following minimum configuration:

- 32-bit 166 MHz Intel Pentium-compatible processor
- 128 MB RAM minimum, 256 MB RAM recommended
- 2 GB hard disk with a minimum of 1 GB free space (additional free space is required if you are installing over a network)
- 12X or faster CD-ROM drive

- Super Video Graphics Array (SVGA) monitor capable of 800 × 600 resolution (1024 × 768 recommended)
- High-density 3.5-inch disk drive, unless your CD-ROM is bootable and supports starting the setup program from a CD-ROM
- Microsoft Mouse or compatible pointing device

Software Requirements

You will need a copy of the Microsoft Windows 2000 Server or Windows 2000 Advanced Server software to complete the procedures in this course. A 120-day evaluation copy of Microsoft Windows 2000 Server is included on the CD-ROM in this training kit.

Caution The 120-day Evaluation Edition provided with this training kit is not the full retail product and is provided only for the purposes of training and evaluation. Microsoft Technical Support does not support this evaluation edition. For additional support information regarding this book and the CD-ROMs (including answers to commonly asked questions about installation and use), visit the Microsoft Press Technical Support Web site at *http://www.microsoft.com/mspress/support*. You can also e-mail TKINPUT@MICROSOFT.COM or send a letter to Microsoft Press, Attn: Microsoft Press Technical Support, One Microsoft Way, Redmond, WA 98502-6399.

About the eBook

The Supplemental Course Materials CD-ROM includes a fully searchable electronic version of the training kit (eBook). To view the eBook, you will need Microsoft Internet Explorer 5.01 or later. Internet Explorer 6 has been included on the Supplemental Course Materials CD-ROM.

▶ **To use the eBook**

1. Insert the Supplemental Course Materials CD-ROM into your CD-ROM drive.

   Note If AutoRun is disabled on your machine, run StartCD.exe or refer to the Readme.txt file in the root folder.

2. Click eBook on the user interface menu and follow the prompts.

   Note You must have the Supplemental Course Materials CD-ROM inserted in your CD-ROM drive to run the eBook.

Setup Instructions

The following information is a list of the tasks you need to perform to prepare your computer to install the evaluation software. If you don't have experience installing Windows 2000 or another network operating system, you might need help from an experienced network administrator. Step-by-step instructions for each task follow.

- Create Windows 2000 Server setup diskettes.
- Run the Windows 2000 Server Pre-Copy and Text Mode Setup Routine.
- Run the graphical user interface (GUI) mode and gathering information phase of Windows 2000 Server Setup.
- Complete the Installing Windows Networking Components phase of Windows 2000 Server Setup.
- Complete the hardware installation phase of Windows 2000 Server Setup.

Note   The installation information provided will help you prepare a computer with the evaluation software. It isn't intended to teach you installation. For comprehensive information on installing Windows 2000 Server, see the *MCSE Training Kit—Microsoft Windows 2000 Server, Second Edition*, also available from Microsoft Press.

Installing Windows 2000 Server

Install Windows 2000 Server on a computer with no formatted partitions. During installation, you can use the Windows 2000 Server Setup program to create a partition on your hard disk, on which you install Windows 2000 Server as a stand-alone server in a workgroup.

▶   **To create Windows 2000 Server setup diskettes**

Complete this procedure on a computer running MS-DOS or any version of Windows with access to the Bootdisk directory on the Windows 2000 Server installation CD-ROM. If your computer is configured with a bootable CD-ROM drive, you can install Windows 2000 without using the Setup disks. To complete this procedure as outlined, bootable CD-ROM support must be disabled in the BIOS.

Important   This procedure requires four formatted 1.44-MB disks. If you use diskettes that contain data, the data will be overwritten without warning.

---

1. Label the four blank, formatted 1.44-MB diskettes as follows:
   - Windows 2000 Server Setup Disk #1
   - Windows 2000 Server Setup Disk #2
   - Windows 2000 Server Setup Disk #3
   - Windows 2000 Server Setup Disk #4

2. Insert the Microsoft Windows 2000 Server CD-ROM into the CD-ROM drive.

3. If the Windows 2000 CD-ROM dialog box appears prompting you to install or upgrade to Windows 2000, click No.

4. Open a command prompt.

5. At the command prompt, change to your CD-ROM drive. For example, if your CD-ROM drive name is E, type **e:** and press Enter.

6. At the command prompt, change to the Bootdisk directory by typing **cd bootdisk** and pressing Enter.

7. If you're creating the setup boot diskettes from a computer running MS-DOS or a Windows 16-bit operating system, type **makeboot a:** (where A: is the name of your floppy disk drive) and press Enter. If you're creating the setup boot diskettes from a computer running Microsoft Windows NT or Windows 2000, type **makebt32 a:** (where A: is the name of your floppy disk drive), and then press Enter. Windows 2000 displays a message indicating that this program creates the four setup disks for installing Windows 2000. It also indicates that four blank, formatted, high-density floppy disks are required.

8. Press any key to continue. Windows 2000 displays a message prompting you to insert the disk that will become the Windows 2000 Setup Boot Disk.

9. Insert the blank formatted diskette labeled Windows 2000 Server Setup Disk #1 into the floppy disk drive and press any key to continue. After Windows 2000 creates the disk image, it displays a message prompting you to insert the diskette labeled Windows 2000 Setup Disk #2.

10. Remove Disk #1, insert the blank formatted diskette labeled Windows 2000 Server Setup Disk #2 into the floppy disk drive, and press any key to continue. After Windows 2000 creates the disk image, it displays a message prompting you to insert the diskette labeled Windows 2000 Setup Disk #3.

11. Remove Disk #2, insert the blank formatted diskette labeled Windows 2000 Server Setup Disk #3 into the floppy disk drive, and press any key to continue. After Windows 2000 creates the disk image, it displays a message prompting you to insert the diskette labeled Windows 2000 Setup Disk #4.

12. Remove Disk #3, insert the blank formatted diskette labeled Windows 2000 Server Setup Disk #4 into the floppy disk drive, and press any key to continue. After Windows 2000 creates the disk image, it displays a message indicating that the imaging process is done.

13. At the command prompt, type **exit** and then press Enter.

14. Remove the disk from the floppy disk drive and the CD-ROM from the CD-ROM drive.

▶   **To run the Windows 2000 Server pre-copy and text mode setup routine**

It's assumed for this procedure that your computer has no operating system installed, the disk isn't partitioned, and bootable CD-ROM support, if available, is disabled.

1. Insert the disk labeled Windows 2000 Server Setup Disk #1 into the floppy disk drive, insert the Windows 2000 Server CD-ROM into the CD-ROM drive, and restart your computer.

    After the computer starts, Windows 2000 Setup displays a brief message that your system configuration is being checked, and then the Windows 2000 Setup screen appears.

    Notice that the gray bar at the bottom of the screen indicates that the computer is being inspected and that the Windows 2000 Executive is loading, which is a minimal version of the Windows 2000 kernel.

2. When prompted, insert Setup Disk #2 into the floppy disk drive and press Enter.

    Notice that Setup indicates that it's loading the hardware abstraction layer (HAL), fonts, local specific data, bus drivers, and other software components to support your computer's motherboard, bus, and other hardware. Setup also loads the Windows 2000 Setup program files.

3. When prompted, insert Setup Disk #3 into the floppy disk drive and press Enter.

    Notice that Setup indicates that it's loading disk drive controller drivers. After the drive controllers load, the setup program initializes drivers appropriate to support access to your disk drives. Setup might pause several times during this process.

4. When prompted, insert Setup Disk #4 into the floppy disk drive and press Enter.

    Setup loads peripheral support drivers, like the floppy disk driver and file systems, and then it initializes the Windows 2000 Executive and loads the rest of the Windows 2000 Setup program.

    If you're installing the evaluation version of Windows 2000, a Setup notification screen appears, informing you that you're about to install an evaluation version of Windows 2000.

5. Read the Setup Notification message and press Enter to continue.

    Setup displays the Welcome To Setup screen. Notice that, in addition to the initial installation of Windows 2000, you can use Windows 2000 Setup to repair or recover a damaged Windows 2000 installation.

6. Read the Welcome To Setup message and press Enter to begin the installation phase of Windows 2000 Setup. Setup displays the License Agreement screen.

7. Read the license agreement, pressing Page Down to scroll down to the bottom of the screen.

8. Select I Accept the Agreement by pressing F8.

   Setup displays the Windows 2000 Server Setup screen, prompting you to select an area of free space or an existing partition on which to install Windows 2000. This stage of setup provides a way for you to create and delete partitions on your hard disk.

   If your computer doesn't contain any disk partitions (as required for this installation), you will notice that the hard disk listed on the screen contains an existing unformatted partition.

9. Make sure that the Unpartitioned space partition is highlighted and then type **c.**

   Setup displays the Windows 2000 Setup screen, confirming that you've chosen to create a new partition in the unpartitioned space and informing you of the minimum and maximum sizes of the partition you might create.

10. Specify the size of the partition you want to create (at least 2048 MB) and press Enter to continue.

    Setup displays the Windows 2000 Setup screen, showing the new partition as C: New (Unformatted).

Note   Although you can create additional partitions from the remaining unpartitioned space during setup, it's recommended that you perform additional partitioning tasks after you install Windows 2000. To partition hard disks after installation, use the Disk Management console.

---

11. Make sure the new partition is highlighted and press Enter.

    You're prompted to select a file system for the partition.

12. Use the arrow keys to select Format The Partition Using The NTFS File System and press Enter.

    The Setup program formats the partition with NTFS. After it formats the partition, Setup examines the hard disk for physical errors that might cause Setup to fail and then copies files to the hard disk. This process takes several minutes.

    Eventually, Setup displays the Windows 2000 Server Setup screen. A red status bar counts down for 15 seconds before Setup restarts the computer.

13. Remove the Setup disk from the floppy disk drive.

Important   If your computer supports booting from the CD-ROM drive and this feature wasn't disabled in the BIOS, the computer could boot from the Windows 2000 Server installation CD-ROM after Windows 2000 Setup restarts. This will cause Setup to start again from the beginning. If this happens, remove the CD-ROM and then restart the computer.

---

14. Setup copies additional files and then restarts your machine and loads the Windows 2000 Setup Wizard.

▶   **To run the GUI mode and gathering information phase of Windows 2000 Server setup**

This procedure begins the graphical portion of Setup on your computer.

1. On the Welcome To The Windows 2000 Setup Wizard page, click Next to begin gathering information about your computer.

   Setup configures NTFS folder and file permissions for the operating system files, detects the hardware devices in the computer, and then installs and configures device drivers to support the detected hardware. This process takes several minutes.

2. On the Regional Settings page, make sure that the system locale, user locale, and keyboard layout are correct for your language and location, and then click Next.

   Note   You can modify regional settings after you install Windows 2000 by using Regional Options in Control Panel.

   Setup displays the Personalize Your Software page, prompting you for your name and organization name. Setup uses your organization name to generate the default computer name. Many applications that you install later will use this information for product registration and document identification.

3. In the Name field, type your name; in the Organization field, type the name of an organization; then click Next.

   Note   If the Your Product Key screen appears, enter the product key located on the CD-ROM label of the Windows 2000 Server Evaluation Edition or the product key listed on the back of your software jewel case.

   Setup displays the Licensing Modes page, prompting you to select a licensing mode. By default, the Per Server licensing mode is selected. Setup prompts you to enter the number of licenses you have purchased for this server.

4. Select the Per Server Number of concurrent connections button, type **5** for the number of concurrent connections, and then click Next.

   Important   Per Server Number of concurrent connections and 5 concurrent connections are suggested values to be used to complete your self-study. Use a legal number of concurrent connections based on the actual licenses you own. You can also choose to use Per Seat instead of Per Server.

Setup displays the Computer Name And Administrator Password page.

Notice that Setup uses your organization name to generate a suggested name for the computer.

5. In the Computer Name field, type **server1**.

Windows 2000 displays the computer name in all capital letters regardless of how it's entered.

Warning   If your computer is on a network, check with the network administrator before assigning a name to your computer.

---

6. In the Administrator Password field and the Confirm Password field, type **password** (all lowercase) and click Next. Passwords are case-sensitive, so make sure you type **password** in all lowercase letters.

Note   Microsoft recommends using complex passwords (one that others can't easily guess) by mixing uppercase and lowercase letters, numbers, and symbols (for example, Lp6*g9).

Setup displays the Windows 2000 Components page, indicating which Windows 2000 system components Setup will install.

7. On the Windows 2000 Components page, click Next.

You can install additional components after you install Windows 2000 by using Add/Remove Programs in Control Panel. Make sure to install only the components selected by default during setup.

If a modem is detected in the computer during setup, Setup displays the Modem Dialing Information page.

8. If the Modem Dialing Information page appears, enter an area code or city code and click Next.

The Date And Time Settings page appears.

Important   Windows 2000 services perform many tasks whose successful completion depends on the computer's time and date settings. Be sure to select the correct time zone for your location.

---

9. Enter the correct Date and Time and Time Zone settings, and then click Next.

The Network Settings page appears and Setup installs networking components.

▶ **To complete the installing Windows networking components phase of Windows 2000 Server setup**

Networking is an integral part of Windows 2000 Server. There are many selections and configurations available. In this procedure, basic networking is configured.

1. On the Networking Settings page, make sure that Typical Settings is selected, and then click Next to begin installing Windows networking components.

   This setting installs networking components that are used to gain access to and share resources on a network and configures Transmission Control Protocol/Internet Protocol (TCP/IP) to automatically obtain an IP address from a DHCP server on the network.

   Setup displays the Workgroup or Computer Domain page, prompting you to join either a workgroup or a domain.

2. On the Workgroup or Computer Domain page, make sure that the button No, This Computer Isn't On A Network or Is On A Network Without A Domain is selected, and that the workgroup name is WORKGROUP, and then click Next.

   Setup displays the Installing Components page, displaying the status as Setup installs and configures the remaining operating system components according to the options you specified. This takes several minutes.

   Setup then displays the Performing Final Tasks page, which shows the status as Setup finishes copying files, making and saving configuration changes, and deleting temporary files. Computers that don't exceed the minimum hardware requirements might take 30 minutes or more to complete this phase of installation.

   Setup then displays the Completing The Windows 2000 Setup Wizard page.

3. Remove the Windows 2000 Server CD-ROM from the CD-ROM drive, and then click Finish.

   Windows 2000 restarts and runs the newly installed version of Windows 2000 Server.

▶ **To complete the hardware installation phase of Windows 2000 Server setup**

During this final phase of installation, any Plug and Play hardware not detected in the previous phases of Setup will be detected.

1. At the completion of the startup phase, log on by pressing Ctrl+Alt+Delete.

2. In the Enter Password dialog box, type **administrator** in the User Name field and type **password** in the Password field.

3. Click OK.

   If Windows 2000 detects hardware that wasn't detected during Setup, the Found New Hardware Wizard screen displays, indicating that Windows 2000 is installing the appropriate drivers.

4. If the Found New Hardware Wizard screen appears, verify that the Restart The Computer When I Click Finish check box is cleared and click Finish to complete the Found New Hardware Wizard.

   Windows 2000 displays the Microsoft Windows 2000 Configure Your Server dialog box. From this dialog box, you can configure a variety of advanced options and services.

5. Select I Will Configure This Server Later, and then click Next.

6. From the next screen that appears, clear the Show This Screen At Startup check box.

7. Close the Configure Your Server screen.

   You have now completed the Windows 2000 Server installation and are logged on as Administrator.

Note   To properly shut down Windows 2000 Server, click Start, choose Shut Down, and then follow the directions that appear.

Warning   If your computers are part of a larger network, you *must* verify with your network administrator that the computer names, domain name, and other information used in setting up Windows 2000 Server as described in this section don't conflict with network operations. If they do conflict, ask your network administrator to provide alternative values.

The Microsoft Certified Professional Program

The Microsoft Certified Professional (MCP) program provides the best method to prove your command of current Microsoft products and technologies. Microsoft, an industry leader in certification, is in the forefront of testing methodology. The exams and corresponding certifications are developed to validate your mastery of critical competencies as you design and develop, or implement and support, solutions with Microsoft products and technologies. Computer professionals who become Microsoft certified are recognized as experts and are sought after industry-wide.

The Microsoft Certified Professional program offers multiple certifications based on specific areas of technical expertise, including:

■ *Microsoft Certified Professional (MCP).*   Demonstrated in-depth knowledge of at least one Windows operating system or architecturally significant platform. An MCP is qualified to implement a Microsoft product or technology as part of a business solution for an organization.

■ *Microsoft Certified Systems Engineer (MCSE) on Windows 2000.*   Qualified to effectively analyze the business requirements, and design and implement the infrastructure for business solutions based on the Windows 2000 platform and Microsoft .NET Enterprise Servers.

- *Microsoft Certified Systems Administrator (MCSA)* on Windows 2000. Individuals who implement, manage, and troubleshoot existing network and system environments based on the Windows 2000 and Windows .NET Server operating systems.

- *Microsoft Certified Database Administrator (MCDBA)* on Microsoft SQL Server 2000. Individuals who derive physical database designs, develop logical data models, create physical databases, create data services by using Transact-SQL, manage and maintain databases, configure and manage security, monitor and optimize databases, and install and configure Microsoft SQL Server.

- *Microsoft Certified Solution Developer (MCSD).* Qualified to design and develop custom business solutions with Microsoft development tools, technologies, and platforms and Windows architecture.

- *Microsoft Certified Trainer (MCT).* Instructionally and technically qualified to deliver Microsoft Official Curriculum through a Microsoft Certified Technical Education Center (CTEC).

Microsoft Certification Benefits

Microsoft certification, one of the most comprehensive certification programs available for assessing and maintaining software-related skills, is a valuable measure of an individual's knowledge and expertise. Microsoft certification is awarded to individuals who have demonstrated their ability to perform specific tasks and implement solutions with Microsoft products. Not only does this provide an objective measure for employers to consider, but it also provides guidance for what an individual should know to be proficient. And as with any skills-assessment and benchmarking measure, certification brings a variety of benefits to the individual and to employers and organizations.

Microsoft Certification Benefits for Individuals

As a Microsoft Certified Professional, you receive many benefits:

- Industry recognition of your knowledge and proficiency with Microsoft products and technologies.

- A Microsoft Developer Network subscription. MCPs receive rebates or discounts on a one-year subscription to the Microsoft Developer Network (*http://msdn.microsoft.com/subscriptions*) during the first year of certification. (Fulfillment details will vary, depending on your location; please see your Welcome Kit.)

- Access to technical and product information direct from Microsoft through a secured area of the MCP Web site (go to *http://www.microsoft.com/traincert/ mcp/mcpsecure.asp*).

- Access to exclusive discounts on products and services from selected companies. Individuals who are currently certified can learn more about exclusive discounts by visiting the MCP secured Web site (go to *http://www.microsoft.com/ traincert/mcp/mcpsecure.asp* and select the "Other Benefits" link).

- MCP logo, certificate, transcript, wallet card, and lapel pin to identify you as a Microsoft Certified Professional (MCP) to colleagues and clients. Electronic files of logos and transcript may be downloaded from the MCP secured Web site upon certification (go to *http://www.microsoft.com/traincert/mcp/ mcpsecure.asp*).

- Invitations to Microsoft conferences, technical training sessions, and special events.

- Free access to *Microsoft Certified Professional Magazine Online*, a career and professional development magazine. Secured content on the *Microsoft Certified Professional Magazine Online* Web site includes the current issue (available only to MCPs), additional online-only content and columns, an MCP-only database, and regular chats with Microsoft and other technical experts.

- Discount on membership to PASS (for MCPs only), the Professional Association for SQL Server. In addition to playing a key role in the only worldwide, user-run SQL Server user group endorsed by Microsoft, members enjoy unique access to a world of educational opportunities (go to *http://www.microsoft.com/ traincert/mcp/mcpsecure.asp*).

An additional benefit is received by Microsoft Certified System Engineers (MCSEs):

- A 50 percent rebate or discount off the estimated retail price of a one-year subscription to *TechNet* or *TechNet Plus* during the first year of certification. (Fulfillment details will vary, depending on your location. Please see your Welcome Kit.) In addition, about 95 percent of the CD-ROM content is available free online at the *TechNet* Web site (*http://www.microsoft.com/technet*).

An additional benefit is received by Microsoft Certified System Database Administrators (MCDBAs):

- A 50 percent rebate or discount off the estimated retail price of a one-year subscription to TechNet or TechNet Plus during the first year of certification. (Fulfillment details will vary, depending on your location. Please see your Welcome Kit.) In addition, about 95 percent of the CD-ROM content is available free online at the TechNet Web site (*http://www.microsoft.com/technet*).

- A one-year subscription to *SQL Server Magazine*. Written by industry experts, the magazine contains technical and how-to tips and advice—a must for anyone working with SQL Server.

You can find a list of benefits for Microsoft Certified Trainers (MCTs) at *http://www.microsoft.com/traincert/mcp/mct/benefits.asp*.

Microsoft Certification Benefits for Employers and Organizations

Through certification, computer professionals can maximize the return on investment in Microsoft technology. Research shows that Microsoft certification provides organizations with:

- Excellent return on training and certification investments by providing a standard method of determining training needs and measuring results
- Increased customer satisfaction and decreased support costs through improved service, increased productivity, and greater technical self-sufficiency
- Reliable benchmark for hiring, promoting, and career planning
- Recognition and rewards for productive employees by validating their expertise
- Retraining options for existing employees so they can work effectively with new technologies
- Assurance of quality when outsourcing computer services

Requirements for Becoming a Microsoft Certified Professional

The certification requirements differ for each certification and are specific to the products and job functions addressed by the certification.

To become a Microsoft Certified Professional, you must pass rigorous certification exams that provide a valid and reliable measure of technical proficiency and expertise. These exams are designed to test your expertise and ability to perform a role or task with a product and are developed with the input of professionals in the industry. Questions in the exams reflect how Microsoft products are used in actual organizations, giving them "real-world" relevance.

- Microsoft Certified Product candidates are required to pass one operating system exam. Candidates may pass additional Microsoft certification exams to further qualify their skills with other Microsoft products, development tools, or desktop applications.
- Microsoft Certified Systems Engineers are required to pass five core exams and two elective exams.
- Microsoft Certified Systems Administrators are required to pass three core exams and one elective exam that provide a valid and reliable measure of technical proficiency and expertise.
- Microsoft Certified Database Administrators are required to pass three core exams and one elective exam that measure technical proficiency and expertise.

- Microsoft Certified Solution Developers are required to pass three core Windows operating system technology exams and one BackOffice technology elective exam.

- Microsoft Certified Trainers are required to meet instructional and technical requirements specific to each Microsoft Official Curriculum course they are certified to deliver. The MCT program requires ongoing training to meet the requirements for the annual renewal of certification. For more information about becoming a Microsoft Certified Trainer, visit *http://www.microsoft.com/ traincert/mcp/mct* or contact a regional service center near you.

Technical Training for Computer Professionals

Technical training is available in a variety of ways, with instructor-led classes, online instruction, or self-paced training available at thousands of locations worldwide.

Self-Paced Training

For motivated learners who are ready for the challenge, self-paced instruction is the most flexible, cost-effective way to increase your knowledge and skills.

A full line of self-paced print and computer-based training materials is available direct from the source—Microsoft Press. Microsoft Official Curriculum courseware kits from Microsoft Press are designed for advanced computer system professionals and are available from Microsoft Press and the Microsoft Developer Division. Self-paced training kits from Microsoft Press feature print-based instructional materials, along with CD-ROM–based product software, multimedia presentations, lab exercises, and practice files. The Mastering Series provides in-depth, interactive training on CD-ROM for experienced developers. They're both great ways to prepare for MCP exams.

Online Training

For a more flexible alternative to instructor-led classes, turn to online instruction. It's as near as the Internet and it's ready whenever you are. Learn at your own pace and on your own schedule in a virtual classroom, often with easy access to an online instructor. Without ever leaving your desk, you can gain the expertise you need. Online instruction covers a variety of Microsoft products and technologies. It includes options ranging from Microsoft Official Curriculum to choices available nowhere else. It's training on demand, with access to learning resources 24 hours a day. Online training is available through Microsoft Certified Technical Education Centers.

Microsoft Certified Technical Education Centers

Microsoft Certified Technical Education Centers (CTECs) are the best source for instructor-led training to help you prepare to become a Microsoft Certified Professional. The Microsoft CTEC program is a worldwide network of qualified technical training organizations that provide authorized delivery of Microsoft Official Curriculum courses by Microsoft Certified Trainers to computer professionals.

For a listing of CTEC locations in the United States and Canada, visit the Web site at *http://www.microsoft.com/traincert/ctec*.

Technical Support

Every effort has been made to ensure the accuracy of this book and the contents of the companion disc. If you have comments, questions, or ideas regarding this book or the companion disc, please send them to Microsoft Press using either of the following methods:

E-mail

TKINPUT@MICROSOFT.COM

Postal Mail

Microsoft Press
Attn: MCSA/MCSE Training Kit—Microsoft Windows 2000
Network Infrastructure Administration Editor
One Microsoft Way
Redmond, WA 98052-6399

The Microsoft Press Web site (*http://www.microsoft.com/mspress/support*) provides corrections for books. Please note that product support is not offered through this Web site. For further information regarding Microsoft software support options, please connect to *http://support.microsoft.com* or call Microsoft Support Network Sales at (800) 936-3500.

Evaluation Edition Software Support

The Evaluation Edition of Windows 2000 Server included with this book is unsupported by both Microsoft and Microsoft Press and should not be used on a primary work computer. For online support information relating to the full version of Windows 2000 Server that might also apply to the Evaluation Edition, you can connect to *http://support.microsoft.com*.

Information about any issues relating to the use of this evaluation edition with this training kit is posted to the Support section of the Microsoft Press Web site (*http://www.microsoft.com/mspress/support*).

For information about ordering the full version of any Microsoft software, please call Microsoft Sales at (800) 426-9400 or visit *http://www.microsoft.com*.

Microsoft®
Windows® 2000
Network Infrastructure
Administration Second Edition

C H A P T E R   1

Introducing Microsoft Windows 2000 Networking

Lesson 1: The OSI Reference Model 4

Lesson 2: Installing and Binding Windows 2000
Network Components 18

About This Chapter

In this chapter you will learn about the basic architectural structure of a data network and the Microsoft Windows 2000 components that populate that structure. A high-level understanding of the networking process is essential for an administrator of a Windows 2000 network. After you learn about the networking components used in Windows 2000, you learn how to install them and bind them together to form a fully functional protocol stack.

Before You Begin

Although a working knowledge of Windows 2000 is helpful, there are no prerequisites for this chapter. However, to perform the exercise in Lesson 2, you must have a Windows 2000 computer with a network interface card (NIC) and a modem.

Lesson 1: The OSI Reference Model

A large part of the Windows 2000 operating system is dedicated to networking components and services, all of which are designed to interoperate with other computers, whether they are running Windows or not. The networking capabilities of Windows 2000 are largely based on industry standards that enable computers of different types to communicate with each other. One of the most commonly used tools for learning about network communications and referencing specific network functions and components is the Open Systems Interconnection (OSI) reference model.

After this lesson, you will be able to

- Understand the concept of data encapsulation
- Describe the functions of the OSI model layers
- Understand the differences between the OSI model and a real world networking architecture

Estimated lesson time: 40 minutes

Introducing the OSI Reference Model

For two people to be able to communicate meaningfully, they must speak the same language. The same is true for two computers on a network. The languages that networked computers use to communicate are called *protocols*; the computers must have protocols in common to be able to communicate. The communication between computers on a network occurs at many levels, and, as a result, the developers of networking protocols split the essential functions into multiple layers, which are implemented by separate protocols. The combination of protocols needed to provide the various levels of communication is collectively known as a *protocol stack*. For communication to occur, the corresponding layers of the stack on the two computers must be running the same protocols at each layer of the stack.

The most common generalized representation of the protocol stack is a seven-layer construction that was defined in a document called "The Basic Reference Model for Open Systems Interconnection," or, more colloquially, the OSI reference model. This document is the result of two separate projects conducted by the International Organization for Standardization (ISO) and the Comité Consultatif International Téléphonique et Télégraphique (CCITT), which is now known as the Telecommunications Standardization Sector of the International Telecommunication Union (ITU-T). The projects were combined in 1983, and the resulting document was published as ISO 7498 by the ISO and as X.200 by the CCITT.

The OSI reference model splits the networking protocol stack into seven layers, as shown in Figure 1.1, with the top of the model representing an application running on the computer and the bottom of the model representing the network medium that connects the computers. Each layer contains specific functions that contribute to the communications process that enables an application on one computer to send data to an application on another computer. The protocols used by the computers perform these functions, and they complement one another to create the protocol stack.

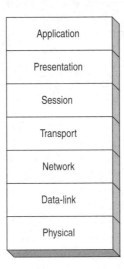

Figure 1.1   The seven layers of the OSI reference model

The protocols operating at adjacent layers of the stack communicate with one another by providing services to, and receiving services from, one another. In this way, data originating at an application at the top of the stack is passed down through the layers until it reaches the network medium. After the data is transmitted over the medium to the destination computer, it is passed up through the layers of the protocol stack to the corresponding application at the top. For the communications to take place, the corresponding layers of the protocol stack on each computer must be running the same (or compatible) protocols.

Understanding Data Encapsulation

The means by which the protocols operating at the various layers of the OSI model process the information they receive from the layer above is called *data encapsulation*. A protocol receiving data from the layer above it encapsulates the data by adding its own information, in the form of a new header (and in some cases, a footer as well). The header consists of *fields* that contain information specific to that protocol that will be read by the corresponding protocol on the destination computer. The information received from the layer above follows the header and becomes the payload in the unit of data created by the protocol. When the data unit is passed down to the layer below it, another protocol encapsulates it again. The header and payload from the protocol above together become the payload of the data unit created by the new protocol when it attaches its own header, as shown in Figure 1.2.

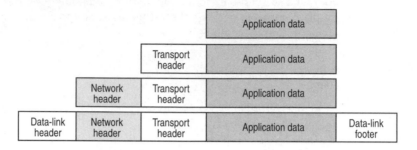

Figure 1.2   The data encapsulation process

The end result of the data encapsulation process is a data packet consisting of the original information generated by the application at the top of the stack, with several protocol headers (and one footer) attached to it, to form a construction like that shown at the bottom of Figure 1.2. This is the protocol data unit that is transmitted over the network to another computer. When the packet arrives at its destination, the protocol at each layer of the stack reads the header information added by the corresponding protocol on the source computer and processes the payload data accordingly. This effectively enables the protocols at each layer of the stack on one computer to communicate with their counterparts on another computer, as shown in Figure 1.3.

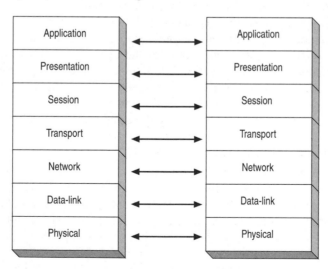

Figure 1.3   Logical communications between the same protocols on different computers

The following sections examine the functions of each layer of the OSI reference model.

The Physical Layer

The physical layer, or layer 1, of the OSI model provides the interface between the computer and the network medium that carries data from one computer to another. In most cases the network medium is a cable, such as a copper local area network (LAN) or telephone cable, but networks can also use various types of fiber-optic cable or wireless media, such as radio waves and infrared transmissions. In a computer, the physical layer takes the form of a network interface adapter (also known as a network interface card, or NIC) or a modem.

At its most basic level, the physical layer defines how data should be encoded into signals suitable for transmission over the network medium. Depending on the type of medium involved, the physical layer protocol describes how the binary data generated by the computer should be converted into electrical voltages, pulses of light, radio transmissions, or whatever form is required. The physical layer hardware then proceeds to transmit those signals.

In addition to the signaling scheme, the physical layer protocol can also define the properties of the network medium itself, such as the types of cables used to build the network and how they should be installed. In the case of LAN protocols, these elements are essential because the physical layer is coupled with the data-link layer protocol. Data-link layer protocols such as Ethernet and Token Ring, for example, perform functions that rely on precise timing of the signal transmissions, and they cannot operate successfully on a physical network with cables that are too long or that do not conform to the specifications the protocol requires. Although these protocols are primarily associated with the data-link layer, they include physical layer parameters that define the types of networks they can utilize.

These days the installation of the physical layer is a task that is increasingly left to specialized contractors. Network administrators who must be familiar with the intricacies of Transmission Control Protocol/Internet Protocol (TCP/IP) and other upper-layer protocols to do their jobs do not necessarily have to know everything there is to know about the physical layer configuration. This is largely because most LANs use unshielded twisted pair (UTP) cable, just like that of telephone systems, and cabling contractors are frequently engaged to install data network cabling at the same time as the telephone network. This is not to say that a typical network administrator can be completely ignorant of the physical layer, however. When troubleshooting networking problems, it is sometimes easy to become engrossed in a search for complex and esoteric causes. In these cases, it is important not to discount the more simple causes, such as a cabling problem, so a working knowledge of the physical layer standards used to build your network is useful, if not essential.

The Data-Link Layer

The data-link layer, layer 2 of the OSI model, is responsible for the final packaging of the application data before it is transmitted over the network medium. A data-link layer protocol receives data units from network layer protocols and encapsulates them for the final time. On a LAN, the data-link layer protocol applies both a header and a footer to form a *frame*, which is, in essence, the envelope used to carry the data to other computers on the network. Like a paper envelope transported by a postal service, the data-link layer protocol header contains the addresses of the computer sending the data and of its recipient. These addresses are found in two of the fields that make up the data-link layer protocol header.

The 6-byte addresses used by the data-link layer protocols on a LAN are hard-coded into the computers' network interface adapters by their manufacturers. These addresses are known as *hardware addresses* or *media access control (MAC) addresses*. Each manufacturer is assigned a 3-byte value called an *organizationally unique identifier (OUI)* by the Institute of Electrical and Electronics Engineers (IEEE). The addresses for the adapters produced by a particular manufacturer consist of its OUI plus a unique 3-byte identifier assigned by the manufacturer. This ensures that every adapter on a network has a unique hardware address.

In addition to this basic addressing, data-link layer protocols can perform a number of other functions, including media access control, protocol identification, and error detection. *Media access control (MAC)* is the process by which a computer gains access to a shared network medium. On most LANs, all the computers are connected to a common baseband medium. A *baseband medium* is one that can carry only one signal at a time, as opposed to a *broadband medium*, which can carry many signals at once. On this type of network, only one computer can transmit data at a time. If two computers were to transmit simultaneously, their signals would collide, causing the data to be lost. The data-link layer protocols used on LANs have a MAC mechanism that defines a method for preventing, minimizing, or recovering from collisions.

For example, Token Ring networks use a MAC mechanism called token passing, in which a small packet called a token circulates around the network. Only the computer in possession of the token is permitted to transmit its data. Because there is only one token, only one computer at a time can transmit data, which prevents collisions. Ethernet networks use a different MAC mechanism called Carrier Sense Multiple Access with Collision Detection (CSMA/CD). Computers using CSMA/CD listen to the network, and if it is free, transmit their data. This is not as sure a method for preventing collisions as token passing; collisions are expected to occur on Ethernet networks. However, the mechanism reduces the number of collisions that would otherwise occur and also provides a means by which the computers can detect the collisions and compensate for them by retransmitting their data. This MAC mechanism is one of the primary reasons why data-link layer LAN protocols are so closely associated with physical layer standards. If an Ethernet network uses the wrong cable or the cable is installed incorrectly, the computers cannot effectively detect collisions and data is lost, greatly reducing the network's efficiency by forcing the protocols at the higher layers to detect the missing packets.

Protocol identification is the process by which the data-link layer protocol identifies the protocol that generated the payload carried in the packet. Computers often run multiple protocols at the network layer, all of which share a single data-link layer protocol. As the network layer protocols pass their data down to the data-link layer, the data-link layer protocol creates a field in the header containing a code that specifies which network layer protocol generated the data in the payload. This is so that the data-link layer protocol on the computer receiving the packet can identify the network layer protocol to which it should pass the incoming data.

Error detection is a function that can be performed at several different layers of the OSI model. The data-link layer protocols used on LANs are unique among the layers in that they include a footer as well as a header. The footer consists of a field called a Frame Check Sequence (FCS), which contains a cyclical redundancy check (CRC) value calculated by the sending computer on the contents of the entire frame. On receipt of the packet, the destination computer performs the same calculation and compares its results to those in the FCS field. If the results match, the packet has been transmitted without error. If the results do not match, the receiving system discards the packet. There is no error correction at the data-link layer; the protocol can detect damaged packets and discard them, but it does not retransmit them. That is left to the protocols operating at the upper layers of the OSI model.

The data-link layer protocols used on LANs are the most complex of the protocols at this layer. Other data-link layer protocols are much simpler. For example, the Serial Line Internet Protocol (SLIP) consists only of a single byte that follows each packet transmitted over a connection. SLIP is used for point-to-point connections between two (and only two) computers, so there is no need for addresses or a MAC mechanism. SLIP has fallen into disuse in recent years because it is too simple and lacks features provided by other protocols, but there are other protocols operating at the data-link layer that are far less complex than Ethernet and Token Ring, such as Point-to-Point Protocol (PPP).

The Network Layer

Data-link layer protocols are used to transmit data between two computers that are directly connected by a LAN or a dedicated link. The destination address in a data-link layer protocol header always identifies a computer on the local network. By contrast, the network layer, layer 3 of the OSI model, is primarily responsible for the end-to-end communications between computers located on different networks. For example, when you use a computer on a LAN to connect to an Internet site with a Web browser, the data-link layer protocol carries your data packets only as far as the router on the network providing access to the Internet. The router then repackages the data, possibly using a different data-link layer protocol, to send it on its way over the next network. The network layer protocol, on the other hand, also encapsulates data using a header that contains Source and Destination Address fields, but these addresses identify the ultimate source and destination of the packet—in other words, the computer running the Web browser and the server on the Internet hosting the target site.

The most common of the network layer protocols, the Internet Protocol (IP), contains its own independent system of addresses. Novell NetWare's Internetwork Packet Exchange (IPX) protocol uses the hardware addresses coded into the computers' network interface adapters, and the NetBIOS Extended User Interface (NetBEUI) protocol provided with Windows uses NetBIOS names as network layer identifiers.

Note   For more information about IP addressing, see Lesson 2 of Chapter 2, "Introducing TCP/IP."

In addition to identifying the ultimate destination of a packet by addressing it, the network layer protocol is also responsible for routing the packet to that destination. A packet traveling through an internetwork to a specific destination is passed from router to router. Each of these routers is responsible for sending the packet on its way using the most efficient path to the destination. Internetworks typically have built-in redundancy that provides multiple paths to a given destination. A router has knowledge of these paths and transmits packets using the path that can get them to the destination in the least amount of time or using the smallest number of intermediate routers.

Note   For more information about routing, see Chapter 6, "Routing IP."

When a router processes an incoming packet, it strips off the data-link layer protocol header and footer and uses the information in the network layer protocol header to determine the best route to the destination. The router then reencapsulates the packet for transmission to its next destination. Because routers function as the interfaces between networks, the packets may be reencapsulated using the same or a different data-link layer protocol.

In addition to addressing and routing, network layer protocols can perform other functions, including fragmentation and protocol identification. *Fragmentation* is necessary when a router connects two networks that support different size packets. When a packet arrives at a router over a Token Ring network, for example, the packet can be up to 4500 bytes long. If the router determines that it must transmit the packet out over an Ethernet network, it has a problem, because Ethernet only supports packets up to 1500 bytes long. To resolve this problem, the router splits the packet into several fragments, each no larger than the maximum transmission unit (MTU) size for the outgoing network. Each fragment is identified by a code that indicates its place in the packet. The router then transmits each fragment in a separate packet.

When the destination computer receives all the fragments, it reassembles them into the original packet. Depending on the configuration of the internetwork, a single packet might be fragmented more than once on the way to the destination. That is, the packet is split into fragments, and then the fragments are themselves split into smaller fragments by another router. The fragments are not reassembled, however, until they reach the packet's final destination.

Protocol identification at the network layer works the same way as at the data-link layer, and for the same reason. Computers can often use multiple transport layer protocols with a single network layer protocol, and the network layer protocol header contains a code specifying which transport layer protocol generated the data carried inside the packet.

The Transport Layer

The transport layer, layer 4 of the OSI reference model, provides functions that complement those of the network layer protocol and help to get the data to the destination in a timely and efficient manner. Generally speaking, there are two types of transport layer protocols: connection-oriented and connectionless. A *connection-oriented* protocol is one in which the source and destination computers exchange a series of messages before they transmit any application data. These messages serve to establish a connection, which confirms that both computers exist, are functioning properly, and are ready to receive and transmit data. Connection-oriented communications are also usually associated with *guaranteed delivery*, a feature in which the computer receiving data returns acknowledgments to the sender on a regular basis, confirming that it has received the data without errors.

Connection-oriented protocols, such as the Transmission Control Protocol (TCP), are typically used to transmit large amounts of data that require extreme accuracy. For example, when transmitting a program file over a network, every bit must be transmitted correctly, or the file will not execute properly. By contrast, a video stream can survive the loss of some bits in transit; the only effect is a momentary lapse in the quality of the display.

When transmitting large amounts of data, it is necessary for the transport layer protocol to split the data stream into pieces called segments, which can fit into single packets. *Segmentation* is a lot like the fragmentation process that occurs at the network layer, but be careful not to confuse the two. Unlike fragmentation, which is performed by the intermediate routers that the packets pass through on their way to their destination, segmentation occurs only at the source of a data transmission. (This is not to say that segments cannot be fragmented by routers during their journey, however; they can.) The sending computer splits the stream into segments of an appropriate size and packages each one in a separate packet. The transport layer protocol header contains a code that identifies each segment so that the destination computer can reassemble them into the original data stream.

Most connection-oriented protocols operating at the transport layer also include a function called flow control. *Flow control* is the ability of the receiving computer to transmit information back to the sender that causes it to modify its transmission rate. The network interface adapter in every networked computer has a memory buffer used to hold incoming packets as they are waiting to be processed. When the buffer in a computer receiving a data transmission approaches fullness, the computer can send flow control information to the sender, ordering it to slow down its transmission rate.

In TCP, flow control is implemented as a field in the protocol header that specifies the number of packets that the computer is capable of receiving. The receiving computer modifies the value of this field in the acknowledgment messages it returns to the sender. When the field's value decreases, the sender knows that the receiver's buffer is filling up faster than it can process the incoming packets, and it slows its transmission rate accordingly. As the value increases again, the sender can ramp up the transmission rate.

All these features provided by connection-oriented protocols come at a price. The protocols generate a great deal of network traffic overhead, both in the form of additional messages used to establish connections and acknowledge transmissions and in additional header fields. The counterpart to a connection-oriented protocol is a *connectionless* protocol, such as TCP/IP's User Datagram Protocol (UDP), which is much simpler and has much lower overhead. IP, at the network layer, is also a connectionless protocol. Connectionless protocols do not transmit connection establishment messages before they transmit application data, nor do they use packet acknowledgments. Connectionless protocols also have no segmentation or flow control. For these reasons, connectionless protocols usually are not suitable for the transmission of large amounts of data requiring extreme accuracy.

For the most part, computers use these protocols for quick exchanges that consist of a single request and reply, such as Domain Name System (DNS) and Dynamic Host Configuration Protocol (DHCP) transactions. The reply message functions as a tacit acknowledgment, and the request is easily retransmitted if no reply is received in a timely manner. Streaming audio and video applications can use connectionless protocols as well because they do not require bit accuracy.

Because they do not have the many complex features of connection-oriented protocols, connectionless protocols have much smaller headers. The UDP header is only 8 bytes, as opposed to 20 for TCP. Even the simplest transport layer protocol, however, has a field in its header that provides protocol identification. Protocol identification at the transport layer is used to identify the application layer protocol that generated the data carried in the packet (because there are no separate session or presentation layer protocols). This completes the path up through the protocol stack that the data takes at the destination computer. The arriving packets are processed by the data-link layer protocol, which passes them up to the appropriate network layer protocol. The network layer protocol then passes the data up to the correct transport layer protocol, which relays it to an application layer protocol.

Transport layer protocols, both connection-oriented and connectionless, can also perform error detection and correction, using a system of transmitted CRC values like those used in the data-link layer. The difference is that the transport layer performs end-to-end error detection, but the data-link layer only checks for errors on local network transmissions. In addition, transport layer protocols are capable of correcting errors as well as detecting them, by transmitting to the sender a list of packets that need to be retransmitted.

Transport layer protocols can perform two types of error correction. Correction of *signaled errors* occurs when a protocol at another layer (such as the data-link layer) informs the transport layer protocol that a specific packet needs to be retransmitted, and the transport layer protocol corrects the error without detecting it on its own. *Unsignaled errors* are those that the transport layer detects on its own and corrects, without the aid of another protocol.

The Session Layer

The lower four layers of the OSI reference model are concerned with getting data from one computer to another over the network. These protocols operating at these layers are designed to overcome the obstacles that can prevent various types of data from being transmitted properly. The session, presentation, and application layers are not concerned with these matters; they assume that the lower-layer protocols are capable of getting data from one computer to another, intact and on time. The top three layers also have less obvious boundaries between them. There are no session and presentation layer protocols; the functions attributed to these layers are incorporated into the application layer protocols.

The session layer performs a large number of functions that aid in the exchange of messages between two computers, which is called a dialog. The two functions most often cited at this layer are dialog separation and dialog control. Dialog separation involves the insertion of a bookmark-like device called a checkpoint into a dialog stream, which enables the communicating computers to perform an action at the same point in the dialog. Dialog control concerns the regulation of the communications between the two computers through the choice of one of two transmission modes: Two-Way Alternate (TWA) mode, in which only one computer can transmit at a time, or Two-Way Simultaneous (TWS) mode, in which either computer can transmit at will. TWS mode presents problems that the session layer has to address, such as whether a reply message was generated before or after the most recently transmitted request.

The Presentation Layer

Compared to the diverse functions performed by the session layer, the presentation layer is relatively simple. One of the primary objectives of most data networks is to enable computers of different types to communicate. The presentation layer provides a translation service that makes this possible. Applications on each computer platform generate network access requests using their own native syntax, which might be different from the syntax used by the application on the destination computer. The syntax can incorporate several elements, include bit-coding formats such as American Standard Code for Information Interchange (ASCII) and Extended Binary Coded Decimal Interchange Code (EBCDIC), compression standards, and encryption algorithms. Before the data generated by the application reaches the transport layer, the computer converts it from its native syntax (called an *abstract syntax*) to a *transfer syntax*, suitable for transmission over the network. The computer receiving the data then performs its own translation on the incoming information, this time converting the transfer syntax to the application's own abstract syntax.

The Application Layer

Application layer protocols form the top of the computer's protocol stack. An application running on a computer uses an application layer protocol to request access to a resource located elsewhere on the network. For example, a Web browser uses the Hypertext Transfer Protocol (HTTP) to generate requests for home pages hosted by Internet servers. The application layer protocol is also the final destination for the data passed up through the stack on the receiving computer.

Little can be said about application layer protocols in general, because there are a great many of them and each is designed to provide highly specialized services required by a particular application or type of application. In some cases, the protocol is virtually indistinguishable from the application itself, as in the case of the File Transfer Protocol (FTP). In other cases, the protocol is a separate entity that many different applications can use. For example, the protocol that enables an application such as a word processor to open a file stored on a network server is part of the computer's operating system. Any application can take advantage of these application layer capabilities and open network files just as though they were stored on a local drive.

Some of the most commonly used application layer protocols are as follows:

- **Hypertext Transfer Protocol (HTTP).**   Used by Web browsers and servers to exchange home page requests and replies
- **File Transfer Protocol (FTP).**   Used to transfer files between computers and perform basic file management tasks
- **Domain Name System (DNS).**   Used to send host name resolution requests and replies to and from DNS servers

- **Dynamic Host Configuration Protocol (DHCP).**   Used to automatically configure the TCP/IP client on network computers
- **Simple Mail Transfer Protocol (SMTP).**   Used by e-mail clients to send messages and to exchange e-mail messages between servers
- **Simple Network Management Protocol (SNMP).**   Used to gather performance information about specific network components and transmit it to a central network management console

Using the OSI Model in the Real World

Originally, the OSI reference model was intended to be a guideline for the creation of a new set of networking protocols that would conform precisely to its seven layers. Those protocols never appeared in a commercial form. The protocols that networks use today are not analogous to the model, for several reasons. The most obvious reason is that the majority of the protocols currently in use, such as TCP/IP and Ethernet, were developed before the OSI model existed and were constructed using their own architectural models. These protocols, therefore, tend to have functions that overlap into multiple OSI model layers. Another reason is that some of the layers, particularly the session and presentation layers, really do not warrant a separate protocol, and creating one would introduce needless additional complexity to the network communications process. The typical protocol stack used by an application running on a networked computer consists of four protocols, such as the example shown in Figure 1.4.

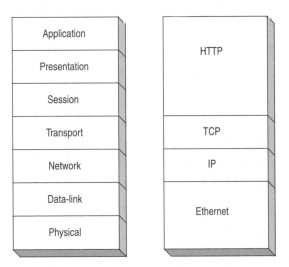

Figure 1.4   The OSI model compared with a real Windows protocol stack

The application layer protocol interacts with the application that needs to communicate with another computer on the network, and typically includes the functions attributed to the presentation and session layers as well. The boundaries of the network and transport layers are the most accurate found in the model. Virtually all computers use two separate protocols that conform relatively rigidly to the functions of the network and transport layers. The functions of the data-link and physical layers are often combined in a single protocol that encompasses all their functions.

The OSI model's value is therefore in its usefulness as a teaching and reference tool. Although there are no separate session or presentation layer protocols, for example, the functions attributed to those layers are essential to network communications. You will often read, in this book and elsewhere, about network protocols or components that operate at particular layers of the model, which helps to break down data networking, a very complex process, into more manageable units.

Lesson Review

1. Which layer of the OSI reference model is responsible for controlling access to the network medium?

2. Which layer of the OSI model is responsible for translating different syntaxes?

3. Which layer of the OSI model identifies a packet's final destination?

4. UDP and IP are both what kind of protocols?

   a. Connection-oriented

   b. Transport layer

   c. Network layer

   d. Connectionless

5. What is the name of the process by which a receiving system instructs a sending system to slow down its transmission rate?

Lesson Summary

- The OSI reference model consists of seven layers: physical, data-link, network, transport, session, presentation, and application.

- The OSI model layers usually do not correspond exactly to the protocol stack running on an actual system.

- The data-link layer protocols often include physical layer specifications.

- The network and transport layer protocols work together to provide a cumulative end-to-end communication service.

- The functions of the session, presentation, and application layers are often combined into a single application layer protocol.

Lesson 2: Installing and Binding Windows 2000 Network Components

The networking concepts you studied in the abstract in the previous lesson, "The OSI Reference Model," are largely realized in Windows 2000 by four components: network adapters, protocols, clients, and services. In this lesson you learn about the functions of these components and how to install them on a Windows 2000 computer.

After this lesson, you will be able to

- List the Windows 2000 networking components
- Install Windows 2000 networking components
- Modify the bindings between Windows 2000 networking components

Estimated lesson time: 25 minutes

Introducing the Windows 2000 Networking Components

The protocol stack on a Windows 2000 computer consists, from the bottom up, of a network interface adapter, one or more protocol modules, one or more clients, and optionally, a collection of services (see Figure 1.5). These components are examined in the following sections.

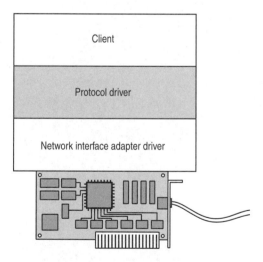

Figure 1.5   The Windows 2000 protocol stack

Network Interface Adapters

A network interface adapter in a Windows 2000 computer typically consists of a NIC and the device driver that the computer needs to communicate with it. These components perform the physical and data-link layer functions of the OSI reference model. For example, the network adapter hardware is responsible for implementing the data-link layer protocol's MAC mechanism and for generating the appropriate signals for transmission over the network medium. A network adapter does not have to be a NIC, however. When you use a modem or other wide area network (WAN) communications device to connect to a network at a remote location, the WAN device is itself functioning as a network adapter and is functionally interchangeable with a NIC.

A computer with a single network interface adapter can handle the data traffic of multiple protocol modules operating above it. The packets generated by the various protocols are combined and transmitted over the single network medium, a process called *multiplexing*. However, it is also possible for a computer to have multiple network adapters connecting it to different networks. The most common configuration is for a computer to have a NIC connecting it to a LAN and a WAN connection to the Internet or another remote network. However, it is also possible for one computer to have multiple NICs installed, enabling it to function as a router that passes data between two networks. When the computer has two or more network adapters, you can configure them to handle the traffic generated by different protocols (enabling you to use one NIC to connect to a TCP/IP network and the other to connect to a NetWare network running IPX, for example), or have both adapters handle all the installed protocols (see Figure 1.6).

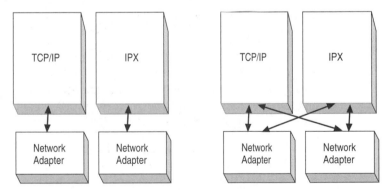

Figure 1.6 Multiplexing and separating traffic with multiple network adapters

Protocols

Computers use many protocols when communicating on a network, but often these protocols are grouped together into cooperative groups, commonly called protocol suites. TCP/IP, for example, is a protocol suite that includes not only TCP and IP, but also many other protocols operating at various layers of the OSI model. Because using TCP/IP requires most or all of the protocols in the suite, Windows 2000 (and most other operating systems) install them as a single entity. When you install the Internet Protocol (TCP/IP) software module on a Windows 2000 computer, you are actually installing the entire TCP/IP protocol suite as well as a variety of related tools and utilities. Therefore, a reference to "installing a protocol" in Windows 2000 means the installation of a single protocol module, which technically implements multiple protocols and applications.

TCP/IP is the default protocol used by Windows 2000. Its functionality falls just above the network adapter and spans the network and transport layers, even reaching as far up as the application layer in some of its components. The primary TCP/IP protocols are IP at the network layer and TCP and UDP at the transport later, but the suite also includes many application and network layer protocols. Windows 2000 also includes two other protocols that are roughly analogous to TCP/IP in their functions.

NWLink is the Microsoft version of the IPX protocols developed by Novell for use with its NetWare operating system. Like TCP/IP, IPX is a protocol suite that consists of the IPX protocol itself, which operates at the network layer, and multiple transport layer protocols, including Sequenced Packet Exchange (SPX) and Network Core Protocol (NCP). NWLink is primarily intended for connecting Windows computers to NetWare networks, but it is also possible to use it for communication between Windows computers.

NetBEUI, the third of the general use protocol modules included with Windows 2000, was the original default networking protocol for the Windows operating systems. Ideal for small LANs, NetBEUI requires no manual configuration and is completely self-adjusting. Unlike TCP/IP and IPX, however, NetBEUI is not routable, which means that it is not suitable for use on internetworks.

The network adapter drivers used by Windows 2000 conform to the *Network Device Interface Specification (NDIS)*, and the boundary between the adapter driver at the data-link layer and the protocol modules at the network layer on a Windows 2000 computer is called the *NDIS boundary layer*. This boundary makes it possible for the computer to use different protocol modules with the same network adapter interchangeably. You can install one, two, or all three of the protocol modules supplied with Windows 2000 and choose which ones to use for specific purposes.

Clients

At the top of the Windows 2000 protocol modules is the transport driver interface (TDI), which performs a function similar to that of the NDIS boundary layer. Above the TDI are the Windows 2000 client modules, which can use any of the protocols installed on the computer. The Client for Microsoft Networks module provides basic Windows network file and print services to the computer, enabling applications to access files and printers on network computers just as if they were installed in the local machine. For NetWare connectivity, Windows 2000 also includes Client Service for NetWare (in Windows 2000 Professional) or Gateway Service for NetWare (in Windows 2000 Server).

Note For more information on the NetWare clients included with Windows 2000, see Lesson 2 in Chapter 4, "NetWare Networking with Windows 2000."

These client modules are based on a component called a *redirector*, which is responsible for evaluating resource access requests and determining whether the requested resource is located on the local machine or on the network. If the latter, the redirector passes the request to the appropriate protocol, starting it on its way down the stack to the network medium.

Services

In Windows terminology, a service is a program that runs continuously on a computer, waiting to satisfy requests for particular functions. For example, on a Windows 2000 computer running Microsoft DNS Server, the DNS server program runs as a service that loads when the computer starts and is ready to service requests from DNS clients at all times. Windows 2000, particularly in its server versions, includes a large collection of services that provides networking functions. By default, Windows 2000 installations include services that provide basic networking functionality, such as the following:

- **Server.**   Enables the computer to share its files and printers with other systems on the network
- **Workstation.**   Makes it possible for applications running on the computer to access resources on other network systems
- **Messenger.**   Enables administrators and applications to send and receive messages
- **Browser.**   Is responsible for compiling and maintaining a list of the resources on the network
- **Netlogon.**   Enables the computer to locate the domain controller on the network and log on to a domain

In addition to these services that are automatically installed with the operating system, Windows 2000 includes many optional services that you can opt to install with the OS or at any time afterward, such as the following:

- **Dynamic Host Configuration Protocol (DHCP).**   The combination of a service and a protocol that enables a Windows 2000 Server computer to automatically assign IP addresses and other configuration parameters to the TCP/IP clients on a network.

- **Domain Name System (DNS).**   A distributed Internet service that enables computers on a network to resolve host names into the IP addresses needed for TCP/IP communications.

- **Windows Internet Name Service (WINS).**   A NetBIOS name server, this is a LAN-based service that enables computers to resolve NetBIOS names into the IP addresses needed for TCP/IP communications.

- **Microsoft Certificate Services.**   Enables you to create and manage the certificate authorities (CAs) that issue digital certificates. Digital certificates are electronic credentials that certify the online identities of individuals, organizations, and computers.

- **Routing and Remote Access Service (RRAS).**   A service that enables a Windows 2000 Server computer to function in a variety of communications roles, including LAN router, remote access server, virtual private network (VPN) server, and network address translation (NAT) server.

- **Internet Information Services (IIS).**   A group of services that enables a Windows 2000 computer to function as a Web, FTP, or news server.

Installing Windows 2000 Networking Components

For a Windows 2000 computer to participate on a network, it must have, at the very least, a network adapter, a protocol, and a client installed. Most of the computers and network interface cards manufactured today conform to the Plug and Play standard, which automates the installation of the network adapter and its device driver. To manually install an adapter, you use the Add/Remove Hardware Control Panel.

For every NIC installed in a Windows 2000 computer, a Local Area Network icon appears in the Network And Dial-Up Connections window, which provides access to the configuration information for the interface. You can also create additional connections in this window using modems and other WAN devices as the network adapters by clicking the Make New Connection icon to launch the Network Connection Wizard.

When you install a NIC in a Windows 2000 computer, or when the Windows 2000 setup program detects one during the operating system installation, the system installs a basic default protocol stack configuration consisting of a device driver for the network adapter, the Client for Microsoft Networks, the Internet Protocol

(TCP/IP) module, and the File and Printer Sharing for Microsoft Networks service, which enables other computers on the network to access the system's files and printers.

To configure the networking components, or to install additional components, you open the Properties dialog box for a particular connection (as shown in Figure 1.7) by right-clicking its icon in the Network And Dial-Up Connections window and selecting Properties from the pop-up menu. The Properties dialog box identifies the network adapter in the Connect Using box and also contains a list of the networking components installed on the computer. You can use the Install and Uninstall buttons to add or remove clients, protocols, and services. Selecting a component and clicking Properties opens a dialog box in which you can configure the properties of that component. The controls in the dialog box vary depending on the component you have selected.

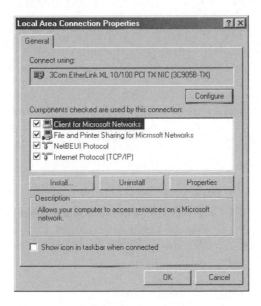

Figure 1.7   The Local Area Connection Properties dialog box

Binding Windows 2000 Networking Components

By default, when you install a networking component, such as a client or protocol module, it is automatically bound to all the other components above and below it. For example, if you install the NWLink protocol module on a computer with two network adapters, both adapters will be configured to use NWLink. You can control the bindings of the various components from the Properties dialog box for each connection. The check boxes next to each of the components in the Properties dialog box indicate which components are bound to the adapter used by that connection. Clear the check box next to a component to unbind it from that connection.

As an example, consider a Windows 2000 computer with both a NIC and a modem installed. You create a new connection so that you can use the modem to connect to the Internet, and you install the NetBEUI protocol for local network communications. By default, the Internet Protocol (TCP/IP) and NetBEUI protocol modules are both bound to the NIC and the modem. However, the modem cannot use NetBEUI when accessing the Internet, and the NIC cannot use TCP/IP on the local network because all the other computers are running NetBEUI only. To conserve system resources and enhance performance, you can unbind TCP/IP from the NIC adapter and unbind NetBEUI from the modem connection.

Exercise 1: Installing and Binding Protocols

In this exercise, you augment the capabilities of the default Windows 2000 networking installation by installing the NetBEUI protocol module. This exercise assumes that you have a Windows 2000 computer with a properly installed NIC and modem, and that you have created an Internet connection using the Network Connection Wizard. It is possible, however, to complete the exercise without actually being connected to a LAN or having a modem physically installed in the computer.

▶ **Procedure 1: Installing the NetBEUI protocol**

In this procedure, you add the NetBEUI protocol module to the computer's network configuration.

1. Click the Start button and select Network And Dial-Up Connections from the Settings menu to display the Network And Dial-Up Connections window.

2. Right-click the Local Area Connection icon and select Properties from the pop-up menu to display the Local Area Connection Properties dialog box. What networking components do you see listed in the dialog box?

3. Click Install to open the Select Network Component Type dialog box.

4. Select Protocol and click Add to open the Select Network Protocol dialog box.

5. Select NetBEUI Protocol and click OK to add the NetBEUI Protocol module to the components list in the Local Area Connection Properties dialog box.

6. Click Close in the Local Area Connection Properties dialog box to install the protocol. You might have to supply the Windows 2000 installation files before rebooting the computer to complete the procedure.

7. Return to the Network And Dial-Up Connections window and open the Properties dialog box for the modem connection you created. What components do you see listed? Why do you see the components you do?

▶ **Procedure 2: Unbinding protocols**

In this procedure, you optimize the performance of the network components by removing selected bindings. The assumption for this procedure is that the computer is connected to a LAN that uses the NetBEUI protocol exclusively, and that uses the modem to dial in to the Internet.

1. Click the Start button and select Network And Dial-Up Connections from the Settings menu to display the Network And Dial-Up Connections window.

2. Right-click the Local Area Connection icon and select Properties from the pop-up menu to display the Local Area Connection Properties dialog box.

3. Clear the check box next to the Internet Protocol (TCP/IP) module and click Close. What does this do, and why would you want to do it?

4. Right-click the icon for the modem connection you created and select Properties from the pop-up menu to display the connection's Properties dialog box.

5. Clear the check box next to the NetBEUI Protocol module and click Close. Why would you want to do this?

Lesson Review

1. What is the protocol traditionally associated with NetWare networking?

   a. NetBEUI

   b. IPX

   c. TCP/IP

   d. Ethernet

2. What is the Windows component that enables an application to access a network resource in the same way as a local one?

   a. Redirector

   b. Protocol

   c. Client

   d. Service

3. Which of the following Windows network components is not required for client functionality?

a. Redirector

b. Service

c. Protocol

d. Network interface adapter driver

4. Which of the following Windows 2000 networking modules do you not install from the Network And Dial-Up Connections dialog box?

a. Services

b. Clients

c. Protocols

d. Network interface adapter drivers

Lesson Summary

- The protocol stack on a Windows 2000 computer consists of network adapters, clients, protocols, and optionally, services.

- Windows 2000 implements entire protocol suites as a single networking component, which makes it possible to install support for all the TCP/IP protocols with one procedure.

- A network adapter in Windows 2000 can be a standard NIC or a WAN device, such as a modem.

- A client redirector is the module that determines whether the resource requested by an application is local or on the network and routes the request accordingly.

- All Windows 2000 networking components are bound to all other components by default, but you can unbind them manually to improve system performance.

CHAPTER 2

Introducing TCP/IP

Lesson 1: TCP/IP Overview **28**

Lesson 2: IP Addressing and Subnetting **47**

Lesson 3: Understanding TCP and UDP **63**

About This Chapter

Transmission Control Protocol/Internet Protocol (TCP/IP) is the suite of protocols most commonly used for computer network communications. In addition to being the common language of the Internet, TCP/IP is the default protocol suite used by virtually all network operating systems for both local area and wide area networking applications. Most of the services covered in Exam 70-216 are based on, or provide functionality to, the TCP/IP protocols. Therefore, a detailed knowledge of the underlying concepts by which TCP/IP supports—and is supported by—these services is essential to your exam preparation regimen.

In this chapter you learn about the architecture of the TCP/IP protocol stack and the basic functions of the main TCP/IP protocols. You also learn how IP addresses and subnet masks are formed and how to create subnets on a TCP/IP network.

Before You Begin

There are no prerequisites for this chapter other than installing Network Monitor, which you need to complete Exercise 1.

Lesson 1: TCP/IP Overview

The TCP/IP protocol suite was developed in the 1970s for use on an experimental packet switching network built for the U.S. Department of Defense. This network, originally called the ARPANET, grew into what we now know as the Internet, and it is still based on the TCP/IP protocols. TCP/IP has also been associated with the UNIX systems since their inception. The primary advantage of the TCP/IP protocols is that they were designed to be used with any computing platform. The ARPANET/Internet was intended from the beginning to be a network that connects many types of computers, so the protocols that the network uses must be adaptable to all of them.

After this lesson, you will be able to

- Compare the layers of the TCP/IP protocol stack with those of the Open Systems Interconnection (OSI) reference model
- List the major protocols of the TCP/IP suite and their functions

Estimated lesson time: 45 minutes

Note *Packet switching* is a term that describes a network in which data is split into discrete units (called packets), each of which is transmitted separately to a destination. After the destination system has received all the packets, it reassembles them into the original data stream. On a packet switching network, it is possible for packets to take different routes to the destination and even to arrive there in a different order from that in which they were sent. The alternative to packet switching is called *circuit switching*, in which a semipermanent connection (called a circuit) is established between the communicating devices. The devices can then transmit data over the circuit continuously and in real time. The telephone system is an example of a circuit switching network.

TCP/IP Standards

In the early days of local area networking, protocols were typically developed for use with specific products, such as the Internetwork Packet Exchange (IPX) protocols designed by Novell for use with NetWare. Because the standards on which these protocols are based are privately held, this type of proprietary networking system is not conducive to use by different types of computers unless the company that owns them wants them to be. The TCP/IP protocols, by contrast, were created with flexibility in mind and have never been the product of a single company. The protocols were developed and are still maintained by ad hoc groups of technicians, many of them working for various major manufacturers of networking products.

A body called the Internet Engineering Task Force (IETF) publishes the TCP/IP standards in documents called *Requests For Comments* (RFCs). The list of RFCs contains documents that define protocol standards in various stages of development, as well as informational, experimental, and historical documents. All the RFCs are in the public domain and are freely available on many Internet Web and File Transfer Protocol (FTP) sites. For links to the standards, see the IETF home page at *www.ietf.org*. The discussions in this book of the protocols and services based on TCP/IP standards include references to the appropriate RFCs, which you can consult for more information.

Note   After a document is published by the IETF as an RFC and assigned a number, that document never changes. If the IETF later publishes a revised version of an RFC, it assigns the document a new number. The RFC-INDEX file, which contains a complete listing of the published documents, also contains cross-references that indicate when RFCs make other documents obsolete or when they have been made obsolete by other documents.

In addition to not being restrained in any way by copyrights, trademarks, or other publishing restrictions, the nonproprietary nature of the TCP/IP standards also means that the protocols are not limited to any particular computing platform, operating system, or hardware implementation. This platform independence was the chief guiding principle of the TCP/IP development effort, and many of the protocol suite's features are designed to make it possible for any computer with networking capabilities to communicate with any other networked computer using TCP/IP.

TCP/IP Architecture

The TCP/IP protocols predate the personal computer, the Ethernet protocol, and most other elements that are today considered the foundations of computer networking, including the OSI reference model. However, the protocols are designed using a layered architecture that is similar in many ways to the OSI model. Splitting the networking functionality of a computer into a stack of separate protocols rather than creating a single monolithic protocol provides several advantages, including the following:

- **Platform independence.**   Separate protocols make it easier to support a variety of computing platforms. Creating or modifying protocols to support new physical layer standards or networking application programming interfaces (APIs) doesn't require modification of the entire protocol stack.

- **Quality of service.**   Having multiple protocols operating at the same layer makes it possible for applications to select the protocol that provides only the level of service required.

- **Simultaneous development.**   Because the stack is split into layers, the development of the various protocols can proceed simultaneously, using personnel who are uniquely qualified in the operations of the particular layers.

The TCP/IP networking model, which is defined in RFC 1122, "Requirements for Internet Hosts—Communication Layers," consists of only four layers, instead of the seven in the OSI reference model. The layers are roughly analogous to the OSI model, as shown in Figure 2.1. When you compare the TCP/IP stack to the OSI model, the session and presentation layers, which are incorporated into the application layer, and the physical layer are missing.

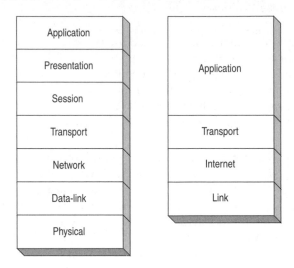

Figure 2.1   The TCP/IP protocol stack compared to the OSI reference model

The physical layer is omitted because this is the area in which platform-specific solutions are required. The interface between the computer and the network must be designed for the type of computer being used, and this goes beyond the hardware-independent nature of the TCP/IP protocols. The result is that although TCP/IP itself can supply most of the protocol stack, it cannot supply all of it. Each computer must have a hardware interface with the network that is designed to work together both with the computer and the TCP/IP protocols. The hardware interface is usually either a network interface card (NIC) in the computer or a wide area network (WAN) device (such as a modem) connected to the computer in some way. The TCP/IP protocols don't impose any limitations on the type of network interface to be used.

The four layers of the TCP/IP protocol stack are as follows:

- **Link.**   The link layer (sometimes called the network interface layer) falls at the bottom of the TCP/IP stack and corresponds to the data-link layer in the OSI model. However, the TCP/IP link layer does not include complex local area network (LAN) protocols such as Ethernet and Token Ring, which are designed for use with specific types of hardware. A computer using one of the data-link protocols has no TCP/IP link layer implementation. The TCP/IP suite does include rudimentary link layer protocols, however, such as the Serial Line Internet Protocol (SLIP) and the Point-to-Point Protocol (PPP), which can be used with many types of network interface hardware, particularly modems and other WAN devices. One other protocol that is sometimes said to function at the link layer is the Address Resolution Protocol (ARP). This is because ARP provides services to the IP protocol operating at the internet layer.

■ **Internet.** The internet layer is equivalent to the network layer of the OSI reference model. The Internet Protocol (IP) is the main TCP/IP protocol at the internet layer and the primary end-to-end data carrier for the entire protocol suite. IP provides features such as data encapsulation, internetwork routing, packet addressing, and fragmentation to the protocols at the transport layer above it. Other, more specialized, protocols also operate at this layer, including the Internet Control Message Protocol (ICMP) and the Internet Group Message Protocol (IGMP), as well as a number of dynamic routing protocols.

Note The word *internet,* in this context, is a generic reference to an internetwork, not to the global network known as the Internet (which is always capitalized). Be careful not to confuse the two.

■ **Transport.** The transport layer equates exactly to the layer of the same name in the OSI reference model. The TCP/IP suite includes two protocols at this layer, the Transmission Control Protocol (TCP) and the User Datagram Protocol (UDP), which provide connection-oriented and connectionless data transfer services, respectively.

■ **Application.** The application layer of the TCP/IP stack can be said to encompass the session, presentation, and application layers of the OSI model. However, this does not mean that all the TCP/IP application layer protocols include all those functions. The protocols at the application layer can take several forms. Some, such as the File Transfer Protocol (FTP), define an entire application themselves, whereas others, such as Hypertext Transfer Protocol (HTTP), are protocols that are designed to provide specific services to other applications.

The layers of the TCP/IP stack relate to each other just as the OSI model layers do. The protocols at each layer provide services to the layer above, which enables an application at the top of the stack to package its data and prepare it for transmission over the network.

TCP/IP Protocols

Figure 2.2 illustrates the primary TCP/IP protocols and their places in the protocol stack. The following sections examine some of the protocols that operate at the various layers.

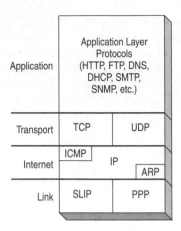

Figure 2.2   The TCP/IP protocols and the protocol stack

Link Layer Protocols

The TCP/IP link layer protocols, SLIP and PPP, support a variety of different network interface hardware implementations, including one of the most common ones, the standard asynchronous dial-up modem used by millions of personal computers to connect to the Internet or another remote network. SLIP and PPP are both known as *end-to-end protocols* because they are used by two computers communicating over a dedicated connection, such as a telephone line. These protocols cannot support computers on a shared network medium, as Ethernet and Token Ring do.

In the case of a modem-equipped computer, TCP/IP provides the entire protocol stack except for the physical layer (and, at times, parts of the application layer). The network, transport, and application layers use the standard TCP/IP protocols, with either SLIP or PPP running at the link layer. The physical layer is implemented by the modem itself, which generally can use a variety of modulation, compression, and error correction protocols, depending on the nature of the connection. In this case the physical layer protocols are implemented totally in the hardware and are completely separate from the link layer and above.

Serial Line Internet Protocol (SLIP)

SLIP is the simplest communication protocol, providing the connected computers with nothing more than a means to determine when the end of a packet has been reached. No actual stand defines the protocol, although the IETF has published RFC 1055, with the rather odd title "A Nonstandard for Transmission of IP Datagrams over Serial Lines." The SLIP frame consists only of a 1-byte end delimiter with the hexadecimal value c0, which the computer transmits at the end of every packet. Some SLIP implementations use two end delimiters per packet, one before and one after, as shown in Figure 2.3. This prevents the receiving computer from interpreting any line noise that occurs between the packets as data.

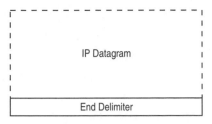

Figure 2.3 The SLIP frame

SLIP provides the connected computers with basic link layer communication capabilities and very low control overhead (1 or 2 bytes per packet, compared with 18 for Ethernet), but nothing more. There is no error correction, so corrupted packets must be detected at the upper layers, and no protocol identification mechanism, so a SLIP connection cannot multiplex network layer protocols. The result of these shortcomings is that SLIP has been all but abandoned in favor of PPP.

Point-to-Point Protocol (PPP)

PPP is the link layer protocol used by most WAN connections today, ranging from dial-up modem connections to leased lines and frame relay installations. The PPP frame (Figure 2.4) is somewhat larger and more complicated than that of SLIP, but it is still not as large as that of an Ethernet or Token Ring frame. One of the main reasons for this is that PPP does not have to include source and destination addresses in every packet. Because protocols like Ethernet support a shared network medium, every packet must be addressed to a specific computer on the network, using the 6-byte hardware addresses coded into the network interface adapters. Modems and most other WAN communication devices don't have their own addresses, and they don't need them. PPP connects two (and only two) computers, so there is no need for them to identify themselves in every packet. The computers can identify themselves once by exchanging IP addresses during the link establishment process, but eliminating the source and destination addresses from the data transmissions saves 12 bytes per packet of control overhead.

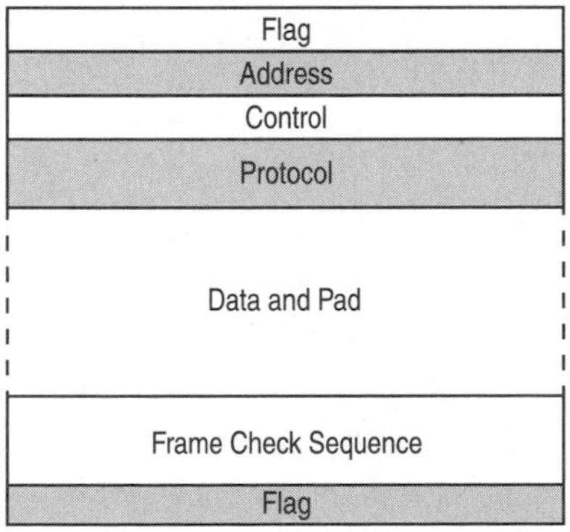

Flag
Address
Control
Protocol
Data and Pad
Frame Check Sequence
Flag

Figure 2.4 The PPP frame

The PPP frame contains the following fields:

- **Flag (1 byte).**   Contains an end delimiter (much like that of SLIP) that indicates that the transmission of a packet is about to begin
- **Address (1 byte).**   Contains a value indicating that the packet is addressed to all recipients
- **Control (1 byte).**   Contains a code indicating that the frame contains an unnumbered information packet
- **Protocol (2 bytes).**   Identifies the protocol (usually operating at the internet layer) that generated the information in the Data field
- **Data and Pad (up to 1500 bytes).**   Contains information generated by the protocol identified in the Protocol field, plus padding if necessary
- **Frame Check Sequence (2 or 4 bytes).**   Contains a checksum value that the receiving system will use to detect transmission errors
- **Flag (1 byte).**   Indicates that the transmission of the packet has been completed

Despite the simplicity of its frame, PPP provides many services, including network layer multiplexing, authentication, and link quality monitoring. These services do not have to be implemented in the frame header, however, because each computer is only communicating with one other computer. Instead of adding bulk to the frame, PPP performs an elaborate connection establishment process before the computer transmits any application data. During this process, the two computers exchange information about their capabilities and negotiate a set of configuration parameters common to both of them.

The connection establishment process involves the use of several different ancillary protocols, including the Link Control Protocol (LCP), authentication protocols such as the Challenge Handshake Authentication Protocol (CHAP) and the Password Authentication Protocol (PAP), and network control protocols, such as the IP Control Protocol (IPCP). These protocols, along with PPP, are defined in separate RFCs, which are listed in Table 2.1.

Table 2.1   PPP Standards Published as RFCs

Document	Title
RFC 1661	The Point-to-Point Protocol (PPP)
RFC 1662	PPP in HDLC-like Framing
RFC 1663	PPP Reliable Transmission
RFC 1332	The PPP Internet Protocol Control Protocol (IPCP)
RFC 1552	The PPP Internetworking Packet Exchange Control Protocol (IPXCP)
RFC 1334	PPP Authentication Protocols
RFC 1994	PPP Challenge Handshake Authentication Protocol (CHAP)
RFC 1989	PPP Link Quality Monitoring

The PPP connection establishment process consists of seven distinct phases, which are as follows:

1. **Link dead.**   The two computers begin in a state where there is no communication between them, until one of the two initiates a physical layer connection, typically by running a program that triggers the network interface hardware. The most common example is the use of a program that causes the modem to dial.

2. **Link establishment.**   After the hardware at both ends has established a physical layer connection, one computer generates a PPP frame containing an LCP Request message. The computers use LCP to negotiate the parameters they will employ during the rest of the PPP session. The message contains a list of options that the computer is capable of using, such as a specific authentication protocol, link quality protocol, header compression, network layer protocols, and so on. The receiving system can then acknowledge the use of these options or deny them and propose a list of its own. Eventually, the two systems agree on a list of options they have in common.

3. **Authentication.**   If the two computers have agreed to the use of a particular authentication protocol during the link establishment phase, they exchange PPP frames that perform a user authentication sequence. Most PPP connections use PAP or CHAP, but there are other authentication protocols as well.

4. **Link quality monitoring.**   If the two computers have negotiated the use of a link quality monitoring protocol during the link establishment phase, an exchange of messages for that protocol occurs after the authentication process is complete.

5. **Network layer protocol configuration.**   For each of the network or internet layer protocols the computers have agreed to use, they perform a separate exchange of messages using the appropriate network control protocols.

6. **Link open.**   When the network control protocol negotiations are complete, the PPP connection is fully established, and the exchange of packets containing application data can begin.

7. **Link termination.**   When the two computers have finished communicating, they sever the PPP connection by exchanging LCP termination messages, after which the systems return to the link dead state.

Internet Protocol (IP)

Regardless of whether a computer is using a TCP/IP protocol at the link layer, IP, operating at the internet layer, is ultimately responsible for the end-to-end communications between the source and destination systems. When IP has encapsulated the information it receives from the transport layer into a unit called a *datagram*, that information remains intact until the packet reaches its final recipient, much as an envelope remains sealed as it winds its way through the postal system.

IP is defined in RFC 791 and is the most important of the TCP/IP protocols. You'll learn a great deal about the specific mechanisms of IP later in this chapter and in other chapters of this book. The four primary functions of IP are

- Encapsulation
- Addressing
- Routing
- Fragmentation

As mentioned earlier, IP is responsible for encapsulating transport layer information into datagrams that remain intact throughout the packet's journey through the internetwork. A link or data-link layer frame, by contrast, is a construction designed solely for transport across a single network, such as from a workstation to a router or from a client computer to an Internet service provider (ISP).

The IP encapsulation process involves the attachment of a 20-byte IP header (Figure 2.5) to transport layer data segments of a length appropriate to the network over which the datagram will be transmitted.

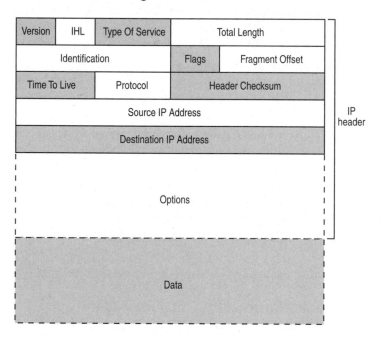

Figure 2.5   The IP datagram format

The IP header consists of the following fields:

- **Version (4 bits).**   Specifies the version of the IP protocol in use. The value for the current implementation is 4, although IPv6 is currently in development.

- **IHL (Internet Header Length) (4 bits).**   Specifies the length of the IP header in 32-bit words. When the header contains no optional fields, the value is 5.

- **TOS (Type of Service) (1 byte).**   Bits 1 through 3 and 8 in the TOS field are unused. Bits 4 through 7 specify the service priority for the datagram.

- **Total Length (2 bytes).**   Specifies the length of the datagram, including all the header fields and the data.

- **Identification (2 bytes).**   Contains a unique value for each datagram, which the destination system uses to associate and reassemble fragments.

- **Flags (3 bits).**   Contains bits used during the datagram fragmentation process. Bit 1 is unused. When bit 2 is set to a value of 1, the datagram cannot be fragmented by any system. A value of 0 in bit 3 indicates that the last fragment of the datagram has been transmitted; a value of 1 indicates that fragments are still awaiting transmission.

- **Fragment Offset (13 bits).**   When a datagram has been fragmented, the Fragment Offset field specifies the location of the current fragment in the datagram.

- **TTL (Time to Live) (1 byte).**   Contains a value that is reduced by one each time the datagram is processed by a router on the way to its destination. If the value reaches 0, the packet is discarded, whether or not it has reached the destination.

- **Protocol (1 byte).**   Identifies the protocol that generated the information in the Data field, using values found in the "Assigned Numbers" RFC (RFC 1700) and the PROTOCOL file found on every TCP/IP system.

- **Header Checksum (2 bytes).**   Contains a checksum value computed on the IP header fields only (not the data), which the destination system uses for error detection.

- **Source IP Address (4 bytes).**   Contains the IP address of the system that originated the datagram.

- **Destination IP Address (4 bytes).**   Contains the IP address of the system that will be the ultimate recipient of the datagram.

- **Options (variable).**   Can contain any of 16 options defined in the "Assigned Numbers" RFC, each of which consists of an option type, option length, and option data subfield.

- **Data (variable).**   Contains the payload of the datagram, usually consisting of information passed down from the transport layer protocols.

The Source IP Address and Destination IP Address fields in every IP header identify the computer that created the datagram and its final recipient. IP addresses are 32-bit values that identify both a particular network interface and the network to which that interface is connected. The IP addressing system is completely separate from the hardware configuration of the networking device and from any other addresses a device might have. For more information about IP addressing, see Lesson 2 of this chapter.

Routing is the process by which IP passes datagrams from system to system until they reach their final destination. A router is a device that connects TCP/IP networks and maintains information about the other routers in its immediate vicinity. When a router receives a packet over one of its network interfaces, it reads the destination IP address and forwards the packet to another router or to the destination system itself. For more information about how IP routes data, see Chapter 6, "Routing IP."

Fragmentation occurs during the routing of packets through an internetwork. The size of the largest packet a network can handle is called its maximum transmission unit (MTU). When a router receives a packet that is too large to be transmitted out over another network, the router splits the datagram into fragments and encapsulates each one in a separate packet. Each fragment of a particular datagram contains the same value for the Identification field in the IP header. The router modifies the values of the bits in the Flags field to indicate whether there are additional fragments to transmit or whether this is the final fragment for the datagram. The router also inserts a value in the Fragment Offset field representing the number of bytes that have been transmitted in the previous fragments. For example, the fragment offset value for the first fragment in a datagram is always zero. If the first fragment is 512 bytes long, the fragment offset value of the second fragment is 513.

As each fragment is transmitted toward the destination, it might reach a router that has to fragment it further, to accommodate a network with an even smaller MTU. Datagrams can be fragmented, and their fragments fragmented, as many times as is necessary on the way to their destination. None of the fragments is reassembled until they all reach the system identified by the Destination IP Address field in their IP headers.

Address Resolution Protocol (ARP)

The source IP address and destination IP address values in the IP header of a particular packet might not represent the same computer as the hardware addresses used in Ethernet and Token Ring headers at the data-link layer. This is because the addresses in the IP header always refer to the packet's original sender and its final recipient. The data-link layer addresses always refer to the packet's most recent sender and its next recipient, either or both of which could be routers along the way to the final destination.

When reconciling the data-link and network layer addresses on a LAN, however, one important question remains. How does IP, after it determines what the packet's next intermediate destination will be, discover the hardware address of that destination, which the data-link layer protocol needs to encapsulate the datagram? The IP routing process works with IP addresses, but at some point the IP address of the packet's next destination must be converted into a data-link layer hardware address.

The answer to this question is found in the Address Resolution Protocol (ARP). ARP is a protocol that is defined in RFC 826, "An Ethernet Address Resolution Protocol," and that operates on the cusp of the internet and link layers. Authorities differ as to exactly where ARP should be located in the protocol stack, but its operation is relatively simple. As the name implies, ARP is a protocol used by LAN computers that resolves IP addresses into the hardware addresses used at the data-link layer. A computer with an IP address of a router or computer that it must resolve generates an ARP Request message containing that IP address and broadcasts it to the local network. All the other TCP/IP systems on the network receive the message and compare the enclosed IP address with their own. The computer using the requested IP address then generates an ARP Reply message containing the hardware address of its network interface adapter and returns it to the sender as a unicast (that is, a transmission addressed to a single destination). The original sender can then use the hardware address from the reply message to address its data-link layer frames to the replying computer.

To reduce the amount of broadcast traffic generated by ARP, TCP/IP systems typically maintain a cache of recently resolved addresses. This way, a computer performing a single transaction consisting of many transmitted packets does not have to repeatedly resolve the same IP address.

Note   You can manipulate the ARP cache on a Microsoft Windows computer using the Arp.exe utility. For more information about using Arp.exe, see Lesson 2 of Chapter 3, "Implementing TCP/IP."

There is another TCP/IP protocol called the Reverse Address Resolution Protocol (RARP) that utilizes the same message formats as ARP, but for the opposite purpose—to request an IP address from a server by furnishing a hardware address. RARP was developed for use by diskless workstations so that they could request and retrieve an IP address from a RARP server on the local network. The protocol is no longer used.

Internet Control Message Protocol (ICMP)

ICMP, as defined in RFC 792, is another internet-layer TCP/IP protocol, but it does not carry application data as IP does. ICMP has two functions: it carries request and reply data for diagnostic programs like ping, and it provides error reporting services for intermediate systems. ICMP messages are carried inside IP datagrams, just like transport layer data.

Note All TCP/IP devices are either intermediate systems or end systems. An *end system* is either the computer that generated a transmission or the ultimate receiver of it. An *intermediate system* is a router that processes a packet and forwards it on its way to the destination.

Because IP is an end-to-end protocol, it is designed so that only the destination system reads the contents of the datagram and processes the data. If an error should occur during the transmission of the packet, preventing it from reaching the destination, the destination system has no way of knowing about the problem or its cause. ICMP enables intermediate systems to report errors back to the end system that generated a packet. For example, if a packet cannot be forwarded to its destination, a router on the path generates a Destination Unreachable message. The problem might be caused by the failure of the end system for which the packet is destined or a router failure that renders the destination network unreachable. There are specific ICMP error messages for various causes of the problem, as well as other messages used when other types of problems occur.

There are three limitations to the generation of ICMP error messages, which are intended to prevent the inundation of a network with ICMP traffic. These limitations are as follows:

- TCP/IP computers do not generate ICMP error messages in response to other ICMP error messages. This is to prevent two computers from continuously sending error messages in response to each other.

- In the event of a fragmentation problem, an ICMP error is generated only for the first fragment of a datagram, not for subsequent fragments.

- TCP/IP computers do not generate ICMP error messages in response to broadcast, multicast, or loopback transmissions, or transmissions with 0.0.0.0 as the source IP address.

ICMP query messages enable TCP/IP computers to perform diagnostic functions, such as testing connections to other systems and requesting and receiving router information. The ping program uses ICMP Echo Request and Echo Reply messages to determine whether the TCP/IP implementation on a particular destination system is functioning properly. A computer transmits an Echo Request message containing a sampling of test data to a particular system, which then replies with an Echo Reply message containing the same data. If the data is received intact in a timely manner, the connection is judged to be functioning properly.

Note For information about TCP and UDP, the transport layer protocols in the TCP/IP suite, see Lesson 3 of this chapter.

Application Layer Protocols

The TCP/IP protocols operating at the application layer are diverse, providing a variety of services to TCP/IP client and server applications. Some of the commonly used TCP/IP application layer protocols are as follows:

- **Hypertext Transfer Protocol (HTTP).**   The protocol used by Web clients and servers to exchange file requests and the files themselves. A client browser opens a TCP connection to a server and requests a particular file, and the server replies by sending that file, which the browser displays as a home page. HTTP messages also contain a variety of fields containing information about the communicating systems.

- **Secure Hypertext Transfer Protocol (S-HTTP or HTTPS).**   A security protocol that works with HTTP to provide server or user authentication and data encryption services to Web client/server transactions.

- **File Transfer Protocol (FTP).**   A protocol used to transfer files between TCP/IP systems. An FTP client can browse through the directory structure of a connected server and select files to download or upload. FTP is unique in that it uses two separate ports for its communications. When an FTP client connects to a server, it uses TCP port 21 to establish a control connection. When the user initiates a file download, the program opens a second connection using port 20 for the data transfer. This data connection is closed automatically when the file transfer is completed, but the control connection remains open until the client explicitly terminates it. FTP is also unusual in that on most TCP/IP systems, the protocol is implemented as a self-contained application, rather than a protocol used by other applications.

- **Trivial File Transfer Protocol (TFTP).**   A minimalized, low-overhead version of FTP that can transfer files across a network but uses the UDP protocol instead of TCP and does not include FTP's authentication and user interface features. TFTP was originally designed for use on diskless workstations that had to download an executable system file from a network server in order to boot.

- **Simple Mail Transfer Protocol (SMTP).**   The protocol that e-mail servers use to transmit messages to each other across a network. E-mail clients also use SMTP to send their outgoing e-mail messages to a server.

- **Post Office Protocol (POP3).**   One of the protocols that e-mail clients use to retrieve their messages from an e-mail server.

- **Internet Mail Access Protocol (IMAP4).**   An e-mail protocol that clients use to access their mail messages on a server. IMAP expands on the capabilities of POP3 by adding services such as the ability to store mail messages permanently on the server in individual folders created by the user, rather than downloading them to an e-mail client.

- **Network Time Protocol (NTP).**   A protocol that enables computers to synchronize their clocks with other computers on the network by exchanging time signals.

- **Domain Name System (DNS).**   TCP/IP systems use DNS to resolve Internet host names into the IP addresses they need to communicate.

- **Dynamic Host Configuration Protocol (DHCP).**   A protocol that network workstations use to request IP addresses and other TCP/IP configuration parameter settings from a server.

- **Simple Network Management Protocol (SNMP).**   A network management protocol used by network administrators to gather information about various components distributed around the network. Remote programs—called agents—gather information and transmit it to a central network management console using SNMP messages.

- **Telnet.**   A command-line terminal emulation program that enables a user to log on to a remote computer on the network and execute commands there.

Exercise 1: Examining ARP Traffic with Network Monitor

In this exercise, you use the Network Monitor application supplied with Windows 2000 Server to capture samples of the ARP messages on your network and examine their contents. This exercise assumes that you have a Windows 2000 Server computer already connected to a LAN, with Network Monitor already installed. For instructions on how to install and use Network Monitor, see Lesson 1 in Chapter 14, "Monitoring Network Activity."

To capture samples of ARP messages and examine their contents, complete the following steps:

1. Click Start and select Network Monitor from the Administrative tools program group. If necessary, select the network interface corresponding to the LAN adapter.

2. Select Start from the Capture menu to begin capturing the packets transmitted over the network.

3. Click Start and select Run from the Start menu to open the Run dialog box.

4. Type the name of another Windows computer on your network in the Open box using Universal Naming Convention (UNC) notation, such as *server*. Click OK. What happens? What is the purpose of this step?

5. Return to the Network Monitor window and select Stop And View from the Capture menu to display a Capture window.

6. Select Filter from the Display menu to open the Display Filter dialog box.

7. Double-click the Protocol==Any branch of the decision tree to open the Expression dialog box.

8. Confirm that the Protocol tab is selected and click Disable All to remove all entries from the Enabled Protocols list.

9. Select ARP_RARP in the Disabled Protocols list and click Enable to add it to the Enabled Protocols list.

10. Click OK to close the Expression dialog box and click OK again to close the Display Filter dialog box. What happens to the Capture window display (see Figure 2.6)?

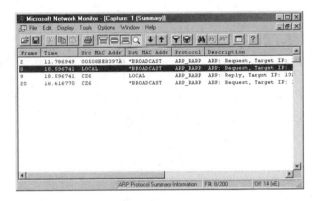

Figure 2.6   The Network Monitor Capture window with a display filter applied

11. In the Capture window, locate a frame entry in which Local appears in the Src MAC Addr column and double-click it to display the contents of the frame, as shown in Figure 2.7.

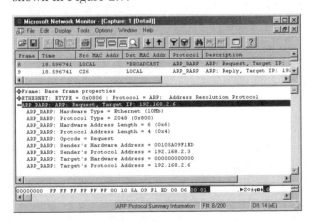

Figure 2.7   An ARP Request message

What type of ARP message is encapsulated in the frame?

What is the destination MAC address for the frame? Why is this?

Notice that the frame contains four address fields, two for the sender's hardware (MAC) and protocol (IP) addresses and two for the target system's hardware and protocol addresses. Which of the four does not contain a value in this packet?

12. Locate a frame farther down in the Capture window with Local in the Dst MAC Addr column. The Src MAC Addr column should contain the name of the computer you typed earlier in the Run dialog box. Click the frame to display its contents, as shown in Figure 2.8.

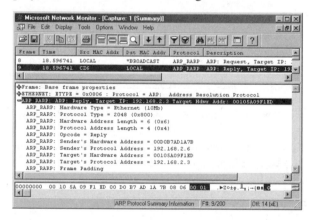

Figure 2.8   An ARP Reply message

What type of ARP message is encapsulated in the frame?

Which of the four address fields in the frame contains the hardware address for the computer whose name you typed earlier in the Run dialog box? Why is this so?

13. Close Network Monitor, answering No when the program prompts you to specify if you want to save the capture.

Exercise 2: TCP/IP Protocols

Match the protocols in the left column with the appropriate descriptions in the right column.

1. DHCP	a. Transmits e-mail messages between servers
2. ARP	b. Routes datagrams to their final destination
3. IP	c. Provides transport layer services
4. POP3	d. Resolves host names into IP addresses
5. SNMP	e. Connects two systems at the link layer
6. ICMP	f. Converts IP addresses into hardware addresses
7. TCP	g. Automatically configures TCP/IP clients
8. DNS	h. Enables e-mail clients to retrieve messages from servers
9. PPP	i. Carries network management data to a central console
10. SMTP	j. Carries error messages from routers to end systems

Lesson Review

1. How does ARP minimize the number of broadcasts it generates?

2. Which of the following fields is blank in an ARP Request message?
   a. Sender Hardware Address
   b. Sender Protocol Address
   c. Target Hardware Address
   d. Target Protocol Address

3. Why are ARP Request messages transmitted as broadcasts?

4. Which of the following fields in an ARP Reply message contains a value supplied by the system transmitting the message?

    a. Sender Hardware Address

    b. Sender Protocol Address

    c. Target Hardware Address

    d. Target Protocol Address

5. Which application layer protocol uses two port numbers at the server?

    a. SMTP

    b. HTTP

    c. DHCP

    d. FTP

Lesson Summary

- The TCP/IP protocols were developed for use on the fledgling Internet and are designed to support systems using any computing platform or operating system.

- The TCP/IP protocol stack consists of four layers: link, internet, transport, and application.

- IP is the primary protocol in the TCP/IP suite, providing functions such as data encapsulation, addressing, routing, and fragmentation.

- IP uses the ARP protocol to resolve IP addresses into the hardware addresses needed for data-link layer protocol communications.

- The ICMP protocol performs numerous functions at the internet layer, including reporting errors and querying systems for information.

- Application layer protocols are not involved in the data transfer processes performed by the lower layers; instead, they enable specific programs and services running on TCP/IP computers to exchange messages.

Lesson 2: IP Addressing and Subnetting

Addressing is one of the main functions of the Internet Protocol (IP), the one that is primarily responsible for the protocol suite's cross-platform interoperability. Every device on a TCP/IP network must have a unique IP address, which enables any other device to send traffic directly to it, even devices on remote networks. In this lesson you learn about the structure of IP addresses and how to assign them to the computers on your network.

After this lesson, you will be able to

- Understand the structure of an IP address
- Describe the function of a subnet mask
- List the three IP address classes
- Create subnets on a network given specific criteria

Estimated lesson time: 60 minutes

IP Address Structure

An IP address is a 32-bit binary value that is typically expressed as four 8-bit decimal numbers, separated by periods, as in 192.168.63.45. This is called *dotted decimal notation*. Each of the four 8-bit values is called an *octet*, or sometimes a *quad* or a *byte*. To convert a binary address into dotted decimal notation, you split the 32 bits into four 8-bit groups and convert each group separately, as follows:

```
   11000000   10101000   00011000   10100111

     192        168         24         167      = 192.168.24.167
```

An 8-bit binary number can have 256 possible values, which are represented in decimal form as the numerals 0 to 255. An IP address can never have a value greater than 255 for one of its octets.

Note The term *octet* is most commonly used in the TCP/IP standards to refer to one of the 8-bit values in an IP address. At the time the protocols were developed, there were still computer systems in common use that used 7-bit bytes, which prevented the use of that term.

An IP address identifies both a specific TCP/IP device (called a *host*) and the network on which the device is located. This is possible because every IP address consists of two parts: a network identifier and a host identifier. The network identifier always precedes the host identifier, but the dividing line between the two can be located anywhere in the 32-bit value. This two-tiered arrangement (a common one on the Internet) is what makes the administration of IP addresses practical on a large scale.

The Internet is by far the largest TCP/IP network in existence, with millions of computers located on thousands of networks around the world. Every one of those computers visible from the Internet has to have a unique IP address. Rather than undertake the monumental task of creating a central registrar to keep track of each of these millions of addresses, a body called the Internet Assigned Numbers Authority (IANA) functions as a registrar for networks, assigning identifiers to networks all over the world. The administrators of the individual networks are then responsible for assigning host identifiers to each computer on their networks.

Splitting addresses into networks and hosts also makes IP routing possible. For a TCP/IP internetwork to function efficiently, the routers that pass data packets between networks do not have to know the exact location of the host for which a packet is ultimately destined. Routers only know what network the host is located on and use information stored in their routing tables to determine how to get the packet to the destination host's network. After the packet is delivered to the destination network, the last router in the path delivers it to the appropriate host.

Network Identifiers

The *network identifier* indicates the TCP/IP hosts that are located on the same physical network. All hosts on the same physical network must be assigned the same network identifier to communicate with each other. If you are running an internetwork that consists of multiple networks connected by routers, a unique network ID is required for each network, including each WAN connection (which is a separate network unto itself). For example, in Figure 2.9, networks 1 and 3 represent two LANs at different locations, each of which is connected to a router. Network 2 represents the WAN connecting the routers and combining the two LANs into an internetwork. Each TCP/IP device on all three networks must have an IP address with the appropriate network identifier for that network.

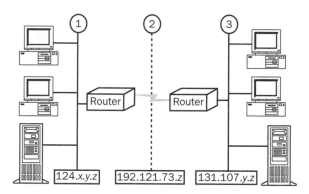

Figure 2.9   Two LANs, connected by routers

The routers in the figure are each connected to two networks and must each have two IP addresses with different network identifiers. This illustrates an important aspect of IP addressing, which is that IP addresses are actually assigned to network interfaces, not necessarily to computers. A computer with more than one network interface (such as two NICs, or one NIC and a modem) must have a separate IP address for each interface.

When a TCP/IP network is to be connected to the Internet, it must use a network address assigned by the IANA. This is to prevent the existence of duplicate IP addresses in the Internet. Today, virtually all network addresses are registered with the IANA by ISPs, which provide them to customers for a fee. If a network is not connected to the Internet, it does not have to use a registered network address.

Host Identifiers

The *host identifier* is a value assigned to a specific network interface connected to a network. Every host identifier assigned to a network interface on a given network must be unique. In other words, you can have duplicate host identifiers on your network, but only if they have different network identifiers. When two computers on a network have exactly the same IP address, usually neither of them functions properly. Windows 2000, as well as some other operating systems, check for a duplicate IP address when the computer starts and, if it finds one, disables the TCP/IP client until a proper address is assigned.

Subnet Masks

Most of the addressing systems used in computer networking use multiple identifiers for a single device. However, in most of these cases, the identifiers are of fixed lengths. For example, the hardware addresses assigned to Ethernet and Token Ring NICs all consist of a 3-byte code that identifies the device's manufacturer and a 3-byte code that identifies the specific device. IP addresses are different, however, in that the network and host identifiers are not always the same length. Depending on the configuration of your internetwork, you can use addresses that support a large number of networks with relatively few hosts per network or a few networks with a large number of hosts on each. You do this by using addresses with different sized identifiers.

The main problem caused by having identifiers of variable lengths is that there is no obvious way to determine where the network identifier in an IP address ends and where the host identifier begins. To resolve this problem, TCP/IP clients always include what is known as a subnet mask with each address. A *subnet mask* is a 32-bit binary value that uses 1s and 0s to designate the network and host identifiers. A 1 indicates a network identifier bit and a 0 indicates a host identifier bit. As with an IP address, the 32 bits are then converted into dotted decimal notation. For example, if the IP address 192.168.24.167 is paired with a subnet mask of 255.255.255.0, this means that the first three octets of the IP address (192.168.24) are the network identifier and the last octet (167) is the host identifier. You know this because when you convert the address and mask to binary form, you see the following:

```
IP Address:    11000000  10101000  00011000  10100111

Subnet Mask:   11111111  11111111  11111111  00000000
```

The presence of the 1 bits in the mask indicates that the corresponding bits in the IP address are the network identifier bits.

IP Address Classes

The IANA assigns network addresses in different classes, based on the number of hosts that the network has to support. The three classes used by standard Internet computers are Class A, Class B, and Class C. The properties of each of these classes are shown in Table 2.2.

Table 2.2   IP Address Classes and their Properties

	Class A	Class B	Class C
Subnet Mask	255.0.0.0	255.255.0.0	255.255.255.0
Values of First Bits	0	10	110
Values of First Byte	1–127	128–191	192–223
Number of Network Bits	8	16	24
Number of Host Bits	24	16	8
Number of Networks	126	16,384	2,097,152
Number of Hosts	16,777,214	65,534	254

Note   In addition to Classes A, B, and C, there are two more classes: D and E. Class D addresses begin with the bit values 1110 and are reserved for use as IP multicast addresses. A multicast transmission is one that addresses a specific group of systems on a network. Class E addresses begin with the bit values 11110 and are as yet unused.

As you can see in the table, the IP addresses for a Class C network use 24 bits for the network identifier and 8 bits for the host identifier. This means that there can be more than 2 million Class C networks on the Internet, and each network can have up to 254 hosts. Because the first 3 bits of a Class C address must have binary values of 110, this makes the range of possible values for the first byte 11000000 to 11011111, which in decimal form is 192 and 223. This means that when you see an IP address in which the value of the first byte falls between 192 and 223, you know you are looking at a Class C address and that the default subnet mask is 255.255.255.0.

IP Addressing Rules

If you noticed that the table states that a Class C address can have up to 254 hosts, you might be wondering what happened to the other two, considering that an 8-bit binary number can have 256 possible values. The reason for this is that there are some additional IP addressing rules that prevent the use of certain address values. These rules are as follows:

- The network identifier cannot have a first byte value of 127. This value is reserved for loopback and diagnostic functions.

- The network identifier and host identifier bits cannot all be 1s. If all bits are set to 1, the address is interpreted as a broadcast rather than an individual host.

- The network identifier and host identifier bits cannot all be 0s. If all bits are set to 0, the address is interpreted to mean "this network only." Some networking systems permit the use of "all zero" addresses for subnets, including Windows 2000 and most routers, but you should be certain that all the equipment on your network supports this feature before you attempt to use these addresses.

The result is that the host identifier in a Class C network can have any value from 00000001 to 11111110, or 1 to 254, because 00000000 (0) and 11111111 (255) are excluded. This makes the general formula for determining the number of network or host identifiers provided by a given number of bits to be $2^x - 2$, where x is the number of bits.

Private Network Addresses

IP addresses that are registered with the IANA are essential for computers that are to be visible from the Internet, such as Web and e-mail servers. However, there are situations in which computers that access the Internet do not require registered addresses, such as when you use network address translation (NAT) or a proxy server to provide users with Internet connectivity. In these cases, you can theoretically use any IP addresses for your network, as long as you follow the standard addressing rules, such as having the same network identifier for all the computers on a single LAN. However, simply choosing network addresses at random can lead to problems. If you happen to select an address that is already registered to another Internet site, for example, your users will have problems accessing that site.

To address this problem, the IANA has allocated specific ranges of IP addresses for use on private networks. These addresses are not registered to any single user and, therefore, will not cause conflicts. Table 2.3 lists the private network addresses for each of the address classes. It is strongly recommended that you use these addresses when building an unregistered network, whether you are currently connecting it to the Internet or not.

Table 2.3   IP Address Ranges for Private Networks

Class	Network Address
A	10.0.0.0 through 10.255.255.255
B	172.16.0.0 through 172.31.255.255
C	192.168.0.0 through 192.168.255.255

Subnetting

If you are an astute reader, there might be a few questions on your mind after your study of Table 2.3. First, if you can tell the class of an IP address from the value of its first byte, why do you need a subnet mask? Second, why do you need Class A addresses that support over 16 million hosts when there is no single network in the world anywhere near that large? The answer to both of these questions is that you can split any existing network into a group of smaller networks using a process called subnetting. *Subnetting* is a procedure in which you borrow a number of bits from the host identifier in an IP address and use them to create a *subnet identifier*, which is a secondary network identifier. Subnetting is the reason Internet network addresses are still available. If you could not subnet the Class A addresses into a large number of smaller networks, most of the host addresses in each Class A network would be wasted.

The simplest type of subnetting is when you take a Class A or B address and borrow an entire byte from the host identifier to form a subnet identifier. For example, if you take a standard Class B network address such as 172.16.0.0, you would normally use the last two bytes for your host identifiers, with a subnet mask of 255.255.0.0. To subnet this address, you can use the third byte for a subnet identifier and the fourth byte for your host identifiers, as follows (where N=network, S=subnet, and H=host):

```
NNNNNNNN NNNNNNNN SSSSSSSS HHHHHHHH
```

The subnet mask value then becomes 255.255.255.0 because the third byte is no longer part of the host identifier.

With the new subnet mask in place, you can then create up to 254 subnets by using various values for the third byte of the address, with up to 254 hosts in each subnet. The first host in the first subnet, for example, would have the IP address 172.16.1.1; the second host in the first subnet would be 172.16.1.2. The first host in the second subnet would be 172.16.2.1; the second host in the second subnet would be 172.16.2.2.

Calculating Subnet Masks

When you create subnets where the boundaries of the subnet identifier fall between bytes, the task of working out the correct IP addresses and subnet masks to use is simple. However, it is possible for the subnet identifier to use any number of bits, and when the boundaries don't fall between bytes, the task of calculating the addresses and mask is more complex. Suppose, for example, you have a Class C network address, such as 192.168.24.0, and you want to create 10 subnets supporting 12 hosts each. You can do this by borrowing 4 bits from the 8-bit host identifier, to create a 4-bit subnet identifier, as follows:

```
NNNNNNNN NNNNNNNN NNNNNNNN SSSSHHHH
```

Because $2^4 - 2 = 14$, the subnet identifier is large enough to support 10 subnets, and the 4 bits left as the host identifier permit up to 14 hosts per subnet. To compute the subnet mask you should use with this arrangement, you add together the number of network and subnet identifier bits and mask them all, resulting in the following binary value:

```
11111111 11111111 11111111 11110000
```

Clearly, the values of the first 3 bytes of the mask are 255.255.255, as always. The fourth byte now has a value of 11110000, which when converted to decimal form, becomes 240. Therefore, the subnet mask you should use with all your IP addresses on this network is 255.255.255.240.

Tip   The easiest way to convert binary values to decimals is, of course, to use a calculator. The Windows Calculator in Scientific mode does this easily. However, when taking the MCSE exam, no such calculator is available, so you better know how to do it by hand. To convert a binary number to a decimal, you assign a numerical value to each bit, starting from the right with 1 and proceeding to the left, doubling the value each time. The values for an 8-bit number are therefore as follows:

```
128  64  32  16  8  4  2  1
```

You then line up the values of your 8-bit binary number with the eight conversion values, as follows:

```
 1   1   1   1   0   0   0   0

128  64  32  16  8   4   2   1
```

Finally, you add together the conversion values for the 1 bits:

```
 1   1   1   1   0   0   0   0

128 +64 +32 +16 +0  +0  +0  +0    =240
```

Therefore, the decimal equivalent to the binary value 11110000 is 240.

Another method for converting the binary value of a subnet mask byte to a decimal is to use the formula $256 - 2^x$, where x is the number of 0s in the byte. As an example, for a byte value of 11000000, the number of 0s in the byte is 6. You subtract 2^6, which is 64, from 256, leaving 192 ($256 - 2^6 = 192$).

Calculating IP Addresses Using the Binary Method

To calculate the IP addresses for the network, you can again work with the binary values. In this example the values for the first 3 bytes in these Class C network addresses are the same for all the hosts:

```
11000000   10101000   00011000

   192         168        24     = 192.168.24
```

To compute the value of the fourth byte, you start with the first possible subnet identifier value, which is 0001, and the first possible host identifier value, which is also 0001. Then, you increment the host identifier values until you use all 4 bits, arriving at the following 14 possible values for the first subnet:

```
0001 0001

0001 0010

0001 0011

0001 0100

0001 0101

0001 0110

0001 0111

0001 1000

0001 1001

0001 1010

0001 1011

0001 1100

0001 1101

0001 1110
```

You then convert each of these 8-bit values into decimal form to achieve the following results:

```
00010001 = 17

00010010 = 18

00010011 = 19
```

```
00010100 = 20
```

```
00010101 = 21
```

```
00010110 = 22
```

```
00010111 = 23
```

```
00011000 = 24
```

```
00011001 = 25
```

```
00011010 = 26
```

```
00011011 = 27
```

```
00011100 = 28
```

```
00011101 = 29
```

```
00011110 = 30
```

Therefore, the IP addresses for your first subnet are as follows:

```
192.168.24.17
```

```
192.168.24.18
```

```
192.168.24.19
```

```
192.168.24.20
```

```
192.168.24.21
```

```
192.168.24.22
```

```
192.168.24.23
```

```
192.168.24.24
```

```
192.168.24.25
```

```
192.168.24.26
```

```
192.168.24.27
```

```
192.168.24.28
```

```
192.168.24.29
```

```
192.168.24.30
```

You then move on to the second subnet, and the third, and the fourth, which results in the following values for the fourth byte:

```
0010 0001 = 33       0011 0001 = 49       0100 0001 = 65

0010 0010 = 34       0011 0010 = 50       0100 0010 = 66

0010 0011 = 35       0011 0011 = 51       0100 0011 = 67

0010 0100 = 36       0011 0100 = 52       0100 0100 = 68

0010 0101 = 37       0011 0101 = 53       0100 0101 = 69

0010 0110 = 38       0011 0110 = 54       0100 0110 = 70

0010 0111 = 39       0011 0111 = 55       0100 0111 = 71

0010 1000 = 40       0011 1000 = 56       0100 1000 = 72

0010 1001 = 41       0011 1001 = 57       0100 1001 = 73

0010 1010 = 42       0011 1010 = 58       0100 1010 = 74

0010 1011 = 43       0011 1011 = 59       0100 1011 = 75

0010 1100 = 44       0011 1100 = 60       0100 1100 - 76

0010 1101 = 45       0011 1101 = 61       0100 1101 = 77

0010 1110 = 46       0011 1110 = 62       0100 1110 = 78
```

By continuing to increment the subnet and host identifiers in this manner, you can determine the range of IP addresses for each of the 14 possible subnets.

Calculating IP Addresses Using the Subtraction Method

The binary calculation method works well, but it is relatively slow and tedious, and it requires many calculations for converting binary values to decimals. When you understand the relationship between the subnet identifier values and the host identifier values, there's another method you can use to calculate the IP addresses much more easily. When you determine the subnet mask you're going to use, you subtract the decimal value of the byte that contains both subnet and host identifier bits from 256 to find your first subnet. Then you increment the result by itself repeatedly until you reach the subnet mask value.

In the previous example, you have decided to use a subnet mask of 255.255.255.240. When you subtract 240 from 256, you get 16, which is your first subnet. You then increment 16 by 16 to get 32, which is your second subnet. You then keep adding 16, to get 48, 64, 80, 96, 112, 128, 144, 160, 176, 192, 208, and 224. These are your 14 subnets. The actual IP addresses for your first subnet would therefore have 17 through 30 as their fourth byte values. The values 16 and 31 are omitted, because these would be addresses with host identifiers that are all 0s and all 1s, respectively. In the same way, the fourth byte values for the second subnet would range from 33 to 46. Notice that these are exactly the same values arrived at earlier using the binary method.

Calculating IP Addresses for a Class B Network

The calculations for subnetting Class A and B addresses work the same way as those for the Class C address in the previous example, except that you usually tend to be working with more bits in either the subnet or host identifier and are therefore dealing with larger numbers of subnets and hosts. For a Class B network address of 172.21.0.0, for example, the default subnet mask is 255.255.0.0, which means that you have 16 network identifier bits and 16 host identifier bits. To subnet this address, you determine how many subnets you need for your network and then calculate the number of subnet identifier bits you need using the formula $2^x - 2$. If you decide that you need 30 subnets to build your network, you arrive at the conclusion that you need 5 subnet identifier bits, because $2^5 - 2 = 30$. This means that you have 11 bits left over for the host identifier, so each of your subnets can have up to 2046 hosts (because $2^{11} - 2 = 2046$).

By borrowing 5 bits from the host identifier for your subnet identifier, you're left with the following binary subnet mask:

```
11111111 11111111 11111000 00000000

NNNNNNNN NNNNNNNN SSSSSHHH HHHHHHHH
```

Converting this mask to decimal form, you compute the value of the third byte by adding together the decimal values for each 1 bit as follows:

```
128+64+32+16+8=248
```

Therefore, the subnet mask for your entire network is 255.255.248.0.

To determine the IP addresses you will use for your computers, you perform the same calculation for the third byte value that you performed for the fourth byte of the Class C address. First, you subtract 248 from 256, leaving 8. This is your first subnet. Incrementing by 8, the second subnet is 16, the third is 24, and so on, up to 240, which is your thirtieth and final subnet. This means that the IP addresses for your first subnet range from 172.21.8.1 to 172.21.15.254. Once again, you omit 172.21.8.0 and 172.21.15.255, because these have host identifiers that are all 0s or all 1s.

When assigning addresses to the hosts on your first subnet, you start with the 172.21.8.1 to 172.21.8.255 range, then move on to 172.21.9.0 to 172.21.9.255, and then continue all the way up to 172.21.15.0 to 172.21.15.254. (Notice that you can use the 0 and 255 values for the fourth byte in these addresses, because some of the host identifier bits are part of the third byte, and they do not contain all 0s or all 1s.) All these 2046 addresses are for the hosts on the first subnet. The remaining 29 subnets on your network would then use the following address ranges:

```
172.21.16.1 to 172.21.23.254

172.21.24.1 to 172.21.31.254

172.21.32.1 to 172.21.39.254

172.21.40.1 to 172.21.47.254

172.21.48.1 to 172.21.55.254

172.21.56.1 to 172.21.63.254

172.21.64.1 to 172.21.71.254

172.21.72.1 to 172.21.79.254

172.21.80.1 to 172.21.87.254

172.21.88.1 to 172.21.95.254

172.21.96.1 to 172.21.103.254

172.21.104.1 to 172.21.111.254

172.21.112.1 to 172.21.119.254

172.21.120.1 to 172.21.127.254

172.21.128.1 to 172.21.135.254

172.21.136.1 to 172.21.143.254

172.21.144.1 to 172.21.151.254

172.21.152.1 to 172.21.159.254

172.21.160.1 to 172.21.167.254

172.21.168.1 to 172.21.175.254

172.21.176.1 to 172.21.183.254

172.21.184.1 to 172.21.191.254

172.21.192.1 to 172.21.199.254
```

```
172.21.200.1 to 172.21.207.254

172.21.208.1 to 172.21.215.254

172.21.216.1 to 172.21.223.254

172.21.224.1 to 172.21.231.254

172.21.232.1 to 172.21.239.254

172.21.240.1 to 172.21.247.254
```

Subnetting Questions in Exam 70-216

A variety of programs are available that can perform subnet calculations for you, which is far easier than manually calculating them yourself. However, Exam 70-216 invariably has a number of questions on IP address subnetting, and you must know how to perform the calculations to answer them correctly. The first step in answering these questions is to understand the notation used on the exam. Users familiar with products by Cisco Systems are probably accustomed to seeing IP address assignments written as a network address followed by a slash and the number of 1 bits in the subnet mask. For example, 192.168.54.0/24 refers to a Class C address with 192.168.54 as the network identifier and a subnet mask of 255.255.255.0. The 24 following the slash indicates the subnet mask value by specifying the number of 1 bits in the mask. In this instance the subnet mask would be as follows:

```
11111111   11111111   11111111   00000000

  255        255        255          0
```

A reference to a network address expressed as 172.18.3.0/19 would refer to a Class B address with 19 one bits in the subnet mask. This means that the address has been subnetted by augmenting the original 16 network identifier bits with 3 bits from the host identifier. The result is 19 one bits in the subnet mask, which yields the decimal value 255.255.224.0. Microsoft now uses this notation in virtually all the subnetting questions on the exam.

In many cases, the questions on the exam ask you to select the appropriate subnet mask for a particular scenario, such as the mask needed to support a particular number of hosts or subnets, or both. A computer on a subnetted network might have the correct IP address, but if its subnet mask is wrong, routers might not be able to forward packets to it and the computer might send packets to the default gateway when they are actually destined for systems on the local network.

Exercise 1: Subnetting a Class B Address

You have been assigned a single Class B network address, 172.28.0.0/16, with which you have to support a large TCP/IP network with 50 subnets of up to 1000 users each. Subnet the address and then answer the following questions.

1. How many bits do you need for the subnet identifier?

2. What subnet mask will you use for the computers?

3. How many hosts will each of your subnets support?

4. Specify the range of IP addresses you can use for your first subnet.

5. Specify the range of IP addresses you can use for your fiftieth subnet.

Lesson Review

1. Which of the following is the proper notation for an unregistered Class C network address?

    a. 192.168.72.0/24

    b. 192.168.0.0/24

    c. 192.24.0.0/16

    d. 192.16.223.0/8

2. You are constructing a new 100-node TCP/IP network that you plan to connect to the Internet. Your ISP has assigned you the network address 192.168.224.0/24. What subnet mask would you use to create four subnets of 25 hosts each?

    a. 255.255.255.0

    b. 255.255.224.0

    c. 255.255.255.224

    d. 255.255.224.255

3. You are the new administrator of a 2000 node network. There is only one router on the entire network, which provides all the computers with Internet access. The company's ISP has assigned the following eight network addresses to them:

10.24.32.0/24

10.24.33.0/24

10.24.34.0/24

10.30.35.0/24

10.30.36.0/24

10.30.37.0/24

10.30.38.0/24

10.30.39.0/24

What subnet mask could you use to minimize the complexity of the routing tables while maintaining the existing Internet connectivity?

a. 255.255.252.0

b. 255.255.255.252

c. 255.255.255.248

d. 255.255.248.0

4. How many host identifier bits do you have left after subnetting a Class A network address using the subnet mask 255.252.0.0?

a. 2

b. 10

c. 18

d. 22

5. Which of the following formulas do you use to determine how many subnets you can create with a given number of bits?

a. $256 - 2^x$

b. $2^x - 256$

c. $2^x - 2$

d. $x^2 - 2$

Lesson Summary

- Every network interface on a TCP/IP network must have a unique 32-bit IP address.

- IP addresses are composed of a network identifier and a host identifier.

- The subnet mask indicates which of the IP address bits function as the network identifier and which as the host identifier.

- To subnet an address, you allocate some of the host identifier bits to form a subnet identifier and modify the subnet mask by changing the values of the allocated bits from 0 to 1.

- The MCSE 70-216 exam expresses network addresses in the form *xxx.xxx.xxx.xxx/yy*, where the *x* values are a network identifier, and the *y* value is the number of 1 bits in the subnet mask.

Lesson 3: Understanding TCP and UDP

The transport layer of the TCP/IP stack contains protocols that work in conjunction with IP to provide a quality of service that a specific application requires. Application layer protocols use either TCP and IP or UDP and IP, depending on a variety of factors, including the amount of data to be transmitted, the tolerance of the target application to lost data, and the need for packet acknowledgments.

After this lesson, you will be able to

- Describe the functions of the TCP protocol
- List the fields in the TCP header
- Understand the TCP connection establishment and termination processes
- Describe how TCP acknowledges packets and performs flow control
- Understand how TCP and UDP use port numbers to identify application layer processes
- Describe the functions of the UDP protocol
- List the fields in the UDP header

Estimated lesson time: 40 minutes

TCP

The *Transmission Control Protocol* (TCP) is a connection-oriented protocol that is defined in RFC 793. TCP provides application layer protocols with a wide variety of services, including the following:

- Guaranteed delivery
- Packet acknowledgment
- Data segmentation
- Flow control
- Error detection
- Application identification

Applications that use the TCP/IP combination generally do so because they have to transmit relatively large amounts of data, which must arrive at the destination with precision. Most applications that transmit files between clients and servers use TCP, such as Web, FTP, and e-mail clients, and operating system network file sharing tools, such as the Windows 2000 Client for Microsoft Networks. Most of the complete files that are transmitted across a network do not fit into a single packet, so it's necessary for the transmitting computer to split the file into separate pieces and transmit each piece in a separate packet. TCP refers to the data stream supplied by the application layer protocol as a *sequence* and each of the pieces as *segments*. When the destination computer receives all the packets that comprise a sequence, it reassembles the segments back into the original file.

In an operation like this, it is usually essential that all the segments arrive at the destination in a timely manner and with every data bit intact. If one segment is missing because a packet is lost or one bit in one of the segments is garbled during the transmission, it is entirely possible that the entire sequence will be rendered useless. TCP provides services that enable the destination system to acknowledge the proper receipt of data segments, detect transmission errors, and signal the sender to retransmit segments that have been damaged or lost.

TCP Encapsulation

As with other protocols in the TCP/IP stack, TCP encapsulates the outgoing data it receives from the layer above it (the application layer) by applying a header to it and passing the data unit down to the layer below (the internet layer). TCP is also responsible for splitting the sequence into segments of the appropriate size and packaging each one separately. For incoming data, TCP receives internet layer datagrams from below, reads the header information, and passes the data inside them up to the appropriate application layer protocol.

Because TCP operates at the transport layer, it transcends the routing functions performed by IP at the internet layer. This means that TCP is strictly an end-to-end protocol. The header formulated by the transmitting computer and the enclosed data are not read or accessed in any way until the packet reaches its final destination.

The TCP header is large, at least 20 bytes long, and provides many functions. The format of the header is illustrated in Figure 2.10.

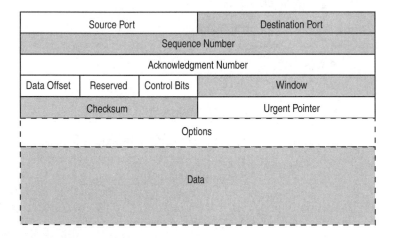

Figure 2.10   The TCP header format

The functions of the header's fields are as follows:

- **Source Port (2 bytes).**   Identifies the application layer process on the transmitting system that generated the information carried in the Data field.

- **Destination Port (2 bytes).**   Identifies the application layer process on the receiving system to which the information in the Data field will be delivered.

- **Sequence Number (4 bytes).**   Identifies the location of the data in this segment in relation to the entire sequence.

- **Acknowledgment Number (4 bytes).**   In acknowledgment (ACK) messages, the Acknowledgment Number field specifies the sequence number of the next segment that the destination system expects to receive.

- **Data Offset (4 bits).**   Specifies the number of 4-byte words in the TCP header.

- **Reserved (6 bits).**   This field is unused.

- **Control Bits (6 bits).**   Contains six flag bits (URG, ACK, PSH, RST, SYN, and FIN) that identify the functions of the message.

- **Window (2 bytes).**   Provides flow control by specifying how many bytes the receiving computer is capable of accepting from the transmitting system.

- **Checksum (2 bytes).**   Contains the results of a cyclical redundancy check (CRC) computation performed by the transmitting system and is used by the receiving system to detect errors in the TCP header, data, and parts of the IP header.

- **Urgent Pointer (2 bytes).**   When the urgent (URG) control bit is present, the Urgent Pointer field indicates which part of the data in the segment the destination system should treat as urgent.

- **Options (variable).**   Can contain information related to optional TCP connection configuration features.

- **Data (variable).**   Can contain one segment of an information sequence generated by an application layer protocol.

TCP Connection Establishment

TCP is called a connection-oriented protocol because the transmitting and receiving computers always establish a connection before they begin sending any application layer information. The connection establishment process is called a *three-way handshake*, because three separate messages are involved in the process. In most cases, TCP opens a separate connection for each file to be transmitted. For example, when you use a Web browser to connect to a server on the Internet, your computer establishes a connection with the server, downloads the home page file specified in the browser's Uniform Resource Locator (URL), and then terminates the connection. If that home page contains graphic images, the browser reads the image links in the home page file and opens a separate connection to the server for each individual image file. As a result, accessing a single Web page with your browser can require many TCP connections.

Note   It is important to remember that TCP connections are only logical connections. The TCP messages are still packaged into IP datagrams at the internet layer and routed to the destination in the usual manner. As with all IP traffic (which is connectionless), the packets can take different routes to the destination and arrive there out of sequence.

A TCP connection is actually two separate connections, with one running in each direction. To establish each one of the connections, a computer transmits a TCP message with the SYN control bit activated. The other computer then replies by sending a message with the ACK control bit activated. To streamline the process into three steps instead of four, the client sends its SYN message and the server replies with a message containing both the ACK and SYN bits. The server is therefore acknowledging the client's connection request and issuing its own connection request, using just one message. The client then replies to the server with an ACK message, and both of the connections are then complete. This three-way handshake is illustrated in Figure 2.11.

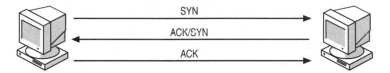

Figure 2.11   The TCP three-way handshake

In addition to verifying the existence and the operational status of the other computer, the connection establishment process also provides the information that the computers will use later to acknowledge transmissions. Each SYN message contains an *initial sequence number (ISN)* in the Sequence Number field, which the computer will use to number the messages it transmits. The computers generate an ISN using an incrementing algorithm that makes it highly improbable for two connections between the same applications on the same computers to select the same number. Each of the computers involved in a TCP connection maintains its own series of sequence numbers, and the exchange of ISNs informs each computer of the ISN that the other computer is using.

Another function of the three-way handshake is for the computers to inform each other of the *maximum segment size (MSS)* they support. The MSS is a value that specifies the size of the segments that each computer will create. The MSS value is based on the data-link layer protocol used by each computer. Each of the computers, when generating its SYN message, includes three additional subfields in the TCP header's Options field, which specify the MSS for that system in bytes.

Ports and Sockets

As with the lower layer protocols, addressing is an important function of TCP. However, getting the packets to the correct computer is the job of the IP protocol at the internet layer. TCP's task is to get the data to the appropriate application on the destination computer. The protocol does this by specifying port numbers in every TCP message. A *port number* is a value assigned to a particular application or process running on a TCP/IP computer. The Source Port field specifies the application that generated the message being transmitted, and the Destination Port field contains the port number of the application on the receiving system. TCP and UDP have separate lists of well-known port numbers; it's possible for a port number to be assigned to one application using TCP and a different application using UDP, although this is rare.

The most commonly used applications have *well-known port* numbers, which are permanently assigned by the IANA and published in the "Assigned Numbers" RFC. Every TCP/IP computer also has a text file on it called Services, which contains a list of well-known ports. Some of the most frequently used well-known ports are listed in Table 2.4.

Table 2.4 Well-Known Port Numbers

Service Name	Port Number	Protocol	Function
ftp-data	20	TCP	FTP data channel; used for transmitting files between systems
ftp	21	TCP	FTP control channel; used for exchanging commands and responses by FTP-connected systems
telnet	23	TCP	Telnet; used to execute commands on network-connected systems
smtp	25	TCP	Simple Mail Transport Protocol; used to send e-mail messages
domain	53	TCP and UDP	DNS; used to receive host name resolution requests from clients
bootps	67	TCP and UDP	Bootstrap Protocol (BOOTP) and Dynamic Host Configuration Protocol (DHCP) servers; used to receive TCP/IP configuration requests from clients
bootpc	68	TCP and UDP	BOOTP and DHCP clients; used to send TCP/IP configuration requests to servers
http	80	TCP	Hypertext Transfer Protocol (HTTP); used by Web servers to receive requests from client browsers
pop3	110	TCP	Post Office Protocol 3 (POP3); used to receive e-mail requests from clients
snmp	161	TCP and UDP	Simple Network Management Protocol (SNMP); used by SNMP agents to transmit status information to a network management console

The reason for having well-known ports is so that applications don't have to explicitly specify a port number for every transmission. Web browsers, for example, automatically send all HTTP messages to port 80 on the Web server because this is the well-known port number for that protocol. To use an alternative port number, you must specify it as part of a URL in the browser.

Therefore, to reach a particular application on a particular computer, a TCP/IP system needs the IP address of the network interface in the computer and the port number associated with the application. The combination of an IP address and a port number is called a socket. Sockets are expressed using the IP address, followed by a colon and then the port number, as in 192.168.21.54:80.

Most of the well-known port numbers are assigned to server applications because clients typically initiate the connection with a server, and not the other way around. In many cases, a client application selects a source port number at random and uses it in its initial connection establishment message to the server. This is called an *ephemeral port number*. The server reads this port number from the message and uses it in all subsequent replies to the client. The well-known port number assignments all use values under 1024, so ephemeral port number assignments always use values higher than 1024.

TCP Packet Acknowledgment

The TCP packet acknowledgment and error correction systems rely on the values of the TCP header's Sequence Number and Acknowledgment Number fields. During the three-way handshake, when the server replies to the client's SYN message, the SYN/ACK message that the server generates contains its own ISN in the Sequence Number field and also a value in its Acknowledgment Number field. This acknowledgment number value is the equivalent of the client's ISN plus one. The function of this field is to inform the other system of what value is expected in the next message's Sequence Number field. If the client's ISN is 1000000, for example, the server's SYN/ACK message contains the value 1000001 in its Acknowledgment Number field. When the client sends its first data message to the server, that message will have the value 1000001 in its Sequence Number field, which is what the server expects.

Note You might wonder why the client's first data message has the sequence number value 1000001 when it previously had to send an ACK message in response to the server's SYN. It might seem that the ACK message should have used sequence number 1000001, but in fact, messages that function solely as acknowledgments do not increment the sequence number counter. The server's SYN/ACK message does increment the counter because of the inclusion of the SYN flag.

When the systems begin to send data, they increment their sequence number values by one for each byte of data they transmit. When a Web browser sends its

URL request to a Web server, for example, its sequence number value is its ISN plus one (1000001), as expected by the server. Assuming that the actual file or Web page requested by the client is 500 bytes (not including the IP or TCP headers), the server will respond to the request message with an ACK message that contains the value 1000501 in its Acknowledgment Number field. This indicates that the server has successfully received 500 bytes of data and is expecting the client's next data packet to have the sequence number 1000501. Because the client has transmitted 500 bytes to the server, it increments its sequence number value by that amount, and the next data message it sends will use the value that the server expects (assuming there are no transmission errors).

The same message numbering process also occurs simultaneously in the other direction. The server has transmitted no data yet, except for its SYN/ACK message, so the ACK generated by the client during the handshake contains the server's ISN plus one. The server's acknowledgment of the client's request contained no data, so the Sequence Number field was not incremented. Therefore, when the server responds to the client's URL request, its first data message will use the same ISN-plus-one value in its Sequence Number field, which is what the client expects.

In the case described here, the file requested by the client's URL request is small and requires only one TCP message, but in most cases the Web server responds by transmitting a Web page, which is likely to require a sequence of TCP messages consisting of multiple segments. The server divides the Web page (which becomes the sequence it is transmitting) into segments no larger than the client's MSS value. As the server begins to transmit the segments, it increments its sequence number value according to the amount of data in each message. For example, if the server's ISN is 20000, the sequence number of its first data message will be 20001. Assuming that the client's MSS is 1000, the server's second data message will have a Sequence Number of 21001, the third will be 22001, and so on.

When the client begins receiving data from the server, the client is responsible for acknowledging the data. TCP uses a system called *delayed acknowledgments*, which means that the computers do not have to generate a separate acknowledgment message for every data message they receive. The intervals at which the systems generate their acknowledgments are left up to the individual TCP implementation. Each acknowledgment message that the client sends in response to the server's data messages has the ACK flag, of course, and the value of its Acknowledgment Number field reflects the number of bytes in the sequence that the client has successfully received.

If the client receives messages that fail the CRC check or fails to receive messages containing some of the segments in the sequence, it signals these failures to the server using the Acknowledgment Number field in the ACK messages. The acknowledgment number value always reflects the number of bytes from the beginning of the sequence that the destination system has received correctly. If, for example, a sequence consists of 10 segments, and all are received correctly except the seventh segment, the recipient's acknowledgment message will contain an acknowledgment number value that reflects the number of bytes in the first six segments only. Segments 8 through 10, even though they were received correctly, are discarded and must be retransmitted along with segment 7. This system is called *positive acknowledgment with retransmission* because the destination system acknowledges only the messages that were sent correctly. A protocol that uses *negative acknowledgement* would assume that all messages have been received correctly except for those that the destination system explicitly lists as having errors.

A system transmitting data maintains a queue of the messages that it has already sent. As the sender receives acknowledgments, it deletes the messages from the queue that are verified as having arrived correctly. Messages that remain in the source system's queue for a predetermined period of time are assumed to have been lost or discarded, and the system automatically retransmits them.

After the server has transmitted all the segments in the sequence that contains the requested Web page and the client acknowledges that it has received all the segments correctly, the systems terminate the connection. If the segments have arrived at their destination out of sequence because of routing conditions, the receiving system uses the values in the Sequence Number field to reassemble them into the proper order.

The HTTP transactions of Web clients and servers are relatively simple. Other types of applications might leave a single TCP connection open for a much longer period of time and perform repeated exchanges of data in both directions. In a case like this, both systems exchange data messages and acknowledgments, with the error detection and correction processes occurring on both sides.

TCP Error Correction

Basically, two things can go wrong during a TCP transaction: messages can arrive in a corrupted state or they can fail to arrive at all. When messages fail to arrive, the lack of acknowledgments from the destination system causes the sender to retransmit the missing messages. If a serious network problem arises that prevents the two systems from exchanging any messages, the TCP connection eventually times out and the entire connection establishment process must start again.

When messages do arrive at their destination, the receiving system checks them for accuracy by performing the same CRC computation that the sender performed before transmitting the data and comparing the results to the value in the Checksum field. If the values don't match, the system discards the message. This is a crucial element of the TCP protocol, because it is the only end-to-end checksum performed on the actual application layer data. IP includes an end-to-end checksum, but only on its header data, and data-link layer protocols like Ethernet and Token Ring contain a checksum, but only for one hop at a time, not for the end-to-end transmission. If the packets pass through a network that doesn't provide a data-link layer checksum, such as a PPP link, it is possible for errors to be introduced that can't be detected at the data-link or network layers.

The checksum performed by TCP is unusual because it is calculated not only on the entire TCP header and the application data, but also on a *pseudo-header.* The pseudo-header consists of the IP header's Source IP Address, Destination IP Address, protocol, and Length fields, plus 1 byte of padding, to bring the total number of bytes to an even 12 (three 4-byte words), as shown in Figure 2.12. The inclusion of the pseudo-header ensures that the datagrams are delivered to the correct computer and the correct transport layer protocol on that computer.

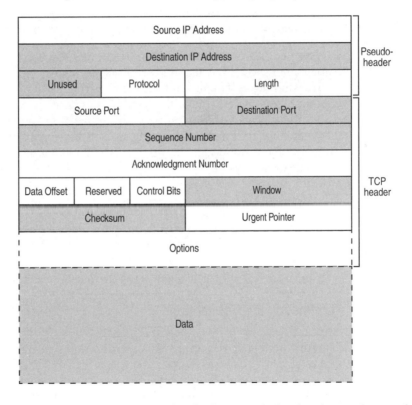

Figure 2.12   TCP computes its checksum on the header, data, and a pseudo-header derived from the IP header

TCP Flow Control

Flow control is the process by which the destination system in a TCP connection provides information to the source system that enables that source system to regulate the speed at which it transmits data.

Each computer has a limited amount of buffer space in which to store incoming data. The data remains in the buffer until the system generates messages acknowledging that data. If the system transmitting the data sends too much information too quickly, the receiver's buffers could fill up, forcing it to discard data. The system receiving the data uses the Window field in its acknowledgment messages to inform the sender of how much buffer space it has available at that time. The transmitting system uses the window value along with the acknowledgment number value to determine what data in the sequence the system is permitted to transmit. For example, if an ACK message contains an acknowledgment number value of 150000 and a window value of 500, the sending system knows that all the data in the sequence through byte 150000 has been received correctly at the destination and that it can now transmit bytes 150001 through 150500. If, by the time the sender transmits those 500 bytes, it has received no additional acknowledgments, it must stop transmitting until the next acknowledgment arrives.

This type of flow control is called a *sliding window* technique. The *offered window* (shown in Figure 2.13) is the series of bytes that the receiving system has permitted the transmitting system to send. As the receiving system acknowledges the incoming bytes, the left side of the window moves to the right, and as the system passes the acknowledged bytes up to the application layer process indicated by the destination port number, the right side of the window moves to the right. Therefore the window can be said to be sliding along the incoming byte stream, from left to right.

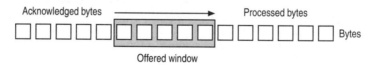

Figure 2.13   The TCP sliding window flow control mechanism

Terminating the Connection

After the systems involved in a TCP connection have finished their exchange of data, they terminate the connection using control messages much like those used in the three-way handshake that established the connection. As with the establishment of the connection, which system initiates the termination sequence depends on the application generating the data. In the case of the Web client/ server transaction used as an example in this lesson, the server begins the termination process by setting the FIN flag in the Control Bits field of its last data message. In other cases, the system initiating the termination process might use a separate message containing the FIN flag and no data.

The system receiving the FIN flag transmits an acknowledgment message and then generates its own message containing a FIN flag, to which the other system must respond with an ACK message. This is necessary because, as shown in the establishment process, the connection runs in both directions, and it is necessary for both systems to terminate their respective connections using a total of four messages (see Figure 2.14). Unlike the connection establishment procedure, the computers can't combine the FIN and ACK flags in the same message, which is why four messages are needed instead of three. There are some occasions when only one of the two connections is terminated and the other is left open. This is called a *half close*.

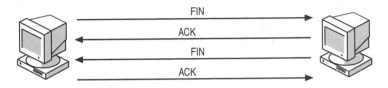

Figure 2.14   The TCP connection termination process

UDP

The *User Datagram Protocol* (UDP) is defined in RFC 768, "User Datagram Protocol." Unlike TCP, UDP is a connectionless protocol that provides no packet acknowledgment, flow control, data segmentation, or guaranteed delivery. As a result, UDP is far simpler than TCP and generates far less overhead. Not only is the UDP header much smaller than that of TCP—8 bytes as opposed to 20 bytes or more—there are no separate control messages, such as those used to establish and terminate connections. UDP transactions typically consist of only two messages—a request and a reply—with the reply functioning as a tacit acknowledgment. For this reason, most of the applications that use UDP must transport only amounts of data small enough to fit into a single message. DNS and DHCP are two of the most common application layer protocols that use UDP. Some applications use UDP to transmit large amounts of data, such as streaming audio and video, but UDP is appropriate for these purposes because this type of data can survive the loss of an occasional packet, whereas a program or data file cannot.

The format of a UDP message is shown in Figure 2.15.

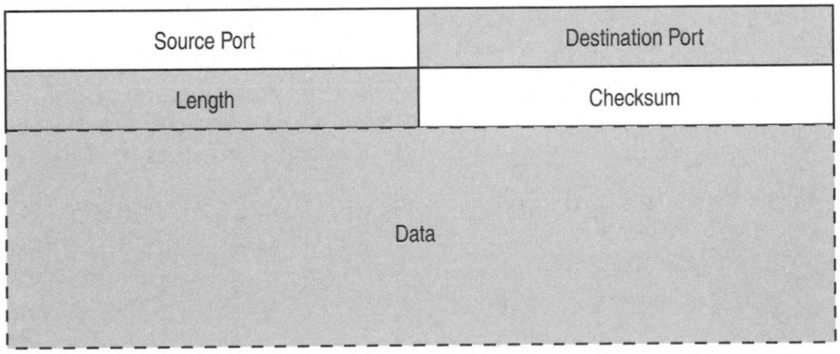

Source Port	Destination Port
Length	Checksum
Data	

Figure 2.15   The UDP message format

The functions of the UDP message fields are as follows:

- **Source Port (2 bytes).**   Identifies the application layer process on the transmitting system that generated the information carried in the Data field
- **Destination Port (2 bytes).**   Identifies the application layer process on the receiving system to which the information in the Data field will be delivered
- **Length (2 bytes).**   Specifies the length of the UDP header and data in bytes
- **Checksum (2 bytes).**   Contains the results of a cyclical redundancy check (CRC) computation performed by the transmitting system and is used by the receiving system to detect errors in the TCP header, data, and parts of the IP header
- **Data (variable).**   Contains the information generated by the application layer process specified in the Source Port field

The Source Port and Destination Port fields in a UDP header perform the same functions as they do in the TCP header. The Length field specifies how much data is included in the UDP message, and the checksum value is computed using the message header, data, and the IP pseudo-header, just as in TCP. The UDP standard specifies that the use of the checksum is optional. The transmitting system fills the Checksum field with zeroes if it is unused. There has been a great deal of debate about whether UDP messages should include checksums. RFC 768 requires all UDP systems to be capable of checking for errors using checksums, and most current implementations do include the checksum computations.

Exercise 1: TCP Header Fields

Match the TCP header field in the left column with the correct description in the right column.

1. Source Port
2. Sequence Number
3. Checksum
4. Window
5. Urgent Pointer

a. Specifies how many bytes the sender can transmit

b. Specifies the number of bytes in the sequence that have been successfully transmitted

c. Specifies the functions of messages used to initiate and terminate connections

d. Contains information for the application layer

e. Specifies which of the bytes in the message should receive special treatment from the receiving system

6. Data Offset

f. Identifies the application or protocol that generated the data carried in the TCP message

7. Destination Port

g. Used to reassemble segments that arrive at the destination out of order

8. Acknowledgment Number

h. Specifies the length of the TCP header

9. Control Bits

i. Contains error detection information

10. Data

j. Specifies the application that will make use of the data in the message

Exercise 2: TCP and UDP Functions

Specify whether each of the following statements describes TCP, UDP, or both.

1. It provides flow control.

2. It is used for DNS communications.

3. It detects transmission errors.

4. It is used to carry DHCP messages.

5. It divides data to be transmitted into segments.

6. It acknowledges transmitted messages.

7. It is used for Web client/server communications.

8. It requires a connection establishment procedure.

9. It contains a Length field.

10. It uses a pseudo-header in its checksums.

Lesson Review

1. In TCP, what does "delayed acknowledgment" mean?

    a. A predetermined time interval must pass before the receiving system can acknowledge a data packet.

    b. Data segments are not acknowledged until the entire sequence has been transmitted.

    c. The receiving system doesn't have to generate a separate acknowledgment message for every segment.

    d. A data segment must be acknowledged before the next segment is transmitted.

2. What does the Data Offset field in the TCP header specify?

    a. The length of the TCP header

    b. The location of the current segment in the sequence

    c. The length of the Data field

    d. The checksum value used for error detection

3. What is the combination of an IP address and a port number called?

    a. A sequence number

    b. A checksum

    c. A data offset

    d. A socket

4. Which of the following TCP/IP systems uses an ephemeral port number?

    a. The client

    b. The server

    c. The system initiating the TCP connection

    d. The system terminating the TCP connection

5. What flag does the first message transmitted in any TCP connection contain?

    a. ACK

    b. SYN

    c. FIN

    d. PSH

6. What TCP header field provides flow control?

    a. Window

    b. Data Offset

    c. Acknowledgment

    d. Sequence Number

7. Which of the following services does the UDP protocol provide?

    a. Flow control

    b. Guaranteed delivery

    c. Error detection

    d. None of the above

Lesson Summary

- TCP is a connection-oriented protocol that provides services such as packet acknowledgment, flow control, error detection and correction, and segmentation.

- Establishing a TCP connection between two systems requires a three-way handshake, during which each computer supplies the other with the sequence number it will assign to its messages, plus its maximum segment size (MSS).

- To transmit large amounts of data over a TCP connection, a system divides a byte stream into multiple segments, each of which is transmitted in a separate message.

- The system receiving the data segments acknowledges them with occasional messages used for that purpose. Unacknowledged messages are eventually retransmitted.

- Acknowledgment messages inform the other system how much data it can transmit. This is called flow control.

- TCP messages contain a checksum that the receiving system uses to detect transmission errors.

- Closing a TCP connection requires the systems to exchange termination (FIN) messages and acknowledgments.

- UDP is a connectionless protocol that provides error detection through checksums, but it provides none of the other services found in TCP.

C H A P T E R   3

Implementing TCP/IP

Lesson 1: Installing and Configuring TCP/IP **80**

Lesson 2: Using the Windows 2000 TCP/IP Tools................. **93**

About This Chapter

Understanding the theory behind the Transmission Control Protocol/Internet Protocol (TCP/IP) suite is an important part of the network administrator's education, but exam 70-216 concentrates as much on practice as theory. This chapter examines the procedures for installing and configuring the TCP/IP protocols on a computer running Microsoft Windows 2000. The procedures for the other Windows operating systems are similar to those for Windows 2000, although the user interface is slightly different.

Before You Begin

No previous knowledge other than a basic familiarity with Windows 2000 controls is needed to perform the procedures in this chapter. However, understanding the place of the TCP/IP protocols in the operating system's protocol stack, as explained in Chapter 1, "Introducing Windows 2000 Networking," and Chapter 2, "Introducing TCP/IP," is important for gaining an overall picture of data networking.

Lesson 1: Installing and Configuring TCP/IP

Windows 2000, like all the current Windows operating systems, provides support for the TCP/IP protocol suite in the form of a single component that you install from the Windows Control Panel. This one component provides support for all the basic protocols needed to transmit data across the network, including the Internet Protocol (IP), the Transmission Control Protocol (TCP), and the User Datagram Protocol (UDP). The TCP/IP client also provides support for ancillary protocols, such as Internet Control Message Protocol (ICMP) and Address Resolution Protocol (ARP), as well as Dynamic Host Configuration Protocol (DHCP), Domain Name System (DNS), and Windows Internet Name Service (WINS) clients.

Note   For more information about the protocols that make up the TCP/IP suite, see Chapter 2, "Introducing TCP/IP."

After this lesson, you will be able to

- Install TCP/IP protocol support on a computer running Windows 2000 Server or Windows 2000 Professional
- Manually configure the TCP/IP client on a Windows 2000 computer
- Configure advanced TCP/IP parameters

Estimated lesson time: 30 minutes

TCP/IP is the default protocol suite in Windows 2000. If the operating system's Setup program detects a network interface adapter in the computer, Plug and Play identifies it, installs the appropriate network adapter driver, and installs the Internet Protocol (TCP/IP), Client for Microsoft Networks, and File and Printer Sharing for Microsoft Networks modules, as shown in Figure 3.1. However, there are occasions when you might have to install the TCP/IP protocols manually.

Figure 3.1   The Local Area Connection Properties dialog box

To manually install the TCP/IP protocols, complete the following steps:

1. In the Start menu's Settings group, select Network And Dial-Up Connections to display the Network And Dial-Up Connections window, as shown in Figure 3.2.

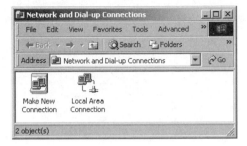

Figure 3.2   The Network And Dial-Up Connections window

2. Right-click the Local Area Connection icon in the Network And Dial-Up Connections window and select Properties from the shortcut menu to display the Local Area Connection Properties dialog box.

Note   If the Network And Dial-Up Connections window does not have a Local Area Connection icon in it, your computer does not have a network adapter driver installed. Use the Add/Remove Hardware window, accessed from the Control Panel, to install the appropriate driver for your network adapter.

3. In the Local Area Connection Properties dialog box, click Install to display the Select Network Component Type dialog box shown in Figure 3.3.

Figure 3.3   The Select Network Component Type dialog box

4. In the component list, select Protocol and click Add to display the Select Network Protocol dialog box shown in Figure 3.4.

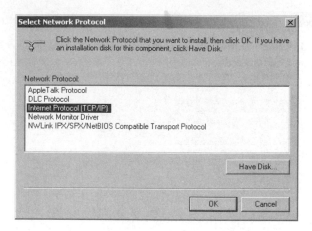

Figure 3.4   The Select Network Protocol dialog box

5. In the protocol listing, select Internet Protocol (TCP/IP) and click OK. This adds the protocol module to the component list in the Local Area Connection Properties dialog box, as shown in Figure 3.5.

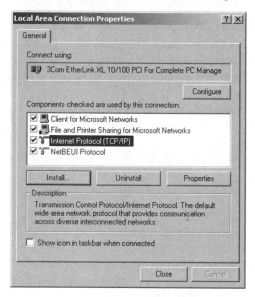

Figure 3.5   The Local Area Connection Properties dialog box with the Internet Protocol (TCP/IP) module added

6. Click Close to install the TCP/IP protocols, bind them to the client and adapter driver already installed on the computer, and copy the TCP/IP utilities to the \Winnt\System32 folder. You might have to insert your Windows 2000 distribution CD-ROM into the drive so the operating system can copy essential files to the computer.

7. After the installation procedure is completed, you must reboot the computer before the new protocols are activated.

Configuring TCP/IP

By default, Windows 2000, like the other Windows operating systems, configures the TCP/IP client to use its DHCP client capabilities to request configuration settings from a DHCP server on the network. However, if no DHCP server is available, someone has to configure the TCP/IP client manually. This lesson examines the process of configuring the various TCP/IP client parameters and the functions of each parameter on the computer and the network.

Configuring Basic TCP/IP Properties

The Local Area Connection Properties dialog box that you used to install the TCP/IP protocols is also where you configure the Windows 2000 TCP/IP client. Use the following procedure to access the TCP/IP client's configuration interface and supply values for its various operational parameters.

Caution   If you plan to experiment with this TCP/IP configuration procedure on a live network, be sure that the values you supply for the TCP/IP parameters, particularly the IP address, are correct for your computer and your network. When incorrectly set, some TCP/IP parameters can prevent your computer from communicating with the network or cause conflicts with other computers on the network, preventing them from functioning properly. If you want to avoid explaining to your boss why he or she couldn't retrieve e-mail this morning, check with your network's administrator before you begin experimenting.

To configure the basic properties of the TCP/IP client, complete the following steps:

1. In the Start menu's Settings group, select Network And Dial-Up Connections to display the Network And Dial-Up Connections window.

2. Right-click the Local Area Connection icon in the Network And Dial-Up Connections window and select Properties from the shortcut menu to display the Local Area Connection Properties dialog box.

3. Select the Internet Protocol (TCP/IP) module in the components list and click Properties to display the Internet Protocol (TCP/IP) Properties dialog box shown in Figure 3.6.

4. Select the Use The Following IP Address option to activate the IP Address, Subnet Mask, and Default Gateway text boxes, which provide the client's manual configuration capability. Although its label does not indicate this, it is the Obtain An IP Address Automatically option that activates the DHCP client.

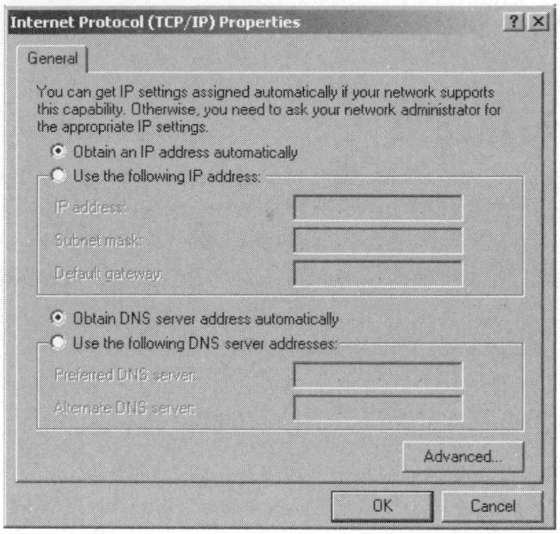

Figure 3.6   The Internet Protocol (TCP/IP) Properties dialog box

5. In the IP text box, enter a valid IP address using the standard dotted decimal notation, as shown in Figure 3.7. The address you supply must be unique on the network and it must conform to the subnet configuration used on your network.

Note   If you don't know anything about the addresses used on your network, ask an administrator to supply you with an IP address you can use. Do not simply select one at random or change the last number of the address used by the computer next to yours.

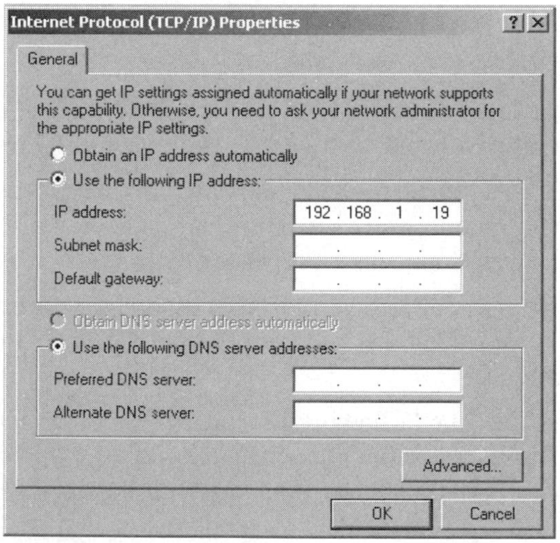

Figure 3.7   Entering a unique IP address into the appropriate text box

Note The IP address and the subnet mask are the only two TCP/IP configuration parameters that are absolutely required for the computer to communicate with the local area network (LAN). Other parameters are required for convenience or for certain types of communication, but they are not essential.

6. In the Subnet Mask text box, type an appropriate mask for the IP address you supplied, as shown in Figure 3.8. Windows 2000 supplies a subnet mask based on your IP address's first byte value. However, if your network is subnetted, the subnet mask value supplied by Windows 2000 might not be correct.

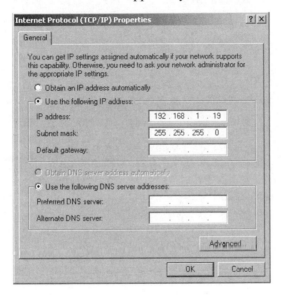

Figure 3.8 Entering an appropriate subnet mask value

Note Windows 2000 determines its value for the Subnet Mask text box by examining the first three bits of the 32-bit IP address you have supplied. If the first bit of the address is a 0, Windows 2000 supplies the subnet mask for a Class A address (255.0.0.0). If the first two bits are 10, Windows assumes the use of a Class B address and supplies a subnet mask of 255.255.0.0. If the first three bits are 110, the subnet mask value is for a Class C address (255.255.255.0). For more information about the nature of IP addresses and subnet masking, see Lesson 2 in Chapter 2, "Introducing TCP/IP."

7. The Default Gateway text box should contain the IP address of the router on the local network that the computer will use to send TCP/IP traffic to destinations on other networks. On a private internetwork, the default gateway is a router that provides access to the other networks. On a stand-alone LAN

connected to the Internet, the default gateway refers to the system that provides the shared Internet connection. If the computer is connected to a LAN that is not part of an internetwork and not connected to the Internet, leave this text box blank.

Note The address that you type into the Default Gateway text box becomes an entry in the computer's routing table with a Network Destination value of 0.0.0.0. You can also create, delete, or modify the default gateway (or any other routing table entry) manually using the Route.exe utility, as explained in Chapter 6, "Routing IP."

8. When you select the Use The Following IP Address option in the Internet Protocol (TCP/IP) Properties dialog box, Windows 2000 deactivates the DHCP client completely, and, as a result, the Obtain DNS Server Address Automatically option becomes unavailable. In the Preferred DNS Server and Alternate DNS Server text boxes, type the IP addresses of the DNS servers that your computer will use to resolve DNS names into IP addresses. The TCP/IP client uses the Alternate DNS Server address only if the primary DNS server is unreachable. If your network is connected to the Internet, you must supply at least one DNS server address to convert the DNS names in your Uniform Resource Locators (URLs) into IP addresses. If your computer is part of a Windows 2000 Active Directory directory service domain, you need to supply the address of a Windows 2000 DNS server or a DNS server that is hosting the zone file for Active Directory on your internetwork. If you are not using Active Directory, the DNS server can be either on your internetwork or that of your Internet service provider (ISP).

9. Click OK to close the Internet Protocol (TCP/IP) Properties dialog box and click OK again to close the Local Area Connection Properties dialog box.

Configuring Advanced TCP/IP Properties

In many cases, a Windows 2000 system needs only the TCP/IP parameters configured in the preceding procedure. However, the Internet Protocol (TCP/IP) Properties dialog box also has an Advanced button that provides access to the Advanced TCP/IP Settings dialog box, in which you can configure a more complete set of TCP/IP parameters, as discussed in the following sections.

The IP Settings Tab

The IP Settings tab of the Advanced TCP/IP Settings dialog box, shown in Figure 3.9, enables you to specify multiple IP addresses and subnet masks for the network interface adapter in your computer, as well as multiple default gateway addresses. Most computers with multiple IP addresses have multiple network interface adapters as well, using one address per network interface adapter. However, there are situations in which a computer might need more than one IP address for a single network interface adapter, such as when a single physical network hosts multiple TCP/IP subnets. In such cases, a computer needs an IP address on each of the two subnets to participate on both.

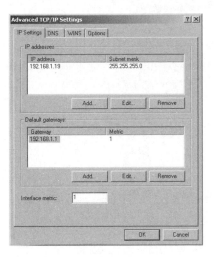

Figure 3.9 The IP Settings tab of the Advanced TCP/IP Settings dialog box

When you open the Advanced TCP/IP Settings dialog box, the parameters you have already configured elsewhere in the Internet Protocol (TCP/IP) Properties dialog box appear in the listings. You can add to the existing settings, modify them, or delete them altogether. To add a new IP address and subnet mask, click Add, type the desired address and mask values in the TCP/IP Address dialog box, and then click Add to add your entries to the IP Addresses list. Windows 2000 supports an unlimited number of IP address/subnet mask combinations for each network interface adapter in the computer.

The procedure for creating additional default gateways is the same as that for adding IP addresses. A computer can use only one default gateway at a time, however, so the ability to specify multiple default gateways in the Advanced TCP/IP Settings dialog box is simply a fault-tolerance mechanism. If the first default gateway in the list is unavailable for any reason, Windows 2000 sends packets to the second address listed. This practice assumes that the computer is connected to a LAN that has multiple routers on it, each of which provides access to the rest of the internetwork.

The DNS Tab

The DNS tab of the Advanced TCP/IP Settings dialog box, shown in Figure 3.10, also provides a fault-tolerance mechanism for the Windows 2000 DNS client. You can specify more than the two DNS server addresses provided in the main Internet Protocol (TCP/IP) Properties dialog box, and you can modify the order in which the computer uses them if one or more of the servers should be unavailable.

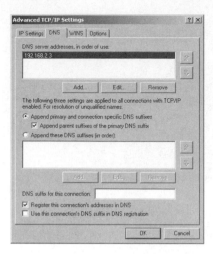

Figure 3.10   The DNS tab of the Advanced TCP/IP Settings dialog box

---

Note   Unlike the IP address, subnet mask, and default gateway settings, which apply only to a specific network interface adapter, the DNS server addresses apply to the entire Windows 2000 TCP/IP client. You cannot specify different DNS server addresses for each network interface adapter.

The other controls in the DNS tab specify how the TCP/IP client resolves unqualified names. An *unqualified name* is an incomplete DNS name that does not indicate the domain in which the host resides. The Windows 2000 TCP/IP client can still resolve these names by appending a suffix to the unqualified name before sending it to the DNS server for resolution. For example, with a properly configured TCP/IP client, you can supply only the name *www* as a URL in your Web browser, and the client appends your company's domain name (for example, *adatum.com*) to the URL as a suffix, resulting in the fully qualified DNS name *www.adatum.com*, which is presumably the name of your network's intranet Web server.

The DNS controls enable you to configure the client to append the primary and connection-specific DNS suffixes to unqualified names, or you can create a list of suffixes that the client will append to unqualified names, one after the other, until the name resolution process succeeds. The primary DNS suffix is the domain name you specify for the computer in the Network Identification tab of the System dialog box, accessed from the Control Panel. This suffix applies to all the computer's network interface adapters. You can create a connection-specific suffix by typing a domain name in the DNS Suffix For This Connection text box in the DNS tab. To create a list of suffixes, select the Append These DNS Suffixes (In Order) option, click Add, type the suffix you want to add to the list, and click Add.

The two check boxes at the bottom of the DNS tab enable you to specify whether the computer should register its DNS name with its designated DNS server. This option requires a DNS server that supports dynamic updates, such as the DNS Server service supplied with Windows 2000 Server. The Register This Connection's Addresses In DNS check box causes Windows 2000 to use the system's primary DNS suffix to register the addresses, and the Use This Connection's DNS Suffix In DNS Registration check box causes the computer to use the connection-specific suffix you've entered in the DNS Suffix For This Connection text box.

Note For more information about DNS, see Chapter 7, "Understanding the Domain Name System," and Chapter 8, "Using the Windows 2000 DNS Server."

The WINS Tab

Windows 2000 includes a WINS client for NetBIOS name resolution, but on a Windows 2000 network that uses Active Directory, WINS is not needed because Active Directory uses DNS names for the computers on the network and relies on DNS for its name resolution services. However, if you run Windows 2000 computers that are members of Microsoft Windows NT domains or that use no directory service at all, you can use the Advanced TCP/IP Settings dialog box's WINS tab, as shown in Figure 3.11, to configure the TCP/IP client to use WINS.

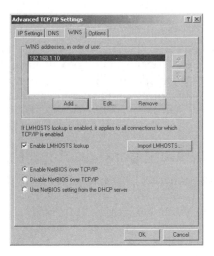

Figure 3.11   The WINS tab of the Advanced TCP/IP Settings dialog box

Click Add in the WINS tab to open the TCP/IP WINS Server dialog box, in which you can specify the address of a WINS server on your network. You can create a list of WINS servers and specify the order in which Windows 2000 should use them. As with the default gateway and DNS server settings, supplying multiple WINS server addresses is a fault-tolerance feature.

The Enable Lmhosts Lookup check box forces the computer to use a file called Lmhosts to resolve NetBIOS names before contacting the designated WINS server. Lmhosts is a text file located in the %systemroot%\System32\ Drivers\Etc folder on the computer's system drive, which contains a list of NetBIOS names and their equivalent IP addresses. Lmhosts functions in much the same way as the Hosts file, which was used for host name resolution before the advent of DNS. Because each computer must have its own Lmhosts file, Windows 2000 enables you to import a file from a network drive to the local computer. To do this, click Import Lmhosts and browse for the desired file.

Using the options at the bottom of the WINS tab, you can specify whether the computer should or should not use NetBIOS over TCP/IP or whether the computer should rely on a DHCP server to specify the NetBIOS setting. Once again, on an all–Windows 2000 network that uses Active Directory, you can disable NetBIOS over TCP/IP because the computers use DNS names instead of NetBIOS names.

Note For more information about NetBIOS naming, name resolution, and WINS, see Chapter 9, "Implementing Windows Internet Name Service."

The Options Tab

The Options tab of the Advanced TCP/IP Settings dialog box contains a list of additional features included with the TCP/IP client. You can select any item in the list and click Properties to open a dialog box that enables you to configure that option. Windows 2000 includes two TCP/IP options: IP Security and TCP/IP Filtering. For information about using these options, see Chapter 10, "Securing Network Protocols."

Exercise 1: TCP/IP Configuration Requirements

For each of the network scenarios listed, specify which of the following TCP/IP parameters (a, b, c, d, e, or a combination of these) you must configure to provide a computer running Windows 2000 with full communications capabilities.

1. A private internetwork using Windows NT domains	a. IP address
2. A single peer-to-peer LAN	b. Subnet mask
3. A corporate internetwork using Active Directory	c. Default gateway
4. A peer-to-peer LAN using a shared Internet connection	d. DNS server address
5. A Windows NT internetwork with a router connected to the Internet	e. WINS server address

Lesson Review

1. Which of the Windows 2000 Control Panel tools do you use to install the TCP/IP client?

2. When performing the TCP/IP installation procedure, what does the lack of a Local Area Connection icon indicate? (Choose all that apply.)

    a. No network interface adapter is installed in the computer.

    b. No network interface adapter driver is installed in the computer.

    c. The network to which the computer is connected does not support TCP/IP.

    d. No DHCP server is on the network.

3. Which of the following components is not installed by default during the Windows 2000 setup process when a Plug and Play network interface adapter is present in the computer?

    a. The NetBIOS Extended User Interface (NetBEUI) Protocol

    b. The Internet Protocol (TCP/IP) module

    c. Client for Microsoft Networks

    d. File and Printer Sharing for Microsoft Networks

4. Which of the following services is not used on a Windows 2000 Active Directory network?

    a. DHCP

    b. WINS

    c. DNS

    d. IPsec

5. What is the function of a DNS suffix?

6. Which of the following is a valid reason for assigning more than one IP address to a single network interface adapter?

    a. To balance the network traffic load between the addresses

    b. To support multiple subnets on one network

    c. To provide fault tolerance

    d. To support both TCP and UDP traffic

7. How many default gateway addresses does a computer need to function on a LAN?

    a. 0

    b. 1

    c. 2

    d. 3

8. How does Windows 2000 supply a subnet mask for the IP address you specify?

    a. By performing a reverse DNS name resolution on the address

    b. By checking the values of the first three address bits

    c. By checking the Hosts file

    d. By querying the directory service

9. What is the function of an Lmhosts file?

Lesson Summary

- The Windows operating systems implement the TCP/IP protocol suite as a single module.

- The default Windows 2000 networking configuration consists of the Internet Protocol (TCP/IP), Client for Microsoft Networks, and File and Printer Sharing for Microsoft Networks modules.

- You install support for the TCP/IP protocols in Windows 2000 using the Local Area Connections Properties dialog box.

- If you don't have DHCP servers on your network, you must configure the TCP/IP client manually.

- Every computer on the network must have a unique IP address and an appropriate subnet mask.

- A default gateway address instructs the computer where to send packets that are destined for other networks.

- The DNS server parameters instruct the computer where to send DNS names for resolution into IP addresses.

- The Advanced TCP/IP Settings dialog box provides access to the complete set of TCP/IP configuration options.

Lesson 2: Using the Windows 2000 TCP/IP Tools

Virtually every operating system with networking capabilities includes support for the TCP/IP protocols, and, in most cases, the TCP/IP implementation also includes an assortment of programs that enable you to gather information about the various protocols and the network. Traditionally, these utilities run from the command line, although graphical versions are sometimes supplied. In many cases, a program uses the same syntax, even on different operating systems. This lesson examines some of the most common TCP/IP utilities and why they are used.

After this lesson, you will be able to

- Describe the functions and syntax of the primary TCP/IP utilities

Estimated lesson time: 30 minutes

Ping

Ping is the most basic of the TCP/IP utilities. Virtually every TCP/IP implementation includes a version of it. On UNIX systems, the program is called ping, and in all versions of the Windows operating system, it is called Ping.exe. NetWare even includes a server-based version called Ping.nlm. Ping can tell you if the TCP/IP stack of another system on the network is functioning normally. The ping program generates a series of Echo Request messages using the Internet Control Message Protocol (ICMP) and transmits them to the computer whose name or IP address you specify on the command line. At its most basic, the syntax of the Ping.exe program is as follows:

```
ping target
```

The *target* variable contains the IP address or name of a computer on the network. You can use either DNS names or NetBIOS names in ping commands. The program resolves the name into an IP address before sending the Echo Request messages, and it then displays the address in its readout. Most ping implementations also have command-line switches that enable you to modify the operational parameters of the program, such as the number of Echo Request messages it generates and the amount of data in each message. The full syntax for the Windows 2000 Ping.exe program is as follows:

```
ping [-t] [-a] [-n count] [-l size] [-f] [-i TTL] [-v TOS] [-r count]
[-s count] [[-j hostlist] | [-k hostlist]] [-w timeout] target
```

- **-t** Causes the program to ping the specified host continuously until you stop it by pressing CTRL+C or CTRL+BREAK.
- **-a** Causes the program to resolve IP addresses supplied as the target variable into hostnames.

- **-n** *count*   Specifies the number of Echo Requests messages the program sends. The default is four.
- **-l** *size*   Specifies how much data (in bytes) the program should include in the payload of the Echo request messages. Possible values range from 0 to 65500.
- **-f**   Prevents the Echo Request messages from being fragmented on the way to their destination.
- **-i** *TTL*   Specifies the Time to Live value for the Echo Request messages.
- **-v** *TOS*   Specifies the Type of Service value for the Echo Request messages.
- **-r** *count*   Causes the program to display the route taken by the Echo Request messages for the specified number of hops.
- **-s** *count*   Causes the program to gather and display time stamps for the specified number of hops.
- **-j** *hostlist*   Enables you to specify a loose source route for the Echo Request messages. The messages must pass through the routers specified in the hostlist variable.
- **-k** *hostlist*   Enables you to specify a strict source route for the Echo Request messages. The messages must pass only through the routers specified in the hostlist variable.
- **-w** *timeout*   Specifies the time that the program should wait for a reply to each Echo Request message.
- *target*   Specifies the name or IP address of the destination system.

Note   Loose source routes and strict source routes are lists of router IP addresses that packets must pass through on their way to a destination. The difference between the two is that for a loose source route, packets can pass through other routers in addition to those listed. A strict source route contains a complete list of all the routers on the path to the destination.

All TCP/IP computers must respond to any Echo Request messages they receive that are addressed to them by generating Echo Reply messages and transmitting them back to the sender. The payload data included in the request message is copied to the replies before they are transmitted. When the pinging computer receives the Echo Reply messages, it produces a display like the following:

```
Pinging cz1 [192.168.2.10] with 32 bytes of data:

Reply from 192.168.2.10: bytes=32 time<10ms TTL=128
Reply from 192.168.2.10: bytes=32 time<10ms TTL=128
Reply from 192.168.2.10: bytes=32 time<10ms TTL=128
Reply from 192.168.2.10: bytes=32 time<10ms TTL=128
```

```
Ping statistics for 192.168.2.10:
  Packets: Sent = 4, Received = 4, Lost = 0 (0% loss),
Approximate round trip times in milli-seconds:
  Minimum = 0ms, Maximum =  0ms, Average =  0ms
```

In the case of the Windows 2000 ping implementation, the display shows the IP address of the computer receiving the Echo Requests, the number of bytes of data included with each request, the elapsed time between the transmission of each request and the receipt of each reply, and the value of the Time to Live (TTL) field in the IP header. In this particular example, the target computer was on the same LAN, so the time measurement is very short—less than 10 milliseconds. When pinging a computer on the Internet, the interval is likely to be longer. A successful use of ping like this one indicates that the target computer's networking hardware is functioning properly, as are the protocols, at least as high as the network layer of the Open Systems Interconnection (OSI) reference model. If the ping test fails, either one or both of the computers is experiencing a problem with its networking hardware or software or some device on the network is blocking ICMP traffic (as some routers are configured to do).

Tracert.exe

Tracert.exe is a variant of the ping program that displays the path that packets take to their destination. Because of the nature of IP routing, paths through an internetwork can change from minute to minute, and Tracert.exe displays a list of the routers that are currently forwarding packets to a particular destination. The program is called traceroute on UNIX systems, Tracert.exe by Windows, and Iptrace.nlm by Novell NetWare.

Tracert.exe uses ICMP Echo Request and Echo Reply messages just like ping, but it modifies the messages by changing the value of the TTL field in the IP header of each message. The TTL field is designed to prevent packets from getting caught in router loops that keep them circulating endlessly around the network. The computer generating the packet normally sets a relatively high value for the TTL field; on Windows systems, the default value is 128. Each router that processes the packet reduces the TTL value by one. If the value reaches zero, the last router discards the packet and transmits an ICMP error message back to the original sender.

When you run Tracert.exe with the name or IP address of a target computer, the program generates its first set of Echo Request messages with TTL values of 1. When the messages arrive at the first router on their path, the router decrements their TTL values to 0, discards the packets, and reports the errors to the sender. The ICMP error messages contain the router's address, which the Tracert.exe program displays as the first hop in the path to the destination. Traceroute's second set of Echo Request messages uses a TTL value of 2, causing the second router on the path to discard the packets and generate error messages. The Echo

Request messages in the third set have a TTL value of 3, and so on. Each set of packets travels one hop farther than the previous set before causing a router to return error messages to the source. The list of routers displayed by the program as the path to the destination is the result of these error messages. The following is an example of the Tracert.exe display:

```
Tracing route to www.adatum.co.uk [10.146.1.1]
over a maximum of 30 hops:
  1   <10 ms     1 ms   <10 ms   192.168.2.99
  2   105 ms    92 ms    98 ms   qrv1-67terminal01.epoch.net [172.24.67.3]
  3   101 ms   110 ms    98 ms   qrv1.epoch.net [172.24.67.1]
  4   123 ms   109 ms   118 ms   svcr03-7b.epoch.net [172.24.103.125]
  5   123 ms   112 ms   114 ms   clsm02-2.epoch.net [172.24.88.26]
  6   136 ms   130 ms   133 ms   sl-0-T3.sprintlink.net [10.228.116.5]
  7   143 ms   126 ms   138 ms   sl-3.sprintlink.net [192.168.5.117]
  8   146 ms   129 ms   133 ms   sl-12-0.sprintlink.net [192.168.5.1]
  9   131 ms   128 ms   139 ms   sl-13-0.sprintlink.net [192.168.18.38]
 10   130 ms   134 ms   134 ms   sl-8-0.sprintlink.net [192.168.7.94]
 11   147 ms   149 ms   152 ms   sl-0.sprintlink.net [192.168.173.10]
 12   154 ms   146 ms   145 ms   ny2-ge021.router.demon.net [172.21.173.121]
 13   230 ms   225 ms   226 ms   tele-ge023.router.demon.net [172.21.173.12]
 14   233 ms   220 ms   226 ms   tele-fxp1.router.demon.net [10.159.252.56]
 15   223 ms   224 ms   224 ms   tele-14.router.demon.net [10.159.254.245]
 16   236 ms   221 ms   226 ms   tele-165.router.demon.net [10.159.36.149]
 17   220 ms   224 ms   210 ms   www.adatum.co.uk [10.146.1.1]
Trace complete.
```

In this example, Tracert.exe is displaying the path between a computer in Pennsylvania and one in the United Kingdom. Each of the entries contains the elapsed times between the transmission and reception of three sets of Echo Request and Echo Reply packets. In this trace you can clearly see the point at which the packets begin traveling across the Atlantic Ocean. At hop 13, the elapsed times increase from approximately 150 to 230 milliseconds (ms) and stay in that range for the subsequent hops. This additional delay of only 80 ms is the time it takes the packets to travel the thousands of miles across the Atlantic Ocean.

Tracert.exe also supports a number of command line parameters. The syntax for the program is as follows:

```
tracert [-d] [-h maxhops] [-j hostlist] [-w timeout] target
```

- **-d** Prevents the program from resolving IP addresses into host names.
- **-h** *maxhops* Imposes a limit on the maximum number of hops the program searches for on the way to the target.

- **-j** *hostlist* Enables you to specify a loose source route to the target.
- **-w** *timeout* Specifies the time that the program should wait for a reply to each Echo Request message.
- *target* Specifies the name or IP address of the destination system.

Tracert.exe can be a handy tool for isolating the location of a network communications problem. Ping simply tells you whether a problem exists; it can't tell you where. A failure to contact a remote computer could be caused by a problem in your workstation, in the remote computer, or in any of the routers in between. Tracert.exe can tell you how far your packets are going before they run into the problem.

Note Because the configuration of the Internet is constantly changing, there is no guarantee that the route displayed by Tracert.exe is completely accurate. The IP datagrams that execute each step of the traceroute process might in fact be taking different routes to the same destination, resulting in the display of a composite route between two points that doesn't actually exist.

Pathping.exe

The Pathping.exe program is a route-tracing tool that combines features of Ping.exe and Tracert.exe with additional information that neither of those tools provides. The pathping command sends packets to each router on the way to a final destination over a period of time and then computes results based on the packets returned from each hop. Because the command shows the degree of packet loss at any given router or link, it is easy to determine which routers or links might be causing network problems.

The syntax for Pathping.exe is as follows:

```
pathping [-n] [-h maxhops] [-g hostlist] [-p period] [-q numqueries]
[-w timeout] [-t] [-R] target
```

- **-n** Prevents the program from resolving IP addresses into host names.
- **-h** *maxhops* Imposes a limit on the maximum number of hops the program searches for on the way to the target.
- **-g** *hostlist* Enables you to specify a loose source route to the target.
- **-p** *period* Specifies a time interval (in milliseconds) that the program should wait in between Echo Request transmissions.
- **-q** *numqueries* Specifies the number of Echo Request messages the program should transmit for each hop.

- **-w** *timeout*   Specifies the time that the program should wait for a reply to each Echo Request message.
- **-t**   Causes the program to test the connectivity to each hop with layer 2 priority tags.
- **-R**   Causes the program to test whether each hop is RSVP aware.
- *target*   Specifies the name or IP address of the destination system.

The following is a typical Pathping.exe report. The compiled statistics that follow the hop list indicate packet loss at each individual router.

```
Tracing route to msw [192.168.54.76]
over a maximum of 30 hops:

0   172.16.87.35
1   172.16.87.218
2   192.68.52.1
3   192.68.80.1
4   192.168.247.14
5   192.168.54.76


Computing statistics for 125 seconds...
                    Source to Here      This Node/Link

   Hop   RTT   Lost/Sent = Pct    Lost/Sent = Pct     Address
    0                                                 172.16.87.35
                                    0/ 100 =   0%      |
    1   41ms    0/ 100 =   0%      0/ 100 =   0%      172.16.87.218
                                   13/ 100 =  13%      |
    2   22ms   16/ 100 =  16%      3/ 100 =   3%      192.68.52.1
                                    0/ 100 =   0%      |
    3   24ms   13/ 100 =  13%      0/ 100 =   0%      192.68.80.1
                                    0/ 100 =   0%      |
    4   21ms   14/ 100 =  14%      1/ 100 =   1%      192.168.247.14
                                    0/ 100 =   0%      |
    5   24ms   13/ 100 =  13%      0/ 100 =   0%      192.168.54.76

Trace complete.
```

When you run Pathping.exe, you first see the results for the route as the program tests it for problems. This is the same path that is shown by the Tracert.exe program. Pathping.exe then displays a busy message for the next 125 seconds (this time varies according to the hop count). During this time, Pathping.exe gathers information from all the routers previously listed and from the links between them. At the end of this period the program displays the test results.

The two rightmost columns—This Node/Link Lost/Sent=Pct and Address—contain the most useful information. The link between 172.16.87.218 (hop 1) and

192.68.52.1 (hop 2) is dropping 13 percent of the packets. All other links are working normally. The routers at hops 2 and 4 also drop packets addressed to them (as shown in the This Node/Link column), but this loss does not affect their forwarding path.

The loss rates displayed for the links (marked as a | in the rightmost column) indicate losses of packets being forwarded along the path. This loss indicates link congestion. The loss rates displayed for routers (indicated by their IP addresses in the rightmost column) indicate that those routers might be overloaded. These congested routers might also be a factor in end-to-end problems, especially if packets are forwarded by software routers.

Ipconfig.exe

The Windows 2000 TCP/IP client includes a program called Ipconfig.exe that displays the current TCP/IP configuration for the computer's network interface adapters. Windows Me, Windows 98, and Windows 95 include a graphical version of the utility, called Winipcfg.exe.

When you run Ipconfig.exe with the /all parameter at the Windows 2000 command line, you see a display like the following:

```
Windows 2000 IP Configuration
  Host Name . . . . . . . . . . . . : cz2-w2ksvr
  Primary DNS Suffix  . . . . . . . : contoso.com
  Node Type . . . . . . . . . . . . : Hybrid
  IP Routing Enabled. . . . . . . . : Yes
  WINS Proxy Enabled. . . . . . . . : No
  DNS Suffix Search List. . . . . . : contoso.com
Ethernet adapter Local Area Connection:
  Connection-specific DNS Suffix  . :
  Description . . . . . . . . . . . : 3Com EtherLink XL 10/100 PCI For
Complete PC Management NIC (3C905C-TX)
  Physical Address. . . . . . . . . : 00-01-02-68-24-DD
  DHCP Enabled. . . . . . . . . . . : No
  IP Address. . . . . . . . . . . . : 192.168.2.2
  Subnet Mask . . . . . . . . . . . : 255.255.255.0
  Default Gateway . . . . . . . . . : 192.168.2.99
  DNS Servers . . . . . . . . . . . : 199.224.86.15
                                      199.224.86.16
```

Running the program with no parameters displays a limited list of configuration data. Running Winipcfg.exe produces a display like the one shown in Figure 3.12.

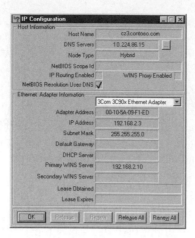

Figure 3.12   The Windows 98 Winipcfg.exe utility

Both Ipconfig.exe and Winipcfg.exe have another function. These utilities are often associated with DHCP because there is no easier way on a Windows system to see what IP address and other parameters the DHCP server has assigned to your computer. However, these programs also enable you to manually release IP addresses obtained through DHCP and renew existing leases. By running Ipconfig.exe with the /release and /renew command-line parameters or by using the Release, Renew, Release All, or Renew All buttons in Winipcfg.exe, you can release or renew the IP address assignment of one of the network interfaces in the computer or for all the interfaces at once.

Arp.exe

The Address Resolution Protocol (ARP) enables a TCP/IP computer to convert IP addresses to the hardware addresses that data-link layer protocols need to transmit frames. IP uses ARP to discover the hardware address to which each of its datagrams will be transmitted. To minimize the amount of network traffic ARP generates, the computer stores the resolved hardware addresses in a cache in system memory. The information remains in the cache for a short period of time (usually between 2 and 10 minutes), in case the computer has additional packets to send to the same address.

Note   For more information about ARP and its function, see Lesson 1 in Chapter 2, "Introducing TCP/IP."

Windows systems include a command-line utility called Arp.exe that you can use to manipulate the contents of the ARP cache. For example, you can use Arp.exe to add the hardware addresses of computers you contact frequently to the cache, thus saving time and network traffic during the connection process. Addresses that you add to the cache manually are static, meaning that they are not deleted after the usual expiration period. The cache is stored in memory only, however, so it is erased when you reboot the computer. If you want to preload the cache whenever you boot your system, you can create a batch file containing Arp.exe commands and execute it from the Windows Startup group.

Arp.exe uses the following syntax:

```
arp [-a {ipaddress}] [-n ipaddress] [-s ipaddress hwaddress {interface}]
[-d ipaddress {interface}]
```

- **-a** {*ipaddress*}   Displays the contents of the ARP cache. The optional *ipaddress* variable specifies the address of a particular cache entry to be displayed.
- **-n** *ipaddress*   Displays the contents of the ARP cache, where *ipaddress* identifies the network interface for which you want to display the cache.
- **-s** *ipaddress hwaddress* {*interface*}   Adds a new entry to the ARP cache, where the *ipaddress* variable contains the IP address of the computer, the *hwaddress* variable contains the hardware address of the same computer, and the *interface* variable contains the IP address of the network interface in the local system for which you want to modify the cache.
- **-d** *ipaddress* {*interface*}   Deletes the entry in the ARP cache that is associated with the computer represented by the *ipaddress* variable. The optional *interface* variable specifies the cache from which the entry should be deleted.

The ARP table of a Windows 2000 computer, as displayed by Arp.exe, appears as follows:

```
Interface: 192.168.2.6 on Interface 0x1000003
  Internet Address      Physical Address      Type
  192.168.2.10          00-50-8b-e8-39-7a      dynamic
  192.168.2.99          08-00-4e-a5-70-0f      dynamic
```

Netstat.exe

Netstat.exe is a command-line program that displays information about the current network connections of a computer running TCP/IP and about the traffic generated by the various TCP/IP protocols. On UNIX computers the program is simply called netstat, and on Windows computers it's called Netstat.exe. The command-line parameters differ for the various implementations of Netstat, but the information they display is roughly the same. The syntax for the Windows version of Netstat.exe is as follows:

```
Netstat [interval] [-a] [-p protocol] [-n] [-e] [-r] [-s]
```

- *interval*   Causes the program to refresh the display at the specified time interval (in seconds) until the user aborts the command.

- **-a**   Causes the program to display the current network connections and the ports that are currently listening for incoming network connections.

- **-p** *protocol*   Causes the program to display the currently active connections for the protocol specified by the *protocol* variable.

- **-n**   When combined with other parameters, this option causes the program to identify computers using IP addresses instead of names.

- **-e**   Causes the program to display incoming and outgoing traffic statistics for the network interface, broken down into bytes, unicast packets, nonunicast packets, discards, errors, and unknown protocols.

- **-r**   Causes the program to display the routing table plus the current active connections.

- **-s**   Causes the program to display detailed network traffic statistics for the IP, ICMP, TCP, and UDP protocols.

The network connection listing displayed by Netstat.exe on a Windows 2000 computer appears as follows:

```
Active Connections

   Proto  Local Address        Foreign Address        State
   TCP    CZ6:epmap            CZ6.contoso.com:0      LISTENING
   TCP    CZ6:microsoft-ds     CZ6.contoso.com:0      LISTENING
   TCP    CZ6:1051             CZ6.contoso.com:0      LISTENING
   TCP    CZ6:1070             CZ6.contoso.com:0      LISTENING
   TCP    CZ6:2883             CZ6.contoso.com:0      LISTENING
   TCP    CZ6:3348             CZ6.contoso.com:0      LISTENING
   TCP    CZ6:3517             CZ6.contoso.com:0      LISTENING
   TCP    CZ6:3907             CZ6.contoso.com:0      LISTENING
   TCP    CZ6:3937             CZ6.contoso.com:0      LISTENING
   TCP    CZ6:3941             CZ6.contoso.com:0      LISTENING
   TCP    CZ6:3952             CZ6.contoso.com:0      LISTENING
   TCP    CZ6:3956             CZ6.contoso.com:0      LISTENING
   TCP    CZ6:4062             CZ6.contoso.com:0      LISTENING
   TCP    CZ6:6103             CZ6.contoso.com:0      LISTENING
   TCP    CZ6:pop3             CZ6.contoso.com:0      LISTENING
   TCP    CZ6:1365             CZ6.contoso.com:pop3   TIME_WAIT
   TCP    CZ6:1367             CZ6.contoso.com:pop3   TIME_WAIT
   TCP    CZ6:netbios-ssn      CZ6.contoso.com:0      LISTENING
   TCP    CZ6:3846             CZ6.contoso.com:0      LISTENING
   TCP    CZ6:3937             CZ10:1026              ESTABLISHED
   TCP    CZ6:3941             CZ10:1232              ESTABLISHED
   TCP    CZ6:3952             CZ10:1026              ESTABLISHED
   TCP    CZ6:3956             CZ10:1232              ESTABLISHED
   TCP    CZ6:4367             CZ6.contoso.com:0      LISTENING
   TCP    CZ6:4367             CZ10:netbios-ssn       ESTABLISHED
   UDP    CZ6:ntp              *:*
   UDP    CZ6:epmap            *:*
   UDP    CZ6:microsoft-ds     *:*
```

```
UDP      CZ6:1026                    *:*
UDP      CZ6:1039                    *:*
UDP      CZ6:1046                    *:*
UDP      CZ6:1193                    *:*
UDP      CZ6:3938                    *:*
UDP      CZ6:3939                    *:*
UDP      CZ6:3953                    *:*
UDP      CZ6:3954                    *:*
UDP      CZ6:2677                    *:*
UDP      CZ6:3879                    *:*
UDP      CZ6:3942                    *:*
UDP      CZ6:netbios-ns              *:*
UDP      CZ6:netbios-dgm             *:*
UDP      CZ6:isakmp                  *:*
```

The interface statistics display looks like this:

```
Interface Statistics

                          Received              Sent
Bytes                    855899622        2031780028
Unicast packets             744616           1304524
Non-unicast packets          50810              1421
Discards                         0                 0
Errors                           0                 0
Unknown protocols            33220
```

Nbtstat.exe

Nbtstat.exe is a Windows command-line program that displays information about the NetBIOS over TCP/IP connections that Windows uses when communicating with other Windows computers on the TCP/IP LAN. The syntax for Nbtstat.exe is as follows:

```
Nbtstat [-a name] [-A ipaddress] [-c] [-n] [-r] [-R] [-s] [-S] [-RR]
```

- **-a** *name*   Causes the program to display the NetBIOS names registered on the computer identified by the *name* variable.

- **-A** *ipaddress*   Causes the program to display the NetBIOS names registered on the computer identified by the *ipaddress* variable.

- **-c**   Causes the program to display the contents of the local computer's NetBIOS name cache.

- **-n**   Causes the program to display the NetBIOS names registered on the local computer.

- **-r**   Causes the program to display the number of NetBIOS names registered and resolved by the local computer, using both broadcasts and WINS.

- **-R**   Causes the program to purge the local computer's NetBIOS name cache of all entries and reloads the Lmhosts file.

- **-s** Causes the program to display a list of the computer's currently active NetBIOS settings (identifying remote computers by name), their current status, and the amount of data transmitted to and received from each system.

- **-S** Causes the program to display a list of the computer's currently active NetBIOS settings (identifying remote computers by IP address), their current status, and the amount of data transmitted to and received from each system.

- **-RR** Causes the program to send name release requests to WINS and then reregister the names.

Caution Unlike the other utilities discussed in this section, the command-line parameters for Nbtstat.exe are case-sensitive.

The NetBIOS cache listing as displayed by Nbtstat.exe on a Windows 2000 computer appears as follows:

```
Local Area Connection:
Node IpAddress: [192.168.2.6] Scope Id: []

    NetBIOS Remote Cache Name Table

    Name            Type        Host Address    Life [sec]
    ---------------------------------------------------------------
    ------------------------------
    CZ10 <20>       UNIQUE      192.168.2.10    345
```

The list of NetBIOS names registered by a computer looks like this:

```
Local Area Connection:
Node IpAddress: [192.168.2.6] Scope Id: []

    NetBIOS Remote Machine Name Table

    Name            Type        Status
    ---------------------------------------------------------------
    ------------------------------
    CZ6 <00>        UNIQUE      Registered
    CONTOSO <00>    GROUP       Registered
    CZ6 <03>        UNIQUE      Registered
    CZ6 <20>        UNIQUE      Registered
    CONTOSO <1E>    GROUP       Registered

    MAC Address = 00-D0-B7-AD-1A-7B
```

Nslookup.exe

Nslookup.exe is a command-line utility that enables you to generate DNS request messages and transmit them to specific DNS servers on the network. The basic syntax of Nslookup.exe is as follows:

```
NSLOOKUP DNSname DNSserver
```

- **DNSname**   Specifies the DNS name that you want to resolve
- **DNSserver**   Specifies the DNS name or IP address of the DNS server that you want to query for the name specified in the *DNSname* variable

The output generated by the program looks like the following:

```
Server:   ns1-dlls.contoso.com
Address:  10.28.65.115

Non-authoritative answer:
Name:     www.contoso.com
Addresses:  10.46.131.91, 10.46.197.102, 10.46.230.218, 10.46.230.229
Aliases:  www.microsoft.com
```

The advantage of Nslookup is that you can test the functionality and the quality of the information on a specific DNS server by specifying it on the command line. By running Nslookup with no command-line parameters, you can use the program in interactive mode, which lets you employ some of its many options.

Telnet.exe

The Telecommunications Network Protocol (Telnet) is a command-line client/ server program that essentially provides remote control capabilities for computers on a network. A user on one computer can run a Telnet client program and connect to the Telnet server on another computer. Once connected, that user can execute commands on the other system and view the results. It's important to distinguish this type of remote control access from simple access to the remote file system. When you use a Telnet connection to execute a program on a remote computer, the program actually runs on the remote computer. By contrast, if you use Windows to connect to a shared drive on another computer and execute a program, the program runs on your computer.

Telnet was originally designed for use on UNIX systems, and it is still an extremely important tool for UNIX network administrators. The various Windows operating systems all include a Telnet client, but only Windows 2000 and later versions have a Telnet server. The syntax for connecting to a Telnet server is as follows:

```
Telnet target
```

Telnet uses a text-based command and response syntax that was the model for several other important application layer protocols, including File Transfer Protocol (FTP), the Hypertext Transfer Protocol (HTTP), and the Simple Mail Transfer Protocol (SMTP). Because all information transmitted during a Telnet session is in clear text, the protocol presents a security hazard when used on unsecured networks.

Ftp.exe

The File Transfer Protocol (FTP) is similar to Telnet, but it is designed for performing file transfers instead of executing remote commands. FTP includes basic file management commands that can create and remove directories, rename and delete files, and manage access permissions. FTP has become a mainstay of Internet communications in recent years, but it also performs a vital role in communications between UNIX computers, all of which have both FTP client and server capabilities. All Windows computers have a character-based FTP client, but FTP server capabilities are built into the Internet Information Services (IIS) application that is included with the Windows 2000 Server product. Many other FTP clients are also available that offer graphical interfaces and other usability features. Generally speaking, Windows computers don't need FTP for communications on a LAN because they can access the shared files on other computers directly. On many UNIX networks, however, FTP is an important tool for transferring files to and from remote computers.

Exercise 1: TCP/IP Utilities

Match the utilities in the left column with their functions in the right column.

1. FTP

a. Provides remote control access to server

2. Ipconfig.exe

b. Displays TCP/IP configuration on a Windows 98 system

3. Tracert.exe

c. Creates cache entries containing IP and hardware addresses

4. Ping.exe

d. Displays NetBIOS connection information

5. Telnet

e. Tests communications between two computers

6. Netstat

f. Transfers files between two computers

7. Winipcfg.exe

g. Displays network traffic statistics

8. Nbtstat.exe

h. Lists the routers forwarding packets to a particular destination

9. Arp.exe

i. Releases and renews IP address assignments on Windows 2000

Lesson Review

1. Which TCP/IP utility should you use to most easily identify which router on your internetwork is malfunctioning?

   a. Ipconfig.exe

   b. Ping

   c. Tracert.exe

   d. Netstat

2. Which of the following protocols does the Ping.exe program never use to carry its messages?

   a. Ethernet

   b. ICMP

   c. IP

   d. UDP

3. Which of the following commands displays the routing table on the local computer?

   a. Arp –r

   b. Netstat –r

   c. Nbtstat –r

   d. Telnet –r

4. Which command would you use to purge the local computer's NetBIOS name cache?

   a. Nbtstat –p

   b. Nbtstat –P

   d. Nbtstat –r

   d. Nbtstat –R

Lesson Summary

- Ping is a utility that tests whether one TCP/IP computer can communicate with another one.

- Tracert.exe and Pathping.exe are both programs that display the path that packets take through a network to reach their destinations.

- Ipconfig.exe and Winipcfg.exe are Windows programs that display information about the computer's TCP/IP configuration and manipulate DHCP IP address assignments.

- Arp.exe enables you to view and modify the contents of the ARP cache maintained by a TCP/IP system.

- Netstat.exe displays information about a computer's TCP/IP connections and the traffic passing over them.

- Nbtstat.exe displays information about NetBIOS connections and their traffic.

- Nslookup.exe enables you to transmit DNS requests to specific servers.

- Telnet is a character-based terminal emulation program that provides remote control access to another computer on the network.

- FTP is a file transfer utility that enables you to manage files and transfer them to and from a remote computer.

C H A P T E R   4

NetWare Networking with Windows 2000

Lesson 1: Introducing IPX and NWLink. **110**

Lesson 2: Using the Windows 2000 NetWare Clients **121**

About This Chapter

Although Microsoft Windows 2000 uses Transmission Control Protocol/Internet Protocol (TCP/IP) as its default protocols for communications with other Windows computers, as well as with UNIX systems and the Internet, many networks still run Novell NetWare servers. NetWare was the market leader in network operating systems long before Windows was introduced and before TCP/IP had become the ubiquitous networking protocol suite. Although the latest versions of NetWare can use TCP/IP, many of the existing installations rely on Novell's own Internetwork Packet Exchange (IPX) protocols. In this chapter, you learn how to provide your network with NetWare connectivity using NWLink, Microsoft's version of IPX.

Before You Begin

To fully understand the concepts in this chapter, you should first study Chapter 1, "Introducing Windows 2000 Networking."

Lesson 1: Introducing IPX and NWLink

Novell developed the IPX protocol suite specifically for use with its NetWare network operating system. Unlike TCP/IP, the IPX standards were not cooperatively developed or published and remain the sole property of Novell. When Microsoft set about integrating networking capabilities into Windows, NetWare compatibility was considered a crucial factor. Originally, it was agreed that Novell would supply a Windows client for NetWare that would be included as part of the Windows product, but after this client failed to materialize, Microsoft developed its own NetWare clients, including a set of protocols it called NWLink, which was designed to be fully compatible with IPX.

After this lesson, you will be able to

- Describe the functions of the IPX protocol suite
- List the primary protocols in the IPX suite
- Describe the format of an IPX, Sequenced Packet Exchange (SPX), and Network Core Protocol (NCP) message
- Explain how IPX is implemented in Windows 2000

Estimated lesson time: 25 minutes

Introducing IPX

In its basic architectural structure, the IPX protocol suite is somewhat similar to TCP/IP. The IPX protocol for which the suite is named is itself a connectionless, network layer protocol that performs most of the same functions that IP does in the TCP/IP suite. Like IP, IPX is responsible for encapsulating transport layer data, addressing it, and routing it to its destination on the network. The primary difference is one of scale. TCP/IP is designed to support any type of computer on any type of network. IPX was designed for use on local area networks (LANs) because NetWare is strictly a LAN operating system.

The most obvious indication of IPX's LAN-centrism is that it does not have its own self-contained address space, as IP does. IPX uses node addresses to identify specific network interfaces on a network and network addresses to identify specific LANs. However, the node addresses are the data-link layer hardware addresses coded into the computers' network interface adapters, and either NetWare randomly assigns network addresses during installation or the network administrator assigns them manually. There is no need for a network registrar or a separate node addressing system with IPX because the protocols are limited to private LANs.

This brings us to the single greatest shortcoming of IPX, which is its incompatibility with the Internet. When NetWare was first developed, the Internet was a small, experimental project, nothing like it is today. When the popularity of the Internet exploded in the mid-1990s, most software manufacturers modified their product lines to make them Internet-compatible. Microsoft, for example, adopted TCP/IP as the default networking protocols for Windows, replacing NetBIOS Extended User Interface (NetBEUI). Novell stuck with its IPX protocols, however, for several more years. It was not until the release of NetWare 5.0 that the operating system could run natively using TCP/IP, eliminating IPX from the network completely. Despite this advance, however, many networks are still running earlier versions of NetWare that need IPX, and NetWare compatibility is still a Windows issue. If you have Novell NetWare servers on your network, you must install additional software components on your Windows systems for them to access resources on those servers.

IPX Protocols

Like TCP/IP, IPX is a protocol suite that consists of several protocols operating at different layers of the Open Systems Interconnection (OSI) reference model, all of which work together to provide a nearly complete protocol stack. Some of the protocols are examined in the following sections.

Data-Link Layer Protocols

IPX has no data-link layer protocols of its own; it relies completely on the standard LAN protocols used at the data-link layers, such as Ethernet and Token Ring. The only important factor when combining Windows and NetWare on the same LAN is the selection of the correct frame type in the NetWare clients and servers. NetWare supports four Ethernet frame types, which are as follows:

- **Ethernet 802.3.** This frame type, also known as "raw Ethernet," was the original default frame type for all NetWare versions up to and including 3.11. This frame lacks any means of identifying the network layer protocol that generated the information in the frame's Data field. Consequently, this frame type can only be used on a NetWare network running only IPX at the network layer. If you have Windows computers running NWLink on your network, you should not use this frame type.

- **Ethernet 802.2.** This frame type, which is the default for NetWare versions 3.12 and later, conforms more precisely to the Ethernet protocol standards published by the Institute of Electrical and Electronics Engineers (IEEE). This means that you can use the frame type with any products that support IPX at the network layer (including Windows). However, the frame type still lacks a network layer protocol identifier, which means that you can't use it on a network running more than one protocol at the network layer, such as a mixed NetWare/Windows network running both IPX and TCP/IP.

- **Ethernet II.** This frame type is defined by the original DIX (Digital Equipment Corporation, Intel Corporation, and Xerox Corporation) Ethernet standard and includes an Ethertype field that specifies what network layer protocol generated the information in the frame's payload. As a result, you can use this frame type on a network running multiple protocols at the network layer, including IPX and TCP/IP. This is the most commonly used frame type on mixed Windows/NetWare networks.

- **Ethernet SNAP.**   This frame type uses the same format as Ethernet 802.2, except that it includes an additional Subnetwork Access Protocol (SNAP) header in the Data field. The SNAP header has a field that identifies the network layer protocol that generated the data carried in the frame, enabling you to use the frame type on networks running TCP/IP, AppleTalk, or both, in addition to IPX.

In most of the NetWare clients used today, the selection of a frame type is automatic and usually reliable. When troubleshooting network communication problems on a Windows/NetWare network, however, it's a good idea to check that the computers are using an appropriate frame type, and that they are all using the same frame type.

Internetwork Packet Exchange

Like IP, IPX is a networking protocol that provides a connectionless datagram transfer service and controls the addressing and routing of data packets within and between networks. The IPX data encapsulation process involves the addition of a 30-byte header to a payload received from a transport layer protocol. The header format is shown in Figure 4.1.

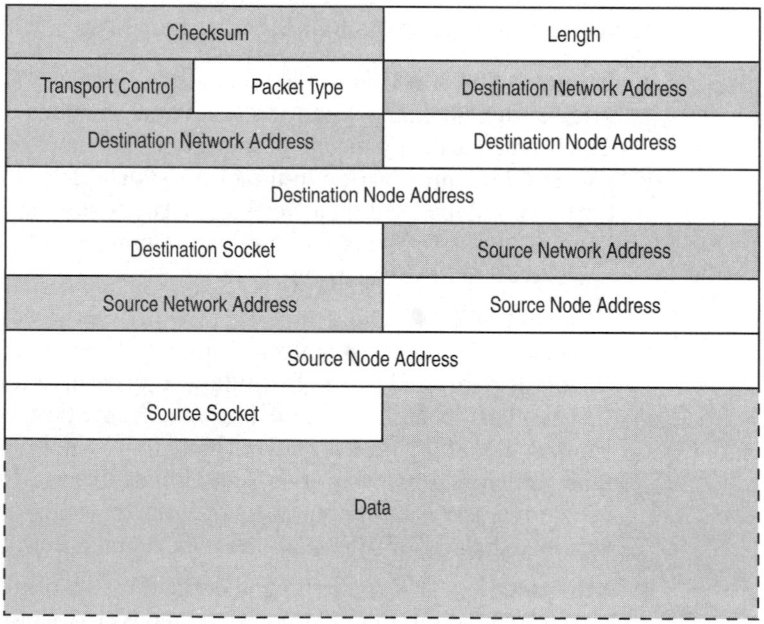

Figure 4.1   The IPX datagram format

The functions of the IPX header fields are as follows:

- **Checksum (2 bytes).** A vestige of the now-unused protocol from which IPX was derived.

- **Length (2 bytes).** Specifies the length of the datagram in bytes, including the IPX header and the data.

- **Transport Control (1 byte).** Also known as the hop count, specifies the number of routers the datagram has passed through on the way to its destination. The computer generating the packet sets the value of this field to 0, and each router increments the field by one as it processes the packet. If the value reaches 16, the packet is discarded.

- **Packet Type (1 byte).** Identifies the upper layer protocol that generated the information carried in the Data field.

- **Destination Network Address (4 bytes).** Identifies the network on which the destination system is located, using a value assigned by the operating system or the administrator during the NetWare installation.

- **Destination Node Address (6 bytes).** Identifies the network interface adapter in the computer to which the data is to be delivered, using the data-link layer protocol hardware address.

- **Destination Socket (2 bytes).** Identifies the application or process on the destination system for which the information in the Data field is intended.

- **Source Network Address (4 bytes).** Identifies the network on which the source system is located, using a value assigned by the operating system or the administrator during the NetWare installation.

- **Source Node Address (6 bytes).** Identifies the network interface adapter in the transmitting computer, using the data-link layer protocol hardware address.

- **Source Socket (2 bytes).** Identifies the application or process on the transmitting system that generated the information in the Data field.

- **Data (variable).** Contains the data generated by the upper layer protocol.

IPX is responsible for end-to-end transmissions across an internetwork and is therefore responsible for network layer addressing and routing, like IP. Both these tasks are somewhat simpler than they are in IP, however, because IPX is working only with private internetworks of limited size. Consider, for example, that IPX discards datagrams after 16 hops, assuming them to be circulating endlessly around the network because of a routing problem. IP datagrams generated by a Windows computer have a Time to Live (TTL) value that enables them to travel as many as 128 hops, because processing by literally dozens of routers is a distinct possibility on the Internet. As with IP, routers on IPX networks use dynamic routing protocols, such as Routing Information Protocol (RIP), to share the routing information they possess.

Sequenced Packet Exchange

SPX is a connection-oriented transport protocol that is often thought of as a frequent partner to IPX, just as TCP is to IP. In fact, the IPX protocol suite is often referred to as the IPX/SPX protocols. However, in actuality, NetWare uses the combination of the IPX and SPX protocols far less frequently than the TCP/IP protocols use TCP and IP together. For example, NetWare's file sharing capability, which generates a substantial amount of the traffic in a typical NetWare network, uses the NetWare Core Protocol (NCP). SPX is relegated to communications between network print devices, remote console sessions, network backups, and other relatively infrequent activities.

Like TCP, SPX provides reliable delivery by assigning sequence numbers to packets and acknowledging specific sequences. A computer receiving SPX data verifies successful delivery of the packets by generating acknowledgment messages and returning them to the sender. If an acknowledgment request brings no response within a specified time, SPX retransmits the request as many as eight times. If no response is received, SPX assumes the connection has failed.

Unlike TCP, the original SPX implementation requires a separate acknowledgment for each data packet. Novell has modified the protocol over the years, adding a packet burst mechanism. Packet burst, also known as burst mode, enables a computer to transmit multiple data packets without requiring that each packet be sequenced and acknowledged individually. By enabling the receiving system to acknowledge multiple packets at once, burst mode can reduce network traffic on most IPX networks. Additionally, the packet burst mechanism monitors dropped packets and retransmits only the missing packets. In Windows 2000, SPX burst mode is enabled by default.

Another enhancement, called SPXII, improves on SPX by enabling it to perform better on high-bandwidth networks. SPXII improves on SPX by allowing a greater number of outstanding packets than SPX and by using larger packets. In SPX there cannot be more than one outstanding unacknowledged packet at any time, whereas in SPXII there can be as many outstanding packets as negotiated by the communicating computers during the establishment of the connection. Also, SPX has a maximum packet size of 576 bytes, whereas SPXII can use the maximum packet size of the data-link layer protocol. For example, on an Ethernet network, SPXII can use packets as large as 1518 bytes.

Because SPX is a connection-oriented protocol, it performs a handshake before transmitting any application data. The header that the protocol adds to the information generated by the application layer protocol is 12 bytes long and is illustrated in Figure 4.2.

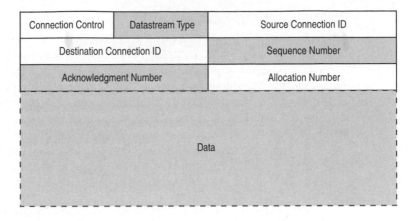

Figure 4.2   The SPX header format

The functions of the SPX header fields are as follows:

- **Connection Control (1 byte).**   Contains a code that helps to regulate the bidirectional flow of data between the computers, indicating, for example, that the packet contains the end of a message, requires an acknowledgment, or is a system packet.

- **Datastream Type (1 byte).**   Indicates the function of the data in the message and the upper layer process for which it is intended.

- **Source Connection ID (2 bytes).**   Contains a unique value used by the source computer to identify this connection, because two computers can have multiple connections open between the same sockets simultaneously.

- **Destination Connection ID (2 bytes).**   Contains the unique value used by the destination computer to identify this connection.

- **Sequence Number (2 bytes).**   Contains a value that identifies this message's place in the sequence of messages that make up the transaction. The destination system uses these values to place the incoming messages in the proper sequence.

- **Acknowledgment Number (2 bytes).**   Contains the sequence number of the next message that the system expects to receive from the connected system, tacitly acknowledging all the packets with lower sequence number values.

- **Allocation Number (2 bytes).**   Provides flow control by specifying the number of packet receive buffers available on the system.

- **Data (variable).**   Contains the information generated by an application layer protocol.

NetWare Core Protocol

NCP is NetWare's primary upper layer protocol and is therefore responsible for the majority of the traffic traveling between clients and servers on most NetWare networks. The protocol carries messages that perform a wide variety of services, including file sharing, printing, directory services communications, messaging, and data synchronization. NCP is difficult to place in the OSI reference model because its functions span the transport, session, presentation, and application layers. However, NCP messages are carried within IPX datagrams, just like those of SPX. There is also a variation on the protocol, called the NetWare Core Packet Burst Protocol (NCPB), which enables a computer to transmit multiple data packets without the need for each one to be acknowledged individually.

NCP uses slightly different headers for request and reply messages. The NCP Request message format is shown in Figure 4.3.

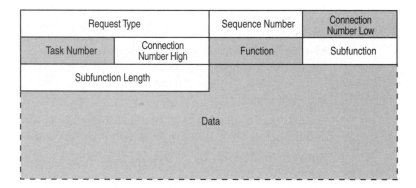

Figure 4.3   The NCP Request message format

The functions of the NCP header fields are as follows:

- **Request Type (2 bytes).**   Specifies the message's basic function.
- **Sequence Number (1 byte).**   Contains a value that identifies this message's place in the sequence of messages that make up the transaction. The destination system uses these values to place the incoming messages in the proper sequence.
- **Connection Number Low (1 byte).**   Contains a value that indicates the number of the client's connection to the server.
- **Task Number (1 byte).**   Contains a unique value that the computers use to associate request messages with replies.
- **Connection Number High (1 byte).**   This field is unused.
- **Function (1 byte).**   Contains a code that indicates the message's specific function.

- **Subfunction (1 byte).**   Contains a code that further defines the message's function.
- **Subfunction Length (2 bytes).**   Specifies the length of the Data field.
- **Data (variable).**   Contains information specific to the type of request, such as the name and location of a file.

The NCP Reply message format is shown in Figure 4.4.

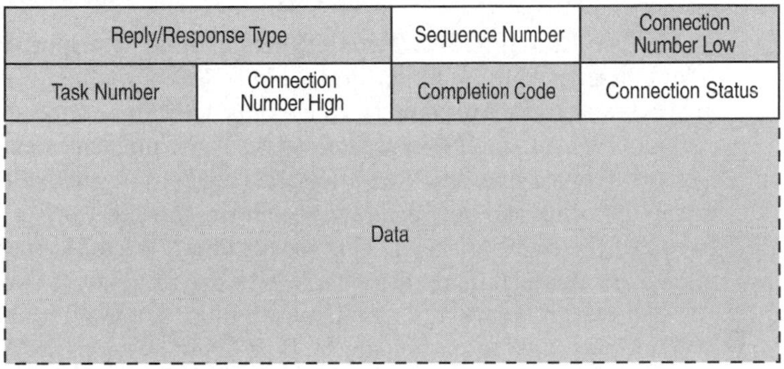

Reply/Response Type		Sequence Number	Connection Number Low
Task Number	Connection Number High	Completion Code	Connection Status
Data			

Figure 4.4   The NCP Reply message format

The functions of the NCP header fields are as follows:

- **Reply/Response Type (2 bytes).**   Specifies the type of reply.
- **Sequence Number (1 byte).**   Contains a value that identifies this message's place in the sequence of messages that make up the transaction. The destination system uses these values to place the incoming messages in the proper sequence.
- **Connection Number Low (1 byte).**   Contains a value that indicates the number of the client's connection to the server.
- **Task Number (1 byte).**   Contains a unique value that the computers use to associate request messages with replies.
- **Connection Number High (1 byte).**   This field is unused.
- **Completion Code (1 byte).**   Specifies whether the associated request succeeded or failed. A value of 0 indicates success; nonzero values indicate failure.
- **Connection Status (1 byte).**   Indicates whether the connection between the client and the server is still active. A value of 0 indicates that the connection is active; a value of 1 indicates that it is not active.
- **Data (variable).**   Contains information transmitted by the server in response to the associated request.

Windows 2000 and NetWare Compatibility

Windows 2000 includes a complete collection of NetWare compatibility components in addition to its Windows networking capability. When you install NWLink on a Windows computer along with an appropriate NetWare client, the computer can access files, printers, and other services on your NetWare servers. The NetWare compatibility components included with Windows 2000 include the NWLink IPX/SPX/NetBIOS Compatible Transport Protocol, a client module, and a Directory Service Migration Tool.

The NWLink IPX/SPX/NetBIOS Compatible Transport Protocol is the IPX counterpart to the Internet Protocol (TCP/IP) module. NWLink provides all network and transport layer services, plus additional upper layer functions as well. The NWLink module is written to the same interfaces as TCP/IP, that is, the Network Device Interface Specification (NDIS) interface at the boundary between the data-link and network layers, and the transport driver interface (TDI) at the top of the transport layer. This means that NWLink can operate parallel to the TCP/IP module, using the same NDIS driver below it and the same client above, as shown in Figure 4.5. One network interface adapter, therefore, can enable Windows 2000 to participate on both Windows and NetWare networks.

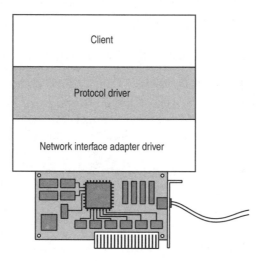

Figure 4.5   NWLink's place in the Windows 2000 networking architecture

In addition to NWLink, Windows 2000 computers also include a NetWare client, which performs roughly the same services as Client for Microsoft Networks, but for NetWare. Windows 2000 Professional comes with Client Service for NetWare (CSNW) and Windows 2000 Server comes with Gateway Service for NetWare

(GSNW). Both of these provide basic client access to NetWare servers, but GSNW includes additional gateway capabilities that CSNW lacks.

You must install NWLink to use Client Service for NetWare or Gateway Service for NetWare to connect to NetWare servers. However, the Windows 2000 NetWare networking components are not your only alternative. Novell also produces its own NetWare client software for Windows, called Novell Client for Windows NT/2000. The Novell client includes its own IPX protocol module, as well as Open Data-link Interface (ODI) network adapter drivers that you can use instead of Windows' own NDIS drivers. ODI drivers are not compatible with the Windows protocol and client modules, however, so you can use them only on a NetWare-only network. NDIS drivers are compatible with both the Windows and Novell networking components, thereby providing your computers with both Windows and NetWare connectivity.

As mentioned earlier, Novell NetWare versions 5.0 and later include native support for TCP/IP, which enables you to eliminate IPX from the network entirely. However, Windows CSNW and GSNW do work with TCP/IP; they require the NWLink protocol module. If you use CSNW and GSNW, you must also enable IPX on your NetWare servers. To access NetWare 5 servers using TCP/IP, you must use Novell Client for Windows NT/2000. In addition, only the Novell client enables you to run NetWare's primary network administration tool, NetWare Administrator.

Exercise 1: IPX Properties

Match the IPX header fields in the left column with the appropriate functions in the right column.

1. Transport Control

    a. Contains a value assigned by the network administrator or the NetWare installation program

2. Source Socket

    b. Is not used in the current IPX protocol implementation

3. Destination Network Address

    c. Has a maximum value of 16.

4. Checksum

    d. Contains a 6-byte value.

5. Source Hardware Address

    e. Identifies the application that generated the packet.

Lesson Review

1. What is the IPX header's equivalent to the TTL field in the IP header?

   a. Packet Type

   b. Transport Control

   c. Checksum

   d. Source Socket

2. Which of the following statements about IPX is untrue?

   a. IPX routes datagrams between different types of networks.

   b. IPX has its own network addressing system.

   c. IPX uses a checksum to verify the proper transmission of data.

   d. The IPX header is larger than the IP header.

3. How many bytes long is the information that IPX uses to identify the datagram's destination computer on a particular network?

   a. 2

   b. 4

   c. 6

   d. 10

4. What is the maximum number of routers that an IPX datagram can pass through on the way to its destination?

   a. 0

   b. 16

   c. 128

   d. 256

Lesson Summary

- IPX is the NetWare equivalent to IP, providing addressing and routing services to NetWare networks.

- The IPX protocol suite consists of the IPX, SPX, and NCP protocols, among others.

- Windows 2000 includes its own version of IPX, called NWLink.

- To identify computers, IPX uses the data-link layer hardware addresses coded into network interface adapters.

- To identify networks, IPX uses network addresses assigned during the NetWare installation.

Lesson 2: Using the Windows 2000 NetWare Clients

To install the NetWare networking components included with Windows 2000, you use the Network and Dial-up Connections Control Panel. When you install the Client Service for NetWare module, Windows 2000 automatically installs the NWLink IPX/SPX/NetBIOS Compatible Transport Protocol module as well because it is required for CSNW to function. You can also install NWLink by itself and use it for Windows communications, but this is rarely done.

After this lesson, you will be able to

- Install Client Service for NetWare
- Configure NWLink and CSNW
- Install Gateway Service for Netware
- Configure the GSNW gateway

Estimated lesson time: 30 minutes

Installing Client Service for NetWare

Before you can install Client Service for NetWare on a Windows 2000 Professional computer, you must have a network interface adapter installed, along with the appropriate device driver. This creates a Local Area Connection icon in the Network And Dial-up Connections window. To install Client Service for NetWare, you need Administrator rights to the computer running Windows 2000 Professional.

To install Client Service for NetWare, use the following procedure:

1. Click Start and select Network And Dial-up Connections from the Settings menu to open the Network And Dial-up Connections window (see Figure 4.6).

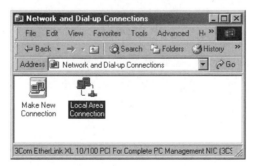

Figure 4.6   The Network And Dial-up Connections window

2. Right-click the Local Area Connection icon and select Properties from the shortcut menu to open the Local Area Connection Properties dialog box (see Figure 4.7).

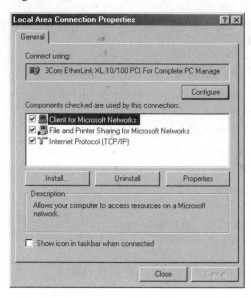

Figure 4.7   The Local Area Connection Properties dialog box

3. In the General tab, click Install to open the Select Network Component Type dialog box (see Figure 4.8).

Figure 4.8   The Select Network Component Type dialog box

4. Select Client, and then click Add to open the Select Network Client dialog box (see Figure 4.9).

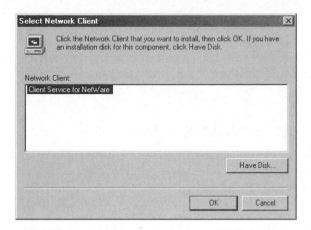

Figure 4.9   The Select Network Client dialog box

5. Click Client Service For NetWare, and then click OK. When asked if you want to restart the computer, click No.

   Back in the Local Area Connection Properties dialog box, notice that the NWLink NetBIOS and NWLink IPX/SPX/NetBIOS Compatible Transport Protocol modules have been automatically installed in addition to Client Services for NetWare.

6. Click OK to complete the installation and close the Local Area Connection Properties dialog box. Restart the computer.

   To confirm that NWLink is working properly, at a command prompt, type **ipxroute config** to display a table with information about the bindings for which NWLink is configured, as illustrated in Figure 4.10.

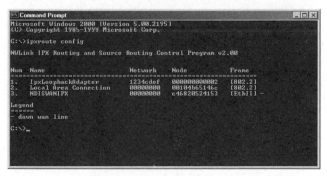

Figure 4.10   NWLink binding information

Tip   If you plan on running a NetWare-only network—that is, one in which your Windows computers access only shared NetWare resources—you can remove the Client for Microsoft Networks and Internet Protocol (TCP/IP) modules from the Local Area Connection Properties dialog box or unbind them from the network adapter.

Configuring NWLink

In most cases you can use the NWLink protocol immediately after installing it, with no additional configuration. However, there are occasions when you might have to modify the default NWLinks settings, and it's a good idea to know what they represent. To configure NWLink, use the following procedure:

1. Click Start and select Network And Dial-up Connections from the Settings menu to open the Network And Dial-up Connections window.

2. Right-click the Local Area Connection icon and select Properties from the shortcut menu to open the Local Area Connection Properties dialog box.

3. Select NWLink IPX/SPX/NetBIOS Compatible Transport Protocol and click Properties to open the NWLink IPX/SPX/NetBIOS Compatible Transport Protocol Properties dialog box (see Figure 4.11).

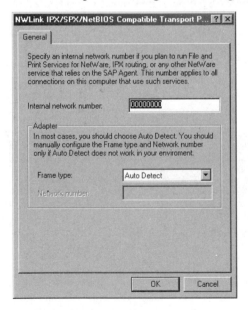

Figure 4.11   The NWLink IPX/SPX/NetBIOS Compatible Transport Protocol Properties dialog box

4. Specify values for any or all of the Internal Network Number, Frame Type, and Network Number settings and click OK to close the NWLink IPX/SPX/ NetBIOS Compatible Transport Protocol Properties dialog box.

5. Click OK to close the Local Area Connection Properties dialog box.

The internal network number is used for internal routing purposes when the computer running Windows 2000 is also hosting IPX services. When calculating the best possible route for transmitting packets to a specified computer, multiple routes with the same route metrics can present ambiguity to computer hosts. When you specify a unique internal network number, you create a virtual network inside the computer. This creates a singular optimum path from the network to the services running on the computer.

As discussed in Lesson 1 of this chapter, the frame type defines the way in which the computer's network adapter formats the NWLink data for transmission over the network. For a Windows 2000 computer to communicate with NetWare servers, it must be configured to use the same frame type as the servers. By default, the NWLink module is configured to automatically detect the frame type used on the network and configure itself accordingly. During the autodetection process, NWLink tries each of the frame types for the data-link layer protocol used by the network interface adapter. For example, on an Ethernet network, NWLink tries the Ethernet 802.2, Ethernet 802.3, Ethernet II, and Ethernet SNAP frame types to see which ones it can use to communicate with the other IPX systems on the network. On computers using Token Ring or Fiber Distributed Data Interface (FDDI), there are two different frame types. When NWLink receives a response from a NetWare server with one of the frame types, it also receives the network number associated with that frame type for the network segment on which the client resides. NWLink then rebinds using the frame types from which it received responses. If NWLink detects no network traffic or if multiple frame types are detected in addition to the 802.2 frame type, NWLink sets the frame type to 802.2.

Occasionally, the autodetection mechanism selects an inappropriate network number and frame type combination for the adapter. Because the mechanism uses the responses it receives from computers on the same network segment, it might select an incorrect frame type and network number if the computers responded with incorrect values. This is usually caused by an incorrect manual setting on another computer on the network.

If the autodetection mechanism selects an inappropriate frame type and network number for a particular adapter, you can manually set a frame type in the NWLink IPX/SPX/NetBIOS Compatible Transport Protocol Properties dialog box. Changing the contents of the Frame Type box to any value but Auto Detect activates the Network Number box, enabling you to specify the network number currently used by the network segment to which the computer is connected. The external network number is a unique number that represents a specific network segment and associated frame type. All computers on the same network segment that use a given frame type must have the same external network number, which must be unique for each network segment. The IPX frame type and network number are set during the initial NetWare server configuration, so it is best to check a NetWare server, rather than another client workstation, to determine the correct Network Number value.

Configuring Client Service for NetWare

When you install the Client Service for NetWare module in the Local Area Connection Properties dialog box, a Select NetWare Logon dialog box appears, as shown in Figure 4.12.

Figure 4.12   The Select NetWare Logon dialog box

In this dialog box, you can specify either a preferred NetWare server to which the client will always connect first, or a default Novell Directory Services (NDS) tree and context that the client will use to log in to the network. You can also specify whether the client should execute the login scripts associated with the user's account. The tree and context define the position of the user object for the user name you use to log on to an NDS tree. A preferred server is the NetWare server to which you are automatically connected when you log on if your network does not use NDS. You set a default tree and context only in an NDS environment; otherwise, you set a preferred server.

You do not have to specify login parameters for the client during the client installation, however. You can access the configuration parameters for Client Service for NetWare at any time through the CSNW Control Panel created during the client installation process. When you double-click the CSNW icon in the Control Panel, you see the dialog box shown in Figure 4.13. In this dialog box, you can set the Preferred Server, Default Tree And Context, and Run Login Script parameters, as well as configure the client's printing behavior.

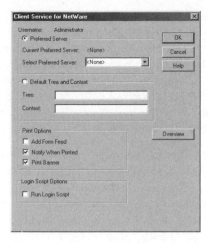

Figure 4.13   The Client Service For NetWare dialog box

Using Gateway Service for NetWare

Installing Client Service for NetWare is one way to provide a Windows 2000 Professional computer with access to NetWare resources on the network, but there is another way. The Gateway Service for NetWare included with Windows 2000 Server is a superset of CSNW. The server computer can access NetWare file and print resources just like a workstation running CSNW, but it can also function as a gateway to those resources, enabling Windows computers to access NetWare resources through the Windows 2000 server.

Gateway Service for NetWare acts as a bridge between the NetBIOS protocol used by the Windows network and the NetWare Core Protocol used by the NetWare network. When you enable a gateway on the network, computers running Microsoft client software can access NetWare files and printers without having to run NetWare client software locally. Figure 4.14 shows an example of a gateway configuration.

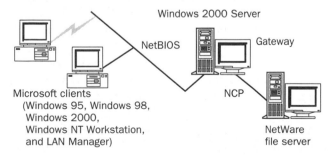

Figure 4.14   A GSNW gateway configuration

For file access, the gateway server maps one of its own drives to the NetWare volume and then shares that drive with other Microsoft clients. The gateway uses a NetWare account on the Windows 2000 Server computer to create a validated connection to the NetWare server. This connection appears on the Windows 2000 Server computer as a normal mapped drive. When you share the mapped drive, it becomes like any other shared Windows network resource. Other computers on the network can access the drive like any other shared Windows resource, without being aware that the shared files and folder are actually stored on a NetWare server.

After the gateway connection between the Windows 2000 server and the NetWare server is established, it is disconnected only if the computer running Windows 2000 Server is turned off, if the administrator disconnects the shared resource or disables the gateway, or if a network problem prevents access to the NetWare server. GSNW is a service that runs continually, so logging off the computer running Windows 2000 Server does not, by itself, disconnect the gateway.

Accessing NetWare resources through a gateway is generally slower and less efficient than accessing them directly using a NetWare client. This is particularly true when you have a large number of clients accessing NetWare resources through the gateway, because all the access requests have to go through one GSNW computer and be transmitted again to the NetWare server. GSNW is intended for servicing clients that require only occasional access to NetWare resources, or for when you are gradually migrating your network from NetWare to Windows 2000 and want to provide users with temporary access to resources on a NetWare server before you move them to a Windows server.

The advantages of GSNW are that you don't have to install a NetWare client and the IPX or NWLink protocols on every computer accessing the NetWare resources, and you don't have to maintain separate accounts for all your users on both Windows and NetWare. This can save network administrators a great deal of work.

Installing Gateway Service for NetWare

You have the option to install Gateway Service for NetWare when you install Windows 2000 Server, or you can install GSNW later. You must be logged on as a member of the Administrators group to install and configure GSNW.

Important Before you install Gateway Service for NetWare on a computer, remove any existing client software that is compatible with NetWare Core Protocol, including any Novell client software, from the computer.

To install Gateway Service for NetWare after the operating system installation, use the following procedure:

1. Click Start and select Network And Dial-up Connections from the Settings menu to open the Network And Dial-up Connections window.

2. Right-click the Local Area Connection icon and select Properties from the shortcut menu to open the Local Area Connection Properties dialog box.

3. In the General tab, click Install to open the Select Network Component Type dialog box.

4. Highlight Client, and then click Add to open the Select Network Client dialog box.

5. Click Gateway (And Client) Service For NetWare, and then click OK. When asked if you want to restart the computer, click No.

   As with CSNW, installing Gateway Service for NetWare also causes Windows 2000 to install the NWLink NetBIOS and NWLink IPX/SPX/NetBIOS Compatible Transport Protocol modules, if they have not been installed already.

6. Click OK to complete the installation and close the Local Area Connection Properties dialog box. Restart the computer.

Configuring Gateway Service for NetWare

As with CSNW, when you install Gateway Service for NetWare, Windows 2000 prompts you to specify a default NDS tree and context or a preferred server. The Gateway Service For NetWare dialog box is illustrated in Figure 4.15.

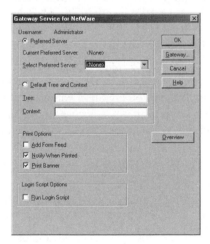

Figure 4.15   Gateway Service For NetWare dialog box

To set a preferred server later, open the GSNW Control Panel to display the Gateway Service For NetWare dialog box, click the Preferred Server option button and, in Select Preferred Server, type the name of the NetWare server you want to use. If you do not want to set a preferred server, click None. You are then logged on to the nearest available NetWare server, and your interaction with the

NetWare network is through that server. If you do not set a preferred server, you are prompted to set one each time you log on.

If you are running NDS on your network, you can specify a default tree and context in place of the preferred server; you cannot configure both. If you select a default tree and context, you can still access NetWare servers that use bindery security. To set a default tree and context, open the GSNW Control Panel, click the Default Tree And Context option button and type the tree name and the context where your user object is located in the Tree and Context boxes.

Creating a Gateway

Before you can create a gateway to NetWare resources using GSNW, you must create a group called NTGATEWAY, either on your preferred NetWare server or in the NDS tree and context you specified. The NTGATEWAY group must also have a user account as a member with the permissions needed to access the NetWare resources you want to share with your Windows users.

The NetWare user account you use to enable gateways can be either an NDS account or a bindery account. If the server will have gateways to both NDS and bindery resources, you should use a bindery account (which can connect to NDS resources using bindery emulation). If you intend to create gateways only to NDS resources, you can use an NDS account.

Enabling Gateways in Windows 2000

Creating a gateway on a Windows 2000 Server computer is a two-step process. First, you enable the gateway, which provides the means for the client to log on to the NetWare resources. When you enable a gateway, you must type the name and password of the user account that has access to the NetWare server and is a member of the NTGATEWAY group. You do this only once for each server that will act as a gateway.

To enable a gateway in Windows 2000 Server, use the following procedure:

1. Click Start, point to Settings, click Control Panel, and then choose Gateway Service For NetWare.

2. Click Gateway to display the Configure Gateway dialog box (see Figure 4.16).

3. Select the Enable Gateway check box. This activates the Gateway Account, Password, and Confirm Password boxes.

4. In the Gateway Account box, type the name of the account you created in the NetWare NTGATEWAY group.

5. In the Password and Confirm Password boxes, type the password for the gateway account. Click OK to close the dialog box.

   You can now share NetWare file and printing resources over a Windows-based network.

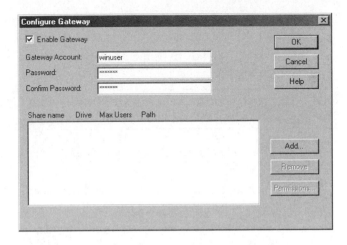

Figure 4.16   The Configure Gateway dialog box

Activating Gateways

The second step in the gateway creation process is to activate a gateway for each volume or printer you want to share. When you activate a gateway, you identify the NetWare resource to be shared and specify the share name that Windows clients will use to access the resource. To activate a gateway for a volume, you use the Gateway Service for NetWare Control Panel. To activate a gateway for a printer, you use the Add Printer Wizard. If you are activating a gateway to an NDS resource and the gateway user is a bindery account, use a bindery context name to identify the resource. If you are using an NDS user account and you do not plan on also creating gateways to bindery resources, specify the NDS resource name.

To activate a gateway to a NetWare file resource, use the following procedure:

1. Click Start, point to Settings, click Control Panel, and then choose Gateway Service For NetWare.
2. Click Gateway to open the Configure Gateway dialog box.
3. Click Add to display the New Share dialog box (see Figure 4.17).

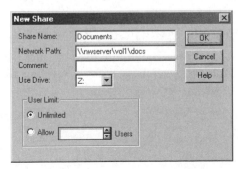

Figure 4.17   The New Share dialog box

4. In the Share Name box, type a share name that Microsoft clients will use to access the NetWare resource.

5. In the Network Path box, type the network path of the NetWare volume or directory you want to share.

Note   When specifying the value for the Network Path field, you use Universal Naming Convention (UNC) notation, as in \\netwareserver\netwarevolume.

6. In Use Drive, type the default drive you want to map to the share, if necessary.

7. Click Unlimited, and then click OK to add the share to the list in the Configure Gateway dialog box.

   You can also click Allow, enter a maximum number of concurrent users, and then click OK.

8. Repeat steps 3 through 7 to create additional shares, or click OK to close the Configure Gateway dialog box.

9. Click OK to close the Gateway Service For NetWare dialog box.

   To activate a gateway to a NetWare printer, you create a network printer in the Printers window in the usual manner, specifying the name of a NetWare printer instead of a Windows printer, and then share the printer from its Properties dialog box.

Securing Gateway Resources

Security for gateway resources is provided on two levels:

- On the computer running Windows 2000 Server and acting as a gateway, you can set share-level permissions for each of the resources made available through the gateway.

- On the NetWare server, the NetWare administrator can assign trustee rights to the user account that is used for the gateway or to the NTGATEWAY group. These rights are enforced for all Microsoft client users who access the resource through the gateway.

Exercise 1: Installing and Configuring NWLink

In this exercise, you install and configure the NWLink IPX/SPX/NetBIOS Compatible Transport Protocol by itself, without a NetWare client. You also change the binding order of the protocols.

1. Click Start and select Network And Dial-Up Connections from the Settings program group.

2. Right-click the Local Area Connection icon and select Properties from the shortcut menu to open the Local Area Connection Properties dialog box. What networking components are currently installed on the computer?

3. Click Add to open the Select Network Component Type dialog box.

4. Select Protocol and then click Add to open the Select Network Protocol dialog box.

5. Select NWLink IPX/SPX/NetBIOS Compatible Transport Protocol, and then click OK to return to the Local Area Connection Properties dialog box. What networking components have been added to the components list?

6. Click OK to close the Local Area Connection Properties dialog box.

7. In the Network And Dial-Up Connections Control Panel, click the Local Area Connection icon and select Advanced Settings from the Advanced menu to open the Advanced Settings dialog box (see Figure 4.18).

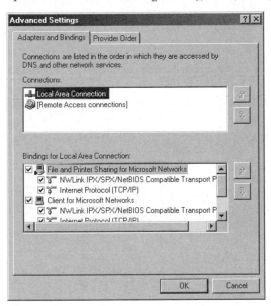

Figure 4.18 The Advanced Settings dialog box

8. Select Local Area Connection in the Connections list. What is the binding order for the File and Printer Sharing for Microsoft Networks module?

9. In the bindings for Local Area Connection list, select NWLink IPX/SPX/ NetBIOS Compatible Transport Protocol and click the down arrow to move it below Internet Protocol (TCP/IP). How does this modify the networking behavior of the computer?

10. Click OK to close the Advanced Settings dialog box.

Lesson Review

1. What is NWLink and how does it relate to Windows 2000?

2. What is SPX?

3. What is Gateway Service for NetWare?

4. When choosing between using Client Service for NetWare and Gateway Service for NetWare, what should you consider?

5. What is the NWLink autodetection mechanism?

6. Which of the following is not true of the SPX protocol?

    a. It is connection-oriented.

    b. It operates at the transport layer only.

    c. Clients use it to access server files.

    d. It provides flow control.

7. At which layers of the OSI reference model does the NCP provide functions?

Lesson Summary

- You install Client Service for NetWare from the Local Area Connection Properties dialog box.

- When you install Client Service for NetWare on Windows 2000, the NWLink IPX/SPX/NetBIOS Compatible Transport Protocol is automatically installed.

- You can configure NWLink to use specific Internal Network Number, Frame Type, and Network Number values.

- Gateway Service for NetWare enables Windows computers to access NetWare resources without having a NetWare client installed.

- You configure GSNW by supplying credentials that enable the Windows 2000 Server computer to access NetWare resources as a client and then creating Windows shares for those resources.

CHAPTER 5

Implementing the Dynamic Host Configuration Protocol

Lesson 1: Introducing DHCP 138

Lesson 2: Using the DHCP Server 152

Lesson 3: Administering DHCP 176

Lesson 4: Troubleshooting DHCP 187

About This Chapter

Dynamic Host Configuration Protocol (DHCP) is a service that enables computers on a network to automatically request and receive Transmission Control Protocol/ Internet Protocol (TCP/IP) configuration settings from a central server, rather than through a manual configuration process. Using DHCP relieves network administrators of several onerous chores, including the assignment and tracking of IP addresses and the need to travel to each computer to configure it individually. In this chapter, you learn how DHCP works and how to implement it on your own network.

Before You Begin

To fully understand the benefits of DHCP, you should be familiar with the TCP/IP protocols and particularly with the IP addressing process, as discussed in Chapter 2, "Introducing TCP/IP." To perform the exercises in this chapter, you must have two Microsoft Windows 2000 computers connected to a local area network (LAN). One of the computers must be running Windows 2000 Server and have Network Monitor installed; the other computer can be running any version of Windows 2000 and must be configured to function as a DHCP client.

Lesson 1: Introducing DHCP

The use of the TCP/IP protocol suite on a private network provides a number of distinct advantages, such as the ability of the protocols to support any computing platform. The main element that provides this cross-platform interoperability is the independent IP addressing scheme that uniquely identifies every computer on the network. Unfortunately, this great advantage is also the cause of a major administrative problem. Assigning unique IP addresses to every computer on a large network is difficult, and manually configuring every computer to use those addresses is extremely time-intensive and labor-intensive. As a solution to this problem, DHCP automates the IP address assignment process and eliminates the need to configure every TCP/IP computer on the network.

After this lesson, you will be able to

- Describe the development of DHCP
- Describe the DHCP message format
- Understand DHCP communications

Estimated lesson time: 45 minutes

Understanding the Origins of DHCP

The roots of DHCP began in the days when it was common to use diskless workstations—that is, computers with no disk drives—on local area networks for economic reasons. To use a diskless workstation on a TCP/IP network, the computer still had to have a unique IP address, so a group of developers created a protocol called the Reverse Address Resolution Protocol (RARP) to make IP address assignment possible. RARP is standardized in a Request For Comments (RFC) document, published by the Internet Engineering Task Force (IETF), called RFC 903. It is closely related to the Address Resolution Protocol (ARP) still used on TCP/IP networks today. The difference between the two is that with RARP, a computer transmits a message containing its data-link layer hardware address to a server and receives in reply a message containing an IP address for it to use. ARP, by contrast, is used to resolve IP addresses into hardware addresses.

A RARP server uses the same message format as ARP and is a simple mechanism for assigning IP addresses over the network. RARP is insufficient for the configuration of a modern TCP/IP client, however, for several reasons. Chief among these is that RARP assigns a workstation an IP address only; it cannot assign a subnet mask or other TCP/IP configuration parameters. Also, an administrator must configure a RARP server with the individual IP address assignments, so it provides no help in tracking address assignments.

The next step in the development of an automated TCP/IP configuration solution is called the Bootstrap Protocol (BOOTP), which is based on a standard published as RFC 951 with extensions in the RFC 1533 and RFC 1542 documents. BOOTP offers several improvements over RARP, including the ability to supply clients with subnet masks, router addresses, and other TCP/IP configuration parameters in addition to IP addresses. Diskless workstations can also download an executable boot file from a BOOTP server using the Trivial File Transfer Protocol (TFTP).

BOOTP messages are carried in User Datagram Protocol (UDP) datagrams, whereas RARP messages are carried directly in data-link layer protocol frames. BOOTP also has a mechanism to support clients on other LANs through the use of *BOOTP relay agents*, which forward messages to a BOOTP server on another network.

The drawback of BOOTP, as with RARP, is that an administrator must create a configuration for each client on the BOOTP server. BOOTP therefore does nothing to prevent configuration errors such as duplicate or incorrect IP addresses.

To address these shortcomings, a group of developers set out to define an improvement to BOOTP that would provide a complete, automated TCP/IP client configuration solution. The result was the Dynamic Host Configuration Protocol (DHCP), as defined in RFC 2131. The developers' design goals in creating DHCP included the following:

- DHCP client computers should require no manual configuration. Each client should be able to discover appropriate local configuration parameters without user intervention and incorporate the parameters into its own configuration.

- DHCP clients should require no manual configuration. Under normal circumstances, the user or network administrator should not have to enter any per-client configuration parameters.

- DHCP should not require a server on each subnet. To allow for scalability and economy, DHCP must be able to function across routers or through the intervention of BOOTP relay agents.

- DHCP clients must be capable of handling multiple responses to a request for configuration parameters. This is to enable the installation of multiple, overlapping DHCP servers to provide fault tolerance and increase performance.

- DHCP must coexist with statically configured, nonparticipating hosts and with existing network protocol implementations.

- DHCP must be capable of providing service to existing BOOTP clients.

- DHCP must be able to ensure that any specific network address will not be in use by more than one DHCP client at a time.

- DHCP clients must retain their configurations across a DHCP client reboot. A DHCP client should, whenever possible, be assigned the same configuration parameters in response to each request.

- DHCP clients must retain their configuration across a DHCP server reboot. Whenever possible, a DHCP client should be assigned the same configuration parameters despite restarts of the DHCP server mechanism.

- DHCP must support fixed or permanent allocation of configuration parameters to specific clients.

The resulting DHCP mechanism is a combination of a client/server application and a protocol that performs two basic tasks: IP address assignment and configuration of other TCP/IP client parameters. As illustrated in Figure 5.1, each time a DHCP client starts, it requests IP addressing information from a DHCP server, including the IP address, the subnet mask, and optional values. The optional values might include a default gateway address, Domain Name System (DNS) address, and Windows Internet Name Service (WINS) server address.

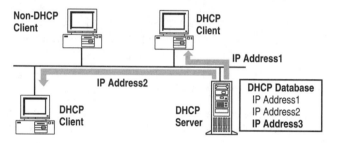

Figure 5.1 How a DHCP client interacts with a DHCP server

When a DHCP server receives a request, it selects IP addressing information from a pool of addresses defined in its database and offers it to the DHCP client. If the client accepts the offer, the IP addressing information is leased to the client for a specified period of time. If no available IP addressing information is in the pool to lease to a client, the client cannot initialize TCP/IP.

Assigning IP Addresses

To assign IP addresses to clients, DHCP uses a pool of addresses called a *scope*. When you configure the DHCP server, you create a scope consisting of a range of IP addresses for each of your subnets. When a DHCP client requests an address from a DHCP server, the server assigns an address from the appropriate scope and updates its internal database to show that address as being in use. This is an improvement over BOOTP, which relies on an administrator to configure the server with an IP address for each client. A DHCP server cannot assign the same IP address to two different computers and continuously maintains a record of addresses currently in use.

To fulfill the developers' intentions, DHCP can assign IP addresses using three methods:

- **Manual allocation.** The assignment of a single predetermined IP address to a specific DHCP client, identified by its data-link layer hardware address. Manual allocation is intended for use on clients that must have particular IP addresses permanently assigned to them, such as Internet servers. Using manual allocation rather than configuring these clients by hand prevents the IP addresses from being duplicated because of human error.

- **Automatic allocation.** The permanent assignment of IP addresses from a scope. When a client is assigned an address, it retains it until an administrator manually changes the configuration. Automatic allocation is intended for networks where client computers are rarely moved between subnets, there is no shortage of IP addresses, and administrators want to minimize the network traffic generated by DHCP.

- **Dynamic allocation.** The assignment of IP addresses from a scope on a leased basis. When a client is assigned an address, a lease timer begins counting down until the lease is renewed by the client or it expires, in which case the IP address is returned to the scope. Dynamic allocation makes it possible for client computers to be moved to other subnets without depleting the supply of IP addresses.

Configuring TCP/IP Parameters

IP address assignment is only a part of DHCP's functionality. To support large network installations, TCP/IP client workstations have to be assigned a subnet mask and usually other settings, such as default gateway and DNS server addresses, as well. DHCP makes this possible by providing support for a large number of options that correspond to the configuration parameters for a wide variety of DHCP client configurations. The object is to provide support for all the possible TCP/IP configuration parameters required by the many computing platforms that use DHCP. DHCP also supports a vendor-specific information option that enables third-party developers and network administrators to create customized options that they can apply to specific clients.

RFC 2132, "DHCP Options and BOOTP Vendor Extensions," contains a list of the options that DHCP server implementations should support. Vendors can submit options designed to support their products for evaluation and inclusion in the document.

DHCP Messaging

DHCP consists of the following three parts:

- A service that responds to DHCP requests from clients and maintains records of IP address assignments

- A client that generates requests for TCP/IP parameters and configures the TCP/IP client
- The protocol that the clients and server use to communicate

DHCP is an application layer protocol that generates messages that are transmitted using UDP. Both the DHCP client and the DHCP server have well-known port numbers assigned to them. The DHCP client uses port 68 and the DHCP server uses port 67. These are the same port numbers used by BOOTP, which is one factor that helps DHCP servers provide support for earlier BOOTP clients.

DHCP clients and servers use just one basic message format for their communications, which is illustrated in Figure 5.2.

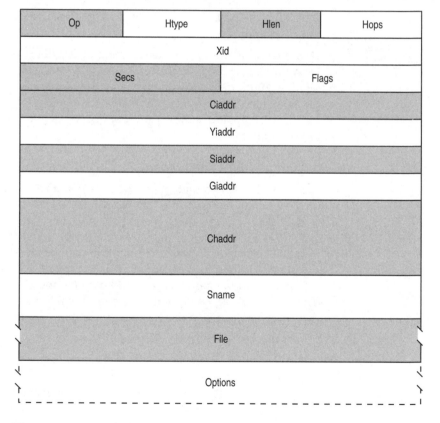

Figure 5.2   The DHCP message format

The functions of the message fields are as follows:

- **Op (1 byte).**   Specifies whether the message originated at a client or a server
- **Htype (1 byte).**   Specifies the type of hardware address in the Chaddr field

- **Hlen (1 byte).**   Specifies the length of the hardware address in the Chaddr field, in bytes

- **Hops (1 byte).**   Specifies the number of routers in the path between the client and the server

- **Xid (4 bytes).**   Contains a transaction identifier used to associate requests and replies

- **Secs (2 bytes).**   Specifies the elapsed time (in seconds) since the beginning of an address allocation or lease renewal process

- **Flags (2 bytes).**   Indicates whether DHCP servers and relay agents should use broadcast transmissions instead of unicast transmissions to communicate with a client

- **Ciaddr (4 bytes).**   Contains the client computer's IP address when it is in the bound, renewal, or rebinding state

- **Yiaddr (4 bytes).**   Contains the IP address being offered to a client by a server

- **Siaddr (4 bytes).**   Specifies the IP address of the next server in a bootstrap sequence; used only when the DHCP server supplies an executable boot file to a diskless workstation

- **Giaddr (4 bytes).**   Contains the IP address of a DHCP relay agent located on a different network, when necessary

- **Chaddr (16 bytes).**   Contains the hardware address of the client system, using the type and length specified in the Htype and Hlen fields

- **Sname (64 bytes).**   Contains either the host name of the DHCP server or overflow data from the Options field

- **File (128 bytes).**   Contains the name and path to an executable boot file for diskless workstations

- **Options (variable).**   Contains a series of DHCP options, which specify the configuration parameters for the client computer

The Options field is where DHCP messages carry all the TCP/IP configuration parameters other than the IP address. The field can contain multiple options, each of which (in most cases) consists of three subfields (see Figure 5.3).

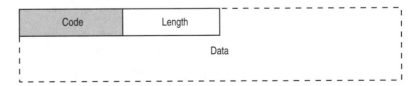

Figure 5.3   The DHCP Option field format

The three subfields of the Options field are as follows:

- **Code (1 byte).** Specifies the function of the option
- **Length (1 byte).** Specifies the length of the Data field
- **Data (variable).** Contains information specific to the option type

DHCP messages can carry a great many options in the Options field, some of which are listed in the following sections.

The Message Type Option

Although it sounds like a contradiction in terms, one option is required in every DHCP message. This is the DHCP Message Type option, which contains a code that specifies the function of each message. This option has eight possible values, as follows:

- **1—DHCPDISCOVER.** Used by clients to request configuration parameters from a DHCP server
- **2—DHCPOFFER.** Used by servers to offer IP addresses to requesting clients
- **3—DHCPREQUEST.** Used by clients to accept or renew an IP address assignment
- **4—DHCPDECLINE.** Used by clients to reject an offered IP address
- **5—DHCPACK.** Used by servers to acknowledge a client's acceptance of an offered IP address
- **6—DHCPNAK.** Used by servers to reject a client's acceptance of an offered IP address
- **7—DHCPRELEASE.** Used by clients to terminate an IP address lease
- **8—DHCPINFORM.** Used by clients to obtain additional TCP/IP configuration parameters from a server

The Pad Option

The Pad option does not use the three subfields listed earlier and does not carry any additional information. The option consists of a 1-byte code field with a value of 0 that the transmitting computer uses to pad out other options so that their boundaries fall between 8-byte words.

The End Option

The End option indicates the end of the Options field.

The Option Overload Option

When a DHCP message includes a large number of options, it can exceed the maximum size of the Options field, which is itself limited by the 576-byte maximum size for an IP datagram. To carry the maximum amount of option information in a message, it's possible for the transmitting system to utilize the Sname and File fields to carry additional options. These two fields are holdovers from BOOTP that are rarely used today. By including the Option Overload option, the transmitting computer can specify whether the Sname field, the File field, or both, carry option information. Together, these two fields can hold an extra 192 bytes of option information.

BOOTP Vendor Information Extensions

RFC 2132 is the latest version of a document that has undergone several revisions and updates over the years. The original version of the document, RFC 1497, contained the most basic of the DHCP options, the ones that you are most likely to use today to support your TCP/IP clients. In addition to the Pad and End options already discussed, these original DHCP options include the following:

- **Subnet Mask.**   Specifies which bits of the IP address identify the host system and which bits identify the network where the host system is located
- **Router.**   Specifies the IP address of the router (or default gateway) on the local network that the client should use to transmit data to systems on other networks
- **Domain Name Server.**   Specifies the IP addresses of the servers that the client will use for DNS name resolution
- **Host Name.**   Specifies the DNS host name that the client system will use
- **Domain Name.**   Specifies the name of the DNS domain in which the system is located

The Vendor-Specific Information Option

The Vendor-Specific Information option is designed to enable third-party developers to use DHCP to deliver configuration information required for their products. The option can itself contain multiple options, each of which has its own Code, Length, and Data field, plus an End option to indicate the end of the vendor-specific options. To ensure that the vendor-specific option information is delivered only to the computers using the vendor's product, you assign a unique value to those systems using the Vendor Class Identifier option in the DHCP messages. You then configure the DHCP clients using the vendor's product with the same class identifier so that they know to process the vendor-specific options.

Other Options

The other options defined in the RFC 2132 document are grouped into several different categories, such as the following:

- **Host-specific IP layer parameters.**   Configure various Internet Protocol settings on the client computer, such as the default Time to Live settings and whether the client system should be configured to route IP packets

- **Interface-specific IP layer parameters.**   Configure settings that are particular to the network interface over which the DHCP message arrives, such as the maximum transmission unit (MTU) size for the interface and the broadcast address it should use

- **Link layer parameters.**   Configure settings specific to the link (or data-link) layer protocol running on the client computer, such as the ARP cache timeout interval and the Ethernet frame type the system should use

- **TCP parameters.**   Configure TCP-specific settings on the client, such as the TCP Time to Live value

- **Application and service parameters.**   Configure settings for specific application layer processes, including the NetBIOS over TCP/IP parameters used to control the use of WINS on Windows systems

- **DHCP extensions.**   Configure settings that control the behavior of the DHCP client itself, such as the length of the DHCP address lease and the renewal and rebinding time values

Although most, if not all, DHCP server implementations support the use of all these options, not all DHCP clients can process them, even if the option represents a configurable parameter on the client computer. In other words, even though you might be able to manually modify the ARP cache timeout setting on a given workstation, this does not necessarily mean that including the DHCP ARP Cache Timeout option in your DHCP messages can automatically configure that setting.

Understanding DHCP Communications

Activating a DHCP client causes it to initiate communications with DHCP servers whenever the computer starts, as illustrated in Figure 5.4. The client generates a series of DHCP packets using the DHCPDISCOVER message type, which it transmits as broadcasts. The function of these messages is to locate DHCP servers and to request an IP address assignment from them. Broadcasts are the client's only option at this point because it has no IP address yet, and it is therefore said to be in the *init* state. Like all broadcasts, these transmissions are limited to the client's local network and, under normal conditions, reach only the DHCP servers located on that network. However, administrators can install a DHCP Relay Agent service on a computer on the LAN, which relays the DHCPDISCOVER messages to DHCP servers on other networks. This enables a single DHCP server to service clients on multiple LANs.

When a DHCP server receives a DHCPDISCOVER message from a client, it generates a response using the DHCPOFFER message type, containing an IP address and whatever other DHCP options the server is configured to supply. How the server transmits the DHCPOFFER message to the client is determined by a variety of factors. Chief among these is the state of the "broadcast bit," which is included in the Flags field of the DHCPDISCOVER message. This bit indicates whether the server should transmit its responses as broadcasts or unicasts. In most cases, the server transmits the DHCPOFFER message as a broadcast, because the client still does not have an IP address that the server can use for a unicast transmission. If the broadcast bit is not enabled, however, the server can generate a unicast transmission, using the IP address it is offering (found in the Yiaddr field) and the data-link layer hardware address specified in the Chaddr field of the DHCPDISCOVER message.

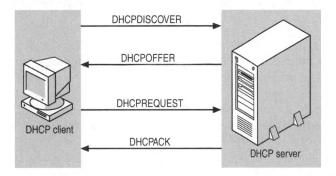

Figure 5.4   DHCP client/server communications

When the server receives the DHCPDISCOVER message through a DHCP relay agent, the server sends the DHCPOFFER message as a unicast to the relay agent address specified in the Giaddr field, and the relay agent either broadcasts or unicasts it to the client, based on the same criteria. It is also possible for a DHCP client to request a specific IP address in its DHCPDISCOVER messages by including an address in the Ciaddr field. The server can then send its DHCPOFFER messages as unicasts directly to the client using that address.

The internal behavior of a server when it offers an IP address and other configuration parameters to a client is left up to the individual implementation. In some cases, the server checks that the address it intends to offer is not already in use by transmitting an Internet Control Message Protocol (ICMP) Echo Request message to that address and then waiting to make sure that no reply arrives. The server also might reserve the offered address until it receives a response from the client.

Because the client broadcasts its DHCPDISCOVER messages, more than one server might receive them, and the client might therefore receive DHCPOFFER responses from multiple servers. After a specified period of time, the client stops its broadcasting and accepts one of the offered IP addresses. To signal its acceptance, the client generates a DHCPREQUEST message, which includes the address of the server from which it is accepting the offer in the Server Identifier option, along with the offered IP address in the Requested IP Address option. The client always transmits the DHCPREQUEST message as a broadcast, both because it is not yet configured to use the offered IP address and to inform the other DHCP servers that it is rejecting their offers.

If the client receives no DHCPOFFER message in response to a DHCPDISCOVER message, it times out and repeats the DHCPDISCOVER broadcast. If, after repeated DHCPDISCOVER broadcasts, the client receives no DHCPOFFER messages in response, the DHCP address assignment procedure is considered to have failed. In some cases, client computers are permitted no further TCP/IP communications except for repeated DHCPDISCOVER broadcasts at regular intervals. In other cases (as with most of the Windows operating systems), the client automatically assigns itself an IP address, which might or might not enable it to interact with other computers on the network.

On receipt of the DHCPREQUEST message, the server whose offer the client is accepting commits the offered IP address and other settings to its database using a combination of the client's hardware address and the offered IP address as a unique identifier for the assignment. This is known as the *lease identification cookie*. To conclude its part of the transaction, the server sends a DHCPACK message to the client, which contains the same offered IP address and other options as in the DHCPOFFER message. This acknowledges the server's completion of the address assignment process. If the server cannot complete the assignment (because it has already assigned the offered IP address to another system, for example), it transmits a DHCPNAK message to the client and the whole process begins again with DHCPDISCOVER broadcasts.

After receiving a DHCPACK message from the server, the client performs a final test by generating a series of ARP broadcasts to ensure that no other system on the network is using the assigned IP address. If the DHCP client receives no response to the ARP transmissions, it configures the TCP/IP client with the IP address and other settings obtained by the server and notes the length of the lease that the server has offered. At this point the client enters what is known as the *bound* state. If another computer on the network does respond to the ARP broadcasts, the client cannot use the offered IP address and transmits a DHCPDECLINE message to the server, nullifying the transaction. The client can then reissue a series of DHCPDISCOVER messages, restarting the whole process.

Note In addition to receiving TCP/IP configuration parameters in the normal manner, it is also possible for a client to request the assignment of the optional parameters without an IP address. This was made possible by the introduction of the DHCPINFORM message type in RFC 2131. In some cases, client computers are already configured with an IP address, but they still need TCP/IP parameters such as default gateway and DNS server addresses. One of the most common scenarios in which this is the case is that of a DHCP server computer itself. DHCP servers cannot themselves be DHCP clients; they must have statically configured IP addresses. A DHCP server that receives a DHCPINFORM message from a client responds with a DHCPACK message containing the options configured for use on that scope, but without an IP address or subnet mask.

DHCP Leasing

The process by which a DHCP server assigns configuration parameters to a client is the same whether the server uses manual, automatic, or dynamic allocation. With manual and automatic allocation, the process described in the previous section is the end of the automated DHCP client/server communications. The client retains the settings assigned to it by the server until someone explicitly changes them or forces a reassignment. However, when the server uses dynamic allocation, the client leases its IP address for a certain period of time (configured at the server) and must periodically renew the lease to continue using it.

The length of an IP address lease is typically measured in days and is usually based on whether computers are frequently moved to different subnets (requiring a new IP address) or whether IP addresses are in short supply. Shorter leases generate more network traffic but enable servers to reclaim unused addresses faster. For a relatively stable network, longer leases reduce the amount of traffic that DHCP generates.

The lease renewal process, illustrated in Figure 5.5, begins when a bound client reaches what is known as the *renewal time value*, or *T1 value*, of its lease. By default, the renewal time value is 50 percent of the lease period. When a client reaches this point, it enters the *renewing* state and begins generating DHCPREQUEST messages. The client transmits the messages to the server that holds the lease as unicasts, unlike the broadcast DHCPREQUEST messages the client generates while in the *init* state. If the server is available to receive the message, it responds with either a DHCPACK message, which renews the lease and restarts the lease time clock, or a DHCPNAK message, which terminates the lease and forces the client to begin the address assignment process again from the beginning. The most common reason for a DHCPNAK message is that the client computer has been moved to a different subnet and its IP address is no longer valid.

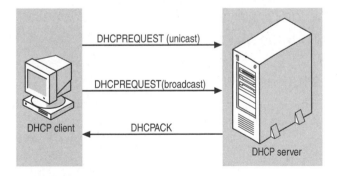

Figure 5.5   The DHCP lease renewal process

If the server does not respond to the DHCPREQUEST unicast message, the client continues to send requests at regular intervals until it reaches the *rebinding time value* or *T2 value*, which defaults to 87.5 percent of the lease period. At this point, the client enters the *rebinding* state and begins transmitting DHCPREQUEST messages as broadcasts, soliciting an address assignment from any DHCP server on the network. Again, a server can respond with either a DHCPACK or DHCPNAK message. If the lease time expires with no response from any DHCP server, the client's IP address is released and all its TCP/IP communication ceases, except for the transmission of DHCPDISCOVER broadcasts.

Releasing an IP Address

It is also possible for a client to terminate an IP address lease at any time by transmitting a DHCPRELEASE message containing the lease identification cookie to the server. On a Windows 2000 system, for example, you can do this manually, using the Ipconfig.exe utility.

Exercise 1: DHCP Message Types

1. Place the following DHCP message types in the order in which a successful IP address assignment procedure uses them.

   a. DHCPACK

   b. DHCPOFFER

   c. DHCPREQUEST

   d. DHCPDISCOVER

2. Place the following DHCP message types in the proper order for an unsuccessful attempt to renew an IP address lease.

   a. DHCPDISCOVER

   b. DHCPREQUEST (broadcast)

   c. DHCPREQUEST (unicast)

   d. DHCPNAK

Lesson Review

1. What happens to a DHCP client when its attempts to renew its IP address lease fail and the lease expires?

2. Which of the following message types is not used during the DHCP lease assignment process?

   a. DHCPDISCOVER

   b. DHCPRELEASE

   c. DHCPOFFER

   d. DHCPREQUEST

3. What is the name of the time during the lease renewal process when a DHCP client begins broadcasting DHCPREQUEST messages?

   a. Lease identification cookie

   b. Rebinding time

   c. Renewal time

   d. Init value

Lesson Summary

- DHCP is a combination of a client, a server, and a protocol that can automatically configure the TCP/IP clients on computers all over the network.

- DHCP is capable of leasing IP addresses from a common pool to client computers, reclaiming them when they are no longer in use, and then returning them to the pool for reassignment.

- In addition to the standard fields, DHCP messages also contain options, such as the message Type option, which describes the function of the message.

- DHCP options contain the parameters used by DHCP clients to configure their TCP/IP clients.

- The DHCP standard provides the ability for third-party vendors to use DHCP to deliver product-specific information to clients.

Lesson 2: Using the DHCP Server

The DHCP standards define precisely the functions of DHCP servers and clients. DHCP clients are nearly always integrated into an operating system's TCP/IP implementation, but DHCP servers are available for many computing platforms, either as integrated components or separate products. All Windows operating systems include a DHCP client, which Windows uses by default. A DHCP server is included with all the Windows 2000 Server and Microsoft Windows NT Server products.

After this lesson, you will be able to

- Install and configure a Windows 2000 DHCP server
- Create and configure scopes
- Configure scope and server options

Estimated lesson time: 60 minutes

Implementing DHCP

Although Windows DHCP clients naturally work well together with DHCP servers, it is also possible for a Windows 2000 DHCP server to support clients running other operating systems and for Windows clients to function with other DHCP server implementations. You can therefore use the Windows 2000 DHCP servers for your entire network, even if you run various client operating systems.

When planning a DHCP implementation, you must consider a number of factors, including the following:

- **The number of clients you intend to support.**   A single DHCP server can theoretically support 1000 scopes with a total of 10,000 clients, depending on the other factors. However, most medium to large networks have at least two DHCP servers so that service can continue if one server fails. To provide fault tolerance, you should divide the range of IP addresses you plan to assign on each subnet between two DHCP servers in an 80/20 split. It is important to understand that DHCP servers do not work together; each server has its own range of addresses to assign. If you configure two DHCP servers with the same identical scope, they will attempt to assign the same IP addresses to clients.

- **The configuration of your internetwork.**   The number of networks that make up your internetwork and the technologies used to connect them can have a great effect on your DHCP implementation. The use of DHCP relay agents prevents you from having to install a DHCP server on every network segment. When branch offices are connected together using relatively slow wide area network (WAN) links, it is generally not a good idea to have DHCP clients that rely on servers at distant locations.

- **The performance capabilities of your servers.**   DHCP is a highly disk-intensive service. If you plan to have DHCP servers with heavy client loads, you should make sure that your server hardware is fast enough to avoid becoming a performance bottleneck. To ensure proper performance, you should plan your server hardware implementation around a worst-case DHCP traffic scenario, such as the end of a brief power outage in which all your client computers are attempting to contact the DHCP server at nearly the same time.

Installing Windows 2000 DHCP Server

Although the DHCP client is an integral part of the Windows operating systems and is installed automatically with the TCP/IP protocols on every computer, installation of Windows 2000 DHCP Server is optional. You can elect to install the DHCP server during the operating system installation, or you can do it any time afterward. The process of installing the DHCP Server included with Windows 2000 and preparing it for use consists of the following steps:

1. Install the DHCP Server software.
2. Authorize the server in the Active Directory service.
3. Create one or more scopes on the server.
4. Configure DHCP options.
5. Activate the scope or scopes.

To install the DHCP Server, use the following procedure:

1. Click Start, point to settings, and select Control Panel.
2. Double-click the Add/Remove Programs icon in the Control Panel to open the Add/Remove Programs dialog box.
3. Click Add/Remove Windows Components to open the Windows Components Wizard (see Figure 5.6).

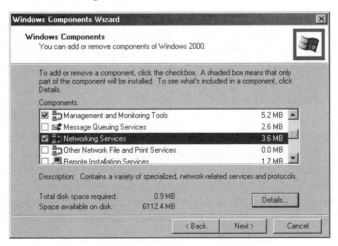

Figure 5.6 The Windows Components Wizard

4. Select Networking Services in the Components list and click Details to open the Networking Services dialog box (see Figure 5.7).

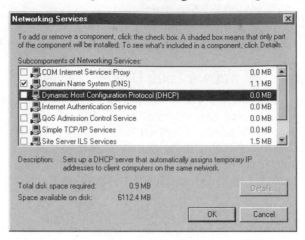

Figure 5.7   The Networking Services dialog box

5. Select the check box next to the Dynamic Host Configuration Protocol (DHCP) entry in the Subcomponents Of Networking Services list and click OK to return to the Windows Components Wizard.

6. Click Next to install the DHCP Server service. You might have to supply your Windows 2000 Server distribution disk.

7. Click Finish to complete the installation and close the Windows Components Wizard.

8. Click Yes in the System Settings Change message box to restart the computer.

When you restart the computer, the DHCP Server service will be running, and it will load every time you restart the server. You can modify the service's startup behavior by opening the Services console and changing its Startup Type value from Automatic to Manual or Disabled.

Authorizing a DHCP Server

The Windows 2000 DHCP Server includes a feature that enables the computer to detect unauthorized DHCP servers, called *rogues*, and prevent them from starting. In the past, the existence of improperly configured DHCP servers on a network was a relatively common problem. The DHCP Server service is easily installed with the Windows 2000 operating system. If someone creates a scope using improper IP addresses or other bad TCP/IP configuration information and activates it, whether out of curiosity, experimentation, or malice, the result can be improperly configured and malfunctioning workstations all over the network.

To prevent rogue DHCP servers from operating on a network, Windows 2000 requires each DHCP Server installation to be authorized with Active Directory. To be authorized, a computer running the DHCP Server service must be either an Active Directory domain controller or a member server.

To authorize a DHCP server, use the following procedure:

1. Log on to the network using an account that is a member of the Enterprise Admins group.
2. Click Start, point to Programs, and select DHCP from the Administrative Tools program group to open the DHCP console (see Figure 5.8).

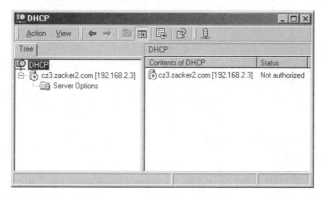

Figure 5.8   The DHCP console with an unauthorized server

3. Select the server you installed on the local computer in the scope pane and select Authorize from the Action menu.
4. Press the F5 key to refresh the server display and then click the DHCP header at the root of the scope tree. Notice that the Status of the server has changed from Not Authorized to Running (see Figure 5.9)

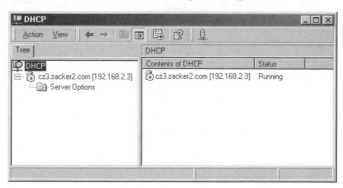

Figure 5.9   The DHCP console with an authorized server

When you authorize a DHCP server, its IP address is added to a list of authorized servers in the Active Directory database. Whenever a Windows 2000 DHCP server starts, it compiles a list of the other DHCP servers on the network by broadcasting DHCPINFORM messages that contain vendor-specific options recognized only by other Windows 2000 DHCP servers. The other servers on the network respond to the DHCPINFORM message with a DHCPACK message, also containing vendor-specific options that supply information about themselves. When the server has compiled a list of the other DHCP servers, it obtains the list of the authorized servers from an Active Directory domain controller. If the server's own address is on the list, it begins to service clients. If the server's address is not on the list, it does not service clients.

Note   This rogue DHCP server detection feature works only with the Windows 2000 version of DHCP Server when the first DHCP server installed on a network is a Windows 2000 server that belongs to an Active Directory domain. If a Windows NT DHCP server or other DHCP server software is running on the network, it cannot be authorized, detected, or prevented from operating.

Creating a Scope

After a DHCP server is authorized, it is capable of functioning on the network, but it cannot actually service DHCP clients until it is configured with a scope of IP addresses to assign. When creating scopes, consider the following restrictions:

- You can create only one scope per subnet on a single DHCP server. If the IP addresses you want to assign are not consecutive, you must create a scope out of the largest possible address range and then exclude specific addresses or address ranges from the scope.

- Reservations must be included in a scope. When using reservations to permanently assign IP addresses to specific computers, do not exclude the reserved addresses from the scope. Excluded addresses are not available for assignment to clients, even using reservations.

- Statically configured IP addresses must not be included in a scope. If you have computers that you've manually configured to use specific IP addresses (without using the DHCP client), you must exclude them from the scope. The DHCP server has no way of knowing that these addresses exist, and if you include them in the scope, the server will attempt to assign them to other clients.

To create a scope, use the following procedure:

1. Click Start, point to Programs, and select DHCP from the Administrative Tools program group to open the DHCP console.
2. Select the entry for your DHCP server in the scope pane and select New Scope from the Action menu to open the New Scope Wizard.

3. Click Next to bypass the Welcome page and proceed to the Scope Name dialog box (see Figure 5.10).

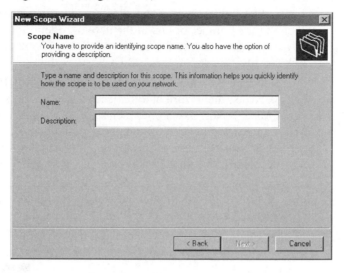

Figure 5.10   The Scope Name dialog box in the New Scope Wizard

4. In the Name and Description boxes, type a name and (optionally) a descriptive string for the scope you are creating. Typically, these fields should identify the subnet that the scope will service. Click Next to proceed to the IP Address Range page (see Figure 5.11).

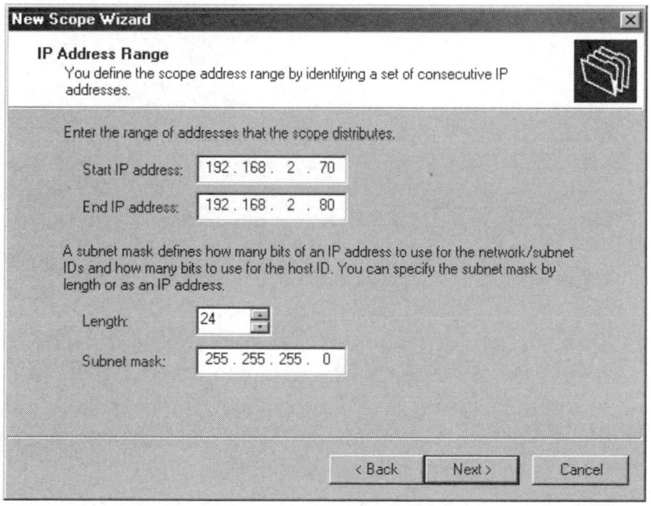

Figure 5.11   The IP Address Range page in the New Scope Wizard

5. Type the beginning and ending IP addresses of the address range you want the DHCP server to assign in the Start IP Address and End IP Address fields.

6. Specify the subnet mask for the addresses that the server will assign either by indicating the number of bits in the network identifier in the Length selector or by typing the mask in the Subnet Mask box using dotted decimal notation. Click Next to proceed to the Add Exclusions dialog box (see Figure 5.12).

When you type the range of IP addresses in the Start IP Address and End IP Address boxes, the wizard automatically supplies values in the Length and Subnet Mask boxes, based on the class of the IP address values you specified. The only time you have to change these default subnet mask values is if you have subnetted your network by using a nonstandard number of bits in the network identifier of your IP addresses.

Note   For more information about IP addressing and subnetting, see Lesson 2 in Chapter 2, "Introducing TCP/IP."

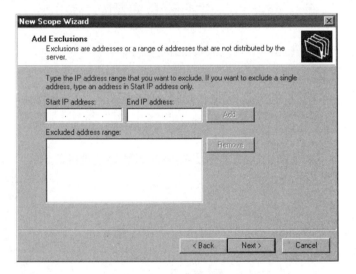

Figure 5.12   The Add Exclusions dialog box in the New Scope Wizard

7. Type a range of addresses that you want to exclude from the range you specified in the IP Address Range page in the Start IP Address and End IP Address box and click Add to add the range to the Excluded Address Range List. Repeat the procedure to exclude additional address ranges. Click Next to proceed to the Lease Duration page (see Figure 5.13).

Excluding multiple address ranges from the IP address range you originally supplied for the scope enables you to select any group of addresses you want for a particular subnet. To exclude a single address from the range, type the same value in the Start IP Address and End IP Address boxes.

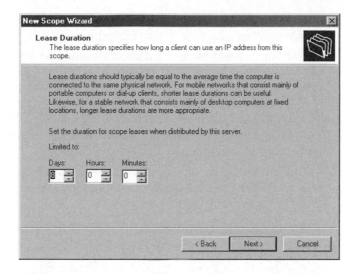

Figure 5.13   The Lease Duration page in the New Scope Wizard

8. Specify the time interval (in days, hours, or minutes, or all three) for the IP address leases the server will assign for this scope. Click Next to proceed to the Configure DHCP Options page (see Figure 5.14).

   The default IP address lease duration is 8 days. For a network in which computers (such as laptops and other portables) are frequently moved to other subnets, you can decrease the lease duration value. For more stable networks, you can increase the value. You cannot configure a scope with an unlimited lease (resulting in automatic allocation) using the New Scope Wizard. You can, however, modify the properties of the scope after you create it to change its lease duration to Unlimited.

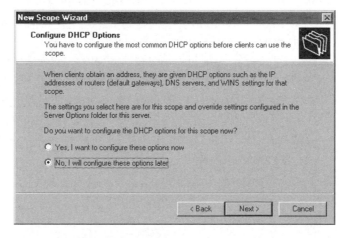

Figure 5.14   The Configure DHCP Options page in the New Scope Wizard

9. Click No, I Will Configure These Options Later and click Next to proceed to the Completing The New Scope Wizard page.

Answering Yes, I Want To Configure These Options Now causes the wizard to display four additional pages, enabling you to configure the Router (Default Gateway), Domain Name and DNS Servers, and WINS Servers options and to activate the scope. These are the most commonly used options on a typical TCP/IP network, and activating the scope completes the process of making the DHCP server functional and active. See the next section in this lesson for more information about configuring these options.

10. Click Finish to close the wizard and create the scope. Notice that the scope now appears in the DHCP console, subordinate to the server on which you created it (see Figure 5.15).

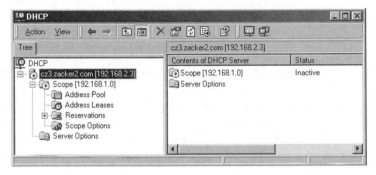

Figure 5.15   The DHCP console with a newly created scope

Activating a Scope

After you have created a scope, you must activate it before the server can use it to assign IP addresses to clients. To activate a scope, use the following procedure:

1. Click Start, point to Programs, and select DHCP from the Administrative Tools program group to open the DHCP console.

2. Select the scope you just created and select Activate from the Action menu. Notice that the status of the scope now shows it as being active (see Figure 5.16).

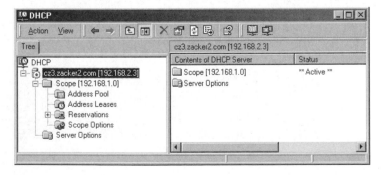

Figure 5.16   The DHCP console with a newly activated scope

Creating a Superscope

A superscope is an administrative grouping of multiple scopes that enables you to support DHCP clients on a single physical network segment that hosts multiple IP subnets. If, for example, you have a large switched network that you've split into five logical subnets, you can create a separate scope for each subnet and then create a superscope with the five scopes as members. Creating the superscope enables you to manage all five of the member scopes as a single administrative entity.

To create a superscope, you select a DHCP server in the DHCP console and select New Superscope from the Action menu. This launches the New Superscope wizard, in which you select the scopes that you want to group together into the superscope. The superscope appears in the scope pane hierarchy as an object beneath the server, with its member scopes subordinate to it. After you've created the superscope, you can activate all the member scopes at one time by simply activating the superscope.

Configuring DHCP Options

Creating a scope enables a DHCP server to assign IP addresses and a subnet mask to the clients on a particular subnet, but the clients' TCP/IP configuration process will not be complete until they receive other parameters, such as a default gateway, as well. As discussed earlier, you can configure the most commonly used DHCP options when you create the scope. However, when you configure the options after creating the scope, you have access to the full range of options supported by the DHCP server.

Windows 2000 DHCP Server enables you to configure DHCP options at the server level or the scope level. If all the DHCP clients on your network will be using the same default gateway, DNS servers, and so on, you can configure server options that apply to all your scopes. If you need to specify different options for the computers on different scopes, you can create scope options that apply only to the client in that scope. If you have some options that apply to all the computers on the network (such as DNS server addresses, for example) and some that are scope-specific (such as default gateway addresses), you can create both server options and scope options; the server will combine them when actually configuring a client computer.

To configure the most commonly used DHCP options, use the following procedure:

1. Click Start, point to Programs, and select DHCP from the Administrative Tools program group to open the DHCP console.

2. Select the Server Options heading or the Scope Options heading beneath a particular scope and select Configure Options from the Action menu to display the Server Options or Scope Options dialog box (see Figure 5.17).

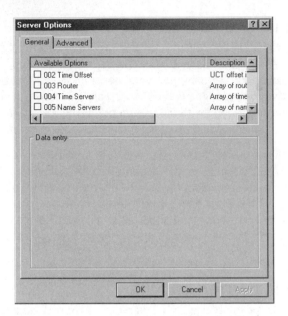

Figure 5.17   The Server Options dialog box

3. Highlight the 003 Router entry in the Available Options list. Notice that additional controls for this particular option appear in the bottom half of the dialog box (see Figure 5.18).

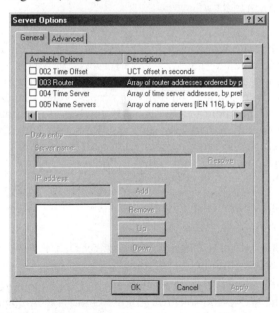

Figure 5.18   The Server Options dialog box with the 003 Router controls displayed

4. Select the check box next to the 003 Router entry. Notice how the Server Name and IP Address fields in the bottom half of the dialog box are now activated (see Figure 5.19).

Many of the various options supported by Windows 2000 DHCP Server require different types of controls to configure them. The controls that appear in the bottom half of the dialog box vary, depending on the option you select.

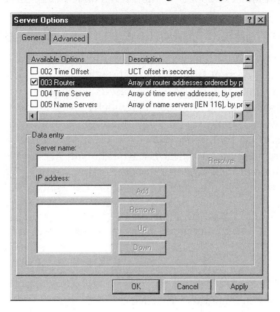

Figure 5.19 The Server Options dialog box with the 003 Router controls activated

5. Type the name of the router that you want the DHCP clients to use as their default gateway in the Server Name box.

If you already know the IP address of the router, you can type it in the IP Address box and proceed to step 8.

6. Click Resolve to resolve the name you supplied into an IP address and add the address to the IP Address box.

7. Click Add to add the IP address to the list of default gateway addresses.

8. Repeat steps 5 through 7 to add additional router addresses to the list.

9. Select the check box next to the 003 DNS Servers entry in the Available Options list. Notice that the controls for this option are the same as those for the 003 Router option. This is because both options require a list of IP addresses that you can either enter directly or resolve from names.

10. Using the same procedure outlined in steps 5 through 7, specify the names or IP addresses of the DNS servers that you want your DHCP clients to use.

11. Scroll down in the Available Options list and select the check box next to the 044 WINS/NBNS Servers option.

12. Using the same procedure outlined in steps 5 through 7, specify the names of IP addresses of the WINS server that you want your DHCP clients to use.

13. Click OK to apply the options you have configured. Notice that the configured options now appear in the details pane of the DHCP console.

Deploying DHCP Options with User Classes

In some cases, you might want to configure certain DHCP clients with parameters that are different from those of the other clients on the same subnet. One example in which this might be the case is when you have a group of laptop computers that are frequently moved throughout your enterprise network. To adequately support these computers, you want to configure them with a short DHCP lease duration, such as four hours. However, specifying a four-hour lease duration for all the computers on your network would result in excessive amounts of DHCP traffic and server disk activity. To address this problem, you can create a separate user class for the laptops and configure DHCP options that apply only to that user class.

The process of assigning option values with user classes consists of three procedures:

- Create a user class
- Configure options for the class
- Configure clients to use the class

To create a new user class, use the following procedure:

1. Click Start, point to Programs, and select DHCP from the Administrative Tools program group to open the DHCP console.

2. Select the server you want to modify and select Define User Classes from the Action menu to open the DHCP User Classes dialog box (see Figure 5.20).

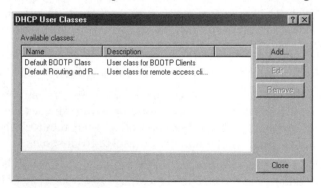

Figure 5.20   The DHCP User Classes dialog box

3. Click Add to open the New Class dialog box (see Figure 5.21).

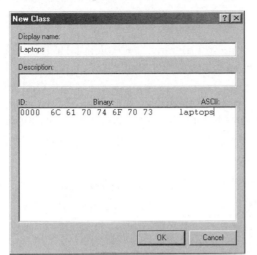

Figure 5.21 The New Class dialog box

4. Type a descriptive name for the class you are creating (such as "Laptops") in the Display Name box. You can add information in the description box.

5. Enter a class ID that the server will use to identify the computers in the class in the box at the bottom of the New Class dialog box. To enter the class ID in hexadecimal form, click the left side of the box. To enter the class ID using ASCII text, click the right side of the box. Whichever notation you use, the dialog box translates it into the other one as you type it in. For the sake of this example, type w2klaptops in the ASCII side of the display.

6. Click OK to create the new class. Notice that the class you've created now appears in the Available Classes list in the DHCP User Classes dialog box (see Figure 5.22).

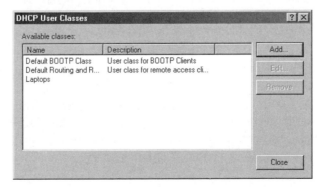

Figure 5.22 The DHCP User Classes dialog box with a newly created class

7. Click Close to close the DHCP User Classes dialog box.

To configure options for the new user class you created, use the following procedure:

1. Click Start, point to Programs, and select DHCP from the Administrative Tools program group to open the DHCP console.

2. Select the Server Options heading or the Scope Options heading beneath a particular scope and select Configure Options from the Action menu to display the Server Options or Scope Options dialog box.

3. Click the Advanced tab to change the appearance of the dialog box to that shown in Figure 5.23.

Figure 5.23   The Advanced tab in the Scope Options dialog box

4. In the User Class box, use the drop-down list to select the user class you created in the previous procedure.

5. Select the DHCP options you want to configure in the Available Options list and configure them in the usual manner.

6. Click OK to configure the options you selected. Notice that the options you configured now appear in the details pane of the DHCP console with the user class you created appearing in the Class column (see Figure 5.24).

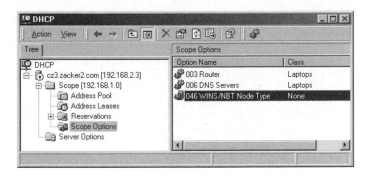

Figure 5.24   User class-specific server options

To configure a DHCP client to be a member of a specific user class, use the following procedure:

1. Open a Command Prompt window on the Windows 2000 client computer.

2. Type the command **ipconfig /setclassid "Local Area Connection"** *classID* at the command prompt, where the *classID* variable contains the class ID (that is, w2klaptops) you specified while creating the user class. If the network interface you want to configure is named differently in the Network And Dial-Up Connections window, replace "Local Area Connection" with the appropriate name.

3. Type the command **ipconfig /renew "Local Area Connection"** to renew the client's DHCP lease, using the class ID you specified to obtain the correct options from the server.

4. Close the Command Prompt window.

Creating a Reservation

Manual IP address allocation is implemented in DHCP Server in the form of reservations, which you create to assign a specific IP address to a specific computer. When you create a reservation, the IP address you specify is always assigned to the same DHCP client. Although it might be just as easy to manually configure a computer with a static IP address, using DHCP reservations is recommended because they prevent the addresses you reserve from being assigned to other computers.

To create a reservation, use the following procedure:

1. Click Start, point to Programs, and select DHCP from the Administrative Tools program group to open the DHCP console.

2. In the scope pane, expand the scope in which you want to create the reservation.

3. Select the Reservations heading and select New Reservation from the Action menu to display the New Reservation dialog box (see Figure 5.25).

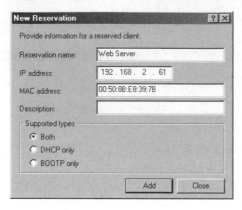

Figure 5.25   The New Reservation dialog box

4. Type a name for the reservation in the Reservation Name box.

5. Type the IP address you want to assign in the IP Address box.

6. Type the data-link layer hardware address of the computer to which you want to assign the IP address in the MAC Address box.

   To determine the hardware address of a Windows 2000 computer, type **ipconfig / all** at the command prompt. To view the hardware address of a remote computer on the network, open the Computer Management console, connect to the desired computer, expand the System Information heading to display the Components/Network/Adapter entry, and view the MAC Address listing in the details pane.

7. Click Add to create the reservation.

8. Repeat steps 4 through 7 to create additional reservations for the scope, or click Close to close the New Reservation dialog box. Notice that the reservations you created now appear in the details pane of the DHCP console (see Figure 5.26).

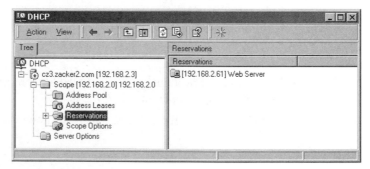

Figure 5.26   The DHCP console with an IP address reservation

Exercise 1: Examining DHCP Traffic

In this exercise, you use the Network Monitor application supplied with Windows 2000 Server to capture samples of DHCP messages on your network and examine their contents. This exercise assumes that you have a Windows 2000 Server computer with Network Monitor installed and connected to a LAN with a DHCP server present. You also need a second Windows 2000 computer configured to function as a DHCP client. For instructions about how to install and use Network Monitor, see Lesson 1 in Chapter 14, "Monitoring Network Activity."

1. On the Windows 2000 DHCP server, click Start and select Network Monitor from the Administrative Tools program group. If necessary, select the network interface corresponding to the LAN adapter.

2. Select Start from the Capture menu to begin capturing the packets transmitted over the network.

3. On the Windows 2000 DHCP client computer, click Start, point to Programs, and select Command Prompt from the accessories program group to open a Command Prompt window.

4. Type **ipconfig /release** at the command prompt.

5. Type **ipconfig /renew** at the command prompt.

6. Return to the Network Monitor window and select Stop And View from the Capture menu to display a Capture window.

7. Select Filter from the Display menu to open the Display Filter dialog box.

8. Double-click the Protocol==Any branch of the decision tree to open the Expression dialog box.

9. Confirm that the Protocol tab is selected and click Disable All to remove all entries from the Enabled Protocols list.

10. Select DHCP in the Disabled Protocols list and click Enable to add it to the Enabled Protocols list.

11. Click OK to close the Expression dialog box and click OK again to close the Display Filter dialog box. What happens to the Capture window display (see Figure 5.27 on the following page)?

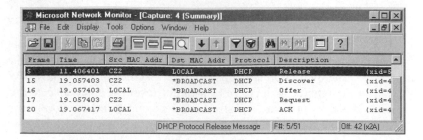

Figure 5.27   The Network Monitor Capture window filtered to display only DHCP messages

12. Double-click the first packet you see with Release in the Description column. In the bottom pane of the Capture window, expand the DHCP portion of the packet to display the message fields, as shown in Figure 5.28.

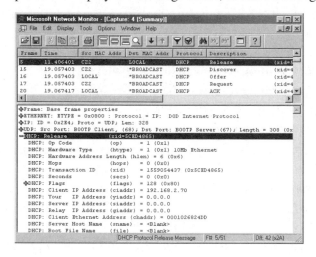

Figure 5.28   A captured DHCPRELEASE message

What caused the DHCPRELEASE message to be generated?

13. Expand the Option Field heading to display the options included in the message (see Figure 5.29).

Notice that the DHCP Message Type option indicates that this is a DHCPRELEASE message.

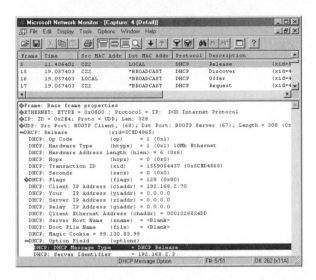

Figure 5.29   The Options field of a DHCPRELEASE packet

14. Click the Discover message that follows the Release message and expand the DHCP message section (see Figure 5.30).

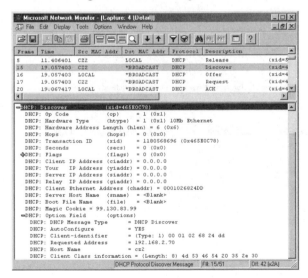

Figure 5.30   A captured DHCPDISCOVER message

What initiated the creation of the DHCPDISCOVER message?

Why do the four IP address fields (Ciaddr, Yiaddr, Siaddr, and Giaddr) all contain values of 0.0.0.0?

15. Expand the Option field.

    Notice that, in this case, the client has included the Requested Address option containing the IP address it had been using up to the time of its recent release. In this DHCP implementation, the client attempts to maintain the use of the same IP address whenever possible.

16. Click the Offer message that follows the Discover message. Expand the message and its Option field (see Figure 5.31).

    What IP address has the server offered the client?

    What are the functions of the options listed in the Option field?

Figure 5.31   A captured DHCPOFFER message

17. Click the Request message that follows the Offer message. Expand the message and its Option field (see Figure 5.32).

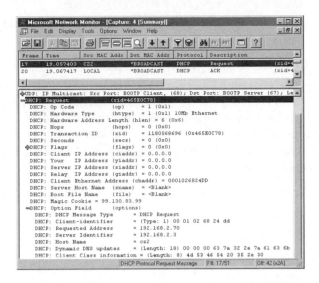

Figure 5.32   A captured DHCPREQUEST message

What is the function of the Client-Identifier option in the Option field?

18. Click the ACK message that follows the Offer message. Expand the message and its Option field (see Figure 5.33).

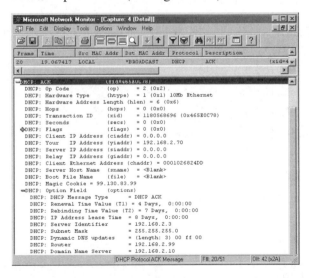

Figure 5.33   A captured DHCPACK message

The DHCPACK message contains all the options that were originally included in the DHCPOFFER message.

19. Close Network Monitor, saving the capture for later study, if you want.

Exercise 2: Configuring Scopes

As the DHCP administrator for your organization, you are creating a scope for your 192.168.6.32/28 subnet. The router functioning as the default gateway for the subnet has been manually configured with the lowest available IP address on the subnet. There are also two Internet servers on the subnet for which you will create reservations using the three highest available IP addresses. Based on this information, answer the following questions.

1. What value should you assign to the Router option for the scope?
   a. 192.168.6.32
   b. 192.168.7.32
   c. 192.168.6.33
   d. 192.168.6.34

2. What IP addresses should you use when creating the reservations for the two Internet servers?
   a. 192.168.6.44 and 192.168.6.45
   b. 192.168.6.45 and 192.168.6.46
   c. 192.168.6.46 and 192.168.6.47
   d. 192.168.6.47 and 192.168.6.48

3. What IP address range should you use when creating the scope for the subnet?
   a. 192.168.6.33–192.168.6.46
   b. 192.168.6.33–192.168.6.44
   c. 192.168.6.34–192.168.6.44
   d. 192.168.6.34–192.168.6.46

Lesson Review

1. What is the function of a user class ID?

2. What type of DHCP messages do servers use to compile a list of the other DHCP servers on the network?

3. For a network with 9000 client workstations on 10 subnets at 6 locations, what is the minimum number of DHCP servers needed to service the entire network?

   a. 1

   b. 6

   c. 9

   d. 10

4. When you create a reservation, how does the DHCP server know which computer should be assigned the IP address you specify?

5. What program do you use to assign a user class to a specific DHCP client interface?

Lesson Summary

- The DHCP Server service is not installed with Windows 2000 by default. You must either select it during the operating system installation or install it manually afterward.

- On a Windows 2000 network using Active Directory, you must authorize a DHCP server before it can service clients.

- You must create a scope for each subnet to be served by a DHCP server, each containing a range of IP addresses to be assigned.

- Class IDs make it possible to assign different DIICP option values to a group of clients on a particular subnet.

- In Windows 2000 DHCP Server, you can configure DHCP options for the entire server or for a specific scope.

- Reservations are IP addresses that are permanently assigned to particular DHCP clients.

Lesson 3: Administering DHCP

In addition to the basic DHCP server configuration tasks examined in Lesson 2 of this chapter, network administrators might have to perform a number of other DHCP-related jobs. This lesson examines some of these tasks.

After this lesson, you will be able to

- Monitor DHCP activity
- Configure the DHCP conflict detection setting
- Compact the DHCP database
- Deploy a DHCP relay agent
- Understand the integration of DHCP and DNS

Estimated lesson time: 30 minutes

Monitoring DHCP Activity

Keeping track of the DHCP servers' status should be a regular concern of a network administrator, and using the DHCP console, you can monitor the address leases and the server status for DHCP servers anywhere on the network. When you install the DHCP Server service on a Windows 2000 Server computer, the DHCP console is installed as well. You can run the DHCP console on another Windows 2000 Server or Windows 2000 Professional computer that is not running the DHCP service by installing Windows 2000 Administration Tools, which are supplied as a Windows Installer Package file called Adminpak.msi on the Windows 2000 Server distribution CD-ROM.

When you launch the DHCP console on a computer running the DHCP service, the local server appears in the scope pane by default. To add DHCP servers to the console, click the DHCP header at the root of the console tree and select Add Server from the Action menu to display the Add Server dialog box (see Figure 5.34).

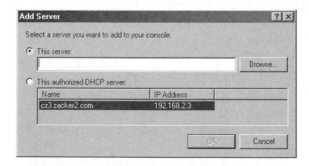

Figure 5.34   The Add Server dialog box

In this dialog box, you can type the name or address of a Windows 2000 Server computer running the DHCP Server service, click Browse to locate a DHCP server, or select one of the authorized servers listed. When you click OK, the server you specified is added to the console tree, and you can access all its functions remotely (assuming you have the appropriate permissions).

To view the addresses currently leased by a DHCP server, select a scope under one of the servers listed in the scope pane and expand it to display the icons beneath it. Click the Address Leases icon, and a list of the current leases appears in the details pane (see Figure 5.35).

Figure 5.35   The DHCP console displaying the Address Leases list for a scope

From the Address Leases list, you can delete any or all of the current leases in order to free up IP addresses for use by other clients. For example, if you move a number of computers to a different subnet and want to reclaim their addresses without waiting for the leases to expire, you can simply delete them from the Address Leases list.

You can also display a statistics window for a particular DHCP server by clicking it in the scope pane and selecting Display Statistics from the Action menu (see Figure 5.36). By default, the display is static; you must refresh it manually by clicking the appropriate button on the Server Statistics dialog box.

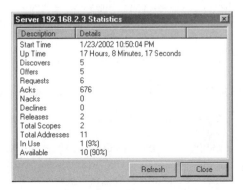

Figure 5.36   The Server Statistics dialog box

To configure the display to refresh itself at regular intervals, click the server and select Properties from the Action menu. In the General tab of the Properties dialog box (see Figure 5.37), select the Automatically Update Statistics Every check box and specify the number of hours or minutes between updates you want to use. Click OK and display the Server Statistics dialog box again.

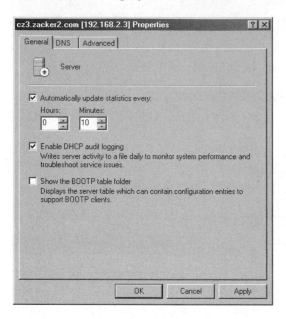

Figure 5.37   A DHCP server's Properties dialog box

Another form of DHCP server monitoring that you can control from a server's Properties dialog box is the DHCP audit logging. By default, Windows 2000 DHCP servers have audit logging enabled. The server maintains a rotating series of log files, named using the days of the week, in the \Winnt\System32\dhcp folder by default. The log files contain entries like the following:

```
63,01/24/02,13:31:00,Restarting rogue detection,,,

51,01/24/02,13:32:01,Authorization succeeded,,contoso.com,

10,01/24/02,14:08:19,Assign,192.168.2.70,cz2.contoso.com,0001026824DD

11,01/24/02,14:08:21,Renew,192.168.2.70,cz2.contoso.com,0001026824DD

12,01/24/02,14:15:38,Release,192.168.2.70,cz2.contoso.com,0001026824DD
```

In addition to these methods, Windows 2000 DHCP Server also includes a set of performance counters that you can use to monitor various types of server activity. By default, these counters are available in the Performance console after you install DHCP service. The DHCP server counters can monitor the following parameters:

- All types of DHCP messages sent and received by the DHCP service
- The average amount of processing time spent by the DHCP server per message packet sent and received
- The number of message packets dropped because of internal delays on the DHCP server computer

Controlling Conflict Detection

By default, Windows 2000 DHCP Server does not use ICMP Echo Request messages (pings) to attempt to detect an IP address conflict before assigning an address to a client. You can modify this behavior by opening the Properties dialog box for a DHCP server and clicking the Advanced tab (see Figure 5.38). In the Conflict Detection Attempts selector, specify the number of pings you want the server to generate before assigning an address. Note, however, that each ping attempt incurs an additional delay of at least one second while the server waits for the ping message to time out. Microsoft recommends a value no higher than 2 for this setting.

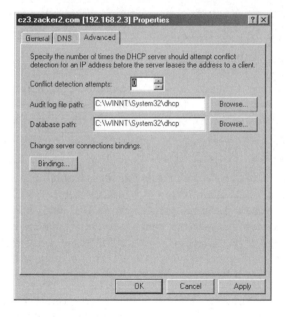

Figure 5.38   The Advanced tab in a DHCP server's Properties dialog box

Note   On a network where DHCP controls all IP address assignments, there is no need to enable this feature. If your network has a mixture of manually configured TCP/IP clients and DHCP clients, enabling conflict detection adds an extra measure of protection.

Compacting the DHCP Database

Windows 2000 DHCP Server uses the Jet storage engine to maintain its database of lease information. The database files are located in the \Winnt\System32\dhcp folder, by default. There is no limit on the size of the database, but as lease records are deleted over time, they leave empty spaces in the database that waste storage space. To remove these empty spaces, the DHCP Server performs an automatic database compaction process after each database update. This automatic process reduces the need for manual compaction but does not completely eliminate it. You can periodically compact the DHCP database using the Jetpack.exe command-line utility included with Windows 2000.

To manually compact the DHCP database, use the following procedure:

1. Open a Command Prompt window on the DHCP server.
2. Change to the \Winnt\System32\dhcp folder on the system drive.
3. To stop the DHCP Server service, type **net stop dhcpserver** at the command prompt.
4. To compact the database, type **jetpack dhcp.mdb tmp.mdb**.
5. To restart the DHCP Server service, type **net start dhcpserver**.
6. Close the Command Prompt window.

The Jetpack.exe program compacts the database by writing all the records it contains to a temporary file called Tmp.mdb, deleting the original Dhcp.mdb file, and then renaming the temporary file with the original file name.

Using DHCP Relay Agents

As mentioned earlier, a DHCP relay agent is a small program that enables a DHCP server to assign TCP/IP configuration setting to clients on another network. Most routers have relay agent capabilities built into them, enabling you to configure them to access your DHCP servers. The standard that defines functionality of a DHCP relay agent is no different from the BOOTP relay agent standard, so a router equipped with a BOOTP relay agent will work with any DHCP server, including a Windows 2000 DHCP server.

A relay agent works by monitoring the network on which it is located for DHCPDISCOVER broadcasts generated by DHCP client. The relay agent itself is configured with the IP addresses of DHCP servers located on other networks, so it can transmit the DHCPDISCOVER messages to the servers as unicasts. Because unicasts are not limited to the local network as broadcasts are, this enables the relay agent to interact with a DHCP server located anywhere on the network. When the server responds to the DHCPDISCOVER messages, it sends its DHCPOFFER messages back to the relay agent, which forwards them to the client as broadcasts. The agent continues in this manner throughout the lease negotiation process, until the client enters the bound state and can communicate with the DHCP server directly.

Windows 2000 includes a DHCP relay agent as part of the Routing and Remote Access (RRAS) service, which the operating system installs automatically when you configure RRAS to function as a router. However, you must configure the relay agent before it will function.

To configure the Windows 2000 DHCP Relay Agent, use the following procedure:

1. Open the Routing and Remote Access console.

2. Expand the icon for the server you want to configure, expand the IP Routing icon, and select the DHCP Relay Agent icon.

3. Select Properties from the Action menu to display the DHCP Relay Agent Properties dialog box (see Figure 5.39).

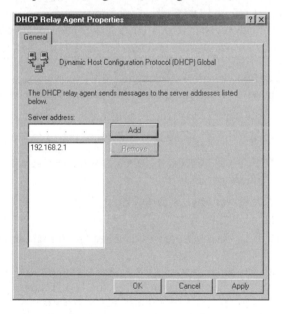

Figure 5.39   The DHCP Relay Agent Properties dialog box

4. Type the IP address of the DHCP server you want the relay agent to use in the Server Address box and click Add.

5. Repeat step 4 to add additional DHCP servers to the list and click OK.

Integrating DHCP with DNS

One of the problems with using a service like DHCP is the possibility that a client's IP address can change, rendering the information in IP address–based services such as DNS obsolete. To overcome this problem, Windows 2000 DHCP Server and Windows 2000 DNS Server both support the dynamic DNS update standard. Dynamic DNS, as defined in RFC 2136, "Dynamic Updates in the Domain Name System," is an extension to the DNS standard that enables a service such as DHCP to send messages to a DNS server that cause it to update the information in its resource records. Before dynamic DNS was developed, all DNS resource records had to be created manually.

Note   Not all DHCP and DNS implementations support dynamic DNS updates. If, for example, your network relies on your Internet service provider's (ISP's) DNS servers, chances are they do not support dynamic DNS or are configured not to permit dynamic updates.

When both DHCP and DNS servers support the dynamic update standard, the DHCP server can register with a DNS server and update pointer (PTR) and address (A) resource records on behalf of its DHCP clients. This process requires the use of a DHCP option called Client FQDN, which enables a client to provide its fully qualified domain name to the DHCP server, as well as instructions for the server about how it should process dynamic DNS updates for the client.

In addition to these client-supplied instructions, you can configure the DHCP server to process the client updates in any of the following ways:

- The DHCP server updates the client's information with the DNS servers only when the client requests it.
- The DHCP server always updates the client's information with the DNS servers, whether the client requests it or not.
- The DHCP server never updates the client's information with the DNS servers.

To configure the behavior of a DHCP server regarding dynamic DNS updates, open a server's Properties dialog box in the DHCP console and click the DNS tab (see Figure 5.40). To configure the server to perform dynamic updates based on the client's requests, select the Automatically Update DHCP Client Information In DNS check box and click the Update DNS Only If DHCP Client Requests option button. To configure the server to always perform dynamic updates, select the Automatically Update DHCP Client Information In DNS check box and click the Always Update DNS option button. To prevent the server from performing any dynamic updates, clear the Automatically Update DHCP Client Information In DNS check box.

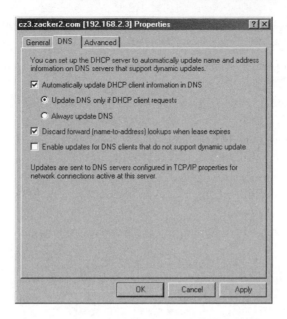

Figure 5.40   The DNS tab of a DHCP server's Properties dialog box

Note   For dynamic DNS updates to occur, the DNS server must also be configured to support them. For more information about the Windows 2000 DNS Server support for dynamic DNS updates, see Lesson 4 in Chapter 8, "Using the Windows 2000 DNS Server."

In this same dialog box, you can also configure two additional options, as follows:

- **Discard Forward (Name-To-Address) Lookups When Lease Expires.**
  When the DHCP server is configured to perform DNS updates, it always sends updates to discard the client's PTR resource record when the lease expires. By default, the server does the same with the client's A resource record, unless you clear this check box.

- **Enable Updates For DNS Clients That Do Not Support Dynamic Update.**
  The DHCP clients in Windows versions prior to Windows 2000 do not themselves support dynamic DNS updates, but when this option is enabled, the Windows 2000 DCP server can identify these clients and perform the updates for them.

Windows 2000 DHCP clients utilize the dynamic DNS update protocol as illustrated in Figure 5.41. The steps of the process are as follows:

1. The client generates a DHCPREQUEST message and transmits it to the DHCP server.

2. The server returns a DHCPACK message to the client, granting it an IP address lease.

3. By default, the client sends a DNS update request to the DNS server for its own forward lookup (A) resource record.

   Alternately, the server can perform this update to the DNS server on behalf of the client if the client and server are configured to do so.

4. The server sends updates for the DHCP client's reverse lookup (PTR) resource record using the process defined by the dynamic DNS update protocol.

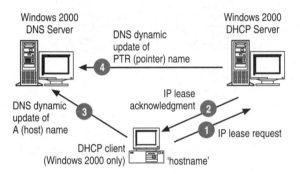

Figure 5.41   A DHCP client interacting with the DNS dynamic update protocol

Earlier versions of Windows DHCP clients do not support the dynamic DNS update process directly and therefore cannot directly interact with the DNS server. For these DHCP clients, updates typically proceed as illustrated in Figure 5.42, using the following steps:

1. The client generates a DHCPREQUEST message and transmits it to the DHCP server.

2. The server returns a DHCPACK message to the client, granting it an IP address lease.

3. The server then sends updates to the DNS server for the client's forward lookup (A) resource record.

4. The server also sends updates for the client's reverse lookup (PTR) resource record.

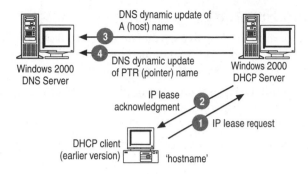

Figure 5.42   DHCP/DNS interaction with earlier Windows clients

Lesson Review

1. You are the administrator of a network that has a Windows 2000 Server computer with RRAS configured to function as the router between Network A and Network B. There is another Windows 2000 server on Network A that is running the Windows 2000 DHCP Server service. As the network is currently configured, the workstations on Network A—all of which are DHCP clients—can access the network. The DHCP clients on Network B cannot. How should you modify the configuration of the router computer to enable the computers on Network B to access the network? (Choose all that apply.)

   a. Configure a DHCP relay agent to run on the interface to Network A.

   b. Configure a DHCP relay agent to run on the interface to Network B.

   c. Create a static route to the IP address of the interface to Network A.

   d. Create a static route to the IP address of the interface to Network B.

   e. Configure the DHCP relay agent in the router with the IP address of the interface to Network B.

   f. Configure the DHCP relay agent in the router with the IP address of the DHCP server on Network A.

2. Describe the integration of DHCP with DNS.

3. What program do you use to compact the DHCP database?

Lesson Summary

- To monitor DHCP activity, you can use the Address Leases list in the DHCP console, the audit logs maintained by the DHCP server, the statistics display for the server, or the DHCP counters in the Performance console.

- By default, DHCP servers do not ping IP addresses before assigning them. However, you can configure the server to issue a specified number of pings for each assigned address at the cost of server delays.

- Large DHCP databases require periodic compaction using the Jetpack.exe utility.

- DHCP relay agents enable clients on one network segment to obtain TCP/IP configuration settings from a server on another network. Windows 2000 includes a DHCP relay agent as part of the RRAS service.

- The DHCP and DNS servers included with Windows 2000 support dynamic DNS updates, which enable DHCP clients and servers to update the resource records on a DNS server as IP address assignments change.

Lesson 4: Troubleshooting DHCP

The most common DHCP client problem is a failure to obtain an IP address or other configuration parameters from the DHCP server during system startup. The most common DHCP server problems are the inability to start the service on the network in a Windows 2000 or Active Directory environment and the failure of clients to obtain TCP/IP configuration parameters from a working server. In this lesson, you learn how to troubleshoot DHCP clients and DHCP servers.

After this lesson, you will be able to

- Identify and solve DHCP client problems
- Identify and solve DHCP server problems

Estimated lesson time: 20 minutes

Preventing DHCP Problems

Many DHCP problems involve incorrect or missing configuration details. To help prevent the most common types of problems, you should do the following:

- **Use the 80/20 design rule for balancing scope distribution of addresses where multiple DHCP servers are deployed to service the same scope.** Using more than one DHCP server on the same subnet provides increased fault tolerance for the DHCP clients located on that subnet. With two DHCP servers, if one server is unavailable, the other server can take its place and continue to lease new addresses or renew existing clients.

- **Use server-side conflict detection on DHCP servers only when it is needed.** Either DHCP servers or clients can use conflict detection to determine whether an IP address is already in use on the network before leasing or using the address.

- **Create reservations on all DHCP servers that can potentially service the reserved client.** You can use a reservation to ensure that a DHCP client computer always receives the same IP address. If a client using a reservation can conceivably contact more than one DHCP server during its startup, you should create an identical reservation for that client on each of the DHCP servers.

- **For server performance, remember that DHCP is disk-intensive and purchase hardware with optimal disk performance characteristics.** DHCP causes frequent and intensive activity on server hard disks. To provide the best performance, consider RAID 0 or RAID 5 solutions when purchasing hardware for your server computer.

- **Keep audit logging enabled for use in troubleshooting.** By default, the DHCP service enables audit logging of service-related events. With Windows 2000 Server, audit logging provides for a long-term service monitoring tool that makes limited and safe use of server disk resources.

Troubleshooting DHCP Clients

Most DHCP-related problems start as a failed IP configuration attempt at a client, so it is good practice to start there. After you have determined that a DHCP-related problem does not originate at the client, check the system event log and DHCP server audit logs for clues. When the DHCP service does not start, these logs generally explain the source of the service failure or shutdown. Further, you can use the Ipconfig.exe utility at the command prompt to get information about the configured TCP/IP parameters on the computer.

The following sections describe common symptoms of DHCP client problems. When a client fails to obtain a TCP/IP configuration, you can use this information to quickly identify the source of the problem.

Invalid IP Address Configuration

If a DHCP client does not have an IP address configured or has an IP address configured as 169.254.x.x, that means that the client was not able to contact a DHCP server and obtain an IP address lease. This is either because of a network communications failure or because the DHCP server was unavailable. If this occurs, you should verify that the client computer has a valid, functioning network connection.

First, check that all the client's network-related hardware devices, such as the cables and network interface adapters, are installed and working properly. Next, check that all the necessary networking software components are installed in the client computer, including the network interface adapter driver, the Client for Microsoft Networks module, and the Internet Protocol (TCP/IP) module. In the Internet Protocol (TCP/IP) Properties dialog box, make sure that Obtain An IP Address Automatically is selected.

One method for checking the networking capabilities of the client computer is to install the NetBIOS Enhanced User Interface (NetBEUI) protocol module. NetBEUI requires no configuration, so simply installing it should enable the computer to communicate with other NetBEUI clients on the network. If the computer can communicate over the network using NetBEUI, you know that the problem lies in the TCP/IP implementation or configuration. If the computer cannot communicate using NetBEUI (assuming that there are other NetBEUI systems on the LAN), you know that the problem lies elsewhere, such as in the network interface adapter, the other networking software components, or the network itself.

Missing Configuration Settings

If a DHCP client is missing configuration settings, the client might be missing DHCP options in its leased configuration, either because the DHCP server is not configured to supply those options, or because the client does not support the options distributed by the server. If this problem occurs on Windows 2000 DHCP clients, verify that the most commonly used and supported options have been configured at either the server or scope level of option assignment. Windows 2000 DHCP Server includes support for numerous options that the Windows 2000 DHCP clients cannot use. These options are intended for DHCP clients running other operating systems. Check the DHCP option settings on the server and make sure that you have selected the appropriate options for your clients.

DHCP Servers Do Not Provide IP Addresses

If DHCP clients are able to access the network but are still unable to obtain IP addresses from a DHCP server, the problem has several possible causes. One cause might be a change in the IP address of the DHCP server. A DHCP server can only service requests for a scope that has a network identifier that is the same as the network identifier of its own IP address. Make sure that the DHCP server IP address falls in the same network range as the scope it is servicing. For example, a server with an IP address in the 192.168.0.0 network cannot assign addresses from scope 10.0.0.0 unless you use superscopes.

Another possible cause of the problem is that the DHCP clients are located on a different LAN from the DHCP server and must go through a router to obtain IP addresses. A DHCP server can provide IP addresses to client computers on other LANs only if a DHCP relay agent is available. Completing the following steps might correct this problem:

1. Configure a DHCP/BOOTP relay agent on the LAN where the clients are located. The relay agent can be on the router itself or on a Windows 2000 Server computer running the Routing and Remote Access Server service.

2. At the DHCP server, configure a scope to match the network address on the other side of the router where the affected clients are located.

3. In the scope, make sure that the subnet mask is correct for the remote network.

4. Do not include this scope (that is, the one for the remote network) in superscopes configured for use on the same local subnet or segment where the DHCP server resides.

Another possibility is that multiple DHCP servers exist on the same LAN. Make sure that you do not configure multiple DHCP servers on the same LAN with scopes that contain the same addresses. You might want to rule out the possibility that one of the DHCP servers in question is a computer running Microsoft Small Business Server. By design, the DHCP service in Small Business Server automatically stops when it detects another DHCP server on the LAN.

Troubleshooting DHCP Servers

When a DHCP server fails to provide leases to its clients, clients most often discover the failure in one of three ways:

- The client might be configured to use an IP address not provided by the server.
- The server sends a negative response to the client, and the client displays an error message indicating that a DHCP server could not be found.
- The server leases an address to the client but the client appears to have other network configuration-based problems, such as the inability to register or resolve DNS or NetBIOS names or to access computers beyond its local network.

The first troubleshooting task is to make sure that the DHCP service is running. You can verify this by opening the DHCP console and attempting to access the server or by opening the Computer Management console and looking at the Services list under Services And Applications. If the DHCP Server service is not started, you can attempt to start it manually using the Start Service button in the console toolbar. However, be sure to take notice of the service's startup type. If the startup type is set to Manual, then it is quite possible that the server computer was restarted and no one started the DHCP Server service. If the startup type is automatic and the service is not running, however, there must be a reason. Either the service failed to start when the computer started, someone manually stopped the service, or it has halted of its own accord. Check the logs in Event Viewer to determine whether the server failed to start or stopped because of a problem elsewhere in the computer, such as a memory shortage.

DHCP Console Incorrectly Reports Lease Expirations

When the DHCP console displays the lease expiration time for reserved clients for a scope, it indicates one of the following:

- If the scope lease time is set to an infinite lease time, the reserved client's lease is also shown as infinite.
- If the scope lease time is set to a finite length of time (such as 8 days), the reserved client's lease uses this same lease time.

The lease term of a DHCP reserved client is determined by the lease assigned to the reservation. To create reserved clients with unlimited lease durations, create a scope with an unlimited lease duration and add reservations to that scope.

DHCP Server Uses Broadcasts to Respond to All Client Messages

The DHCP server uses broadcast transmissions to respond to all client configuration request messages, regardless of how each DHCP client has set the broadcast bit flag. DHCP clients can set the broadcast flag (the first bit in the 16-bit Flags field in the DHCP message header) when sending DHCPDISCOVER messages to indicate to the DHCP server that it should address its DHCPOFFER messages to the limited broadcast address (255.255.255.255).

By default, the DHCP server in Windows NT Server 3.51 and earlier versions ignored the broadcast flag in DHCPDISCOVER messages and sent all DHCPOFFER replies as broadcasts. This behavior is implemented on the server to avoid problems that can result from clients not being able to receive or process a unicast response without a complete TCP/IP configuration.

Starting with Windows NT Server 4, the DHCP service still attempts to transmit all DHCP responses to the limited broadcast address, unless support for unicast responses is explicitly enabled by setting the value of the IgnoreBroadcastFlag registry entry to 1. This registry entry is located in HKEY_LOCAL_MACHINE\System\CurrentControlSet\Services\DHCPServer\Parameters\IgnoreBroadcastFlag. When set to 1, the computer ignores the broadcast flag in client requests and broadcasts all DHCPOFFER responses. When the registry entry is set to 0, the server adjusts its transmission behavior (whether to broadcast or not) based on the value of the broadcast bit flag in the client's DHCPDISCOVER request. If this flag is set in the request, the server transmits its responses to the limited local broadcast address. If the flag is not set in the request, the server transmits its responses directly to the client as unicasts.

DHCP Server Fails to Issue Address Leases for a New Scope

There are situations in which you might want to assign new IP addresses to all the DHCP clients on a particular network. You might have obtained a registered class of IP addresses for your network, or you might be changing the address class to accommodate more computers or more networks. To do this, you create a new scope on your DHCP server containing a range of new addresses. In this type of situation, you want clients to obtain leases in the new scope instead of using the earlier scope to obtain or renew their leases. When all clients are actively obtaining leases in the new scope, you intend to remove the existing scope. However, when you activate the new scope, you find that the DHCP clients do not obtain leases from the newly defined scope.

When superscopes are not available or not used, only a single DHCP scope can be active on the network at one time. If more than one scope is defined and activated on the DHCP server, the server uses only one scope to provide leases to clients. The active scope that the DHCP server used for distributing leases is determined by the network identifier in the first IP address assigned to the DHCP server's network interface adapter hardware. The DHCP server always uses the scope with the same network identifier as its own IP address. You can configure additional IP addresses for a network interface using the IP Settings tab in the Advanced TCP/IP Properties dialog box, but these addresses have no effect on the DHCP server's scope selection.

You can resolve this problem in the following ways:

- Configure the DHCP server to use a superscope that includes the earlier scope and the new scope.

- Change the primary IP address—that is, the address assigned in the Internet Protocol (TCP/IP) Properties dialog box for the DHCP server's network adapter to an IP address that has the same network identifier as the new scope. If necessary, you can maintain the prior address that was first assigned as an active IP address for the server computer by moving it to the list of multiple IP addresses maintained in the Advanced TCP/IP Properties tab.

Lesson Review

1. How can you force a DHCP server to assign new IP addresses with a different network identifier to all the clients on the network?

2. What type of messages, broadcast or unicast, do Windows 2000 DHCP servers use to send DHCPOFFER messages in response to DHCPDISCOVER messages, by default?

3. What is the most common symptom of DHCP-related problems?

Lesson Summary

- Most DHCP problems manifest as a failure of DHCP clients to obtain IP addresses and other TCP/IP configuration parameters from a DHCP server.

- Windows 2000 DHCP clients that fail to contact a DHCP server have an IP address of 169.254.x.x assigned to them by the Windows Automatic Private IP Addressing (APIPA) feature.

- A DHCP server can only service requests for a scope with the same network identifier as its own IP address.

- The Windows 2000 DHCP Server service always responds to DHCPDISCOVER messages with broadcast transmissions, unless you change its default behavior by modifying the Windows 2000 registry.

- A DHCP server configured with multiple scopes uses the network identifier of its own IP address to determine which scope to use when servicing clients.

C H A P T E R   6

Routing IP

Lesson 1: Understanding IP Routing. **194**

Lesson 2: Routing with RRAS **207**

Lesson 3: Using Dynamic Routing Protocols. **224**

About This Chapter

At its simplest, a router is a network layer device that connects two networks and relays traffic from one to the other. Routers are the building blocks of an internetwork (literally a network of networks), which enables a computer on one network to communicate with a computer on any other network. On a small internetwork, routing is a relatively simple process, but on larger networks, and particularly the Internet, it can be extraordinarily complex. In this chapter you study the underlying concepts of Internet Protocol (IP) networking and then examine the tools that perform routing tasks on a Microsoft Windows 2000 network.

Before You Begin

This chapter requires an understanding of the TCP/IP protocols, as discussed in Chapter 2, "Introducing TCP/IP," and of the Open Systems Interconnection (OSI) reference model, as described in Lesson 1 of Chapter 1, "Introducing Windows 2000 Networking."

Lesson 1: Understanding IP Routing

For a data packet to travel from one computer to another across an internetwork, in most cases it must pass through a number of routers on its way. The only time that routers are not involved is when the packet's destination is located on the same network segment as its source. Routing is a network layer process. In the Transmission Control Protocol/Internet Protocol (TCP/IP) protocol suite, it is the IP, running at the network layer, that is responsible for routing packets to their destinations.

After this lesson, you will be able to

- Understand the basic functions of a router
- List the information stored in a routing table
- Understand how a router uses the information stored in a routing table

Estimated lesson time: 40 minutes

Routing Principles

As discussed in Lesson 1 of Chapter 1, "Introducing Windows 2000 Networking," the network layer is primarily responsible for end-to-end-communications on an internetwork. Data-link layer protocols transmit packets only to other systems on the same network and are completely unaware of the other networks that make up the internetwork. Network layer protocols such as IP, however, are responsible for seeing to it that packets make their complete journey from source to destination intact. This task requires network layer protocols to have knowledge of the other networks around them.

The router is a device with two or more network interfaces, with each one connected to a different network. The basic function of the router is to receive data packets over one network interface and transmit them out through another. When a router processes packets, they travel up through the protocol stack no higher than the network layer and then travel down again to be retransmitted, as shown in Figure 6.1. For this reason, routers are sometimes referred to as *intermediate systems*. On the computer that originally transmitted the packet and on the computer that is its final destination, the packet is processed by the entire protocol stack, encompassing all seven layers of the OSI model. The source and destination computers are called *end systems*.

Note   The term *internetwork* refers to any collection of two or more networks connected by routers and is not to be confused with the Internet, which is an example of an internetwork. The term network is used more loosely, sometimes referring to an internetwork but most often referring to a single network segment, which could be a local area network (LAN) or wide area network (WAN) link.

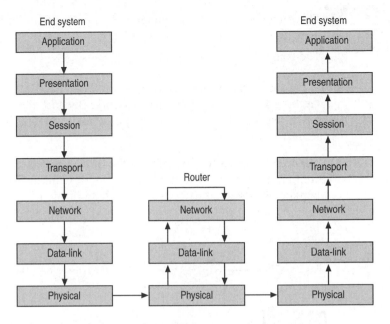

Figure 6.1   Routers as intermediate systems, processing packets no higher than the network layer

On the simplest possible internetwork, one composed of only two network segments (see Figure 6.2), routing is easy.

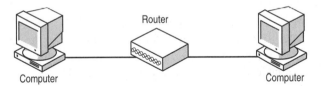

Figure 6.2   A simple, two-segment internetwork with one router

The routing process consists of the following steps:

1. A packet arrives over one network interface.
2. The router strips off the data-link layer frame used to transmit the datagram over the incoming network.
3. The router reads the Destination IP Address value in the IP header.
4. If the destination is a computer on the same network as the one that originally transmitted it, the router discards the packet.
5. If the destination is a computer on the other network, the router transmits it out through the other network interface.

6. The router repackages the datagram by encapsulating it in a new data-link layer frame, suitable for the outgoing network.

7. The router transmits the packet.

In this example, the router has to make only one decision—whether to discard a packet or transmit it over the other network. Because the internetwork consists of only two segments, there is only one possible destination for each packet, which is the destination end system.

On a more complex network, such as the three-segment internetwork shown in Figure 6.3, the process is slightly more complex. In this internetwork, two routers connect the three networks in daisy-chain fashion.

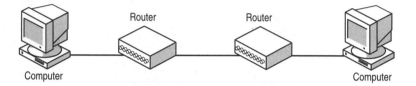

Figure 6.3   An internetwork composed of three networks and two routers

Each time one of the routers receives a packet, the decision-making process consists of three alternatives instead of two, as follows:

- If the destination is a computer on the same network as the one that originally transmitted it, the router discards the packet.

- If the destination is a computer on the other network to which the router is attached, the router transmits the packet directly to the destination end-system. This is called a *direct route*, because the data-link layer destination address is the same as the network layer destination address.

- If the destination is a computer on a network to which the router is not attached, the router transmits the packet to the other router. This is an *indirect route*, because the data-link layer destination is different from that of the network layer.

A router has direct knowledge only of the networks connected to its interfaces. If a packet is destined for a computer on a network to which the router is not connected, the router must transmit the packet to another router, which will perform the same process. In the case of a three-segment network like this, there are only two routers, so if the destination is on an unknown network, there is only one possible place to send the packet.

When the internetwork is larger still, such as the five-segment, three-router internetwork shown in Figure 6.4, the routing process is further complicated by the fact that when a packet's destination is a computer on an unknown network, the router can forward it to any one of several other routers. On the network shown in the figure, for example, when Computer 1 generates a packet that is destined for Computer 3, the packet goes to Router A first. Router A has no direct knowledge of the network where Computer 3 is located, so it must forward the packet to another router. However, two other routers are on the internetwork, and only one of them provides access to the network with Computer 3 on it. The most complex part of the routing process is deciding where to send each individual packet next.

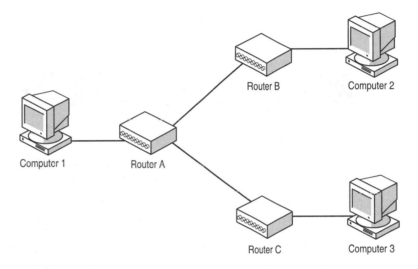

Figure 6.4 A five-segment internetwork with three routers

Large internetworks are often designed with redundant paths so that traffic can always reach its destination, even if a router fails. This means that when selecting the next intermediate destination for a packet, a router can choose from multiple paths, some of which might be more efficient than others. Therefore, each router must make an intelligent routing decision when processing each packet in order to get the packet to its destination as quickly as possible.

Routing Tables

To make their routing decisions, routers need information about networks other than those to which they are attached. This information is stored in what is known as a *routing table*, which every TCP/IP computer maintains. A routing table is a list of possible destinations with the information needed to transmit data to each destination in the most efficient manner possible. The exact appearance of the routing table varies on different computing platforms; a Windows 2000 routing table appears as follows:

Network Address	Netmask	Gateway Address	Interface	Metric
0.0.0.0	0.0.0.0	192.168.2.99	192.168.2.2	1
127.0.0.0	255.0.0.0	127.0.0.1	127.0.0.1	1
192.168.2.0	255.255.255.0	192.168.2.2	192.168.2.2	1
192.168.2.2	255.255.255.255	127.0.0.1	127.0.0.1	1
192.168.2.255	255.255.255.255	192.168.2.2	192.168.2.2	1
224.0.0.0	224.0.0.0	192.168.2.2	192.168.2.2	1
255.255.255.255	255.255.255.255	192.168.2.2	192.168.2.2	1

Tip   To display the routing table on any Windows computer with TCP/IP installed, type **route print** at the command prompt.

The functions of the columns in the table are as follows:

- **Network Address.**   Specifies the address of the network or host for which routing information is provided in the other columns.
- **Netmask.**   Specifies the subnet mask to be applied to the value in the Network Address column. As with any subnet mask, the system uses the Netmask value to determine which bits of the Network Address value function as the network identifier and which function as the host identifier.
- **Gateway Address.**   Specifies the IP address of the router that the system should use to send datagrams to the network or host identified in the Network Address column. On a LAN, the data-link layer hardware address for the system identified by the Gateway Address value will become the Destination Address in the packet's data-link layer protocol header.
- **Interface.**   Specifies the IP address of the network interface adapter that the computer should use to transmit packets to the system identified in the Gateway Address column.
- **Metric.**   Contains a value that enables the system to compare the relative efficiency of routes to the same destination.

Workstation Routing

This sample routing table contains the typical entries for a TCP/IP workstation that is not functioning as a router. The value 0.0.0.0 in the Network Address column, found in the first entry in the table, identifies the default gateway entry. The *default gateway* is the router on the LAN that the system uses when no routing table entries match the Destination IP Address of an outgoing packet. Even if multiple routers are available on the local network, a routing table can have only one functional default gateway entry. On a typical workstation that is not a router, the majority of packets go to the default gateway; only packets destined for systems on the local network do not use this router. The Gateway Address column in the default gateway entry contains the IP address of a router on the local network, and the Interface column contains the IP address of the network interface adapter that connects the system to the network.

Note   In TCP/IP terminology, the term *gateway* is synonymous with the term *router*. However, this is not the case in other networking disciplines, in which a gateway can refer to a different device that connects networks at the application layer instead of the network layer.

The second entry in the sample routing table contains a special IP address that is designated as the TCP/IP loopback address. IP automatically routes all packets destined for any address on the 127.0.0.0 network right back to the incoming packet queue on the same computer. The packets never reach the data-link layer or leave the computer. The entry ensures this by specifying that the system should use its own loopback address (127.0.0.1) as the "router" to the destination.

The IP address of the network interface adapter in the computer to which this routing table belongs is 192.168.2.2. Therefore, the third entry in the sample routing table contains the address of the local network on which the computer is located. The Network Address and Netmask values indicate that it is a Class C network with the address 192.168.2.0. This is the entry that the system uses for direct routes when it transmits packets to other systems on the local network. The Gateway Address and Interface columns both contain the IP address of the network interface adapter for the computer, indicating that the computer should use itself as the gateway. In other words, the computer should transmit the data-link layer frames to the same computer identified by the Destination IP Address value in the datagrams.

The fourth entry in the sample routing table contains the host address of the computer itself. It instructs the system to transmit data addressed to itself to the loopback address. IP always searches the routing table for host address entries before network address entries, so when processing any packets addressed to the computer's own address (192.168.2.2), IP would select this entry before the entry above it, which specifies the system's network address.

The fifth and seventh entries in the sample routing table contain broadcast addresses, both the generic IP broadcast address (255.255.255.255) and the local network's broadcast address (192.168.2.255). In both these cases, packets are transmitted to the computers on the local network, so the system again uses itself as a gateway. The sixth entry in the sample routing table contains the network address for the multicast addresses designated by the Internet Assigned Numbers Authority (IANA) for specific purposes.

On a TCP/IP computer functioning as a router, the routing table is usually longer and more complex. In addition to the entries described earlier, a router's routing table also includes entries for other networks and hosts on the internetwork. The information in these entries enables the router to decide which of the other available routers it should use to reach the destination and which of its network interfaces it should use to access that router.

Router Routing

A router on the same network as the computer in the previous example might have the following additional entries in its routing table:

Network Address	Netmask	Gateway Address	Interface	Metric
192.168.3.0	255.255.255.0	192.168.3.1	192.168.3.1	1
192.168.3.1	255.255.255.255	127.0.0.1	127.0.0.1	1
192.168.4.0	255.255.255.0	192.168.2.3	192.168.2.1	1
192.168.4.0	255.255.255.0	192.168.3.6	192.168.3.1	2
192.168.5.0	255.255.255.0	192.168.3.6	192.168.3.1	2

The first entry indicates that to reach the 192.168.3.0 network, the router should use a gateway with the address 192.168.3.1. However, since the Interface value is also 192.168.3.1, you can deduce that this router is directly connected to the 192.168.3.0 network and this entry provides for direct routes to computers on that network. As in the previous example, the following entry instructs the router to send all traffic addressed to its own network interface to the loopback address.

The third and fourth entries provide instructions for the router to access the 192.168.4.0 network. In this case, there are two possible routes to this network, one using the router's 192.168.2.1 interface to access another router with the address 192.168.2.3 and a second using the 192.168.3.1 interface to access a router with the address 192.168.3.6. The difference between these two routes is indicated by the respective values in the Metric column. The actual significance of the Metric value can vary depending on how the routing table entries are created, but in most cases the value reflects the number of hops needed to reach the destination. Each router that processes a packet is considered to be one hop, so these entries indicate that packets transmitted to the 192.168.4.0 network through the 192.168.2.3 gateway require one hop but packets using the 192.168.3.6 gateway are two hops away. When a router has two entries for the same destination in its routing table, it always uses the one with the lower Metric value.

The entry for the 192.168.5.0 network indicates that the router must again use the 192.168.3.6 gateway and that the destination is again two hops away. However, in this case this is the only known route to the destination, so the router must use it.

Selecting a Route

Each time a router processes a packet, it accesses its routing table and utilizes the information there according to the sequence shown in Figure 6.5.

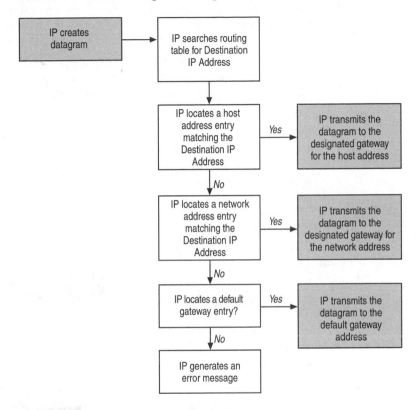

Figure 6.5 The IP routing process

The steps of the routing table procedure are as follows:

1. The router reads the value of the Destination IP Address field in the packet's IP header and compares it with the routing table, looking for a host address with the same value. A host address entry in the table has a full IP address in the Network Address column and the value 255.255.255.255 in the Netmask column.

2. If no host address entry in the routing table exactly matches the Destination IP Address value, the router then scans the routing table's Network Address and Netmask columns for an entry that matches the destination address's network identifier. If more than one entry in the routing table contains the desired network identifiers, the router uses the entry with the lower value in the Metric column.

3. If no table entries match the network identifier of the destination IP address, the router searches for a default gateway entry that has a value of 0.0.0.0 in the Network Address and Netmask columns.

4. If there is no default gateway entry, the router generates an Internet Control Message Protocol (ICMP) Destination Unreachable error message and transmits it back to the end-system that transmitted the datagram.

5. If the router locates a viable routing table entry, it prepares to transmit the datagram to the router identified in the Gateway Address column. The system consults the Address Resolution Protocol (ARP) cache or performs an ARP transaction to obtain the data-link layer hardware address of the router.

6. When it has the hardware address, the router passes it and the datagram down to the data-link layer protocol associated with the address specified in the Interface column. The data-link layer protocol constructs a frame using the destination router's hardware address in its Destination Address field and transmits it out over the designated interface.

Routing Table Creation

Although the previous sections describe how TCP/IP computers use routing tables to forward packets to their destinations, the question remains—how does the information get into the routing table? In the example of a workstation routing table shown earlier, the computer itself automatically creates the entries. The default gateway address is supplied as part of the TCP/IP client configuration, and the local network and local host entries are derived from the computer's own IP address. The routing table in a router, however, contains entries that the computer cannot derive from its own configuration because they contain information about remote networks.

Entries can be created in a router's routing table in two ways: manually and automatically. The manual method is called *static routing* and consists of an administrator using a program to create table entries. The automatic method is called *dynamic routing* and involves the use of a specialized routing protocol. Dynamic routing protocols enable routers to transmit the contents of their routing tables to other routers, thereby providing them with information about remote parts of the internetwork. Each router has first-hand information about the networks to which it is connected and creates routing table entries for those networks. The router then transmits those table entries (along with the rest of its routing table) to other routers on the local network. The routers receiving the dynamic routing information add the new entries to their own routing tables, modifying the Gateway Address, Interface, and Metric information as needed. These routers then share the entries with other routers, and so on. Eventually, all the routers have knowledge of the entire internetwork.

Note On the Internet, the IP routing process is still more complicated because there is no way for every router on the Internet to maintain information about every other router. The routing tables would be enormous and the traffic generated by the dynamic routing protocols would flood the network. For a discussion of how routing is handled on extremely large internetworks, such as the Internet, see Lesson 3 of this chapter.

For a small internetwork that does not often change, static routing can be an effective routing solution. Administrators create the required entries on each router's routing table, and no further adjustment is necessary. Also, routing protocols generate no additional network traffic.

On a large internetwork, dynamic routing is all but essential. With a large number of routers, you have a large number of routing tables and a large number of entries in each table. Creating those entries manually on each router would be a large and complex task. Another advantage of dynamic routing, in addition to reducing the network administrator's workload, is that it automatically compensates for changes in the network infrastructure. If a particular router goes down, for example, its failure to communicate with the other routers nearby means that it will eventually be deleted from their routing tables and packets will take different routes to their destinations. If and when that router comes back online, it resumes communications with the other routers and is again added to their tables. The process by which the routers compensate for a change of the internetwork configuration is called *convergence*. An internetwork as large as the Internet could not exist without dynamic routing because it would be all but impossible for administrators to keep up with the constant configuration changes occurring on the network.

Routing Hardware

Although the basic functions performed by a router are the same, routers themselves can take many different forms. On large internetworks and the Internet, a router is typically a dedicated hardware device with multiple network interfaces. The most elaborate type of router, found in corporate data centers, consists of a rack-mounted frame with slots for network interface modules of various types. Because routers function at the network layer of the OSI model, the data-link layer protocol used by a network is irrelevant to the routing function. Therefore, the various network interfaces in a router can use the same or different data-link layer protocols. Modular routers enable network administrators to customize the unit to their network configuration so that they can join networks using different LAN and WAN protocols together into an internetwork.

Note Most of the private networks constructed today use switches to connect LANs instead of routers. Routing is primarily used for WAN connections. A switch is a data-link layer device that looks much like a hub. The difference between a hub and a switch is that a hub receives data packets through one port and forwards them out through all the other ports and a switch receives incoming data through one port and forwards it out only through the port providing access to the destination system. The result is that each pair of computers on a switched network has what amounts to a dedicated, full-bandwidth connection between them. There is therefore no contention for the network medium, no collisions, and no need for media access control. By eliminating the shared network medium, switching joins the individual LANs into one large network. Data-link layer switching requires much less processing than network layer routing, which makes a switched network faster, more efficient, and considerably less expensive than a routed network of the same configuration.

Modular routers are intended for high-end installations, and by the time you purchase the frame, network interface modules, and other components you would need for a large corporate internetwork, the total price can easily approach six figures. As you move down the price scale, you find stand-alone units that are preconfigured with specific interface combinations. These devices might or might not be rack-mounted and are generally less expensive than modular routers, but they can still cost many thousands of dollars.

A more common type of hardware router today is one that connects a LAN to another network using a WAN link. These devices are frequently marketed as Internet routers because they are often used to provide LAN users with Internet access. In this type of router, one of the network interfaces is a standard LAN adapter using a protocol such as Ethernet and the other is a WAN adapter using any of several media, such as a dial-up modem connection or a leased line. Regardless of the data-link layer protocol used to connect to each network, the routing process is the same.

Because Internet access is an all but ubiquitous service on networks today, routers of this type are available at all levels of price and complexity, ranging from expensive units designed to connect a large internetwork to the Internet using a leased line or other high-speed technology to inexpensive models intended for use with modems on home or small business networks. This type of router often includes additional features apart from basic routing capabilities, such as network address translation (NAT) and other firewall technologies that protect the network from Internet-based intruders.

Note For more information about NAT, see Chapter 12, "Using Network Address Translation."

Routing Software

Although many of the routers in use today are dedicated hardware devices, it is also possible to implement all the processing capabilities a router needs in software. A computer with two or more network interfaces (called a *multihomed* computer) can function as a router, in addition to its other capabilities. Many network operating systems, including Windows 2000 Server, are capable of routing IP and other network layer protocols, such as Internetwork Packet Exchange (IPX). The Routing and Remote Access Service (RRAS) included with Windows 2000 Server enables the computer to function in a variety of roles—as a router connecting two LANs, a router connecting a LAN and a remote network, a remote access server, and a NAT server, among others.

On an even smaller scale, there are software products that you can use to share an Internet connection with other users on a home or small office LAN, such as the Internet Connection Sharing (ICS) feature in Windows XP and Windows 2000 Professional. These products enable a computer with a standard LAN interface card and a modem to route IP traffic between the local network and the network of an Internet service provider (ISP).

Exercise 1: Routing Tables

Place the following steps of the routing table search process in the proper order.

1. Default gateway search

2. Host address search

3. Network address search

Lesson Review

1. What type of route does a packet use if its Destination IP Address and data-link layer Destination Address values refer to different computers?

    a. The default gateway

    b. A direct route

    c. The default route

    d. An indirect route

2. What is a TCP/IP system with interfaces to two different networks called?

    a. A bridge

    b. Multihomed

    c. A switch

    d. All of the above

3. In a Windows routing table, what column contains the address of the router that should be used to reach a particular network or host?

    a. Network Address

    b. Netmask

    c. Gateway Address

    d. Interface

4. What does a router do when it fails to find a routing table entry for a particular network or host?

5. In a Windows routing table, what is the Network Destination value for the default gateway entry?

    a. 0.0.0.0

    b. The address of the network to which the router is connected

    c. 255.255.255.255

    d. The address of the router's network interface

Lesson Summary

- Routing is one of the complicated functions of IP. Routers receive packets and forward them to their destinations.

- Complex internetworks can have redundant routers that provide multiple paths to the same destination. The job of a router is to forward packets using the most efficient path.

- Routers store information about the network in a routing table. When forwarding a packet, the router searches the table for a route to each destination and transmits the packet to the appropriate destination.

- When a router fails to locate a route to a particular destination in the table, it sends the packet to the designated default gateway.

- A router can be a stand-alone hardware device, an operating system, or a separate software product.

Lesson 2: Routing with RRAS

Virtually all the routing-related functions in Windows 2000 Server are built into the Routing and Remote Access Service (RRAS). You can configure this service to perform a variety of routing-related tasks that enable the server to perform a variety of network communication functions.

After this lesson, you will be able to

- Configure RRAS
- Create a demand-dial routing interface
- Create static route entries in the routing table

Estimated lesson time: 30 minutes

Configuring RRAS

All versions of Windows 2000 Server install RRAS by default with the operating system, but they do not configure or activate it. This is because RRAS can perform a variety of functions, and Windows 2000 leaves it up to the system admin istrator to select one. You must configure the service manually using the RRAS console, which provides access to wizards that aid in the process.

To configure RRAS to provide basic IP routing between two existing network interfaces, use the following procedure:

1. Click Start and launch the Routing and Remote Access console from the Administrative tools program group to display the console shown in Figure 6.6.

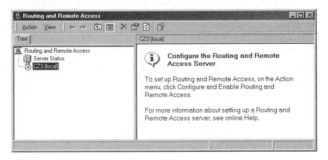

Figure 6.6   The default Routing and Remote Access console

2. Select the server in the scope pane and select Configure And Enable Routing And Remote Access from the Action menu to launch the Routing And Remote Access Server Setup Wizard.

3. Click Next to bypass the Welcome page and proceed to the Common Configurations page (see Figure 6.7).

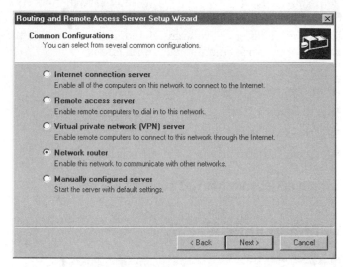

Figure 6.7   The Common Configurations page in the Routing And Remote Access Server Setup Wizard

4. Click the Network Router option button and click Next to proceed to the Routed Protocols page (see Figure 6.8).

The protocols currently installed on the computer are shown in the Protocols box.

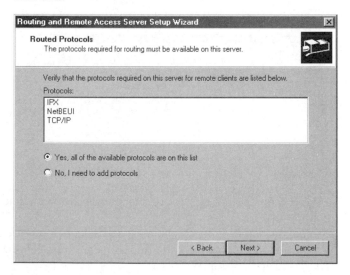

Figure 6.8   The Routed Protocols page in the Routing And Remote Access Server Setup Wizard

5. If TCP/IP appears in the Protocols box, confirm that Yes, All Of The Available Protocols Are On This List is selected and click Next to proceed to the Demand-Dial Connections page (see Figure 6.9).

If you want to route protocols that do not appear in the list, click No, I Need To Add Protocols, and then click Next. This closes the wizard so you can install the required protocols using the Network And Dial-up Communications Control Panel before you attempt to configure RRAS again.

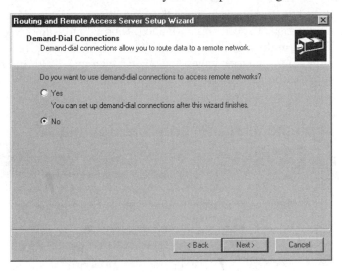

Figure 6.9   The Demand-Dial Connections page in the Routing And Remote Access Server Setup Wizard

6. Click No and click the Next button to proceed to the Completing The Routing And Remote Access Server Setup Wizard page.

Clicking Yes causes the Demand Dial Interface Wizard to launch when the Routing And Remote Access Server Setup Wizard is completed.

7. Click Finish to complete the configuration process and close the wizard. The Routing And Remote Access console now appears as shown in Figure 6.10.

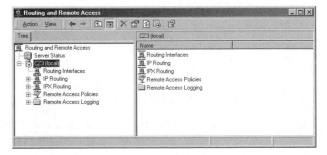

Figure 6.10   The Routing And Remote Access Console for a configured router

After you have configured RRAS in this manner, the service is ready to route traffic between networks using two standard network interface adapters. If the adapters are properly installed, two dedicated Local Area Connection entries appear in the details pane of the RRAS console when you click the Routing Interfaces icon.

Manually Configuring RRAS

It is also possible to activate RRAS without configuring it to perform any particular task. To do this, you launch Routing and Remote Access Server Setup Wizard in the usual manner and select Manually Configured Server in the Common Configurations page. The wizard then installs all the main RRAS components without configuring them and terminates. When the RRAS service starts, you can manually configure the components to perform the tasks you need.

Implementing Demand-Dial Routing

RRAS can route traffic between two LANs, when the computer has two network interface adapters installed, or between a LAN and a remote network, using one network interface adapter and a WAN connection. In the latter case, you must create a demand-dial interface for the WAN connection, which can be a dial-up modem, Integrated Services Digital Network (ISDN) adapter, or other communications device. A *demand-dial interface* is one in which the interface is activated only when the routing table shows that this interface is needed to reach the IP destination address. For example, when you use a modem for a demand-dial connection, a user generating traffic that is destined for the remote network causes RRAS to initiate the dial-up process, connecting the server to the network and then transmitting the data.

RRAS can use a demand-dial interface to connect to a network at one of your company's other locations or to connect to the Internet through an ISP's network. The only differences between the Network Router option and the Internet Connection Server option in the Routing and Remote Access Server Setup Wizard's Common Configurations page are the use of a demand-dial interface and certain additional services, such as NAT.

You can create a demand-dial interface either by answering Yes on the Demand-Dial Connections page of the Routing and Remote Access Server Setup Wizard or after completing the RRAS Network Router configuration process by using the following procedure:

1. Click Start and open the Routing And Remote Access console from the Administrative tools program group.
2. Select the RRAS server icon in the scope pane and select Properties from the Action menu to open the server's Properties dialog box (see Figure 6.11).

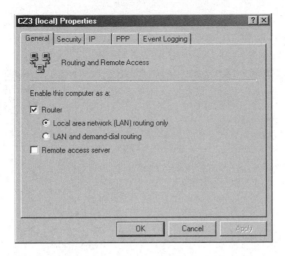

Figure 6.11   The RRAS server Properties dialog box

3. On the General tab, confirm that the Router check box is selected and click the LAN And Demand-Dial Routing option button.

4. Click OK. A Routing And Remote Access message box appears, informing you that the configuration change you are making requires the RRAS service to be stopped and restarted.

5. Click Yes to stop and start the RRAS service.

6. Select the Routing Interfaces icon beneath the server icon in the scope pane and select New Demand Dial Interface from the Action menu to launch the Demand Dial Interface Wizard.

7. Click Next to bypass the Welcome page and proceed to the Interface Name page (see Figure 6.12).

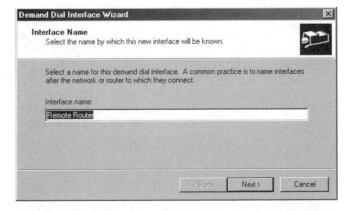

Figure 6.12   The Interface Name page in the Demand Dial Interface Wizard

8. Type a name by which the demand-dial interface will be identified in the RRAS console in the Interface Name box. Click Next to proceed to the Connection Type page (see Figure 6.13).

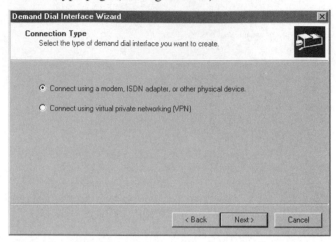

Figure 6.13   The Connection Type page in the Demand Dial Interface Wizard

9. Click the Connect Using A Modem, ISDN Adapter, Or Other Physical Device option button and click Next to proceed to the Phone Number page (see Figure 6.14).

If more than one communications device is available on the computer, a Select A Device page appears, enabling you to choose one.

Click Connect Using Virtual Private Networking to configure a virtual private network (VPN) link to the remote network, using either the Point-to-Point Tunneling Protocol (PPTP) or the Layer 2 Tunneling Protocol (L2TP). For information on VPNs, see Chapter 11, "Using the Remote Access Service."

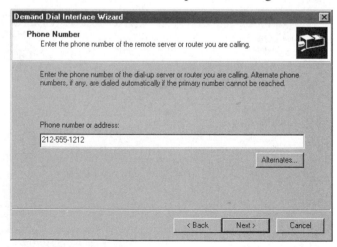

Figure 6.14   The Phone Number page in the Demand Dial Interface Wizard

10. Type the telephone number of the remote access server or router on the remote network in the Phone Number Or Address box and click Next to proceed to the Protocols And Security page (see Figure 6.15).

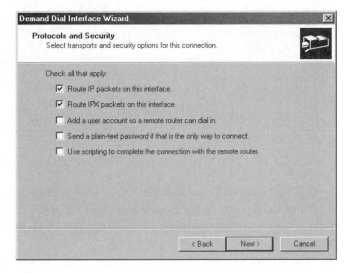

Figure 6.15   The Protocols And Security page in the Demand Dial Interface Wizard

11. Select the appropriate check boxes to enable the following features, and then click Next to proceed to the Dial Out Credentials page (see Figure 6.16).

- **Route IP Packets On This Interface.**   Enables RRAS to route IP datagrams

- **Route IPX Packets On This Interface.**   Enables RRAS to route IPX datagrams

- **Add A User Account So A Remote Router Can Dial In.**   Adds a Dial In Credentials page to the wizard, enabling you to specify a password that the remote server can use to connect to the RRAS server

- **Send A Plain-Text Password If That Is The Only Way To Connect.** Enables RRAS to use unencrypted passwords when it cannot negotiate the use of a more secure authentication protocol with the remote access server or router

- **Use Scripting To Complete The Connection With The Remote Router.** Enables the use of scripts to control the connection process

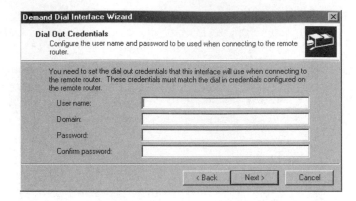

Figure 6.16   The Dial Out Credentials page in the Demand Dial Interface Wizard

12. Type the credentials needed for RRAS to log on to the remote access server or router in the User Name, Domain, Password, and Confirm Password boxes. Click Next to proceed to the Completing The Demand Dial Interface Wizard page.

13. Click Finish to close the wizard and create the new demand-dial interface. The interface now appears in the list of LAN And Demand-Dial Interfaces in the RRAS console's details pane.

After you have created the demand-dial interface, you create a static route to specify when RRAS should use it. You can also create filters for the interface that impose limits on the types of TCP/IP traffic that can use it, based on IP addresses or protocols, and specify the times of day that the interface is operative.

Configuring Demand-Dial Interfaces

After you create a demand-dial interface, you can configure many parameters to control the connection process, set the TCP/IP parameters, and secure the communications between the networks. To configure a demand-dial interface, you select it in the Routing Interfaces list and select Properties from the Action menu to display a dialog box like that shown in Figure 6.17.

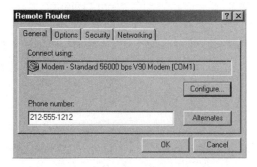

Figure 6.17   The Properties dialog box for a demand-dial interface

Configuring Dialing Properties

To configure properties that control the process by which RRAS connects to a remote access server or router, click the Options tab in the Properties dialog box (see Figure 6.18). In the Connection Type box, you can specify whether the interface uses demand-dial or is persistent, meaning that it stays connected continuously. The Idle Time Before Hanging Up drop-down list enables you to specify the amount of time an interface with no traffic passing through it should remain connected. On a modem interface, selecting a high value minimizes the delay incurred waiting for the modem to dial and connect; a low value minimizes the telephone charges.

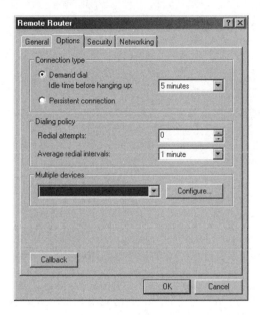

Figure 6.18 The Options tab of a demand-dial interface's Properties dialog box

In the Dialing Policy box, you can specify how many times RRAS should redial when trying to connect to a remote access server or router and how long the interval between redial attempts should be. The Multiple Devices box enables you to specify when RRAS should utilize multiple WAN connections to increase available bandwidth. Click Callback to configure RRAS to hang up its connection to the remote access server or router after requesting that it be called back at a specific number.

Configuring TCP/IP Settings

Click the Networking tab in an interface's Properties dialog box (see Figure 6.19) to configure the TCP/IP parameters that the interface uses. Click Settings to control the parameters used when establishing a Point-to-Point Protocol (PPP) connection, such as whether to use Link Control Protocol (LCP) extensions, Van Jacobsen header compression, and multilink connections. Click Properties to open a standard Internet Protocol (TCP/IP) Properties dialog box, in which you can specify an IP address, subnet mask, and other parameters for the interface or configure it to use the Dynamic Host Configuration Protocol (DHCP) to obtain parameter settings.

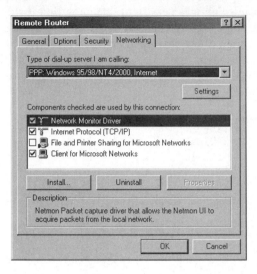

Figure 6.19   The Networking tab of a demand-dial interface's Properties dialog box

Configuring Security

The Security tab in the Properties dialog box (see Figure 6.20) enables you to specify whether you want to require the use of encrypted passwords or data encryption, or both, on the interface. Select the Advanced (Custom Settings) option button and click Settings to open an Advanced Security Settings dialog box, in which you can select a specific authentication protocol and configure a data encryption policy.

Figure 6.20   The Security tab of a demand-dial interface's Properties dialog box

Creating Static Routes

When you have configured RRAS to function as a router, it's time to populate the computer's routing table. As discussed in Lesson 1 of this chapter, a router can use either static or dynamic routing. In this section, you learn how to manually create static entries in the computer's routing table. In Lesson 3 you learn how to use dynamic routing protocols to build a routing table.

Configuring Static Routes Using the RRAS Console

When the RRAS service is configured and running, you can use the RRAS console to view the computer's routing table and manage its entries. To view the routing table, expand the IP Routing icon, select Static Routes, and select Show IP Routing Table from the Action menu to display the IP Routing Table window shown in Figure 6.21.

Destination	Network mask	Gateway	Interface	Metric	Protocol
0.0.0.0	0.0.0.0	192.168.2.99	Local Area Connection	1	Network management
127.0.0.0	255.0.0.0	127.0.0.1	Loopback	1	Local
127.0.0.1	255.255.255.255	127.0.0.1	Loopback	1	Local
192.168.2.0	255.255.255.0	192.168.2.3	Local Area Connection	1	Local
192.168.2.3	255.255.255.255	127.0.0.1	Loopback	1	Local
224.0.0.0	240.0.0.0	192.168.2.3	Local Area Connection	1	Local
255.255.255.255	255.255.255.255	192.168.2.3	Local Area Connection	1	Local

Figure 6.21   The IP Routing Table window

To create a new entry in the routing table, use the following procedure:

1. Click Start and open the Routing And Remote Access console from the Administrative tools program group.

2. Expand the server icon, and then the IP Routing icon.

3. Select the Static Routes icon and select New Static Route from the Action menu to display the Static Route dialog box (see Figure 6.22).

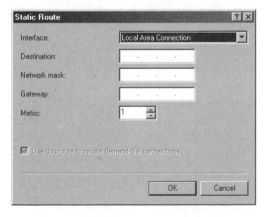

Figure 6.22   The Static Route dialog box

4. Using the Interface Selector, select the interface that you want the computer to use to reach the destination.

5. The Interface selector contains all the network interfaces found in the RRAS Routing Interfaces header (except for the Loopback interface).

6. In the Destination box, type the address of the network or host for which the entry will provide routing information.

7. In the Network Mask box, type the subnet mask to be associated with the destination address.

8. In the Gateway box, specify the address of the router that RRAS should use to send traffic to the destination.

9. In the Metric field, type a value that indicates the relative efficiency of the route.

   The metrics you select for your static routes do not have to reflect any specific physical condition; the values are significant only in relation to the metrics of the other routes in the table. For example, if you have a high-speed WAN connection to a particular remote network and you want to create a backup connection using a modem, you can assign the higher speed route a lower Metric value so that RRAS will use it first.

10. Select the Use This Route To Initiate Demand-Dial Connections check box if you want traffic going to the specified destination to trigger a demand-dial connection.

11. Click OK to close the dialog box and add the new entry to the routing table.

Note Although the RRAS console enables you to modify and delete the static route entries you have created, it does not permit you to modify the table entries that are automatically created by the TCP/IP client. To modify or delete these entries, you must use either the standard TCP/IP configuration settings in the Network And Dial-up Connections Control Panel or the Route.exe program, the latter of which provides full access to all the entries in the routing table.

Using Route.exe

As mentioned in Lesson 1, every TCP/IP computer has a routing table, even those not functioning as routers. All the current Windows operating systems include a command-line utility called Route.exe with their TCP/IP clients that enables you to view and manage the entire contents of the computer's routing table. The syntax for Route.exe is as follows:

```
route [-f] [-p] command [destination] [MASK netmask] [gateway] [METRIC
metric] [IF interface]
```

- **–f** This parameter deletes all the entries from the routing table. When used with the Add command, it deletes the entire table before adding the new entry.

- **–p**   When used with the Add command, this parameter creates a persistent route entry in the table. A persistent route is one that remains in the table permanently, even after the system is restarted. When –p is used with the Print command, the system displays only persistent routes.

- *Command*   This variable contains a keyword that specifies the function of the command.

- *Destination*   This variable specifies the network or host address of the table entry being managed.

- **MASK** *netmask*   The variable *netmask* specifies the subnet mask to be applied to the address specified in the *destination* variable.

- *Gateway*   This variable specifies the address of the router that the system should use to reach the host or network specified by the *destination* variable.

- **METRIC** *metric*   The variable *metric* specifies a value that indicates the relative efficiency of the route in the table entry.

- **IF** *interface*   The variable *interface* specifies the address of the network interface adapter that the system should use to reach the router specified by the *gateway* variable.

Route.exe's *command* variable takes one of four values, which are as follows:

- **Print.**   Displays the contents of the routing table. When used with the –p parameter, it displays only the persistent routes in the routing table.

- **Add.**   Creates a new entry in the routing table.

- **Delete.**   Deletes an existing entry from the routing table.

- **Change.**   Modifies the parameters of an entry in the routing table.

The Route Print command displays the current contents of the routing table. To delete an entry, you use the Route Delete command with a *destination* parameter to identify the entry you want to remove. To create a new entry in the table, you use the Route Add command with parameters that specify the values for the entry. The Route Change command works in the same way, except that it modifies the table entry specified by the *destination* variable. The *destination* variable is the address of the network or host for which you are providing routing information. The other parameters contain the subnet mask, gateway address, interface address, and metric information, as described in Lesson 1 of this chapter. For example, using the network configuration shown in Figure 6.23 to create an entry that informs the Windows 2000 system labeled Router A of the existence of Router B on the same LAN, you would execute a Route.exe command like the following at the Router A system's command line:

```
ROUTE ADD 192.168.5.0 MASK 255.255.255.0 192.168.2.7 IF 192.168.2.2
METRIC 1
```

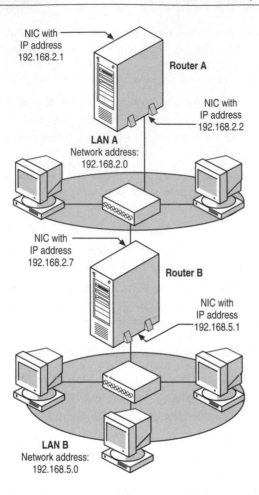

Figure 6.23   Using static routing to forward internetwork traffic

The functions of the Route.exe parameters in this particular command are as follows:

- **ADD**   Indicates that the program should create a new entry in the existing routing table
- **192.168.5.0**   The address of the other network to which Router B provides access
- **MASK 255.255.255.0**   The subnet mask to be applied to the destination address, which in this case indicates that the address represents an unsubnetted Class C network
- **192.168.2.7**   The address of the network interface adapter with which Router B is connected to the same network as Router A

- **IF 192.168.2.2**   The address of the network interface adapter in Router A that provides access to the network it shares with Router B
- **METRIC 1**   Indicates that the destination network is one hop away

This new routing table entry essentially tells Router A that when it has traffic to send to any computer on the network with the address 192.168.5.0, it should send the traffic to the router with the address 192.168.2.7 using the Router A network interface adapter with the address 192.168.2.2.

Exercise 1: Configuring RRAS

1. You are the network administrator of a corporate network that consists of three subnets connected by a single router. The router has three network interface adapters installed, which are configured as follows:

   - Subnet A: IP address 10.60.4.1, subnet mask 255.255.255.0
   - Subnet B: IP address 10.60.5.1, subnet mask 255.255.255.0
   - Subnet C: IP address 10.60.6.2, subnet mask 255.255.255.0

   Subnet B and Subnet C both contain client computers. Subnet A does not. Subnet B and Subnet C each contain a Windows 2000 DHCP server that is responsible for assigning IP addresses to client computers on the local subnet only. The scope properties on the two DHCP servers are as follows:

   - Subnet B scope: Start IP Address 10.60.5.100, End IP Address 10.60.5.254, Subnet Mask 255.255.255.0
   - Subnet C scope, Start IP Address 10.60.6.100, End IP Address 10.60.6.254, Subnet Mask 255.255.0.0

   Subnet A contains a Web server and provides the entire internetwork with Internet connectivity. However, the network is experiencing connectivity problems. Clients on Subnet B can communicate with any host on their own subnet, but they cannot communicate with hosts on Subnet C. Clients on Subnet C cannot communicate with hosts on Subnet B, but they can successfully connect to Subnet A. What should you do to correct this problem?

   a. Delete and re-create the scope on the Subnet B DHCP server to reflect the correct subnet mask
   b. Modify the routing table on the router to enable routing from Subnet B to Subnet A and Subnet C
   c. Delete and re-create the scope on the Subnet C DHCP server to reflect the correct subnet mask
   d. Modify the routing table on each Subnet B host computer to enable direct connectivity to hosts on Subnet A and Subnet C
   e. Delete and re-create the scopes on both the Subnet B and Subnet C DHCP servers to reflect the same configuration information for both subnets

2. Your Windows 2000 network has three subnets, A, B, and C. Subnet A is located at the corporate headquarters, and Subnet C is located at a remote office. Subnet B is a WAN link that connects a router on Subnet A to a router at Subnet C. Both routers are Windows 2000 Servers using demand-dial connections for the WAN link. Router AB connects Subnet A to Subnet B, and Router BC connects Subnet B to Subnet C. What two steps must you take to allow a client on Subnet C to access a share on Subnet A? (Choose all that apply.)

   a. Configure a static route for Subnet A on the demand-dial interface of Router AB

   b. Configure a static route for Subnet B on the demand-dial interface of Router BC

   c. Configure a static route for Subnet C on the demand-dial interface of Router BC

   d. Configure a static route for Subnet A on the demand-dial interface of Router BC

   e. Configure a static route for Subnet B on the demand-dial interface of Router AB

   f. Configure a static route for Subnet C on the demand-dial interface of Router AB

Lesson Review

1. Which of the configuration tasks must you perform after creating a demand-dial interface in RRAS?

   a. Specify an IP address for the interface

   b. Create a static routing table entry for the interface

   c. Select an authentication protocol for the interface connection

   d. Specify the number of redial attempts the interface should perform

2. A demand-dial interface enables RRAS to route traffic between which types of network interfaces? (Choose all that apply.)

   a. Two LANs

   b. A LAN and a modem connection

   c. Two modem connections

   d. A LAN and a VPN

3. Which of the following statements regarding this Route.exe command is not true?

```
ROUTE ADD 171.29.0.0 MASK 255.255.0.0 171.29.32.19 IF 171.29.32.19
METRIC 1
```

a. The destination is a network to which the computer is directly connected.

b. The command is using an incorrect subnet mask.

c. The gateway used by the route is on the same network as the computer whose routing table this is.

d. It should not be necessary to run this command on the computer.

Lesson Summary

■ For Windows 2000 to function as a router, you must configure and start the Routing and Remote Access Service.

■ RRAS supports a variety of functions, including standard network routing and Internet access routing.

■ RRAS can route traffic between standard network interface adapters or between network interface adapters and WAN connections.

■ To route LAN traffic to a WAN connection, you must create and configure a demand-dial interface in RRAS.

■ You can create static routing table entries on a Windows 2000 Server computer using the RRAS console or the Route.exe command-line utility.

Lesson 3: Using Dynamic Routing Protocols

Dynamic routing is essentially the glue that holds a large internetwork together. Without it, network administrators would be faced with the difficult task of creating static routing table entries on every one of their routers, and even worse, updating all those routing tables whenever the configuration of the network changes. In this lesson you learn how dynamic routing works and how to implement it on your Windows 2000 network.

After this lesson, you will be able to

- Understand how dynamic routing works on the Internet
- Install and configure RIP
- Install and configure OSPF

Estimated lesson time: 40 minutes

Dynamic Routing Protocols

Dynamic routing uses specialized routing protocols to gather and share routing information. The two routing protocols supported by RRAS (and by most other hardware and software routers) are the Routing Information Protocol (RIP) and the Open Shortest Path First (OSPF) protocol. RIP is the simplest and most popular routing protocol used today, but OSPF is designed to address some of RIP's shortcomings and is becoming more common. A typical Windows 2000 internetwork runs one or the other of these protocol on all its routers, enabling them to continually share their routing table information. If a router on the internetwork should fail, the other routers notice the absence of its routing protocol messages and, after a specified period, remove it from their routing tables. This prevents the other routers on the internetwork from sending packets to a router that is not functioning.

RIP and OSPF are both *interior routing protocols* designed to provide dynamic routing services within an internetwork. As a Windows 2000 network administrator, these are likely to be the only routing protocols you ever use. Interior routing refers to the sharing of routing table information within a private internetwork. If you run RIP on your Windows 2000 internetwork, for example, all your routers share their routing tables with one another by regularly transmitting them in RIP messages. If your internetwork is connected to the Internet, your RIP traffic does not pass through the router providing the Internet connection. This is only logical, because if every internetwork advertised its routes on the Internet, there would be no bandwidth left for any other types of traffic, and the routing tables in the Internet routers would become so large that the systems would grind to a halt.

To prevent its saturation with routing protocol traffic, the Internet is broken up into administrative units called *autonomous systems.* Each autonomous system (AS) is theoretically a group of networks controlled by a single administrative body and running an interior routing protocol throughout it. An AS on the Internet must have a registered number assigned to it by the IANA in much the same way as network IP addresses are registered. In actuality, it is rare for a single organization to run its own AS. You can run whatever interior routing protocol you choose on your internetwork and still be part of a larger AS without even being aware of it.

The interior routing protocol communications within an AS are invisible to systems outside it. However, ASs still share routing information with other ASs, using exterior routing protocols such as the Border Gateway Protocol (BGP) or the Exterior Gateway Protocol (EGP). Typically, a small subset of the routers in an AS are configured to run both interior and exterior routing protocols to provide routing information to other nearby ASs, as shown in Figure 6.24. These are called *border routers.* This two-tiered distribution of the Internet dynamic routing effort is comparable to the way that IP addresses and Domain Name System (DNS) names are split, the former into network addresses and host addresses and the latter into domain names and host names.

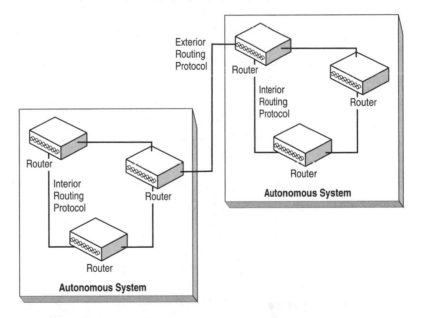

Figure 6.24   Interior and exterior routing protocols

On a smaller scale, border routing can also refer to any router providing an internetwork with access to other internetworks. For example, a Windows 2000 internetwork might have internal routers connecting its many networks and a single border router that provides Internet connectivity.

Note The term *border routing* also comes into play with the OSPF routing protocol, with which you can split an internetwork into discrete areas, which are connected using area border routers. See "Understanding OSPF" later in this lesson for more information.

Understanding RIP

RIP is the most commonly used interior routing protocol in the TCP/IP suite and on networks around the world. Originally designed for UNIX systems in the form of a daemon called *routed* (pronounced *route-dee*), RIP was eventually ported to many other platforms and standardized in Request for Comments (RFC) 1058 by the Internet Engineering Task Force (IETF). Some years later, RIP was updated to a version 2, which was published as RFC 2453.

Most RIP exchanges are based on two message types: requests and replies. Both are packaged in User Datagram Protocol (UDP) packets addressed to the well-known port number 520. When a RIP router starts, it generates a RIP request message and transmits it as a broadcast over all its network interfaces. Upon receiving the broadcast, every other router that supports RIP on either network generates a reply message that contains its routing table information. A RIP reply message can contain up to 25 routes, each of which is 20 bytes long, as shown in Figure 6.25. If the routing table on the replying router contains more than 25 entries, the router generates multiple reply messages until it has transmitted the entire contents of the table. When the original router receives the replies, it integrates the routes they contain into its own routing table.

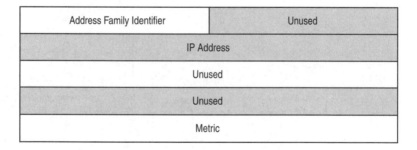

Figure 6.25   A RIP version 1 route

The metric value included with each routing table entry determines the efficiency of the route based on the number of hops required to reach the destination. When routers receive routing table entries from other routers using RIP, they increment the value of the metric for each route to reflect the additional hop required to reach the destination. The maximum value for a metric in a RIP message is 15. Routing that uses metrics based on the number of hops to the destination is called *distance vector routing*.

After their initial exchange of messages, RIP routers transmit periodic updates by default, to ensure that all the other routers on the networks to which they are connected have current information. If a RIP-supplied routing table entry is not refreshed on a regular basis, the router assumes that the entry is no longer viable, increases its metric to 16 (an illegal value that prevents the route from being used), and eventually removes it from the table completely.

This frequent retransmission of routing data is the main reason that RIP is criticized. The protocol generates a large amount of redundant broadcast traffic. In addition, the message format does not support the inclusion of a subnet mask for each route. Instead, RIP applies the subnet mask of the interface over which it receives each route, which might not always be accurate. RIP version 2 is designed to address these problems.

The primary difference between RIP 1 and RIP 2 is the format of the routes included in the reply messages. The RIP 2 message is no larger than that of RIP 1, but it makes use of the empty fields in the RIP 1 message by including additional information about each route. The format of a RIP version 2 route is shown in Figure 6.26.

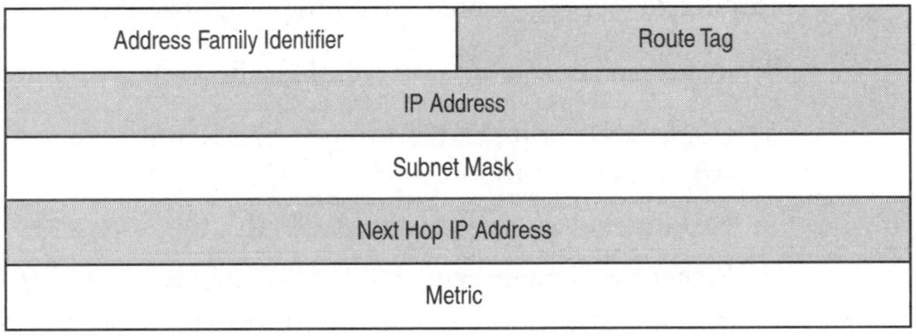

Address Family Identifier	Route Tag
IP Address	
Subnet Mask	
Next Hop IP Address	
Metric	

Figure 6.26   A RIP version 2 route

The functions of the RIP version 2 route fields are as follows:

- **Address Family Identifier (2 bytes).**   Contains a code that identifies the network layer protocol for which routing information is being provided. The code for IP is 2. (RIP supports other protocols besides IP, such as IPX.)

- **Route Tag (2 bytes).**   Contains an autonomous system number that enables RIP to communicate with exterior routing protocols.

- **IP Address (4 bytes).**   Specifies the address of the network or host for which routing information is being provided.

- **Subnet Mask (4 bytes).**   Contains the subnet mask that the router should apply to the IP Address value.

- **Next Hop IP Address (4 bytes).**   Specifies the address of the gateway that the router should use to forward traffic to the network or host specified in the IP Address field.

- **Metric (4 bytes).**   Contains a value that specifies the relative efficiency of the route.

The other main difference between RIP version 1 and RIP version 2 is that the latter supports the use of multicast transmissions. A multicast address is a single address that represents a group of computers on the network. By using a multicast address that represents all the routers on the network instead of broadcasts, the amount of extraneous traffic processed by the other computers is greatly reduced.

Installing RIP

To use RIP on a Windows 2000 network, you must install the protocol in RRAS, and bind it to the computer's network interfaces. After you have installed and configured RIP, it requires little or no monitoring. In fact, since RRAS does not provide a means to modify the RIP information in the routing table, there is little that you can do once it is operating. (You can still modify the routing table using Route.exe, but you should have little or no need to.)

To install and configure RIP, use the following procedure:

1. Click Start and open the Routing and Remote Access console from the Administrative tools program group.

2. Expand the server icon and the IP Routing icon.

3. Select the General icon and then select New Routing Protocol from the Action menu to display the New Routing Protocol dialog box (see Figure 6.27).

Figure 6.27   The New Routing Protocol dialog box

4. Select RIP Version 2 For Internet Protocol in the Routing Protocols list and click OK. A new RIP icon appears beneath the IP Routing icon.

5. Select the RIP icon and then select New Interface from the Action menu to display the New Interface For RIP Version 2 For Internet Protocol dialog box (see Figure 6.28).

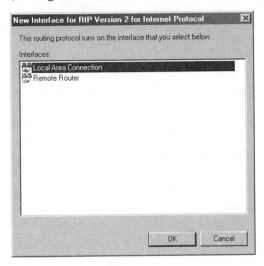

Figure 6.28   The New Interface For RIP Version 2 For Internet Protocol dialog box

6. Select an interface on which you want to use RIP in the Interfaces list and click OK to open a RIP Properties dialog box for that interface (see Figure 6.29).

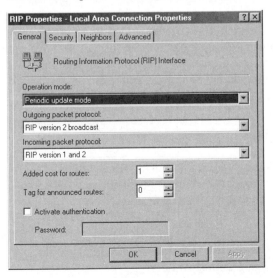

Figure 6.29   The RIP Properties dialog box for a Local Area Connection interface

7. Select the Operation mode for the RIP on the selected interface using the drop-down list provided.

When you use RIP on a LAN interface, the default setting is *Periodic Update Mode*, which maintains the routing table in the manner described earlier. RRAS flags the table entries it receives from other routers as RIP routes and leaves them in the table only as long as the other routers remain present on the network. If RRAS fails to receive periodic updates from a specific router, it deletes the table entries derived from that router. Periodic Update Mode is not suitable for demand-dial interfaces, however, because you don't want RIP updates to trigger a remote connection every few minutes. Therefore, when you install RIP on a demand-dial interface, the default setting is *Auto-Static Update Mode*. In Auto-Static Update Mode, RRAS only broadcasts its routing table entries when explicitly asked to by another router. In addition, RRAS flags the routing table entries it receives from other routers as static routes, which remain in the table permanently until an administrator deletes them. You can modify the default mode as needed.

8. In the Outgoing Packet Protocol drop-down list, specify the type of RIP messages RRAS should transmit over the interface, choosing from the following options:

- **RIP Version 1 Broadcast.**   Causes RRAS to transmit RIP messages as broadcasts using the version 1 format. Use this option when RRAS must interact with other routers that support only RIP version 1.

- **RIP Version 2 Broadcast (default).**   Causes RRAS to transmit RIP messages as broadcasts using the version 2 format. Use this option when RRAS must interact with other RRAS systems or routers that support RIP version 2.

- **RIP Version 2 Multicast.**   Causes RRAS to transmit RIP messages as multicasts using the version 2 format. Use this option when RRAS must interact with other RRAS systems or routers that support RIP version 2 and you want to minimize the amount of broadcast traffic on your networks.

- **Silent RIP.**   Causes RRAS not to generate any outgoing RIP traffic but does leave the service capable of processing and utilizing incoming RIP messages.

Note   To use multicast transmissions with RIP, you must install the Internet Group Membership Protocol (IGMP) as a RRAS routing protocol and configure it to function on the desired interfaces.

---

9. Specify the type of incoming RIP messages that RRAS should process from the interface in the Incoming Packet Protocol drop-down list, choosing from the following options:

- **Ignore Incoming Packets.**   Prevents RRAS from processing any incoming RIP packets, despite the Outgoing Packet Protocol value

- **RIP Version 1.** Enables RRAS to process only incoming messages that use the RIP version 1 format

- **RIP Version 2.** Enables RRAS to process only incoming messages that use the RIP version 2 format

- **RIP Version 1 And 2 (default).** Enables RRAS to process incoming messages that use both the RIP version 1 and RIP version 2 formats

10. Specify the factor by which RRAS should augment the metric value of incoming RIP routes in the Added Cost For Routes selector.

11. Click OK to configure RIP for the selected interface.

If you want to use RIP on more than one of your networks, you must add and configure each interface separately. In addition to the parameters already covered, you can also use the RIP Properties dialog box for an interface to configure a number of other features, including the following tabs:

- **General.** Since it uses plain text passwords, this option does not provide a significant degree of security, but it does let you enable your RRAS RIP routers to identify themselves during their communications. To enable this feature, you must supply the same password for all your RRAS routers using RIP.

- **Security.** This optional feature enables you to specify the routes that can be added to the routing table as the result of incoming RIP messages and that RRAS can advertise in its outgoing RIP messages.

- **Neighbors.** This option enables you to specify the IP addresses of other RIP routers with which you want RRAS to interact, either in addition to or instead of its usual broadcast/multicast behavior.

- **Advanced.** In this tab you can specify the interval at which RRAS should transmit its RIP announcements (30 seconds by default), the time before RIP routes expire (180 seconds by default), and the time before expired routes are removed from the routing table (120 seconds by default). These controls are available only when the RIP interface is operating in Periodic Update Mode. Other controls in this tab specify when RIP generates update messages and implement RIP's routing loop detection capabilities.

Understanding OSPF

Judging routes by the number of hops required to reach a destination, as in distance vector routing, is not always very efficient. A hop can refer to anything from a Gigabit Ethernet connection at 1000 megabits per second (Mbps) to a dial-up modem line at 56 kilobits per second (Kbps). As a result, it is entirely possible for traffic moving over a route with a smaller number of hops to take longer than one with more hops. There is another type of routing called *link-state routing* that measures the actual properties of each connection and stores the information in a database that is shared among the routers on the network. The most common interior routing protocol that uses this method is OSPF, as defined in RFC 2328. OSPF uses a formula called the Dijkstra algorithm to rate the efficiency of a route based on several criteria in addition to the hop count, including the transmission speed of the link, delays caused by network traffic congestion, and a route cost value specified by the network administrator.

The link state routing used by OSPF is more complex than distance vector routing and requires more processing by the routers themselves, but it is far more precise in its determination of a route's relative efficiency, and it enables the routers to compensate for changes in the network configuration more quickly. OSPF also uses less network bandwidth than RIP because it generates messages only when network conditions change, unlike RIP, which continually retransmits the same routing information.

With OSPF it is possible to split an autonomous system into discrete units called areas. An *area* is a group of networks within an internetwork joined to other areas with *backbones*. Most OSPF routers are configured to maintain routing information only about the networks in the local area. For routing communications between areas, there are special OSPF routers called area border routers. The use of areas provides OSPF with greater scalability, enabling it to service larger internetworks without generating inordinate amounts of traffic. For a relatively small internetwork, RIP is usually preferable because it is easier to set up and run, but OSPF is becoming increasingly popular on larger internetworks.

Installing OSPF

The process of installing the OSPF protocol is the same as that of RIP, as outlined in the previous section. You add the protocol to the RRAS console and create interfaces on which you want to use it. To configure the OSPF protocol itself, you select its icon in the scope pane of the RRAS console and select Properties from the Action menu to display the OSPF Properties dialog box shown in Figure 6.30.

In the OSPF Properties dialog box you can configure the parameters in the following tabs:

- **General.** In addition to setting event logging options for OSPF, you can specify an IP address by which the router will identify itself and indicate whether RRAS should function as an OSPF autonomous system boundary router. Enabling this latter option causes RRAS to advertise the routes it obtains from methods other than OSPF (such as RIP and static routes) to other autonomous systems.

- **Areas.** In this tab you create and configure the OSPF areas that make up your internetwork. Creating a new area or configuring an existing one opens an OSPF Area configuration dialog box in which you specify ranges of addresses that fall in the area.

- **Virtual Interfaces.** In this tab you can create virtual links between pairs of OSPF area border routers that are not both directly connected to the backbone.
- **External Routing.** This tab, which is activated only when you select the Enable Autonomous System Boundary Router check box, enables you to specify exactly which other types of routing data you want RRAS to share with other autonomous systems.

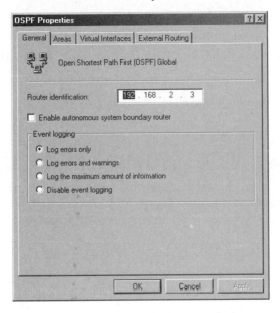

Figure 6.30   The OSPF Properties dialog box

Exercise 1: Configuring RRAS

You are the network administrator of a branch office for a large corporation. Your network is connected to the corporate headquarters using a Windows 2000 RRAS server at each site configured with a demand-dial interface using ISDN. Your network regularly exchanges sensitive company data, e-mail, and application traffic with computers at the corporate headquarters. Your goals when configuring the RRAS server are as follows:

- All data transmitted over the ISDN link should be secure.
- Rogue routers should be prevented from exchanging router information with either router.
- Both routers should be able to validate each other.
- Both routers should automatically maintain up-to-date routing tables.
- Traffic over the ISDN link during peak business hours should be minimized.

In attempting to achieve these goals, you take the following actions:

- Enable MS-CHAP as the authentication protocol on both RRAS servers.
- Enable OSPF on the demand-dial interfaces.
- Set the Require Encryption option on both RRAS servers.

Which results do these actions produce? (Choose all that apply.)

a. All data transmitted over the connection is secure.

b. Prevent rogue routers from exchanging router information with either router.

c. Both routers will be able to validate each other.

d. Both routers maintain up-to-date routing tables.

e. Traffic over the link during peak business hours will be minimized.

Exercise 2: Static and Dynamic Routing

Specify whether each of the following terms is associated with static routing, dynamic routing, both, or neither.

1. Routed
2. Default gateway
3. Convergence
4. Route.exe
5. Link-state routing
6. Routing and Remote Access
7. Distance vector routing
8. Route Add
9. Autonomous system
10. Metric

Lesson Review

1. Which of the following is not a dynamic routing protocol?

    a. OSPF

    b. RIP

    c. ICMP

    d. EGP

2. What is the name for the use of metrics based on the number of hops between a source and a destination?

   a. Distance vector routing

   b. Loose source routing

   c. Link-state routing

   d. OSPF routing

3. What is the primary difference between OSPF and RIP?

4. Which of the following fields is not included in a RIP version 1 route?

   a. Metric

   b. Subnet Mask

   c. IP Address

   d. Address Family Identifier

5. What is the primary criticism leveled at RIP?

6. What is the name of the process of updating routing tables to reflect changes in the network?

   a. Divergence

   b. Link-state routing

   c. Minimal routing

   d. Convergence

7. On a Windows 2000 Professional computer, what command do you use to display the contents of the routing table?

8. The Next Hop IP Address in a RIP version 2 route ends up in which column of a Windows routing table?

   a. Network Destination

   b. Netmask

   c. Gateway

   d. Interface

Lesson Summary

- Dynamic routing enables routers to share the information in their tables with the other routers on the network.

- The Internet is divided into autonomous systems, which are administrative divisions designed to limit the propagation of local routing information.

- Routers within autonomous systems use internal routing protocols to exchange routing information. Routing communications between autonomous systems uses exterior routing protocols.

- RIP is the most common routing protocol used today; it relies predominantly on broadcast transmissions to share routing table information and uses the number of hops to the destination as its metric.

- OSPF is a more advanced routing protocol that uses link-state routing, which measures the actual efficiency of a route rather than simply counting the number of hops.

C H A P T E R   7

Understanding the Domain Name System

Lesson 1: IP Host Naming and DNS **238**

Lesson 2: Resolving Host Names with DNS **251**

Lesson 3: Planning a DNS Implementation **263**

About This Chapter

The Domain Name System (DNS) is a distributed database used on Transmission Control Protocol/Internet Protocol (TCP/IP) networks to translate computer names (host names) to IP addresses. DNS is integral to the operation of a Microsoft Windows 2000 Active directory network, and access to a DNS server is required for any computer accessing the Internet. This chapter introduces you to the DNS name space and its origins and explains how a DNS server works together with other DNS servers to resolve the host name of any computer on the Internet.

Before You Begin

This chapter requires an understanding of the TCP/IP protocols, as provided in Chapter 2, "Introducing TCP/IP."

Lesson 1: IP Host Naming and DNS

The TCP/IP protocols, and particularly the Internet Protocol (IP), are completely reliant on IP addresses to identify computers on a network and transmit data to them. However, IP addresses are difficult for people to remember. To simplify the interaction between users and TCP/IP computers, the developers of the TCP/IP protocols began assigning friendly names to TCP/IP hosts, which they naturally called host names.

After this lesson, you will be able to

- Understand the function of a host table
- Recount the origins of the DNS
- Describe the three components of the DNS

Estimated lesson time: 40 minutes

Using Host Tables

A *host name* is simply a word that stands for a particular IP address. As originally implemented, each computer on the ARPANET, the experimental network that grew into today's Internet, was assigned a single word as a host name, which people could use in place of the IP address in the computer's interface. The use of host names does not affect TCP/IP communications in the least. IP still uses IP addresses in its packet headers to identify the source and destination of a transmission. For the host names to function with the IP addresses and the existing TCP/IP protocols, however, there has to be a means of converting a host name supplied by a user into the IP address required by the protocols.

The process of converting a host name into an IP address is called *name resolution*, and the first name resolution mechanism used by TCP/IP computers was a simple file called a host table. A *host table* is simply a list of IP addresses and their equivalent host names. In the early days of TCP/IP, every computer had its own host table. When an application was designed to accept host names as identifiers for other computers in its user interface, it would resolve each name by looking it up in the table and then using the equivalent IP address to initiate communications with the other computer.

The host table took the form of a plain text file called Hosts, and it still does to this day. Every TCP/IP computer still has a Hosts file, although few of them use it anymore. The Hosts file consists of nothing more than a list of IP addresses, one to a line, with the equivalent host name for each address on the same line, separated by at least one space. An example of a Hosts file is as follows:

```
172.16.94.97      server1      # source server
10.25.63.10       client23     # x client host
127.0.0.1         localhost
```

The pound character (#) indicates the beginning of a comment area. All characters following the pound sign on a single line are ignored. In this example, the host name server1 is assigned to a computer with the IP address 172.16.94.97. The "source server" reference is a comment that is included only to further identify the computer in question. The last entry in the example assigns the host name localhost to the TCP/IP loopback address (127.0.0.1). All traffic addressed to this name or address is fed directly back into the incoming IP queue without ever leaving the system.

The advantages of using a host table for name resolution are that it is simple and very fast, because the table is stored on the computer's local drive. You can still use a host table today to resolve frequently used host names. On a computer running Windows 2000, the table is called hosts, and it is located in the *systemroot*\system32\drivers\etc folder. You can modify the file by adding entries using any text editor (such as the Windows 2000 Notepad.exe).

The disadvantages of host tables as a general-purpose name resolution mechanism outweigh their advantages, however. In the early days of the ARPANET, the entire network consisted of a few dozen computers. The operators of those computers each chose their own host name. The host table was brief and easily maintained, with the network's users informally notifying each other of new names to be added to their tables. As the network began to grow, the ARPANET's administrators decided to create a central registry for the host names. The Network Information Center (NIC) at Stanford Research Institute (SRI) in Menlo Park, CA was chosen to maintain the master Hosts file for all the computers on the ARPANET. System administrators all over the network would send their new host names (which they still chose themselves) to SRI, who would add them to the master host table. Network users would then download the latest version of the Hosts file periodically and copy it to their systems.

Although this was an adequate solution at first, it gradually became untenable as the network continued to grow. The number of additions to the Hosts file increased, making it difficult for SRI to keep up with the changes, and the number of users downloading the file created an excessive amount of network traffic. Name conflicts also became a problem, as users assigned host names to their computers without checking to see whether another computer was already using the same name.

With our knowledge of the Internet as it exists today, it is easy to see why the use of host tables for name resolution could only be a temporary solution. A single host table listing the names and addresses of all the computers on the Internet today would be enormous and would change thousands of times per second. Clearly, a more efficient solution was needed, and this led to the Domain Name System (DNS).

Designing the DNS

The developers responsible for the ARPANET decided that maintaining an extensive list of IP addresses and domains for the network required a distributed database, one that would avoid the maintenance and traffic problems inherent in a single data store. The objectives of the project were to create a means for administrators to assign host names to their computers without duplicating the names of other systems and to store those names in a database distributed among servers all over the network, so as to avoid creating a traffic bottleneck or a single point of failure. In addition to a means for managing host names, a need was also recognized at the time for a standardized system for naming and accessing electronic mailboxes. It was hoped that both needs could be satisfied with a single solution.

The result of the project was the Domain Name System (DNS), which was originally standardized in two Request For Comments (RFC) documents published in 1983 by the Internet Engineering Task Force (IETF)—RFC 882, "Domain Names: Concepts and Facilities," and RFC 883, "Domain Names: Implementation Specification." These documents were updated and published in 1987 as RFC 1034 and RFC 1035 and later ratified as IETF standards. Numerous other RFCs have been published since then, containing updates and revisions to the DNS, some of which are crucial to the use of DNS on Windows 2000 networks. Some of these additional documents are as follows:

- **RFC 1101.**   "DNS Encoding of Network Names and Other Types"
- **RFC 1183.**   "New DNS RR Definitions"
- **RFC 1348.**   "DNS NSAP RRs"
- **RFC 1794.**   "DNS Support for Load Balancing"
- **RFC 1876.**   "A Means for Expressing Location Information in the Domain Name System"
- **RFC 1982.**   "Serial Number Arithmetic"
- **RFC 1995.**   "Incremental Zone Transfer in DNS"
- **RFC 1996.**   "A Mechanism for Prompt Notification of Zone Changes (DNS NOTIFY)"
- **RFC 2052.**   "A DNS RR for Specifying the Location of Services (DNS SRV)"
- **RFC 2136.**   "Dynamic Updates in the Domain Name System (DNS UPDATE)"
- **RFC 2137.**   "Secure Domain Name System Dynamic Update"
- **RFC 2181.**   "Clarifications to the DNS Specification"
- **RFC 2308.**   "Negative Caching of DNS Queries (DNS NCACHE)"
- **RFC 2535.**   "Domain Name System Security Extensions"

The DNS consists of three elements, which are as follows:

- **The domain name space.**   A specification for a tree-structured name space in which each branch of the tree identifies a domain and contains an information set. Query operations are attempts to retrieve specific information from a particular set.

- **Name servers.**   Applications running on server computers that maintain information about the domain tree structure and contain authoritative information about specific areas of that structure. The application is capable of responding to queries for information about the areas for which it is the authority and also has pointers to other name servers that enable it to access information about any other area of the tree.

- **Resolvers.**   Client programs that generate requests for DNS information and send them to name servers for fulfillment. A resolver has direct access to at least one name server and can also process referrals to direct its queries to other name servers when necessary.

Introducing the Domain Name Space

The use of single words for host names was a convenient solution at first, but there is no way for a name resolution system to use single word names and still fulfill the objectives for the creation of the DNS. For administrators to be able to select names for their systems without the possibility of name duplication, an expanded name space is needed. Taking a page from the IP address assignment system, the developers of the DNS decided to create a name space with two administrative levels, one of which is assigned by a central registrar and the other of which is controlled by the individual network administrator. In the same way that network administrators register a network IP address with the Internet Assigned Numbers Authority (IANA) and assign host addresses themselves, they register a network name (called a *domain*) and are free to assign host names within that domain.

The domain name space is the naming scheme that provides the hierarchical structure for the DNS database. The basic structural unit of the DNS name space is the domain, and each domain consists of a number of hosts. A domain is an administrative entity that does not necessarily correspond to an IP network address or any other TCP/IP communications element. The DNS name space is completely independent of the IP addressing system.

The domain name space uses a tree configuration, much like a directory tree, with a root domain at the top and multiple layers of branches stemming off of the root. When expressed as a name, a domain consists of the root, represented by a period, plus the names assigned to the units at each layer of the tree representing a particular location in the DNS hierarchy, all separated by periods. Unlike

IP addresses, which run from left to right, domain names run from right to left. In the domain name *microsoft.com*, for example, the word *com* represents the first layer beneath the root of the tree, called the top-level domain. The word *microsoft* is the second-level domain, found beneath *com* at the second layer of the tree.

As you add more domains to the DNS hierarchy, the name of each child domain (or subdomain) precedes that of its parent domain. Consequently, a domain's name identifies its position in the DNS tree. Each domain, at the second layer or below, can contain any number of hosts, the names of which are assigned by the owner of the domain. The host name is a single name, just as it was originally designed, that precedes the domain name, and it is again separated by a period. The combination of a host name and all its domain names up to the root is called a *fully qualified domain name (FQDN)*, or more colloquially, a *DNS name*.

For example, in Figure 7.1 the FQDN *computer1.sales.microsoft.com* identifies a computer with the host name *computer1* as being in the *sales* third-level domain. The *sales* domain is a subdomain of the *microsoft* domain and *microsoft* is a subdomain of the *com* domain. As the figure illustrates, the hierarchical structure of the domain name space consists of a root domain, top-level domains, second-level domains, and host names, at minimum. Additional domain levels are possible as long as the names remain within the limits established by the DNS standards. The various elements of the DNS name space are described in more detail in the following sections.

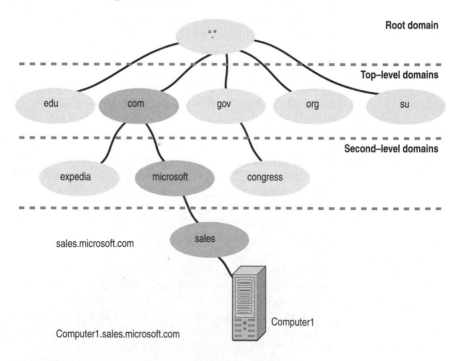

Figure 7.1   The hierarchical structure of the DNS name space

> **Note**   The term *domain*, in the context of DNS, has a different meaning than it does when used in the Windows 2000 and Microsoft Windows NT directory services. A Windows 2000 domain is a grouping of Windows computers and devices that are administered as a unit. In DNS, a domain is a group of hosts and possibly subdomains that represent a partition in the DNS database.

Root Domain

The root domain is located at the top of the DNS hierarchy and is represented as a period (.) at the right side of an FQDN. Although they are rarely written as such, every FQDN should technically end with a period, representing the root domain, as in the following example:

```
sales.microsoft.com.
```

The root domain is the authority for information about the top-level DNS domains. When a DNS name server has no information about any of the domains specified in a name it is trying to resolve, it begins by sending a query to one of the root name servers. Every DNS name server has a file containing the names and addresses of the current root name servers. On Windows 2000 computers the file is called Cache.dns. These are the only other name servers that a new DNS server knows about when it begins operating.

The current root name servers, as listed in the Windows 2000 Cache.dns file, are as follows:

```
@                         NS  m.root-servers.net.
m.root-servers.net        A   202.12.27.33

@                         NS  i.root-servers.net.
i.root-servers.net        A   192.36.148.17

@                         NS  e.root-servers.net.
e.root-servers.net        A   192.203.230.10

@                         NS  d.root-servers.net.
d.root-servers.net        A   128.8.10.90

@                         NS  a.root-servers.net.
a.root-servers.net        A   198.41.0.4

@                         NS  h.root-servers.net.
h.root-servers.net        A   128.63.2.53

@                         NS  c.root-servers.net.
c.root-servers.net        A   192.33.4.12

@                         NS  g.root-servers.net.
g.root-servers.net        A   192.112.36.4
```

```
@                          NS  f.root-servers.net.
f.root-servers.net         A   192.5.5.241

@                          NS  b.root-servers.net.
b.root-servers.net         A   128.9.0.107

@                          NS  j.root-servers.net.
j.root-servers.net         A   198.41.0.10

@                          NS  k.root-servers.net.
k.root-servers.net         A   193.0.14.129

@                          NS  l.root-servers.net.
l.root-servers.net         A   198.32.64.12
```

Top-Level Domains

The first word on the right side of an FQDN (just to the left of the theoretical root period) is the top-level domain name. Top-level domains are codes, usually consisting of two, three, or four characters, that represent either the type of resources the domain contains or the location of the domain. Top-level domains are not available for registration by private networks but instead function as the registrars for second-level domains, which are available to private networks.

The seven original top-level domains, and the resources they represent, are as follows:

- **com**   Commercial organizations
- **edu**   Four-year, degree-granting educational institutions in North America
- **gov**   United States government institutions
- **int**   Organizations established by international treaty
- **mil**   United States military organizations
- **net**   Networking organizations
- **org**   Noncommercial organizations

In addition to these seven, most of the countries/regions of the world are represented by two-letter top-level domain names, such as *fr* for France and *de* for Germany (Deutschland). There is also a special second-level domain called *in-addr.arpa*, which is used exclusively for reverse name lookups (as explained later in this chapter).

Note   A list of the two-letter top-level domain names for registered countries/ regions is available at *www.din.de/gremien/nas/nabd/iso3166ma/codlstp1/ en_listp1.html*.

Generally speaking, it is the *com*, *net*, and *org* domains that most businesses and individuals use to register their own second-level domains. Originally, these three top-level domains were serviced by a single body, called the Internet Network Information Center (InterNIC, later known as Network Solutions, Inc., and now owned by VeriSign), which was solely responsible for handling registrations and arbitrating disputes between name-holders. Since 1998, however, other organizations have been granted the right to register names in these domains and domain registration has grown into a competitive business, with various companies offering cut-rate prices on registrations. An organization called the Internet Corporation for Assigned Names and Numbers (ICANN) is responsible for the accreditation of domain name registrars. Although many organizations are now registering names in the com, net, and org domains, they are still not permitted to duplicate names within a particular top-level domain.

Despite what seem to be strictly defined functions of the *org* and *net* domains, no documentation of your noncommercial or network-related status is needed to register a second-level domain of these types. The *edu*, *gov*, *int*, and *mil* domains, however, are closely held and strictly regulated and are not available to the average commercial user.

The *com* top-level domain is by far the most popular on the Internet, which has led to a depletion of quality names and a good deal of litigation between parties who believe that they have a right to a particular name. There have been numerous attempts over the years to mitigate this problem (and to cash in on registration revenue) by introducing additional top-level domain names. Several new top-level domains are now available for registration, such as *biz* and *info*, and several small countries/regions have heavily promoted the registration of names in their top-level domains as a commercial enterprise. None of these rival the *com* domain in popularity, however, and it remains to be seen whether these new domains will gain in popularity.

Note   As with many technological achievements, the DNS has grown from an academic phenomenon to a commercial one, giving rise to a new class of Internet profiteers called "domain speculators." These are people who register large numbers of domain names that they think will be valuable to someone in the future, hoping to sell the rights to the name at inflated prices later. There are also people who use the domain registration system rather unscrupulously by registering names that are common misspellings of their competitors' names, hoping to draw their competitors' traffic to their own sites.

Second-Level Domains

The second-level domain is the second word from the right side in an FQDN and represents the network belonging to a particular individual, company, or other organization. Second-level domain names are easily obtained from a top-level domain registrar for a modest annual fee, usually $20 to $40 per year. A second-level domain can contain both hosts and subdomains. For example, the *microsoft.com* domain can contain computers such as *ftp.microsoft.com* and subdomains such as *sales.microsoft.com*. The subdomain *sales.microsoft.com* can also contain hosts such as *printserver1.sales.microsoft.com*.

The administrative structure of the DNS name space is similar to that of the IP addressing system. After you obtain an IP network address, you are free to create subnets and host addresses on that network. In the same way, after you register a second-level domain name with one of the Internet registrars, you are free to create as many subdomains and hosts as you wish in that domain.

Host Names

Host names refer to specific computers or other TCP/IP devices on the Internet or a private network. For example, in Figure 7.1, Computer1 is a host name. A host name is the leftmost word in an FQDN, which describes the exact position of a host within the domain hierarchy. In the figure, computer1.sales.microsoft.com. (including the end period, which represents the root domain) is an FQDN. DNS uses a host's FQDN to resolve a name to an IP address.

Domain Naming Guidelines

When you create subdomains and hosts within your own second-level domain, consider the following domain guidelines and standard naming conventions:

- **Limit the number of domain levels.**   Typically, DNS host entries should be three or four levels down the DNS hierarchy and no more than five levels down the hierarchy. As the number of levels increases, so do the administrative tasks.

- **Use unique names.**   Each subdomain must have a unique name within its parent domain to ensure that the name is unique throughout the DNS name space.

- **Use simple names.**   Simple and precise domain names are easier for users to remember and they enable users to search intuitively and locate Web sites or other computers on the Internet or an intranet.

- **Avoid lengthy domain names.**   Domain names at a particular level can be up to 63 characters long, including the following period. The total length of an FQDN cannot exceed 255 characters.

- **Use standard DNS characters.**   DNS names are not case-sensitive and can include letters, numbers, and dashes, but they can not contain spaces or punctuation symbols.

Zones

A *zone* represents a discrete portion of the name space for a particular domain. Zones provide a way to partition the domain name space into manageable sections. You can create multiple zones in the name space of a single domain to distribute administrative tasks to different users or groups. For example, Figure 7.2 depicts the microsoft.com domain name space divided into two zones. The two zones enable one administrator to manage the microsoft.com and sales.microsoft.com domains and another administrator to manage the development.microsoft.com domain.

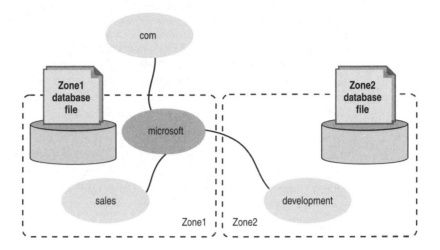

Figure 7.2   Domain name space divided into zones

A zone must encompass a contiguous area of a domain's name space. For example, as the figure shows, you can create a zone for sales.microsoft.com and the parent domain microsoft.com because these zones are contiguous. However, you cannot create a zone that consists of only the sales.microsoft.com domain and the development.microsoft.com domain because these two domains are not contiguous.

The name–to–IP-address mappings for a zone are stored in the zone database file. Each zone is anchored to a specific domain, referred to as the zone's root domain. The zone database file does not necessarily contain information for all subdomains of the zone's root domain, only those within the zone.

In Figure 7.2, the root domain for Zone1 is microsoft.com, and its zone file contains the name–to–IP-address mappings for the microsoft.com and sales.microsoft.com domains. The root domain for Zone2 is development.microsoft.com, and its zone file contains the name–to–IP-address mappings for the development.microsoft.com domain only. The zone file for Zone1 does not contain the name–to–IP-address mappings for the development.microsoft.com domain, although development is a subdomain of the microsoft.com domain.

Understanding Domain Name Servers

A DNS name server stores the zone database file. Name servers can store data for one zone or multiple zones. A name server is said to have authority for the domain name space that the zone encompasses. Having authority for a zone means that the name server is the ultimate resource for information about the hosts in that zone. Name servers trying to resolve the name of a host in a particular zone send their requests to the authoritative name server for that zone. This storage of the DNS information on servers located all over the Internet is why the DNS is known as a distributed database.

There are DNS name servers on the Internet that are the authorities for all the domains at every level. The root domain name servers are the authorities for information about the top-level domains, and the name servers for the top-level domains are the authorities for information about the second-level domains. This makes it possible for any DNS name server to locate information about any domain by tracing it from the root of the DNS tree.

To host a domain, you must have access to two DNS name servers to function as the authorities for that domain. You don't have to actually run the DNS servers on your network. Many domain owners use the DNS servers of their Internet service provider (ISP) for this purpose. There must also be at least one name server for every zone in a domain. However, a zone can have multiple name servers associated with it. One of these servers contains the master zone database file, which is also referred to as the *primary zone database file*, for that zone. The server containing the primary zone database file is called the *primary master name server* for the zone.

When you make changes to a zone, such as adding subdomains or hosts, you modify the primary zone database file. Any other name servers associated with the zone act as backups to the name server containing the primary zone database file. These are called *secondary master name servers* and they contain a *secondary zone database file*. Having multiple name servers provides several advantages, including the following:

- **Performing zone transfers.**   A secondary master name server obtains a copy of the zone database file from another name server, called its *master server*. This is known as a *zone transfer*. The master server can be the primary master for the zone or another secondary master. Secondary master name servers periodically query their master servers for updated zone data.

- **Providing redundancy.**   If the name server containing the primary zone database file fails, the additional name servers can provide the name resolution service to the network.

- **Improving access speed for remote locations.**   If a number of clients are in remote locations, you can use additional name servers to reduce the query traffic across slow wide area network (WAN) links.

- **Reducing loads.**   The additional name servers reduce the load on the name server containing the primary zone database file. Windows 2000 also supports directory-integrated zone storage by using the Active Directory database to store the zone information. Zones stored in this way are located in the Active Directory tree under the domain object container. Each directory-integrated zone is stored in a DNS zone container object identified by the name you choose for the zone when you create it.

A DNS server does not have to be an authority for a zone in order to function. You can install a DNS server on your network for the sole purpose of serving your TCP/IP clients. This is called a *caching-only server*.

The fundamental unit of storage in the DNS database is the resource record. A resource record, in its simplest form, is a host name and its equivalent IP address, but other types of resource records contain different types of information used by DNS name servers and resolvers.

Note   For more information about resource records, see Lesson 3 in Chapter 8, "Using the Windows 2000 DNS Server."

Understanding Resolvers

Resolver is the technical term for the DNS client built into every TCP/IP implementation. The resolver is, in almost every case, a set of operating system routines that enable any application to resolve DNS names by generating DNS requests and transmitting them to a specified DNS name server. On receiving the resolved name and its accompanying address from the DNS server, the resolver feeds it to the application, which initiates normal TCP/IP communications. The resolver can also retransmit its requests when no response is forthcoming and relay error messages received from the server to the application.

Exercise 1: Understanding DNS Terminology

Match the terms in the left column with the definitions in the right column.

1. Zone transfer

2. Caching-only server

3. Primary zone database file

4. Second-level domain

5. in-addr.arpa

a. Is not the authority for a zone

b. Contains both subdomains and hosts

c. Provides redundancy

d. Is used for reverse name resolution

e. Contains changes made to the zone database

Lesson Review

1. Name the three components of the DNS.

2. List three reasons to have a secondary name server.

3. What does the first word in a full DNS name identify?
    a. The top-level domain
    b. The second-level domain
    c. The DNS server
    d. The host

4. Describe the difference between a domain and a zone.

5. What is the portion of the DNS name space that is stored in a DNS name server?
    a. A host
    b. A domain
    c. A zone
    d. A root name

Lesson Summary

- The original TCP/IP name resolution mechanism was the host table, which is a list of host names and IP addresses stored on each computer.
- DNS name resolution is the process of resolving host and domain names to IP addresses.
- The DNS name space consists of multiple levels of domains, each of which can contain subdomains and hosts.
- A DNS name server contains one or more zones, each of which is a segment of the DNS name space consisting of one or more domains.
- A resolver is the DNS client routine built into a TCP/IP stack that enables applications to send name resolution requests to DNS servers.

Lesson 2: Resolving Host Names with DNS

DNS name resolution is something like looking up a name in a telephone book. Every name is associated with a number (that is, an IP address) and the DNS is the master directory for all the names and numbers. As with looking up a telephone number, however, you can't find the listing for a specific DNS name unless you are looking in the right book. The DNS name listings are distributed among thousands of name servers, just as the telephone listings are published in hundreds of telephone books. The similarity ends here, however, because the DNS enables you to resolve any name in the entire tree by sending a request to any server. This lesson examines how DNS name servers work together to provide a unified name resolution service for the entire Internet.

After this lesson, you will be able to

- Describe the format of DNS message
- Understand the difference between recursive and iterative queries
- Describe the DNS name resolution process
- Understand how reverse name lookups work

Estimated lesson time: 40 minutes

DNS Messaging

DNS is an application layer protocol that most commonly uses the User Datagram Protocol (UDP) for its communications. The well-known port number 53 is assigned to the DNS name server process for both UDP and the Transmission Control Protocol (TCP). If a DNS message is truncated because it contains more data than can fit in a UDP packet, the computers open a TCP connection to resend the data.

All communications between DNS name servers, and between name servers and resolvers, use a single message format for both requests and replies. The DNS message consists of a 12-byte header followed by four sections, which are as follows:

- **Question.**   Specifies the information being requested from the destination server.
- **Answer.**   Consists of resource records containing the information requested in the Question section.
- **Authority.**   Consists of resource records identifying the authority for the information requested in the Question section.
- **Additional.**   Consists of resource records containing additional information furnished in response to the request in the Question section.

The DNS Message Header

The format of the DNS header is illustrated in Figure 7.3.

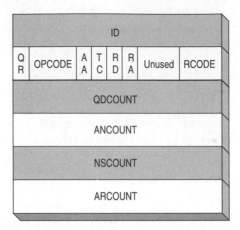

Figure 7.3   The DNS message header format

The functions of the fields are as follows:

- **ID (2 bytes).**   Contains a value unique to each transaction that the computers use to associate requests with replies.
- **FLAGS (2 bytes).**   Contains a number of 1-bit and 4-bit codes that are used to specify the function and properties of the message. The function of the bits are as follows:
  - **Bit 1—QR.**   This bit indicates whether the message is a query or a response.
  - **Bits 2–5—OPCODE.**   In query messages, these bits indicate whether the message contains a standard (name to address) query, an inverse (address to name) query, or a server status request.
  - **Bit 6—AA (Authoritative Answer).**   This bit indicates that the message is a response that contains information from the authoritative source for the zone or domain in which the requested name is located.
  - **Bit 7—TC (Truncation).**   This bit indicates that the message has been truncated because it contains too much information to fit in a UDP packet.
  - **Bit 8—RD (Recursion Desired).**   In a query message, this bit specifies whether the message contains a recursive or an iterative query. In a response message, the bit indicates whether the message contains a response to an iterative or recursive query.
  - **Bit 9—RA (Recursion Available).**   This bit indicates whether the server is configured to process recursive queries.

- **Bits 10–12.** Unused.
- **Bits 13–16—RCODE (Response Code).** In a response message, these bits indicate whether an error has occurred and contain a code specifying the type of error, such as an improperly formatted query, a failure of the server to process the query, a failure to locate the requested name in the zone or domain, or a refusal of the server to process the query because of security restrictions.
- **QDCOUNT (2 bytes).** Specifies the number of entries in the Question section.
- **ANCOUNT (2 bytes).** Specifies the number of entries in the Answer section.
- **NSCOUNT (2 bytes).** Specifies the number of name server resource records in the Authority section.
- **ARCOUNT (2 bytes).** Specifies the number of entries in the Additional section.

The DNS Question Section

The Question section of a DNS message contains the number of entries specified in the header's QDCOUNT field. In most cases there is only one entry. The format of each entry is illustrated in Figure 7.4.

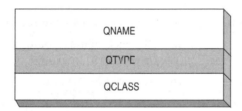

Figure 7.4 The DNS Question section format

The functions of the fields are as follows:

- **QNAME (variable).** Contains the DNS name to be resolved
- **QTYPE (2 bytes).** Specifies the type of resource record being requested
- **QCLASS (2 bytes).** Specifies the class of the resource record being requested

The DNS Response Sections

The Answer, Authority, and Additional sections of a DNS message all contain resource records, the numbers of which are specified in the header's ANCOUNT, NSCOUNT, and ARCOUNT fields. The format for each resource record is shown in Figure 7.5.

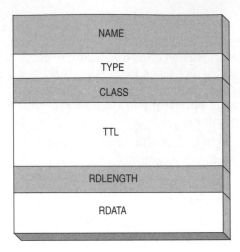

Figure 7.5   The DNS message's resource record format

The functions of the fields are as follows:

- **NAME (variable).**   Contains the DNS name about which information is being supplied
- **TYPE (2 bytes).**   Specifies the type of resource record the entry contains
- **CLASS (2 bytes).**   Specifies the class of the resource record the entry contains
- **TTL (4 bytes).**   Specifies the amount of time (in seconds) that the resource record should remain in the cache of the server to which it is being supplied
- **RDLENGTH (2 bytes).**   Specifies the length of the RDATA field in bytes
- **RDATA (variable).**   Contains the resource record information, the nature of which is dependent on its TYPE and CLASS

DNS Request Types

DNS transactions, whether between two name servers or between a client and a server, typically consist of a single query and a single reply. The entire name resolution process might involve several transactions between various pairs of computers, but each individual transaction consists of only two messages. There are two types of DNS queries, as indicated by the value of bit 8 in the DNS message header's FLAGS field.

A *recursive query* is one in which the name server receiving the message accepts full responsibility for delivering a reply containing a resolved DNS name to the system that generated the message. In nearly all cases, the resolver in a DNS client always sends recursive queries to its designated DNS name server. The name server must then do whatever is necessary to resolve the requested name, whether that includes sending queries to other name servers or simply replying using its own authoritative information. When the server responds to the recursive query, it sends a reply message back to the resolver that either contains the resolved name or an error message stating why the name could not be resolved.

The other type of query message is an *iterative query* (sometimes called a nonrecursive query). When a name server receives an iterative query, it responds immediately with the best information that it has in its possession. If the server is the authority for the name or has the name in its cache, it replies with the resolution information. If the server cannot resolve the name itself, it might respond by identifying another server that is the authority for the requested name. In any case, the name server receiving an iterative query is not responsible for searching for the name by sending its own queries to other servers. Typically, DNS name servers use iterative queries when requesting information from other servers. It is considered improper for a name server to transfer the entire burden of resolving a name to another server by transmitting a recursive query.

The exception to this policy is when you explicitly configure a DNS server to send recursive queries to another server. A name server configured to receive recursive queries from other servers in this way is called a *forwarder*. Forwarders are generally used in cases in which conditions make it difficult for a name server to perform the repeated server-to-server transactions needed to resolve a name. For example, if your organization has a number of branch offices with their own DNS servers and relatively slow Internet connections, you might configure the remote DNS servers to send their name resolution requests using recursive queries to a DNS server functioning as a forwarder at the corporate headquarters, which has a high-speed connection to the Internet. The forwarder can then perform the name resolution process much more quickly and respond to the server at the branch office. The branch office server then replies to the resolver on the client that originated the name resolution request.

A server that is configured to rely completely on a forwarder is called a *subordinate* (previously known as slave) or is said to operate in *exclusive mode*. A server running in *nonexclusive mode* makes its own attempts to resolve the requested name if the forwarder should fail.

Resolving a Name

The DNS name resolution process occurs whenever a user specifies a DNS host or domain name in an application. For example, when you connect to the Microsoft Web site, you use the name www.microsoft.com, which represents a particular computer (called www) in a second-level domain (called microsoft.com). Before sending any messages to the www.microsoft.com server, your Web browser uses the DNS resolver to convert the name www.microsoft.com to its associated IP address. This type of name-to-address resolution is called a *forward lookup query*. The address mapping for www.microsoft.com comes from the DNS name server that is the authority for the microsoft.com domain. The process of resolving the name consists of getting the DNS request message generated by the resolver to the authoritative server for the microsoft.com domain and then getting a reply back to the resolver.

DNS name servers can resolve both forward and reverse lookup queries. A forward lookup query resolves a name to an IP address, and a reverse lookup query resolves an IP address to a name. A name server can resolve queries only for names in a zone for which it is the authority. If a name server cannot resolve the query itself, it passes the query to other name servers in an effort to find the one that can resolve the query. The first name server then stores the query results in its cache so that it can respond to future requests for that name itself, thereby reducing the DNS traffic on the network. The forward lookup process for a host name is illustrated in Figure 7.6.

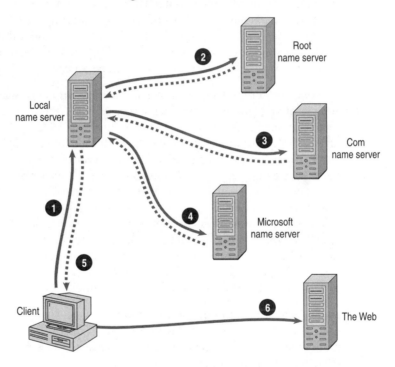

Figure 7.6   Resolving a forward lookup query

The forward lookup process for a host name consists of the following steps:

1. The resolver on the DNS client generates a recursive query for the name www.microsoft.com and transmits it to its local DNS name server, the IP address for which is specified in its TCP/IP configuration.

2. The local name server checks its zone database file to determine whether it contains the authoritative name–to–IP-address mapping for the name requested by the client. Because the local name server does not have authority for the microsoft.com domain, it sends an iterative query to one of the DNS root servers, requesting resolution of the host name. The root name server sends a referral back to the name servers that are authoritative for the com top-level domain.

3. The local name server then sends an iterative query to one of the com name servers, which responds with a referral to the name servers that are authoritative for the microsoft.com domain.

4. The local name server then sends an iterative query to the authoritative name server for microsoft.com. Because the Microsoft name server has authority for that portion of the domain name space, it looks up the requested name in the appropriate zone database file and returns the host resource record for www.microsoft.com (which contains the IP address associated with the name) to the local name server.

5. The local name server sends the resource record for www.microsoft.com in a DNS reply message to the resolver on the client computer.

6. The resolver on the client computer reads the IP address for www.microsoft.com from the resource record and supplies it to the application. The name resolution process is now complete, and the application can now access www.microsoft.com using its IP address.

Note   In many instances, the forward lookup procedure is abbreviated considerably, either by the use of cached DNS information stored in one of the name servers (as described in the next section) or by the combination of name server roles. For example, the DNS root name servers are also the authoritative servers for com and several other top-level domains. This means that the initial query sent to the root name server in the previous example would actually result in an authoritative reply containing the microsoft.com name server address rather than requiring two separate message transactions. If the requested name was in a top-level domain for which the root name servers are not the authorities, however, the referral process would proceed as described.

Name Server Caching

A DNS name resolution process does not always require the entire process described in the previous section. In some cases name servers are able to use information they have already retrieved from other name servers instead of issuing a query for the same information. When a name server processes a recursive query, it often needs to perform several DNS message transactions with various other name servers to resolve the requested name. With each query, the name server discovers information about other name servers that have authority for a portion of the DNS name space. The name server stores these query results in a cache on the computer's local drive for later use.

When a name server receives a response to one of its queries, it caches the resource records included in the reply for a specified amount of time, referred to as the Time to Live (TTL). The authoritative server for the zone that sent the reply specifies the length of the TTL interval. When the name server receiving the reply caches the resource records, the TTL starts counting down from its original value. When the TTL expires, the name server deletes the resource records from its cache. Caching query results enables the name server to quickly resolve other queries for the same names or for names in the same domain.

Caching not only speeds up the name resolution process, it also reduces the amount of DNS traffic on the Internet. The root name servers, being at the top of the DNS tree, are in the greatest danger of becoming a bottleneck for the whole system. These servers handle many thousands of requests per hour; if all the other name servers on the Internet suddenly stopped caching, the number of requests going to the root name, servers would increase enormously, possibly bringing them to a halt.

The cache in a DNS name server does not have to contain the resource record for the exact name requested to be useful. If a user attempts to connect to a computer called ftp.microsoft.com, for example, the fact that the DNS name server recently resolved www.microsoft.com means that it has the IP address of the authoritative name server for microsoft.com in its cache. Even though the DNS server can't fetch the actual resource record for ftp.microsoft.com from its cache, it can retrieve information that enables it to send a single iterative query right to the authoritative name server for microsoft.com rather than sending three successive queries to a root name server, the com server, and the microsoft.com server.

In addition to caching specific resource records, many DNS name servers are equipped with a feature called negative caching. *Negative caching* occurs when a name server maintains records of its inability to resolve names. The server does this so that when a client requests the resolution of a name that its local server recently failed to resolve because it didn't exist in the authoritative server's zone database file, the local server can immediately return an error to the client rather than go through the entire name resolution process over again only to have it fail again.

The TTL value specified by authoritative DNS name servers is critical to the operation of the caching system. Large TTL values cause resource records to remain in server caches for extended periods of time. The drawback of this is that if the resource record information ever changes, it takes longer for the existing information to expire from caches all over the Internet. If you use a short TTL value for the records on your zones, you increase the amount of DNS traffic generated by requests for the names in those records.

Performing Reverse Name Lookups

A reverse name lookup occurs when a client's resolver sends a query containing an IP address to its DNS name server and requests the name associated with that address. Troubleshooting tools, such as the Windows 2000 Nslookup.exe command-line utility, use reverse name lookups to report back to the user with a host name instead of an IP address. In addition, certain applications implement security features based on their ability to connect to names, not IP addresses.

It might seem at first that the reverse name lookup process should be easy. If a DNS resource record contains both the name and the IP address of a computer, searching for the IP address should be as easy as searching for the name. This is true when you are performing a reverse name lookup on a single DNS name server. If the address you are seeking to resolve is not located on the local server, however, the question suddenly arises of where to send the query next. Because the DNS name space is indexed by name and not by IP address, a reverse name lookup performed using the standard domain structure would require an exhaustive search of every domain name on every DNS name server. This is obviously not practical. To resolve this problem, the designers of the DNS created a special reverse lookup domain called in-addr.arpa.

The in-addr.arpa domain follows the same hierarchical naming scheme as the rest of the domain name space; however, it is based on IP addresses, not domain names. As shown in Figure 7.7, the in-addr domain is a subdomain of arpa, and in-addr itself has 256 third-level subdomains, which are named with the numbers 0 to 255. Each of those 256 third-level domains has 256 fourth-level subdomains named in the same way, and each of the fourth-level domains has 256 fifth level subdomains. At the sixth level of the hierarchy are 256 possible hosts for each subdomain, which are again named using the numbers 0 to 256.

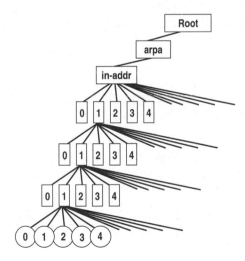

Figure 7.7   The in-addr.arpa domain

Using this domain structure, it is possible to express any IP address in terms of an FQDN in the in-addr.arpa domain. For example, the IP address 192.168.54.217 would exist in the DNS tree as a host with the FQDN 217.54.168.192.in-addr.arpa. Notice that the order of the four decimal values is reversed in the FQDN. This is because in the DNS name space, the most significant bit is on the right, and in the IP address hierarchy, it is on the left. The DNS host name of the computer in question is 217, and the host identifier of the computer is also 217.

Using this reverse lookup domain structure, a resolver on a client computer can take an IP address furnished by an application and generate a DNS query message with the address formatted as an FQDN in the in-addr-arpa domain. The name resolution process can then proceed in the normal manner, except that the name server is requested to supply a special type of resource record that contains an address-to-name mapping called a Pointer (PTR) resource record instead of one that contains a name-to-address mapping.

Exercise 1: Understanding DNS Communications

A company called Lucerne Publishing has registered the lucernepublishing.com second-level domain. The company has also created three subdomains named for their branch offices, called sf.lucernepublishing.com, la.lucernepublishing.com, and ny.lucernepublishing.com. The DNS name servers that are the designated authorities for the domain are called ns1.lucernepublishing.com and ns2.lucernepublishing.com.

The ns1 server is located in San Francisco and is the authority for a zone containing the lucernepublishing.com domain and the sf and la subdomains. The ns2 server is located in Los Angeles and contains a secondary zone database file for the ns1 server's zone. A third DNS name server, called ns3 and located in New York, is the authority for a zone containing only the ny.lucernepublishing.com subdomain.

Each of the three offices has its own intranet Web server with the names www.sf.lucernepublishing.com, www.la.lucernepublishing.com, and www.ny.lucernepublishing.com, respectively. All the workstations in the three offices are configured to use their local name server as their default DNS server.

Given this information, describe the sequence of DNS message transactions that occurs as a user in the New York office connects to each of the three Web servers in turn (keeping in mind that the root name servers are also the authorities for the com top-level domain).

1. Which of the following sequences of DNS name servers are involved when a user in the New York office attempts to connect to the New York Web server?

   a. ns3

   b. ns3, root name server, ns1, ns3

   c. ns3, root name server, ns1

   d. ns3, ns1, ns3

2. Which of the following sequences of DNS name servers are involved when a user in the New York office attempts to connect to the Los Angeles Web server?

   a. ns3, ns2

   b. ns3, root name server, ns1, ns2

   c. ns3, root name server, ns1

   d. ns3, root name server, ns2

3. Which of the following sequences of DNS name servers are involved when a user in the Los Angeles office attempts to connect to the New York Web server?

   a. ns2, root name server, ns3

   b. ns2, ns3

   c. ns2, root name server, ns1, ns3

   d. ns2, ns1, ns3

Lesson Review

1. What is the name of the DNS domain that contains address-to-name mappings?

2. Describe the difference between a primary master name server, a secondary master name server, and a master name server.

3. What is the host name of a DNS FQDN formed by the reverse name mapping of the IP address 10.56.128.65?

   a. 65

   b. in-addr

   c. 10

   d. arpa

Lesson Summary

- DNS is an application layer protocol that primarily uses UDP and well-known port 53 for its messaging. TCP messaging is possible when a DNS server must transmit longer messages.

- All DNS messages consist of a header and four sections: Question, Answer, Authority, and Additional.

- DNS client resolvers send recursive queries to their name servers. DNS name servers send iterative queries to other servers.

- In the DNS name resolution process, a resolver's local name server sends queries to other name servers to locate the authority for the requested domain.

- DNS name servers cache the information they receive from other servers to speed up the name resolution process and reduce DNS traffic.

- DNS name servers perform reverse name lookups using a special domain called in-addr.arpa that contains numbered subdomains.

Lesson 3: Planning a DNS Implementation

The DNS server configuration for your internetwork should depend on several factors, such as the size of your organization, the locations of your offices, and your fault tolerance requirements. This lesson gives you an idea of how to configure DNS for your internetwork, and it contains scenarios that measure your network planning knowledge prior to installing DNS.

After this lesson, you will be able to

- Register a DNS server with the parent domain
- Estimate the number of DNS name servers, domains, and zones needed for a network

Estimated lesson time: 40 minutes

DNS Considerations

Although a Windows 2000 network running the Active Directory service requires a DNS server, as do clients with access to the Internet, the DNS server itself does not have to run on a Windows 2000 server. In fact, the DNS server does not even have to be on your local network. As long as you can configure Windows 2000 to reference a valid DNS server that supports the necessary record types, such as one hosted by your ISP, you can provide the required name resolution capabilities to Windows 2000. However, with the increased functionality provided by the version of DNS included with Windows 2000, you might decide it is worthwhile to install and configure your own DNS server.

If your organization, regardless of size, wants to own a second-level domain name, you must register the name with an appropriate registrar for the top-level domain, providing it with the IP addresses of at least two DNS servers that will be the authorities for the name you choose. You can also set up additional DNS servers within your organization that are independent of the Internet.

For reliability and redundancy, Microsoft recommends that you deploy at least two DNS servers per domain—a primary master and a secondary master name server. The primary master name server maintains the primary zone database file containing the information about the computers in the domain and replicates it to the secondary master name server using zone transfers. This replication enables clients all over the Internet to resolve names in the domain even if one of the name servers is unavailable. You can configure the zone transfer schedule depending on how often names change in the domain. Transfers should occur frequently enough to keep both servers synchronized nearly all the time. However, excessive replication can increase network traffic and the processing burden on the name server.

Exercise 1: Implementing DNS

In this exercise, you work through three DNS implementation scenarios. In each scenario, you estimate the number of DNS name servers, domains, and zones needed for a network. Each scenario describes a company that is migrating to Windows 2000 and wants to implement directory services. You answer some questions involved in drafting a DNS network design for each company using unique criteria. The purpose of these exercises is to measure your network planning knowledge prior to installing DNS. This can serve as a baseline to measure how much you have learned by the time you complete this training kit and can help you start thinking about how to best implement DNS on your own organization's internetwork.

Scenario 1: Designing DNS for a Small Network

Northwind Traders is in the process of replacing its older minicomputer with a local area network running Windows 2000. Most of the company's employees access the minicomputer using terminal devices. Some users have computers with Intel Pentium processors, which are not currently networked. The company has already purchased the hardware for the migration.

The network will be used for basic file and print sharing and will also have one Windows 2000 server running Microsoft SQL Server. The majority of users will need access to the computer running SQL Server. Desktop applications will be installed on the local computers, but all data files will be stored on the servers.

The company would also like all users to be connected to the Internet so the employees can send and receive e-mail.

Draft a network design using the criteria shown in Table 7.1.

Table 7.1   Network Design Criteria

Environmental Components	Detail
Users	100
Locations	Single office
Administration	One full-time administrator
Servers	3 computers: Two 1 GHz Pentium III systems with 512 megabytes (MB) of RAM, 80 gigabyte (GB) hard disk; one 2.0 gigahertz (GHz) Pentium 4 with 1 GB of RAM dedicated to SQL Server
Clients	All Pentium III and 4 computers running Windows 2000 Professional
Microsoft BackOffice applications	Microsoft SQL Server and DNS
Server usage	SQL Server database access; basic file and print services; Internet access

The design you create should take the following factors into account:

- Number of users
- Number of administrative units
- Number of sites

Based on these design objectives, answer the following questions:

1. How many DNS domains will you need to configure?

2. How many subdomains will you need to configure?

3. How many zones will you need to configure?

4. How many primary name servers will you need to configure?

5. How many secondary name servers will you need to configure?

6. How many DNS cache-only servers will you need to configure?

Scenario 2: Designing DNS for a Medium-Size Network

You are consulting for Northwind Traders, which has 8795 users. There are 8000 users located in four primary sites, with the remaining employees located in 10 branch offices in major U.S. cities. The company has decided to upgrade its existing LANs to Windows 2000 Server. The organization has also decided to centralize all user accounts in a single location at the corporate headquarters.

As illustrated in Figure 7.8, the four primary sites are connected by T1 lines. The branch offices are connected to the nearest primary site by 56 kilobits per second (Kbps) lines.

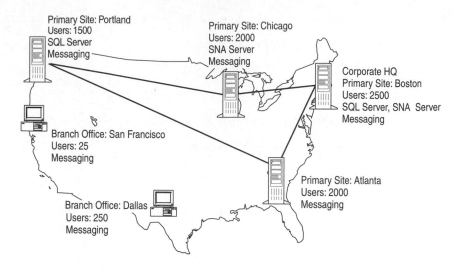

Figure 7.8   Connection of headquarters

Three of the four primary sites are independent business units and operate independently of the others. The fourth is the corporate headquarters. Branch offices have between 25 and 250 users needing access to all four of the primary sites but seldom needing access to the other branch offices.

In addition to the 10 branch offices, you have discovered that the company has a temporary research location employing 10 people. This site has one server that connects to Boston using dial-on-demand routers. This site is expected to be shut down within six months. It is a stand-alone operation requiring connectivity for messaging only.

Primary sites will continue to maintain their own equipment and the equipment of the branch offices connected to them. Currently, bandwidth utilization is at 60 percent during peak times. Future network growth is expected to be minimal for the next 12 to 18 months.

Other branch offices include: Los Angeles, 40 users; Salt Lake City, 25 users; Montreal, 30 users; New Orleans, 25 users; Kansas City, 25 users; Washington, DC, 100 users; Denver, 200 users; Miami, 75 users.

Draft a network design using the criteria shown in Table 7.2.

Table 7.2   Network Design Criteria

Environmental Components	Detail
Users	8795
Locations	Four primary sites, with 10 branch sites in major cities in the United States. No plans for opening any international locations.
Administration	Full-time administrators at each of the four primary sites. Some of the smaller sites have part-time administrators.
Number of name servers	To be determined.
Number of caching-only servers	DNS caching-only servers are needed in each of the remote locations for the same zone.
Clients	Various Pentium computers running Windows 2000 Professional.
Server applications	Microsoft SQL Server, Microsoft Exchange, DNS, file and print services.

The design you create should take the following factors into account:

- Number of users
- Number of administrative units
- Number of sites
- Speed and quality of links connecting sites
- Available bandwidth on links
- Expected changes to network
- Line of business applications

Based on these design objectives, answer the following questions:

1. How many DNS domains must you create?

2. How many subdomains do you need?

3. How many zones should you create?

4. How many primary master name servers do you need?

5. How many secondary master name servers do you need?

6. How many caching-only servers do you need?

7. Use the following mileage chart to design a zone/branch office configuration based on the geographical proximity between each primary site and branch office. Branch offices should be in the same zone as the nearest primary site.

Mileage Chart	Atlanta	Boston	Chicago	Portland, OR
Dallas	807	1817	934	2110
Denver	1400	1987	1014	1300
Kansas City	809	1454	497	1800
Los Angeles	2195	3050	2093	1143
Miami	665	1540	1358	3300
Montreal	1232	322	846	2695
New Orleans	494	1534	927	2508
Salt Lake City	1902	2403	1429	800
San Francisco	2525	3162	2187	700
Washington, DC	632	435	685	2700

Scenario 3: Designing DNS for a Large Network

Northwind Traders has 60,000 users located around the world. The corporate headquarters is in Geneva, Switzerland. The headquarters for North and South America is in New York City. The Australia and Asia headquarters is in Singapore. Each of the regional headquarters will maintain total control of the users within its area. Users require access to resources in the other regional headquarters. The three regional headquarters sites are connected by T1 lines.

Each of the three regional headquarters has line-of-business applications that must be available to all sites within its areas as well as to the other regional head-quarters. The Malaysian and Australian subsidiaries have major manufacturing sites to which all regional subsidiaries need access.

These line-of-business applications are all running on Windows 2000 servers. These computers must be configured as servers within the domains. The links between Singapore, Australia, and Malaysia typically operate at 90 percent utilization. The Asia and Australia region has 10 subsidiaries comprising Australia, China, Indonesia, Japan, Korea, Malaysia, New Zealand, Singapore, and Thailand.

Because of import restrictions with some of the subsidiaries, it has been decided to give control of the equipment to each subsidiary and to have a resource domain in each subsidiary. Lately, most of the computers the subsidiaries have purchased are running Windows 2000 Professional. The company has authorized the deployment of redundant hardware where it can be justified.

To keep this scenario to a reasonable length and complexity, the questions and answers deal only with the Asia and Australia region.

Draft a network design using the criteria in Table 7.3.

Table 7.3   Network Design Criteria

Environmental Components	Detail
Users in Asia and Australia domain	25,000 evenly distributed across all the subsidiaries
Locations	Regional headquarters in Singapore; 10 subsidiaries in Australia, China, Indonesia, Japan, Korea, Malaysia, New Zealand, Singapore, and Thailand
Administration	Full-time administrators at the regional headquarters and each of the subsidiaries
Number of domains	To be determined
Clients	Various Pentium computers running Windows 2000 Professional
Server applications	Microsoft SQL Server, Microsoft SNA Server, Microsoft Systems Management Server, Messaging, DNS
Number of cache servers	To be determined

The design you create for the Asia and Australia region must take the following factors into account:

- Number of users
- Number of administrative units
- Number of sites
- Speed and quality of links connecting sites
- Available bandwidth on links
- Expected changes to network
- Line of business applications

Based on these design objectives, answer the following questions:

1. How many new DNS domains do you need?

2. How many subdomains must you create?

3. How many zones must you create?

4. How many primary master name servers do you need?

5. How many secondary master name servers do you need?

6. How many DNS caching-only servers should you create?

Lesson Review

1. What is the primary reason for creating a secondary master name server?

2. What are the primary reasons for creating caching-only DNS servers?

3. What is the primary factor of an internetwork's design that makes the deployment of additional DNS name servers necessary?

Lesson Summary

- Windows 2000 requires access to a DNS server to provide complete directory service and Internet functionality.

- The DNS servers for your network can be local or provided remotely by your ISP.

- The DNS implementation included in Windows 2000 has additional features beyond those of traditional DNS servers.

- Microsoft recommends the use of at least two DNS servers per domain—a primary master and a secondary master name server.

- The DNS implementation for a particular network should be based on a variety of factors, including the number of users, the number of sites, the locations of the sites, the speed of the links between the sites, and the access to different sites required by the users.

CHAPTER 8

Using the Windows 2000 DNS Server

Lesson 1: Installing and Configuring Windows 2000 DNS 274

Lesson 2: Working with Zones 280

Lesson 3: Working with Resource Records 294

Lesson 4: Configuring Zone Transfers 303

Lesson 5: Monitoring and Troubleshooting DNS 310

About This Chapter

In the previous chapter you learned about the theory underlying the Domain Name System (DNS). In this chapter you put this theory to practice by installing DNS Server on a Microsoft Windows 2000 Server computer and configuring it to service your domain.

Before You Begin

This chapter requires an understanding of the concepts discussed in Chapter 7, "Understanding the Domain Name System," as well as familiarity with Transmission Control Protocol/Internet Protocol (TCP/IP) communications, as described in Chapter 2, "Introducing TCP/IP."

Lesson 1: Installing and Configuring Windows 2000 DNS

All the Windows 2000 Server products include the DNS Server service, which can provide the DNS services required by the Active Directory service, also included with Windows 2000 Server, as well as host an Internet domain. Virtually all network operating systems are capable of running a DNS server, using either a program supplied with the operating system or a third-party product, and virtually all DNS servers are designed to conform to the standards published by the Internet Engineering Task Force (IETF). This means that the Windows 2000 DNS Server can interact with all the other DNS servers operating on the Internet, regardless of the software products they use and the platform on which they are running.

After this lesson, you will be able to

- Install Windows 2000 DNS Server on a Windows 2000 computer
- Understand the functions and benefits of a caching-only server
- Perform a test query on a Windows 2000 DNS Server installation

Estimated lesson time: 20 minutes

Installing DNS Server

You can install the Windows 2000 DNS Server in three ways: selecting it during the Windows 2000 operating system installation, allowing the Active Directory Installation Wizard to install it along with the Active Directory service, or manually installing it using the Add/Remove Programs Control Panel.

Active Directory service relies on the DNS name space in the same way that Windows versions prior to Windows 2000 rely on the NetBIOS name space. To use Active Directory service on your network, you must have a DNS server that supports the SRV resource record defined in Request For Comments 2052, "A DNS RR for Specifying the Location of Services (DNS SRV)." This is the only one of the relatively new DNS features that Active Directory service requires. Many of the DNS implementations used on the Internet do not support this resource record, which is the main reason most Active Directory installations run Windows 2000 DNS Server on the local network. To use your Internet service provider's (ISP's) DNS servers to support Active Directory service, you must make sure that the implementation they are using supports RFC 2052 and that you have the access needed to create the appropriate resource records on the server. In most cases it is easier to run your own.

As with the Dynamic Host Configuration Protocol (DHCP) and the Windows Internet Name Service (WINS), you must configure the computer running Windows 2000 DNS Server with a static Internet Protocol (IP) address, not one assigned by a DHCP server. In addition, you should configure the server's TCP/IP properties so that the Preferred DNS Server setting points back to the server. In other words, the DNS server computer should use itself as its own DNS server.

To install the Windows 2000 DNS Server, use the following procedure:

1. On a computer running Windows 2000 Server, log on as Administrator.
2. Click Start, point to Settings, and click Control Panel.
3. Double-click the Add/Remove Programs icon, and then click Add/Remove Windows Components to display the Windows Components page of the Windows Component Wizard, as shown in Figure 8.1.

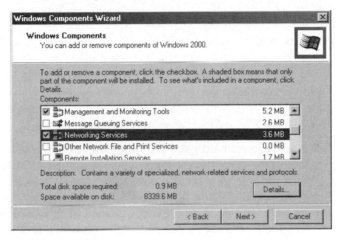

Figure 8.1   The Windows Component page

4. In the Components list, select Networking Services.
5. Click Details to display the Networking Services dialog box.
6. In the Subcomponents Of Networking Services list, shown in Figure 8.2, select the Domain Name System (DNS) check box.

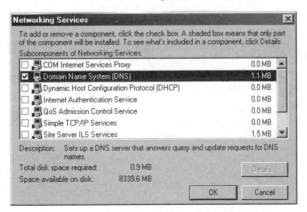

Figure 8.2   The Subcomponents Of Networking Services list

7. Click OK, and then click Next. If prompted, type the full path to the Windows 2000 distribution files and click Continue. Windows 2000 then copies the required files to your hard disk.

8. Click Finish to close the Windows Components Wizard.

Installing DNS Server creates the *systemroot*\System32\dns folder (C:\Winnt\System32\DNS, by default), which contains the DNS database files. Generally, you do not need to edit the DNS database files. However, you might use them to troubleshoot DNS. The DNS Server service provides a set of sample files, which are added to the *systemroot*\System32\DNS\Samples folder after you have installed the DNS Server service. It is traditional for DNS servers to store their data in text files on the local drive. The Windows 2000 DNS Server implementation does not have to do this, but it can use text files that are compatible with other DNS server implementations, particularly one of the earliest server programs, Berkeley Internet Name Domain (BIND).

BIND reads server configuration parameters from a text file called BOOT whenever the server starts. The primary function of the BOOT file is to specify the names of the other text files containing DNS data. Windows 2000 DNS Server does not require a BOOT file, but it can utilize one, which facilitates migration from BIND. The only active text file created by DNS Server is the Cache.dns file, which contains the names and addresses of the root name servers used to resolve names not located in a local zone.

Note   Although Windows 2000 DNS Server comes configured with the names and addresses of the root name servers that were active when the product was released, these addresses can change over time. To keep the list of root name servers updated, the DNS server transmits a query to the first root name server in the list every time it starts, requesting a list of the servers that are currently authoritative for the root domain.

In addition to installing and starting the DNS Server service, the installation process installs the DNS console (as shown in Figure 8.3) and adds a shortcut for the console to the Administrative Tools program group on the Start menu. You can use the DNS console to manage all functions of local and remote DNS name servers. The installation also adds the following key for the DNS Server service to the Windows 2000 registry: HKEY_LOCAL_MACHINE\System\CurrentControlSet\Services\DNS.

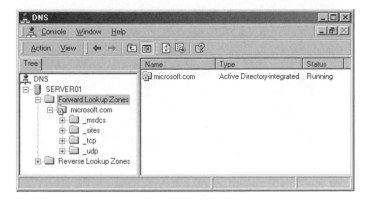

Figure 8.3   The DNS console

Implementing a Caching-Only Server

Although all DNS name servers cache queries that they have resolved, caching-only servers are DNS name servers that only perform queries, cache the answers, and return the results. A caching-only server is not the authority for any domain and does not contain any zone information. The only name resolution information a caching-only server contains is that which it has cached while resolving queries.

The primary benefit provided by a caching-only server is that it provides a local name resolution service for DNS clients, even when not hosting a domain. Because caching-only servers have no zone files, they do not generate any zone transfer traffic on the network. However, there is one disadvantage: When a caching-only server initially starts, it has no cached information and must refer all queries to other DNS servers until it builds up information of its own.

When you complete the DNS Server installation described in the previous section, the computer is ready to function as a caching-only server, as long as it has access to the Internet. The server comes configured with the names and addresses of the current root name servers, which it can use to resolve any name supplied to it by a client. To view or modify the list of root servers, you use the following procedure:

1. Click Start and launch the DNS console from the Administrative Tools program group.

2. Select the server icon in the scope pane and select Properties from the Action menu to open the Properties dialog box.

3. Click the Root Hints tab to display the dialog box shown in Figure 8.4. Using the controls provided, you can add root name servers to the list as well as modify or delete existing entries.

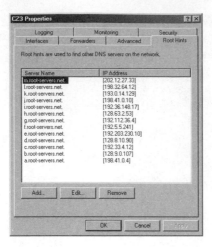

Figure 8.4   The Root Hints tab in a DNS server's Properties dialog box

Exercise 1: Testing a Simple Query on a DNS Server

In this exercise, you use the DNS console to perform a test query on your DNS server.

1. Click Start, point to Programs, point to Administrative Tools, and then click DNS.

2. In the scope pane, select the DNS server icon and select Properties from the Action menu to open the Properties dialog box.

3. Click the Monitoring tab, as shown in Figure 8.5.

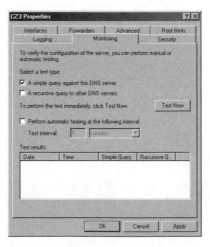

Figure 8.5   The Monitoring tab of a DNS server's Properties dialog box

4. Select the A Simple Query Against This DNS Server check box.

5. Click Test Now. Results of the test query appear in the Test Results box.

6. Click OK to close the DNS server's Properties dialog box.

Lesson Review

1. Which of the following active files is created by default during the installation of Windows 2000 DNS Server?

   a. BOOT

   b. Boot.dns

   d. CACHE

   d. Cache.dns

2. Which of the following best describes the function of a caching-only server?

   a. A caching-only server is one that uses a Cache.dns file to configure itself.

   b. A caching-only server is the authority for only a single zone.

   c. A caching-only server is not the authority for any domain or zone.

   d. A caching-only server maintains a zone database but does not service client name resolution requests.

3. What is BIND?

Lesson Summary

- The Windows 2000 Server computer must have a static IP address and should be configured to use its own DNS Server service as its primary DNS server.

- DNS Server can be installed with the Windows 2000 Server operating system, by the Active Directory Installation Wizard, or with the Add/Remove Programs Control Panel.

- The Active Directory service requires a DNS server that supports the SVR resource record defined in RFC 2052.

- Windows 2000 DNS Server supports the BOOT file format used by BIND and other DNS server products.

- A caching-only DNS name server is one that exists only to service client requests and is not the authority for any domain or zone.

Lesson 2: Working with Zones

DNS servers enable you to divide the DNS name space into zones that store name information about one or more DNS domains. The zone becomes the authoritative source for information about each DNS name included in it. This lesson introduces you to DNS zones and shows you how to create and configure them in Windows 2000 DNS Server.

After this lesson, you will be able to

- Identify zone types
- List the benefits of Active Directory integrated zones
- Create zones
- Explain zone delegation
- Configure Dynamic Domain Name System (DDNS) for a zone

Estimated lesson time: 40 minutes

Creating a Zone

When you install a DNS server for the purpose of servicing a domain, you must always create at least one zone. You can create a single zone that contains the entire area of the DNS space for which you are the authority, or you can choose to divide your domain by creating multiple subdomains and placing them in different zones. You might want to divide your domain into multiple zones for the following reasons:

- **Administrative delegation.**   When you create multiple zones, you can grant different people permission to manage them, thereby dividing the DNS administration chores.
- **Performance enhancement.**   Creating multiple zones and storing them on different DNS servers can divide the name resolution traffic burden among your servers or local area networks (LANs).
- **Fault tolerance.**   Dividing your domain into zones stored on different servers enables DNS to continue servicing clients, even when a server fails.
- **Name space expansion.**   Creating subdomains in different zones is an easy way to accommodate the opening of a new branch office or site.

To create a zone in DNS Server, you use the DNS console, which is installed by default with the DNS Server service. You can use the DNS console to manage the local DNS server or any other DNS server on your network (assuming you have the appropriate permissions). To run the DNS console from a computer running Windows 2000 that is not running the DNS Server service, you can install the

Adminpak.msi package from the \I386 folder on the Windows 2000 Server installation CD-ROM.

To create a zone, use the following procedure:

1. Click Start, and from the Administrative Tools program group, select DNS to open the DNS console.

2. Expand the DNS server icon.

3. Select the Forward Lookup Zone folder and select New Zone from the Action menu to launch the New Zone Wizard.

   Forward lookup zones contain name–to–IP-address mappings, and reverse lookup zones contain IP-address–to–name mappings. You must create each type of zone separately if you want clients to be able to perform both forward and reverse lookups. Later, when you create Host (A) resource records in the forward lookup zone, which contain name–to–IP-address mappings, the DNS console enables you to create pointer (PTR) records, which are reverse lookup records containing IP-address–to–name mappings, at the same time—provided you have already created an appropriate reverse lookup zone.

Note   When you install Active Directory service using the Active Directory Installation Wizard and allow the wizard to install and configure DNS Server, the wizard automatically creates a forward lookup zone based on the domain name you specified for the server.

---

4. Click Next to bypass the Welcome page and proceed to the Zone Type page, shown in Figure 8.6.

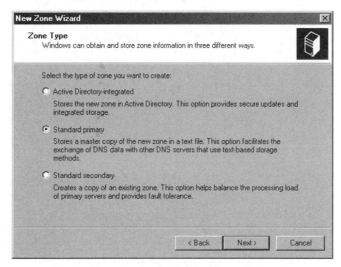

Figure 8.6   The Zone Type page in the New Zone Wizard

5. Select the type of zone you want to create by selecting the appropriate option. Then, click Next to proceed to the Zone Name page, shown in Figure 8.7. The available zone types are as follows:

- **Active Directory–integrated.**   The master copy of a new zone. The zone uses the Active Directory database to store and replicate the zone files. This type of zone is recommended for installations in which DNS Server supports an Active Directory network.

- **Standard primary.**   The master copy of a new zone with its information stored in a standard text file, just like BIND and many other DNS server implementations. You administer and maintain a primary zone on the computer where you created it.

- **Standard secondary.**   A replica of an existing zone. Secondary zones are read-only and are stored in standard text files. You must create a primary zone before you can create a secondary zone. When creating a secondary zone, you specify the DNS server, called the master server, that will transfer the primary zone information to the name server containing the standard secondary zone. You create a secondary zone to provide fault tolerance and to reduce the traffic load on the name server containing the primary zone database file.

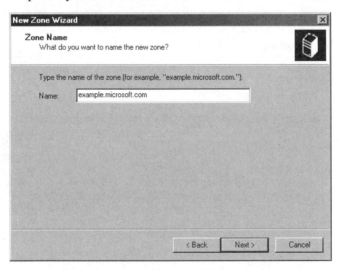

Figure 8.7   The Zone Name page in the New Zone Wizard

6. Type the name you want to assign to the zone in the Name text box. Click Next to proceed to the Zone File page, shown in Figure 8.8.

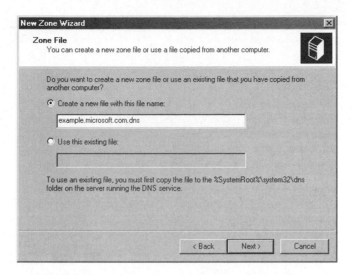

Figure 8.8   The Zone File page in the New Zone Wizard

Typically, a zone is named after the highest domain in the hierarchy that the zone encompasses—that is, the root domain for the zone. As an example, for a zone that encompasses both the microsoft.com and sales.microsoft.com domains, the traditional zone name would be microsoft.com.

Note   If you elected to create an Active Directory–integrated zone, clicking Next takes you to the Completing The New Zone Wizard page. Proceed to step 9.

7. If you elected to create a standard primary zone, you must specify the name of the text file in which you want to store the zone database. By default, the New Zone Wizard offers to create a file named for the zone, with a .dns extension.

   This page does not appear if you elected to create an Active Directory–integrated zone (because the DNS information is stored in the Active Directory database, and no information is needed) or a standard secondary zone. Click Next to proceed to the next page.

   When migrating a zone from another server, you can import the existing zone file. To use an existing DNS database file instead of creating a new one, select Use This Existing File and type the name of the file you want to use in the text box provided. The file you specify must already exist in the *systemroot*\ System32\DNS folder (C:\Winnt\System32\DNS, by default).

8. If you elected to create a standard secondary zone, the Master DNS Servers page appears, as shown in Figure 8.9. Type the IP address of the DNS server containing the master zone database file for the zone in the IP Address text box, or click Browse to select a server, and then click Add. You can repeat this process to add more DNS servers to the list. Click Next to continue.

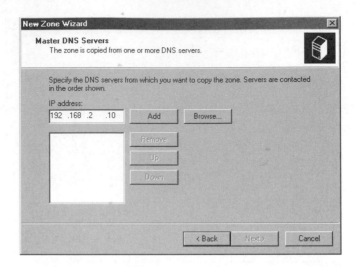

Figure 8.9   The Master DNS Servers page in the New Zone Wizard

9. In the Completing The New Zone Wizard page, click Finish to close the wizard and create the zone, using the parameters you provided.

Note   When you create a reverse lookup zone, the procedure is largely the same, except for the addition of a Reverse Lookup Zone page, shown in Figure 8.10, where you specify the network identifier for the reverse lookup zone you want to create. When you type the network identifier part of an IP address, the wizard automatically reverses the order of the bytes and adds the in-addr.arpa domain name, as shown in the Reverse Lookup Zone Name text box.

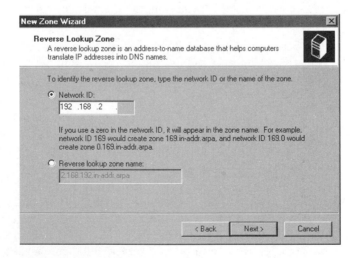

Figure 8.10   The Reverse Lookup Zone page in the New Zone Wizard

Creating Active Directory-Integrated Zones

For networks deploying DNS to support Active Directory service, directory-integrated primary zones are strongly recommended and provide the following benefits:

- Multiple-master update and enhanced security based on the capabilities of Active Directory service.

    In a standard zone storage model, DNS updates are performed using the single-master update model. In this model, a single authoritative DNS server for a zone is designated as the primary source for the zone. This server maintains the master copy of the zone database in a local text file. With this model, the primary server for the zone represents a single fixed point of failure. If this server is not available, update requests from DNS clients are not processed for the zone.

    With directory-integrated storage, dynamic updates to DNS are performed based on a multiple-master update model. In this model, any authoritative DNS server (such as a domain controller running the DNS Server service) can function as the primary source for the zone. Because the master copy of the zone is maintained in the Active Directory database, which is fully replicated to all domain controllers, the zone can be updated by the DNS Server service at any domain controller in the domain. With the multiple-master update model, any of the primary servers for the directory-integrated zone can process requests from DNS clients to update the zone as long as a domain controller is available on the network.

    Also, when using directory-integrated zones, you can use access control lists (ACLs) to provide granular access to either the zone or a specified resource record in the zone. For example, you can use the ACL for a specific domain name in the zone to specify that only certain DNS clients be permitted to perform dynamic updates or to authorize only a secure group such as domain administrators with permissions for updating zone or record properties. This security feature is not available with standard primary zones.

- Zones are replicated and synchronized to new domain controllers automatically whenever a new zone is added to an Active Directory domain.

    Although you can selectively remove the DNS Server service from a domain controller, the directory-integrated zones are already stored at each domain controller, so zone storage and management do not require additional resources. Also, the methods used to synchronize the directory-stored information offer performance improvement over standard zone update methods, which can potentially require transfer of the entire zone.

- Simplified planning and administration for both DNS and Active Directory.

    When name spaces are stored and replicated separately (for example, one for DNS storage and replication and another for Active Directory service), an additional level of administrative complexity is added to the planning and design process for your network. By integrating DNS storage into Active Directory service, you can unify the management of storage and replication for both DNS and Active Directory information into a single administrative entity.

- Directory replication is faster and more efficient than standard DNS replication.

Because Active Directory replication processing is performed on a per-property basis, only the relevant changes are propagated to the other domain controllers. This enables the updates for directory-stored zones to occur using the minimum amount of network traffic.

Delegating Zones

A zone starts as the storage database for a single DNS domain name. If you add subdomains below the domain you specified when you created the zone, these subdomains can either be part of the same zone or part of another zone. When you add a subdomain, you can configure it to be managed and included as part of the original zone records or delegated away to another zone created to support the subdomain.

For example, Figure 8.11 shows the microsoft.com domain. When you create a zone for the microsoft.com domain on a single DNS server, that one zone contains the entire microsoft.com name space. If, at a later time, you expand the microsoft.com domain by adding subdomains, those subdomains must either be included in the microsoft.com zone or delegated away to another zone. In the figure, the *example* subdomain was added to the microsoft.com domain, and a new example.microsoft.com zone was created to support the example.microsoft.com subdomain.

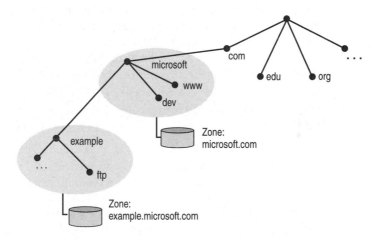

Figure 8.11   Delegating a new subdomain to a new zone

When you delegate zones within a domain's name space, you must also create Name Server (NS) resource records to point to the authoritative DNS server for the new zone. This is necessary both to transfer authority and to provide correct referrals to other DNS servers and clients of the servers being made authoritative for the new zone. The New Delegation Wizard is available to assist in delegation of zones.

Note For more information about creating NS and other resource records, see Lesson 3 of this chapter.

Before you can delegate a zone, you must first create the new subdomains that will be in the new zone within the existing zone. To create a new subdomain, use the following procedure:

1. Click Start and from the Administrative Tools program group, open the DNS console.
2. Select an existing zone in the DNS console and select New Domain from the Action menu to open the New Domain dialog box.
3. Type the name you want to use for the subdomain in the Type The New Domain Name box and click OK.

The new subdomain appears in the console beneath the existing domain. At this point, the new subdomain is part of the same zone. You can create resource records in the new subdomain, just as you would in its parent.

To create a zone delegation, use the following procedure:

1. Click Start and from the Administrative Tools program group, open the DNS console.
2. In the DNS console's scope pane, select the parent domain for the subdomain you want to delegate and select New Delegation from the Action menu to launch the New Delegation Wizard.
3. Click Next to bypass the Welcome page and display the Delegated Domain Name page, shown in Figure 8.12.

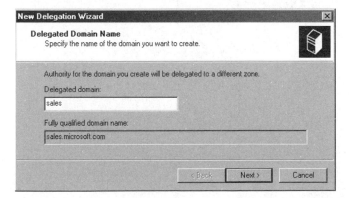

Figure 8.12 The Delegated Domain Name page of the New Delegation Wizard

4. Type the name of the subdomain you want to delegate. The wizard automatically displays the fully qualified domain name (FQDN) for the name you specify.

5. Click Next to proceed to the Name Servers page, shown in Figure 8.13.

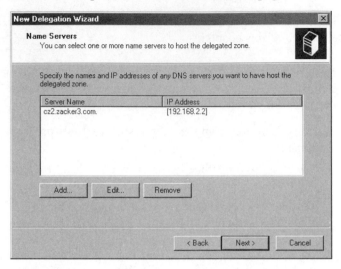

Figure 8.13   The Name Servers page of the New Delegation Wizard

6. Click Add to display the New Resource Record dialog box with a Name Server (NS) tab, as shown in Figure 8.14.

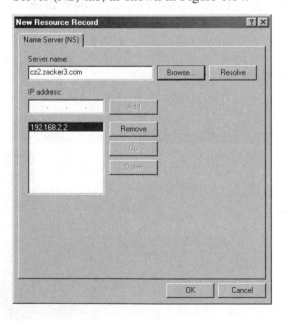

Figure 8.14   The New Resource Record dialog box

7. Type the name of the server to host the delegated zone in the Server Name text box and click Resolve to obtain its IP address, or click Browse to select a server. Then click OK to close the dialog box.

8. Click Next in the Name Servers page, and then click Finish.

The wizard creates the delegated zone in the DNS scope pane and populates it with an NS record identifying the name server that will be the authority for the new zone. If you specified the name and address of the same server that hosts the original zone, you can proceed to create other resource records in the subdomain you added before the delegation. If you specified the name and address of a different name server, you must create the zone on that server before you can create resource records in it. The NS record you created for the delegated zone with the wizard enables the authoritative server for the domain to refer queries to the authoritative server for the subdomain.

Configuring Dynamic Updates

Windows 2000 DNS Server includes a dynamic update capability, as defined in RFC 2136, "Dynamic Updates in the Domain Name System (DNS UPDATE)." Until dynamic updates were developed, name registration on DNS server was strictly manual; an administrator had to manually update the zone database file on the primary name server by creating new resource records or modifying existing ones. With dynamic updates, name servers and clients within a network can automatically update the zone database files, as shown in Figure 8.15.

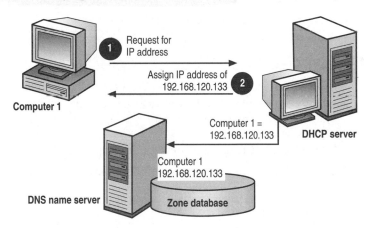

Figure 8.15 Dynamic updates changes the zone database when IP addresses change

You can configure a list of authorized servers to initiate dynamic updates. This list can include secondary name servers, domain controllers, and other servers that perform network registration for clients, such as servers running the DHCP service or WINS.

Dynamic updates interact with the DHCP Server service to maintain synchronized name–to–IP-address mappings for network hosts. By default, the DHCP Server service enables clients to add their own Host (A) resource records to the zone, and the DHCP service itself adds the pointer (PTR) resource record to the zone. The DHCP service cleans up both the A and PTR resource records in the zone when the lease expires.

To configure a zone to use dynamic updates, use the following procedure:

1. Click Start and from the Administrative Tools program group, open the DHCP console.

2. Select the forward or reverse lookup zone that you want to configure and select Properties in the Action menu.

3. In the General tab, in the Allow Dynamic Updates list, choose one of the following options:

   ■ **No.**   Prevents all dynamic updates for this zone from occurring.

   ■ **Yes.**   Permits all dynamic updates for this zone to occur.

   ■ **Only Secure Updates.**   Permits only the dynamic updates that use secure DNS to occur for this zone. This is the preferred option.

   The Only Secure Updates option appears only if the zone type is Active Directory–integrated. If you select the Only Secure Updates option, the requester's permission to update the records in the zone database is tested using mechanisms defined in RFC 2137, "Secure Domain Name System Dynamic Update."

4. Click OK to close the Properties dialog box.

Exercise 1: Configuring Zones

In this exercise, you create zones on a DNS server. In the first two procedures, you create a forward and a reverse lookup zone. In Procedure 3, you configure the zones you created in Procedures 1 and 2 to use dynamic updates.

▶ **Procedure 1: Creating a forward lookup zone**

To create a forward lookup zone, complete the following steps:

1. Click Start, and from the Administrative Tools program group, select DNS to open the DNS console.

2. Double-click the name of your computer to display the Forward Lookup Zones and Reverse Lookup Zones folders.

3. Right-click the icon for your server and from the pop-up menu, choose New Zone to activate the New Zone Wizard.

4. Click Next to display the Zone Type page.

5. Ensure that Standard Primary is selected, and then click Next to display the Forward Or Reverse Lookup Zone page.

6. Ensure that Forward Lookup Zone is selected, and then click Next to display the Zone Name page.

7. Type **training.microsoft.com** in the Name text box and click Next to display the Zone File page.

Important If you are on a production network, check with your network administrator to make sure you can use this as your DNS domain name.

---

8. Ensure that Create A New File With This File Name is selected and that the name of the file to be created is Training.microsoft.com.dns. (If you did not use training.microsoft.com as the domain name in step 7, the name of the file will be the domain name you typed in step 7 with a .dns extension.) Click Next to display the Completing The New Zone Wizard page.

9. Review the information in the Completing The New Zone Wizard page, and then click Finish.

▶ **Procedure 2: Creating a reverse lookup zone**

To create a reverse lookup zone, complete the following steps:

1. Right-click the icon for your server and, from the pop-up menu, choose New Zone to activate the New Zone Wizard.

2. Click Next to display the Zone Type page.

3. Ensure that Standard Primary is selected, and then click Next to display the Forward Or Reverse Lookup Zone page.

4. Ensure that Reverse Lookup Zone is selected, and then click Next to display the Reverse Lookup Zone page.

5. Ensure that Network ID is selected, and type the network identifier for your network's IP addresses in the Network ID text box. For example, if the IP address of your server is 192.168.18.43, with a subnet mask of 255.255.255.0, type **192.168.18** in the Network ID text box. What happens when you enter the network identifier?

6. Click Next to display the Zone File page.

7. Ensure that Create A New File With This File Name is selected. What value appears in the box provided?

8. Click Next to display the Completing The New Zone Wizard page.

9. Review the information in the Completing The New Zone Wizard page, and then click Finish.

▶ **Procedure 3: Configuring zones to use dynamic updates**

To configure the DNS Server service to permit dynamic updates for forward and reverse lookup zones, complete the following steps:

1. In the DNS scope pane, expand the icon representing your server.

2. Expand Forward Lookup Zones, and then double-click training.microsoft.com. (If you did not use training.microsoft.com as your DNS domain name, double-click your DNS domain name.)

3. Right-click training.microsoft.com (or your DNS domain name) and from the pop-up menu, choose Properties to display the training.microsoft.com Properties dialog box. (If you did not use training.microsoft.com as your DNS domain name, the name of the dialog box reflects your DNS domain name.)

4. In the Allow Dynamic Updates list in the General tab, select Yes, and then click OK. This configures dynamic updates for the forward lookup zone.

5. Double-click Reverse Lookup Zones.

6. Right-click the reverse lookup zone you created in Procedure 2 and, from the pop-up menu, choose Properties to display the Properties dialog box for your subnet.

7. In the Allow Dynamic Updates list in the General tab, select Yes, and then click OK. This configures dynamic updates for the reverse lookup zone.

Lesson Review

1. What are the advantages of using the Active Directory–integrated zone type?

2. What must be done when you delegate zones within a namespace?

3. How do dynamic updates improve the efficiency of Windows 2000 DNS Server?

Lesson Summary

- DNS servers enable you to divide the DNS name space into zones that store name information about one or more DNS domains.

- DNS servers can have forward lookup zones for name–to–IP-address mappings and reverse lookup zones for IP-address–to–name mappings.

- You can create three types of zones: Active Directory–integrated zones, standard primary zones, and standard secondary zones.

- Delegating zones enables you to accommodate the creation of new subdomains by adding them to different zones.

- Dynamic updates enable computers on the network to automatically modify their resource records, preventing administrators from having to change them manually.

Lesson 3: Working with Resource Records

The actual information in a DNS zone database file is stored in units called resource records. *Resource records* are entries in the zone database file that associate DNS names to related data for a given network resource, such as an IP address. This lesson examines the various types of resource records used in the DNS database and the process of creating them using Windows 2000 DNS Server.

After this lesson, you will be able to

- List the most commonly used DNS resource records
- View the contents of a resource record
- Create a resource record

Estimated lesson time: 20 minutes

Understanding Resource Record Types

DNS servers use many types of resource records. When you create a zone, DNS automatically adds two resource records to the zone: the Start of Authority (SOA) record and the Name Server (NS) record. The functions of these resource records, as well as those of the other most common types of records, are listed in the following sections. The fields described in these sections are carried in the RDATA field of a resource record entry in a DNS message and typically provide information that relates to the DNS name of the system in question, as identified in the NAME field.

Note For more information about the DNS message format, see Lesson 2 in Chapter 7, "Understanding the Domain Name System."

Start of Authority (SOA)

The SOA resource record identifies which name server is the authoritative source of information for data within this domain. The first record in the zone database file must be an SOA record. In Windows 2000 DNS Server, SOA records are created automatically with default values when you create a new zone. Later, you can modify the individual field values as needed.

Unlike most resource records, the RDATA field of the SOA resource record contains a variety of subfields, most of which are used for name server maintenance operations. These subfields are as follows, listed using the name by which they are known in the DNS console interface, followed by the field name as specified in RFC 1035, in parentheses:

- **Serial number (SERIAL).** Contains a version number for the original copy of the zone.

- **Primary Server (MNAME).** Contains the FQDN of the DNS name server that is the primary source of data for the zone.

- **Responsible Person (RNAME).** Contains the name of the mailbox belonging to the person responsible for the administration of the zone.

- **Refresh Interval (REFRESH).** Specifies the time interval (in seconds) at which secondary master name servers must verify the accuracy of their data.

- **Retry Interval (RETRY).** Specifies the time interval (in seconds) at which secondary master name servers retry their zone transfer operations after an initial transfer failure.

- **Expires After (EXPIRE).** Specifies the time interval after which a secondary master name server removes records from its zone database file when they are not successfully refreshed by a zone transfer.

- **Minimum (default) TTL (MINIMUM).** Specifies the lower end of the range of Time to Live (TTL) values supplied with every resource record furnished by the zone. A server receiving resources records from this zone saves them in its cache for a period of time between this MINIMUM field value and a maximum value specified in the TTL field of the resource record itself.

Name Server (NS)

The NS resource record identifies the name server that is the authority for the particular zone or domain. The RDATA field for this resource record consists of a single DNSNAME subfield containing the name of a DNS name server. Windows 2000 DNS Server creates an NS resource records by default in every new zone. When you create subdomains and delegate them into different zones, NS records enable the name server to refer queries to the authoritative name server for a subdomain.

Host (A)

The A (for Address) resource record is the fundamental data unit of the DNS. This resource record has a single ADDRESS subfield in the RDATA field, which contains the IP address associated with the system identified in the NAME field. Host resource records provide the name–to–IP-address mappings that DNS name servers use to perform their primary function, name resolution.

Alias (CNAME)

The CNAME (for Canonical Name) resource record is used to specify an alias, or alternative name, for the system specified in the NAME field. The RDATA field contains a single CNAME subfield that holds another name, in the standard DNS naming format. You create CNAME resource records to use more than one name to point to a single IP address. For example, you can host a File Transfer Protocol (FTP) server, such as *ftp.microsoft.com*, and a Web server, such as *www.microsoft.com*, on the same computer by creating an A record in the microsoft.com domain for the host name www and a CNAME record equating the host name ftp with the A record for www.

Host Information (HINFO)

The HINFO resource record contains two subfields in the RDATA field, called CPU and OS, that contain values identifying the processor type and operating system used by the computer specified in the NAME field. You can use this record type as a low-cost resource-tracking tool.

Mail Exchanger (MX)

A secondary, but crucial, function of the DNS is the direction of e-mail messages to the appropriate mail server. The DNS standards define a variety of obsolete and experimental resource records devoted to e-mail functions, but the resource record in general use today for e-mail is the MX record. The RDATA field in this resource record contains two subfields, called PREFERENCE and EXCHANGE. The PREFERENCE subfield contains an integer value that indicates the relative priority of this resource record as compared to others of the same type and class in the same domain. Lower values indicate higher priorities. The EXCHANGE subfield contains the name of a computer that is capable of acting as an e-mail server for the domain specified in the NAME field.

Pointer (PTR)

The PTR resource record is the functional opposite of the A record, providing an IP-address–to–name mapping for the system identified in the NAME field using an in-addr.arpa domain name. The RDATA field consists of a single PTRDNAME subfield, containing the FQDN of the system identified by the IP address in the NAME field. When you create the appropriate reverse lookup zone on your Windows 2000 DNS Server, you can create PTR resource records automatically with your A records.

Service (SRV)

The SRV resource record is a relatively new addition to the DNS defined in RFC 2052, which enables clients to locate servers that are providing a particular service. Windows 2000 Active Directory clients rely on the SRV resource record to locate the domain controllers they need to validate logon requests. The SRV record uses a different resource record format in the DNS message, which consists of the following fields:

- **SERVICE.** Contains the name of the service sought by the client, using the symbolic name published locally (such as in the Services file included with every TCP/IP implementation) or in the "Assigned Numbers" RFC (currently RFC 1700).

- **PROTO.** Specifies a protocol (typically TCP or User Datagram Protocol [UDP]) that the service is expected to use.

- **NAME.**   Specifies the name of the domain in which the service is operating. Unlike other resource records, the SRV record is indexed using the value of the SERVICE field and not that of the NAME field.

- **TTL.**   As in other resource record types, specifies the amount of time (in seconds) that the resource record should remain in the cache of the server to which it is being supplied.

- **CLASS.**   As in other resource record types, specifies the class of the resource record the entry contains.

- **PRIORITY.**   As with the PREFERENCE subfield in the MX resource record, contains an integer that indicates the relative value of this record when compared to others of the same type. Lower values indicate higher priorities.

- **WEIGHT.**   Can contain a value that functions as a load-balancing mechanism when there are multiple SRV resource records with the same priority value. The probability of a client selecting this resource record should be proportional to its weight value, which can range from 1 to 65,535. A value of 0 in this field disables load balancing.

- **PORT.**   Contains an integer that identifies the TCP or UDP port number of the service, using either a well-known port number or one assigned by an administrator.

- **TARGET.**   Contains the domain name in which the host running the service resides. The name server hosting the SRV record must also have a corresponding A record for this domain name, which can be included in the Additional section of the DS message containing the SRV record.

Viewing Resource Records

To view the information in a resource record, use the following procedure:

1. Click Start and from the Administrative Tools program group, open the DNS console.

2. In the DNS console's scope pane, select the zone for which you want to view a resource record.

3. In the details pane, select the record you want to view and select Properties from the Action menu to display the Properties dialog box.

   The Properties dialog box for each resource record contains a tab that is named for the record type, which contains the information stored in that particular type of record. For example, the Properties dialog box for an A record (see Figure 8.16) contains only the IP address associated with the record's host name. By contrast, the Properties dialog box for an SOA record (see Figure 8.17) contains all the configuration parameters listed earlier in this lesson, including the TTL for the zone.

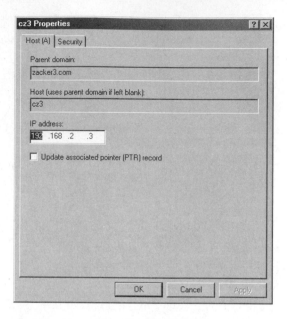

Figure 8.16   The Properties dialog box for a Host (A) record

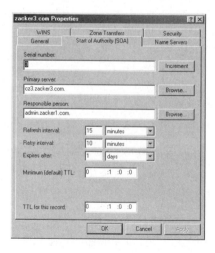

Figure 8.17   The Properties dialog box for a Start of Authority (SOA) record

4. When you have finished viewing the record, click OK.

Creating Resource Records

The process of creating a resource record varies depending on the type of record you want to create. As you have seen, different resource record types perform different functions and contain different types and amounts of information.

Creating an A record is simply a matter of supplying a host name and an IP address, whereas other record types contain a lot more data. To create a new resource record in the DNS console, right-click the zone in which you want to locate the record and choose the appropriate command from the pop-up menu, as shown in Figure 8.18.

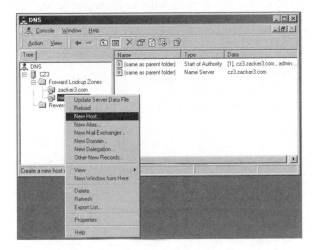

Figure 8.18   The pop-up menu for a DNS zone

The pop-up menu commands vary depending on whether you have selected a forward lookup zone or a reverse lookup zone. When you choose Other New Records from the pop-up menu, the DNS console open the Resource Record Type dialog box, shown in Figure 8.19, which contains a list of all the resource records you can create.

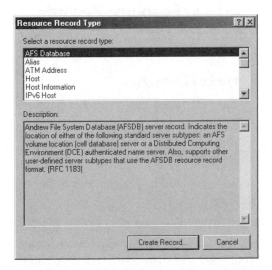

Figure 8.19   The Resource Record Type dialog box

When you select a record type, you see a New Resource Record dialog box, an example of which is shown in Figure 8.20, which contains fields for the information carried by that type of record. After supplying the requested information in the boxes provided, click OK to create the record, which appears in the details pane of the DNS console under the appropriate zone.

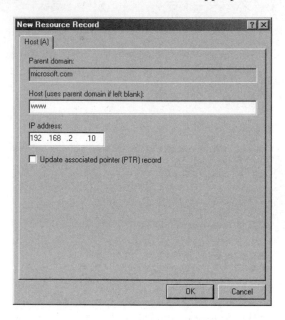

Figure 8.20   The New Resource Record dialog box for a Host (A) record

Exercise 1: Adding Resource Records

In this exercise, you practice adding resource records for forward and reverse lookup zones.

▶ **Procedure 1: Creating a host record**

To add a Host record to the zone you created in Exercise 1 of Lesson 2, complete the following steps:

1. Click Start and, from the Administrative Tools program group, select DNS to display the DNS console.

2. Double-click the name of your computer to display the Forward Lookup Zones and Reverse Lookup Zones folders.

3. Double-click the Forward Lookup Zones folder to display the zones on the server.

4. Right-click the zone you created in Exercise 1, Procedure 1 of Lesson 2, and from the pop-up menu, choose New Host. What happens?

5. Type **server1** in the Name text box.

6. Type a valid, unused IP address on your network in the IP Address text box.

7. Click Add Host.

8. Type **server2** in the Name text box.

9. Type a different, valid, unused IP address on your network in the IP Address text box.

10. Select the Create Associated Pointer (PTR) Record check box.

11. Click Add Host.

12. Click Done.

▶ **Procedure 2: Viewing resource records**

To view the resource records you just created, complete the following steps:

1. From the Action menu, select Refresh.

2. Click the icon for the forward lookup zone in which you created the Host (A) resource records. What do you see in the zone?

3. Click the icon for the reverse lookup zone corresponding to the forward lookup zone you created. What do you see and why?

▶ **Procedure 3: Creating a PTR record manually**

To create a PTR resource record for the host name server1, complete the following steps:

1. In the scope pane, click Reverse Lookup Zones.

2. Right-click the zone you created in Exercise 1, Procedure 2 of Lesson 2 and from the pop-up menu, choose New Pointer to display the New Resource Record dialog box.

3. Enter the host identifier you assigned to the server1 resource record in the Host IP Number text box.

4. In the Host Name text box, type **server1.microsoft.com**. Remember to include the trailing period.

5. Click OK. A pointer record appears in the details pane.

6. Close the DNS console.

Lesson Review

1. What type of resource record do you create to represent a domain controller on a Windows 2000 network?

2. Which two types of resource records can contain the same IP address and host name?

   a. SOA and A

   b. PTR and A

   c. A and CNAME

   d. PTR and CNAME

3. Which resource records does the DNS console create automatically when you create a forward lookup zone?

Lesson Summary

- A Domain Name System (DNS) zone database file can contain many types of resource records, including host (A), pointer (PTR), and alias (CNAME) records.

- The information stored in the various resource record types varies, depending on the record type.

- Host (A) records contain the basic name–to–IP-address mappings that DNS uses to resolve names.

- Pointer (PTR) records contain the IP-address–to–name mappings used for reverse name lookups.

- Mail Exchanger (MX) and Service (SRV) records identify the mail servers and domain controllers on a Windows network, respectively.

Lesson 4: Configuring Zone Transfers

This lesson introduces the concepts of zone replication and transfer. *Zone transfer* is the process by which DNS servers interact to maintain and synchronize authoritative name data.

After this lesson, you will be able to
- Explain the purpose of zone transfers
- Configure zone transfers

Estimated lesson time: 20 minutes

Zone Replication and Zone Transfers

Because of the important role that zones play in DNS, it is intended that they be available from more than one DNS server on the network to provide fault tolerance when resolving name queries. Otherwise, if a zone exists on a single server and that server is not responding, queries for names in the zone can fail. For additional servers to host a zone, their zone data must be identical. To prevent administrators from having to modify the zone database file manually on all their DNS servers whenever they add, remove, or change a resource record, DNS uses zone transfers to synchronize all the copies of the zone.

When structuring your zones, there are several good reasons to use additional DNS servers for zone replication, including the following:

- Adding DNS servers provides zone redundancy, enabling DNS clients to resolve names in the zone, even if the primary server for the zone stops responding.

- Adding DNS servers can reduce DNS network traffic. For example, adding a DNS server to the opposite side of a low-speed wide area network (WAN) link can be useful in managing and reducing WAN traffic.

- Adding secondary servers can reduce the processing load on the primary server for a zone.

When you add a new DNS server to the network and configure it as a new secondary master name server for an existing zone, the server performs a *full zone transfer (AXFR)* to obtain a full copy of all resource records for the zone. Some DNS server implementations also use this same full transfer method when the zone requires updating after changes are made to the primary zone database file. The Windows 2000 DNS Server service supports *incremental zone transfer (IXFR)*, a revised DNS zone transfer process for intermediate changes.

Incremental Zone Transfers

IXFR is an additional DNS standard for replicating DNS zones defined in RFC 1995, "Incremental Zone Transfer in DNS," that provides a more efficient method of propagating zone changes and updates. In earlier DNS implementations, any request for an update of zone data required a full transfer of the entire zone database using an AXFR query. With incremental transfers, DNS servers use an IXFR query instead. IFXR enables the secondary master name server to pull only those zone changes it needs to synchronize its copy of the zone with its source, either a primary master or another secondary master copy of the zone maintained by another DNS server.

With IXFR zone transfers, the servers first determine the differences between the source and replicated versions of the zone. If the zones are identified to be the same version—as indicated by the SERIAL field in the SOA resource record of each zone—no transfer occurs. If the serial number for the zone at the primary master server is greater than the serial number at the requesting secondary master server, the primary master performs a transfer of only those changes made for each incremental version of the zone. For an IXFR query to succeed and a transfer to occur, the primary master name server for the zone must keep a history of incremental zone changes to use when answering these queries. The incremental transfer process requires substantially less traffic on a network and zone transfers are completed much faster.

Example of a Zone Transfer

In addition to a manual initiation, a zone transfer occurs during any of the following scenarios:

- When starting the DNS Server service on the secondary master name server for a zone
- When the refresh interval time expires for the zone
- When changes are made to a primary master name server that is configured with a notify list

Zone transfers are always initiated by the secondary master server for a zone and sent to the DNS server configured as its master server. This master server can be any other DNS name server that hosts the zone, either a primary master or another secondary master server. When the master server receives the request for the zone, it can reply with either a partial or full transfer of the zone.

As shown in Figure 8.21, zone transfers between servers follow an ordered process. This process varies depending on whether a zone has been previously replicated or if the servers are performing an initial replication of a new zone.

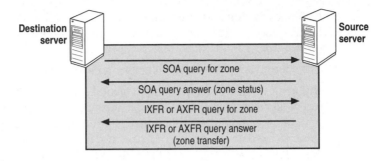

Figure 8.21   Zone transfer process

In this example, the following sequence illustrates the process for a zone transfer between a requesting secondary master name server for a zone—the destination server—and its master server, another DNS server that hosts the zone.

1. During its initial configuration, the destination server sends an initial (AXFR) transfer request for the zone to the DNS server configured as its source for the zone.

2. The source server responds and transfers the entire zone database to the destination server.

   The zone is delivered to the destination server with its version established by use of the SERIAL field in the properties of the SOA resource record. The SOA record also contains a refresh interval (15 minutes, by default), which indicates when the destination server should next request renewal of the zone with the source server.

3. When the refresh interval expires, the destination server requests renewal of the zone from the source server with a query for the source server's SOA resource record.

4. The source server responds to the query for its SOA record.

   This response contains the serial number for the zone in its current state at the source server.

5. The destination server checks the serial number of the SOA record in the response and determines how to renew the zone.

   If the value of the serial number in the SOA response is equal to its current local serial number, the destination server concludes that the zone is the same at both servers and a zone transfer is not needed. The destination server then renews the zone by resetting its refresh interval based on the value of the field in the SOA response from its source server. If the value of the serial number in the SOA response is higher than the current local serial number, the destination server concludes that the zone has been updated and that a transfer is needed.

6. If the destination server concludes that the zone has changed, it sends an IXFR query to the source server containing its current local value for the serial number in the SOA record for the zone.

7. The source server responds with either an incremental or full transfer of the zone.

   If the source server supports incremental transfer by maintaining a history of recent and incremental zone changes for modified resource records, it can answer with an incremental (IXFR) transfer of the zone. If the source server does not support incremental transfer or does not have a history of zone changes, it can, alternatively, answer with a full (AXFR) transfer of the zone instead.

Note   For Windows 2000 Server, incremental zone transfer through IXFR query is supported. For earlier versions of the DNS Server service running in Windows NT Server 4.0, and for many other DNS server implementations, incremental zone transfer is not available and only full-zone (AXFR) queries and transfers are used to replicate zones.

Zone Transfer Security

The DNS console enables you to specify the servers allowed to participate in zone transfers. This can help prevent an undesired attempt by an unknown or unapproved DNS server to pull, or request, zone updates.

To specify the servers allowed to participate in zone transfers, use the following procedure:

1. Click Start, point to Programs, point to Administrative Tools, and then click DNS.

2. In the DNS console's scope pane, select the zone for which you want to set up zone transfers and select Properties from the Action menu to open the Properties dialog box.

3. Click the Zone Transfers tab (see Figure 8.22).

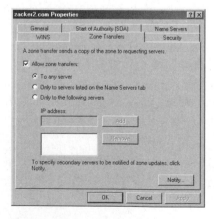

Figure 8.22   The Zone Transfers tab of a zone's Properties dialog box

4. Specify the servers for which you want to allow zone transfers by clicking the appropriate option button, and, if necessary, typing the servers' IP addresses in the IP Address box and clicking Add for each one.

5. Click OK to close the Properties dialog box.

DNS Notification

The DNS Server service supports DNS notification, which is an updated revision to the DNS standard specification, published as RFC 1996, "A Mechanism for Prompt Notification of Zone Changes (DNS NOTIFY)." DNS notification implements a push mechanism that notifies a select set of secondary master name servers for a zone when that zone is updated. The notified servers can then initiate the zone transfer process and pull changes from the notifying server to update the zone.

Use DNS notification only to notify DNS servers that are operating as secondary master servers for a zone. For replication of Active Directory–integrated zones, DNS notification is not needed. This is because any DNS servers that load a zone from Active Directory automatically poll the directory approximately once every 15 minutes (depending on the SOA refresh interval setting) to update and refresh the zone. In these cases, configuring a notification list can actually degrade system performance by causing unnecessary additional transfer requests for the updated zone.

The typical DNS notify process begins when the local zone on a DNS server acting as a source for the zone to other servers is updated (by addition, deletion, or modification of resource records). When the zone is updated at the source, the SERIAL field value in the SOA record also updates, indicating a new local version of the zone. The source server then sends a notify message to the other servers specified in the Notify dialog box. All secondary master servers that receive the notification message respond by initiating a zone transfer request back to the notifying server. The normal zone transfer process can then continue as described earlier in this lesson.

To specify the servers to be notified, use the following procedure:

1. Click Start, point to Programs, point to Administrative Tools, and then click DNS.

2. In the DNS console's scope pane, select the zone for which you want to set up zone transfers and select Properties from the Action menu to open the Properties dialog box.

3. Select the Zone Transfers tab, and then click Notify.

4. In the Notify dialog box (see Figure 8.23), specify the secondary servers to be notified when the zone changes by clicking the appropriate option button, and, if necessary, typing the servers' IP addresses in the IP Address box and clicking Add for each one.

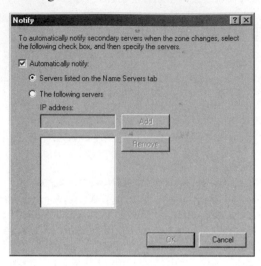

Figure 8.23   The Notify dialog box

5. Click OK to close the Properties dialog box.

Lesson Review

1. What is the purpose of the SOA resource record?

2. Why is an IXFR query more efficient than an AFXR query?

3. What is the purpose of DNS notification?

Lesson Summary

- Zone transfers are required to replicate and synchronize all copies of the zone used at each DNS server configured to host the zone.

- Earlier DNS server implementations always perform a full transfer of the entire zone database. However, the DNS Server service included with Windows 2000 Server supports incremental zone transfers, which can transfer only the data that has changed since the previous transfer.

- The Windows 2000 DNS console enables you to specify which DNS servers should receive zone transfers from a primary server.

- Under normal conditions, secondary DNS servers request zone transfers from primary servers at regular intervals.

- DNS notification is a feature that enables DNS primary servers to inform secondary servers when database changes have been made and a transfer is required.

Lesson 5: Monitoring and Troubleshooting DNS

This lesson explains the monitoring options available for Windows 2000 DNS Server and also describes some of the problems you might encounter, along with possible solutions.

After this lesson, you will be able to

- Monitor DNS server
- Troubleshoot common DNS problems

Estimated lesson time: 20 minutes

Monitoring DNS Servers

Windows 2000 Server includes four options for monitoring DNS Server activities:

- Submitting queries to the server
- Default logging of DNS server event messages to the DNS server log
- Performance counters
- Optional debug options for trace logging to a text file on the DNS server computer

Querying the DNS Server

The DNS console enables you to monitor the DNS Server service by performing both simple and recursive queries. To do this, use the following procedure:

1. Click Start, point to Programs, point to Administrative Tools, and then click DNS.

2. In the DNS console's scope pane, select the name server on which you want to perform the test and select Properties from the Action menu to open the Properties dialog box.

3. Click the Monitoring tab. Select one of the following check boxes to specify the type of query you want to use:

   - **Simple Query.**   Select this type of query to perform a simple query test of the DNS server. This is a local test that uses the DNS client on this computer to query the name server.

   - **Recursive Query.**   Select this type of query to perform a more complex, recursive query test of the name server. This query tests the name server by forwarding a recursive query to another name server.

4. Select Test Now to perform a test immediately. You can also select the Perform Automatic Testing At The Following Interval check box and specify a time interval to trigger regular tests.

5. Click OK to close the Properties dialog box.

DNS Server Event Logging

For Windows 2000 Server, DNS server event messages are kept separate from events generated by other applications and services in the DNS Server log, which you can examine using the Event Viewer console, as shown in Figure 8.24. The DNS Server log contains basic predetermined events logged by the DNS Server service, such as when the DNS server starts and stops.

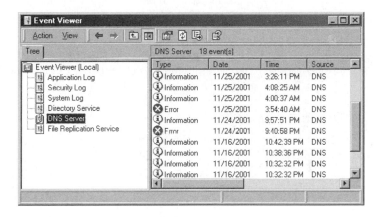

Figure 8.24   The DNS Server log as displayed in Event Viewer

You can also use Event Viewer to view and monitor client-related DNS events. These events appear in the System log and are generated by the DNS Client service on all computers running Windows 2000.

Monitoring DNS Server Performance

Because DNS servers are of critical importance in most environments, monitoring their performance can provide a useful benchmark for predicting, estimating, and optimizing DNS server performance. In addition, you can quickly identify degraded server performance either over time or during periods of peak activity. Windows 2000 Server provides a set of DNS server performance counters that you can use with System Monitor to measure and monitor various aspects of server activity. These counters are as follows:

- Overall DNS server performance statistics, such as the number of overall queries and responses processed by a DNS server

- UDP or TCP counters, for measuring DNS queries and responses that are processed using either of these transport protocols, respectively

- Dynamic update and secure dynamic update counters, for measuring registration and update activity generated by dynamic clients

- Memory usage counters, for measuring system memory usage and memory allocation patterns created by operating the server computer as a Windows 2000 DNS Server

- Recursive lookup counters, for measuring queries and responses when the DNS Server service uses recursion to look up and fully resolve DNS names on behalf of requesting clients

- WINS lookup counters, for measuring queries and responses made to WINS servers when using the WINS lookup integration features of the DNS Server service

- Zone transfer counters, including specific counters for measuring all-zone transfer (AXFR), incremental zone transfer (IXFR), and DNS zone update notification activity

Debug Options

The DNS console also enables you to set additional logging options to create a temporary trace log as a text-based file of DNS server activity for debugging purposes. To configure the logging options, use the following procedure:

1. Click Start, point to Programs, point to Administrative Tools, and then click DNS.

2. In the DNS console's scope pane, select the name server on which you want to perform the test and select Properties from the Action menu to open the Properties dialog box.

3. Click the Logging tab to display the controls shown in Figure 8.25.

Figure 8.25   The Logging tab of a DNS server's Properties dialog box

4. Select from the following check boxes to specify the type of events you want to log:

- **Query.**   Logs queries received by the DNS Server service from clients
- **Notify.**   Logs notification messages received by the DNS Server service from other servers
- **Update.**   Logs dynamic updates received by the DNS Server service from other computers
- **Questions.**   Logs the contents of the question section for each DNS query message processed by the DNS Server service
- **Answers.**   Logs the contents of the answer section for each DNS query message processed by the DNS Server service
- **Send.**   Logs the number of DNS query messages sent by the DNS Server service
- **Receive.**   Logs the number of DNS query messages received by the DNS Server service
- **UDP.**   Logs the number of DNS requests received by the DNS Server service over a UDP port
- **TCP.**   Logs the number of DNS requests received by the DNS Server service over a TCP port
- **Full Packets.**   Logs the number of full packets written and sent by the DNS Server service
- **Write Through.**   Logs the number of packets written through by the DNS Server service and back to the zone

5. Click OK to close the Properties dialog box. The information for the options you selected is stored in the Dns.log file in the *systemroot*\System32\dns folder (C:\Winnt\System32\dns, by default).

By default, all debug logging options are disabled. When selectively enabled, the DNS Server service can perform additional trace-level logging of selected types of events or messages for general troubleshooting and debugging of the server. Debug logging can be resource-intensive, however, affecting overall server performance and consuming disk space. Therefore, you should use it only temporarily when you need more detailed information about server performance.

DNS Troubleshooting Scenarios

Table 8.1 describes some zone problems you might encounter and possible solutions to these problems, and Table 8.2 describes some problems you might encounter with dynamic updates along with possible solutions to these problems.

Table 8.1   Troubleshooting Scenarios for Zone Problems

Cause	Solution
Symptom: A zone transfer fails to occur	
The DNS Server service is stopped or the zone is paused.	Verify that the master (source) and secondary master (destination) DNS servers involved in the zone transfer are both started and that the zone is not paused at either server.
The DNS servers used during a transfer do not have network connectivity with each other.	Eliminate the possibility of a basic network connectivity problem between the two servers. Using the ping command, ping each DNS server by its IP address from its remote counterpart. Both ping tests should succeed. If not, investigate and resolve intermediate network connectivity issues.
The SOA serial number is the same at both the source and destination servers. Because the value is the same at both servers, no zone transfer occurs between the servers.	Using the DNS console, perform the following tasks: In the Start Of Authority (SOA) tab, increase the value of the serial number for the zone at the master server (source) to a number greater than the value at the applicable secondary server (destination). Initiate zone transfer at the secondary server.
The master server (source) and its targeted secondary server (destination) are having inter-operability-related problems.	Investigate possible causes for any problems related to interoperability between Windows 2000 DNS servers and other DNS servers running different implementations, such as an earlier version of the BIND distribution.
The zone has resource records or other data that the DNS server cannot interpret.	Verify that the zone does not contain incompatible data, such as unsupported resource record types or data errors. Also, verify that the server has not been configured in advance to prevent loading a zone when bad data is found and investigate its method for checking names. You can configure these settings using the DNS console.
Authoritative zone data is incorrect.	If a zone transfer continues to fail, ensure that the zone does not contain nonstandard data. To determine if erroneous zone data is a likely source for a failed zone transfer, look in the DNS Server event log for messages.
Symptom: Zone delegation does not function properly	
Zone delegations are not configured correctly.	Review how to use zone delegations and revise your zone configurations as needed.

Table 8.2   Troubleshooting Scenarios for Dynamic Updates

Cause	Solution
Symptom: The client is not performing dynamic updates	
The client (or its DHCP server) does not support the use of dynamic update.	Verify that your clients or servers support dynamic update using the options for dynamic update support provided in Windows 2000. For client computers to be registered and updated dynamically with a DNS server, either install or upgrade client computers to Windows 2000 or install and use a Windows 2000 DHCP server on your network to lease addresses to client computers.
The client was not able to register and update with the DNS server because of missing or incomplete DNS configuration.	Verify that the client is fully and correctly configured for DNS, and update its configuration as needed. To update the DNS configuration for a client, either configure a primary DNS suffix at the client computer for static TCP/IP clients or configure a connection-specific DNS suffix for use at one of the installed network connections at the client computer.
The DNS client attempted to update its information with the DNS server but failed because of a problem related to the server.	If a client can reach its preferred and alternate DNS servers as configured, it is likely that the cause of its failed updates can be found elsewhere. At Windows 2000 client computers, use Event Viewer to check the System log for any event messages that explain why attempts by the client to dynamically update its host (A) or pointer (PTR) resource records failed.
The DNS server does not support dynamic updates.	Verify that the DNS server used by the client can support the dynamic update standard. For Windows servers, only the version of Windows 2000 DNS Server included with Windows 2000 supports dynamic updates; earlier versions, such as the one provided with Windows NT 4.0 Server, do not.
The DNS server supports dynamic updates but is not configured to accept them.	Verify that the primary zone where clients require updates is configured to allow dynamic updates. For Windows 2000 DNS servers, the default for a new primary zone is to not accept dynamic updates. At the DNS server that loads the applicable primary zone, modify zone properties to allow updates.
The zone database is not available.	Verify that the zone exists. Verify that the zone is available for update. For a standard primary zone, verify that the zone file exists at the server and that the zone is not paused. Secondary zones do not support dynamic updates. For Active Directory–integrated zones, verify that the DNS server is running as a domain controller and has access to the Active Directory database where zone data is stored.

Lesson Review

1. What is the difference between a simple query and a recursive query?

2. Give three reasons why a zone transfer might fail to occur.

3. What is the first thing to check if dynamic updates fail to occur?

Lesson Summary

- The Monitor tab in a Domain Name System (DNS) server's Properties dialog box enables you to send simple and recursive queries to the server.

- Event Viewer contains a separate DNS Server log on Windows 2000 Server computers with the DNS Server service installed.

- The Logging tab in a DNS server's Properties dialog box enables you to select specific server activities to monitor in a separate log file.

- Zone transfers can fail for a variety of reasons, including network failures and invalid or unsupported data stored in the zone database.

- One of the common causes of dynamic update failures is lack of support for the dynamic update standard by all the computers involved.

CHAPTER 9

Implementing Windows Internet Name Service

Lesson 1: Introducing NetBIOS 318

Lesson 2: WINS Name Registration and Resolution 335

Lesson 3: Implementing WINS 345

Lesson 4: Configuring WINS Replication 356

About This Chapter

In Chapter 7, "Understanding the Domain Name System," and Chapter 8, "Using the Windows 2000 DNS Server," you learned about the DNS name space, which both the Active Directory service and the Internet rely on to identify computers and their locations. However, there is another name space, called the Network Basic Input/Output System or NetBIOS, that Microsoft Windows versions prior to Windows 2000 use for roughly the same purpose. The computer name that you supply when installing a pre–Windows 2000 computer is in fact a NetBIOS name, which the operating system uses to uniquely identify the system on the network. The Windows Internet Name Service (WINS) is a NetBIOS name server application that these computers use to resolve NetBIOS names into the Internet Protocol (IP) addresses needed for Transmission Control Protocol/Internet Protocol (TCP/IP) communications.

Before You Begin

This chapter requires an understanding of the TCP/IP protocols, as discussed in Chapter 2, "Introducing TCP/IP." A familiarity with the Domain Name System (DNS), as discussed in Chapter 7, "Understanding the Domain Name System," is also helpful. To perform the exercises in this chapter, you need a Windows 2000 server computer with Microsoft Dynamic Host Configuration Protocol (DHCP) Service installed, and (optionally) a second Windows 2000 client computer.

Lesson 1: Introducing NetBIOS

In 1993, when Microsoft first introduced networking into the Windows operating systems, it relied on the NetBIOS Extended User Interface (NetBEUI) protocol for all communications, and NetBEUI relies on the NetBIOS name space as the sole identifier of the computers on the network. In later years, as TCP/IP came to be the dominant protocol suite for all types of computer networking, Microsoft replaced NetBEUI as the default Windows networking protocol with TCP/IP but retained the NetBIOS name space. To make this conversion possible, Microsoft used the standards published by the Internet Engineering Task Force (IETF) that define the use of NetBIOS on a TCP/IP network. These standards are Request for Comments (RFC) 1001, "Protocol Standard for a NetBIOS Service on a TCP/UDP Transport: Concepts and Methods," and RFC 1002, "Protocol Standard for a NetBIOS Service on a TCP/UDP Transport: Detailed Specifications." The resulting implementation is more commonly called NetBIOS over TCP/IP (NetBT).

After this lesson, you will be able to

- Describe the NetBIOS name space
- Create an Lmhosts file
- Understand the broadcast NetBIOS name resolution mechanism
- List the NetBIOS node types

Estimated lesson time: 45 minutes

NetBIOS is an application programming interface (API) that enables user applications to submit network input/output (I/O) and control directives to underlying network protocols. An application program that uses the NetBIOS interface API for network communication can run on any protocol that supports the NetBIOS interface. NetBIOS provides commands and support for the following services:

- Network name registration and verification
- Session establishment and termination
- Reliable connection-oriented session data transfer
- Unreliable connectionless datagram data transfer
- Support protocol (driver) and adapter monitoring and management

NetBIOS Naming

The NetBIOS name space was originally designed to be the only means of identifying specific computers used on a network. On Windows networks that use NetBEUI as their protocol, for example, computers have no addresses; the NetBIOS name is a computer's only identifier. The NetBIOS name itself is a 16-byte character string assigned by a network administrator to a particular entity on a network.

The NetBIOS name is either a unique (exclusive) or group (nonexclusive) name. Unique names are typically used to send network communication to a specific process on a computer. Group names are used to send information to multiple computers at one time.

Note   Windows 2000 uses DNS for name resolution by default; on a network consisting only of Windows 2000 computers, NetBIOS is not needed at all. All the Windows 2000 operating systems include NetBIOS client capabilities (including a WINS client), and all the Windows 2000 Server operating systems include a WINS server, only for reasons of interoperability with computers running earlier versions of Windows.

To identify the type of resource a Windows NetBIOS name identifies, the sixteenth character of the name is reserved for a resource identifier code, the most common of which are listed in Table 9.1. This leaves 15 characters for the NetBIOS name itself. Names shorter than 15 characters are padded out with spaces (after the name) to ensure that the resource identifier code always appears as the sixteenth character.

Table 9.1   Windows NetBIOS Resource Identifier Codes

Resource Identifier (hex)	Resource Type	Function
00	Unique	Workstation Service
01	Unique	Messenger Service
01	Group	Master Browser
03	Unique	Messenger Service
06	Unique	RAS Server Service
1F	Unique	NetDDE Service
20	Unique	File Server Service
21	Unique	RAS Client Service
22	Unique	Microsoft Exchange Interchange (MSMail Connector)
23	Unique	Microsoft Exchange Store
24	Unique	Microsoft Exchange Directory
30	Unique	Modem Sharing Server Service
31	Unique	Modem Sharing Client Service
43	Unique	SMS Clients Remote Control
44	Unique	SMS Administrators Remote Control Tool
45	Unique	SMS Clients Remote Chat
46	Unique	SMS Clients Remote Transfer
87	Unique	Microsoft Exchange MTA

(continued)

Table 9.1   *(continued)*

Resource Identifier (hex)	Resource Type	Function
6A	Unique	Microsoft Exchange IMC
BE	Unique	Network Monitor Agent
BF	Unique	Network Monitor Application
03	Unique	Messenger Service
00	Group	Domain Name
1B	Unique	Domain Master Browser
1C	Group	Domain Controllers
1D	Unique	Master Browser
1E	Group	Browser Service Elections
1C	Group	Internet Information Services (IIS)
00	Unique	IIS

Computers on a Windows network have a single NetBIOS name but can use several resource identifiers. For example, if you use the Windows Nbtstat.exe utility to list the local NetBIOS names used by a typical Windows 2000 Professional installation, you see a display like the following:

```
Node IpAddress: [192.168.2.7] Scope Id: []
            NetBIOS Local Name Table

    Name             Type      Status
    ---------------------------------------
    CZ7         <00>   UNIQUE   Registered
    CONTOSO     <00>   GROUP    Registered
    CZ7         <03>   UNIQUE   Registered
    CZ7$        <03>   UNIQUE   Registered
    CZ7         <20>   UNIQUE   Registered
    CONTOSO     <1E>   GROUP    Registered
    MLEE        <03>   UNIQUE   Registered
```

The NetBIOS name you assigned during the operating system installation (which in this case is CZ7) appears three times, with three different resource identifiers, 00, 03, and 20, in angle brackets following the name. The 00 identifier represents the Workstation service running on the computer, which enables you to access shared resources on other Windows systems, and the 20 identifier represents the Server service, which enables the computer to share its own resources. The 03 identifier represents the Windows Messenger service, which provides communications between computers on the network. Of the other entries, the name CONTOSO is the NetBIOS equivalent of the domain to which the computer belongs (notice that these two entries use group and not unique names), and MLEE is the name of the user logged on to the domain.

As with any other mechanism used to identify computers on the network, the NetBIOS name assigned to a computer must be unique. However, when you compare NetBIOS names with DNS names or with IP addresses, it's clear that the NetBIOS names are far less complex. This is because the NetBIOS name space consists of only a single level; there are no separate domain and host names, as in a DNS name. Because the NetBIOS name space is flat (as opposed to being hierarchical), only one computer on the network can use a particular name. In a hierarchical name space like that of DNS, it is possible for two hosts to have the same name as long as they are in different domains. This limitation of the NetBIOS name space limits its usefulness to a relatively small network, but the DNS is almost infinitely scalable.

Registering and Resolving Names

As it was originally used with NetBEUI, the NetBIOS name space was a suitable solution for a small local area network (LAN), but it could never support the large enterprise internetworks of today. Using the NetBIOS name space with TCP/IP instead of NetBEUI provides the scalability inherent in the hierarchical addressing system of the Internet Protocol. Ultimately, the relationship between NetBIOS names and IP addresses is similar to that between DNS names and IP addresses. NetBIOS provides users with friendly names for the computers on the network, but before any application layer communication between systems can begin, the names must be resolved into the IP addresses needed for TCP/IP communications.

Two basic functions are involved in the use of NetBIOS names with TCP/IP—name registration and name resolution. As with DNS, *name resolution* is the process by which a computer uses a name to discover the IP address associated with that name. The NetBIOS name resolution mechanism on a Windows network can take the form of a lookup table or a communications process. *Name registration* is the process that enables a computer to use a particular name, either by adding it to a lookup table or by ensuring that no other computer is using that name, or both.

Because NetBIOS names are limited in scale compared to DNS names, there are more NetBIOS name resolution mechanisms that computers running Windows operating systems can use than there are DNS name resolution mechanisms, and each name resolution mechanism has its own form of name registration. These NetBIOS name resolution mechanisms are as follows, and are discussed in detail in the remainder of this lesson and in the next one:

- NetBIOS name caching
- Lmhosts files
- Broadcast transmissions
- WINS
- DNS and Hosts files

NetBIOS Name Caching

DNS name servers maintain a cache in which they store information about recently resolved names. With NetBIOS, it is the individual computer that caches name resolution data. Every computer running the Windows operating system that uses NetBIOS maintains a NetBIOS name cache in memory that contains the names it has recently resolved (by any means) and their related IP addresses. Entries remain in the NetBIOS name cache for a relatively short period of time (10 minutes for Windows 2000, by default), but because it is accessed from memory, the cache is the fastest NetBIOS name resolution mechanism by far. No matter what other mechanism the computer is configured to use, it always checks the cache first to see if the requested name is present. This prevents a client computer from having to repeatedly resolve the same name to perform an extended transaction with another system.

To view the current contents of the NetBIOS name cache, you can use the Windows 2000 Nbtstat.exe command-line utility with the –c switch to produce a display like the following:

```
Node IpAddress: [192.168.2.5]   Scope Id: []
                   NetBIOS Remote Cache Name Table

    Name            Type        Host Address        Life [sec]
    ---------------------------------------------------------
    CZ3     <20>  UNIQUE        192.168.2.3         360
    CZ1     <20>  UNIQUE        192.168.2.10        360
    CZ1     <00>  UNIQUE        192.168.2.10        360
    CZ1     <03>  UNIQUE        192.168.2.10        360
```

Name registration for the cache is, for the most part, automatic. Resolving a NetBIOS name by any means causes the name and its IP address to be added to the cache for later use. When the entry's lifetime is expired, it is automatically removed from the cache.

Cache name registration is not limited to the automatic process, however. It is possible to manually load the NetBIOS name cache using specially tagged entries in an Lmhosts file (as described in the next section). When you preload the cache from an Lmhosts file, the entries you create do not have a limited life like the automatically created ones. You can therefore accelerate the name resolution process permanently for certain systems by loading the cache in this manner.

Unlike the other NetBIOS name resolution mechanisms included with Windows, the user cannot control cache name resolution. A computer running the Windows operating system using NetBIOS always checks the name cache before using any other form of name resolution.

Using Lmhosts

The Lmhosts file is the NetBIOS equivalent of the Hosts file sometimes used by DNS clients (and used by all TCP/IP systems before the introduction of DNS). As with Hosts, Lmhosts is a lookup table stored on a local drive that contains a list of names and their equivalent IP addresses. The differences between Lmhosts and Hosts are that Lmhosts is for NetBIOS names and not host names and that Lmhosts includes a number of optional tags that perform other functions.

In the days before WINS, the main function of the Lmhosts file was to provide name resolution for computers on different LANs in cases where broadcast transmissions were used as the primary NetBIOS name resolution mechanism. Because the broadcast method can resolve only the names of computers on the local network, an Lmhosts file containing the names and addresses of key servers on other networks was needed to resolve their names. Today, WINS is the preferred internetwork name resolution mechanism, and Lmhosts is used less often. However, you can still use Lmhosts as a fallback when WINS and other name resolution mechanisms fail.

In addition to its ability to resolve the NetBIOS names of computers anywhere on an internetwork, the other advantage of Lmhosts is that the file is stored locally and requires no network communications of any kind to resolve a name. This makes the name resolution process faster than that of any other mechanism except for the NetBIOS name cache (which is stored in memory). The disadvantage of Lmhosts, as with Hosts, is that the name registration process is manual; you must create the individual name/address entries in the file on every computer that requires them.

Implementing Lmhosts

The format of a standard Lmhosts entry is the same as that of a Hosts entry: the IP address comes first, followed by the NetBIOS name, separated by at least one space, as in the following example:

```
102.54.94.97       rhino

102.54.94.123      popular

102.54.94.117      localsrv
```

The use of an Lmhosts file for name resolution is optional on all computers running a Windows operating system. In Windows 2000, you enable the use of Lmhosts by executing the following procedure:

1. Click Start, point to Settings, and select Network And Dial-up Connections to open the Network And Dial-up Connections window.
2. Select the Local Area Connection icon and select Properties from the File menu to open the Local Area Connection Properties dialog box (see Figure 9.1).

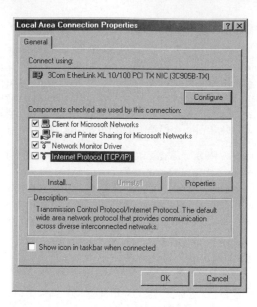

Figure 9.1   The Local Area Connection Properties dialog box

3. On the General tab, select Internet Protocol (TCP/IP) in the components list and click Properties to open the Internet Protocol (TCP/IP) Properties dialog box (see Figure 9.2).

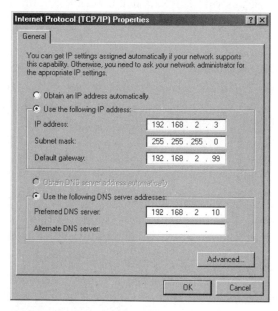

Figure 9.2   The Internet Protocol (TCP/IP) Properties dialog box

4. Click Advanced to open the Advanced TCP/IP Settings dialog box (see Figure 9.3).

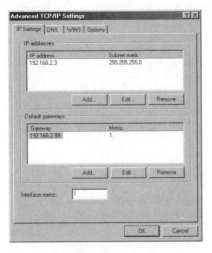

Figure 9.3   The Advanced TCP/IP Settings dialog box

5. Click the WINS tab to display the dialog box shown in Figure 9.4.

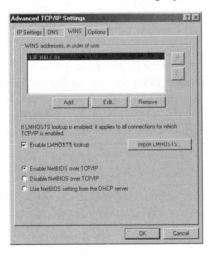

Figure 9.4   The WINS tab of the Advanced TCP/IP Settings dialog box

6. Select the Enable LMHOSTS Lookup check box. Click OK three times to close the dialog boxes you opened.

Enabling the use of the Lmhosts file in this way causes Windows to use it to resolve NetBIOS names when the other name resolution mechanisms have failed.

An additional feature in the WINS tab of the Advanced TCP/IP Settings dialog box makes the deployment of Lmhosts files on a network easier. By clicking the Import LMHOSTS button, you can browse to the location of an Lmhosts file on a network drive and import its information into the computer's own Lmhosts file. This enables you to maintain one file in a central location and use it to update all the computers on your network.

Note   You can click the Disable NetBIOS Over TCP/IP option button to completely disable NetBIOS on the computer, but you should do this only if you are running a network that consists only of Windows 2000 systems.

Using Lmhosts Tags

In addition to simple name and IP address listings, an Lmhosts file can also contain specially tagged entries that perform other functions, such as preloading the NetBIOS name cache. The tags, in most cases, appear after the IP address and NetBIOS name of a standard Lmhosts entry, and are preceded by a pound (#) symbol. The various Lmhosts tags and their functions are as follows:

- **#PRE.**   Part of a NetBIOS name–to–IP-address mapping entry that causes that entry to be preloaded into the NetBIOS name cache, as in the following example: (By default, entries are not preloaded into the name cache but are parsed only after WINS and name query broadcasts fail to resolve a name.)

  ```
  192.168.94.97      rhino          #PRE
  ```

- **#DOM:*domain*.**   Part of a NetBIOS name–to–IP-address mapping entry that indicates that the IP address belongs to a domain controller in the domain specified by *domain*. This keyword affects how the Browser and Logon services behave in a routed TCP/IP environment on a pre–Windows 2000 domain network. To preload a #DOM entry, the #PRE tag must precede the #DOM tag, as in the following example:

  ```
  192.168.94.97      rhino          #PRE #DOM:networking
  ```

- **#INCLUDE *filename*.**   Forces the system to seek the file specified by the *filename* variable and parse it as if it were local. Specifying a Universal Naming Convention (UNC) *filename* value enables you to use a centralized Lmhosts file on a server, as in the following example: (If the server on which the specified file name exists is located on another LAN, you must add a preloaded entry for the server (using the #PRE tag) before the #INCLUDE entry.)

  ```
  #INCLUDE \\rhino\public\lmhosts
  ```

- **#BEGIN_ALTERNATE.**   Used to group multiple #INCLUDE statements. Any single successful #INCLUDE statement falling between a #BEGIN_ALTERNATE and an #END_ALTERNATE tag causes the group to succeed.

- **#END_ALTERNATE.**　Used to mark the end of an #INCLUDE statement grouping, as in the following example:

```
#BEGIN_ALTERNATE
#INCLUDE \\rhino\public\lmhosts
#INCLUDE \\localsrv\public\lmhosts
#END_ALTERNATE
```

- **#0x*nn*.**　Provides support for nonprinting characters in NetBIOS names. Enclose the NetBIOS name in double quotation marks and use the notation \0x*nn*, where *nn* is the hexadecimal value for the nonprinting character. This enables custom applications that use special names to function properly in routed topologies. Note that the hexadecimal notation applies only to one character in the name. The name should be padded with blanks so that the special character appears as the sixteenth character in the string, as in the following example:

```
192.168.94.102   "appname  \0x14"
```

- **#MH.**　Part of a NetBIOS name–to–IP-address mapping entry that defines the entry as a unique name that can have more than one address. The maximum number of addresses that can be assigned to a unique name is 25. The number of entries is equal to the number of network interface adapters in a multihomed computer.

- **#SG:*name*.**　Part of a NetBIOS name–to–IP-address mapping entry that associates that entry with a user-defined special (Internet) group specified by *name*. The #SG keyword defines Internet groups by using a NetBIOS name that has 0x20 in the sixteenth byte. A special group is limited to 25 members.

Using Broadcast Transmissions

The original NetBIOS name resolution mechanism used by Windows involves the transmission of broadcast messages to the local network. NetBEUI networks use this method to discover the hardware addresses associated with specific NetBIOS names, and Windows TCP/IP networks not running WINS use it to resolve NetBIOS names into IP addresses. The process is similar to that of the Address Resolution Protocol (ARP) described in Lesson 1 of Chapter 2, "Introducing TCP/IP." A computer that needs information about a specific system on the network but is unable to address it directly generates a series of broadcast transmissions containing information about the target system that the computer does have. On receiving the broadcasts, the system possessing that information is then obligated to respond with a reply containing additional data.

In the case of NetBIOS name resolution, the messages involved use a format defined in the NetBT standards. The computer wanting to resolve a NetBIOS name generates a NAME QUERY REQUEST message containing the name to be resolved and broadcasts it in the local network. The message is packaged in a

User Datagram Protocol (UDP) packet and addressed to the well-known port number 137. Every computer running Windows on the network that is configured to use NetBIOS receives the broadcast transmissions and reads the NetBIOS name enclosed within them. If a computer detects its own NetBIOS name in the message, it replies to the sender with a POSITIVE NAME QUERY RESPONSE message containing its IP address, as shown in Figure 9.5. All the other computers that don't recognize the NetBIOS name in the NAME QUERY REQUEST message simply discard it.

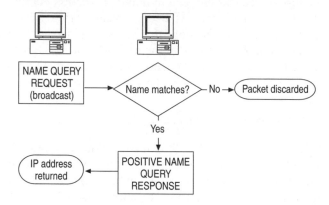

Figure 9.5   The NetBIOS broadcast name resolution process

Computers running Windows operating systems that use broadcast transmissions for NetBIOS name resolution also use a similar method for name registration. In this case, because there is no central table of NetBIOS names, the purpose of the name registration process is simply to ensure that no two computers on the same network are using the same NetBIOS name. The name registration procedure occurs each time a computer using NetBIOS starts on the network. The process begins with the computer generating a NAME REGISTRATION REQUEST message containing its own NetBIOS name and broadcasting it over the network three times, at 250 millisecond intervals. The computers receiving the broadcasts process them in the same way that they do NAME QUERY REQUESTS. If a computer recognizes its own NetBIOS name in a NAME REGISTRATION REQUEST message, it responds by transmitting a NEGATIVE NAME REGISTRATION RESPONSE to the original computer as a unicast. This message denies the name registration and causes the computer to prompt the user for a different NetBIOS name (see Figure 9.6).

When the computer trying to register its name receives no responses to its broadcasts, it generates a NAME OVERWRITE DEMAND message and broadcasts it over the network. This is the computer declaring in effect that it is taking possession of the name. No replies to this message are expected.

The broadcast transmission method is a simple but effective name resolution mechanism that is well suited to small network installations. However, it suffers from several important drawbacks. The primary disadvantage of broadcast name resolution is that broadcast transmissions are limited to the local network, making it impossible for a computer to resolve the names of computers on other networks using this method. As mentioned earlier, it is possible to use an Lmhosts file to resolve the names of computers on other networks when the broadcast method fails, but the maintenance of the Lmhosts tables can increase the administration overhead of the network significantly.

Another significant drawback of broadcast name resolution is the resources it consumes. Broadcasts are inherently inefficient, and NetBT broadcasts particularly so. Every NAME REGISTRATION REQUEST and NAME QUERY REQUEST transmitted by a NetBIOS client must be processed by every computer on the network. The data-link layer protocol on each computer receives the packet and passes it up through the protocol stack all the way to the NetBIOS interface, where the system then decides whether to respond to the message or discard it. The majority of the broadcast messages are discarded by each computer, meaning that the bandwidth and CPU time used to process them is wasted.

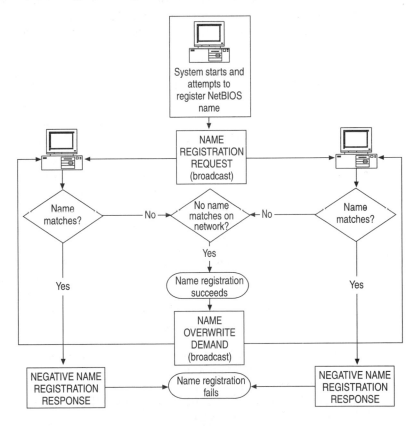

Figure 9.6 The NetBIOS broadcast name registration process

Using NetBIOS Name Servers

The solution to the limitations of the broadcast and Lmhosts NetBIOS name resolution mechanisms is the use of a NetBIOS name server (NBNS), as defined in the NetBT standards. WINS is the NBNS included with the Windows server operating systems. A NetBIOS name server automatically registers the NetBIOS names and IP addresses of all the computers on the network (which eliminates the need for manual name registration) as Lmhosts. NetBIOS name servers also use unicast transmissions for all their communications, which eliminates the traffic and processing problems of broadcast name resolution. You will learn more about NetBIOS name servers and WINS in Lesson 2 of this chapter.

Understanding NetBIOS Node Types

All the Windows name resolution mechanisms have their advantages and disadvantages, but you are not limited to using only one of them. The NetBT standards define a series of node types, each of which consists of a number of NetBIOS name resolution mechanisms that the computer uses in a particular order. The idea is for each mechanism to act as a fallback for its predecessor, providing the system with every opportunity to resolve a specific name.

The three node types defined in the NetBT standards are as follows:

- **B node (broadcast node).**   Calls for the use of the broadcast method for NetBIOS name registration and resolution exclusively.

- **P node (point-to-point node).**   Calls for the use of NetBIOS name servers (that is, WINS servers) for NetBIOS name registration and resolution exclusively.

- **M node (mixed mode node).**   Calls for the exclusive use of the broadcast method for name registration. For NetBIOS name resolution, this type of node uses broadcasts first, and if the broadcast method fails to resolve a name, uses a NetBIOS name server.

Microsoft Node Types

When Microsoft designed WINS to function as a NetBIOS name server, it became clear that these three node types were inadequate. The b node and p node types had no fallbacks, and the m node type is designed to use an NBNS only for resolving names of computers on other networks. To address these shortcomings, Microsoft developed its own additional node types, which are as follows:

- **Modified b node.**   Calls for the exclusive use of the broadcast method for name registration. For name resolution, this type of node uses broadcasts first and the Lmhosts file if broadcasts fail to resolve a name. This is the default node type for a computer running the Windows operating system that is not configured to use WINS.

- **H node (hybrid node).**   Calls for the exclusive use of NetBIOS name servers for name registration. For name resolution, this type of node uses NetBIOS name servers first and the broadcast method if the NetBIOS name servers fail to resolve the name or are unavailable. The system then reverts to using the name servers as soon as they become available again. This is the default node type for a WINS-enabled client.

- **Microsoft-enhanced h node.**   The various Windows versions include options that can supplement an h node system with alternatives such as Lmhosts name resolution, Windows Sockets calls to a DNS server, and a Hosts file, all to be used if both WINS servers and broadcasts fail to resolve a name.

When a computer running Windows 2000 has all possible name resolution options enabled, the process of resolving the name proceeds as illustrated in Figure 9.7.

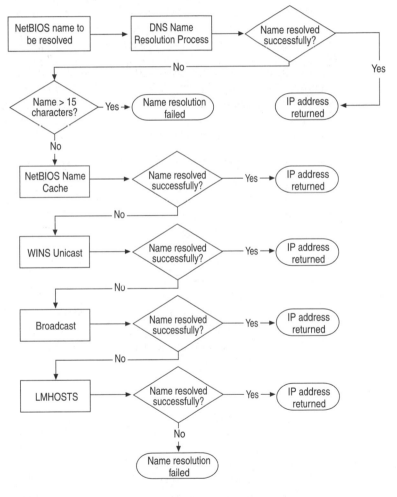

Figure 9.7   The Microsoft-enhanced h node NetBIOS name resolution process

Windows 2000 always attempts to perform a DNS name resolution first. If DNS fails to resolve a name and that name is more than 15 characters long, then the name resolution process is said to have failed. If the name has fewer than 15 characters, the NetBIOS name resolution process begins. In Windows NT, the process is slightly different. A Windows NT computer uses the length of the name to be resolved to determine whether it should perform a DNS or NetBIOS name resolution first.

Setting Node Types

In most cases where you use NetBIOS on a Windows 2000 network, you don't have to configure the node type of your computers directly. The act of specifying the IP addresses for WINS servers in the Internet Protocol (TCP/IP) Properties dialog box or supplying WINS server addresses using a Dynamic Host Configuration Protocol (DHCP) server converts a default b node system into an h node, and enabling Lmhosts as a fallback converts a b node into a modified b node and an h node into a Microsoft-enhanced h node.

However, it is possible to explicitly set the node type for a computer running a Windows operating system either manually, by modifying the registry, or by using DHCP. These are the only means of configuring a computer to use a non-standard node type, such as a p node or m node. To specify a node type by modifying the registry, you create a registry entry called NodeType in the following key:

```
HKEY_LOCAL_MACHINE\System\CurrentControlSet\Services\NetBT\Parameters
```

Then you assign one of the following REG_DWORD values to the new entry:

- 0x00000001 for b node
- 0x00000002 for p node
- 0x00000004 for m node
- 0x00000008 for h node

It is easier, however, to specify a node type by using DHCP. To do this, you set the WINS/NBT Node Type option (option 046). You must also set the WINS/NBNS Servers option (option 044) if the node type you specify requires WINS server addresses.

Exercise 1: NetBIOS Name Resolution Concepts

Match the terms in the left column with the appropriate descriptions in the right column.

1. M node

   a. Default name resolution mechanism for computers running the Windows operating system that are not configured to use WINS

2. NetBIOS name cache

   b. Uses broadcast name resolution, with WINS as a fallback

3. Broadcast name resolution

   c. Fallback name resolution mechanism for a modified b node computer

4. H node

   d. First non-DNS name resolution mechanism used by all computers running the Windows operating system

5. Lmhosts

   e. Uses WINS name resolution, with broadcasts as a fallback

Lesson Review

1. What is the function of a WINS server?

   a. To convert IP addresses into hardware addresses

   b. To convert host names into IP addresses

   c. To convert IP addresses into host names

   d. To convert NetBIOS names into IP addresses

2. You are the administrator of a Windows NT network that uses the broadcast method for NetBIOS name resolution, with a centrally located Lmhosts file as a fallback, for the resolution of server names on other networks. When the primary domain controller (Server1) for the Sales domain on your network malfunctions, you decide to promote one of your backup domain controllers (Server3) to primary domain controller (PDC) status. In addition to removing the entry for Server1 from the Lmhosts file, which of the following other entries should you add?

   a. 192.168.43.56 Server3 #DOM:Sales

   b. 192.168.43.56 Server3 #PRE #DOM:Sales

   c. 192.168.43.56 Server3 #DOMAIN:Sales

   d. 192.168.43.56 #PRE Server3 #DOM:Sales

3. Which of the following name resolution mechanisms can resolve only the names of computers on the local network?

    a. NetBIOS name cache

    b. Lmhosts

    c. Broadcast name resolution

    d. WINS

4. Which of the following is the fastest NetBIOS name resolution mechanism?

    a. NetBIOS name cache

    b. Lmhosts

    c. Broadcast name resolution

    d. WINS

5. Which of the following node types can use an Lmhosts file for NetBIOS name resolution?

    a. B node

    b. Modified b node

    c. M node

    d. H node

Lesson Summary

- Prior to Windows 2000, Windows networks used NetBIOS names to identify themselves on the network. Windows 2000 networks now use DNS.

- To use NetBIOS names on a TCP/IP network, a mechanism must be available to resolve NetBIOS names into IP addresses.

- Lmhosts is a lookup table stored on a computer's local drive that contains NetBIOS names and their appropriate IP addresses.

- Broadcast name resolution uses messages transmitted to all the computers on the local network to discover the one computer using a particular NetBIOS name.

- WINS is a NetBIOS name server that enables computers to resolve NetBIOS names using unicast instead of broadcast transmissions.

- The node type of a NetBIOS computer specifies the name resolution mechanisms it uses and the order in which it uses them.

Lesson 2: WINS Name Registration and Resolution

Although Windows 2000 does not use NetBIOS by default, the Windows 2000 Server operating systems still include the WINS service to support clients running earlier versions of Windows. WINS is a NetBIOS name server that provides name registration and resolution services for NetBIOS clients anywhere on a network, preventing them from having to use broadcast transmissions and eliminating the need for administrators to maintain Lmhosts files.

After this lesson, you will be able to

- Understand the difference between WINS messaging and broadcast messaging
- Describe the WINS name registration process
- Describe the WINS name resolution process
- Diagram the NetBT message format

Estimated lesson time: 20 minutes

Understanding WINS Messaging

WINS uses the same message formats as broadcast name resolution, but all the transmissions are unicasts, which means that only the WINS client and server expend processing resources during the name registration and resolution processes. Unicast transmissions are also not limited by network boundaries, meaning that one WINS server can service clients all over an internetwork. WINS also requires no configuration or administrative maintenance to perform its basic tasks. The result is that WINS is the most efficient of the NetBIOS name resolution mechanisms by far.

A WINS client can communicate with WINS servers using unicast transmissions because it is already configured with the IP addresses of one or more WINS servers as part of its TCP/IP configuration. You configure a WINS client either by manually specifying the WINS server addresses in the WINS tab of the Advanced TCP/IP Settings dialog box (as shown earlier in Figure 9.3) or by supplying them using DHCP. After the computer is configured to function as a WINS client, it can communicate directly with its designated WINS server.

WINS Name Registration

On a WINS network, every client configured with WINS server addresses performs a name registration procedure as the system starts. This procedure adds the client's NetBIOS name and IP address to the WINS server's database so that other computers on the network can resolve the name. The WINS server also checks the NetBIOS name against its database to ensure that no two computers on the network are using the same NetBIOS name.

The WINS name registration process is initiated by the client, which transmits a NAME REGISTRATION REQUEST message to the first address in its list of WINS servers. As stated earlier, the client sends this message as a unicast in a UDP packet addressed to port number 137. If the WINS server is available to process the message, it checks to see if another computer has already registered the client's NetBIOS name. If the name does not exist in the WINS database, the server adds a NetBIOS name–to–IP-address mapping to its database and returns a POSITIVE NAME REGISTRATION RESPONSE message to the client, also as a unicast. This response message includes a Time to Live (TTL) value, which is the amount of time that the NetBIOS name will stay registered to the client without being renewed.

One of the advantages of WINS over other types of name servers, such as DNS, is that a WINS client automatically updates the WINS server database whenever its IP address changes. For example, when you move a client computer to a different subnet and DHCP assigns it a new address, the WINS database is automatically updated with the new information.

When a WINS client attempts to register a name that is already in the WINS database, the WINS server performs a name challenge procedure to ensure that the name is actually still in use. If you move a computer to a different subnet and assign it a new IP address, its NetBIOS name might still be in the WINS database. The name challenge process enables WINS to recognize that these two NetBIOS name registrations belong to the same computer, despite the different IP address, and to remove the old record from the database.

The name challenge (illustrated in Figure 9.8) begins with the WINS server transmitting a series of NAME QUERY REQUEST messages to the currently registered owner of the NetBIOS name, using the IP addresses in the existing database record. If the name's current owner responds to the server with a POSITIVE NAME QUERY RESPONSE message, the server sends a NEGATIVE NAME REGISTRATION RESPONSE message to the new applicant, denying the name registration and forcing the user at the client computer to choose a new NetBIOS name. If the WINS server does not receive a response after transmitting three NAME QUERY REQUEST messages at 500-millisecond intervals, or if the currently registered name owner responds with a NEGATIVE NAME QUERY RESPONSE message, indicating that it is no longer using the name, the server purges the name from its database and assigns it to the new client.

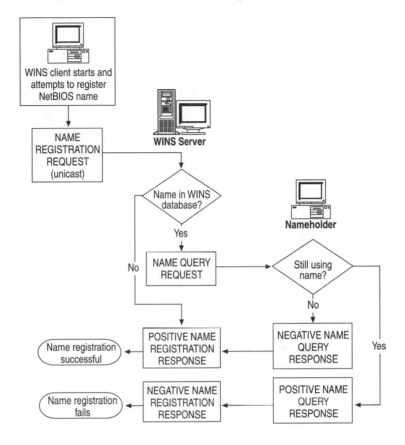

Figure 9.8   The WINS name challenge process

WINS Name Renewal

To prevent leaving obsolete information in the database, WINS servers register all NetBIOS names for a specified interval, the TTL, which is six days by default. This way, other computers can use the same name later if the original owner stops using it. Because WINS NetBIOS name registrations are temporary, the WINS clients must periodically renew their names or the leases will expire.

Each time a WINS client computer restarts and registers its name with the WINS server, the TTL interval is reset. If the client remains logged on to the network continuously for half of the TTL interval (three days, by default), it begins transmitting NAME REFRESH REQUEST messages to the WINS server. The server then replies with a POSITIVE NAME REFRESH RESPONSE message, which resets the TTL timer, or with a NEGATIVE NAME REFRESH RESPONSE message, which cancels the name registration and forces the client to register a different NetBIOS name.

If the client receives no response from the server, it repeats its request every two minutes until half of the remaining TTL interval has passed. The client then switches to the second WINS server specified in its configuration and transmits the same NAME REFRESH REQUEST messages. Once again, if the client receives no response, it retransmits every two minutes until half of the remaining TTL interval has expired. The renewal process continues in this way, switching WINS servers every time the client reaches half of the remaining TTL value. If the TTL period expires without the client receiving a response from a WINS server, the client reverts to broadcast name registration.

WINS Name Release

As part of a WINS client's system shutdown sequence, the computer transmits a NAME RELEASE REQUEST message to the WINS server, indicating that it is no longer using its registered NetBIOS name. This enables the WINS server to reassign the name to another client that might attempt to register it. The server responds to the request with either a POSITIVE NAME RELEASE RESPONSE message, indicating that the server has successfully released the name, or a NEGATIVE NAME RELEASE RESPONSE message, which only occurs when the record for the NetBIOS name contains a different IP address than that of the computer sending the message.

WINS Name Resolution

The WINS name resolution process (as illustrated in Figure 9.9) enables WINS clients to retrieve the IP addresses associated with NetBIOS names far more efficiently than the broadcast name resolution mechanism. As always, when a WINS client initiates the process of communicating with another NetBIOS computer, it first checks its NetBIOS name cache to see if there is an entry for the desired name. If the client cannot resolve the name from its cache, it transmits a NAME QUERY REQUEST message to its primary WINS server. The WINS server searches its database for a NetBIOS name–to–IP-address mapping for the name specified in the query and returns the IP address to the WINS client in a POSITIVE NAME QUERY RESPONSE message. If the requested name does not exist in the WINS database, the server transmits a NEGATIVE NAME QUERY RESPONSE back to the client.

If the WINS server experiences a delay in responding to the client's request, it might send a series of WAIT FOR ACKNOWLEDGEMENT RESPONSE (WACK) messages to prevent the client from timing out. If the client receives no response at all from the WINS server after a given amount of time, it switches to the next WINS server address that it is configured to use (if there is one) and transmits another series of NAME QUERY REQUEST messages. This process is repeated until the client has sent messages to all the configured WINS servers (up to 12, in the case of Windows 2000). If there is still no response, or if any of the servers transmits a NEGATIVE NAME QUERY RESPONSE message, the client switches to an alternate NetBIOS name resolution mechanism, such as broadcast query messages, as defined by its node type. If there is no alternative name resolution method, the name resolution process is said to have failed.

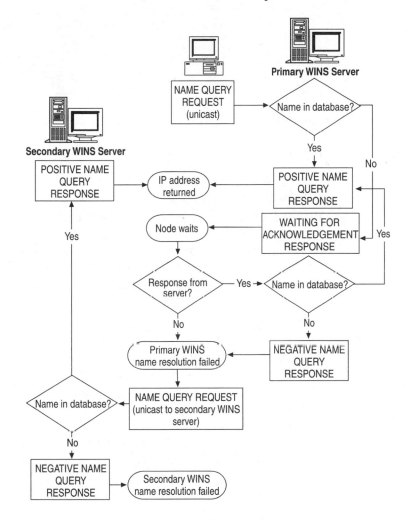

Figure 9.9   The WINS name resolution process

Understanding the NetBT Message Formats

The NetBT messages used in WINS communications are derived from the DNS packet format, with additional types and codes added to support NetBIOS functions. As with DNS, the message consists of a header and four sections called Question, Answer, Authority, and Additional. WINS uses only the header and the Question and Answer sections, however.

The Header Section

The format of the NetBT message header is illustrated in Figure 9.10.

NAME_TRN_ID		OPCODE	NM_FLAGS	RCODE
QDCOUNT		ANCOUNT		
NSCOUNT		ARCOUNT		

Figure 9.10   The NetBT message header format

The functions of the fields are as follows:

- **NAME_TRN_ID (2 bytes).**   Contains a transaction identifier that computers use to match request messages with responses.

- **OPCODE (5 bits).**   The first bit of the OPCODE field is the R flag, which specifies whether the message is a request or a response. The remaining four bits specify the type of message contained in the packet, using values representing the following types: query, registration, release, WACK, or refresh.

- **NM_FLAGS (7 bits).**   Contains seven one-bit flags with the following functions:

  - **Bit 1—AA (Authoritative Answer).**   Specifies whether a response message contains information furnished by an authoritative source. In request messages (where the R flag in the OPCODE field is 0), the value of this flag is always 0. WINS servers always set the value of this flag to 1.

  - **Bit 2—TC (Truncation).**   Specifies whether the message had to be truncated to fit into a UDP datagram; serves as a signal to retransmit using TCP. Because packet length is not a problem in NetBIOS Name Service messaging, the value of this flag is always 0.

  - **Bit 3—RD (Recursion Desired).**   Used in request messages to obtain information about the NetBIOS name server's recursive capabilities. Windows clients always set this flag to a value of 1, indicating that recursion is desired.

  - **Bit 4—RA (Recursion Available).**   Used in response messages to indicate that the NetBIOS name server supports recursive queries, registrations, and releases. For most types of messages (WACK messages are the exception), WINS servers set this value to 1, indicating that recursion is available.

  - **Bit 5.**   Unused.

  - **Bit 6.**   Unused.

  - **Bit 7—B (Broadcast).**   Specifies whether the packet was broadcast or unicast. In WINS messaging, the value of this bit is always 0, indicating unicast messaging. The messages used in broadcast name registration and resolution always have a value of 1 for this bit.

- **RCODE (4 bits).**   Used in response packets to specify the results of a particular request, using the following codes:
  - **0.**   No Error
  - **1—FMT_ERR.**   Format Error (the request was formatted incorrectly)
  - **2—SRV_ERR.**   Server Failure (the request could not be processed because of a malfunction of the NetBIOS name server)
  - **3—NAM_ERR.**   Name Error (the requested name does not exist in the name server)
  - **4—IMP_ERR.**   Unsupported Request Error (used only when a NetBIOS name server is challenged by an update type registration request)
  - **5—RFS_ERR.**   Refused Error (policy prevents the server from registering the requested name to this host)
  - **6—ACT_ERR.**   Active Error (the requested name is already registered to another node)
  - **7—CFT_ERR.**   Name in Conflict Error (a unique NetBIOS name is already owned by another node)
- **QDCOUNT (2 bytes).**   Specifies the number of entries in the Question section of the message. NetBT messages always contain only one entry in the Question section.
- **ANCOUNT (2 bytes).**   Specifies the number of resource records in the Answer section of the message. NetBT messages always contain only one entry in the Answer section.
- **NSCOUNT (2 bytes).**   Specifies the number of resource records in the Authority section of the message. The Authority section is not used in NetBT messages.
- **NRCOUNT (2 bytes).**   Specifies the number of resource records in the Additional section of the message. The Additional section is not used in NetBT messages.

By examining the values of the header fields in a NetBT message, you can determine its function. For example, when a message has a value of 0 for its R flag, indicating that it is a request message, a value of 0 for its OPCODE field, indicating that it is a query message, a B flag value of 0, indicating that it is a unicast message, and a QDCOUNT value of 1, indicating that there is one entry in the Question section, you can deduce that the message is a NAME QUERY REQUEST directed at a WINS server. A POSITIVE NAME QUERY RESPONSE from the WINS server back to the client would change the R flag value to 1, the QDCOUNT value to 0, and the ANCOUNT value to 1, indicating that the message is a response containing one entry in the Answer section. A NEGATIVE NAME QUERY RESPONSE would have a value of 0 in both the QDCOUNT and ANCOUNT fields and an RCODE value of 3, indicating that the name resolution attempt failed because the requested name did not exist in the WINS database.

The Question Section

The Question section of a NetBT message typically contains a NetBIOS name to be registered or resolved. Only the following message types contain information in the Question section:

- NAME REGISTRATION REQUEST
- NAME REFRESH REQUEST
- NAME RELEASE REQUEST
- NAME OVERWRITE DEMAND
- NAME QUERY REQUEST

When the Question section contains information, the value of the QDCOUNT field in the header is set to 1, and three additional fields appear immediately after the header. The format of the Question section is shown in Figure 9.11.

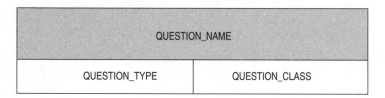

Figure 9.11   The NetBT message's Question section format

The functions of the fields are as follows:

- **QUESTION_NAME (variable).**   Contains the NetBIOS name that the message is intended to register or resolve.
- **QUESTION_TYPE (2 bytes).**   Contains a code that specifies the type of request in the message. The most common value for a WINS messages 0x0020, indicating that the message is a request for a NetBIOS Name Service resource record.
- **QUESTION_CLASS (2 bytes).**   Contains a code that specifies the class of the request, for which only one possible value exists: 0x0001, indicating the Internet class.

The Answer Section

As with DNS, a NetBT message contains three sections that can carry the NetBIOS equivalent of a DNS resource record: the Answer, Authority, and Additional sections. However, NetBT messages on a Windows network never need to carry more than one resource record, so they only use the Answer section, and the maximum possible value of the header's ANCOUNT field is 1.

The only NetBT messages that contain information in the Answer section are the positive response and WACK messages, as follows:

- POSITIVE NAME REGISTRATION RESPONSE
- POSITIVE NAME QUERY RESPONSE
- POSITIVE NAME REFRESH RESPONSE
- POSITIVE NAME RELEASE RESPONSE
- WAIT FOR ACKNOWLEDGEMENT RESPONSE

A NetBT message containing an Answer section includes the resource record fields illustrated in Figure 9.12, which immediately follow the message header.

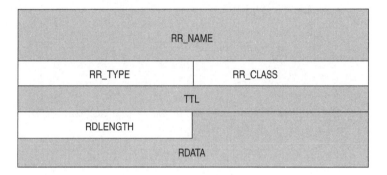

Figure 9.12   The NetBT message's Answer section format

The functions of the fields in the Answer section are as follows:

- **RR_NAME (variable).**   Contains the NetBIOS name from the QUESTION_NAME field in the request message to which this is the response.
- **RR_TYPE (2 bytes).**   Contains a code that specifies the type of resource record in the Answer section. The most common value on a WINS network is 0x0020, indicating that the message contains a NetBIOS name service resource record.
- **RR_CLASS (2 bytes).**   Contains a code that specifies the class of the resource record in the Answer section, for which only one possible value exists: 0x0001, indicating the Internet class.
- **TTL (4 bytes).**   Specifies the Time to Live for the information in the resource record.
- **RDLENGTH (2 bytes).**   Specifies the number of bytes in the RDATA field.

- **RDATA (variable).** Contains the IP address of the system with which the NetBIOS name in the RR_NAME field is associated. When the RR_TYPE field contains the code indicating the presence of a NetBIOS name service resource record (as WINS server responses do), the RDATA field begins with 16 NB_FLAGS bits, broken down as follows:
  - **Bit 1—G (Group Name Flag).** Specifies whether the name supplied in the RR_NAME field is a unique or group NetBIOS name
  - **Bits 2–3—ONT (Owner Node Type).** Specifies the node type of the system identified in the RR_NAME field
  - **Bits 4–16.** Unused

Lesson Review

1. List two reasons why WINS is an improvement over the broadcast name resolution method.

2. What is the name of the property that determines when a WINS client should renew its name registration?

3. When does a WINS name release occur?

Lesson Summary

- Windows Internet Name Service (WINS) is a Network Basic Input/Output System (NetBIOS) name server application that can provide NetBIOS name registration and resolution services for an entire Windows network.

- WINS is an improvement over broadcast name resolution because it uses only unicast transmissions, which reduces the amount of network traffic generated by the name resolution process.

- During the WINS name registration process, a client supplies its name to a WINS server to ensure that it is not already in use.

- WINS clients register their names for a given period of time, after which they have to either renew the name or lose the registration.

- WINS messages use the same basic format as DNS messages, with additional types and codes specific to NetBIOS functions.

Lesson 3: Implementing WINS

If your network consists solely of Windows 2000 computers and you are using the Active Directory service, you have no need for NetBIOS names or WINS. In fact, you can disable NetBIOS on all your Windows 2000 computers to eliminate the overhead needed to maintain NetBIOS compatibility. However, if you have computers running earlier versions of Windows or other operating systems that use the NetBIOS name space, you should leave NetBIOS enabled on the Windows 2000 computers, and you can benefit from having at least one WINS server on your network.

After this lesson, you will be able to

- Install a WINS server
- Configure a TCP/IP client to use WINS
- Create a static mapping
- Configure a WINS proxy agent

Estimated lesson time: 30 minutes

Installing a WINS Server

WINS is supplied with the Windows 2000 Server operating system, but it is not installed by default. You can opt to install WINS with the operating system, or you can install it separately later, using the Add/Remove Programs Control Panel. Although a WINS server requires a computer running Windows 2000 Server, the server does not have to be a domain controller. In addition, the server must be configured with a static IP address, subnet mask, and default gateway. Do not use DHCP to configure the TCP/IP configuration parameters for a WINS server.

To install the WINS service, use the following procedure:

1. On a computer running Windows 2000 Server, log on as Administrator.
2. Click Start, point to Settings, and click Control Panel.
3. Double-click the Add/Remove Programs icon, and then click Add/Remove Windows Components (see Figure 9.13) to activate the Windows Components Wizard.
4. In the Components list, scroll down to select Networking Services.
5. Click Details to open the Networking Services dialog box.

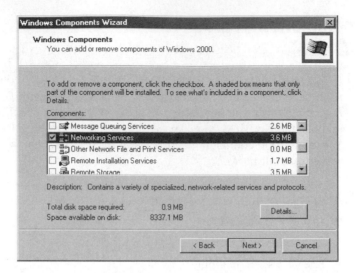

Figure 9.13   The Windows Components page of the Windows Components Wizard

6. In the Subcomponents Of Networking Services list, shown in Figure 9.14, select the Windows Internet Name Service (WINS) check box.

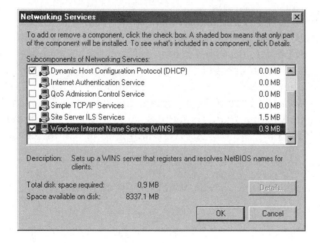

Figure 9.14   The Subcomponents Of Networking Services list in the Networking Services dialog box

7. Click OK, and then click Next. If prompted, type the full path to the Windows 2000 distribution files and click Continue. Required files are copied to your hard disk.

8. Click Finish to close the Windows Components Wizard.

Note   After you install the WINS Service on the computer running Windows 2000 Server, you should configure the server to function as a WINS client (as described later in this lesson), with itself as the WINS server.

When you install WINS on a computer running Windows 2000, the WINS snap-in, as shown in Figure 9.15, is added to the Administrative Tools program group. The WINS snap-in provides access to detailed information about the WINS servers on a network and enables you to view the contents of the WINS database, search for specific entries, and perform all WINS management and configuration tasks. You can access the WINS snap-in as a stand-alone Microsoft Management Console (MMC) or through the Computer Management console, under Services And Applications.

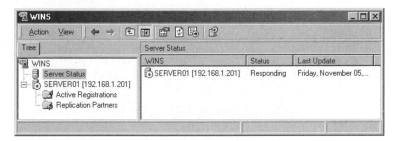

Figure 9.15   The WINS snap-in

Configuring a Windows 2000 WINS Client

Although Windows 2000 does not need WINS to access other Windows 2000 resources on the network, it does need it to access resources on computers running earlier versions of Windows. You must also configure the WINS server itself to be a WINS client.

To configure a Windows 2000 computer to function as a WINS client, use the following procedure:

1. Log on as Administrator.
2. Click Start, point to Settings, and click Networking And Dial-Up Connections.
3. Right-click the Local Area Connection icon and from the pop-up menu, choose Properties to display the Local Area Connection Properties dialog box.
4. Select Internet Protocol (TCP/IP) and click Properties to display the Internet Protocol (TCP/IP) Properties dialog box.
5. Click Advanced to display the Advanced TCP/IP Settings dialog box and then click the WINS tab.

6. Click Add to display the TCP/IP WINS Server dialog box, shown in Figure 9.16.

Figure 9.16   The TCP/IP WINS Server dialog box

7. Type the IP address of a WINS server on your network in the WINS Server text box and click Add.

8. Repeat steps 6 and 7 to add other WINS servers to the configuration, if desired. The Windows 2000 WINS client can support up to 12 server addresses.

9. Click OK to close the Advanced TCP/IP Settings dialog box.

10. Click OK to close the Internet Protocol (TCP/IP) Properties dialog box.

11. Click OK to close the Local Area Connection Properties dialog box.

Supporting Non-WINS Clients

In a WINS environment, you can provide support for non-WINS clients in two ways: by using static mappings and by configuring a WINS proxy agent, as described in the following sections.

Using Static Mappings

On a network that includes NetBIOS computers that are not WINS clients, you can configure a static NetBIOS name–to–IP-address mapping for each non-WINS client. This ensures that WINS clients can resolve the NetBIOS names of the non-WINS computers.

Note   If you have DHCP clients that require static mappings, you must create IP address reservations for them on the DHCP server so that their IP addresses are always the same.

To configure a static mapping for a non-WINS client, use the following procedure:

1. Click Start and from the Administrative Tools program group, open the WINS console.

2. Expand the icon for your WINS server and select Active Registrations.

3. From the Action menu, select New Static Mapping to display the New Static Mapping dialog box, as shown in Figure 9.17.

4. Type the NetBIOS name of the computer you want to create a mapping for in the Computer Name text box.

Figure 9.17   The New Static Mapping dialog box

5. Select the type of mapping you want to create in the Type drop-down list. The available options are as follows:

- **Unique.**   A unique name that maps to a single IP address.

- **Group.**   A name that maps to a group. When adding an entry to a group using the WINS snap-in, enter the computer name and IP address. The IP addresses of group members are not stored in the WINS database, so there is no limit to the number of members you can add.

- **Domain Name.**   A NetBIOS name–to–IP-address mapping with 0x1C as the sixteenth byte. A domain group stores up to 25 addresses for members. For registrations after the address limit has been reached, WINS overwrites a replica address or, if none is present, the oldest registration.

- **Internet Group.**   User-defined groups that you use to group resources, such as printers, for reference and browsing. An Internet group can store up to 25 addresses for members. A dynamic member, however, does not replace a static member that you add by using the WINS snap-in or by importing the Lmhosts file.

- **Multihomed.**   A unique name that can have more than one address. Use this option for computers with multiple network adapter cards. You can register up to 25 multihomed addresses. For registrations after the address limit has been reached, WINS overwrites a replica address or, if none is present, it overwrites the oldest registration.

6. Type the IP address that you want to map to the NetBIOS name you selected in the IP Address text box.

7. Click OK to create the static mapping.

Note The WINS snap-in adds a static mapping to the WINS database when you click OK. If you enter incorrect information for a static mapping, you must delete that mapping and then create a new one.

Configuring a WINS Proxy Agent

A WINS proxy agent extends the name resolution capabilities of the WINS server to non-WINS clients by listening for broadcast name registration and name resolution requests and then forwarding them to a WINS server. When a non-WINS client broadcasts a NAME REGISTRATION REQUEST message, the WINS proxy agent forwards the request to the WINS server to verify that no other WINS client has registered that name. The WINS server does not register the NetBIOS name, it only verifies it. When a WINS proxy agent detects a NAME QUERY REQUEST broadcast, it checks its NetBIOS name cache and attempts to resolve the name. If the name is not in the cache, the proxy agent sends the request to a WINS server. The WINS server then responds to the WINS proxy agent with the IP address for the requested NetBIOS name. The WINS proxy agent returns this information to the non-WINS client.

To configure a WINS proxy agent, edit the registry on a WINS client computer by setting the value for the EnableProxy entry to 1, and then restart the computer. The EnableProxy entry is located in the registry under the subkey HKEY_LOCAL_MACHINE\SYSTEM\CurrentControlSet\Services\NetBT\Parameters.

Maintaining the WINS Database

The WINS server included with Windows 2000 stores information about the computers on the network in a database. As with many databases, the process of adding and removing records can leave empty spaces that waste storage space. To eliminate this wasted space, you should periodically compact the WINS database using the Jetpack.exe utility included with Windows 2000.

To manually compact the WINS database, use the following procedure:

1. Open a Command Prompt window on the WINS server.

2. Change to the *systemroot*\System32\wins folder on the system drive.

3. Stop the WINS Server service by typing **net stop wins** at the command prompt.

4. Compact the database by typing **jetpack wins.mdb tmp.mdb** at the command prompt.

5. Restart the WINS Server service by typing **net start wins** at the command prompt.

6. Close the Command Prompt window.

The Jetpack.exe program compacts the database by writing all the records it contains to a temporary file called Tmp.mdb, deleting the original Wins.mdb file, and then renaming the temporary file back to the original file name.

You can also configure a Windows 2000 WINS server to back up its database whenever the service is stopped. To do this, use the following procedure:

1. Click Start and select WINS from the Administrative tools program group.

2. Select the WINS server in the scope pane and select Properties from the Action menu to display the server's Properties dialog box, as shown in Figure 9.18.

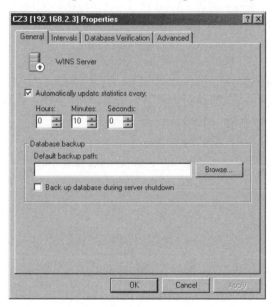

Figure 9.18   The Properties dialog box for a WINS server

3. On the General tab, type the path to the folder where you want the WINS server to back up its database in the Default Backup Path box.

4. Select the Back Up Database During Server Shutdown check box and click OK.

Exercise 1: Installing and Configuring WINS

In this exercise, you install WINS on your Windows 2000 server and then configure your DHCP server to provide a primary WINS server address to clients on the network.

▶ **Procedure 1: Installing WINS**

To install WINS on a Windows 2000 server, complete the following steps:

1. Log on to the server as Administrator.
2. Click Start, point to Settings, and then click Control Panel.
3. Double-click Add/Remove Programs to display the Add/Remove Programs dialog box.
4. Click Add/Remote Windows Components in the left pane to activate the Windows Components Wizard.
5. In the Components list, select Networking Services, but do not select or clear the check box to the left of this option.
6. Click Details to display the Networking Services dialog box.
7. In the Subcomponents Of Networking Services list, select the Windows Internet Name Service (WINS) check box.
8. Click OK to display the Windows Components page.
9. Click Next. The Configuring Components page makes the configuration changes you requested. A File Copy box appears as WINS files are copied into the operating system folders. Insert the Windows 2000 Server CD-ROM into the drive if you are prompted to do so. The Completing The Windows Components Wizard page appears.
10. Click Finish.
11. Close the Add/Remove Programs window.
12. Close Control Panel.

▶ **Procedure 2: Configuring DHCP to support WINS**

In this procedure, you configure the DHCP service to deliver a WINS server address to DHCP clients on the network. This procedure assumes that the DHCP service is already installed and configured with a scope on your server. To give you practice with setting server options, you use the server options node. You could also configure these settings as scope options if you want them to apply only to a specific scope.

1. Click Start and from the Administrative Tools program group, open the DHCP console.
2. In the scope pane, right-click the Server Options icon and from the pop-up menu, choose Configure Options to open the Server Options dialog box.

3. Scroll down to 044 WINS/NBNS Servers, and then select this check box.

4. In the Server Name text box, type the name of your WINS server, and then click Resolve. What happens?

5. Click Add.

6. In the Available Options list, scroll down to 046 WINS/NBT Node Type and select this check box.

7. In the Byte text box, type **8** so that the text box entry reads 0x8. The value 0x8 sets the node type to h node. What does this mean?

8. Click OK. What happens?

9. Close the DHCP console.

▶ **Procedure 3: Testing WINS settings (optional)**

In this procedure, you release and renew the DHCP lease on a client workstation. Then you load the WINS console on your server to verify the registration of the client in the WINS database.

1. On a Windows 2000 DHCP client workstation connected to the same network as your WINS/DHCP server, open a command prompt.

2. Type **ipconfig /release**, and then press ENTER. What happens?

3. Type **ipconfig /renew**, and then press ENTER. What happens?

4. Type **ipconfig /all | more**, and then press ENTER.

5. Press ENTER as necessary so that you can see the settings for *<adapter type>* adapter Local Area Connection.

6. Notice that Node Type is set to Hybrid. Hybrid is equivalent to h node. Also notice that the primary WINS server is set to the IP address of your WINS server.

7. Close the command prompt on the client.

8. On your WINS server, click Start, point to Programs, and from the Administrative Tools program group, select WINS to display the WINS snap-in.

9. Maximize the WINS snap-in.

10. Expand the icon for your WINS server and then click Active Registrations.

    From the Action menu, select Find By Name to display the Find By Name dialog box.

11. In the Find Names Beginning With text box, type the first three letters of the client computer's NetBIOS name and then click Find Now.

    Under Record Name, your client appears with three entries, which are the services that broadcast the client's name onto the network. The first entry, 00h, is the NetBIOS computer name. 03h is used for sending and receiving broadcast messages. 20h is used for share access by other computers on the network.

12. Close the WINS snap-in.

Lesson Review

1. You are the administrator of a network that consists of computers running a variety of operating systems, including Windows 2000 Server, Windows 2000 Professional, Windows 95, Windows 98, and OS/2 with Microsoft LAN Manager version 2.2c, all on the same subnet with a single WINS server. The OS/2 computers are running a NetBIOS application, and you want them to be able to use NetBIOS names to access the computers running Windows operating systems on the network, but OS/2 does not include a WINS client. What should you do to enable the applications on the OS/2 computers to resolve NetBIOS names using the WINS database?

    a. Install a DHCP relay agent on the network.

    b. Configure one of the other computers running Windows on the network to function as a proxy agent.

    c. Configure the OS/2 computer to function as a WINS proxy agent.

    d. Add static mappings for the OS/2 computers to the WINS database.

2. You are the administrator of a routed network with 6 Windows 2000 computers and 250 Window workstations on various subnets. After installing the WINS service on one of the Windows 2000 servers and configuring your DHCP server to supply the WINS server address to all your clients, you discover that the computers on the same subnet as the WINS server all function normally, but that the computers on the other subnets cannot access file and print services running on the computer running the WINS server. All other TCP/IP connectivity, such as Internet access, is not affected. What should you do?

    a. Install WINS proxy agents on the remote subnets.

    b. Configure the computers on the remote subnets to use DNS for name resolution instead of WINS.

    c. Enable dynamic updates on the WINS server.

    d. Configure the WINS server to use its own IP address as its WINS client address.

3. How do you manually compact the database on a Windows 2000 WINS server?

   a. Use the Compact command and specify the *systemroot*\System32\wins folder.

   b. Stop the WINS server. Run the Jetpack.exe utility with the name of the database file. Restart the WINS server.

   c. Back up the WINS database. Use Jetpack.exe to compact the copy of the database. Perform an authoritative restore of the backup.

   d. Stop the WINS server. Use the Compact command to compress the database. Restart the WINS server.

4. On a mixed Windows and UNIX network, you deploy a WINS server to provide NetBIOS name resolution services and configure the WINS clients accordingly. Later, you discover that the computers running Windows operating systems on the network cannot access UNIX resources by using their NetBIOS names. What should you do to resolve the problem?

   a. Install a WINS proxy agent on one of the other computers running Windows.

   b. Install a WINS proxy agent on one of the UNIX computers.

   c. Create static mappings for the UNIX computers on the WINS server.

   d. Create static mappings for the WINS server on the UNIX computers.

5. How do you configure a Windows 2000 WINS server to back up its database automatically?

   a. Use the Jetpack.exe utility from the command line.

   b. Specify a backup folder in the WINS server's Properties dialog box.

   c. Use a third-party backup utility to back up the Sysvol folder.

   d. Use the file replication service to replicate the WINS database to a different location.

Lesson Summary

- Windows 2000 Server includes the WINS server but does not install it by default. To install it manually, you use the Add/Remove Programs Control Panel.

- You cannot use the DHCP client on the computer running the WINS server. You must statically configure the IP address.

- A WINS server must be configured to use itself as its own WINS server.

- To enable non-WINS clients to resolve NetBIOS names using WINS, you create a WINS proxy server.

- To enable WINS clients to resolve the NetBIOS names of non-WINS computers, you create static mappings in the WINS database.

Lesson 4: Configuring WINS Replication

Unlike DHCP servers, which always operate independently, all the WINS servers on an internetwork can be configured to work together if you fully replicate their database entries with other WINS servers. This ensures that a name registered with one WINS server is eventually replicated to all other WINS servers on the network. This lesson explains how WINS replicates its database entries and how you can configure the replication process.

After this lesson, you will be able to

- Add a replication partner
- Perform WINS database replication

Estimated lesson time: 20 minutes

Replication Overview

WINS database replication occurs whenever the database changes, including when a NetBIOS name is released. Replicating databases enables a WINS server to resolve the NetBIOS names of hosts registered with another WINS server. For example, if a host that is registered with a WINS server on its local network wants to communicate with a host that is registered with a different WINS server on another network, the NetBIOS name of the destination computer cannot be resolved unless the two WINS servers have replicated their databases with each other.

To replicate database entries, each WINS server must be configured as either a pull or a push partner with at least one other WINS server. You configure the WINS partnerships using the WINS console. A *push partner* is a WINS server that sends a message to its pull partners notifying them when its WINS database has changed. When a WINS server's pull partners respond to the message with a replication request, the WINS server sends (pushes) a copy of its new database entries to its pull partners. A *pull partner* is a WINS server that requests new database entries from its push partners by requesting entries with a higher version number than the entries it received during the last replication.

Note   WINS servers replicate only the new entries in their database. They do not transmit the entire WINS database every time that replication occurs.

Configuring a WINS Server as a Push or Pull Partner

Determining whether to configure a WINS server as a pull partner or push partner depends on your network environment. Remember the following rules when configuring WINS server replication:

- Configure a push partner when servers are connected by fast links, because push replication occurs when a specified number of updated WINS database entries is reached.

- Configure a pull partner between sites, especially across slow links, because pull replication can be configured to occur at specific intervals.

- Configure each server to be both a push and pull partner to replicate database entries between them.

- Every WINS server must be both a push partner and a pull partner for the replication to be complete, but not necessarily with each other.

In Figure 9.19, all WINS servers at both the Sydney and Seattle sites push their new database entries to a single server at their local site. The server at each site that receives the push replication is configured for pull replication with its counterpart at the other site. This is because the network link between Sydney and Seattle is relatively slow, and you can configure pull replication to occur when the link is used the least, such as during off-peak hours. The single server at each site is then also configured to push the database entries it receives from the other site to all the local WINS servers. This ensures that all the WINS servers on the network are updated regularly.

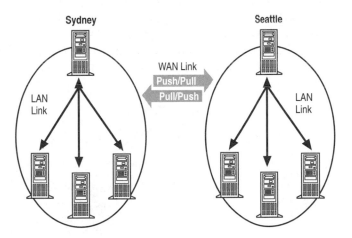

Figure 9.19 WINS push and pull partner configuration

Another common WINS configuration is the use of a ring replication topology, as shown in Figure 9.20. Each WINS server is configured to be a push partner of its clockwise neighbor in the ring and a pull partner of its counterclockwise neighbor. This illustrates that although each WINS server must be both a push and a pull partner, you do not have to pair the servers off and make them push and pull partners of each other.

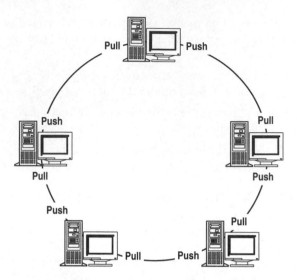

Figure 9.20   A WINS ring replication topology

One of the potential problems with this configuration on a network with wide area network (WAN) links, however, is that the failure of a single WAN link can prevent all the WINS servers from being properly replicated. One solution to this problem is creating two counter-rotating rings using different links, as shown in Figure 9.21. This replication topology provides greater fault tolerance because multiple link failures would have to occur for the replication process to be interrupted.

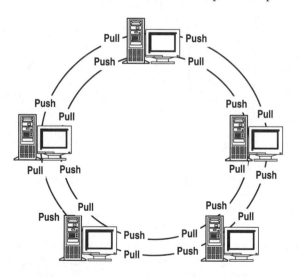

Figure 9.21   A WINS double ring replication topology

Planning How Many WINS Servers to Use

On a smaller network, a single WINS server can adequately service up to 10,000 clients for NetBIOS name resolution requests. To provide fault tolerance, you can configure a second computer to function as a backup WINS server. If you use only two WINS servers, you can easily set them up as replication partners of each other. For simple replication between two servers, one server should be set as a pull partner and the other as a push partner. Replication can be either manual or automatic, which you can configure in the Advanced tab of the Replication Partner Properties dialog box by selecting the Enable Automatic Partner Configuration check box.

A larger network sometimes requires more WINS servers for several reasons including, most important, the number of client connections per server. The number of users that each WINS server can support varies with usage patterns, data storage, and the processing capabilities of the WINS server computer. Some enterprise network environments require more robust hardware to handle WINS activity, so you might benefit from upgrading the server computer. When planning your servers, remember that each WINS server can simultaneously handle hundreds of registrations and queries per second. You can create any number of WINS servers for fault tolerance purposes. However, you should avoid deploying large numbers of WINS servers unless they are necessary. By limiting the number of WINS servers on your network, you minimize the traffic that results from replication, provide more effective NetBIOS name resolution, and reduce administrative requirements.

Initiating Database Replication

Database replication requires that you configure at least one push partner and one pull partner. There are four methods of initiating the replication of the WINS database:

- At system startup. After a replication partner is configured, by default WINS automatically pulls database entries each time WINS is started. You can also configure the WINS server to push on system startup.
- At a configured interval, such as every five hours.
- When a WINS server has reached a configured threshold for the number of registrations and modifications to the WINS database. When the threshold (the update count setting) is reached, the WINS server notifies all its pull partners, which then request the new entries.
- By forcing replication in the WINS console, as illustrated in Figure 9.22.

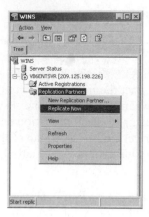

Figure 9.22   Forcing WINS database replication

WINS Automatic Replication Partners

If your network supports multicasting, you can configure the WINS server to automatically find other WINS servers on the network by multicasting to the IP address 224.0.1.24. This multicasting occurs by default every 40 minutes. Any WINS servers found on the network are automatically configured as push and pull replication partners, with pull replication set to occur every two hours. If network routers do not support multicasting, the WINS server finds only other WINS servers on its subnet. Automatic WINS server partnerships are turned off by default.

Configuring WINS Database Replication

To configure a WINS server to perform database replication with another WINS server, use the following procedure:

1. Log on to the computer running WINS as Administrator.

2. Click Start and from the Administrative Tools program group, open the WINS console.

3. Right-click the Replication Partners folder under your WINS server, and then from the pop-up menu, choose New Replication Partner to display the New Replication Partner dialog box, shown in Figure 9.23.

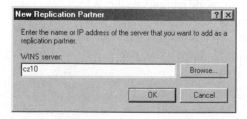

Figure 9.23   The New Replication Partner dialog box

4. Type the NetBIOS name or IP address of another WINS server on the network in the WINS Server text box, or click Browse to select a server, and then click OK.

The Replication Partners list appears in the details pane of the console with the server you specified added to the list, as shown in Figure 9.24.

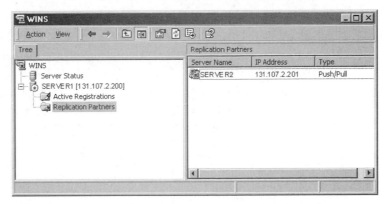

Figure 9.24   Replication partners listed in the WINS administrative console

5. Right-click the replication partner that you just added in the details pane, and from the pop-up menu, choose Properties to display the Server Properties dialog box.

6. Click the Advanced tab, shown in Figure 9.25.

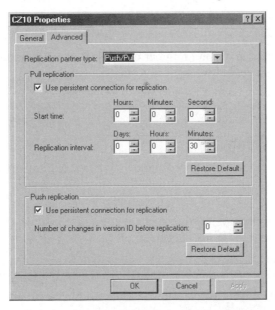

Figure 9.25   The Advanced tab of the Properties dialog box for a WINS replication partner

7. In the Replication Partner Type drop-down list box, select Push/Pull. The pull replication interval is set for 30 minutes by default.

8. In the Push Replication box, set the value in the Number Of Changes In Version ID Before Replication box to 5.

   You can modify the push and pull replication intervals as needed.

9. Click OK to close the Properties dialog box.

10. Repeat the entire process (steps 1 through 8) for the partner WINS server on your network.

After you have configured your WINS servers to be replication partners, you can force the replication process to commence by right-clicking the Replication Partners folder for one of your servers and, from the pop-up menu, selecting Replicate Now.

Lesson Review

1. What is the difference between the replication configuration parameters of push and pull partners?

2. Which type of replication partnership is preferable when traversing a slow WAN link?

3. What is the minimum number of WINS servers required to support a 5000 node routed network in a single location?

Lesson Summary

- When you have multiple Windows Internet Name Service (WINS) servers on a network, you must configure them to replicate their databases so that complete connectivity is provided for all clients.

- A pull replication partner sends requests for new database information to other servers at scheduled intervals.

- A push replication partner sends new database information to other servers when a specified number of database changes has occurred.

- When deploying WINS on a network with wide area network (WAN) links, you should minimize the number of replication partnerships that traverse the links to reduce network traffic.

- A single WINS server can service up to 10,000 clients.

C H A P T E R   1 0

Securing Network Protocols

Lesson 1: Using Packet Filters **364**

Lesson 2: Using IPsec **377**

Lesson 3: Deploying IPsec **390**

About This Chapter

Microsoft Windows 2000 includes a large number of security mechanisms, including NTFS permissions, the Kerberos authentication protocol, and the Encrypting File System, but these mechanisms are designed primarily to protect the resources stored on Windows 2000 computers; they are not involved in the network transmissions themselves. However, Windows 2000 does include two mechanisms that directly involve the transmission of data over the network: Transmission Control Protocol/Internet Protocol (TCP/IP) packet filters and the IP security (IPsec) protocol. In this chapter you learn how these two features work and how to implement them on your network.

Before You Begin

This chapter requires an understanding of the TCP/IP protocols, as discussed in Chapter 2, "Introducing TCP/IP." To perform the exercises in this chapter, you need two Windows 2000 computers connected to the same local area network (LAN).

Lesson 1: Using Packet Filters

A Windows 2000 computer running TCP/IP is, by default, open to many types of attacks from outside parties. This is particularly true if the computer is connected to the Internet. Unscrupulous intruders can attempt to gain access to the system to try to access confidential files, deny legitimate users access to services provided by the computer, or simply to cause any damage they can. You can use a variety of techniques to prevent unauthorized access to a computer running Windows 2000. These techniques are collectively referred to as firewall mechanisms. One of the most commonly used firewall mechanisms is packet filtering, which is the process of blocking certain packets incoming over a network interface based on specific criteria.

After this lesson, you will be able to

- Understand the uses of packet filtering
- List the various types of packet filters
- Configure Windows 2000 TCP/IP client packet filters
- Configure Routing and Remote Access Services (RRAS) packet filters

Estimated lesson time: 30 minutes

Understanding Packet Filtering

Packet filtering enables you to control which data packets are permitted to enter a computer, based on TCP/IP criteria such as port and protocol numbers. The system examines each packet arriving over the network interface and either admits it or discards it based on the values of specific fields in the protocol headers. This enables you to prevent specific types of traffic from entering the computer. For example, if you have a Windows 2000 computer that is configured to function as a Web server, you can create a filter that only enables packets addressed to port number 80 (the well-known port for the Hypertext Transfer Protocol [HTTP] used by Web servers) to enter the computer. This means that any attempts to access the computer using other application layer protocols (such as Telnet, for example) will fail because those packets use different port numbers and will be discarded by the filter.

Packet filters can often be inclusive or exclusive, meaning that the filter configuration you create can either specify the traffic to be blocked or the traffic to be permitted. In other words, you can use the filter for traffic addressed to port 80 described earlier to permit only Web traffic to enter the computer or to admit all packets except those addressed to port 80.

Packet filtering is a security technique most commonly used by routers or by dedicated firewalls that are used to isolate a private network from the Internet. However, Windows 2000 has rudimentary packet filtering capabilities built into its TCP/IP client that you can use to protect an individual computer. Windows 2000

Routing and Remote Access Service (RRAS) includes a more comprehensive packet filtering mechanism that you can use to set filters for specific network interfaces and for incoming or outgoing traffic. Effective packet filtering requires an understanding of how the TCP/IP protocols work and of how potential intruders think. In many cases a network administrator who uses packet filtering plays a continual game of cat and mouse with his or her nemesis, repeatedly modifying the filter configuration to block the latest security holes exploited by the intruder.

Packet filtering can occur at any one of several layers of the Open Systems Interconnection (OSI) reference model. The packet-filtering mechanism included with Windows 2000 is relatively limited, but a full-featured firewall can filter packets based on any of the following characteristics:

- **Hardware addresses.**   Packet filtering based on hardware addresses enables only certain computers to transmit data through the filter. This type of filtering isn't usually used to protect networks from unauthorized Internet access, but you can use this technique in an internal firewall to permit only specific computers to access a particular network. The advantage of this type of filtering is that it is more difficult for intruders to masquerade as another user. It is a simple matter to change the Internet Protocol (IP) address of a computer to masquerade as another system, but because hardware addresses are coded into network interface adapters, they cannot be changed as easily.

- **IP addresses.**   You can use IP address filtering to permit only traffic destined to, or originating from, specific addresses to pass through the filter. If, for example, you have a single public Web server on your private network, you can configure a packet filter in your router or firewall to admit only the Internet traffic that is destined for that server's IP address to your network. This can prevent Internet users from accessing any of the other computers on the network in any way.

- **Protocol identifiers.**   The IP header's Protocol field contains a code specifying the protocol that generated the payload carried in the datagram. Windows 2000 can filter packets based on this code, enabling only Transmission Control Protocol (TCP), User Datagram Protocol (UDP), Internet Control Message Protocol (ICMP) packets, or all three, to enter the system. With this capability, you can limit the potentially dangerous traffic reaching a computer or a network. One of the most common Internet firewall protocol filter configurations is to allow only TCP traffic to reach the network. This enables the network's users to access common Internet applications, such as Web servers, e-mail, and File Transfer Protocol (FTP) servers, while preventing the entry of UDP and ICMP traffic onto the network, which blocks many of the tools used for denial of service attacks and other intrusions.

- **Port numbers.**   The port number fields in the TCP and UDP headers identifies the application that generated the data carried in a packet. By filtering packets based on the source or destination port number, you can be more specific in the types of traffic you allow into a computer or onto a network. This is called *service-dependent filtering*. For example, you can configure a firewall to permit network users to access the Internet using ports 110 and 25 (the well-known port numbers used for incoming and outgoing e-mail) but deny them Internet access using port 80 (the port number used to access Web servers).

The strength of the firewall protection provided by packet filtering is its ability to combine the various types of filters. For example, you might want to permit Telnet traffic into your network from the Internet so that network support personnel can remotely administer certain computers. However, leaving port 23 (the Telnet port) open to all Internet users is a potentially disastrous security breach. Therefore, you can combine the port number filter with an IP address filter to permit only certain computers (those of the network administrators) to access the network using the Telnet port.

Packet-filtering capabilities usually are included in router products, whether the router is a stand-alone hardware device or a software product like Windows 2000. The RRAS packet filters built into Windows 2000 Server are designed to prevent unwanted traffic from passing through a Windows 2000 computer configured to function as a router. The packet filters in the Windows 2000 TCP/IP client are included in all versions of Windows 2000 and are designed to filter only traffic that is destined for one of the computer's network interfaces. These filters are designed to protect that computer alone and cannot be used to filter routed traffic.

The main drawback of packet filtering is that it requires a detailed understanding of TCP/IP communications and the ways of the criminal mind. Using packet filters to protect your network means participating in an ongoing battle of wits with those who would infiltrate your network. Potential intruders are constantly inventing new techniques to defeat standard packet filter configurations, and you must be ready to modify your filters to counteract these techniques.

Another important consideration when using packet filters is to keep from inhibiting communications required by the computer or the network. Many types of communication often occur on a network at once, and using filters to block all but a specific few application protocols can easily cause more problems than it prevents. When creating filters, the fundamental paradox is that using exclusive filters to block specific protocols is less likely to cause problems with other communications but is inherently less secure than using inclusive filters to specify the only protocols that are permitted onto the network. You should have a complete understanding of all the normal traffic passing through the router before you attempt to block any of it using packet filters.

When you use packet filtering on a router, you introduce an extra level of processing overhead, as the router must run each packet through the entire list of filters. This extra processing usually does not have a major effect on the router's throughput unless you create an excessively large number of filtering rules. A very complex system of filters can conceivably slow the router down, thereby inhibiting the network access speed.

Important   The inclusion of packet filtering in Windows 2000 means that you might be able to provide sufficient protection for your network without incurring the additional expense of a separate firewall product. However, firewall products are usually designed with preset configurations that protect against specific types of intrusion. Their creators typically have a greater understanding of the criminal mind that spends its time trying to infiltrate other people's networks. The Windows 2000 packet filtering mechanisms, although effective, are not preconfigured and include very little guidance on their effective use. In most cases, professional administrators seeking serious protection for a network opt for a separate, more comprehensive firewall product.

Configuring Packet Filters in the TCP/IP Client

By creating packet filters on a Windows 2000 computer at the TCP/IP client level, you can restrict the types of traffic that reach the computer through any of its interfaces. You cannot filter ICMP traffic using this implementation, nor can you create filters for routed traffic or create exclusive filters (that is, filters specifying the traffic that is to be blocked). You can only specify the protocols or ports, or both, that the computer is to leave open.

To configure TCP/IP client packet filtering, use the following procedure:

1. Click Start, point to Settings, and select Network And Dial-up Connections to display the Network And Dial-up Connections window.

2. Select the Local Area Connection icon and select Properties from the File menu to display the Local Area Connection properties dialog box (see Figure 10.1).

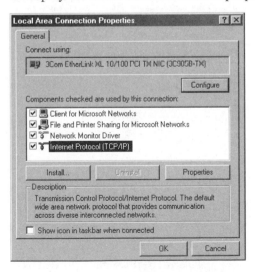

Figure 10.1   The Local Area Connection Properties dialog box

3. Select Internet Protocol (TCP/IP) and click Properties to open the Internet Protocol (TCP/IP) Properties dialog box (see Figure 10.2).

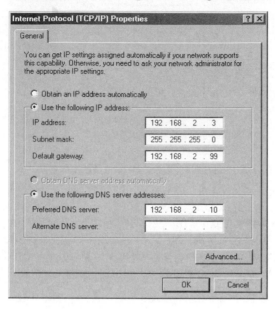

Figure 10.2   The Internet Protocol (TCP/IP) Properties dialog box

4. Click Advanced to open the Advanced TCP/IP Settings dialog box and click the Options tab (see Figure 10.3).

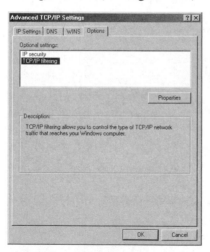

Figure 10.3   The Advanced TCP/IP Settings dialog box

5. Select TCP/IP Filtering and click Properties to open the TCP/IP Filtering dialog box (see Figure 10.4).

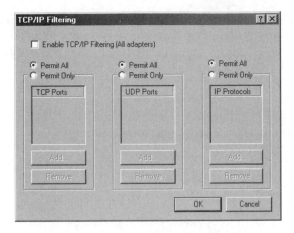

Figure 10.4   The TCP/IP Filtering dialog box

6. Select the Enable TCP/IP Filtering (All Adapters) check box if you want to apply your filters to all the computer's network interfaces.

7. To create a packet filter based on TCP port numbers, click the Permit Only option button to activate the TCP Ports list (see Figure 10.5).

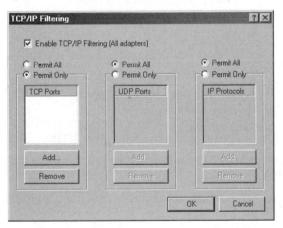

Figure 10.5   The TCP Filtering dialog box with the TCP Ports list activated

8. Click Add to open the Add Filter dialog box and type a port number in the TCP Port box.

9. Click OK to add the port to the TCP Ports list.

   The TCP Ports and UDP Ports lists use the well-known port numbers for applications and services, as defined in the "Assigned Numbers" Request for Comments (RFC) document published by the Internet Engineering Task Force

(IETF). For a partial list of port numbers, see the Services file in the *systemroot*\system32\drivers\etc folder on any Windows 2000 computer. Some of the most commonly used TCP ports are as follows:

- **20.** FTP-data
- **21.** FTP-control
- **23.** Telnet
- **25.** Simple Mail Transfer Protocol (SMTP)
- **53.** Domain Name System (DNS)
- **80.** Hypertext Transfer Protocol (HTTP)
- **110.** Post Office Protocol, Version 3 (POP3)

Some of the most common UDP ports are as follows:

- **53.** Domain Name System (DNS)
- **67.** Dynamic Host Configuration Protocol (DHCP) and Bootstrap Protocol (BOOTP) Server
- **68.** Dynamic Host Configuration Protocol (DHCP) and Bootstrap Protocol (BOOTP) Client
- **137.** NetBIOS Name Server (WINS)
- **161.** Simple Network Management Protocol (SNMP)
- **162.** SNMP Traps

10. Repeat steps 8 and 9 to add TCP port numbers to the filter.

11. To create a packet filter based on UDP port numbers, click the Permit Only option button to activate the UDP Ports list and repeat steps 8 and 9.

12. To create a packet filter based on the Protocol field of the IP header, click the Permit Only option button to activate the IP Protocols list.

13. Click Add to open the Add Filter dialog box and type a protocol number in the IP Protocol box.

As with port numbers, the codes representing the protocols that IP datagrams can carry are published in the "Assigned Numbers" RFC. A list of the protocol codes also appears in the Protocol file, found in the *systemroot*\system32\drivers\etc folder on any Windows 2000 computer. The most common protocol codes are as follows:

- **0.** Internet Protocol
- **1.** Internet Control Message Protocol
- **6.** Transmission Control Protocol
- **17.** User Datagram Protocol

However, specifying the value 1 will have no effect because the TCP/IP client's filtering mechanism cannot block ICMP traffic. If you want to filter ICMP traffic, you must use the filtering capabilities of RRAS.

14. Click OK to add the protocol to the IP Protocols list.

15. Click OK to set the filters you have created and close the TCP/IP Filtering dialog box.

16. Close all the dialog boxes you opened and restart the computer when you are prompted to do so.

Configuring Packet Filters in RRAS

To create packet filters in RRAS, you must first configure the service to function as an IP router, as described in Lesson 2 of Chapter 6, "Routing IP," and then create interfaces for the connections that provide access to the networks being routed. You can then create packet filters for each interface using the following procedure:

1. Click Start, and then select Routing And Remote Access from the Administrative Tools program group to open the RRAS console (see Figure 10.6).

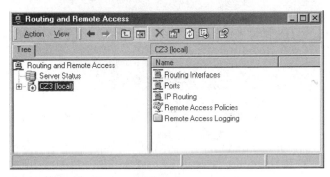

Figure 10.6 The RRAS console

2. Expand the server icon and then the IP Routing icon. Select the General icon to display the list of interfaces in the details pane (see Figure 10.7).

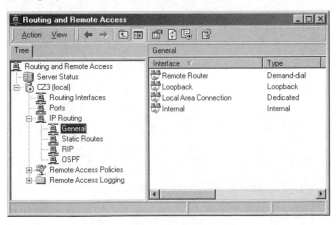

Figure 10.7 The list of interfaces for an RRAS server

3. Select one of the interfaces in the list and select Properties from the Action menu to display the Properties dialog box for the interface (see Figure 10.8).

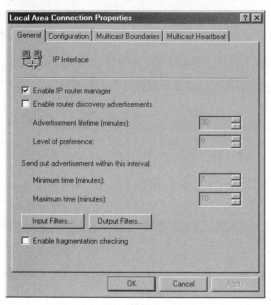

Figure 10.8   The Properties dialog box for an RRAS interface

4. Click either Input Filters or Output Filters, depending on whether you want to create filters for incoming or outgoing traffic on the selected interface. This displays either an Input Filters (see Figure 10.9) or Output Filters dialog box.

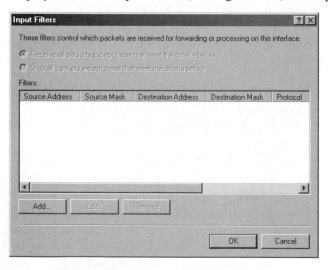

Figure 10.9   The RRAS Input Filters dialog box

5. Click Add to open the Add IP Filter dialog box (see Figure 10.10).

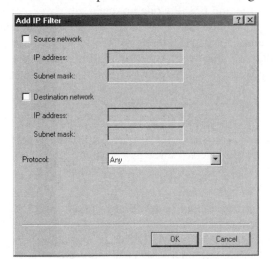

Figure 10.10   The Add IP Filter dialog box

6. Select the Source Network check box to create a filter that evaluates packets based on the network from which they are arriving. This activates the IP Address and Subnet Mask boxes, in which you specify the IP address and mask of the network or host whose traffic you want to filter. Use a Subnet Mask value of 255.255.255.255 when creating a filter for a host IP address.

7. Select the Destination Network check box to create a filter that evaluates packets based on the network to which they are going. Type IP Address and Subnet Mask values for the network whose traffic you want to filter in the boxes provided.

8. Select an entry in the Protocol drop-down list. Most of the entries cause additional fields to appear in the dialog box, in which you can specify the precise criteria to be filtered. The values in the Protocol list are as follows:

   ■ **TCP.**   Select this option to filter TCP traffic originating from or destined for specific ports. Selecting this option displays Source Port and Destination Port boxes, in which you can specify port values. If you leave these fields blank, they default to a value of 0, meaning all ports.

   ■ **TCP (established).**   Select this option to filter traffic for TCP connections established by or with the RRAS router. The Source Port and Destination Port fields function in the same way as those for the TCP option.

   ■ **UDP.**   Select this option to filter TCP traffic originating from, or destined for, specific ports. The Source Port and Destination Port fields function in the same way as those for the TCP option.

- **ICMP.** Select this option to filter ICMP traffic. This option displays ICMP Type and ICMP Code boxes in which you can specify values that define particular types of ICMP traffic. Table 10.1 contains the type and code values for ICMP messages. If you leave these fields blank, they default to a value of 255, meaning all message types.

- **Any (default).** Select this option to filter all IP traffic.

- **Other.** Select this option to specify a protocol other than TCP, UDP, or ICMP, using the protocol codes defined in the "Assigned Numbers" RFC.

9. Click OK to add the new filter to the list on the Input Filters or Output Filters dialog box. Repeat steps 5 through 8 to create additional filters. You must create separate filters to block traffic for multiple networks or multiple ports using the same protocol.

10. Click the appropriate option button to indicate whether you want the filters you have created to be inclusive or exclusive. The Receive All Packets Except Those That Meet The Criteria Below option creates exclusive filters and the Drop All Packets Except Those That Meet The Criteria Below option creates inclusive filters.

11. Click OK to close the Input Filters or Output Filters dialog box.

Table 10.1   Type and Code Values for ICMP Messages

Type	Code	Function
0	0	Echo Reply
3	0	Network Unreachable
3	1	Host Unreachable
3	2	Protocol Unreachable
3	3	Port Unreachable
3	4	Fragmentation Needed and Don't Fragment Flag Was Set
3	5	Source Route Failed
3	6	Destination Network Unknown
3	7	Destination Host Unknown
3	8	Source Host Isolated
3	9	Communication with Destination Network is Administratively Prohibited
3	10	Communication with Destination Host is Administratively Prohibited
3	11	Destination Network Unreachable for Type of Service
3	12	Destination Host Unreachable for Type of Service
4	0	Source Quench
5	0	Redirect Datagram for the Network (or Subnet)
5	1	Redirect Datagram for the Host

(continued)

Table 10.1   *(continued)*

Type	Code	Function
5	2	Redirect Datagram for the Type of Service and Network
5	3	Redirect Datagram for the Type of Service and Host
8	0	Echo Request
9	0	Router Advertisement
10	0	Router Solicitation
11	0	Time to Live Exceeded in Transit
11	1	Fragment Reassembly Time Exceeded
12	0	Pointer Indicates the Error
12	1	Missing a Required Option
12	2	Bad Length
13	0	Timestamp
14	0	Timestamp Reply
15	0	Information Request
16	0	Information Reply
17	0	Address Mask Request
18	0	Address Mask Reply
30	0	Traceroute
31	0	Datagram Conversion Error
32	0	Mobile Host Redirect
33	0	IPv6 Where-are-you
34	0	IPv6 I-am-here
35	0	Mobile Registration Request
36	0	Mobile Registration Reply

Lesson Review

1. Which of the following criteria are used to filter packets in service-dependent filtering?

    a. Hardware addresses

    b. IP addresses

    c. Protocol identifiers

    d. Port numbers

2. Under what conditions can packet filtering slow down network performance?

3. Which of the following can you do with RRAS packet filters that you can't do with Windows TCP/IP client packet filters? (Choose all that apply.)

   a. Create separate filters for each of the computer's network interfaces

   b. Apply one set of filters to all the computer's network interfaces

   c. Apply filters to traffic routed by the computer

   d. Filter ICMP traffic

Lesson Summary

- Packet filtering is a mechanism that protects a computer or a network by reading the protocol header information of incoming packets and rejecting those that do not meet certain criteria.

- You can use packet filtering to protect systems on your network from damaging traffic generated by potential intruders.

- A packet-filtering mechanism can evaluate traffic based on hardware addresses, IP addresses, protocol identifiers, port numbers, or a combination of the four.

- Windows 2000 includes a TCP/IP-filtering mechanism as part of its TCP/IP client that enables you to specify the ports and protocols that packets must use to be admitted into the system.

- RRAS includes its own separate packet-filtering mechanism, which provides greater flexibility.

Lesson 2: Using IPsec

As stated earlier, most of the security mechanisms included with Windows 2000 are designed to protect the resources stored on the computer. Windows 2000 uses access control lists (ACLs) to determine who has access to files and other resources and authentication protocols to verify the identities of users. Newer technologies such as the Encrypting File System (EFS) and smart card authentication enhance these capabilities, but none of them do anything to protect data as it is transmitted over a network. The primary means of securing network data in Windows 2000 is the IP Security protocol, more commonly known as IPsec.

After this lesson, you will be able to

- Explain the ways in which network communications can be compromised

- Describe how IPsec protects network communications

- Describe the Authentication Header (AH) and Encapsulating Security Payload (ESP) packet formats

- Understand the difference between IPsec's transport and tunnel modes

Estimated lesson time: 30 minutes

Securing IP Communications

Windows 2000 can protect the files stored on its drives by encrypting them and placing them behind a wall of permissions, but when a network user attempts to access a file, the server accesses it with the user's credentials and decrypts it before sending it on its way over the network. The data, as transmitted over the network, is left completely unprotected and vulnerable to a variety of attacks. On today's large enterprise networks, the Internet is not the only source of potential intruders. Internal users might attempt to access sensitive data in many ways, including the following:

- **Packet capturing.**   Capturing packets using a protocol analyzer is a useful way of learning about how networks function and a valuable troubleshooting tool. You learn more about using the Windows 2000 protocol analyzer, called Network Monitor, later in this book. However, the ability to capture packets as they are transmitted over the network and to study their contents also makes the data carried inside the packets vulnerable to interception by unauthorized users. Windows 2000 Network Monitor is capable only of capturing packets generated by or addressed to the computer on which it is running. However, the full version of Network Monitor included in Microsoft Systems Management Server, as well as many other protocol analyzer products, is capable of switching a network interface adapter into *promiscuous mode*, meaning that the adapter reads and processes all the packets on the network and not just those addressed to it. This means that a single protocol analyzer can capture the packets generated by users all over the network, including those containing sensitive data, and examine their contents.

- **Data modification.**   When unauthorized users gain access to unprotected packets by capturing them with a protocol analyzer, they not only can read the data in the packets, but they can also modify the data and send it on to the original recipient. The receiver of the packet has no way of knowing that the data has been modified and might take inappropriate action based on the intruder's actions instead of those of the original sender.

- **Spoofing.**   Spoofing is the process by which an unauthorized user masquerades as another user, typically by using the other user's IP address. Every data packet on a TCP/IP network has a source IP address and a destination IP address in its IP header. When two computers initiate a client/server connection over the network, they typically use a TCP connection, which involves the exchange of sequence numbers, which are integers that the computers use to number their packets. An intruder attempting to impersonate another user will typically capture a sample of the genuine packets exchanged by the connected computers and use the header information in them to create bogus packets of his or her own, using the genuine computer's IP address and sequence numbers but with the intruder's own version of the data. At the same time, the intruder might prevent the victim from communicating with the other computer by setting up a denial of service attack. After the intruder has successfully begun to spoof a victim, the intruder can receive data that was meant for the victim, gain access to the victim's resources, and even generate messages of his or her own using the victim's identity.

- **Password compromise.**   Virtually all network operating systems rely heavily on user names and passwords to secure their resources, and in most cases this means that the passwords have to be transmitted over the network. A few applications, such as FTP, transmit passwords in clear text, meaning that anyone capturing a packet containing an FTP password can simply read it in the protocol analyzer and use it again. This is why network administrators are urged never to use their administrative accounts for everyday user tasks, such as accessing FTP servers. After an intruder captures the administrative password from an FTP session, the intruder can access any of the resources available to that account. Many other applications use encrypted passwords, but in some cases it is possible to use the password in its encrypted form to gain access to protected resources. A spoofed packet containing an intercepted password, for example, can provide access to protected resources, even if the spoofer doesn't know the unencrypted password.

- **Denial of service attacks.**   A denial of service attack occurs when a user floods a network or computer with traffic, preventing it from performing its normal tasks. There are many types of denial of service attacks, typically taking advantage of normal TCP/IP procedures. For example, by sending continuous streams of TCP connection requests from many clients to a particular server, it is possible to prevent actual clients from connecting. The same end can be accomplished with a continuous series of pings or other transmissions. This type of attack is often used as a form of harrassment, but it can also function as a distraction to prevent network administrators from noticing a different type of attack.

- **Key compromise.**   In the same way that unauthorized users can discover passwords in captured packets, they can also discover keys used to encrypt data. Depending on the type of encryption used, the keys might or might not be useful to the intruder. For example, the Windows 2000 public key infrastructure uses separate keys to encrypt and decrypt data, so capturing an encryption key does not help you to read data encrypted with that key. However, other forms of encryption use single keys, and their interception can compromise sensitive data.

- **Application layer attack.**   In some cases attacks are directed not at the network's underlying communications technology, but at an application itself. Vulnerabilities in applications can enable intruders to modify program or data files or to introduce damaging software, such as viruses, worms, and Trojan horses. Server applications that are open to Internet access (such as Web servers) are particularly vulnerable to this type of attack.

One way of preventing many of these types of attacks is to physically protect the network from intrusion. You can take steps to ensure that unauthorized users do not have access to workstations and safeguard the network cables to prevent intruders from tapping into them and adding an unauthorized workstation. For example, government agencies that require absolute security for their networks run their cables inside sealed metal conduits and might use smart cards or biometric sensors to restrict workstation access to authorized personnel. These are extraordinary measures, however, that are not practical for the average business network.

Advantages of IPsec

Instead of securing the network itself, you can secure the data transmitted over a Windows 2000 network using IPsec. IPsec is a series of standards that provide a means for encrypting IP datagrams before they are transmitted over the network. Because IP is responsible for carrying all application data on a TCP/IP network, this type of encryption can protect all types of sensitive data and eliminate vulnerability to all the types of attacks listed earlier. Intruders still might be able to capture packets as they travel over the network, but since they cannot decrypt any of the data inside the packets, they cannot make use of the information.

The network layer of the OSI reference model (where IP operates) is the perfect place to situate an encryption mechanism of this type. As you have learned in Chapter 2, "Introducing TCP/IP," IP is the primary end-to-end protocol in the TCP/IP suite, meaning that it is responsible for carrying data generated by the source system all the way to its final destination. Therefore, if you encrypt an IP datagram at its source using IPsec, it does not have to be decrypted until it reaches its final destination. The result is that the routers functioning as the intermediate systems in the internetwork communications process do not have to support IPsec, so you can freely deploy it on local area, wide area, remote access, and virtual private network connections. Routers receive datagrams that are already encrypted and simply forward them on to their next interim destination, still in their encrypted form. As long as both the source and destination computers support IPsec, secured communications can occur.

Encrypting network transmissions at the data-link layer would require routers to decrypt every packet and then re-encrypt it again for transmission. This would not only greatly increase the processing burden on the routers, it would also force you to upgrade or replace all the routers with models that support IPsec. Encrypting data at the network layer also means that all the workstation's transmissions are encrypted (with the exception of a few specialized protocols, such as the Address Resolution Protocol), regardless of the application that generated them.

Most of the other encryption protocols designed to protect transmitted data operate at the application layer and are limited to specific services. The primary function of the Secure Sockets Layer (SSL) protocol, for example, is to encrypt transmissions between Web clients and servers. This requires both the client and the server to be modified to support SSL. Applications need not be modified to use IPsec, however, because all application layer processes are completed before the data reaches the network layer, where IPsec encrypts it. IPsec is therefore completely transparent to all processes operating above the network layer, including all TCP, UDP, and ICMP functions.

IPsec Functions

The encryption that IPsec uses to protect transmitted data is based on either the Data Encryption Algorithm (DES) or the Triple Data Encryption (3DES) algorithm. These are both *symmetric encryption algorithms*, meaning that both the computers involved in a connection possess the key used to encrypt and decrypt the data. Both algorithms encrypt 64-bit blocks of data, with the 3DES algorithm processing each block three times for additional protection.

In addition to this encryption (or because of it), IPsec also provides the following additional security functions:

- **Nonrepudiation.**   As part of its encryption capability, IPsec effectively prevents users from denying that they sent a particular message and from masquerading as other users and sending messages on their behalf. By using public key technology and digital signatures, IPsec verifies that each message originated from the actual sender and not from an imposter.

- **Authentication.**   IPsec supports a variety of authentication mechanisms, including Kerberos authentication, digital signatures based on public key certificates, and preshared key authentication, which enable a computer to verify the identity of another user before initiating communications with that user.

- **Antireplay.**   Traffic analysis is the process of making an educated guess about what information a packet contains, even when its contents are encrypted and unreadable. For example, in many cases a potential intruder might assume that the first packets exchanged by two computers contain authentication messages and try to make use of them to gain access to secured resources without decrypting them. To prevent this, IPsec uses a technique called Cipher Block Chaining (CBC) in combination with the DES or 3DES excryption algorithm and a unique value for each packet called an initialization vector. The result of this technique is that no two packets encrypted with IPsec are identical, even when they contain exactly the same message. Intruders therefore cannot use traffic analysis to make use of undecrypted packets.

- **Packet filtering.**   IPsec includes its own packet-filtering mechanism that enables administrators to block traffic based on IP addresses, protocols, ports, or all three, therefore preventing intruders from initiating denial of service attacks. See Lesson 1 of this chapter for more information on packet filtering.

- **Integrity.**   IPsec prevents intruders from modifying the contents of a packet by including a special signature called an integrity check value (ICV). An ICV is a cryptographic checksum that functions much like the cyclical redundancy checks used by networking protocols for error detection. The computer sending a packet runs it through a hashing algorithm such as Message Digest 5 (MD5) or Secure Hash Algorithm 1 (SHA1) and appends the resulting signature to the packet. This signature (or *message digest*) is essentially a summary of the packet's contents, but there is no way to recreate the message using the digest (which is why it is also called a *one-way transform*). When the packet arrives at its final destination, the receiving system performs the same computation and compares its results to the signature included in the packet. If the two signatures match, the packet has arrived at the destination unmodified. Any attempt to alter the packet's contents will cause a discrepancy in the signatures.

Taken together, these protection mechanisms prevent potential intruders from using any of the methods listed earlier in this lesson to compromise the security of the network. An unauthorized user with a protocol analyzer can still capture packets as they are transmitted over the network, but the user cannot:

- Read a packet's contents, because it is encrypted

- Modify a packet's contents, because of the inclusion of a Hash Message Authentication Code (HMAC)

- Spoof a recipient by assuming another user's identity, because of the authentication mechanisms

- Discover passwords and keys, or reuse undecrypted packets, because of the CBC mechanism

- Inhibit network functionality using denial of service attacks, because of the packet-filtering capability

IPsec Standards

IPsec is based on a series of RFC documents that are in the process of being ratified as standards by the IETF. RFC 2411, "IP Security Document Roadmap," explains how the technologies defined in the various other documents work together. The RFCs pertaining to IPsec are as follows:

- **RFC 2411.**   IP Security Document Roadmap
- **RFC 2401.**   Security Architecture for the Internet Protocol
- **RFC 2402.**   IP Authentication Header
- **RFC 2403.**   The Use of HMAC-MD5-96 Within ESP and AH
- **RFC 2404.**   The Use of HMAC-SHA-1-96 Within ESP and AH
- **RFC 2405.**   The ESP DES-CBC Cipher Algorithm with Explicit IV
- **RFC 2406.**   IP Encapsulating Security Payload (ESP)
- **RFC 2407.**   The Internet IP Security Domain of Interpretation for ISAKMP
- **RFC 2408.**   Internet Security Association and Key Management Protocol (ISAKMP)
- **RFC 2409.**   The Internet Key Exchange (IKE)
- **RFC 2410.**   The NULL Encryption Algorithm and Its Use with IPsec
- **RFC 2412.**   The OAKLEY Key Determination Protocol
- **RFC 2709.**   Security Model with Tunnel-mode IPsec for NAT Domains
- **RFC 3104.**   RSIP Support for End-to-End IPsec

IPsec Protocols

IPsec uses two different protocols to provide systems with varying levels of security: IP Authentication Header (AH) and IP Encapsulating Security Payload (ESP). These protocols are described in the following sections.

IP Authentication Header

The IP Authentication Header (AH) protocol is defined in RFC 2402 and is designed to provide authentication, antireplay, and integrity services for IP datagrams, but it does not encrypt the data. The intention is for the protocol to provide basic security services with a relatively low overhead in processing and control traffic. You can use AH alone in situations requiring a modest amount of security or in combination with ESP for full protection. When you use AH alone, you can be certain that the messages exchanged by two connected systems have not been modified and that each packet definitely originated at the source specified in the IP header, but there is no guarantee that a third party has not intercepted the messages and read their contents.

Unlike many TCP/IP protocols, AH provides a service to another protocol, in this case IP, without encapsulating it. AH has its own header, but on a system configured to use IPsec, the AH header is inserted after the IP header and before the IP Data field (which typically contains a TCP, UDP, or ICMP message with its own header). Therefore, in a TCP packet, the AH header falls between the IP and TCP headers, as shown in Figure 10.11. If a computer is configured to use ESP as well as AH, the ESP header typically follows the AH header.

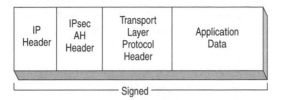

Figure 10.11   The AH header location in a typical IP datagram

---

Note   The positions of the AH and ESP headers described assume that IPsec is operating in transport mode and not tunnel mode. More information about these modes is provided later in this lesson.

The IP header includes a Protocol field that contains a code that usually identifies the protocol that generated the message carried in the datagram. The most common values for this code are 6 for TCP, 17 for UDP, and 1 for ICMP. However, the actual function of the Protocol field is to identify the protocol that generated the header immediately following the IP header. In a typical IP datagram, a TCP, UDP, or ICMP header follows the IP header, but the addition of the AH header immediately following the IP header forces the value of the Protocol field to change. In an IPsec packet, the Protocol field in the IP header has a value of 51, and the task of identifying the protocol that generated the datagram message is left to the Next Header field in the AH header. The format of the AH header is shown in Figure 10.12.

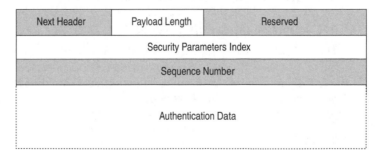

Figure 10.12   The AH header format

The functions of the fields are as follows:

- **Next Header (1 byte).** Identifies the protocol whose header immediately follows the AH header, using the standard values defined in the "Assigned Numbers" RFC. If the system is using the ESP protocol in addition to AH, the ESP header follows the AH header, so the value of this field is 50. If the system is not using ESP, the value of this field represents the protocol that generated the message carried in the datagram, such as TCP, UDP, or ICMP.

- **Payload Length (1 byte).** Specifies the total length of the AH header in 4-byte words minus 2 (to conform to the standard defining IPv6 extension headers, of which AH is one).

- **Reserved (2 bytes).** Unused.

- **Security Parameters Index (4 bytes).** Contains an arbitrary value that, with the packet's destination IP address and its security protocol (AH, in this case), identifies the security association for the datagram. A *security association* is a negotiated agreement between two computers on the security measures they will use to protect the data they intend to transmit.

- **Sequence Number (4 bytes).** Contains a value that starts at 1 and is incremented for every packet using a particular security association. This field provides the protocol's antireplay service. If the destination system receives multiple packets with the same sequence number value and using the same security association, it assumes that the duplicates are an attempt to replay previous packets and discards them.

- **Authentication Data and Padding (variable).** Contains the ICV that is calculated by the transmitting system, based on all the IP header fields that are immutable in transit or predictable in value; the entire AH header, including the Authentication Data field (which is set to a value of zero for this purpose); and the upper-level protocol header and data that follow the AH field. The receiving system uses the ICV to verify the packet's integrity by performing the same calculation and comparing the results with this value. The length of the value must be a multiple of 32 bits; the field might contain padding to bring its length up to the next 32-bit boundary.

IP Encapsulating Security Payload

The IP Encapsulating Security Payload (ESP) protocol is responsible for providing the actual encryption of the data carried in IP packets, as well as authentication, integrity, and antireplay services. ESP differs from the AH protocol (which simply adds a header to the IP datagram) by encapsulating the IP Data field within a header and a trailer, as shown in Figure 10.13.

All the data following the ESP header and up to and including the ESP trailer is encrypted to protect it from unauthorized access. This includes the entire header generated by the TCP, UDP, or ICMP protocol, plus any application layer data that was encapsulated by the transport layer protocol. ESP also uses all this information to compute an ICV, which is included in its header. Unlike AH, however, ESP does not include any part of the IP header in its ICV, which means that it is possible for someone to modify the contents of this header without the ESP implementation on the receiving system being able to detect it. This is one of the reasons why using both AH and ESP together is recommended in situations requiring maximum security.

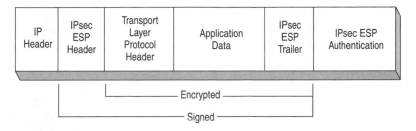

Figure 10.13 An IP datagram with the ESP header and trailer

When using ESP without AH, the Protocol field in the IP header contains a value of 50, because ESP supplies the header immediately following the IP header. ESP has a Next Header field that contains a code identifying the protocol that generated the information in the IP datagram's original Data field. When using both AH and ESP, the value in the IP header's Protocol field is 51, pointing to the AH header. The AH header's Next Header field then has a value of 50, pointing to the ESP header, and the ESP header's Next Header field contains the value for the TCP, UDP, or ICMP protocol that generated the datagram's original message.

The format of the ESP message, which includes original contents of the IP datagram's Data field, is shown in Figure 10.14.

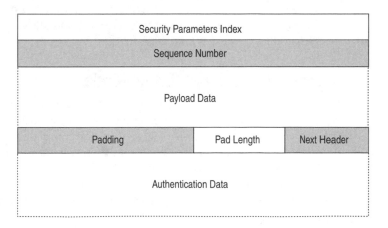

Figure 10.14 The ESP message format

The functions of the fields are as follows:

- **Security Parameters Index (4 bytes).**   Contains an arbitrary value that, with the packet's destination IP address and its security protocol (ESP, in this case), identifies the security association for the datagram. A *security association* is a negotiated agreement between two computers on the security measures they will use to protect the data they intend to transmit.

- **Sequence Number (4 bytes).**   Contains a value that starts at 1 and is incremented for every packet using a particular security association. This field provides the protocol's antireplay service. If the destination system receives multiple packets with the same sequence number value and using the same security association, it assumes that the duplicates are an attempt to replay previous packets and discards them.

- **Payload Data and Padding (variable).**   Contains the IP datagram's original Data field, including the TCP, UDP, or ICMP header, plus the original application layer message. This field also contains sufficient padding to ensure that the following Pad Length and Next Header fields are right-aligned on a 32-bit word. This is done so that the Authentication Data field can begin on a 32-bit boundary.

- **Pad Length (1 byte).**   Specifies the number of bytes of padding appended to the Payload Data field.

- **Next Header (1 byte).**   Identifies the protocol whose header immediately follows the ESP header, using the standard values defined in the "Assigned Numbers" RFC.

- **Authentication Data (variable).**   This field is optional, and, when present, it contains an ICV based on all the fields ranging from the end of the beginning of the ESP header to the end of the ESP trailer, excluding the Authentication Data field. The receiving system uses the ICV to verify the packet's integrity by performing the same calculation and comparing the results with this value. The field must begin on a 32-bit boundary, which is the reason for the padding in the Payload Data field.

Transport Mode and Tunnel Mode

IPsec is capable of functioning in two modes: transport mode and tunnel mode. All the discussion of IPsec in this lesson so far is specific to transport mode. *Transport mode* is used to provide security for computers on a LAN or connected by private wide area network (WAN) links. To function in transport mode, both of the end systems (the source and the destination of the packets) must support IPsec, but as explained earlier, the intermediate systems (routers) don't have to support it because they simply forward the packets in the normal manner, without decrypting them.

IPsec's *tunnel mode* is intended primarily for use on gateway-to-gateway connections, such as virtual private networking links, which require the greatest possible security. The primary difference between tunnel mode and transport mode is the packet format. In tunnel mode, IPsec creates an entirely new datagram, which it uses to completely encapsulate the original datagram, as shown in Figure 10.15.

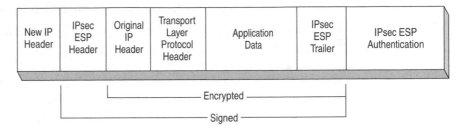

Figure 10.15 An IPsec tunnel mode packet

The "inner" IP header is the header from the original datagram, which remains unchanged. The ESP header and trailer surround the original datagram and are themselves preceded by a new, "outer" IP header. This outer header is designed to get the packet only from one end of the gateway connection to the other. Although the source IP address and destination IP address of the inner IP header continue to reflect the ultimate source and destination of the packet, the outer header contains the IP addresses of the two gateways that form the endpoints of the tunnel.

When IPsec is operating in tunnel mode, only the two gateways have to support IPsec communications. In the case of a virtual private network (VPN) connection like that shown in Figure 10.16, for example, the source computer generates an IP standard datagram and sends it over the LAN to the local gateway. The gateway, which is configured to use IPsec in tunnel mode, encapsulates the original datagram within an ESP header and trailer, and then adds a new, outer IP header, encrypting an ICV on the entire original datagram in the process. After transmitting the now secure packet over the VPN link, the gateway at the other end decrypts the data, performs whatever integrity checks are needed, and strips off the outer IP header and the ESP header and trailer, restoring the datagram to its original form. The gateway then transmits the original datagram to its final destination in the normal manner. The two end systems never see the encrypted packets and don't have to support IPsec. In fact, the end systems don't even have to be using TCP/IP.

Figure 10.16 An IPsec VPN connection

L2TP Tunneling

As you have seen, tunneling is the process of creating a secure communications conduit through an inherently insecure network. IPsec has the capability to form tunnels and encrypt the data passing through them. However, it is also possible in many cases to use another protocol, such as the Layer 2 Tunneling Protocol (L2TP) to form the tunnel, while IPsec continues to provide the data encryption service.

L2TP is a protocol defined in RFC 2661 that is a combination of the Point-to-Point Tunneling Protocol (PPTP) and the Cisco Systems Layer 2 Forwarding (L2F) protocol. L2TP encapsulates Point-to-Point Protocol (PPP) frames, such as those used by Dial-Up Networking and WAN connections inside UDP datagrams, as shown in Figure 10.17. It doesn't matter whether the original data being transmitted through the tunnel uses TCP or UDP at the transport layer; each separate datagram is packaged in yet another UDP datagram before transmission.

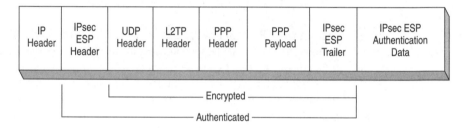

Figure 10.17   The L2TP packet format

L2TP can encapsulate datagrams to form a tunnel, but it cannot encrypt them itself; it uses IPsec's ESP protocol to encrypt and authenticate the UDP datagrams it creates to protect them from compromise by unauthorized users. Although it is possible to create L2TP tunnels without encryption, this defeats the reason for creating a VPN connection in the first place, because the data inside the tunnel is not secured.

Exercise 1: Understanding IPsec Terminology

Match the terms in the left column with the definitions in the right column.

1. ESP

2. Security association

3. AH

4. L2TP

5. Transport mode

a. Protects the IP header against modification

b. Requires end system support for IPsec

c. Provides tunneling without encryption

d. Uses a header and a footer to encapsulate the datagram's payload

e. Specifies the security mechanisms used by two connected computers

Lesson Review

1. Which of the following protocols do not provide encryption services? (Choose all that apply.)

   a. AH

   b. ESP

   c. L2TP

   d. ICMP

2. Which of the following statements are true about IPsec's tunnel mode?

   a. Tunnel mode requires all end systems and intermediate systems to support IPsec.

   b. ESP in tunnel mode encapsulates the datagram's original IP header.

   c. The two IP headers in a tunnel mode IPsec packet have the same source IP address and destination IP address values.

   d. Tunnel mode requires a separate protocol, such as L2TP, to provide encryption services.

3. How does IPsec provide protection against denial of service attacks?

Lesson Summary

- Protocol analyzers are useful network administration tools, but they also open a network up to many forms of intrusion, including password and key compromise, data modification, spoofing, and packet replay.

- IPsec is a series of standards that define a methodology for protecting data as it is transmitted over the network using signatures and encryption.

- The Authentication Header (AH) protocol provides authentication, antireplay, and integrity services for IP datagrams.

- The Encapsulating Security Payload (ESP) protocol provides some of the same functions as AH, plus data encryption.

- IPsec is capable of operating in transport mode and tunnel mode. Transport mode is intended for LAN communications and tunnel mode for gateway-to-gateway links.

Lesson 3: Deploying IPsec

In this lesson, you learn how to configure the computers on your network to use IPsec and how to create policies that enforce its use.

After this lesson, you will be able to

- List the components involved in IPsec communications
- Create an IPsec policy
- Create IPsec rules, filter lists, and filter actions
- Configure IPsec to operate in tunnel mode

Estimated lesson time: 50 minutes

IPsec Components

The administrative elements of the Windows 2000 IPsec implementation are the IPsec policies that specify when and how network communications should be protected using IPsec and the IP Security Policies console, which is a Microsoft Management Console (MMC) extension snap-in that you use to create and configure the policies. IPsec uses policies to store the configuration information for its various security services. Network administrators can then associate the policies with Active Directory objects such as users and groups to deploy them on the network.

Windows 2000 computers also include the following runtime components:

- **IPsec Policy Agent Service.** The function of the IPsec Policy Agent service, which runs on every Windows 2000 computer, is to access the IPsec policy information stored in the Active Directory or the local system registry and forward the information to the IPsec driver.

- **Internet Key Exchange (IKE).** The IKE, as defined in RFC 2409, is the protocol that IPsec computers use to create a security association (SA) and agree on the keys that two systems will use to encrypt their data for transmission. RFC 2409 defines a two-phase process for the IKE negotiation process, in which the first phase consists of the establishment of a secure, authenticated communications channel between the systems called the Phase 1 SA. This involves the negotiation of the encryption algorithm, hashing algorithm, and authentication method that the systems will use, followed by the authentication process itself. The second phase is the establishment of two Phase 2 SAs for the IPsec service, one inbound and one outbound, including the negotiation of the IPsec protocols to be used (AH or ESP, or both), the hash algorithm (MD5 or SHA1), and the encryption algorithm (DES or 3DES), as well as the exchange or refreshing of authentication and encryption key material.

- **IPsec Driver.**   The IPsec driver is responsible for performing the actual encapsulation, encryption, and verification processes required for secure communications. The driver receives a list of IP filters from the IPsec policy that it uses to determine exactly what types of communications should be secured and how it should secure them. The driver then monitors the network's communications and compares them to the filter list. When the driver detects outbound packets that match an entry in the filter list, it triggers the IKE key exchange process with the destination system. After the IKE protocol has established the SAs with the other system, the driver adds the appropriate AH or ESP protocol headers, or both, to the packets and performs whatever encryption is needed. For incoming packets, the IPsec driver checks the signatures by performing the same ICV computations as the sending system and comparing them to the values in the packets and then performs any decryption that is necessary.

When all the IPsec components are in place, a typical communications exchange proceeds as follows:

1. The user on Computer A is working in an application that generates a message to be sent to Computer B.

2. The IPsec driver on Computer A compares the outgoing message's destination IP address or protocol, or both, against the IP filter list in the currently active IPsec policy.

3. If the IPsec policy specifies that communications between Computer A and Computer B should be secured, the IPsec driver instructs the IKE to commence negotiations with Computer B.

4. Computer B's IKE receives a message from Computer A's IKE requesting a secure negotiation.

5. The two computers negotiate a Phase 1 SA and two Phase 2 SAs, one inbound and one outbound.

6. Using the parameters agreed upon for the outbound Phase 2 SA, the IPsec driver on Computer A calculates an integrity signature for the outgoing data, encrypts it, and constructs the IPsec packets by adding the appropriate fields to the IP datagrams.

7. Computer A transmits the completed packets to Computer B, which passes them to its own IPsec driver.

8. Using the parameters of the inbound SA, Computer B's IPsec driver decrypts the data and verifies the packet's integrity by recomputing the signature and comparing it to the results in the packet.

9. The IPsec driver on Computer B passes the decrypted data to the TCP/IP stack, which in turn passes it up to the application that is the final destination of the message.

Deploying IPsec

The first (and arguably the most important) step in deploying IPsec on your network is to assess the needs of your users and determine exactly what communications need to be secured and how secure they need to be. It is relatively easy to secure all communications with IPsec, using the maximum amount of protection available, but this increases the burden on your computers and your network in several ways. Encryption is a highly processor-intensive task, and configuring your computers to encrypt every packet can greatly increase the number of processor cycles devoted to the networking process, which means that less processor time is available for other tasks, such as running applications. IPsec also increases the amount of traffic on your network in the form of additional headers added to every packet and the extra messages used to perform IKE negotiations. The combination of the additional processor burden on each computer and the additional network traffic generated by all the computers could cause a noticeable degradation in the performance of your network.

IPsec is extremely flexible in its configuration. You can specify which pairs of computers or networks you want to use to secure communications, whether the security should be mandatory or optional, and whether they should use AH protection only or add encryption using ESP as well. In most cases, the simplest deployment method is to select the specific computers or networks that you want to secure. You do this by creating filters that use IP addresses to decide whether or not specific packets should be secured. For example, you can configure a database server that hosts extremely sensitive information to require IPsec security for all its client communications by creating a filter that specifies all IP addresses. Alternatively, you can create a filter that calls for the use of IPsec security only when the server is communicating with specific clients or with specific networks.

One of the most important factors to consider when deciding on an IPsec deployment strategy is the use of other operating systems on your network. Versions of Windows prior to Windows 2000 do not support IPsec, so if you run earlier Windows operating systems on your network, you should be careful not to make the use of IPsec mandatory. This is particularly true for computers that host critical network services, such as the Dynamic Host Configuration Protocol (DHCP), the Domain Name System (DNS), and the Windows Internet Name Service (WINS).

Running IPsec Policy Management

To deploy IPsec on a Windows 2000 network, you create policies using the IP Security Policy snap-in. By default, Windows 2000 includes the IP Security Policies On Local Machine snap-in in the Local Security Settings console, which you can access by selecting Local Security Policy from the Start menu's Administrative Tools program group. You can also open the console manually by running Mmc.exe and adding the IP Security Policy Management snap-in or by opening the Group Policy console for an Active Directory container. When you select IP Security Policies On Local Machine in the scope pane of the Local Security Settings console (as shown in Figure 10.18), you see the three policies created on the system by default.

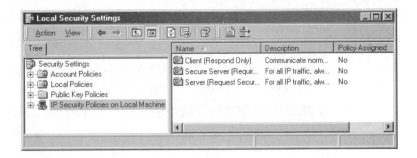

Figure 10.18   The IP Security Policies snap-in

The three policies are as follows:

- **Client (Respond Only).**   Configures the computer to use IPsec security only when another computer requests it. The local system never requires security and initiates a negotiation only in response to another computer's request. This policy is intended for client systems that you want to use additional security whenever another system needs it, such as when the client is connecting to a server that contains sensitive information.

- **Secure Server (Require Security).**   Configures the computer to require IPsec security for all communications and to deny all connections to systems that do not support IPsec. This policy is intended for a server that contains sensitive data or for a gateway system used to establish VPN connections.

- **Server (Request Security).**   Configures the computer to request the use of IPsec security from all other systems but not to require it. If the other system supports IPsec, a secured connection is established. If the other system does not support IPsec, a standard, unsecured connection is permitted. The typical use for this policy would be for a server that you want to use IPsec whenever possible, but which also has to service pre–Windows 2000 clients that do not have IPsec capabilities.

The default IPsec policies are all deactivated by default, as you can tell from the No in the Policy Assigned column in the details pane. You can activate a policy by selecting it and then selecting Assign from the Action menu or by clicking the Assign This Policy button on the console's toolbar.

Creating a New Policy

To configure the local system to use IPsec, you can activate one of the default policies as it is, modify its properties, or create new policies for your own use. To create a new policy on the local system, use the following procedure:

1. Click Start and select Local Security Policy from the Administrative tools program group to open the Local Security Settings console.

2. Select the IP Security Policies On Local Machine icon in the scope pane and select Create IP Security Policy from the Action menu to launch the IP Security Policy Wizard.

3. Click Next to bypass the Welcome page and proceed to the IP Security Policy Name page (see Figure 10.19).

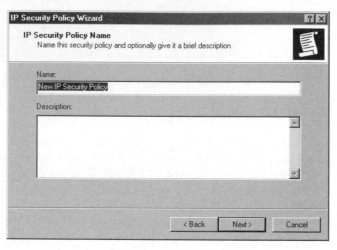

Figure 10.19   The IP Security Policy Name page in the IP Security Policy Wizard

4. Specify a name for the new policy in the Name box and add a description, if desired. Click Next to proceed to the Requests For Secure Communication page (see Figure 10.20).

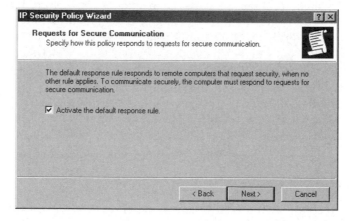

Figure 10.20   The Requests For Secure Communication page in the IP Security Policy Wizard

5. Select the Activate The Default Response Rule check box if you want the computer to respond to requests for secure communications from other

systems. Click Next to proceed to the Default Response Rule Authentication Method page (see Figure 10.21).

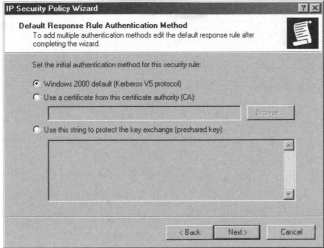

Figure 10.21 The Default Response Rule Authentication Method page in the IP Security Policy Wizard

6. Specify the authentication method that you want the policy to use by choosing from the following options. Click Next to proceed to the Completing The IP Security Policy Wizard page.

- Windows 2000 Default (Kerberos V5 Protocol)
- Use A Certificate From This Certificate Authority (CA)
- Use This String To Protect The Key Exchange (Preshared Key)

Windows 2000 IPsec uses Kerberos V5 for authentication by default, but you can also elect to use a certificate obtained from a third-party certificate authority or from the Windows 2000 CA. The third option is the use of an alphanumeric string that you specify in the box provided. This string functions as a preshared key for the communicating systems as long as you configure all the other computers that will be communicating with this system to use the exact same string. This method is designed for use with non–Windows 2000 computers that support IPsec but do not support Kerberos V5 authentication.

7. Select the Edit Properties check box to configure the new policy further after the wizard is completed. Click Finish to close the wizard and create the new policy, which appears in the details pane of the Local Security Settings console.

Creating Policies in Active Directory

The procedure in the preceding section describes the process of creating a policy for a local system, but you can also create IPsec policies and apply them to domain, organizational unit, or site objects in the Active Directory service using group policies. To do this, use the following procedure:

1. Click Start and open the Active Directory Users And Computers console from the Administrative Tools program group. (To apply an IPsec policy to a site object, open the Active Directory Sites And Services console instead.)

2. Select the domain, organizational unit, or site object to which you want to apply an IPsec policy and select Properties from the Action menu to open the Properties dialog box for the object.

3. Click the Group Policy tab in the Properties dialog box.

4. Select an entry in the group Policy Object Links list and click Edit to open the Group Policy console. You can also create a new group policy by clicking Add.

5. In the console's scope pane, browse through the Computer Configuration, Windows Settings, and Security Settings headings and select the IP Security Policies On Active Directory icon. Notice that the same three default IPsec policies that you saw in the Local Security Settings console appear here as well.

6. Select Create IP Security Policy from the Action menu to launch the same IP Security Policy Wizard as in the Local Security Settings console.

7. Complete the wizard using the same steps as the previous procedure.

Configuring IPsec Policies

IPsec policies are composed of three basic elements: rules, IP filter lists, and filter actions. A rule is a combination of an IP filter list and a filter action that determines when and how security is to be used. A filter list is a selection of IP addresses, protocols, or ports, or a combination of the three, that identify the computers to which the rule is to be applied. A filter action defines the type of security that is imposed when the rule is applied.

For example, the Server (Request Security) policy contains the rules shown in Figure 10.22. The first filter list specifies that all IP traffic should have this rule imposed on it and the filter action for the rule calls for the system to request (but not require) the use of IPsec security. You can modify the filter list to apply the rule only to specific IP addresses and modify the filter action to require security instead of only request it. You can also configure other parameters to modify the security measures that the rule invokes. The following sections examine the processes for creating and modifying these various elements.

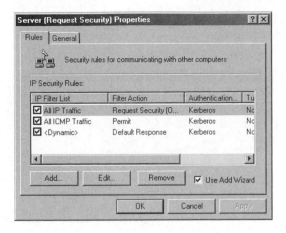

Figure 10.22 The Server (Request Security) Properties dialog box

Creating a Rule

After you have created an IPsec policy, you control all its configuration parameters from its Properties dialog box, which you access by selecting the policy and then selecting Properties from the Action menu. When you click Add on the Rules page of a policy's Properties dialog box, the console launches the Security Rule Wizard by default. (You can also bypass the wizard and create rules directly by clearing the Use Add Wizard check box.)

To create a rule with the wizard, use the following procedure:

1. Select an IPsec policy and then select Properties from the Action menu to open the policy's Properties dialog box.
2. In the Rules tab, click Add (ensuring that the Use Add Wizard check box is selected) to launch the Create IP Security Rule Wizard.
3. Click Next to bypass the Welcome page and proceed to the Tunnel Endpoint page (see Figure 10.23).

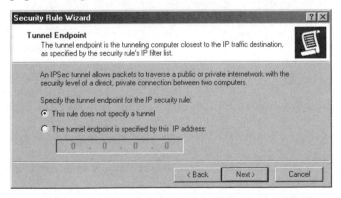

Figure 10.23 The Tunnel Endpoint page in the Create IP Security Rule wizard

4. Click This Rule Does Not Specify A Tunnel, unless you are planning to use IPsec in tunnel mode. Click Next to proceed to the Network Type page (see Figure 10.24).

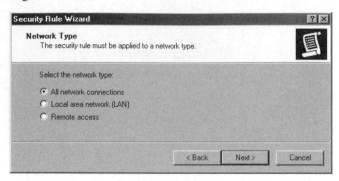

Figure 10.24   The Network Type page in the Create IP Security Rule wizard

5. Specify whether you want the rule to apply to:

   ▪ All Network Connections

   ▪ Local Area Network (LAN) connections only

   ▪ Remote Access connections only

   Click Next to proceed to the Authentication Method page.

6. Specify an authentication method for the rule, using the same options as those shown in Figure 10.21. Click Next to proceed to the IP Filter List page (see Figure 10.25).

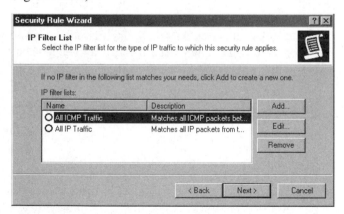

Figure 10.25   The IP Filter List page in the Create IP Security Rule wizard

7. Select one of the default IP filter lists or create one of your own by clicking the Add button. (More information on creating filter lists appears later in this lesson.) Click Next to proceed to the Filter Action page (see Figure 10.26).

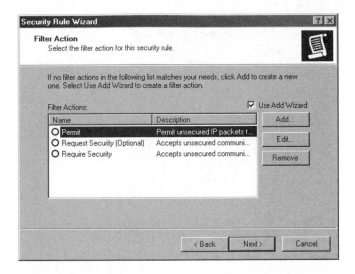

Figure 10.26   The Filter Action page in the Create IP Security Rule wizard

8. Select one of the default filter actions or create one of your own by clicking the Add button. (More information on creating filter actions appears later in this lesson.) Click Next to proceed to the Completing The New Rule Wizard page.

9. Select the Edit Properties check box to configure the new rule after the wizard is completed. Click Finish to close the wizard and create the new rule, which appears in the IP Security Rules list.

You can repeat this procedure to create as many rules in a policy as you need, and activate or deactivate them as needed using the check boxes in the policy's IP Security Rules list. More than one rule can be active at the same time, enabling you to define different security scenarios for various types of communications.

Creating a Filter List

You can create filter lists and filter actions during the rule creation process or afterward by selecting a rule and clicking Edit to open its Properties dialog box (see Figure 10.27). The filter lists define which communications the rule should secure, and the IP Filter List page of the dialog box contains two default filters: All IP Traffic and All ICMP Traffic. Unless you want to apply the rule to all the computer's IP or ICMP traffic, you should create new filter lists or modify the existing ones.

Important   The filter lists used by IPsec are maintained independently of the rules that use them. When you create a new filter list for a rule, that list becomes available to all the other rules on the system. When you modify an existing filter list, those modifications affect all the rules that are currently using that filter list. You should consider the relationships between your rules and your filter lists carefully before you make any modifications to the default filter lists.

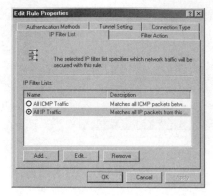

Figure 10.27   The Properties dialog box for a rule

When you click the Add button in the IP Filter List tab of a rule's Properties dialog box or click Edit to modify an existing filter list, you see the IP Filter List dialog box shown in Figure 10.28. This dialog box summarizes all the filter list's properties. You select the types of communications that you want to secure by adding entries to the Filters box, using either the IP Filter Wizard or a Filter Properties dialog box, depending on whether or not you select the Use Add Wizard check box.

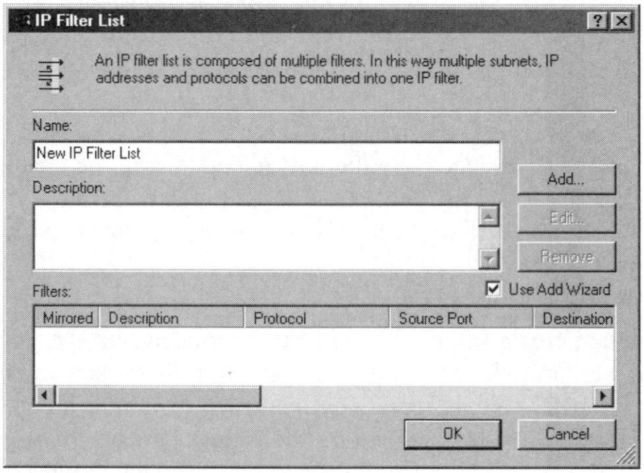

Figure 10.28   The IP Filter List dialog box

The IP Filter Wizard automatically creates mirrored filters—that is, filters that apply to traffic moving in both directions. If you want to create separate rules for the traffic traveling in each direction, you can either use the wizard to create the filter and then modify it to disable the mirroring option or manually create the filter without mirroring. This is the only significant difference between using the wizard to create a filter list and doing it manually.

When you create a filter without the wizard, you see a Filter Properties dialog box like that shown in Figure 10.29. On the Addressing page, the Mirrored check box enables you to specify whether the filter should operate symmetrically. You then identify the computers involved in the communications you want to secure by specifying parameters for the source and destination systems.

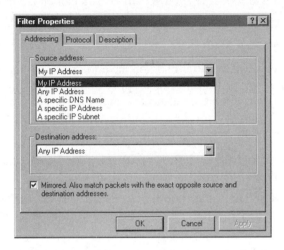

Figure 10.29   The Filter Properties dialog box

These parameters are as follows:

- **My IP Address.**   Refers to the system's current IP address, enabling you to secure all traffic originating from or directed to the system.

- **Any IP Address.**   Refers to any valid IP address, enabling you to secure the traffic originating from or directed to any system on the network.

- **A Specific DNS Name.**   Generates a Host Name box, in which you can specify the DNS name of any system on the network instead of its IP address. You can use this option to secure communications with specific systems whose IP addresses might change (because of DHCP address assignments, for example).

- **A Specific IP Address.**   Generates IP Address and Subnet Mask boxes, in which you can specify a particular host address whose traffic you want to secure.

- **A Specific IP Subnet.**   Also generates IP Address and Subnet Mask boxes, in which you can specify a particular network address whose traffic you want to secure.

On the dialog box's Protocol page, you specify the type of traffic that you want to secure. By default, the filter secures all traffic, but you can select a specific protocol to limit the security to certain applications. When you select the TCP or UDP protocol, you can also specify the port numbers you want to secure. If, for example, you want to secure all Internet e-mail communications, you would select the TCP protocol and port numbers 25 and 110, which are the well-known port numbers for the Simple Mail Transport Protocol (SMTP) and the Post Office Protocol (POP3) used by most Internet e-mail clients. Of course, you must be certain that the e-mail servers support IPsec as well.

After you have created the filter, it appears in the IP Filter List dialog box with a summary of the properties you specified. You can create multiple filters in a list, all of which are applied when you select that filter list to be used by a rule.

Creating a Filter Action

After you've created a filter list, you have to create a filter action that specifies the type of security the rule should apply to the traffic conforming to the list. Once again, you can use a wizard to create the filter action or do it manually. The Filter Action page of the rule's Properties dialog box lists three filter actions that are created by default, which are as follows:

- **Permit.**   Allows the traffic specified by the filter list to proceed without requesting security of any kind.
- **Request Security (Optional).**   Causes the system to request security for the traffic specified by the filter list but enables it to proceed even if the other system does not support IPsec.
- **Require Security.**   Requires security for the traffic specified by the filter list and refuses communications with systems that do not support IPsec.

Although you can create a filter action manually, the IP Security Filter Action Wizard provides additional guidance and explanation that simplifies the process. To create a filter action using the IP Security Filter Action Wizard, use the following procedure:

1. Open the Properties dialog box for a rule and click the Filter Action tab (see Figure 10.30).

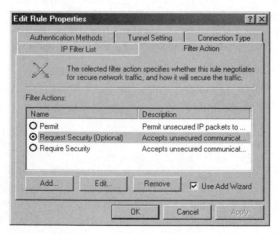

Figure 10.30   The Filter Action tab of a rule's Properties dialog box

2. Click Add, ensuring that the Use Add Wizard check box is selected, to launch the IP Security Filter Action Wizard.

3. Click Next to bypass the Welcome page and proceed to the Filter Action Name page (see Figure 10.31).

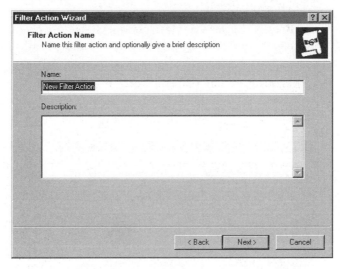

Figure 10.31   The Filter Action Name page of the IP Security Filter Action Wizard

4. Specify a name for the new filter action policy in the Name box and add a description, if desired. Click Next to proceed to the Filter Action General Options page (see Figure 10.32).

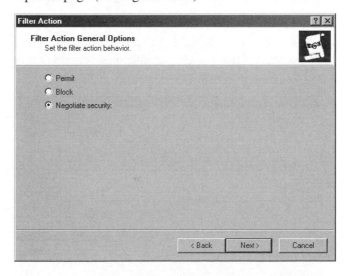

Figure 10.32   The Filter Action General Options page of the IP Security Filter Action Wizard

5. Specify which action you want the rule to take for the systems that conform to the filter list, choosing from the following options:

- **Permit.** Causes the rule to allow any communication between the systems specified in the IP filter list to occur without IPsec security or negotiation of any kind.

- **Block.** Causes the rule to prevent all security negotiation and all communication from occurring between the systems specified in the IP filter list.

- **Negotiate Security.** Enables the systems specified in the IP filter list to negotiate a common set of security parameters.

Click Next to proceed to the Communicating With Computers That Do Not Support IPsec page (see Figure 10.33).

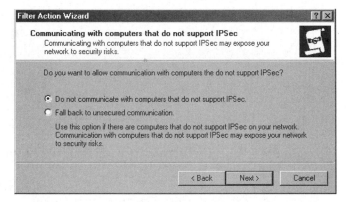

Figure 10.33 The Communicating With Computers That Do Not Support IPsec page of the IP Security Filter Action Wizard

6. Specify whether you want to block all communications with computers that do not support IPsec or permit unsecured communications when IPsec is unsupported. Click Next to proceed to the IP Traffic Security page (see Figure 10.34).

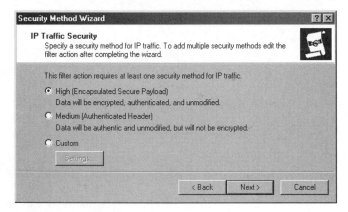

Figure 10.34 The IP Traffic Security page of the IP Security Filter Action Wizard

7. Specify the security method the rule should use for communications between the systems that conform to the filter list, choosing from the following options:

- **High (Encapsulated Secure Payload).**   Causes the data to be authenticated and encrypted and ensures that it arrives at its destination unmodified.

- **Medium (Authenticated Header).**   Authenticates the data and ensures that it arrives unmodified but does not encrypt it.

- **Custom.**   By selecting this option and clicking Settings to display the Custom Security Method Settings dialog box (see Figure 10.35), you can specify which IPsec protocols to use, and which algorithms to use with each protocol.

Click Next to proceed to the Completing The IP Security Filter Action Wizard page.

Figure 10.35   The Custom Security Method Settings dialog box

8. Click Finish to create the new filter action and close the wizard.

When you have completed creating and configuring the rules, filter lists, and filter actions for your system, you are ready to activate them. Be sure that the appropriate filter list is associated with each rule you plan to use and that you activate the rules you want to use for each policy by filling the check boxes in the rules list of the policy's Properties dialog box. Finally, you must activate your policies by assigning them, using the Assign button on the MMC toolbar or the Assign menu item.

Configuring IPsec for Tunnel Mode

Configuring IPsec to use tunnel mode is simply a matter of specifying the IP address of the tunnel endpoint when you are creating the rules on the computers that form the two ends of the tunnel, as shown in Figure 10.36. When creating a tunnel, you should not use the mirror option when creating your filter lists. Instead, you must create two filter lists at each end of tunnel, one for inbound traffic and one for outbound traffic.

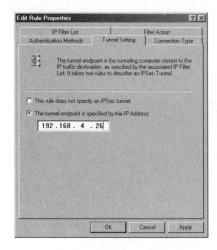

Figure 10.36   The Properties dialog box for a rule with tunnel mode activated

Exercise 1: Using IPsec

In this exercise, you activate one of the default IPsec policies on a Windows 2000 computer and then demonstrate that communications with another computer on the network are blocked. You then enable IPsec on the other computer and demonstrate that communications are now possible. For this exercise, you need two Windows 2000 computers connected to the same LAN.

▶ **Procedure 1: Testing communications**

In this procedure, you verify that the network is functioning properly and that the two computers can communicate.

1. Open a command prompt window on one of the computers.

2. At the command prompt, type **ping *ipaddress***, where *ipaddress* is the address of the other computer, and then press ENTER. What happens?

3. Close the command prompt window.

▶   **Procedure 2: Enabling IPsec**

In this procedure, you enable IPsec on one of the two computers, configuring it to require secured communications.

1. Click Start and select Local Security Policy from the Administrative Tools program group to open the Local Security Settings console.

2. Select IP Security Policies On Local Machine in the scope pane.

3. Select the Secure Server (Require Security) policy in the details pane and select Properties from the Action menu.

4. In the Secure Server (Require Security) Properties dialog box, click Add to launch the Security Rule Wizard.

5. At the Welcome page, click Next.

6. At the Tunnel Endpoint page, click Next.

7. At the Network Type page, click Next.

8. At the Authentication Method page, click the Use This String To Protect The Key Exchange (Preshared Key) option button. Type **MSPRESS** in the scroll box, and then click Next.

9. At the IP Filter List page, click All ICMP Traffic, and then click Next.

10. At the Filter Action page, click Require Security, and then click Next.

11. Click Finish to close the wizard.

12. Now that you have created a restrictive filter list, clear all the default filter lists in the IP Security Rules list.

13. Close the Secure Server (Require Security) Properties dialog box.

14. Select the Secure Server (Require Security) policy in the console's details pane and select Assign from the Action menu.

▶   **Procedure 3: Testing IPsec**

In this procedure you retest the network connection and configure the other computer to use IPsec.

1. Test the network connection by repeating Procedure 1. What happens? Why?

2. Now, repeat Procedure 2 on the second computer and test the network connection again. What happens now? Why?

3. To configure the computers to communicate normally again, unassign the Secure Server (Require Security) policy on both computers.

Lesson Review

1. What is the function of an IPsec filter list?

2. Which of the following IPsec components must be assigned before secured communications can take place?

   a. Policies

   b. Rules

   c. Filter lists

   d. Filter actions

3. Which of the following actions is the best way to create an IPsec rule that will secure all Internet e-mail traffic to your external mail servers?

   a. Enable the Secure Server (Require Security) policy.

   b. Create a new IPsec policy that uses the addresses of the external servers as destinations with the All IP traffic filter list and the Require Security action.

   c. Create a new IPsec policy that uses the addresses of the external servers as destinations and uses a filter list that specifies TCP ports 25 and 110.

   d. Modify the All IP Traffic filter list to specify the addresses of the external mail servers as the only destinations.

Lesson Summary

- The Windows 2000 IPsec implementation consists of an IPsec Policy Agent service, an Internet Key Exchange, and an IPsec driver.

- You configure all IPsec parameters using the IP Security Policies MMC snap-in.

- To implement IPsec on Windows 2000, you create policies, rules, filter lists, and filter actions.

- The IP Security Policies snap-in includes wizards that simplify the process of configuring the IPsec components.

- After creating policies, you must assign them before they become operational.

C H A P T E R   1 1

Using the Remote Access Service

Lesson 1: Introducing the Remote Access Service **410**

Lesson 2: Configuring a Remote Access Server **422**

Lesson 3: Managing Remote Access Security **433**

Lesson 4: Virtual Private Networking **451**

About This Chapter

In Chapter 6, "Routing IP," you learned how to configure Microsoft Windows 2000 Routing and Remote Access Service (RRAS) to function as an Internet Protocol (IP) router, either connecting two local area networks (LANs) or connecting a LAN to a wide area network (WAN) and forwarding traffic between the two. RRAS can also function as a remote access server, enabling clients at distant locations to access the Windows 2000 server and the LAN to which it is connected, using dial-up connections or other WAN technologies, such as Integrated Services Digital Network (ISDN). RRAS also provides support for virtual private networks (VPNs), which enable a client at a remote location to communicate with the remote access server using a secured connection through the Internet.

Before You Begin

This chapter requires a basic understanding of TCP/IP communications as discussed in Chapter 2, "Introducing TCP/IP," and of the Point-to-Point Protocol in particular. It is also helpful to have an introduction to Windows 2000 RRAS, as discussed in Chapter 6, "Routing IP."

Lesson 1: Introducing the Remote Access Service

Windows 2000 remote access technology enables remote clients to connect to corporate networks or to the Internet. This lesson provides an overview of remote access and the process of configuring RRAS to function as a remote access server. Hereafter, the acronym RAS is used to refer to the Remote Access Service component of RRAS.

After this lesson, you will be able to

- Describe how remote access works, including dial-in remote access connections and remote access security
- Configure and enable Windows 2000 RRAS

Estimated lesson time: 20 minutes

Overview of Remote Access

In Windows 2000 RAS, remote access clients are connected to either the remote access server's resources only (which is sometimes called *point-to-point remote access connectivity*), or they are connected to the RAS server's resources and the resources of the network to which the server is connected (which is called *point-to-LAN remote access connectivity*). The latter type of connection enables remote access clients to access network resources as if they were directly attached to the network.

A Windows 2000 RAS server provides two remote access connection methods:

- **Dial-in remote access.**   A remote access client uses the telecommunications infrastructure to create a temporary physical circuit to a port on a remote access server. After the physical circuit is created, the two computers can negotiate the rest of the connection parameters.

- **Virtual private network (VPN) remote access.**   A client uses an Internet Protocol (IP) internetwork (typically the Internet) to create a virtual point-to-point connection with a remote access server acting as the VPN server. After the virtual point-to-point connection is created, the two computers can negotiate the rest of the connection parameters.

Note   This lesson focuses primarily on dial-in remote access; however, many of the topics discussed here also apply to VPN remote access. For more information about VPNs, see Lesson 4 later in this chapter.

Dial-In Remote Access Connections

A dial-in remote access connection consists of a remote access client, a remote access server, and a WAN infrastructure, as shown in Figure 11.1. The physical or logical connection between the remote access server and the remote access client is facilitated by dial-in equipment installed at the client and server sites and by the telecommunications network. The nature of the dial-in equipment and tele-communications network varies depending on the type of connection being made.

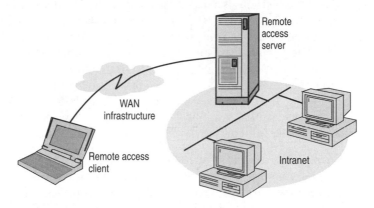

Figure 11.1   Elements of a dial-in remote access connection

The most common type of WAN connection used by RAS is the Public Switched Telephone Network (PSTN), also known as Plain Old Telephone Service (POTS). PSTN is the standard analog telephone system designed to carry only the frequencies necessary to distinguish human voices. Because the PSTN was not designed for data transmissions, the maximum bit rate that a PSTN connection can support is limited. Dial-in equipment consists of analog modems for the remote access client and the remote access server, as shown in Figure 11.2. For large organizations, the remote access server is attached to a modem array that can contain dozens or hundreds of modems, each of which can service a different client. With analog modems at both ends of the connection, the maximum bit rate supported by PSTN connections is 33,600 bits per second, or 33.6 kilobits per second (Kbps). The 56-Kbps modems commonly used today require a digital connection on the server side and are able to achieve higher transmission speeds for traffic from the server to the client. Client-to-server traffic is still limited to 33.6 Kbps, however.

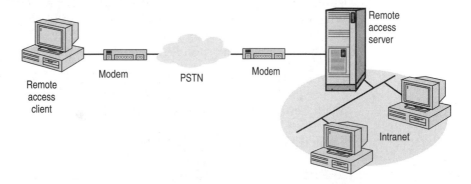

Figure 11.2   Dial-in equipment and WAN infrastructure for PSTN connections

Integrated Services Digital Network (ISDN) is another form of dial-up connection that provides greater transmission speeds and an all-digital connection. Originally designed as a digital replacement for the analog telephone network, ISDN never achieved any significant popularity until the explosive growth of the Internet in the mid-1990s led to an increasing demand for higher bandwidth connections. The standard ISDN installation in the United States is called the Basic Rate Interface (BRI) and consists of two 64-Kbps B channels and one 16-Kbps D channel, the latter of which is used exclusively for control traffic. This combination is sometimes called 2B+D. It is possible to combine the two B channels into one 128-Kbps data pipe or use them separately with different devices, such as ISDN telephones and fax machines. In practice, however, ISDN is rarely used for voice traffic in the United States.

Unlike most other high-speed WAN technologies, ISDN is a dial-up service that enables you to connect to different destinations as needed. The connection process is extremely fast, taking about half a second, as opposed to the lengthy dial, ring, and modem negotiation sequence on standard PSTN connections. ISDN is not a portable technology, even though it uses the same cables as PSTN connections. An ISDN connection requires the installation of special equipment to provide its higher speeds. Despite its attributes, ISDN still has not achieved great popularity because of its relatively high cost-per-megabit of transmission speed and its relatively difficult installation. However, it does provide a higher-speed alternative for RAS connections that functions with RRAS just as PSTN dial-ups do. Generally speaking, the dial-in RAS architecture is the same, whatever type of WAN technology is providing the connection between the client and the server.

Remote Access Protocols

Remote access protocols control the establishment of connections and the transmission of data over the WAN links connecting RAS clients and servers. The operating system and LAN protocols used on remote access clients and servers dictate which remote access protocol your clients can use. In nearly all cases, RAS connections use the Point-to-Point Protocol (PPP) for WAN communications because PPP includes mechanisms that provide security and support for multiple protocols at the network layer. Older RAS protocols used with earlier Windows RAS implementations, such as the Serial Line Internet Protocol (SLIP) and Asynchronous NetBIOS Enhanced User Interface (NetBEUI), have fallen into disuse because they do not provide these features.

After the WAN connection is established between the RAS client and server, the client can access server resources using PPP. For the client to access resources on the network to which the server is attached, the server functions as a router between the PPP connection and a standard LAN protocol, such as Ethernet or Token Ring. Both PPP and the LAN protocols provide support for all the standard network layer protocols, such as TCP/IP, Internetwork Packet Exchange (IPX), NetBEUI, and AppleTalk. This enables the RAS client to access virtually any type of resource on the server's network, just as if the computer were directly connected to the LAN. The only perceivable difference is the speed of the connection, which is much slower than a standard LAN connection.

Note For more information on PPP, see Lesson 1 in Chapter 2, "Introducing TCP/IP."

Remote Access Security

As with any technology that opens a network up to outside users, security is an important consideration. Windows 2000 remote access offers a wide range of security features, including user authentication, mutual authentication, data encryption, callback, caller ID, remote access account lockout, and access control.

User Authentication

The most basic form of security for any network connection is authentication, which is the exchange and verification of credentials that identify the user to the network. To prevent credentials (such as passwords) from being intercepted by third parties, Windows 2000 RAS supports a variety of authentication protocols that encrypt the user's credentials before transmitting them over the network. When a client establishes a connection with a RAS server using PPP, the two computers negotiate the use of a specific authentication protocol that controls how the user credentials are exchanged. The authentication protocols supported by Windows 2000 RAS are as follows:

- **Password Authentication Protocol (PAP).** An unsecured authentication protocol, meaning that it transmits the user's credentials in clear text. Anyone capturing network packets with a protocol analyzer (such as the Windows 2000 Server Network Monitor) can read a user's account name and password from the PAP messages and use them to gain access to secured resources. PAP also has no means for a client and a server to authenticate each other. PAP typically is used only when the RAS client and server have no other authentication protocols in common. To protect your users' passwords from being compromised, you can disable the use of PAP on your RAS server. When you do this, clients that do not support one of the more advanced authentication protocols are unable to connect to the server.

- **Shiva Password Authentication Protocol (SPAP).** A variant of PAP designed for use with Shiva remote networking products (now owned by Intel). Windows clients connecting to a Shiva server device or Shiva clients connecting to a Windows 2000 RAS server use SPAP to transmit their user credentials over the network connection in encrypted form. SPAP is more secure than PAP, but it uses a reversible form of encryption that makes the data packets containing the user credentials subject to replay. *Replay* occurs when a potential intruder takes a packet containing an encrypted password and uses it to access unauthorized resources without decrypting the contents.

- **Challenge Handshake Authentication Protocol (CHAP).** An authentication protocol that uses the Message Digest 5 (MD5) hashing algorithm to encrypt the authentication information. The server sends a message called a challenge to the client in encrypted form, and the client must decrypt it and transmit the appropriate response back to the server. Because CHAP never transmits passwords in clear text, the credentials remain secure during the authentication process. Windows 2000 RAS servers support CHAP so that non-Microsoft clients can access the server. Windows 2000 clients access Windows 2000 RAS servers using MS-CHAP.

- **Microsoft Challenge Handshake Authentication Protocol (MS-CHAP) version 1 and version 2.** An extension of the CHAP authentication protocol that provides greater security and support for the use of Windows authentication information. MS-CHAP is also the only authentication protocol supported by Windows 2000 that enables users to change their passwords during the logon process. In an MS-CHAP version 1 authentication, the server sends a challenge to the client that contains a session identifier and an arbitrary challenge string. The client's response contains the user's account name, plus a nonreversible encryption of the challenge string, the session identifier, and the user's password. The server then evaluates the response and either grants or denies access. MS-CHAP version 2 provides even greater security by supporting mutual authentication, separate encryption keys for transmitted and received data, and keys that are based on the user's password plus an arbitrary challenge string so that each time a user connects with the same password, the encryption key is different. The MS-CHAP v2 authentication process proceeds in the same way as the version 1 process, except that the client's response to the server's challenge contains an arbitrary peer challenge string for the authentication of the server, in addition to the other components. When the server responds to the client's authentication attempt, it includes an encrypted string of its own. The client then verifies the authentication of the server, after which the connection is established.

- **Extensible Authentication Protocol (EAP).** A protocol that enables RAS clients and servers to negotiate the use of any authentication mechanism that the two have in common. EAP makes it possible for the client and server to conduct an open-ended conversation in which the server issues individual requests for authentication information and the client responds to each request. As the server processes each response, it advances the client to the next authentication level. When all the requests have been satisfied, the client is fully authenticated and access is granted. The authentication mechanisms used by EAP are called EAP types; for authentication to occur, the client and server must support the same type. Windows 2000 RAS includes two EAP types: EAP-MD5 CHAP, which is identical to PPP-based CHAP except that the challenges and responses are transmitted in EAP messages, and EAP-Transport Level Security (TLS), which is used for certificate-based authentication, such as a network that uses smart cards. Windows 2000 RAS also includes a mechanism that makes it possible for a server to forward EAP authentication messages of any type to a Remote Authentication Dial-In User Service (RADIUS) server.

You can configure a Windows 2000 RAS server to use any or all of these authentication methods. If the remote access does not support any of the authentication protocols that the server is configured to use, the connection is denied.

Mutual Authentication

As mentioned earlier, mutual authentication is obtained by authenticating both ends of the connection through the exchange of encrypted user credentials. This is possible through the use of PPP with MS-CHAP version 2 or with EAP-TLS. During the mutual authentication procedure, the remote access client authenticates itself to the RAS server, and then the RAS server authenticates itself to the remote access client.

Data Encryption

Data encryption encodes the data sent between the remote access client and the RAS server. However, remote access data encryption provides protection only on the WAN link between the RAS client and server. If end-to-end encryption is needed, such as between a RAS client and another computer on the server network, you can use the IP Security (IPsec) extensions to create an encrypted end-to-end connection after establishing the RAS connection.

Data encryption on a remote access connection is based on a secret encryption key known to the RAS server and the client. This shared secret key is generated during the user authentication process. Data encryption is possible over dial-in remote access links when using PPP along with EAP-TLS or MS-CHAP. As with authentication, you can configure the RAS server to require data encryption. If the remote access client cannot perform the required encryption, the connection attempt is rejected.

Callback

With callback, the remote client dials into the RAS server, authenticates itself, and then severs the connection. The server then calls the client back and reestablishes the connection. You can configure the server to call the client back at a preset number or at a number specified by the client during the initial call. This enables a traveling user to dial in and have the RAS server call back the remote access client at the current location, saving telephone charges. When you configure the server to always call the client back at the same number, you prevent unauthorized users from connecting to the server using different telephone numbers.

Caller ID

RAS can use caller ID to verify that a call from a client is coming from a specified phone number. You configure caller ID as part of the dial-in properties of the user account. If the caller ID number of the incoming connection for that user does not match the configured caller ID, the connection is denied.

Remote Access Account Lockout

The remote access account lockout feature enabled in the registry on the server providing authentication specifies how many failed remote access authentication attempts a user is permitted before the server denies remote access. Remote access account lockout is especially important for VPN connections over the Internet. Malicious Internet users can attempt to access an organization's intranet by repeatedly sending credentials (a valid user name and a guessed password) during the VPN connection authentication process. With remote access account lockout enabled, this type of attack is thwarted after a specified number of failed attempts.

Access Control

In addition to the various connection techniques described in the previous sections, you can also control remote client access to your network in other ways. You can configure individual Windows 2000 user accounts to permit or deny remote network access, and you can create remote access policies to control whether remote users can access a server, based on a variety of criteria. For more information on creating remote access policies, see Lesson 3 later in this chapter.

Installing a Remote Access Server

The Routing and Remote Access Service is responsible for all remote access functions in Windows 2000 Server. Although RRAS is installed with the operating system by default, you must configure and enable the service before you can perform the more specific tasks described in this chapter. Just as you configured RRAS to function as a router in Chapter 6, "Routing IP," you can configure it to function as a remote access server.

To configure RRAS as a remote access server, use the following procedure:

1. Click Start and, from the Administrative Tools program group, open the Routing and Remote Access console.

2. Select the icon for your server in the scope pane and select Configure And Enable Routing And Remote Access from the Action menu to launch the Routing and Remote Access Server Setup Wizard.

3. Click Next to bypass the Welcome page and proceed to the Common Configurations page, as shown in Figure 11.3.

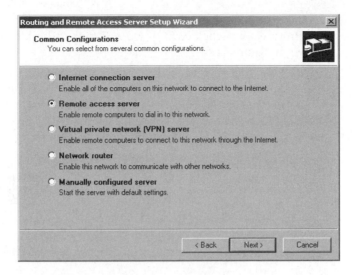

Figure 11.3   The Common Configurations page of the Routing and Remote Access
Server Setup Wizard

4. Select the Remote Access Server option button and click Next to proceed to
   the Remote Client Protocols page shown in Figure 11.4.

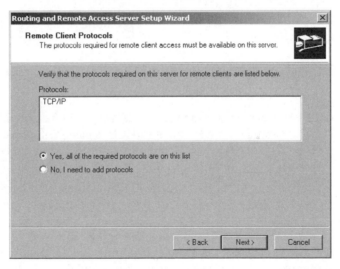

Figure 11.4   The Remote Client Protocols page of the Routing and Remote Access
Server Setup Wizard

5. If all the protocols you want your remote access clients to be able to use appear in the Protocols list, click Next to proceed to the IP Address Assignment page shown in Figure 11.5.

If you want your remote access clients to be able to use protocols not in the list, click No, I Need To Add Protocols and click Next. This terminates the wizard, so that you can add the protocols from the Network And Dial-up Connections Control Panel. After you have installed the protocols you need, you can relaunch the wizard and start the configuration process again.

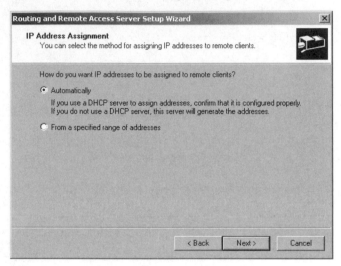

Figure 11.5   The IP Address Assignment page of the Routing and Remote Access Server Setup Wizard

6. If you want the server to assign addresses on its own or by using Dynamic Host Configuration Protocol (DHCP), select Automatically and then click Next to proceed to the Managing Multiple Remote Access Servers page, as shown in Figure 11.6.

If you want to specify a range of addresses to be allotted to remote access users, select From A Specified Range Of Addresses, and then click Next to proceed to the Address Range Assignment page (see Figure 11.7). Click New to open a New Address Range dialog box in which you can specify a Start IP Address and End IP Address for the range. (Be sure that the range of addresses you specify is not already allotted to a DHCP server.) When you have specified an address range, click OK to close the dialog box and click Next to proceed to the Managing Multiple Remote Access Servers page.

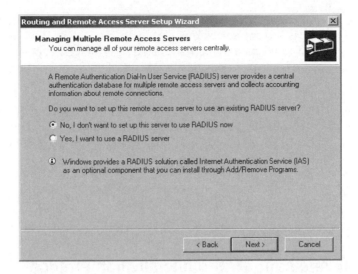

Figure 11.6   The Managing Multiple Remote Access Servers page of the Routing
and Remote Access Server Setup Wizard

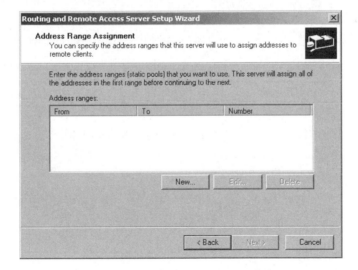

Figure 11.7   The Address Range Assignment page of the Routing and Remote
Access Server Setup Wizard

7. Select No, I Don't Want To Set Up This Server To Use RADIUS Now, and
then click Next to proceed to the Completing The Routing And Remote Access
Server Setup Wizard page.

If you want to use a RADIUS central authentication database for your remote access servers, select Yes, I Want To Use A RADIUS Server, and then click Next to proceed to the RADIUS Server Selection page, in which you can identify the primary and alternate RADIUS servers you want to use.

8. Click Finish to complete the configuration process.

If you elect to use DHCP to assign IP addresses to your remote access clients, the wizard displays a message box reminding you to configure the DHCP Relay Agent included in RRAS. Click OK to close the message box and start RRAS.

Note For more information on using DHCP with RRAS, see Lesson 2 later in this chapter.

Exercise 1: RAS Authentication Protocols

Match the protocols in the left column with the descriptions in the right column.

1. CHAP   a. Included with Windows 2000 RAS to support non-Windows RAS clients

2. EAP   b. Transmits passwords in clear text

3. SPAP   c. Enables users to change passwords during logon

4. MS-CHAP   d. Enables the RAS client and server to have an open conversation

5. PAP   e. Designed for use with Shiva products

Lesson Review

1. You are the network administrator for a financial firm that is deploying a Windows 2000 RAS server. To provide the greatest possible security, the company has issued smart cards to all remote users. Which of the following authentication protocols should you use on the RAS server?

   a. MS-CHAP v2

   b. EAP-TLS

   c. CHAP

   d. EAP-MD5 CHAP

2. In a RAS installation that provides point-to-LAN remote access connectivity, which of the following functions does the RAS server perform? (Choose all that apply.)

   a. Bridge

   b. File server

   c. Router

   d. Authentication server

3. How does the RAS callback feature provide additional security?

4. Which of the following is the primary protocol that Windows 2000 RAS uses for its WAN connections?

   a. VPN

   b. SLIP

   c. Asynchronous NetBEUI

   d. PPP

Lesson Summary

- Windows 2000 remote access provides two different types of remote access connectivity: dial-in remote access and virtual private network (VPN) remote access.

- A dial-in remote access connection consists of a remote access client, a remote access server, and a wide area network (WAN) infrastructure.

- Remote access protocols, such as Point-to-Point Protocol (PPP), control the connection establishment and transmission of data over WAN links.

- Windows 2000 remote access supports the following local area network (LAN) protocols: Transmission Control Protocol/Internet Protocol (TCP/IP), Internetwork Packet Exchange (IPX), AppleTalk, and NetBIOS Enhanced User Interface (NetBEUI).

- Windows 2000 remote access offers a wide range of security features, including secure user authentication, mutual authentication, data encryption, callback, caller ID, and remote access account lockout.

Lesson 2: Configuring a Remote Access Server

After you have completed the process of configuring RRAS to function as a RAS server using the Routing and Remote Access Server Setup Wizard, you can configure the RAS server's properties, ports, and other options.

After this lesson, you will be able to

- Configure RAS server properties
- Enable and disable specific network layer protocols
- Configure remote access device properties

Estimated lesson time: 15 minutes

When you configure RRAS to function as a RAS server, many of the RRAS elements are the same as those you created when configuring RRAS to function as a simple router in Chapter 6, "Routing IP." This is because the various RRAS configurations you can choose from the Routing and Remote Access Server Setup Wizard's Common Configurations page are not all that different, nor are they mutually exclusive. Many of them use the same components, and, as you will see in this lesson, enable you to modify the function of the RRAS service without disabling it (causing you to lose the parameters you have configured) and then reconfiguring it.

Configuring RAS Server Properties

The Properties dialog box for a RAS server contains controls that you can use to configure specific general functions of the server, as well as the functions of specific protocols. Many of the basic parameters you configure prior to letting clients use the RAS server are located in this dialog box. To open the Properties dialog box for a RAS server, select the server in the scope pane of the RRAS console and select Properties from the Action menu.

Configuring General Options

In the General tab of the Properties dialog box (see Figure 11.8), you can activate and deactivate the RAS function of the server and control its routing functions. The Remote Access Server check box is enabled by default, indicating that RRAS is currently functioning as a RAS server. You can disable all RAS functionality by clearing this check box, which doesn't affect any other of the server's configuration parameters.

This tab also contains controls that let you enable or disable the RRAS routing functions. Selecting the Router check box activates the Local Area Network (LAN) Routing Only and LAN And Demand-Dial Routing option buttons, with which you specify what kind of router you want RRAS to be. Disabling the RAS function and enabling routing in this tab is the equivalent of disabling the entire

RRAS configuration and reconfiguring it as a network router using the Routing and Remote Access Server Setup Wizard, except that none of your other settings are lost.

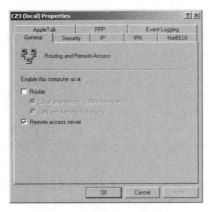

Figure 11.8   The General tab of a RAS server's Properties dialog box

Configuring Security Options

The Security tab in the Properties dialog box contains controls that enable you to specify the types of authentication you want the RAS server to use. For more information about these and other security settings, see Lesson 3 of this chapter.

Configuring PPP Options

The PPP tab in the server's Properties dialog box (see Figure 11.9) enables you to configure the Point-to-Point Protocol features that are available to your RAS users. The settings in this tab are global; they affect all RAS users. If you want to configure these options for specific users, you can do so using remote access policies.

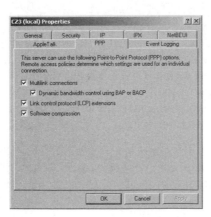

Figure 11.9   The PPP tab of a RAS server's Properties dialog box

The options in the PPP tab are as follows:

- **Multilink connections.**   A RRAS feature that makes it possible to combine the bandwidth of two or more dial-up connections into a single link. See "Using Multilink" later in this lesson for more information on using this feature.

- **Link Control Protocol (LCP) Extensions.**   A protocol used by PPP to negotiate the parameters of a connection between two systems. The functionality of the protocol has been enhanced over the years by the publication of supplemental documents defining extensions that provide additional connection options, such as the transmission of Time Remaining and Identification packets. By default, RRAS enables the use of these extensions because some of its functions require them, particularly the callback feature. Leave this option enabled unless your clients are using older PPP implementations that do not support the extensions.

- **Software Compression.**   Enables the use of the Microsoft Point-to-Point Compression (MPPC) protocol, which compresses the data transmitted over remote access (or demand-dial) connections. Asynchronous modems typically provide their own hardware compression capabilities, but MPPC functions as a fallback in the event that the two modems involved in a connection cannot agree on the use of a specific hardware compression algorithm.

Configuring Network Layer Protocol Options

When you configure RRAS to function as a RAS server, the Routing and Remote Access Server Setup Wizard detects the protocol modules installed on the computer and configures RRAS to use each one. This is why the wizard gives you the opportunity to abort the process and install additional protocols before completing the configuration, if you need them. The Properties dialog box for the RAS server contains a tab for each of the installed protocols, enabling you to configure each one independently.

Configuring IP Options

The Internet Protocol (IP) is by far the most popular of the network layer protocols used for remote access, and the IP tab in the Properties dialog box (see Figure 11.10) provides controls that enable and disable the IP functionality of the RAS server. The Enable IP Routing check box, which is enabled by default, makes it possible for clients connected to the RAS server to access other resources on the network using the RRAS computer as a router. If you want to limit your users' access to resources on the RRAS computer itself, clear this check box.

The Allow IP-Based Remote Access And Demand-Dial Connections check box controls IP connectivity for remote access users. Clearing this check box prevents users from connecting to the server using the IP protocol. Although most RAS servers are used to support IP clients, there might be cases in which you don't want users connecting with IP. Obviously, if RAS is going to function at all, you must enable at least one of the other protocols if you disable IP.

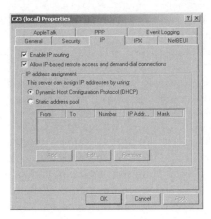

Figure 11.10   The IP tab of a RAS server's Properties dialog box

The IP Address Assignment box is where you specify how RAS clients will receive IP addresses from the server. You had the opportunity to configure this option during the initial configuration of the RAS server, but here you can modify your settings by clicking the appropriate option button to select either DHCP address assignments or a static address pool. If you elect to use an address pool, you can modify your address ranges as needed using these controls to support additional users or to reclaim addresses for other purposes.

Configuring IPX Options

The IPX tab in the server's Properties dialog box (see Figure 11.11) is similar to that of IP. The Allow IPX-Based Remote Access And Demand-Dial Connections check box enables clients to connect to the server using the IPX protocol, and the Enable Network Access For Remote Clients And Demand-Dial Connections check box specifies whether RRAS should function as an IPX router, enabling clients to access other IPX resources on the network.

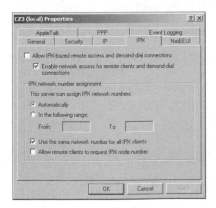

Figure 11.11   The IPX tab of a RAS server's Properties dialog box

IPX uses network and node addresses, just as IP addresses have network and host identifiers. The remaining controls in the IPX tab specify how the RAS server should assign addresses to IP clients. The default setting enables the server to assign network address values to IPX clients automatically, and this is generally the best option to choose. However, you can also click the In The Following Range option button and specify a range of network addresses in the From and To boxes.

The Use The Same Network Number For All IPX Clients check box is enabled by default and causes the server to provide all IPX clients with immediate access to all IPX resources by putting them on the same network. The Allow Remote Clients To Request IPX Node Number check box is disabled by default, and in most cases it should remain so. When this option is enabled, a client can connect to the server and request any node address, even one used by another device. This is a potential security hazard that is best avoided by leaving this option disabled.

Configuring NetBEUI Options

The NetBEUI tab (see Figure 11.12) has only two options, enabling you to specify whether or not clients should be able to connect to the server using the NetBEUI protocol, and, if they should, whether they should have access to the entire network or just to resources on the RAS server.

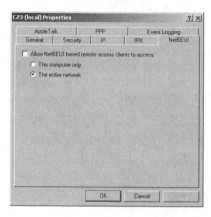

Figure 11.12   The NetBEUI tab of a RAS server's Properties dialog box

The AppleTalk tab is simpler still, providing only a single Enables AppleTalk Remote Access check box that you can use to enable or disable client access using the AppleTalk protocol.

Configuring Event Logging Options

The Event Logging tab contains controls that you can use to specify whether the RAS server should maintain a log and what information should be included in it. For more information about using logs to monitor RAS activities, see Lesson 2 in Chapter 14, "Monitoring Network Activity."

Allowing Inbound Connections

When you configure RRAS to function as a RAS server, the Routing and Remote Access Server Setup Wizard automatically creates five Point-to-Point Tunneling Protocol (PPTP) and five Layer 2 Tunneling Protocol (L2TP) ports, as illustrated in Figure 11.13, as well as a parallel port. If any modems are installed in the computer at the time that the wizard runs, a port entry for each modem is created as well. The number of VPN ports that are available to any remote access server is not limited by the hardware and can be augmented as needed. You learn more about using VPN ports later in this chapter.

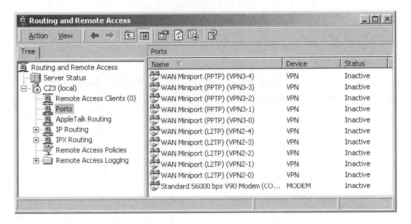

Figure 11.13 A RAS server's Ports list

To configure the individual ports in a RAS server, select the Ports icon and select Properties from the Action menu to display the Ports Properties dialog box (see Figure 11.14). Select one of the devices in the list and click Configure to display a Configure Device dialog box like that shown in Figure 11.15.

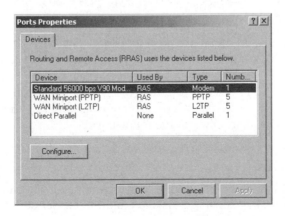

Figure 11.14 The Ports Properties dialog box

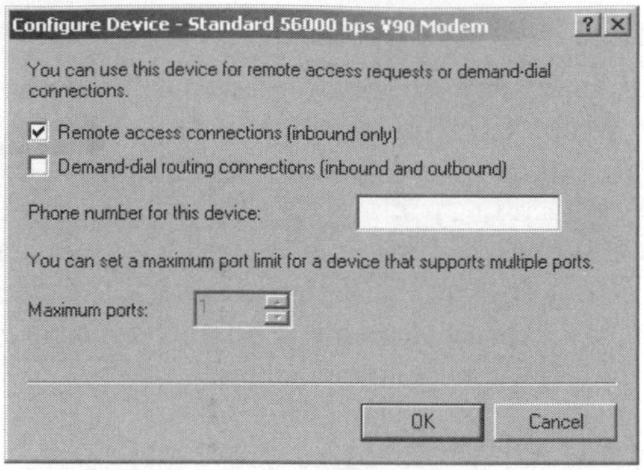

Figure 11.15   A Configure Device dialog box

For each device, you can specify whether only inbound calls should be permitted or both inbound and outbound calls. You can also specify the device's phone number, which the server uses as the Called Station ID during remote access policy evaluations. You can also specify the number of ports supported by the connected device if it has multiport capabilities.

Using Multilink

Multilink is a technique that enables a RAS client to connect to a RAS server using multiple communications links, combining their bandwidth into a single, logical data pipe. Originally designed for use with ISDN, multilink is equally capable of combining the bandwidth of multiple modem connections to provide users with a higher-speed connection to a server. To use multilink, both the RAS client and the RAS server must support it (as the Windows 2000 client and server do), and you must have all the hardware necessary to implement multiple communications links installed on both computers. For example, the minimum multilink configuration would be for the client and the server computers each to have two modems installed on different ports and two telephone lines available.

Multilink is based on the Request for Comments (RFC) 1990 standard entitled "The PPP Multilink Protocol (MP)," published by the Internet Engineering Task Force (IETF). Multilink is based on an extension to the Link Control Protocol (LCP), which PPP uses to negotiate the type of connection that will be established between two computers. The computer initiating the connection includes an LCP option that indicates the following:

- That the computer is capable of combining multiple physical links into one logical link
- That the computer is capable of receiving upper-layer data packets that have been fragmented using a special multilink header defined in the standard

- That the computer is capable of receiving packets of a size specified in the option (which might be larger than the maximum receive unit for one of the physical links)

After the two computers have successfully negotiated the use of multilink, they are free to transmit packets that have been encapsulated and possibly fragmented using the multilink header. In multilink communications, network layer datagrams are formed in the usual manner (although they can be larger than those used on a single link) and encapsulated by PPP. The PPP packet is then broken up into fragments small enough to be transmitted over a single physical link, and a new PPP header consisting of a multilink protocol identifier and a multilink header is added to each fragment. The multilink header consists of a sequence number and two flags that indicate whether the fragment contains the beginning or the ending of a packet. The individual fragments can then be transmitted over different physical links and reassembled when they reach the destination.

To use multilink, both the RAS client and the RAS server must be capable of supporting the option and configured to use it. In a Windows 2000 RAS server, you do this by selecting the Multilink Connections check box in the PPP tab in the server's Properties dialog box.

You can also select the Dynamic Bandwidth Control Using BAP Or BACP check box. The Bandwidth Allocation Protocol (BAP) and the Bandwidth Allocation Control Protocol (BACP), as defined in RFC 2125, are protocols that implement a method for dynamically allocating bandwidth on a multilink connection. BAP manages the number of links in a logical multilink connection (called a bundle), and BACP defines messages that are used to add links to, and remove them from, a bundle. Selecting this check box enables the use of these protocols. You can also configure BAP settings for specific connections by setting options in the remote access profile associated with a specific remote access policy, as shown in Figure 11.16. In this dialog box, you specify a percentage and a time interval that represent the point at which the server should disable one of the links in the bundle.

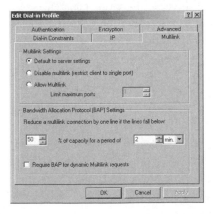

Figure 11.16   The Multilink tab of the Edit Dial-In Profile dialog box

Using RRAS with DHCP

When a Routing and Remote Access address pool is configured to use DHCP, no DHCP packets go over the wire to the clients. RRAS uses DHCP to lease addresses in blocks of 10, stores them in the registry, and allocates them to clients as needed. When all the addresses in the initial pool are allocated, RRAS leases another block of 10. RRAS server releases the DHCP addresses when the service is shut down. You can modify the number of addresses that RRAS leases by modifying the value of the InitialAddressPoolSize in the registry, which is located in the following key: \System\CurrentControlSet\Services\RemoteAccess\Parameters\Ip. The value of the InitialAddressPoolSize entry is the number of DHCP leases that RRAS initially reserves.

To use DHCP with RRAS, the server running RRAS must have access to a DHCP server. If a DHCP server is on the local network or running on the same computer, RRAS can access it using broadcasts, like any DHCP client. If no DHCP server is on the local network, then you must have a DHCP relay agent, which is a program that receives the broadcast transmissions generated by DHCP clients and forwards them to a DHCP server on another network as unicasts. RRAS includes a DHCP relay agent, but to use it you must first configure it with the IP addresses of one or more DHCP servers on other networks. The procedure for configuring a DHCP relay agent is in Lesson 3 of Chapter 5, "Implementing the Dynamic Host Configuration Protocol."

Exercise 1: Configuring a RAS Server

In this exercise you configure RRAS to function as a RAS server and configure its properties. For this exercise, you need a modem-equipped Windows 2000 Server computer with TCP/IP and NetBEUI installed.

1. Click Start and, from the Administrative Tools program group, open the Routing and Remote Access console.

2. Select the icon for the server in the scope pane and select Configure And Enable Routing And Remote Access from the Action menu to launch the Routing and Remote Access Server Setup Wizard.

3. Click Next to bypass the Welcome page.

4. Select the Remote Access Server option button on the Common Configurations page and click Next.

5. Click Next on the Remote Client Protocols page.

6. Click From A Specified Range Of Addresses on the IP Address Assignment page and click Next.

7. Click New and type a range of valid IP addresses for your network into the Start IP Address and End IP Address boxes. Click OK, and then click Next.

8. Click Next to bypass the Managing Multiple Remote Access Servers page.

9. Click Finish to complete the wizard.

10. Select the Ports icon in the RRAS console. What do you see in the details pane?

11. Select the server icon in the RRAS console and select Properties from the Action menu.

12. Click the IP tab. Is remote network access using IP enabled? How can you tell?

13. Click the IPX tab. Is remote access using IPX enabled? How can you tell?

14. Clear the Allow IPX-Based Remote Access And Demand-Dial Connections and Enable Network Access For Remote Clients And Demand-Dial Connections check boxes.

15. Click the NetBEUI tab and clear the Allow NetBEUI Based Remote Access Clients To Access check box.

16. Click the PPP tab and clear the Multilink Connections check box.

17. Click OK to close the Properties dialog box.

Lesson Review

1. How do you configure RAS to permit only inbound connections on a specific modem?

2. Which of the following RAS parameters enables the callback feature?

   a. LCP Extensions

   b. Software compression

   c. Multilink

   d. MPPC

3. Which of the following protocols require RAS clients to have addresses? (Choose all that apply.)

   a. IP

   b. IPX

   c. NetBEUI

   e. AppleTalk

Lesson Summary

- A RAS server's Properties dialog box contains controls that configure the individual protocols used by RAS.

- Each of the installed network layer protocols has a tab in the Properties dialog box, where you can specify whether RAS should use that protocol.

- You can limit remote access using IP, IPX, or NetBEUI to resources on the server itself, or grant users access to the network.

- The PPP tab provides access to advanced PPP features that you can disable to provide compatibility with older PPP implementations.

- The Ports list contains entries for each of the remote access devices on the computer, which you can configure to allow inbound connections only, or both inbound and outbound connections.

Lesson 3: Managing Remote Access Security

Remote access is an inherently dangerous feature because it is designed to enable users to access the network from any location using standard off-the-shelf equipment. This opens the network up to possible unauthorized access by anyone with a computer and modem. As a result, security is always one of the most important factors in deploying RAS on a network, and Windows 2000 provides a variety of mechanisms that you can use to control which users have remote access to the network as well as when and how to verify their identities.

After this lesson, you will be able to

- Select the authentication protocols used by a RAS server
- Control RAS server access using account properties
- Create a remote access policy
- Configure a remote access profile

Estimated lesson time: 45 minutes

Configuring Authentication

Authentication is the only means a RAS server has of knowing who is trying to connect to the network and whether the users are actually who they say they are. You learned about some of the dangers inherent in the authentication process earlier in this chapter and in Chapter 10, "Securing Network Protocols." Most authentication is based on passwords, and passwords can be stolen or intercepted in a variety of ways. The authentication protocols you select for use with RAS determine how passwords are stored and transmitted over the network.

To select the authentication protocols your RAS server should use, open the server's Properties dialog box (as shown in the previous lesson) and click the Security tab (see Figure 11.17). In the Authentication Provider selector, you specify whether you want Windows itself to provide authentication services for RAS or use a RADIUS server for authentication.

The Remote Authentication Dial-In User Service (RADIUS) is an industry standard protocol for providing centralized authentication, authorization, and accounting services for remote access networking. RADIUS is used primarily by Internet service providers (ISPs) and other organizations that maintain large numbers of RAS servers. By having a central RADIUS server perform all authentication, you enable your users to access any one of your RAS servers without having to create and configure individual accounts for every user on each server. Remote access servers such as Windows 2000 RAS function as RADIUS clients, sending their user and connection information to a RADIUS server, which authenticates the users. Windows 2000 Server includes a RADIUS server implementation called Internet Authentication Service (IAS).

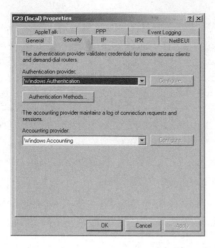

Figure 11.17 The Security tab in a RAS server's Properties dialog box

When you select the RADIUS Authentication option, the Configure button is activated, providing access to the RADIUS Authentication dialog box (see Figure 11.18). This dialog box enables you to specify the RADIUS servers you want RAS to use and other connection properties in the Add RADIUS Server dialog box (see Figure 11.19). After you do this, no further authentication configuration is needed in RAS. You specify the authentication protocols you want to use and configure their properties in the RADIUS server.

Figure 11.18 The RADIUS Authentication dialog box

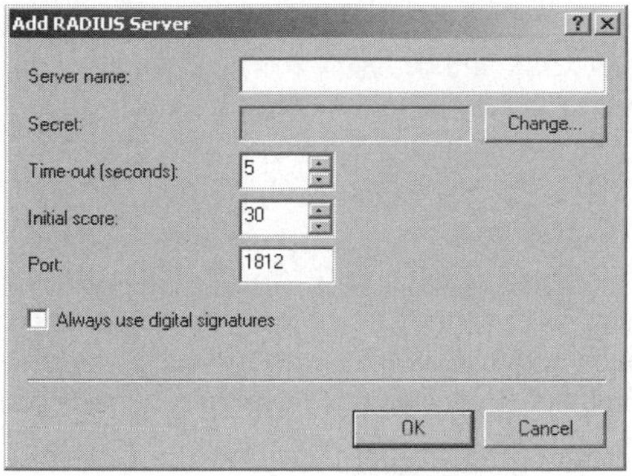

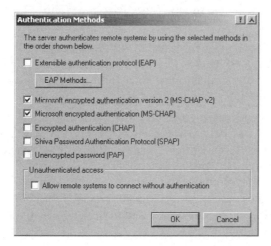

Figure 11.19   The Add RADIUS Server dialog box

When you select the Windows Authentication option, you click the Authentication Methods button to open the Authentication Methods dialog box (see Figure 11.20). In this dialog box you select the authentication protocols that you want Windows to use. RAS clients and servers always negotiate the use of the protocol providing the greatest security that they have in common. You can select several of the supported protocols to enable clients on various platforms to access the server, or you select a single protocol, which prevents all clients not supporting that protocol from connecting to the server. The protocol options are as follows:

Figure 11.20   The Authentication Methods dialog box

- **Extensible Authentication Protocol (EAP).**   An open-ended system that makes it possible for RAS to use third-party authentication protocols, as well as those supplied with Windows 2000. To use EAP, you must select this check box and click the EAP Methods button to open the EAP Methods dialog box. This dialog box contains a list of the EAP methods installed on the system. When using certificate-based authentication mechanisms (such as smart cards) or third-party authentication protocols, you must enable EAP. Otherwise, you can achieve virtually the same degree of security with the other authentication protocols.

- **Microsoft Encrypted Authentication Version 2 (MS-CHAP v2).** The simplest and most secure option to use when your clients are running Windows 2000. The encryption and mutual authentication makes it difficult for intruders to penetrate this protocol using standard techniques such as packet capturing and replay.

- **Microsoft Encrypted Authentication (MS-CHAP).** Windows 2000 RAS includes support for the MS-CHAP v1 authentication protocol so that Windows computers using LAN Manager authentication (such as Windows 95 and Windows NT 3.51) can connect to the server. The use of MS-CHAP v2 wherever possible is preferable, however, because of its support for mutual authentication, separate transmit and receive encryption keys, and its antireplay mechanism.

- **Encrypted Authentication (CHAP).** CHAP is a serviceable authentication protocol for clients that do not support MS-CHAP, but it requires special configuration on the RAS server because CHAP requires access to the users' passwords and Windows 2000 doesn't store the passwords in a form that is usable to CHAP. To use CHAP, you must first enable it here and in your remote access policies. Then you must modify the group policy governing your users by activating the Store Password Using Reversible Encryption For All Users password policy. Finally, every user's password must be reset or changed so that it is stored using the newly specified reversible encryption.

- **Shiva Password Authentication Protocol (SPAP).** SPAP is not a particularly secure authentication protocol, and you should use it only when it is required to support Shiva products.

- **Unencrypted Password (PAP).** Because PAP transmits passwords in clear text, it provides virtually no security against the determined intruder, but it is better than no password at all. Depending on how sensitive the information stored on your network is, you might want to use PAP as the final fallback for users who cannot connect using any other authentication protocol. However, you should be careful not to use administrative accounts for remote access when PAP is enabled because compromising their passwords could have disastrous consequences.

- **Allow Remote Systems To Connect Without Authentication.** Windows 2000 RAS provides this option to enable connections to the server with no authentication at all, but this means that anyone can access the server—and possibly the network. The use of this option is strongly discouraged.

After you have selected the authentication protocol or protocols you want to use, click OK to close the Authentication Methods dialog box and click OK again to close the Properties dialog box for the server.

Controlling User Access

After you have specified how the RAS server will authenticate users, it is time to specify which users will be allowed remote access to the server. In Windows 2000 a RAS server accepts connections based on the dial-in properties of each user account and on the server's remote access policies. These elements are discussed in the following sections.

Managing User Account Dial-In Properties

Every Windows 2000 Server computer that is not a domain controller has the ability to maintain a database of local user accounts, which you can use to regulate access to the RAS service running on that server. However, rather than maintaining separate accounts for the same users on different servers and trying to keep all the accounts simultaneously current, most administrators set up a master account database in the Active Directory service, or, alternatively, on a RADIUS server. This enables the RAS server to send the authentication credentials to a central authenticating device and reduces the maintenance burden for the network's administrators.

Each user account on a stand-alone Windows 2000 server or in the Active Directory database contains a set of dial-in properties that a RAS server uses when allowing or denying a connection attempt made by a user. For a stand-alone server, you set the dial-in properties using the Local Users and Groups snap-in by accessing the Dial-In tab of the user account's Properties dialog box. On an Active Directory network, you set the dial-in properties using the Active Directory Users and Computers console by accessing the Dial-In tab of the Properties dialog box for the user object (which is identical to the tab of the same name in Local Users and Groups), as shown in Figure 11.21.

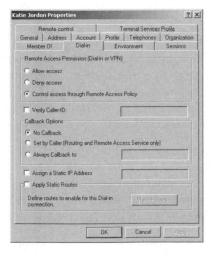

Figure 11.21   The Dial-In tab of an Active Directory user's Properties dialog box

The Dial-In tab includes the following options:

- **Remote Access Permission (Dial-In Or VPN).** You use this property to specify whether remote access should be explicitly allowed, explicitly denied, or determined by remote access policies. If access is explicitly allowed, remote access policy conditions, user account properties, or profile properties can still deny the connection attempt. The Control Access Through Remote Access Policy option is available only on user accounts in a Windows 2000 native-mode domain or for local accounts on stand-alone Windows 2000 computers.

- **Verify Caller ID.** If this check box is selected, the server verifies the caller's phone number using caller ID. If the caller's phone number does not match the configured phone number, the connection attempt is denied.

- **Callback Options.** If this property is enabled, the server calls the client back during the connection establishment process at a telephone number specified by the caller or preset by the network administrator.

- **Assign A Static IP Address.** If this check box is selected, you can supply a specific IP address that the RAS server will assign to the user during the connection establishment process.

- **Apply Static Routes.** If this check box is selected, you can define a series of static IP routes that are added to the routing table of the remote access server when a connection is made. This setting is designed for accounts that Windows 2000 routers use for demand-dial routing.

Note For a user account in a Windows 2000 mixed-mode domain or a Microsoft Windows NT 4 domain, only the Allow Access and Deny Access options in the Remote Access Permission (Dial-In Or VPN) box and the options in the Callback Options box are available.

Using Remote Access Policies

A *remote access policy* is a set of conditions that determines which users are able to connect to a remote access server and a series of connection parameters that define the characteristics of the incoming connection. You can use remote access policies to impose connection parameters such as maximum session time, idle disconnect time, required secure authentication methods, and required encryption.

By creating multiple remote access policies, you can apply different sets of conditions to different remote access clients, or you can apply different requirements to the same remote access client based on the parameters of the connection attempt. For example, you can create multiple remote access policies that require clients to meet conditions like the following:

- Allow or deny connections if the user account belongs to a specific group

- Define access times and maximum session times for different user accounts based on group membership

- Configure different authentication methods for dial-in and VPN remote access clients

- Configure different authentication or encryption settings for PPTP or L2TP connections

One typical example of policy-based access control is to grant access through group membership. For example, you create a Windows 2000 group with a name such as DialUpUsers, whose members are those users who are to be allowed dial-in remote access. You then create a remote access policy that grants dial-in remote access only to members of the DialUpUsers group.

It is possible to control user access to a RAS server using remote access policies only on a stand-alone Windows 2000 server or a native mode Active Directory domain. You cannot use remote access policies on a mixed mode domain.

Note A mixed mode Active Directory domain is one that can use Windows NT servers as domain controllers. By default, all Active Directory domains use mixed mode. If all the domain controllers for a particular domain are running Windows 2000, then you can switch the domain into native mode (using the Active Directory Domains and Trusts console), which provides additional capabilities, such as nested groups and remote access policies. Note, however, that the switch to native mode operates is one-way. You cannot switch a native mode domain back to mixed mode.

To control user access to a RAS server with remote access policies, you must first open the Properties dialog box for each RAS user's account and, in the Dial-In tab, select the Control Access Through Remote Access Policy option. You then define the new remote access policies that allow or deny access to the RAS server based on your needs. You create and configure remote access policies in the Remote Access Policy node of the Routing and Remote Access console, as shown in Figure 11.22.

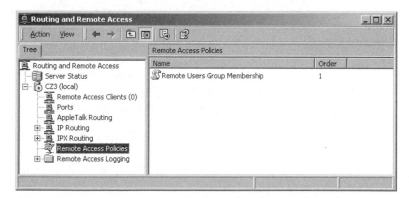

Figure 11.22 The Remote Access Policies node in the Routing and Remote Access snap-in

The Remote Access Policies node appears in the Routing and Remote Access console whenever the Authentication Provider field in the Security tab of the server's Properties dialog box is set to Windows Authentication. When the authentication provider is set to RADIUS Authentication, you configure policies from the RADIUS authentication provider interface instead. One policy always appears by default: Allow Access If Dial-in Permission Is Enabled. This policy provides RAS users with default access to the server until you create new, more restrictive policies.

To create a new remote access policy, use the following procedure:

1. Click Start and, from the Administrative Tools program group, open the Routing and Remote Access console.

2. Select the Remote Access Policies node and select New Remote Access Policy from the Action menu to display the Add Remote Access Policy Wizard, as shown in Figure 11.23.

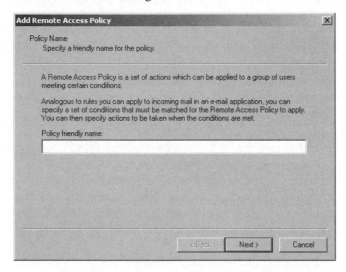

Figure 11.23   The Policy Name page of the Add Remote Access Policy Wizard

3. Type the name by which the policy will be listed in the Routing and Remote Access console in the Policy Friendly Name text box and click Next to proceed to the Conditions page (see Figure 11.24).

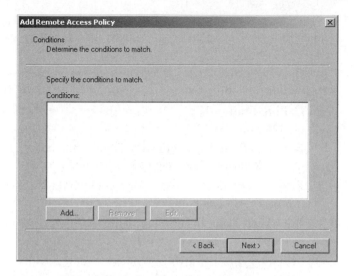

Figure 11.24 The Conditions page of the Add Remote Access Policy Wizard

4. Click Add to add a condition. The Select Attribute dialog box opens, as shown in Figure 11.25.

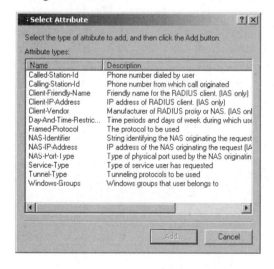

Figure 11.25 The Select Attribute dialog box

5. Select one of the following entries from the Attribute Types list and click Add to open a new dialog box containing controls that are specific to the attribute type you selected.

- **Called-Station-ID.**   Allows or denies server access based on the phone number dialed by the user, as determined by Caller ID.

- **Calling-Station-ID.**   Allows or denies server access based on the phone number from which the call originated, as determined by Caller ID.

- **Day-and-Time-Restrictions.**   Defines the hours of the day or the days of the week during which the user is granted access to the server.

- **Framed-Protocol.**   Allows or denies server access based on the data-link layer protocol (such as PPP) used by the client to connect to the server.

- **NAS-Port-Type.**   Allows or denies access based on the server port (such as modem or VPN) over which the connection arrived.

- **Service-Type.**   Allows or denies server access based on the logon service requested by the user (such as Authenticate Only or Callback).

- **Tunnel-Type.**   For VPN connections, allows or denies access based on the protocol creating the tunnel used by the client to access the server.

- **Windows-Groups.**   Allows or denies server access based on the Windows groups to which the user belongs. This is by far the most useful and commonly used attribute type.

The typical attribute dialog box contains a list of elements, such as protocols, port types, service types, or groups, from which you can choose those that you want incoming connections to use. An example is shown in Figure 11.26.

Note   The other attribute types that appear in the list are for use only with the IAS RADIUS server.

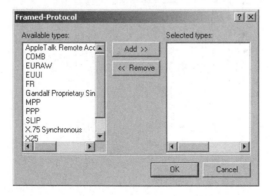

Figure 11.26   The Framed-Protocol dialog box

6. Configure the attribute you selected in its dialog box and click OK.

7. Repeat steps 4 through 6 to create additional conditions, if desired. Then click Next to display the Permissions page (see Figure 11.27).

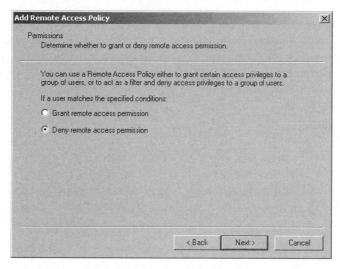

Figure 11.27   The Permissions page of the Add Remote Access Policy Wizard

8. Select the appropriate option to specify whether you want to use the policy to grant or deny remote access permission, and then click Next to display the User Profile page (see Figure 11.28).

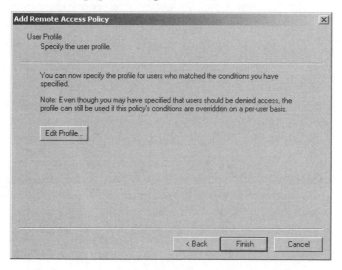

Figure 11.28   The User Profile page of the Add Remote Access Policy Wizard

9. If desired, click Edit Profile to modify the dial-in profile for the users that match the conditions you specified.

10. Click Finish to create the remote access policy.

When you have multiple remote access policies configured, the server evaluates each user attempting to connect by comparing it to each policy in turn, based on the order numbers appearing in the Remote Access Policies list. A connection can be denied by any one of the policies in the list when the user fails to meet its criteria. You can modify the order of the list by selecting a policy and then selecting Move Up or Move Down from the Action menu.

When a user attempts to connect to the server, RAS accepts or rejects the connection attempt using the following logic (policy evaluation order):

1. Check the first policy in the ordered list of remote access policies. If no policies are in the list, reject the connection attempt.

2. If all the conditions of the policy do not match the connection attempt, go to the next policy. If there are no more policies, reject the connection attempt.

3. If all the conditions of the policy match the connection attempt, check the remote access permission setting for the user attempting the connection.

   ▪ If Deny Access is selected, reject the connection attempt.

   ▪ If Allow Access is selected, apply the user account properties and profile properties.

      ▪ If the connection attempt does not match the settings of the user account properties and profile properties, reject the connection attempt.

      ▪ If the connection attempt matches the settings of the user account properties and profile properties, accept the connection attempt.

   ▪ If Control Access Through Remote Access Policy is selected, check the remote access permission setting of the policy.

      ▪ If Deny Remote Access Permission is selected, reject the connection attempt.

      ▪ If Grant Remote Access Permission is selected, apply the user account properties and profile properties.

4. If the connection attempt does not match the settings of the user account properties and profile properties, reject the connection attempt. If the connection attempt matches the settings of the user account properties and profile properties, accept the connection attempt.

Figure 11.29 shows the logic of remote access policies and user account settings.

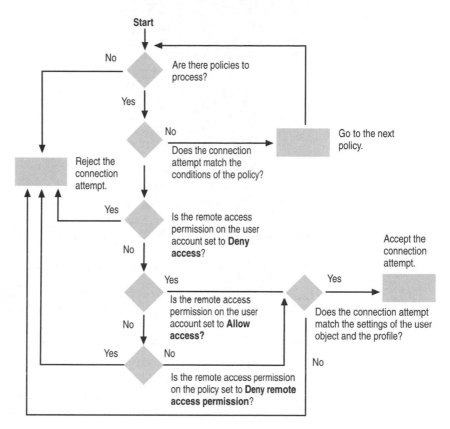

Figure 11.29   Using remote access policies and user account settings to accept a connection attempt

Defining a Remote Access Profile

A remote access profile is a group of connection configuration settings, associated with a remote access policy, that the RAS server applies to all users who meet the policy restrictions and are granted a connection to the server. You can edit the remote access profile associated with a new policy when you create it or later by selecting an entry in the Remote Access Policies list, selecting Properties from the Action menu, and then clicking Edit Profile in the policy's Properties dialog box to open an Edit Dial-in Profile dialog box (see Figure 11.30).

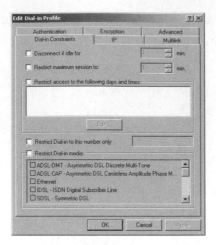

Figure 11.30   The Edit Dial-In Profile dialog box

This dialog box contains six tabs, which are as follows:

- **Dial-in Constraints.**   Contains controls that set limits on the time of day the user can connect to the server, the time the user can remain connected, and the time the user can remain connected while idle. You can also restrict connections to a specific server phone number and dial-in medium.

- **IP.**   Contains controls that specify whether the server or the client should supply the client's IP address and also enables you to create incoming and outgoing packet filters using the same interface as the one described in "Configuring Packet Filters in RRAS," in Lesson 1 of Chapter 10, "Securing Network Protocols."

- **Multilink.**   Contains controls that enable you to control whether the connected client uses multilink and, if so, how many ports the client is permitted to use. You can also configure the Bandwidth Allocation Protocol (BAP) settings for the client. See Lesson 2 of this chapter for more information about using multilink.

- **Authentication.**   Enables you to specify the authentication protocols that RAS should support for this particular connection. The controls are the same as those in the Authentication Methods dialog box, described earlier in this lesson.

- **Encryption.**   In this tab, you specify the types of encryption that the RAS server should support for this connection. The options are as follows:

  - **No Encryption.**   Enables users to connect with no encryption. Clearing this check box causes the server to reject unencrypted connections.

  - **Basic.**   Provides support for IPsec 56-bit Data Encryption Standard (DES) and Microsoft Point-to-Point Encryption (MPPE) 40-bit data encryption.

- **Strong.**   Provides support for IPsec 56-bit DES and MPPE 56-bit data encryption.

- **Strongest.**   Provides support for IPsec Triple DES (3DES) and MPPE 128-bit data encryption.

- **Advanced.**   Enables you to define dozens of additional parameters that enable the RAS server to interact with a RADIUS server on the network. Some of the parameters are generic RADIUS attributes, and others are specific to individual manufacturer's products.

Exercise 1: Creating a Remote Access Policy

In this exercise, you create a new user object and grant that user remote access to your RAS server with a remote access policy.

▶ **Procedure 1: Creating a new user and group**

In this procedure, you create a new user account, add it to a new group, and configure the account to use remote access policies.

1. Log on to your server as Administrator.

2. Click Start and select Active Directory Users And Computers from the Administrative tools program group.

   On a stand-alone server, you can also perform these account management tasks in the Local Users and Groups snap-in, accessed from the Computer Management console.

3. Select the Users container and click the Create A New User In The Current Container button in the toolbar to open the New-Object-User dialog box.

4. Type **Katie** in the First Name text box and **Jordan** in the Last Name text box. Type **kjordan** in the User Logon Name text box.

5. Click Next twice, and then click Finish to create the user object.

6. Click the Create A New Group In The Current Container button in the toolbar to open the New Object-Group dialog box.

7. Type **Remote Users** in the Group Name text box and click OK to create the group object.

8. Select the Katie Jordan user object you created and select Properties from the Action menu to open the Katie Jordan Properties dialog box.

9. Click the Member Of tab and click Add to open the Select groups dialog box.

10. Select the Remote Users group, click Add, and then click OK to add Katie Jordan to the Remote Users group.

11. Click the Dial-In tab and click the Control Access Through Remote Access Policy option button. Why is this step essential to this exercise?

12. Click OK to close the dialog box.

▶   **Procedure 2: Creating a remote access policy**

1. Click Start and select Routing And Remote Access from the Administrative tools program group to open the Routing and Remote Access console.

2. Select the Remote Access Policies node and select New Remote Access Policy from the Action menu to open the Add Remote Access Policy wizard.

3. Type **Remote Users Group Membership** in the Policy Friendly Name dialog box and click Next to proceed to the Conditions page.

4. Click Add and select Windows-Groups in the Select Attribute dialog box. Click Add to open the Groups dialog box.

5. Click Add in the Groups dialog box to open the Select Groups dialog box.

6. Select Remote Users from the group list, click Add, and then click OK to add Remote Users to the Groups dialog box.

7. Click OK to create an entry on the Conditions page. Click Next to proceed to the Permissions page.

8. Click Grant Remote Access Permission, and then click Next to proceed to the User Profile page. What would happen when Katie Jordan tried to connect to the RAS server if you selected the Deny Remote Access Permission option?

What would happen if you selected the Deny Remote Access Permission option in the new policy and then reversed the order of the two policies in the list?

9. Click Finish to add the new policy to the Remote Access Policies list.

Lesson Review

1. You are the new administrator of a network that is setting up a RAS server to provide remote access to a large number of home users with various types of computers. When some of the users report being unable to connect to the RAS server, you discover that the only authentication protocol their RAS clients support that uses encrypted passwords is CHAP. To accommodate these

users, you enable the use of CHAP in the RAS server's Properties dialog box. However, the users are still unable to connect to the server. Which of the following steps should you take to provide these users with RAS access? (Choose all that apply.)

a. Add support for MS-CHAP in the server's Properties dialog box.

b. Disable the Link Control Protocol (LCP) Extensions option in the server's Properties dialog box.

c. Modify the users' accounts by enabling the Store Passwords Using Reversible Encryption option.

d. Modify the users' accounts by enabling the User Must Change Password At Next Logon option.

2. You are creating new remote access policies on a RAS server to restrict server access to specific groups at specific times of the day. What should you do to the default Allow Access If Dial-In Permission Is Enabled policy to prevent it from interfering with your new policies?

a. Delete the default policy.

b. After creating your new policies, move the default policy to the bottom of the list.

c. After creating your new policies, make sure that the default policy remains at the top of the list.

d. Nothing. The default policy will not interfere with your new policies.

3. You are the administrator of a RAS installation that must service two groups of users: traveling salespeople who dial in from various locations at any time of the day or night and customers who dial in from their offices during business hours to check the status of their orders. To ensure the security of the network, you have been instructed to use callbacks and access time restrictions wherever possible. Which of the following settings should you configure to increase network security? (Choose all that apply.)

a. Enable the Always Callback To option for all dial-in users.

b. Create a separate user group for the customers.

c. Create a remote access policy granting server access to users that meet Windows-Groups and Day-And-Time-Restrictions conditions.

d. Enable the Set By Caller callback option for the salespeople.

e. Enable the Always Callback To option for customers only.

Lesson Summary

- You configure a RAS server to use specific authentication protocols based on the capabilities of your clients.

- Windows 2000 clients typically use MS-CHAP v2 authentication or EAP.

- You can grant users access to a RAS server by modifying their user account properties.

- A remote access policy is a group of criteria that a user connection must meet before being granted access to a RAS server.

- A remote access profile is a group of parameter settings associated with a remote access policy that are applied to a connection once it has been granted access to the server.

Lesson 4: Virtual Private Networking

A VPN is a connection between two computers across an internetwork or the Internet that enables them to communicate in a manner that mimics the properties of a dedicated private network. In most cases, a VPN is functionally similar to a WAN connection, except that the Internet functions as the network medium. In this lesson, you learn about VPNs in a routed environment and with the Internet.

After this lesson, you will be able to

- Understand the concepts behind virtual private networking
- Describe the functions of a tunneling protocol
- Configure a VPN server
- Configure a VPN client

Estimated lesson time: 30 minutes

Implementing a VPN

Virtual private networking was developed as a means to provide users with a relatively low-cost method of connecting to a network at a remote location, as shown in Figure 11.31. VPNs enable users working at home or on the road to connect securely to a remote corporate server using the routing infrastructure provided by a public internetwork such as the Internet. From the user's perspective, the VPN is a point-to-point connection between the user's computer and a corporate server. The nature of the intermediate internetwork (also called the *transit internetwork*) is irrelevant because it appears as if the data is being sent over a dedicated private link.

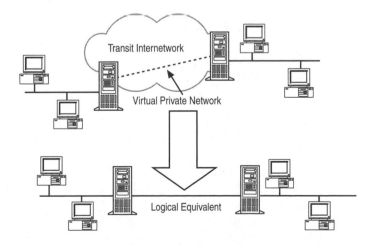

Figure 11.31   Virtual private networking

The traditional method by which a traveling employee in a distant city connects to the home office network is by dialing in to a RAS server using a standard modem connection. However, this practice can result in considerable long-distance telephone charges. A VPN enables both the client and server computers to connect to the Internet using a local Internet service provider (ISP), keeping the telephone charges to a minimum. The client then establishes a connection to the server across the Internet, and the server provides routed access to the corporate network. The connection across the transit internetwork appears to the user as a virtual network interface providing private network communication over a public internetwork, hence the term virtual private network.

The problem with using the Internet for private network communications in this manner is, of course, security. For the client and server to exchange confidential information over a public internetwork like the Internet, a mechanism for securing the data is needed. The method used by VPNs is called *tunneling*.

Tunneling Basics

Tunneling, also known as *encapsulation*, is a method of using an internetwork infrastructure to transfer a payload (see Figure 11.32). The payload might be the frames (or packets) generated by another protocol, such as PPP, or even a LAN protocol, such as Ethernet. Instead of transmitting the frame as produced by the originating node, the frame is encapsulated with an additional header generated by a tunneling protocol. The additional header provides routing information so that the encapsulated payload can traverse the intermediate internetwork. The encapsulated packets are then routed between the tunnel endpoints over the transit internetwork. After the encapsulated frames reach their destination on the transit internetwork, the frame is de-encapsulated and forwarded to its final destination.

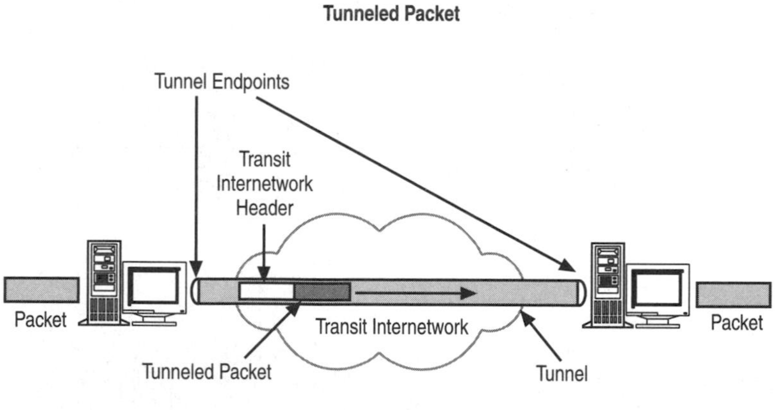

Figure 11.32   A VPN tunnel

This entire process (the encapsulation and transmission of packets) is known as tunneling. The logical path by which the encapsulated packets travel through the transit internetwork is called a tunnel. The name is derived from the way that the tunneling protocol creates a secure conduit (or tunnel) between two points on the transit internetwork. The original frame produced by the sending computer passes through the tunnel without being accessed or modified in any way so that the information inside remains intact. The tunneling protocol also encrypts the original frame. Therefore, even if someone intercepts the packets as they pass over the Internet, that person cannot read the information inside.

Tunnel Maintenance and Data Transfer

Tunneling protocols are responsible for two primary functions in a VPN: *tunnel maintenance*, which is the process of creating and managing the tunnel through the transit internetwork, and *data transfer*, which is the transmission of encapsulated data through the tunnel. The collective functionality of a tunnel maintenance protocol and a tunnel data transfer protocol is known as a tunneling protocol. For a tunnel to be established, both the tunnel client and the tunnel server must be using the same tunneling protocol. The two most popular tunneling protocols used in VPNs are PPTP and L2TP, which are discussed in more detail later in this lesson.

A tunnel maintenance protocol is the mechanism that VPN computers use to manage the tunnel. For some tunneling protocols, such as PPTP and L2TP, a tunnel is similar to a session: both endpoints of the tunnel must agree to the tunnel and be aware of its presence. However, unlike a session, a tunnel does not guarantee reliable data delivery. Data transferred through the tunnel is typically sent by a datagram-based protocol such as the User Datagram Protocol (UDP) when L2TP is used, and a modified Generic Routing Encapsulation (GRE) protocol with PPTP. In some cases, the tunneling protocols use a separate protocol, such as the Transmission Control Protocol (TCP), for tunnel management.

Before they transfer any application data, a VPN client and server must create a tunnel. The tunnel client initiates this process, and the tunnel server at the other end receives the connection request. To create the tunnel, the two computers perform a connection establishment process similar to that used for a PPP connection. The tunnel server requests that the tunnel client authenticate itself. Once validated by the tunnel server, the connection is granted and the tunnel formed; data transfer through the tunnel can then begin.

A tunnel data transfer protocol encapsulates the data to be transferred through the tunnel. When the VPN client sends a payload to the server, the client adds a tunnel data transfer protocol header to the payload. The resulting encapsulated payload is transmitted across the transit internetwork and routed to the server. The server at the other end of the tunnel accepts the packets, removes the tunnel data transfer protocol header, and then forwards the payload to the appropriate destination on the private network. Information sent by the server to the VPN client behaves similarly.

For some tunneling technologies, such as PPTP and L2TP, once the tunnel has been created it must be maintained. Each end of the tunnel must be aware of the status of the other end in case of a connection fault. Tunnel maintenance is typically performed through a keep-alive process that periodically polls the other end of the tunnel when no data is being transferred. Certain tunneling technologies also allow either end of the tunnel to gracefully terminate the tunnel through an exchange of tunnel termination messages.

The most popular tunneling protocols used to create VPNs are PPTP, L2TP, the IPsec, and IP-in-IP (IP-IP), as described in the following sections.

Point-to-Point Tunneling Protocol

PPTP is an extension of PPP that encapsulates PPP frames into IP datagrams for transmission over an IP internetwork such as the Internet. PPTP can also be used in private LAN-to-LAN networking. PPTP uses a TCP connection for tunnel maintenance and modified GRE-encapsulated PPP frames for tunneled data. The payloads of the encapsulated PPP frames can be encrypted and compressed.

PPTP tunnels are authenticated using the same authentication mechanisms as PPP connections, such as PAP, CHAP, MS-CHAP, or EAP. PPTP also inherits encryption and compression of PPP payloads from PPP. In Windows 2000, PPP encryption can be used only when the authentication protocol is EAP-TLS or MS-CHAP. PPP encryption provides confidentiality between the endpoints of the tunnel only. If stronger security or end-to-end security is needed, IPsec is the preferred tunneling protocol. Figure 11.33 shows a fully constructed PPTP packet, with the original application data encrypted and encapsulated by PPP and then the PPP frame encapsulated in turn by the GRE and IP headers. The IP datagram is then packaged for transmission over the transit internetwork inside another data-link layer frame.

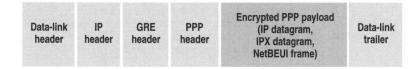

| Data-link header | IP header | GRE header | PPP header | Encrypted PPP payload (IP datagram, IPX datagram, NetBEUI frame) | Data-link trailer |

Figure 11.33   A PPTP packet showing the encrypted data being sent, including header and trailer information

Layer 2 Tunneling Protocol

L2TP is a combination of PPTP and Layer 2 Forwarding (L2F), a technology developed by Cisco Corporation. L2TP is a hybrid of the best features of PPTP and L2F.

L2TP is a network protocol that encapsulates PPP frames to be sent over IP, X.25, frame relay, or Asynchronous Transfer Mode (ATM) networks. When utilizing IP as its datagram transport, L2TP can function as a tunneling protocol over the Internet, or it can be used in private LAN-to-LAN networking.

L2TP uses UDP and a series of L2TP messages for tunnel maintenance. L2TP also uses UDP to send L2TP-encapsulated PPP frames as the tunneled data. The payloads of encapsulated PPP frames can be both encrypted and compressed. Windows 2000 uses IPsec to encrypt the data inside L2TP packets instead of using PPP encryption. However, it is possible for other implementations of L2TP to use PPP encryption. Figure 11.34 shows an L2TP packet prepared to be sent using IPsec authentication and encryption settings over a point-to-point WAN connection, such as a dial-in line. The processing steps are shown in the figure.

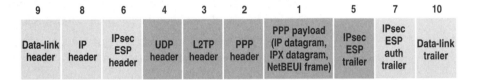

Figure 11.34   L2TP packet showing encrypted data with IPsec authentication, an additional IP header, and data-link header and trailer information

Steps 1 through 4 show normal processing prior to IPsec encapsulation. The application information becomes the payload of a PPP frame, which is then encapsulated by L2TP and UDP. Steps 5 through 7 show the IPsec processing, in which the entire UDP datagram is encapsulated and encrypted by IPsec's Encapsulating Security Payload (ESP) protocol. The remaining steps (8 through 10) show the normal encapsulation of the IPsec information in an IP datagram and a data-link layer frame, both of which are necessary to send the packet on the network to its final destination.

L2TP is similar to PPTP in function. An L2TP tunnel is created between the L2TP client and an L2TP server. The client might already be attached to an IP internetwork (such as a LAN) that can reach the tunnel server, or a client might have to dial in to an ISP to establish IP connectivity (for dial-in Internet users).

Creation of L2TP tunnels must be authenticated using the same authentication mechanisms as PPP connections (PAP, CHAP, MS-CHAP, or EAP). L2TP inherits PPP compression but not encryption because PPP encryption does not meet the security requirements of L2TP. PPP encryption could provide confidentiality but would not provide per-packet authentication, integrity, or replay protection. IPsec provides data encryption for L2TP.

PPTP versus L2TP

Both PPTP and L2TP use PPP for point-to-point WAN connections to provide an initial envelope for the data and then to append additional headers for transport through the transit internetwork. However, there are some differences between PPTP and L2TP, as follows:

- PPTP requires the transit internetwork to use IP. L2TP requires only that the tunnel medium provide packet-oriented point-to-point connectivity. L2TP can run over IP (using UDP), frame relay permanent virtual circuits, X.25 virtual circuits, or ATM virtual circuits.

- L2TP provides header compression capability. When header compression is enabled, L2TP operates with 4 bytes of overhead, compared to 6 bytes for PPTP.

- L2TP also provides tunnel authentication, whereas PPTP does not. However, when either PPTP or L2TP is run over IPsec, it provides tunnel authentication, making layer 2 tunnel authentication unnecessary.

- PPTP uses PPP encryption and L2TP does not. Windows 2000 L2TP implementation requires IPsec for encryption.

IPsec

IPsec, a layer 3 tunneling protocol, is a series of standards that support the secured transfer of information across an IP internetwork. The IPsec ESP protocol, when running in Tunnel mode, supports the encapsulation and encryption of entire IP datagrams for secure transfer across a private or public IP internetwork. With IPsec in Tunnel mode, a complete IP datagram is encapsulated and encrypted with ESP. The result is then encapsulated—using a plain text IP header—and transmitted over the transit internetwork.

On receipt of the encrypted datagram, the tunnel server processes and discards the plain text IP header and authenticates and decrypts the ESP and IP packet. The IP packet is then processed normally, which might include routing the packet to its final destination.

IP-IP

IP-in-IP, or IP-IP, is a simple network layer tunneling technique. IP-IP creates a virtual network by encapsulating an IP packet with an additional IP header. The primary use of IP-IP is for tunneling multicast traffic over sections of a network that do not support multicast routing. The IP-IP packet structure consists of the outer IP header, the tunnel header, the inner IP header, and the IP payload.

The IP payload includes everything normally included in an IP datagram. This could be a TCP, UDP, or Internet Control Message Protocol (ICMP) header, plus application layer data. A limited form of tunnel maintenance is achieved using standard ICMP messages, which enable the tunnel to do tunnel maximum transmission unit (MTU) discovery and detect congestion and routing failures.

Integrating a VPN in a Routed Environment

In some corporate internetworks (see Figure 11.35), the data of a particular department (such as the accounting or human resources department) is so sensitive that the department's LAN is physically disconnected from the rest of the corporate internetwork. Although this protects the department's data, it creates information accessibility problems for users who are not physically connected to that LAN.

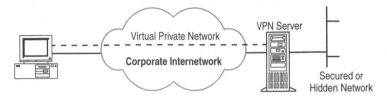

Figure 11.35   A VPN on a corporate internetwork

VPNs enable the department's LAN to be physically connected to the corporate internetwork but separated by a VPN server. Note, however, that the VPN server is not acting as a router between the corporate internetwork and the department LAN. Users on the corporate internetwork having the appropriate credentials (based on a need-to-know policy within the company) can establish a VPN with the VPN server and gain access to the protected resources of the department. Additionally, all communication across the VPN can be encrypted for data confidentiality. For those users without proper credentials, the department LAN is essentially hidden from view.

Integrating VPN Servers with the Internet

Rather than having remote users make long-distance calls to a corporate or outsourced RAS server, the users call their local ISP. Using the connection to the ISP, a VPN is created between the dial-in user and the corporate VPN server across the Internet (see Figure 11.36).

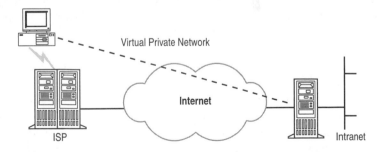

Figure 11.36   Remote access over the Internet

To connect to a network over the Internet (see Figure 11.37), you have two options:

- **Branch office using dedicated lines.**   Rather than using conventional methods such as frame relay, both the branch office and the corporate hub routers are connected to the Internet using a local dedicated circuit and local ISP. Utilizing the local ISP connections, a VPN is created between the branch office router and corporate hub router across the Internet.

- **Branch office using a dial-in line.**   Rather than having a router at the branch office make a long-distance call to a RAS server, the router at the branch office calls its local ISP. From the connection to the local ISP, a VPN is created between the branch office router and the corporate hub router across the Internet.

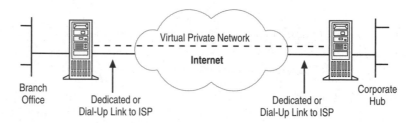

Figure 11.37   A VPN over the Internet

For VPN connections to be reliably available, the corporate router acting as a VPN server must be connected to a local ISP using a dedicated line. The VPN server must be listening 24 hours a day for incoming VPN traffic. Although this is possible with a dial-in connection, it is less reliable because ISPs typically use dynamically assigned IP addresses and the connection might not be persistent.

Managing Virtual Private Networking

Earlier in this chapter, you learned how to manage Windows 2000 remote access. In many ways, the management of VPNs is similar to managing remote access. Virtual private networking must be managed just like any other network resource, and VPN security issues must be managed carefully, particularly with Internet VPN connections.

Managing Users

Because it is not practical to have separate user accounts on separate servers for the same user, most administrators set up a master account database in the Active Directory service or on a RADIUS server. As with RAS, this enables the VPN server to send the authentication credentials to a central authenticating device. The same user account is therefore used for both dial-in remote access and VPN-based remote access.

Managing Addresses and Name Servers

Like RAS, the VPN server must have IP addresses available to assign them to the VPN server's virtual interface and to VPN clients during the IP Control Protocol (IPCP) negotiation phase of the connection process. By default, the IP addresses assigned to VPN clients by Windows 2000–based VPN servers are obtained through DHCP. You can also configure a static IP address pool for address assignments. You must also configure the VPN server with the addresses of name resolution servers, such as Domain Name System (DNS) and Windows Internet Name Service (WINS) server addresses, to assign to the VPN client during IPCP negotiation.

Managing Access

In Windows 2000 you configure the dial-in properties on user accounts and remote access policies to manage access for both dial-in networking and VPN connections. If you are managing remote access on a user basis in the Dial-In tab of the user's Properties dialog box for those user accounts that are allowed to create VPN connections, select the Allow Access option.

If you are managing remote access on a group basis, select the Control Access Through Remote Access Policy option on all user accounts. Create a Windows 2000 group with members who are allowed to create VPN connections. If the VPN server allows only VPN connections, delete the default Allow Access If Dial-In Permission Is Enabled remote access policy. Then create a new policy with a descriptive name such as *VPN Access If Member Of VPN-Allowed Group* and configure the policy to allow access to members of the appropriate group. If the VPN server also allows dial-in networking remote access services, do not delete the default policy; instead, move it so that it is the last policy to be evaluated.

Exercise 1: Creating a VPN Connection

In this exercise you configure RRAS to function as a VPN server and then configure a VPN client. Finally, you use the client to connect to the VPN server, establishing a secure connection on your local network. This exercise requires two Windows 2000 computers on the same LAN, one of which is the Windows 2000 RAS server you configured in Exercise 1 of Lesson 2 (which can also function as a VPN server without modification). You must also have created the user and group objects and the remote access policy detailed in Exercise 1 of Lesson 3.

▶ **Procedure 1: Creating users**

In this procedure you create the user accounts that you will use to connect to your VPN server.

1. Log on to your server as Administrator.

2. Click Start and select Active Directory Users And Computers from the Administrative tools program group.

On a stand-alone server, you can also perform these account management tasks in the Local Users and Groups snap-in, which you access from the Computer Management console.

3. Select the Users container and click the Create A New User In The Current Container button in the toolbar to open the New-Object-User dialog box.

4. Type **Mark** in the First Name box and **Lee** in the Last Name box. Type **mlee** in the User Logon Name box.

5. Click Next twice, and then click Finish to create the user object.

6. Repeat steps 3 through 5 to create another user with the name **Sharon Hoepf** and the User Logon Name shoepf.

7. Double-click the Mark Lee user object to open its Properties dialog box.

8. Click the Dial-in tab, click the Allow Access option button, and then click OK.

9. Double-click the Sharon Hoepf user object to open its Properties dialog box.

10. Click the Dial-In tab, click the Deny Access option button, and then click OK.

▶ **Procedure 2: Configuring a VPN client**

To configure a Windows 2000 workstation to function as a VPN client, complete the following steps. This procedure requires a second computer running Windows 2000 on the same network you configured as the VPN server in Procedure 1.

1. Click Start and, from the Settings group, select Network And Dial-Up Connections to open the Network And Dial-Up Connections window.

2. Double-click the Make New Connection icon to launch the Network Connection Wizard.

3. Click Next to bypass the Welcome page and proceed to the Network Connection Type page.

4. Click Connect To A Private Network Through The Internet and click Next to proceed to the Destination Address page.

   Despite the name of this option, in this exercise you will be using the client to connect to a VPN server on your local network, rather than connecting through the Internet.

5. Type the IP address of your VPN server in the Host Name Or IP Address text box and click Next to proceed to the Connection Availability page.

   If the Connection Availability page does not appear, proceed to step 6.

6. Make sure the For All Users option is selected and click Next to proceed to the Internet Connection Sharing page.

   By selecting the Only For Myself option in the Connection Availability page, you store the connection in your user profile, which prevents other users from accessing it.

7. Click Next to proceed to the Completing The Network Connection Wizard page.

8. Type **VPN Connection** and click Finish to create the connection. The Connect VPN Connection page appears. Click Cancel.

► **Procedure 3: Establishing a VPN connection**

To use the VPN client you just configured to connect to your VPN server on the local network, complete the following steps:

1. Click Start and, from the Settings group, select Network And Dial-Up Connections to open the Network And Dial-Up Connections window.

2. Double-click the VPN Connection icon to display the Connect VPN Connection dialog box.

3. Type shoepf in the User Name text box and click Connect. What happens? Why?

4. Click Cancel to abort the connection attempt.

5. Double-click the VPN Connection icon to display the Connect VPN Connection dialog box.

6. Type **mlee** in the User Name text box and click Connect. What happens? Why?

7. Return to the computer running the RRAS service and in the Routing and Remote Access console, from the Action menu, select Refresh.

8. Expand the Remote Access Clients node in the scope pane. What do you see?

9. In the Remote Access Clients list, double-click the mlee entry to display a Status dialog box. Notice that the statistics for the connection are displayed, including the number of bytes and frames transmitted and received by the server.

10. Click Disconnect to close the VPN connection.

11. Back on the client computer, double-click the VPN Connection icon again to display the Connect VPN Connection dialog box.

12. Type **kjordan** in the User Name text box and click Connect. What happens? Why?

Lesson Review

1. How is the Deny Access remote access permission (in mixed mode or native mode) similar in function to the native-mode domain default remote access policy?

2. List the four tunneling protocols that VPNs can use.

3. How does virtual private networking reduce the cost of supporting remote access clients?

Lesson Summary

- A virtual private network (VPN) mimics the properties of a dedicated private network, allowing data to be transferred between two computers across an internetwork, such as the Internet.

- Branch offices can use two different methods to connect to a network over the Internet: dedicated lines or dial-in lines.

- VPNs use tunneling to transfer data. A tunneling protocol is made up of a tunnel maintenance protocol and a tunnel data transfer protocol.

- You can also use VPNs to provide secured communication between computers on a local network.

- The primary protocols used by Windows 2000 for VPN access are Point-to-Point Tunneling Protocol (PPTP), Layer 2 Tunneling Protocol (L2TP), Internet Protocol Security (IPsec), and IP-in-IP (IP-IP).

C H A P T E R   1 2

Using Network Address Translation

Lesson 1: Introducing NAT **464**

Lesson 2: Installing and Configuring NAT **472**

Lesson 3: Installing Internet Connection Sharing **492**

About This Chapter

In Chapter 6, "Routing IP," you learned how to configure the Routing and Remote Access Service (RRAS) on a Microsoft Windows NT Server computer to function as a router. In Chapter 11, "Using the Remote Access Service," you learned how to use RRAS to support remote network clients using wide area network (WAN) connections, such as dial-up modems. In this chapter you learn about a third RRAS function, network address translation (NAT), which enables you to provide Internet access to your network clients without assigning them registered IP addresses.

Before You Begin

This chapter requires an understanding of basic Transmission Control Protocol/Internet Protocol (TCP/IP) communications, as described in Chapter 2, "Introducing TCP/IP," and of the uses for the Windows 2000 Routing and Remote Access Service (RRAS), as described in Chapter 6, "Routing IP," and Chapter 11, "Using the Remote Access Service."

Lesson 1: Introducing NAT

Internet access is an all but ubiquitous requirement for today's networks. Applications such as e-mail and the Web are vital business tools that millions of people use every day, but connecting a network to the Internet is an inherently dangerous process, and the network's administrators must consider the security issues carefully. In this lesson, you learn about one of the most popular techniques for protecting an Internet-connected network from outside intrusion.

After this lesson, you will be able to

- Describe the difference between registered and unregistered IP addresses
- Understand the problems involved in connecting an unregistered network to the Internet
- Describe how NAT enables unregistered computers to access the Internet
- List the components of a NAT implementation
- Understand the function of a NAT editor

Estimated lesson time: 30 minutes

Routing to the Internet

To connect a private network to the Internet, or to any other network, for that matter, you must have a router that is configured to forward data packets back and forth between the networks. Routers are often specialized, stand-alone hardware devices that are designed to provide this function and other related services. As you learned in Chapter 6, "Routing IP," however, you can also install the RRAS service on a Windows 2000 Server equipped with two or more network interfaces and configure the computer to function as a router.

The danger inherent in connecting a network to the Internet using a standard router is that the same technology that enables your network users to see and access computers on the Internet also enables users on the Internet to see and possibly access your computers. A normal routed connection to the Internet requires you to supply all your computers with registered Internet Protocol (IP) addresses. As explained in Chapter 2, "Introducing TCP/IP," a registered IP address is one that has been obtained from the Internet Assigned Numbers Authority (IANA). The IANA is responsible for registering network IP addresses to specific organizations so that there is no address duplication on the Internet.

Although registered IP addresses ultimately come from the IANA, in practice you obtain a block of addresses from your Internet service provider (ISP). Your ISP might have registered addresses with the IANA or might have obtained them from another ISP. The source does not matter, as long as the addresses you obtain are not being used by anyone else on the Internet. In most cases, you pay a fee for the registered addresses or obtain them as part of a package with an Internet connection. After you have the registered IP addresses, you can assign them to the computers on your network, either by manually configuring the Transmission Control Protocol/Internet Protocol (TCP/IP) clients or by using a Dynamic Host Configuration Protocol (DHCP) server.

When you have configured your computers with registered IP addresses, you use a router to connect your network to the Internet. To use RRAS as an Internet router, you must have a Windows 2000 Server computer with a standard local area network (LAN) connection and another connection to your ISP. The ISP connection can use a dial-up modem, Integrated Services Digital Network (ISDN), a cable modem, a leased line, or any other type of WAN technology. After the router is connected to the Internet, the computers on your network actually become part of the Internet. Your users can now access Internet services, but at the same time, those registered IP addresses are visible to any other user anywhere on the Internet. Some measure of protection is provided by share passwords, NTFS permissions, and other Windows security features, but the bottom line is that when your computers are visible to the Internet, someone will eventually find a way to break into them.

The alternative to this type of routed Internet connection is to use unregistered addresses instead of registered ones. Unregistered addresses are those that are free for anyone to use, without informing an ISP or the IANA. To avoid duplicating addresses that are already owned by other networks, the IANA has reserved three address ranges (listed in Table 2.3 in Chapter 2, "Introducing TCP/IP") for use by unregistered networks. Because the addresses in these ranges are not associated with any specific network, they are invisible from the Internet. Internet users cannot send packets to a computer using an unregistered address, so they cannot penetrate its security.

The problem with this arrangement is that using unregistered addresses makes computers inaccessible to all Internet systems, not just potential intruders. For example, a Web browser running on an unregistered computer can send a request to a Web server on the Internet, but the Web server cannot send a reply back to the browser because it cannot send traffic to the unregistered address. The solution to this problem is to use a service like *network address translation (NAT)*, which makes the unregistered computers appear as though they are accessible from the Internet.

Understanding NAT

The entire purpose of NAT is to enable networks to use unregistered IP addresses and still participate on the Internet. The computers on a network using NAT still have unregistered IP addresses and are still invisible to the Internet. It is only through an intervening service such as NAT that the private network computers can access Internet servers and receive replies from them.

NAT is a service built into a router that modifies the header information in IP datagrams before sending them on to their destinations. In a standard (nontranslating) router, the only changes made to the datagram during the routing process are of the IP header's Time to Live value (which indicates the number of routers the packet has passed through), and, in relatively rare cases, of certain optional fields. A router that uses NAT modifies the most crucial header fields in the datagram, the Source IP Address and Destination IP Address fields in the IP header and, in some cases, the Source Port and Destination Port fields in the transport-layer protocol header.

When a client application such as a Web browser running on a computer with an unregistered IP address generates an Internet service request, it sends the resulting message packets to its default gateway, which is the router on the network providing access to the Internet. This is normal behavior, no matter what type of IP address the client is using. The packets generated by the client computer have the system's unregistered address in the Source IP Address field of the IP header and an ephemeral port number chosen by the client at random in the Source Port field. The destination IP address is the address of the Web server and the destination port value is 80, the well-known port for the Hypertext Transfer Protocol (HTTP) used by Web servers.

Note   Well-known port numbers are typically associated with the server part of a network application. In most cases, the client initiating a transaction with the server chooses a port number at random for its own use. This is called an ephemeral port number and always has a value greater than 1024 (to avoid conflicts with well-known port numbers). The server reads the client's ephemeral port number in the request packets and uses it as the destination port when generating its reply messages. For more information on port numbers, see Lesson 3 in Chapter 2, "Introducing TCP/IP."

The NAT router, like all routers, has at least two network interfaces. One of the interfaces is connected to the local network, and in this case it has an unregistered IP address so it can participate on that network. The other interface must have a registered IP address because it is directly connected to the Internet through an ISP. The two network connections make it possible for the router to forward packets it receives from the local (unregistered) network to the destination Web server on the Internet. The Web server can receive the requests and process them, but without NAT, the replies that the server generates are directed to the client's unregistered address, which doesn't exist on the Internet. Client/server traffic originating on the unregistered network, therefore, can move in one direction only.

On a translated network (see Figure 12.1), the router still has one registered IP address and one unregistered one, but it is also running a NAT service. On receiving the requests from the client, the NAT service reads headers in each packet and creates an entry in a NAT table that contains the following information:

- The destination address for the packet (found in the Destination IP Address field)
- The destination port (typically the well-known port number associated with an Internet server)
- The packet's source address (which is the unregistered IP address of the client computer)
- A substitute ephemeral port number chosen at random by the NAT server

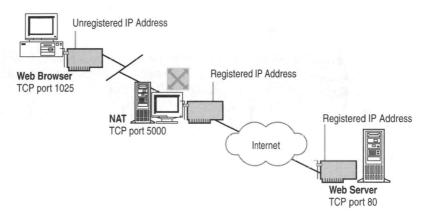

Figure 12.1   Using NAT to transparently connect an intranet to the Internet

The NAT router then modifies the header fields in the packets by substituting its own registered IP address for the client's unregistered address and the substitute port number it has selected for the one generated by the client computer. The router also recalculates the checksum values for the headers to reflect the datagram's changed contents and then forwards the packets to the Web server on the Internet in the normal manner. The server, having no knowledge of the client on the unregistered network, processes the requests that seem to have originated from the NAT router's address and port number and returns its replies to that address and port. The NAT router receives the reply packets from the Web server and then, using the information in the NAT table entry, performs the same translation in reverse, substituting the client's private address for its own registered address and the client's ephemeral port number for its own, and finally transmits the reply packets to the client.

To the Web client, it appears as though it is communicating directly with the Internet server. To the Web server, it appears as though it is communicating directly with a client (actually the NAT router) using a registered address. To other users on the Internet, only the router appears to exist. The actual client is totally hidden and protected from unauthorized access.

Consider a business network with a fleet of computers connecting to the Internet. The business would normally have to obtain a registered IP address for each computer on the network from its ISP. With a router using NAT, however, the business can use unregistered addresses for its computers and have NAT map those unregistered addresses to a single registered IP address assigned to the router by its ISP. For example, if a business is using the 192.168.0.0 private network for its intranet and has been granted the public IP address of 206.73.118.54 by its ISP, the NAT server can map all the private IP addresses on network 192.168.0.0 to the public IP address 207.73.118.54.

NAT Components

NAT implementations can take several forms. The service can be integrated into a hardware device, such as an Internet access router; take the form of a separate software product, such as a software router; or be integrated into an operating system, as is the case with Windows 2000. The core component of any NAT implementation is the *translation component*—that is, the network address translator itself, the service that actually modifies the packet headers as they are being routed to their destinations and keeps track of the clients and their Internet transactions. Every NAT implementation has a translator, but some have a variety of other components as well.

High-end hardware routers designed to provide Internet access to large enterprise networks typically have only the translation capabilities because the designers expect the network to implement any other services that are needed on other computers. The translation process itself already adds a significant extra burden to the router on a busy network, and including additional services would increase the cost of an already expensive component and create a single point of failure. NAT implementations that are intended for use on relatively small networks, however, often include other services that simplify the process of deploying an Internet access solution for the entire network. These products are typically designed to be "all-in-one" Internet access solutions and include an IP addressing component and a name resolution component.

The *IP addressing component* is a simplified DHCP server, which is configured to supply the client computers on the network with an unregistered IP address, an appropriate subnet mask, a default gateway address (which is the address of the NAT router itself), and a Domain Name System (DNS) server address. The TCP/IP client on all Windows computers is configured to obtain its configuration settings from a DHCP server by default, so building a small network for the purpose of sharing an Internet connection can often be a simple matter of installing network interface cards and plugging the computers into a hub. The NAT server takes care of all client configuration tasks.

The *name resolution component* of the NAT router is either a caching-only DNS server or a DNS proxy. In either case, the DNS service in the NAT router receives the recursive name resolution queries generated by the clients and attempts to resolve them. The difference between a caching-only DNS server and a DNS proxy is that the caching-only server sends iterative queries to other DNS servers in an attempt to resolve the name specified by the client. A DNS proxy receives the recursive queries from the clients and then sends recursive queries of its own to another DNS server on the Internet, as specified in the router's configuration parameters.

Note A recursive DNS query is one that passes the full responsibility for resolving the specified name to the destination server. An iterative query is a simple request for information stored in the destination server's cache. For more information on DNS query types, see Lesson 2 in Chapter 7, "Understanding the Domain Name System."

Static and Dynamic Address Mapping

NAT can use either static or dynamic mapping. A static mapping is a configuration that always maps traffic in a specific way. You can map all traffic to and from a specific private network location to a specific Internet location. For example, to run an Internet Web server on a computer on your private network, you create a static mapping that always associates the unregistered IP address of the Web server to a particular registered IP address so that Internet users can always access the server at the same address.

Dynamic mappings are created when users on the unregistered network initiate traffic with Internet locations, such as when a Web browser connects to a server on the Internet. The NAT router automatically adds these mappings to its NAT table and refreshes them with each use so that it can successfully forward the replies from the server to the client. Dynamic mappings that are not refreshed are removed from the NAT table after a specified amount of time. For TCP connections, the default time-out is 24 hours. For User Datagram Protocol (UDP) traffic, the default time-out is 1 minute.

NAT Editors

By default, a NAT server translates only IP addresses and the port numbers in TCP and UDP headers, which alone makes it compatible with many Internet applications. If the packets generated by an application contain IP address and port information only in the IP and TCP/UDP headers, as is the case with HTTP traffic, for example, NAT can translate the packets, enabling the client and the server to communicate transparently. There are applications and protocols, however, that carry IP addresses or port numbers in places other than the IP, TCP, and UDP headers. The File Transfer Protocol (FTP), for example, stores IP addresses in the FTP header for the FTP port command. If the NAT server does not properly translate this IP address, connectivity problems can occur. Additionally, in the case of FTP, because the protocol is text-based, the IP address is stored in dotted-decimal format, and the number of digits in the FTP header's translated IP address is not predictable. The NAT server must be able to compensate.

When the NAT router must translate packet information outside of the IP, TCP, and UDP headers, a NAT editor is required on the router. A *NAT editor* is an installable component, transparent to end users, that can properly modify otherwise non-translatable payloads so that they can be forwarded between unregistered and registered networks. The Windows 2000 NAT implementation includes built-in NAT editors for the following protocols:

- FTP
- Internet Control Message Protocol (ICMP)
- Point-to-Point Tunneling Protocol (PPTP)
- NetBIOS over TCP/IP (NetBT)

Additionally, the NAT routing protocol includes proxy software for the following protocols:

- H.323
- Direct Play
- Lightweight Directory Access Protocol (LDAP)–based Internet Locator Service (ILS) registration
- Remote procedure call (RPC)

Exercise 1: Understanding NAT Communications

Put the following steps of the NAT communication process into the correct order.

1. The NAT router transmits the packet to the Internet server.
2. The Internet server transmits a reply message.
3. The client receives a message from the NAT router.
4. The NAT router creates a NAT table entry.
5. The NAT router puts an unregistered address into the packet's Destination IP Address field.
6. The client transmits a request to its default gateway.
7. The NAT router puts a registered IP address into the packet's Source IP Address field.

Lesson Review

1. Which of the following best describes the function of a NAT editor?

    a. A NAT editor enables you to manually configure static address mappings.

    b. A NAT editor modifies the IP addresses and port numbers in TCP, UDP, and IP headers.

    c. A NAT editor modifies IP addresses and port numbers outside of TCP, UDP, and IP headers.

    d. A NAT editor assigns unregistered IP addresses to client computers.

2. Which of the following elements is not stored in a NAT table entry?

    a. The ephemeral port number selected by the client

    b. The client computer's unregistered IP address

    c. The ephemeral port number selected by the NAT router

    d. The IP address of the destination Internet server

3. What is the function of a static address mapping?

Lesson Summary

- Registered IP addresses are visible from the Internet; unregistered IP addresses are not.

- Connecting a registered network to the Internet opens the network up to possible intrusion by unauthorized users.

- NAT is a service that enables computers with unregistered IP addresses to access the Internet.

- NAT works by modifying the header information in the packets generated by the unregistered computers.

- By substituting its own registered IP address for the client's unregistered address, A NAT router performs a transaction with an Internet server and relays the responses back to the client.

Lesson 2: Installing and Configuring NAT

Windows 2000 includes two NAT implementations. One, called Internet Connection Sharing (ICS), is part of the TCP/IP client and is included in all Windows 2000 versions. You learn more about ICS is Lesson 3 of this chapter. The other implementation is a full-featured NAT server that is incorporated into the Routing and Remote Access Service (RRAS) found in all versions of Windows 2000 Server. In this lesson, you learn how to install the RRAS NAT server.

After this lesson, you will be able to

- Install NAT while configuring RRAS
- Install NAT on an existing RRAS server
- Configure NAT properties

Estimated lesson time: 50 minutes

Implementing NAT

In RRAS, NAT is implemented as a routing protocol. On a Windows 2000 Server computer where RRAS has not yet been activated, you can configure RRAS as an Internet connection server using the Routing and Remote Access Server Setup Wizard, which installs NAT at the same time and configures RRAS to use it. If you have already configured RRAS, you can install NAT separately and configure it to work with your existing router configuration.

Installing NAT with RRAS

On a Windows 2000 Server computer where RRAS is not yet configured and activated, you can implement NAT for a dial-in connection to the Internet using the following procedure:

1. Click Start and, from the Administrative Tools program group, open the Routing and Remote Access console.

2. Select the node for your server in the scope pane and from the Action menu, select Configure And Enable Routing And Remote Access to launch the Routing and Remote Access Server Setup Wizard.

3. Click Next to bypass the Welcome page and proceed to the Common Configurations page, shown in Figure 12.2.

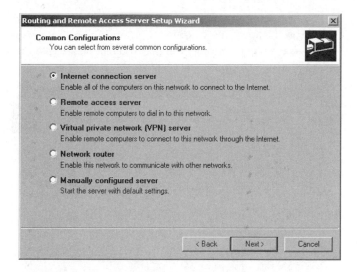

Figure 12.2   The Common Configurations page of the Routing and Remote Access
Server Setup Wizard

4. Select Internet Connection Server, and then click Next to proceed to the
Internet Connection Server Setup page shown in Figure 12.3.

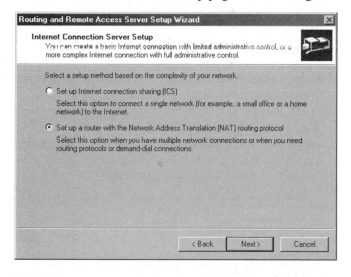

Figure 12.3   The Internet Connection Server Setup page of the Routing and Remote
Access Server Setup Wizard

5. Select Set Up A Router With The Network Address Translation (NAT) Routing
Protocol, and then click Next to proceed to the Internet Connection page, as
shown in Figure 12.4.

This is the only real option presented on this page, since selecting the Set Up Internet Connection Sharing (ICS) option button causes the wizard to display a message box informing you that you can only configure ICS from the Network and Dial-Up Connections Control Panel.

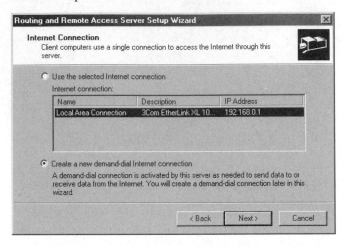

Figure 12.4   The Internet Connection page of the Routing and Remote Access Server Setup Wizard

6. Select Create A New Demand-Dial Internet Connection, and then click Next to proceed to the Applying Changes page shown in Figure 12.5.

   If you plan to use a dial-in connection to the Internet, select Create A New Demand-Dial Internet Connection. A demand-dial connection is one in which any attempt to access the Internet by a client on the network causes the server to dial in to the ISP and connect to the Internet. If your connection to the Internet is a permanent connection that appears in Windows 2000 as a LAN interface, such as a Digital Subscriber Line (DSL) or cable modem connection, select Use The Selected Internet Connection and select the network interface providing Internet access in the Internet Connection list.

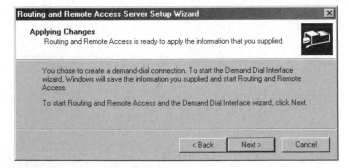

Figure 12.5   The Applying Changes page of the Routing and Remote Access Server Setup Wizard

7. Click Next to start the RRAS service and launch the Demand Dial Interface Wizard.

   The Applying Changes page informs you that the Routing and Remote Access Server Setup Wizard is saving your settings and launching the new wizard to create a demand dial connection.

8. Click Next to bypass the Welcome To The Demand Dial Interface Wizard page and proceed to the Interface Name page shown in Figure 12.6.

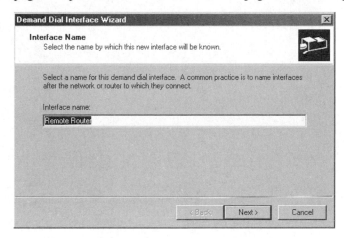

Figure 12.6   The Interface Name page of the Demand Dial Interface Wizard

9. Type a name for the new connection in the Interface Name text box and click Next to proceed to the Connection Type page shown in Figure 12.7.

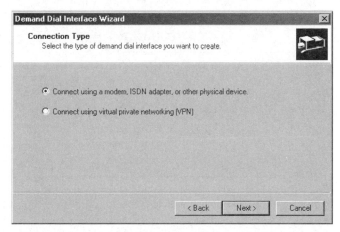

Figure 12.7   The Connection Type page of the Demand Dial Interface Wizard

10. Select Connect Using A Modem, ISDN Adapter, Or Other Physical Device and then click Next to proceed to the Select A Device page shown in Figure 12.8.

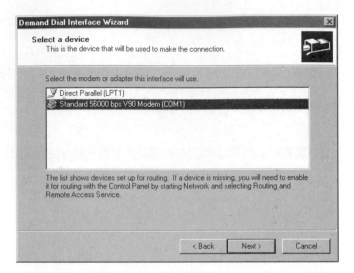

Figure 12.8   The Select A Device page of the Demand Dial Interface Wizard

11. Select the modem or other installed device you want the computer to use to connect to the Internet and click Next to proceed to the Phone Number page, as shown in Figure 12.9.

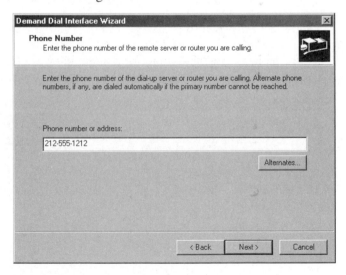

Figure 12.9   The Phone Number page of the Demand Dial Interface Wizard

12. Type the number that you want the modem to dial in the Phone Number Or Address text box and click Next to proceed to the Protocols And Security page shown in Figure 12.10.

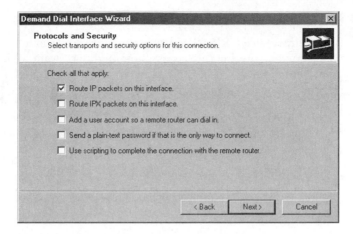

Figure 12.10   The Protocols And Security page of the Demand Dial Interface Wizard

13. Click Next to accept the default settings and proceed to the Dial Out Credentials page shown in Figure 12.11.

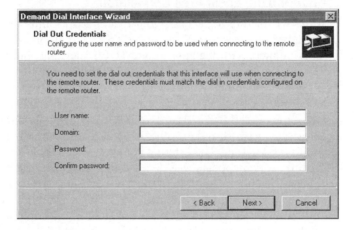

Figure 12.11   The Dial Out Credentials page of the Demand Dial Interface Wizard

14. Type the user name, domain name (if necessary), and password needed to connect to the ISP's server. Then click Next to proceed to the Completing The Demand Dial Interface Wizard page.

15. Click Finish. The Demand Dial Interface Wizard closes and the Completing The Routing And Remote Access Server Setup Wizard page appears.

16. Click Finish.

Configuring RRAS to Use NAT

If you already have RRAS activated on your server and configured to provide your network with Internet access, you might not want to deactivate it (causing your configuration settings to be lost) in order to add NAT. You can install NAT in your existing configuration and configure RRAS to use it by performing the following procedures:

- Configure the computer's local area connection to use an unregistered IP address
- Create a static route for the interface providing Internet access
- Install the NAT routing protocol
- Create one NAT interface for the local network connection and one for the demand-dial interface

The Routing and Remote Access Server Setup Wizard automatically performs all these tasks when you use it to create an Internet connection server configuration. To perform them manually, use the procedures in the following sections.

Configuring the Local Area Connection

To use NAT for Internet access, your local network must be configured to use unregistered IP addresses. You can use DHCP to automatically configure your client computers with the appropriate TCP/IP settings, but for the RRAS server itself, you must configure the TCP/IP client manually. If your Windows 2000 server has RRAS already activated, then you must have two network interfaces installed in the computer. One interface is a standard network interface adapter (usually a network interface card, or NIC) that provides the connection to your local (private) network and the other is a WAN connection to an ISP that provides access to the Internet. The Internet connection can take the form of a modem or ISDN link, which appears as a demand-dial interface in RRAS or a connection to a particular telephone number in the Network and Dial-Up Connections window, or it can use a second network interface adapter, as in the case of a cable modem or DSL connection. If two NICs are installed in the computer, both show up as Local Area Connection icons in the Network and Dial-Up Connections window. Be sure to configure the one that provides the connection to your local network, not the one providing the Internet connection.

The interface providing the connection to your local network must be configured to use an IP address in one of the following three address ranges:

- 10.0.0.0 – 10.255.255.255
- 172.16.0.0 – 172.31.255.255
- 192.168.0.0 – 192.168.255.255

These are the address ranges the IANA has allocated for use by private networks. You can select addresses in these ranges from Class A, B, or C for your network and create your own subnets, if needed, as long as you use the appropriate subnet mask. Be sure to decide on a subnetting arrangement that provides you with sufficient addresses for all computers on your network. If your computers are currently using registered IP addresses, you will have to change them to unregistered ones so that they can use the NAT router, but that can come later.

Note   See Lesson 2 in Chapter 2, "Introducing TCP/IP," for more information about IP addresses and subnetting.

After you have assigned an appropriate unregistered IP address and subnet mask to the RRAS server, be sure that the Default Gateway field in the TCP/IP configuration is left blank.Because the RRAS server itself will be providing access to the Internet, there is no need for a default gateway setting here.

Creating a Static Route

For RRAS to send all nonlocal traffic over the interface providing Internet access, you must create a static route in RRAS, using the following procedure:

1. Click Start and open the Routing and Remote Access console from the Administrative tools program group.

2. Expand the icon for your server and then expand the IP Routing node (see Figure 12.12).

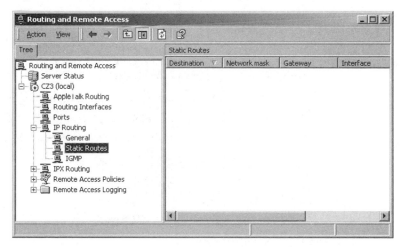

Figure 12.12   The Routing and Remote Access Console, with the Static Routes node highlighted

3. Select the Static Routes node and select New Static Route from the Action menu to display the Static Route dialog box (see Figure 12.13).

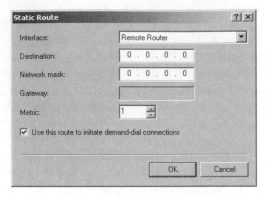

Figure 12.13   The Static Route dialog box

4. From the Interface drop-down menu, select the name that you assigned to the demand-dial connection providing access to the Internet.

5. Type **0.0.0.0** in the Destination box.

6. Type **0.0.0.0** in the Network Mask box.

7. Click OK to close the dialog box and create the static route.

Installing the NAT Routing Protocol

To install the NAT routing protocol on an existing RRAS server, use the following procedure:

1. Click Start and open the Routing and Remote Access console from the Administrative tools program group.

2. Expand the icon for your server and then expand the IP Routing node.

3. Select the General node and select New Routing Protocol from the Action menu to display the New Routing Protocol dialog box (see Figure 12.14).

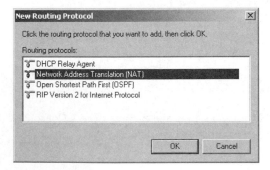

Figure 12.14   The New Routing Protocol dialog box

4. Select Network Address Translation from the Routing Protocols list and click OK to add the protocol to the IP Routing node.

Creating NAT Interfaces

As with the other routing protocols supported by RRAS, you must create a NAT interface for each of the computer's network connections before NAT can process the packets transmitted over them. To create the network interfaces, use the following procedure:

1. Select the Network Address Translation (NAT) node in the scope pane of the Routing and Remote Access console and select New Interface from the Action menu to display the New Interface For Network Address Translation dialog box (see Figure 12.15).

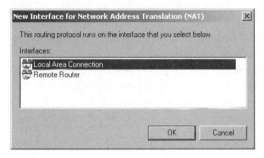

Figure 12.15   The New Interface For Network Address Translation Properties dialog box

2. Select the Local Area Connection entry in the Interfaces list that provides access to your local (private) network and click OK to open the Network Address Translation Properties dialog box (see Figure 12.16).

Figure 12.16   The Network Address Translation Properties dialog box

3. Verify that the Private Interface Connected To Private Network option button is selected and click OK to create the interface.

4. Repeat step 1 to open another instance of the New Interface For Network Address Translation dialog box.

5. Select the interface that provides access to the Internet in the Interfaces list and click OK to open the Network Address Translation Properties dialog box again.

6. Verify that the Public Interface Connected To The Internet option button is selected and that the Translate TCP/UDP Headers check box is selected.

7. Click OK to create the interface.

Configuring NAT Interface Properties

After you create a NAT interface, you can configure its properties at any time by selecting the interface in the details pane of the Routing and Remote Access console and selecting Properties from the Action menu to display the Properties dialog box. For the interface that provides access to your local network, the only configurable option is whether the interface represents the connection to your private network or to the Internet. You should not change this value unless you incorrectly configured the interface when you created it.

The Properties dialog box for the NAT interface representing the Internet connection contains two additional tabs that enable you to configure the IP addresses and ports that NAT will use when translating packets. The functions of these tabs are described in the following sections.

Creating an Address Pool

When you click the Address Pool tab (as shown in Figure 12.17), you see controls that enable you to specify the registered IP addresses that you want NAT to use when translating the packets generated by your network's clients.

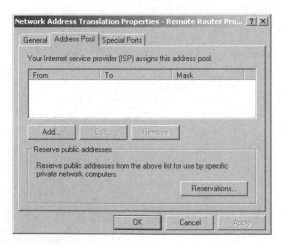

Figure 12.17   The Address Pool tab of a NAT interface's Properties dialog box

Small networks, and particularly ICS installations, typically use a single registered IP address, assigned by the ISP, for all the clients on the private network. If you have multiple registered IP addresses available to you, however, you can configure NAT to use them by clicking the Add button to open an Add Address Pool dialog box (see Figure 12.18). In this dialog box, you can specify a range of IP addresses, or a single address (by just using the Start Address box), along with a subnet mask. You can create as many ranges in your address pool as you need to support your IP addresses.

Figure 12.18   The Add Address Pool dialog box

The primary reason for creating an address pool is to assign specific registered IP addresses to certain unregistered computers on your network. For example, if you have a Web server on your private network that you want to be accessible by clients on the Internet, you can allocate one of the registered addresses in the pool to the Web server's unregistered address so that the NAT router forwards all incoming traffic for that registered address to the Web server. This procedure creates a permanent entry in the router's NAT table so that it always processes traffic sent to the registered address you specify in the same way.

To reserve an IP address, use the following procedure:

1. Click Start and open the Routing and Remote Access console from the Administrative tools program group.

2. Expand the node for your RRAS server and browse to the Network Address Translation (NAT) node.

3. Select the NAT interface representing the server's connection to the Internet and select Properties from the Action menu to open the Properties dialog box for the interface.

4. Click the Address Pool tab.

   If you have not yet created an address pool, you must do so before creating IP address reservations.

5. Click Reservations to open the Reserve Addresses dialog box (see Figure 12.19).

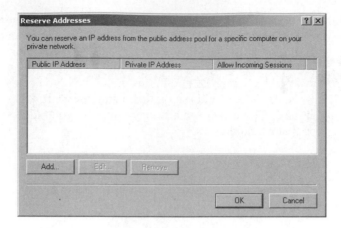

Figure 12.19   The Reserve Addresses dialog box

6. Click Add to open an Add Reservation dialog box (see Figure 12.20).

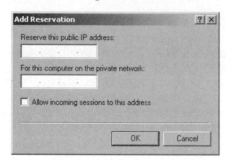

Figure 12.20   The Add Reservation dialog box

7. Type the registered address you want to use in the Reserve This Public IP Address box and the address of the unregistered computer you want to assign it to in the For This Computer On The Private Network box.

   The registered IP address you supply must be in the address pool you have already configured.

8. Select the Allow Incoming Sessions To This Address check box.

   If you don't select this check box, clients on the Internet will not be able to initiate communications with the computer using the unregistered address you have specified.

9. Click OK to create the reservation.

10. Repeat steps 6 through 9 to create additional reservations if necessary.

11. Click OK twice to close the Reserve Addresses dialog box and the Properties dialog box.

Creating Special Ports

The Special Ports tab in the interface's Properties dialog box enables you to create permanent mappings at the port level, rather than at the IP address level. This enables you to direct the traffic arriving at a specific port on one of your registered IP addresses to a specific port an any one of your unregistered network computers. You can, for example, map all HTTP traffic arriving over the Internet interface to a single Web server on your local network by mapping port 80 for all your registered addresses to port 80 on a specific unregistered address.

To create a special port mapping, use the following procedure:

1. Open the Properties dialog box for the NAT interface representing the server's connection to the Internet.
2. Click the Special Ports tab (see Figure 12.21).

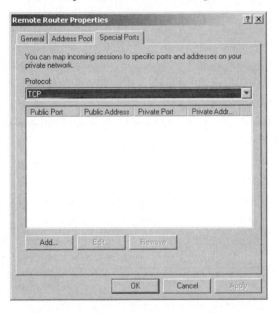

Figure 12.21   The Special Ports tab of a NAT interface's Properties dialog box

3. Select the protocol (TCP or UDP) for which you want to create a port mapping in the Protocol drop-down list.
4. Click Add to open the Add Special Port dialog box (see Figure 12.22).
5. In the Public Address box, specify whether you want to map a port for the entire interface or for one specific IP address. If the latter, type the registered IP address in the box provided.
6. Type the port number in the incoming packets that you want to map in the Incoming Port box.

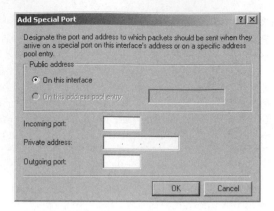

Figure 12.22   The Add Special Port dialog box

7. Type the unregistered IP address of the computer you want to receive the mapped packets in the Private Address box.

8. In the Outgoing Port box, type the port number that the computers on the local (private) network will use for outbound traffic.

9. Click OK to create the port mapping.

10. Repeat steps 3 through 9 to create additional mappings, if necessary.

11. Click OK to close the Properties dialog box.

Configuring NAT Properties

In addition to the properties for specific NAT interfaces, you can also configure properties for NAT itself, by selecting the Network Address Translation (NAT) node in the Routing and Remote Access console's scope pane and selecting Properties from the Action menu to display the Network Address Translation (NAT) Properties dialog box (see Figure 12.23).

Figure 12.23   The Network Address Translation (NAT) Properties dialog box

In the General tab you configure the logging options for the NAT protocol by specifying the amount of NAT information that RRAS should save to the log. In the Translation tab you can specify the amount of time that TCP and UDP entries should remain in the NAT table. By clicking the Applications button in the Translation tab, you open an Applications dialog box in which you can create mappings to support specific applications that use nonstandard port numbers.

Configuring IP Addressing

In the Address Assignment tab (as shown in Figure 12.24), you can enable NAT's ability to automatically configure clients on the unregistered network with the IP addresses and other settings they need to utilize the NAT router. This feature is a simplified subset of the DHCP server included with Windows 2000 Server. If you have already deployed a DHCP server on your network (either on the server running NAT or elsewhere), you do not need to activate NAT's Address Assignment function.

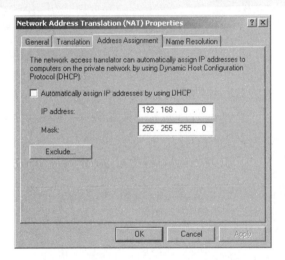

Figure 12.24   The Address Assignment tab of the Network Address Translation (NAT) Properties dialog box

The Address Assignment function is simple to deploy, and it provides few customizable settings. Selecting the Automatically Assign IP Addresses By Using DHCP check box enables the feature. The IP Address box contains the private Class C network address 192.168.0.0 by default, with a Mask value of 255.255.255.0. You can modify the address or the mask as needed, and you can click the Exclude button to prevent specific addresses on the network from being assigned by DHCP. If you plan to create IP address mappings so that specific computers on your unregistered network are accessible from the Internet, you must configure the TCP/IP settings on those unregistered computers manually and exclude the addresses you assign them from assignment by any DHCP server on your network.

In addition to IP addresses and a subnet mask, this DHCP implementation supplies clients with a default gateway address and also a DNS server address (if the NAT name resolution components is enabled), both of which are the address of the NAT router itself and cannot be modified. If you want to use settings other than these defaults, you must use the full Windows 2000 DHCP Server product, as described in Chapter 5, "Implementing the Dynamic Host Configuration Protocol."

Configuring Name Resolution

In the Name Resolution tab (see Figure 12.25), you specify whether you want to activate the DNS proxy provided by the NAT protocol. When you activate this feature by selecting the Clients Using Domain Name System (DNS) check box, NAT's address assignment component supplies clients with the NAT router's IP address as a DNS server address. The NAT router, upon receiving name resolution requests from clients, passes them on to the DNS server specified in the RRAS computer's own TCP/IP configuration. By selecting the Connect To The Public Network When A Name Needs To Be Resolved check box, you can control whether a demand-dial connection is triggered by DNS name resolution requests.

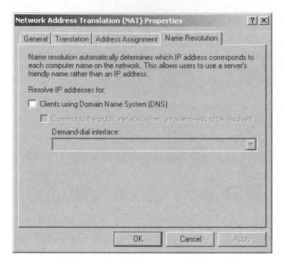

Figure 12.25   The Name Resolution tab of the Network Address Translation (NAT) Properties dialog box

If you decide not to use the DNS proxy included with NAT, you must supply each of your clients with an alternative DNS server address, either by manually configuring them or using a full DHCP implementation.

Exercise 1: Configuring a NAT Installation

You are a network administrator assigned the task of providing the users on your company's network with access to the Internet. In the interest of security, you decide to use the NAT routing protocol in RRAS. The NAT configuration is as follows:

- The RRAS server's interface to the local network has an IP address of 192.168.10.1 and a subnet mask of 255.255.255.0. The computer's DNS server address is 192.168.6.2.

- All client computers on the local network are configured to obtain TCP/IP configuration parameters using DHCP.

- The NAT address assignment component is enabled, with an IP Address value of 192.168.10.0 and a Mask value of 255.255.255.0. The IP addresses 192.168.10.1 through 192.168.10.10 are excluded from assignment.

- You create a demand-dial interface called Remote Router, which provides the Internet connection and has an address pool consisting of 10 registered IP addresses, 207.209.68.45 through 207.209.68.54, assigned by the company's ISP.

1. What IP addresses will the RRAS server assign to the client computers on the local network?

   a. 192.168.10.1 through 192.168.10.10

   b. 192.168.10.11 through 192.168.10.255

   c. 207.209.68.45 through 207.209.68.54

   d. 207.209.68.1 through 207.209.68.44 and 207.209.68.55 through 207.209.68.255

2. When you enable NAT's name resolution component, what DNS server address will be supplied to the client computers?

   a. 192.168.10.1

   b. 192.168.6.2

   c. x.y.z.45

   d. A DNS server address supplied by the ISP when the demand-dial interface connects.

3. What parameters should you use when creating the static route to the Internet?

   a. Interface: Local Area Connection
      Destination: 192.168.10.0
      Network Mask: 255.255.255.0
      Gateway: 192.168.10.1

   b. Interface: Remote Router
      Destination: 0.0.0.0
      Network Mask: 255.255.255.0
      Gateway: x.y.z.45

   c. Interface: Local Area Connection
      Destination: 192.168.10.1
      Network Mask: 255.255.255.0
      Gateway: None

   d. Interface: Remote Router
      Destination: 0.0.0.0
      Network Mask: 0.0.0.0
      Gateway: None

Lesson Review

1. You are the administrator of an unregistered network that uses NAT to access the Internet. You are deploying a Web server hosting a company home page on the local network, and you want users on the Internet to be able to access it. Which of the following tasks must you perform to make this possible? (Choose all that apply.)

   a. Create an address pool containing two or more registered IP addresses assigned by your ISP.

   b. Create a static route for the interface providing Internet access in which the value of the Destination field is the registered IP address you want Internet clients to use to access the Web server, and the Gateway value is the RRAS server's registered IP address.

   c. Create a reservation using one of the registered IP addresses assigned by your ISP and the Web server's unregistered IP address.

   d. Configure the Web server to use multiple IP addresses, one of which is unregistered and one of which is a registered address assigned by your ISP.

2. On an unregistered network using NAT and a cable modem to access the Internet, users on the client computers cannot access Internet servers using fully qualified domain names (FQDNs). However, they can access the same

servers using IP addresses. When you investigate the problem, you discover that the Windows 2000 Server computer functioning as the NAT router can access Internet servers using both IP addresses and FQDNs. Which of the following could be the cause of the problem? (Choose all that apply.)

a. The RRAS computer does not have a DNS server address specified in its TCP/IP configuration.

b. The name resolution component of the NAT protocol is disabled.

c. There is no RRAS filter in place allowing DNS packets to pass to the Internet.

d. The Connect To The Public Network When A Name Needs To Be Resolved check box in the Name Resolution tab of the Network Address Translation (NAT) Properties dialog box is not selected.

3. You are deploying NAT on a Windows 2000 Server computer with a NIC connection to the local network and a demand-dial connection to an ISP. The IP address of the local network connection is 10.5.87.2. The registered IP address assigned by your ISP is x.y.z.172. When you open the Network Address Translation (NAT) Properties dialog box and click the Address Assignment tab, what value do you see in the IP Address box?

a. 0.0.0.0

b. 10.0.0.0

c. x.y.z.0

d. 192.168.0.0

Lesson Summary

- Using the Routing and Remote Access Server Setup Wizard, you can configure RRAS to use NAT at the same time that you configure the router.

- NAT is implemented in RRAS as a routing protocol, which you can install on an existing RRAS server.

- For RRAS to use RAS, you must create NAT interfaces for the unregistered network and Internet connections and create a static route on the Internet interface.

- NAT includes a simplified DHCP server that automatically configures network clients to use the NAT router. You can specify the IP addresses that this DHCP implementation assigns, but you cannot configure any of the other options.

- NAT includes a DNS proxy that receives name resolution requests from clients on the network and forwards them to another DNS server.

Lesson 3: Installing Internet Connection Sharing

Internet Connection Sharing (ICS) is another method you can use to provide all the users on a network with Internet access using a single dial-up connection. ICS is really just another implementation of NAT, one that is easier to set up but less customizable than the NAT protocol included in RRAS. In this lesson you learn about the differences between ICS and NAT and how to implement ICS on a Windows 2000 computer.

After this lesson, you will be able to

- List the differences between Windows 2000 ICS and NAT
- Configure a network connection to use ICS
- Configure ICS properties

Estimated lesson time: 15 minutes

Differentiating ICS and NAT

Both ICS and the NAT protocol included in RRAS use the same network address translation technique to enable computers with unregistered IP addresses to share an Internet connection. ICS differs from NAT mainly in that it is a "light" version of the protocol that is far simpler to install and use, but which is also less flexible. Some of the differences between the two are as follows:

- ICS is included in all versions of Windows 2000, including Windows 2000 Professional, but NAT is part of RRAS, which is included only in the Windows 2000 server operating systems.

- ICS is activated through the Network and Dial-Up Connections Control Panel, but you install and configure NAT using the Routing and Remote Access console.

- ICS can use only a single registered IP address when translating the Internet packets generated by an unregistered network. NAT can use multiple IP addresses.

- With NAT, you can map specific registered IP addresses to specific unregistered addresses to make a computer on the unregistered network accessible to Internet clients. ICS cannot do this.

- ICS can link only one LAN to one registered IP address; NAT can support multiple LANs with different IP addresses.

- ICS automatically uses its address assignment component using a fixed range of unregistered IP addresses. With NAT, you can control whether to use address assignment and specify the addresses to be assigned.

Installing ICS

As with any other NAT implementation, to use ICS your computer must have two network interfaces. One interface connects to the local network and the other to an ISP. The local network connection must use a standard NIC, and the Internet connection can use a dial-up modem or a NIC-based interface (such as a cable modem or DSL connection). Assuming that you have these two connections in place, the process of installing ICS couldn't be simpler; you only have to select one check box.

To install ICS on a Windows 2000 computer, use the following procedure:

1. Click Start, point to Settings, and select Network And Dial-Up Connections to open the Network and Dial-Up Connections window.

2. Click the icon representing the connection to your ISP (the connection you want to share) and select Properties from the File menu to open the Properties dialog box for the connection.

   If you are using a dial-up connection to the Internet, the icon representing the connection is labeled using a name that you assigned when you created the connection. If your Internet connection uses a NIC, the icon is labeled Local Area Connection, possibly with a numeral as well. The NIC connection to your local network is labeled the same way. Be sure to select the correct connection before you proceed to enable ICS.

3. Click the Sharing tab to display the controls shown in Figure 12.26.

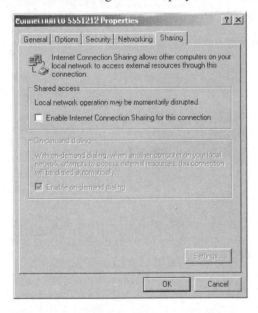

Figure 12.26   The Sharing tab of a connection's Properties dialog box

4. Select the Enable Internet Connection Sharing For This Connection check box.

The For This Connection selector lists all the local area connections in your Network and Dial-Up Connections window. If you have more than one, select the one representing the local network with which you want to share the Internet connection.

5. If you are using a dial-up connection to the Internet, verify that the Enable On-Demand Dialing check box is selected.

By default, ICS causes dial-up Internet connections to use on-demand dialing so that any user on the network can trigger a connection to the Internet on the ICS computer by attempting to access an Internet service. You can disable on-demand dialing by clearing this check box, but if you do, the user on the ICS computer must initiate a connection to the Internet before anyone on the network can access Internet services.

6. Click OK to close the connection's Properties dialog box.

Although the process is invisible to the user, activating ICS on a Windows 2000 computer performs a number of configuration tasks behind the scenes. Sharing an Internet connection with ICS causes Windows to do the following:

- The ICS service is started and configured to load automatically when Windows 2000 starts.

- The Local Area Connection you selected in the For Local Network box in the Sharing tab of the connection's Properties dialog box is reconfigured with an IP address of 192.168.0.1 and a subnet mask of 255.255.255.0.

- The ICS address allocation component is enabled and configured to provide DHCP clients with IP addresses ranging from 192.168.0.2 to 192.168.0.254 and a subnet mask of 255.255.255.0. Both the default gateway and the DNS server value supplied to the clients are the address of the computer running ICS. There is no way to modify the allocated settings or disable the address allocation component without disabling ICS.

- The ICS name resolution component is enabled, which causes the ICS computer to function as a DNS proxy, receiving DNS name resolution requests from clients and forwarding them to the DNS server the computer is configured to use.

The only remaining task needed to get ICS up and functioning is to make sure that all the client computers on the network have properly installed network interfaces and that they are configured to obtain their TCP/IP configuration settings using DHCP.

Configuring ICS

ICS is preconfigured to provide clients with standard Internet connectivity. However, once you have enabled ICS, you can configure the service to support other applications by clicking the Settings button in the Sharing tab of your Internet connection's Properties dialog box. This opens the Internet Connection Sharing Settings dialog box, as shown in Figure 12.27.

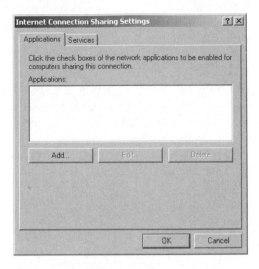

Figure 12.27   The Internet Connection Sharing Settings dialog box

Using the Applications Tab

In the Applications tab, you can create port mappings for outbound traffic to support applications with unusual communications requirements. To create a mapping, click the Add button to open the Internet Connection Sharing Application dialog box (see Figure 12.28). After typing the name of the application in the Name Of Application box, you specify the port number your client computers will use when connecting to a server on the Internet that is running the application in the Remote Server Port Number box. Click the TCP or UDP option button to specify which transport-layer protocol the outbound messages should use.

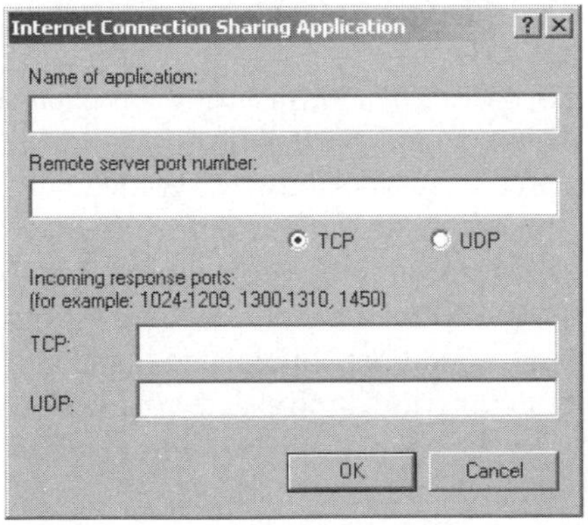

Figure 12.28   The Internet Connection Sharing Application dialog box

In the Incoming Response Ports boxes, you specify which port numbers the Internet server should use when sending traffic back to the clients on your network. You can supply multiple port numbers in both the TCP and UDP boxes. Click OK to create the application entry. You can create as many application mappings as you need to support your clients.

Using the Services Tab

In the Services tab of the Internet Connection Sharing Settings dialog box (see Figure 12.29), you can configure ICS to permit Internet users to access services on your unregistered network. The Services list contains six of the most common applications you might want to share with Internet users. You can enable any of these applications by selecting its check box, which opens an Internet Connection Sharing Service dialog box, where you must identify the computer on your private network that you want to receive all traffic going to the well-known port number associated with that application.

Figure 12.29   The Services tab of the Internet Connection Sharing Settings dialog box

In addition to the six preconfigured services, you can create additional ones of your own by clicking the Add button in the Services tab to display a blank Internet Connection Sharing Service dialog box (see Figure 12.30). Here, you type a name for the service in the Name Of Service text box, specify the port number the service uses in the Service Port Number box, specify whether the service uses TCP or UDP by clicking the appropriate option button, and type the DNS name or IP address of the computer on your unregistered network that you want to receive the traffic in the Name Or Address Of Server Computer On Private Network text box. Clicking OK creates a new entry in the Services list using your parameters.

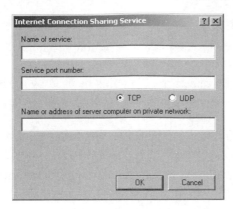

Figure 12.30   The Internet Connection Sharing Service dialog box

Lesson Review

1. Which of the following configuration tasks are not automatically performed when you activate ICS on a Windows 2000 computer? (Choose all that apply.)

   a. The IP address of the Local Area Connection on the ISC computer is configured as 192.168.0.1.

   b. The client computers on the local network are configured to obtain TCP/IP settings using DHCP.

   c. The ICS computer is configured to process client name resolution requests.

   d. The ICS computer is configured to satisfy FTP requests generated by Internet users.

2. How does the address assignment component in ICS differ from the one in NAT?

3. Which of the following tasks must you perform before enabling ICS on a Windows 2000 computer?

   a. Start the DHCP service.

   b. Create a connection providing Internet access.

   c. Configure the Local Area Connection with the IP address 192.168.0.1.

   d. Obtain a registered IP address from your ISP.

Lesson Summary

- ICS is a stripped down version of NAT that is designed to enable a single LAN to share an Internet connection.

- ICS automatically selects the IP addresses used by the unregistered network and activates the address assignment component used to configure the client computers.

- ICS can share an Internet connection with only one LAN, using one registered IP address.

- On a computer with properly configured interfaces to the local network and to the Internet, selecting one check box is all that is needed to enable ICS.

- You can configure ICS to support nonstandard port mappings and make services on the unregistered network accessible to Internet users.

C H A P T E R   1 3

Implementing Certificate Services

Lesson 1: Introducing Certificates 500

**Lesson 2: Installing and Configuring Microsoft
            Certificate Services** 509

Lesson 3: Managing Certificates 525

About This Chapter

Security is a primary consideration in Microsoft Windows 2000, and digital certificates are one of the most important tools used to maintain that security. In this chapter you learn about the public key technology that underlies the digital certificates used by Windows 2000, as well as how to install, configure, and use the certificate authority included with Windows 2000 Server, which is called Microsoft Certificate Services.

Before You Begin

There are no prerequisites for this chapter.

Lesson 1: Introducing Certificates

Many of the Windows 2000 security mechanisms rely on encryption to prevent unauthorized users or processes from reading confidential data. Encrypting and decrypting data requires a *key*, which is a set of instructions describing how the data is encoded. One system uses a key to encrypt data, and another system uses a key to decrypt it. When different computers perform the encryption and decryption processes, an exchange of keys is necessary for communication to occur. Digital certificates are a method of packaging encryption keys and other information for transmission over a network. Many Windows 2000 programs and services use certificates to provide security, including the Kerberos authentication protocol, the Internet Protocol security (IPsec) extensions, the encrypting file system (EFS), and Internet Information Services (IIS).

After this lesson, you will be able to

- Understand the use of encryption keys
- List the uses of digital certificates
- Describe the various types of certificate authorities
- Understand the certificate creation process

Estimated lesson time: 20 minutes

Understanding Encryption Keys

Encryption is simply a mechanism for encoding data by substituting one string of characters for another string of characters. One of the simplest types of encryption is called a letter transposition code, in which each letter in the alphabet is replaced by another letter. For example, the letter a might be replaced by the letter p, the letter b by the letter m, the letter c by the letter h, and so on. In encrypted form, a simple message such as "hello world" would appear as "ftggl slngo." The recipient of the message, in order to understand its contents, must have the list of letter transpositions used to create the code. This list is the key for this particular form of encryption. A code this simple is actually easy to break without the key, but the concept is the same in more complex encryption schemes. The recipient must be furnished with the key to decrypt the message.

The problem with this type of encryption is that the exchange of keys is a point of vulnerability. If the key should be intercepted or stolen by an unauthorized person, the code is compromised. For this reason, this type of encryption is called *secret key encryption*. Secret key encryption can be a highly secure method of communication, as long as there is an absolutely secure means for distributing and storing the keys. Government agencies that use this type of encryption to secure their communications distribute CD-ROMs full of prearranged encryption keys to their correspondents well in advance. These keys are stored securely and are used only to encrypt and decrypt messages. Because the keys are never transmitted over the medium used to send a message, the communications system remains secure.

Using secret key encryption on a data network would require the keys to be transmitted over the network at some time, which compromises the whole system. Windows 2000, therefore, uses a different type of encryption, which is based on what it calls the *public key infrastructure (PKI)*. For every code in the PKI there are two separate encryption keys: a public key and a private key. As the names imply, *public keys* are freely available to anyone and can be transmitted over the network. *Private keys* are held only by one person or system and are never transmitted over the network.

The basic concept of the PKI is that one key is used to encrypt data and the other is used to decrypt it. The encryption key cannot decrypt the data that it has encrypted. For example, if Mike wants to send a private message to Shelly, he obtains Shelly's public key, uses it to encrypt the message, and then transmits it to Shelly over the network. To read the message, Shelly must first use her private key to decrypt it. Because no one else has the private key, no one else can read the message. Because the public key cannot be used to decrypt the data that it has encrypted, potential intruders intercepting the public key on the way to Mike's computer gain nothing except the means to encrypt their own messages.

The public and private keys can also work in the opposite direction. Shelly can encrypt a message using her private key and send it to Mike, who then decrypts it using Shelly's public key. This is not a method for preventing other users from reading the message because anyone can obtain Shelly's public key, but it does prove that it was Shelly who sent the message because any message that can be decrypted using her public key must have been encrypted with her private key.

Therefore, by using public and private keys, the Windows 2000 PKI provides the following security services:

- **Encryption.**   As described earlier, encryption is the protection of data through cryptographic encoding. To send data in encrypted form, a system uses the intended recipient's public key to encode the data. Once encoded, only the recipient's private key can decrypt the data and render it readable. As long as the private key remains private, anyone with access to the recipient's public key can encrypt data, but only the recipient can decrypt it.

- **Signing.**   Encrypting data using a private key makes it readable by anyone in possession of the corresponding public key. This does not provide any protection for the data (because anyone can obtain the public key), but the fact that the public key can decrypt the data verifies that the private key was used to encrypt it. Because only the holder of the private key can encrypt data so that it is readable with the public key, this confirms that the data originated from the reputed source.

Note Although it is possible to encrypt an entire message to provide a digital signature, this practice is not practical most of the time. In most cases, hashes are used; they are much shorter and provide a much smaller set of data for someone trying to determine the other person's private key by means of brute force.

- **Authentication.** It is possible to use public and private keys to verify the identity of another user or computer. One method is to encrypt a challenge message using a system's public key and then transmit it. If the receiving system is capable of reading the message and replying to it, this indicates that it is in possession of the private key and is therefore the intended recipient of the message.

- **Verification.** To ensure that data is not modified while en route to its destination, the transmitting system runs the data through a hash algorithm that creates a string (called a hash) that is unique to the data sample. The system then encrypts the data, along with the hash, using its private key. The receiving system decrypts the data using the sender's public key and then performs the same hash computation. If the hash string included in the message is the same as the one generated by the recipient, the data is verified as not having changed.

- **Nonrepudiation.** In addition to verifying the source of a message, encrypting it with a private key can also serve as legal proof of a document's source, much as a signature on a paper document does. This prevents a person from denying that he or she sent the message at a later time.

Understanding Certificates

Each user or computer that participates in the Windows PKI is assigned a public key and a private key. The private key remains on the computer and is never transmitted over the network. However, for the PKI to function properly, there must be a means of distributing public keys in a controlled and verified manner. The entire system would be compromised if you could not be certain that the public key you have been given for a particular user is not genuine. Digital certificates are the mechanisms used to distribute public keys over the network.

A *digital certificate* is a document that attests to the binding of a public key to an entity. The main purpose of a certificate is to generate confidence that the public key contained in the certificate actually belongs to the entity named in the certificate. A digital certificate consists of the public key itself, plus a collection of attributes that contains information about the owner of the public key, such as the owner's name and contact information. Certificates are issued by a *certificate authority (CA)*.

A CA is an organization or a program that is trusted to issue valid certificates for individual users. Some CAs are commercial companies, such as VeriSign and Thawte, but Windows 2000 Server also includes a CA program of its own, called Microsoft Certificate Services (MCS). Like a notary public, a CA is responsible for verifying that the people to whom they issue certificates are actually who they say they are. Whether you use a commercial CA or run your own depends on the type of data you are trying to protect. If you want to ensure that the e-mail traffic for a private company is secure, you can use MCS. A software developer distributing applications to customers is more likely to use a commercial CA. The object is for the CA to be trusted by everyone involved in the secure transactions.

Certificate Contents

The format for the certificates used by Windows 2000 and by most commercial CAs is defined by the X.509 standard, which is published by the Telecommunication Standardization Sector of the International Telecommunication Union (ITU-T). The attributes included in a certificate vary according to its function, but all X.509 certificates contain at least the following attributes:

- Version
- Serial Number
- Signature Algorithm ID
- Issuer Name
- Validity Period
- Subject (user) Name
- Subject Public Key Information
- Issuer Unique Identifier
- Subject Unique Identifier
- Extensions
- Signature on the above fields

CA Types

The Windows PKI supports two types of CAs—enterprise CAs and stand-alone CAs. An *enterprise CA* is one that stores its information in the Active Directory database and is used to issue certificates to users, computers, or other CAs within the organization. All users and computers in the domain where an enterprise CA is installed automatically trust that CA. *Stand-alone CAs* store their own information and are intended for use in organizations that will be issuing certificates to users or computers outside the company. Although enterprise CAs and stand-alone CAs function similarly, there are some important differences between the two. When an enterprise CA generates a certificate, it stores it in the Active Directory service, from which any user on the network can access it. Stand-alone CAs don't publish the certificates they generate; you are responsible for distributing them to the users that need them.

In an enterprise, the most trusted CA is called the *enterprise root CA*. There can be more than one enterprise root CA in a Windows 2000 domain, but there can be only one enterprise root CA in any given hierarchy. All other CAs in the hierarchy are called *enterprise subordinate CAs*. An organization should set up an enterprise root CA if the CA will be issuing certificates to users and computers within the organization. In large organizations, the enterprise root CA is used only to issue certificates to subordinate CAs. The subordinate CAs then issue certificates to users and computers. Isolating the root CA from the end users in this manner helps to protect it from attempts to compromise its private key. In fact, for maximum security, some organizations keep the root CA offline once it has issued certificates to the subordinate CAs.

Despite their name, stand-alone CAs can also function in a hierarchy. A *stand-alone root CA* is the top of a CA trust hierarchy. The stand-alone root CA requires administrative privileges on the local server but does not need access to the Active Directory service. A *stand-alone subordinate CA* is one that either operates as a solitary certificate server or exists in a CA hierarchy by obtaining its certificate from a superior CA, such as a stand-alone root. As with the enterprise hierarchy, a stand-alone root CA typically issues certificates only to subordinate CAs.

Creating Certificates

The process by which a user requests a certificate and a CA generates one consists of the following basic steps:

1. **Generating keys.**   The applicant generates public and private keys or is assigned a key pair by some authority in the applicant's organization.

2. **Collecting required information.**   The applicant collects whatever information the CA requires to issue a certificate. The information could include the applicant's e-mail address, birth certificate, fingerprints, notarized documents—whatever the CA needs to be certain that the applicant is who he or she claims to be. CAs with stringent identification requirements produce certificates with high assurance—that is, their certificates generate a high level of confidence. CAs themselves are said to be of high, medium, or low assurance.

3. **Requesting the certificate.**   The applicant sends a certificate request, consisting of the public key and the additional required information, to the CA.

The certificate request might be encrypted using the CA's own public key. In many cases, requests are submitted using e-mail, but requests can also be sent by postal or courier service, for example, when the certificate request itself must be notarized.

4. **Verifying the information.**   The CA uses a policy module to process the applicant's certificate request. A *policy module* is a set of rules that the CA uses to determine whether it should approve the request, deny it, or mark it as pending for later review by a network administrator. The policy module also adds an attribute to the certificate containing the source of the CA's own certificate. This enables users to verify the newly issued certificate by checking the credentials of the CA that issued it. As with the identification requirements, the rules in a CA's policy module influence the amount of confidence generated by the certificates it issues.

5. **Creating the certificate.**   The CA creates a digital document containing the applicant's public key and other appropriate information and signs it using its own private key. The signed document is the certificate. The signature of the CA authenticates the binding of the subject's name to the subject's public key and enables anyone receiving the certificate to verify its source by obtaining the CA's public key.

6. **Sending or posting the certificate.**   The CA uses an *exit module* to determine how it should make the new certificate available to the applicant. Depending on the CA type, the exit module might cause the CA to publish the new certificate in the Active Directory service, send it to the applicant in an e-mail message, or store it in a specified folder.

CAs must themselves be trustworthy if their certificates are to be trusted. Because anyone can become a CA, certificates are only as trustworthy as the authority that issues the underlying keys. For this reason, CAs have their own certificates, which can be issued by another CA that is higher up in a CA hierarchy. There can be any number of levels in a CA hierarchy, but there must eventually be an ultimate authority. The CA at the top of the hierarchy is called the root certificate authority, and it is the only CA in the hierarchy that can sign its own certificate.

When you use a single MCS as the CA for a relatively small organization, there is no hierarchy, and the sole CA is obviously the root certificate authority. However, for a large enterprise, you can create multiple CAs and build a hierarchy of your own, with the first CA functioning as the root and issuing certificates for the other CAs.

Certificate Templates

When a CA generates a certificate, it uses a certificate template to determine what attributes it should include and what values it should provide for the essential attributes. The template used to create the certificate depends on its function.

Windows 2000 provides many certificate templates with Microsoft Certificate Services, including the following:

- **Administrator.**   Used for authenticating clients and for EFS, secure mail, certificate trust list (CTL) signing, and code signing.

- **Authenticated Session.**   Used for authenticating clients.

- **Basic EFS.**   Used for EFS operations.

- **CEP Encryption (offline request).**   Used to enroll Cisco Systems, Inc., routers for IPsec authentication certificates from a Windows 2000 CA.

- **Code Signing.**   Used for code signing operations.

- **Computer.**   Used for authenticating clients and servers.

- **Domain Controller.**   Used for authenticating domain controllers. When an enterprise CA is installed, this certificate type is installed automatically on domain controllers to support the public key operations that are required when domain controllers are supporting Certificate Services.

- **EFS Recovery Agent.**   Used for EFS encrypted-data recovery operations.

- **Enrollment Agent.**   Used for authenticating administrators that request certificates on behalf of smart card users.

- **Enrollment Agent (computer).**   Used for authenticating services that request certificates on behalf of other computers.

- **Exchange Enrollment Agent (offline request).**   Used for authenticating Microsoft Exchange Server administrators that request certificates on behalf of secure mail users.

- **Exchange Signature Only (offline request).**   Used by Exchange Server for client authentication and secure mail (used for signing only).

- **Exchange User (offline request).**   Used by Exchange Server for client authentication and secure mail (used for both signing and confidentiality of mail).

- **IPsec.**   Used for IPsec authentication.

- **IPsec (offline request).**   Used for IPsec authentication.

- **Root Certification Authority.**   Used for root CA installation operations. (This certificate template cannot be issued from a CA and is used only when installing root CAs.)

- **Router (offline request).**   Used for authentication of routers.

- **Smart Card Logon.**   Used for client authentication and logging on with a smart card.

- **Smart Card User.**   Used for client authentication, secure mail, and logging on with a smart card.

- **Subordinate Certification Authority (offline request).**   Used to issue certificates for subordinate CAs.
- **Trust List Signing.**   Used to sign CTLs.
- **User.**   Used for client authentication, EFS, and secure mail (used for both signing and confidentiality of mail).
- **User Signature Only.**   Used for client authentication and secure mail (used for signing only).
- **Web Server (offline request).**   Used for Web server authentication.

Exercise 1: Understanding Certificates and Encryption

Match the terms in the left column with the definitions in the right column.

1. Policy module

2. Private key

3. Certificate template

4. Exit module

5. Stand-alone CA

a. Encrypts or decrypts data, but not both

b. Issues certificates to users outside the organization

c. Specifies where to store newly created certificates

d. Determines whether a certificate request should be approved or denied

e. Specifies the attributes to be included in new certificates.

Lesson Review

1. What are certificates and what is their purpose?

2. What is a certificate authority (CA) and what does it do?

3. What are the four types of Microsoft certificate authorities?

Lesson Summary

- Secret key encryption uses one key to both encode and decode data. The key must be distributed to any user intending to decide encrypted data.

- Public key encryption uses separate keys for encryption and decryption, a public key and a private key. The public key is freely distributed, but the private key is never transmitted over the network.

- Data encrypted with a user's public key can only be decrypted with that user's private key.

- Users can also encrypt data with their private keys, which can be decoded with their public keys. This does not provide security, but it does verify the source of the coded data.

- A certificate is a digital document that contains a user's public key, plus attributes containing other information.

- A certificate authority (CA) is a program or organization that is responsible for issuing certificates to applicants after an investigation of their credentials.

Lesson 2: Installing and Configuring Microsoft Certificate Services

Windows 2000 Server includes its own CA, called Microsoft Certificate Services (MCS). MCS is not installed by default; you must install and configure it before it becomes functional. In this lesson you learn how to install and configure MCS and how to use the Certificates and Certification Authority snap-ins.

After this lesson, you will be able to

- Install Microsoft Certificate Services
- Configure MCS using the Certification Authority console
- Back up and restore a CA's database

Estimated lesson time: 30 minutes

Preparing to Install MCS

Before you install MCS, you must decide what type of CA you want to install, enterprise or stand-alone, because you cannot change the type after the installation is completed. You must also decide whether to install a root CA or a subordinate CA. The first CA you install, either enterprise or stand-alone, must be a root, but after that you can decide whether to create additional root CAs or subordinate CAs. Before you can install an enterprise root CA or enterprise subordinate CA, you must have Active Directory installed on your network and a Domain Name System (DNS) server available that supports SRV resource records. An enterprise CA can run on either a domain controller or a member server.

You should also decide what cryptographic service providers (CSPs) you want to use with Certificate Services. A CSP is a library of cryptographic information that provides a programming interface called the CryptoAPI. Applications running on the computer can make calls to the CryptoAPI to request encryption services. The CSPs you elect to use with the CryptoAPI determine how data is encrypted on the system. Windows 2000 includes a set of CSPs that you can choose from when installing Certificate Services (as long as you select the Advanced Options check box), or you can install additional CSPs obtained from third parties.

Note   When you install Service Pack 2 on a Windows 2000 computer, the CSPs are permanently upgraded to provide 128-bit high encryption by default, as opposed to the standard 56-bit encryption included with the original Windows 2000 release. Even if you uninstall the service pack, the high-encryption CSPs remain in place. Installing this service pack is strongly recommended before you install Certificate Services.

Protecting a CA

CAs are high-value resources, and it is often desirable to provide them with a high degree of protection. Specific actions that you should consider include:

- **Physical protection.**   Because CAs represent highly trusted entities within an enterprise, they should be protected from tampering. This requirement is dependent on the inherent value of the certification made by the CA. Physical isolation of the CA server in a facility accessible only to security administrators can dramatically reduce the possibility of such physical attacks.

- **Key management.**   The CA's private key provides the basis for trust in the certification process and should be secured from tampering. Cryptographic hardware modules (accessible to Certificate Services through a CryptoAPI CSP) can provide tamper-resistant key storage and isolate the cryptographic operations from other software running on the server. This significantly reduces the likelihood of a CA key being compromised.

- **Restoration.**   Loss of a CA—because of hardware failure, for example—can create a number of administrative and operational problems and prevent revocation of existing certificates. Certificate Services supports backup of a CA instance so it can be restored later. This is an important part of the overall CA management process.

Installing Certificate Services

To install Microsoft Certificate Services, use the following procedure:

1. Click Start, point to Settings, and select Control Panel.

2. Double-click the Add/Remove Programs icon to display the Add/Remove Programs dialog box.

3. Click Add/Remove Windows Components to launch the Windows Components Wizard (see Figure 13.1).

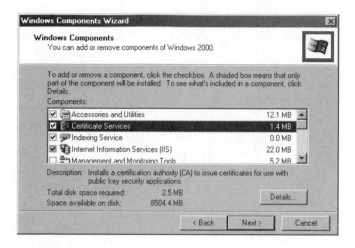

Figure 13.1   The Windows Components Wizard

4. Select the Certificate Services check box in the Components list on the Windows Components page and click Next. The wizard displays a Microsoft Certificate Services message box stating that you cannot rename the computer and you cannot join it to or remove it from a domain after you have installed Certificate Services.

5. Click Yes to proceed to the Certification Authority Type page (see Figure 13.2).

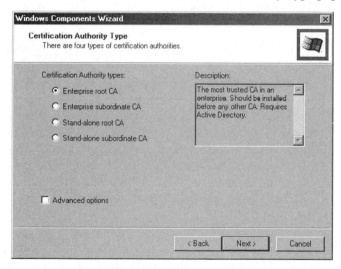

Figure 13.2   The Certification Authority Type page of the Windows Components Wizard

6. Select the type of CA you want to install (enterprise or stand-alone, root or subordinate). Select the Advanced Options check box if you want to view or modify the CSPs used by the CA. Click Next to proceed to the Public And Private Key Pair page (see Figure 13.3) if you selected the Advanced Options box; if not, clicking Next proceeds to the CA Identifying Information page (skip to step 8).

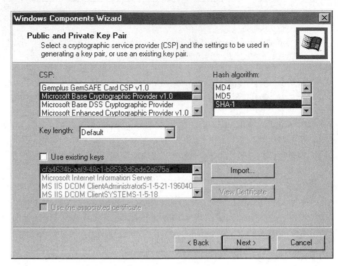

Figure 13.3 The Public And Private Key Pair page of the Windows Components Wizard

7. On the Public And Private Key Page you can select the CSP that Certificate Services will use to encrypt data and the hash algorithm used to create digital signatures. The default settings provide sufficient protection and interoperability for most environments. You should be familiar with the capabilities of the alternate CSPs and hash algorithms before you change these settings. The Key Length selector enables you to specify an alternate length for the encryption keys used by Certificate Services; the default value is 1024, but you can select values up to 4096. Selecting the Use Existing Keys check box enables you to reuse a pair of public and private keys for the CA. Click Next to proceed to the CA Identifying Information page (see Figure 13.4).

8. Type the name you want to assign to the CA in the CA Name field. In addition to the CA name (which is required), you should also supply additional information about the CA and the organization running it, particularly an e-mail address where applicants can send certificate requests. In the Valid For selector, you can specify the length of time that the CA's own certificate remains operational. The default value is two years.

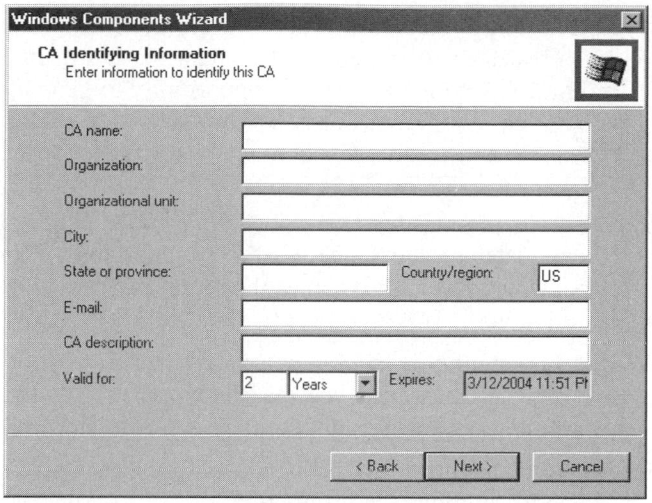

Figure 13.4 The CA Identifying Information page of the Windows Components Wizard

Important Avoid using symbols and special characters in the descriptive information you supply because the CA must encode them using unicode, which can prevent some applications from processing the certificates issues by the CA properly.

Click Next to proceed to the Data Storage Location page (see Figure 13.5).

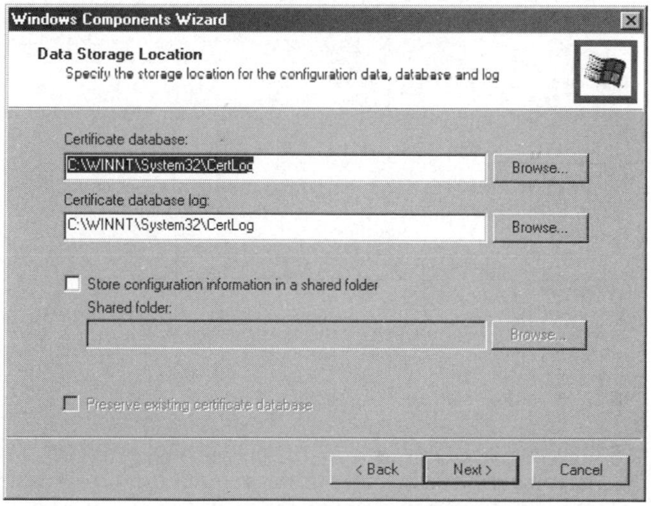

Figure 13.5 The Data Storage Location page of the Windows Components Wizard

---

Note   When you create a root CA, the Certificate Services installation process creates a self-signed certificate for the CA itself. When you create a subordinate CA, you are given the opportunity to generate a certificate request and submit it to a root CA or another subordinate CA. A certificate must be obtained from another CA before a subordinate CA can become operational.

---

9. Click Next to use the default locations for the certificate database and the certificate database log. Click Next to continue to the Configuring Components page, where the wizard copies the required files for the Certificate Services installation.

   If IIS is running on the computer, a Microsoft Certificate Services message box appears, informing you that the wizard must stop the IIS services before proceeding with the installation. Click OK to stop the services and continue.

10. When the Completing The Windows Components Wizard page appears, click Finish to complete the installation.

11. Click Close to close the Add/Remove Programs dialog box.

Configuring a CA

Installing Certificate Services creates a shortcut to the Certification Authority console in the Start menu's Administrative Tools program group. You use this console to configure and manage the CA you've just installed. When you launch the Certification Authority console, you see an interface like that shown in Figure 13.6, with an icon representing your CA and five folders beneath it.

Figure 13.6   The Certification Authority console

The five folders are as follows:

- **Revoked Certificates.**   Contains all the certificates that the CA has revoked. Certificates added to this folder remain there permanently. You cannot reactivate a certificate that has been revoked.

- **Issued Certificates.**   Contains a list of all the certificates the CA has issued. From this list you can view the certificates or revoke them.

- **Pending Requests.**   On a stand-alone CA, this folder contains a list of the certificate requests that have been assigned a "pending" status while they wait for an administrator to approve or deny them. Enterprise CAs always process requests automatically, so this folder is always empty.

- **Failed Requests.**   Contains a list of the certificate requests that have been denied, either automatically by the CA itself or manually by an administrator.

- **Policy Settings.**   Contains a list of the certificate templates that the CA can use to create different types of certificates.

As with most Microsoft Management Console (MMC) consoles, the primary interface you use to configure the CA service is its Properties dialog box. When you select the icon for the CA in the scope pane of the Certification Authority console and select Properties from the Action menu, you see the Properties dialog box shown in Figure 13.7.

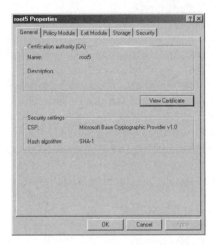

Figure 13.7   The General tab of a CA's Properties dialog box

The General Tab

The General tab in the Properties dialog box does not contain controls that modify the behavior of the CA, but it does display information about it, including the name and description you assigned while installing Certificate Services and the CSP and hash algorithm you elected to use. Clicking View Certificate displays the Certificate dialog box. This certificate is the CA's own, issued by the CA itself in the case of a root CA and issued by another CA in the case of a subordinate. You can see in the figure that this certificate was issued to the CA called root5 by the CA called root5.

The Policy Module Tab

In the Policy Module tab (see Figure 13.8), you can select the policy module that the CA uses to decide whether or not to issue a certificate to an applicant. In most cases, Windows 2000 CAs use the Enterprise and Stand-Alone Policy Module included with the operating system. However, if you have written your own policy module or purchased one from a third party, you can click Select to open the Set Active Policy Module dialog box, where you can select the module you want to use.

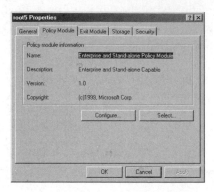

Figure 13.8   The Policy Module tab of a CA's Properties dialog box

Clicking the Configure button opens a Properties dialog box that you can use to configure the selected policy module. In the Default Action tab (see Figure 13.9), you specify how the CA should react when it receives a valid request for a certificate. In an enterprise CA, the Always Issue The Certificate option is the default and the only available option. In a stand-alone CA, you can configure the policy module to always issue the certificate or to set the request's status to "pending" until an administrator reviews the application and manually issues the certificate.

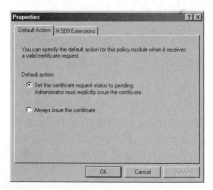

Figure 13.9   The Default Action tab of a policy module's Properties dialog box

In the X.509 Extensions tab (see Figure 13.10), you can specify additional paths to the locations where certificate revocation lists (CRLs) are stored and where users can access the CA's own certificate, which is called the Authority Information Access (AIA) location. These paths are included in all certificates issued by the CA. By default, MCS uses Uniform Resource Locators (URLs) with Hypertext Transfer Protocol (HTTP) and Lightweight Directory Access Protocol (LDAP) references, but you can also add file system URLs to the lists.

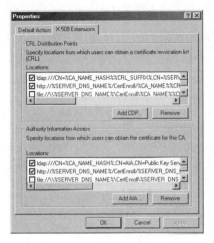

Figure 13.10   The X.509 Extensions tab of a policy module's Properties dialog box

The Exit Module Tab

In the Exit Module tab (see Figure 13.11), you can perform the same basic functions as in the Policy Module tab. The Add and Remove buttons enable you to select the exit modules used by the CA. Clicking the Configure button opens a Properties dialog box, in which you can specify where the CA should publish the certificates that it creates—in the Active Directory database or in the computer's file system.

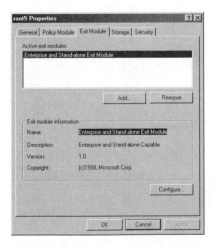

Figure 13.11   The Exit Module tab of a CA's Properties dialog box

The Storage Tab

The Storage tab (see Figure 13.12) is primarily informational, displaying the folders where you elected to store the certificate database and the request log. When you create a stand-alone CA on a computer with access to the Active Directory service, the Active Directory check box is activated, enabling you to store the CA data in the Active Directory database instead of the specified paths.

Figure 13.12   The Storage tab of a CA's Properties dialog box

The Security Tab

As with virtually every other element of the Windows 2000 operating system, you can control who has access to the CA using a Security tab, as shown in Figure 13.13. The standard permissions enable you to specify who can manage the CA, who can enroll with (request certificates from) the CA, and who can read the certificates issued by the CA. By clicking Advanced, you can set more granular permissions.

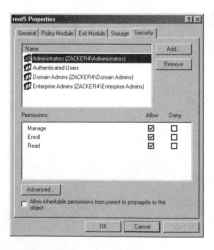

Figure 13.13   The Security tab of a CA's Properties dialog box

Backing Up and Restoring a CA

When a network relies on locally issued certificates for its security, the CA data becomes a critically important resource that must be protected against loss or damage. Because the Certificate Services database is perpetually in an open state when the service is running, it is not possible to back it up using a standard application, such as the Windows 2000 Backup program, without help. The Certification Authority console includes a backup mechanism that you can use to work around this limitation. The Backup CA function of the Certification Authority console does not actually create an offline backup of the CA's data; it only copies the data to another folder on the computer's hard disk. Making this copy requires the CA service to be shut down momentarily and then restarted. After the copy of the CA data is made, you can back it up to tape or another medium in the normal manner, using the Backup program in Windows 2000 or a third-party backup product.

Backing Up a CA

To prepare a CA for backup by making a copy of its database, use the following procedure:

1. Click Start and select Certification Authority from the Administrative Tools program group to open the Certification Authority console.

2. Select the icon for the CA and then, from the Action menu, point to All Tasks, and select Backup CA to launch the Certification Authority Backup Wizard.

3. Click Next to bypass the Welcome page and proceed to the Items To Back Up page (see Figure 13.14).

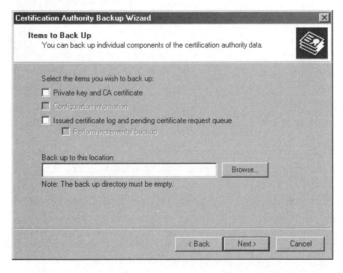

Figure 13.14   The Items To Back Up page in the Certification Authority Backup Wizard

4. Select the check boxes next to the items you want to back up.

   Selecting the Perform Incremental Backup check box causes the wizard to back up everything that has changed since the last backup.

5. Type the path to the destination folder where you want to store the backup copy of the CA database in the Back Up To This Location box or click Browse to select a folder. Click Next to proceed to the next page.

   Note   The folder you specify must be empty. If the folder you specify does not exist, the wizard offers to create it for you.

   If you selected the Private Key And CA Certificate check box on the Items To Back Up page, clicking Next takes you to the Select A Password page (see Figure 13.15). If you did not select this check box, the wizard proceeds to the Completing The Certification Authority Backup Wizard page, in which case you should skip to step 7.

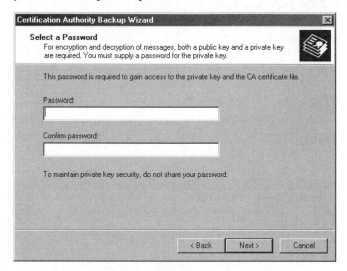

Figure 13.15   The Select A Password page in the Certification Authority Backup Wizard

6. Type the password you want to use to secure the CA's private key and certificate in the Password box and again in the Confirm Password box. Click Next to proceed to the Completing The Certification Authority Backup Wizard page.

7. Click Finish to close the wizard and perform the backup.

   When the wizard performs the backup, it creates a folder called DataBase in the destination folder you specified in the wizard. This folder contains the CA database and all the other information being backed up, except for the CA's private key and certificate (if selected), which are saved to a file in the destination directory that has the CA's name, with a p12 extension.

8. Use a standard backup program, such as Windows 2000 Backup, to copy the destination folder you specified to an offline medium, such as a magnetic tape drive.

Restoring the CA Database

To restore the CA database and other information, use the following procedure:

1. Use your backup program to restore the destination folder to your hard disk from the tape or other medium you used to back it up.

2. Click Start and select Certification Authority from the Administration Tools program group to open the Certification Authority console.

3. Select the icon for the CA and then, from the Action menu, point to All Tasks, and select Restore CA to launch the Certification Authority Restore Wizard.

4. Click Next to bypass the Welcome page and proceed to the Items To Restore page (see Figure 13.16).

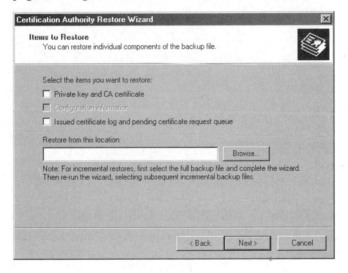

Figure 13.16   The Items To Restore page in the Certification Authority Backup Wizard

5. Select the check boxes next to the items you want to restore.

6. Type the path to the destination folder you just restored from tape in the Restore From This Location text box or click Browse to select a folder. Click Next to proceed to the next page.

If you selected the Private Key And CA Certificate check box on the Items To Restore page, clicking Next takes you to the Provide Password page (see Figure 13.17). If you did not select this check box, the wizard proceeds to the Completing The Certification Authority Restore Wizard page, in which case you should skip to step 8.

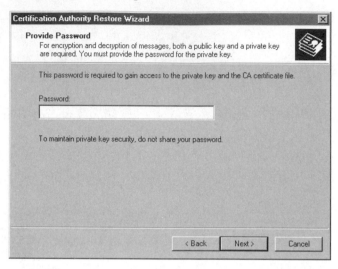

Figure 13.17   The Provide Password page in the Certification Authority Backup Wizard

7. Type the password you used to secure the CA's private key and certificate during the backup. Click Next to proceed to the Completing The Certification Authority Restore Wizard page.

8. Click Finish to close the wizard and perform the restore.

Exercise 1: Installing a Stand-Alone CA

In this exercise, you install a stand-alone root CA on a Windows 2000 Server computer.

1. Click Start, point to Settings, and select Control Panel.

2. Double-click the Add/Remove Programs icon.

3. Click Add/Remove Windows Components.

4. Select the box next to Certificate Services, and then click Next.

5. In the Certification Authority Type page, click the Stand-Alone Root CA option button, and then click Next.

6. On the CA Identifying Information page, type **TestCA** in the CA name box. Click Next.

7. On the Data Storage Location page, use the default paths for the certificate database and the certificate database log. Click Next.

During the CA installation process, you might need to click OK to stop the World Wide Web Publishing Service and provide the location of the Windows 2000 installation files.

8. Click Finish.

9. Click Close to close the Add/Remove Programs window.

Lesson Review

1. A Java software development company sells its products over the Web using credit cards and allows clients to download Web browser applications immediately after completing the e-commerce transaction. The company has an enterprise root CA, which has issued a certificate for their enterprise subordinate CA, which the company uses to secure the credit card transactions. However, some of the customers are complaining that they cannot run the Web applications because they are not digitally signed. What should the company do to add digital signing capabilities to its Web site?

   a. Request a Code Signing certificate from the enterprise root CA.

   b. Request a User Signature Only certificate from the enterprise subordinate CA.

   c. Request a Code Signing certificate from a commercial CA.

   d. Request a User Signature Only certificate from the enterprise root CA.

2. A network administrator running Windows 2000 servers without Active Directory installs a stand-alone root CA on one of the network's computers. Some weeks later, she is instructed to deploy Active Directory on the same computer. What must she do to the CA to make this possible?

   a. Revoke all the certificates issued by the CA and then reissue them after installing Active Directory.

   b. Select the Active Directory check box in the Storage tab of the CA's Properties dialog box.

   c. Obtain a new certificate for the CA.

   d. Uninstall the CA and reinstall it.

3. After installing a stand-alone root CA on a Windows 2000 Server computer, the network administrator is dismayed to find that users have been requesting certificates, but no one has been receiving them. What is the most likely cause of the problem?

   a. The exit module is improperly configured and is publishing the certificates in the wrong place.

   b. The CA's own certificate is invalid; one must be obtained from a commercial CA.

   c. The certificate requests are being held in the "pending" queue until an administrator manually approves them.

   d. The users have been sending their requests to the wrong CA.

Lesson Summary

- Before installing an enterprise CA, you must install and configure the Active Directory service.

- To create a CA on a Windows 2000 Server computer, you use the Add/Remove Programs Control Panel to install Microsoft Certificate Services.

- After you have installed MCS, you use the Certification Authority console to manage the CA.

- The Properties dialog box for the CA contains controls that enable you to modify the behavior of the policy and exit modules, as well as control access to the CA.

- To back up a CA, you must first use the Backup CA function in the Certification Authority console to create a copy of the CA database and other information.

Lesson 3: Managing Certificates

After you have installed a CA and configured it to your needs, users can proceed to request certificates from it. Using the Certification Authority console, you can monitor the CA's activities, approve and revoke certificates, and perform other maintenance tasks.

After this lesson, you will be able to

- List the certificate enrollment methods supported by Microsoft Certificate Services
- Create a Certificates console
- Request a certificate from a CA
- Revoke certificates
- Remove EFS recovery keys

Estimated lesson time: 30 minutes

Certificate Enrollment

The process by which a user obtains a digital certificate is called *certificate enrollment*. The Windows 2000 PKI supports certificate enrollment to Microsoft Certificate Services enterprise CAs, stand-alone CAs, or third-party, commercial CAs. The support for certificate enrollment is implemented in a transport-independent manner and is based on use of industry-standard messages, such as public key cryptography standards (PKCS) #10 certificate request messages and PKCS #7 responses, which contain the resulting certificate or certificate chain. The PKI supports multiple enrollment methods, including Web-based enrollment, an enrollment wizard, and policy-driven autoenrollment that occurs as part of a user's logon processing.

Certificates Snap-In Enrollment

Certificate Services supports client certificate enrollment using an MMC snap-in called Certificates that is included with all versions of Windows 2000. With the Certificates snap-in, you can view and manage all the information in your certificates store, as well as request new certificates from a CA using the Certificate Request Wizard. You learn more about using the Certificates snap-in later in this lesson.

Web-Based Enrollment

The Web-based enrollment process begins with a client submitting a certificate request and ends with the installation of the certificate in the client application. When you install Certificate Services as outlined in Lesson 2 of this chapter, you are actually installing two separate software modules—the Certificate Services

CA and the Certificate Services Web Enrollment Support module. The Web En-rollment module is a Web site that is added to the computer's IIS installation (see Figure 13.18), which provides forms-based access to the CA. The Certificate Ser-vices enrollment interface is accessible at the following URL: *http://servername/ certsrv/default.asp*, where *servername* is the NetBIOS name of the computer on which Certificate Services is running.

Figure 13.18   The Certificate Services Web page

Note   You can elect not to install the Certificate Services Web Enrollment Support module during the CA installation by clicking the Details button on the Windows Components page in the Windows Components Wizard and clearing the Certifi-cate Services Web Enrollment Support check box.

Automated Enrollment

You can use the Automatic Certificate Request Setup Wizard (available from the Automatic Certificate Request Settings node in the Group Policy console's Com-puter Configuration/Windows Settings/Security Settings/Public Key Policies node) to configure autoenrollment for computer certificates. Autoenrollment is not available for user certificates and does not function unless an enterprise CA is online to process certificate requests. You can configure autoenrollment for Computer, Domain Controller, and IPsec certificates.

When you configure autoenrollment, the specified certificate types are issued automatically to all computers that are within the scope of the group policy and to all computers that have the Enroll permission for that certificate type. Auto-enrollment certificates are issued the next time the computer logs on to the network.

> **Tip**   You configure permissions for the various certificate types using the Active Directory Sites and Services console. Open the console, select Show Services Node from the View menu, and then expand the Services folder to locate the Public Key Services/Certificate Templates folder. Select one of the templates in the details pane and use the Security tab in its Properties dialog box to set the permissions.

This mechanism is not a replacement for the enterprise CA issuing policy but is integrated with it. The CA service receives a set of certificate types as part of its policy object. The Enterprise Policy Module uses these to define the types of certificates the CA is allowed to issue. The CA rejects requests for certificates that fail to match these criteria.

Creating the Certificates Console

In addition to the Certification Authority console, there is a certificate-related Microsoft Management Console (MMC) snap-in called Certificates, which you use to manage the certificates themselves. Windows 2000 does not have a shortcut to a Certificates console by default, so you must create one by using the following procedure:

1. Click Start and select Run to open the Run dialog box.

2. Type **mmc** in the Open text box and click OK to open a blank MMC console (see Figure 13.19).

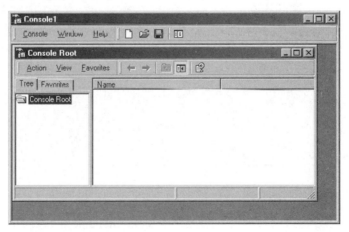

Figure 13.19   A blank MMC console

3. Select Add/Remove Snap-In from the Console menu to display the Add/Remove Snap-In dialog box (see Figure 13.20).

Figure 13.20   The Add/Remove Snap-In dialog box

4. Click Add to open the Add Standalone Snap-In dialog box (see Figure 13.21).

Figure 13.21   The Add Standalone Snap-In dialog box

5. Select Certificates from Available Standalone Snap-Ins and click Add to open a Certificates Snap-In dialog box (see Figure 13.22).

6. Click one of the option buttons to specify whether you want the console to manage certificates for your user account, the service account, or the computer account. Click Finish to close the dialog box.

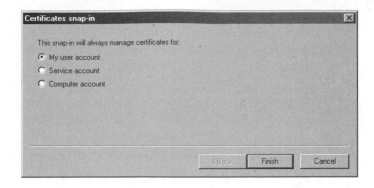

Figure 13.22   The Certificates Snap-In dialog box

7. Click Close to close the Add Standalone Snap-In dialog box.

8. Click OK to close the Add/Remove Snap-In dialog box.

Using the Certificates Console

You use the Certificates console to manage the database of certificates, called the *certificate store*, that Windows 2000 creates for every user and computer account. After you have added the certificate snap-in to an MMC console, you see the interface shown in Figure 13.23.

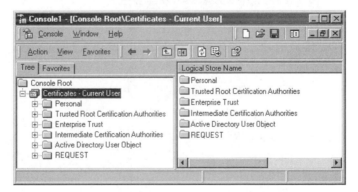

Figure 13.23   The Certificates console

Under the Certificates node, the following folders appear:

- **Personal.**   Contains a Certificates folder holding all the certificates that have been issued to your user account or that you have imported.

- **Trusted Root Certification Authorities.**   Contains a Certificates folder holding a list of the commercial root CAs that your user account is configured to trust. Having trust in a CA means that you count on the CA to properly evaluate certificate requests and reject those that do not meet specified criteria, as well as to revoke certificates that are no longer valid and publish a certificate revocation list (CRL). Your ability to modify the contents of this folder depends on the group policy object settings that apply to your user account. If you add a root CA certificate to this folder, all the computer's users will trust that CA.

- **Enterprise Trust.**   This is a container for *certificate trust lists (CTLs).* A CTL is a list of self-signed certificates issued by other root CAs that the PKI administrator has decided are trustworthy.

- **Intermediate Certification Authorities.**   Contains a Certificates folder and a Certificate Revocation List folder, which hold certificates and CRLs issued by other CAs.

- **Active Directory User Object.**   Contains certificates associated with your user object that are published in the Active Directory database.

- **REQUEST.**   Contains pending or rejected certificate requests.

Viewing Certificates

To view any of the certificates in your store, you simply double-click it or select it and choose Open from the Action menu to display a Certificate dialog box like the one shown in Figure 13.24. This is the format that Windows 2000 uses whenever it displays a certificate.

Figure 13.24   The Certificate dialog box

The General tab of the Certificate dialog box displays basic information about the certificate, such as its uses, the name of the CA that issued it, and the dates during which it is valid. Clicking the Details tab (see Figure 13.25) displays a complete list of the certificate's attributes, including the CSP and hash algorithm used to create the certificate and the locations of the issuing CA's CRL distribution point and AIA path. Clicking the Certification Path tab displays the hierarchical path of the certificate's authorities up to its ultimate root CA.

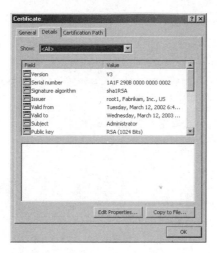

Figure 13.25   The Details tab of the Certificate dialog box

Every certificate also has a Properties dialog box (see Figure 13.26), which you can open by selecting the certificate and choosing Properties from the Action menu. In this dialog box you can supply a friendly name and descriptive information for the certificate. More important, you can modify the purposes for which the certificate can be used. You can enable or disable all the certificate's functions or, by clicking the Enable Only The Following Purposes option button, enable or disable the certificate's individual functions.

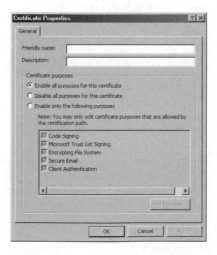

Figure 13.26   A certificate's Properties dialog box

Requesting Certificates

To request a certificate from a CA using the certificates console, use the following procedure:

1. Open the Certificates snap-in.

2. Select the Personal folder, point to All Tasks in the Action menu, and select Request New Certificate to open the Certificate Request Wizard.

3. Click Next to bypass the Welcome page and display the Certificate Template page (see Figure 13.27).

Figure 13.27   The Certificate Template page of the Certificate Request Wizard

4. Select the template that you want the CA to use to create the certificate from the Certificate templates list and select the Advanced Options check box. Click Next to proceed to the Cryptographic Service Provider page (see Figure 13.28).

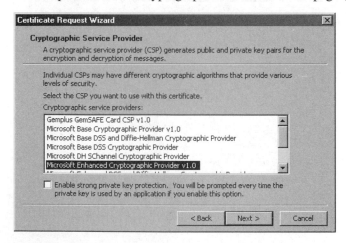

Figure 13.28   The Cryptographic Service Provider page of the Certificate Request Wizard

To skip the Cryptographic Service Provider and Certification Authority pages, clear the Advanced Options check box.

5. Select the CSP you want the CA to use to create the certificate from the Cryptographic Service Providers list and click next to proceed to the Certification Authority page (see Figure 13.29).

Figure 13.29 The Certification Authority page of the Certificate Request Wizard

6. If you want a CA other than the one specified in the CA box to receive the certificate request, click Browse to open a Select Certification Authority dialog box, where you can select one of the other CAs on your network. Click Next to proceed to the Certificate Friendly Name And Description page (see Figure 13.30).

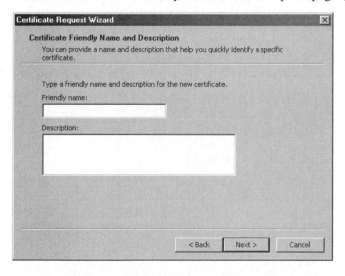

Figure 13.30 The Certificate Friendly Name And Description page of the Certificate Request Wizard

7. Type the name you want to assign to the certificate in the Friendly Name text box and enter any descriptive text you want in the Description text box. Click Next to proceed to the Completing The Certificate Request Wizard page.

8. Click Finish to close the wizard and submit a certificate request to the CA.

A Certificate Request Wizard message box appears. If you sent the request to an enterprise CA, the message box typically states that the request was successful and provides buttons enabling you to view the certificate or install it on your computer. If you sent the request to a subordinate CA, the request is typically flagged as pending, and no response is forthcoming until an administrator approves or denies it.

Revoking Certificates

Revoking certificates is just as important a part of managing a CA as issuing them. You can revoke certificates for many reasons, the most common of which are that the user to whom the certificate was issued has left the organization or that the user's private key was compromised. Whatever the reason, you want to be careful when revoking certificates—once they are revoked, you cannot unrevoke them.

To revoke a certificate, use the following procedure:

1. Click Start and select Certification Authority from the Administrative Tools program group to open the Certification Authority console.

2. In the scope pane, select the Issued Certificates folder under the CA that issued the certificate you want to revoke.

3. Select the certificate you want to revoke in the details pane.

4. Point to All Tasks in the Action menu and select Revoke Certificate to open the Certificate Revocation dialog box (see Figure 13.31).

Figure 13.31   The Certificate Revocation dialog box

5. Select a reason for revoking the certificate in the Reason Code drop-down list (if desired), and click Yes to revoke the certificate.

Notice that the certificate you selected is moved immediately from the Issued Certificates folder to the Revoked certificates folder.

When you revoke a certificate, its serial number is automatically added to the CRL maintained by the CA. Regular publication of the CRL ensures that certificates that have been revoked cannot be used to access confidential resources. The CA publishes its CRL according to a schedule that you can define by selecting the Revoked Certificates folder in the Certification Authority console and selecting Properties from the Action menu to display the Revoked Certificates Properties dialog box shown in Figure 13.32. In this dialog box you can view the time at which the next publication of the CRL is to occur and modify the interval between CRL publications from its default value of one week. The locations where the CA publishes the CRL (called the CRL distribution points, or CDPs), are specified in the X.509 Extensions tab of the CA policy module's Properties dialog box, as shown in Lesson 2 of this chapter.

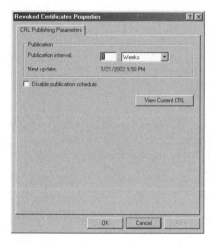

Figure 13.32   The Revoked Certificates Properties dialog box

In addition to scheduling the publication of the CRL, you can also publish it immediately by selecting the Revoked Certificates folder, pointing to All Tasks in the Action menu, and choosing Publish.

Removing EFS Recovery Keys

The Windows 2000 Encrypting File System (EFS) protects files stored on NTFS drives by encrypting them using a key belonging to their owners. The owners can read the contents of their files, but other users cannot. However, EFS actually encrypts the key used to protect the files more than once. In addition to the owner, the Administrator user (on the local machine) or the Domain Administrator user (in a domain) is designated an *EFS recovery agent*, which enables the user to access EFS-encrypted files belonging to other users in case their owners should ever be unable or unavailable to decrypt them. Administrators can also designate other users as EFS recovery agents by adding them to a group policy object (GPO) controlling the domain, site, or organizational unit in which the users reside.

For EFS to function, there must be at least one recovery agent, in addition to the owner, with access to the encrypted files. Deleting the EFS recovery keys in a GPO disables EFS within the scope of that GPO. To remove the EFS recovery keys, you open a group policy object for a local computer, domain, site, or organizational unit and expand your way down the scope pane to the Computer Configuration/Windows Settings/Security Settings/Public Key Policies node. Select the Encrypted Data Recovery Agents folder and choose Delete Policy from the Action menu.

Exercise 1: Requesting a Certificate Using the CA Web Interface

To request and install a certificate from the stand-alone root CA you installed in Exercise 1 of Lesson 2, use the following procedures:

▶ **Procedure 1: Requesting a certificate**

In this procedure, you issue a request for a certificate and send it to your CA using the Web interface.

1. Open Internet Explorer and type the URL **http://*servername*/certsrv/default.asp** in the Address box, where *servername* is the name of the computer running Certificate Services. Press the ENTER key.

2. On the Welcome page, confirm that the Request A Certificate option button is selected and click Next.

3. On the Choose Request Type page, confirm that the User Certificate Request option button is selected and that Web Browser Certificate is selected. Click Next.

4. On the Web Browser Certificate–Identifying Information page, type your name and your e-mail address in the boxes provided. Click Submit. What happens?

5. Close Internet Explorer.

▶ **Procedure 2: Approving a certificate request**

In this procedure you approve the request that you just submitted to the CA.

1. Click Start and select Certification Authority from the Administrative Tools program group to launch the Certification Authority console.

2. In the scope pane, select the Pending Requests folder.

3. In the details pane, select the certificate request you just submitted.

4. In the Action menu, point to All Tasks and select Issue. What happens?

▶ **Procedure 3: Checking the status of a certificate request**

In this procedure you use the CA's Web interface to check the status of the certificate request you sent and install the issued certificate.

1. Open Internet Explorer and type the URL **http://*servername*/certsrv/default.asp** in the Address box, where *servername* is the name of the computer running Certificate Services. Press the ENTER key.

2. On the Welcome page, click the Check On A Pending Certificate option button and click Next.

3. On the Check On A Pending Certificate Request page, verify that a Web Browser Certificate entry with today's date is selected in the Please Select The Certificate Request You Want To Check box. Click Next. What happens?

4. Click the Install This Certificate link. A Certificate Installed page appears, stating that the certificate has been successfully installed.

5. Close Internet Explorer.

Lesson Review

1. You are the administrator of a Windows 2000 network using certificates to secure e-mail communications. One of your users believes that his private key has been compromised. Which of the following steps should you take to address the situation? (Choose all that apply.)

   a. Revoke the user's existing certificate.

   b. Issue a new certificate to the user.

   c. Publish the CRL for the CA that issued the user's certificate.

   d. Uninstall and reinstall the CA.

2. How do you prevent specific users from requesting certain types of certificates from a CA?

3. As the administrator responsible for managing your company's CA, you immediately revoke the certificates of users who leave the company and regularly publish the CRL. A month after leaving, however, one of the former employees has decided to come back to the company. What do you do to reinstate the user's credentials?

   a. Move the user's certificate from the Revoked Certificates folder to the Issued Certificates folder in the Certification Authority console.

   b. Issue the user a new certificate.

   c. Restore the user's certificate from a backup.

   d. Delete the user's certificate listing from the CRL.

Lesson Summary

- Users can request certificates from a CA using the Certificates console or the CA's Web interface.

- In the Certificates console, you can view the certificates in your certificate store, modify the purposes for which they are used, and request new certificates from a CA.

- You revoke certificates using the Certification Authority console when a user's private key is compromised or when the user leaves the organization.

- A certificate revocation list (CRL) is a regularly published document containing the serial numbers of all the certificates you have revoked.

- For EFS to function, there must be at least one designated EFS recovery agent. Deleting the EFS recovery keys in a group policy object disables EFS for the scope of that object.

C H A P T E R   1 4

Monitoring Network Activity

Lesson 1: Monitoring Windows 2000 Activity **540**

Lesson 2: Monitoring Network Services **561**

Lesson 3: Using Network Monitor **574**

About This Chapter

In this book you have learned about many of the different network protocols and services used by Microsoft Windows 2000 and how to implement them. When these protocols and services are operational, it is up to the network administrator to monitor their continued operation. This chapter examines the various tools you can use to monitor the operations of a Windows 2000 computer and the activities of your network's users.

Before You Begin

This chapter contains information about monitoring the various protocols and services introduced throughout this book. A familiarity with each service is needed to understand the value of the monitoring features.

Lesson 1: Monitoring Windows 2000 Activity

Windows 2000 includes a number of multipurpose tools that you can use to monitor the various processes running on the computer. Tools like Event Viewer, the Performance console, and the Shared Folders snap-in should be familiar to every administrator of a Windows 2000 network, as they provide essential information about the ongoing activities of the computer and the network.

After this lesson, you will be able to

- Use Event Viewer to monitor system activity
- Use the Performance console
- Use the Shared Folders snap-in

Estimated lesson time: 45 minutes

Using Event Viewer

Windows 2000, by default, tracks various system events and stores information about them in a series of logs. Event Viewer is a program that enables you to view these logs using a single interface. In addition, you can use Event Viewer to perform a variety of other tasks, including viewing the information gathered as a result of setting audit policies, as well as searching for specific events within log files.

By default, all Windows 2000 computers maintain three logs that are accessible using Event Viewer:

- **System log.** Contains information about events generated by Windows 2000 components, such as services and device drivers. For example, a failure of a service to start or a driver to load during system startup is recorded in the system log. Windows 2000 chooses the types of events recorded in this log. This is the primary Windows 2000 log; you should always view this log first when looking for information about Windows 2000 system problems.

- **Security log.** Contains information about security-related events, such as failed logons, attempts to access protected resources, such as shares and file system elements, and success or failure of audited events. Windows 2000, in its default configuration, does not record information in the security log. The events that Windows 2000 records in this log are a result of the audit policies you must specify using the Group Policy console. By default, only members of the Administrators group can view this log.

- **Application log.** Contains information about specific programs running on the computer, as determined by the application developer.

When you install optional services on a computer running Windows 2000, the system sometimes creates additional logs as well. When you promote a computer running Windows 2000 Server to a domain controller (installing the Microsoft Domain Name System [DNS] service in the process), three additional logs are added to Event Viewer:

- **Directory service log.**   Contains information about Active Directory service events

- **File replication service log.**   Contains information about the success or failure of file replication activities

- **DNS server log.**   Contains information about the status and operations of the DNS service

Viewing Event Logs

Event Viewer is a Microsoft Management Console (MMC) snap-in that you can access in a variety of ways. The simplest method for viewing the contents of the Windows 2000 event logs is to select Event Viewer from the Administrative Tools program group on the Start menu, which opens the Event Viewer console shown in Figure 14.1. You can also access Event Viewer by opening the Computer Management console from the Administrative Tools program group or by adding it to a customized MMC console of your own.

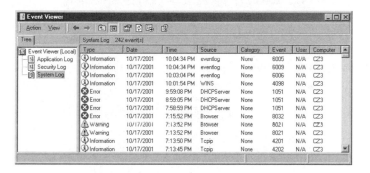

Figure 14.1   The Windows 2000 Event Viewer console

The scope pane of the Event Viewer console lists the various logs maintained by the computer. Selecting one of the logs displays its events in chronological order (most recent first) in the details pane. You can re-sort the list by clicking any of the column headings. Each event in a log is flagged with a type indicator, which can have any of the values shown in Table 14.1.

Table 14.1   Windows 2000 Event Types

Event Type	Icon	Description
Error		A significant problem, such as loss of data or loss of functionality
Warning		An event that might not be significant, but that might indicate a future problem
Information		An event that describes the successful operation of an application, driver, or service
Success audit		An audited security access attempt that succeeds
Failure audit		An audited security access attempt that fails

Every logged event is summarized in the details pane with the date and time that the event occurred, plus an event number and the software module associated with the incident. Double-click an event to display an Event Properties dialog box like that shown in Figure 14.2. This dialog box contains a more complete description of the event, plus any related raw data.

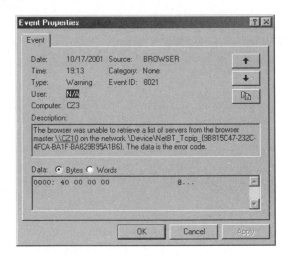

Figure 14.2   An Event Properties dialog box

Locating Events

When you first start Event Viewer, it automatically displays all events that are recorded in the selected log. When a Windows 2000 computer has been operational for some time, the logs can grow quite large. However, many of the event entries are Information items that are the result of normal everyday activities. To limit the display of what appears in the log so that you can focus on the important events, use the Filter command to select the events you want to see. To implement filters in Event Viewer, from the View menu, choose Filter to display the Filter tab of the System Log Properties dialog box, as shown in Figure 14.3. In this dialog box, you can specify the event types you want to display and select other event criteria to reduce the event list to a manageable size.

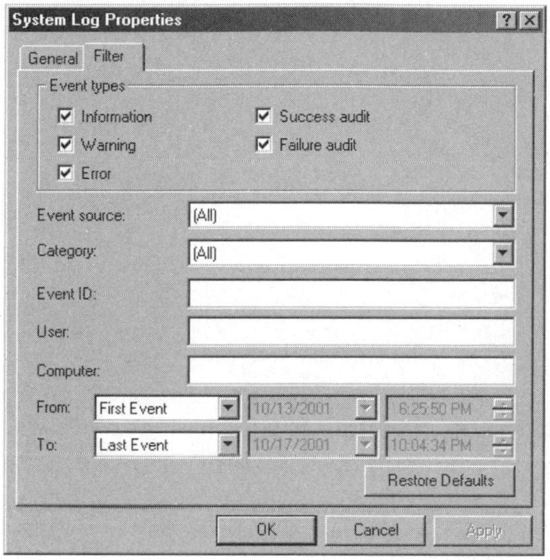

Figure 14.3 The Event Viewer Filter tab

Similarly, you can choose Find from the View menu to perform a search on a log for particular events, using the Find dialog box shown in Figure 14.4.

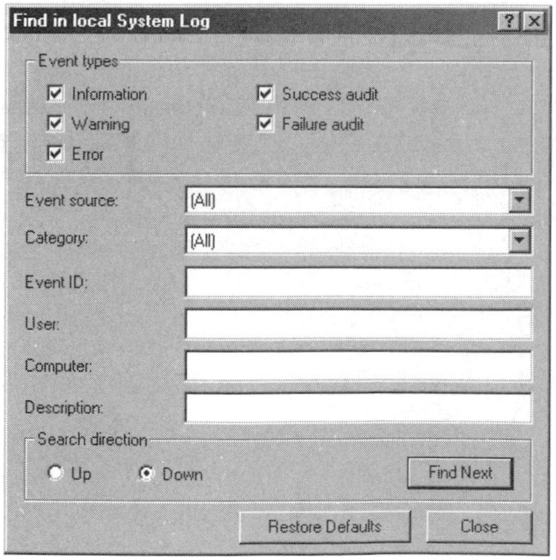

Figure 14.4 The Event Viewer Find dialog box

Table 14.2 lists the various criteria you can use to create filters for and perform searches on an event log.

Table 14.2   Options for Filtering and Finding Events

Option	Description
From and To	The date range for which to view events (Filter tab only).
Event Types	The types of events to view.
Event Source	The software or component driver that logged the event.
Category	The type of event, such as a logon or logoff attempt or a system event.
Event ID	An event number to identify the event. This number helps product support representatives track events.
User	A user logon name.
Computer	A computer name.
Description	The text that is in the description of the event (Find dialog box only).
Search Direction	The direction (up or down) in which to search the log (Find dialog box only).

Accessing Remote Event Logs

As with many MMC snap-ins, you can use Event Viewer to view the logs on other Windows 2000 computers as well as the computer on which you are working. To perform this task, in the scope pane, select the Event Viewer (Local) icon and choose Connect To Another Computer from the Action menu. In the Select Computer dialog box, specify the name of the computer whose event logs you want to see.

Using the Performance Console

Performance is a built-in MMC console accessible from the Administrative Tools program group, which contains two preinstalled snap-ins, one called System Monitor and the other called Performance Logs And Alerts (see Figure 14.5). The System Monitor snap-in enables you to collect and view real-time data about the performance of the computer's memory, disks, processor, network interfaces, and other components in graph, histogram, or report form. The Performance Logs and Alerts snap-in enables you to collect performance data from local or remote computers, as well as configure logs to record performance data and set system alerts that notify you when a specific counter indicates a value above or below a defined threshold.

Monitoring system performance is an important part of maintaining and administering your Windows 2000 Server installation. You can use performance data for the following purposes:

- To understand your workload and its effect on your system resources

- To observe changes and trends in workloads and resource use so that you can plan for future upgrades
- To test configuration changes or other tuning efforts by monitoring the results
- To diagnose problems and target components or processes for optimization

Figure 14.5   The Windows 2000 Performance console

Using the System Monitor Snap-In

In Windows 2000, the System Monitor snap-in has replaced the Performance Monitor application from Windows NT. With System Monitor, you can measure the performance of your own computer or of other computers on a network. System Monitor enables you to perform the following tasks:

- Collect and view real-time performance data on a local computer or from remote computers
- View data collected either currently or previously in a counter log
- Present data in a printable graph, histogram, or report view
- Incorporate System Monitor functionality into Microsoft Word or other applications in the Microsoft Office suite by means of automation
- Create Hypertext Markup Language (HTML) pages from performance views
- Create reusable monitoring configurations that can be installed on other computers that use MMC

With System Monitor, you can collect and view extensive data about hardware resource use and the activity of system services on the computers you administer. You can define the data you want the graph to collect in the following ways:

- **Type of data.**   To select the data to be collected, you can specify one or more *counters*, which are instances of performance objects. Some objects (such as the memory object) provide system resource counters; others provide counters on the operation of applications or services.

- **Source of data.** System Monitor can collect data from your local computer or from other computers on the network for which you have the appropriate permissions. (By default, membership in the Administrators group is required.) In addition, you can include real-time data or data collected previously and saved in counter logs.

- **Sampling parameters.** System Monitor supports manual, on-demand sampling or automatic sampling based on the time interval you specify. When viewing logged data, you can also choose starting and stopping times so that you can view data spanning a specific time range.

When you open the Performance console, it shows the two snap-ins in the scope pane. System Monitor is selected by default, and a blank graph view and a toolbar appear in the details pane. After you add counters to the graph, System Monitor begins charting counter values in this graph area, as shown in Figure 14.6. As the figure illustrates, the System Monitor interface has three main areas: the graph area, the legend, and the value bar.

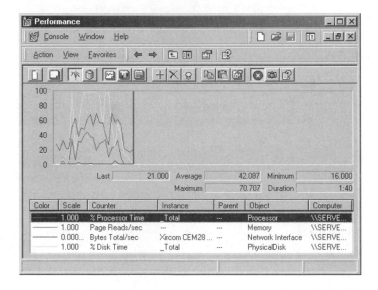

Figure 14.6 The System Monitor snap-in charting counter values in the graph view

You can choose to have the data in the graph area updated automatically or on demand. For updating on demand, use the Update Data toolbar button to start and stop the collection intervals. Click Clear Display to remove all data from the display. To add counters to the graph, click Add to display the Add Counters dialog box, as shown in Figure 14.7. Make a selection in the Performance Object drop-down list, and a list of the counters for that object is displayed underneath. You can then select the counters you want to display or choose to display all the counters for the object. Selecting large numbers of counters is generally not a good idea because it makes the resulting graph difficult to read. The number of counters you can comfortably display depends on the size of your monitor and the screen resolution you are using.

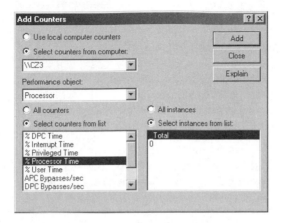

Figure 14.7   The Add Counters dialog box

The movement of the timer bar (the vertical line crossing the entire graph) indicates the passing of each update interval. Regardless of the update interval, the view shows up to 100 data samples. System Monitor compresses log data as necessary to fit it in the display. To see the compressed data in a log, click Properties (the fourth toolbar icon from the right), click the Source tab, select a log file, and then select a shorter time range. Shorter time ranges contain less data, so the system is less likely to eliminate data points.

You can also define the following attributes of the graph:

- Type of display, with options for graph, histogram, or report
- Background color of the details pane and of the data display area
- Size, type, and style of font used to show text in the display
- Color, width, and style of line used to chart data

The names and associated information for the counters you select are shown in the legend, the set of columns beneath the graph. The legend displays the following information:

- **Object.**   A logical collection of counters associated with a resource or service that can be monitored.
- **Counter.**   A data item associated with an object. For each counter selected, System Monitor presents a value corresponding to a particular aspect of the performance defined for the object.

■ **Instance.**   A term used to distinguish between multiple occurrences of the same counter on a computer. Note that by default counter instances are listed by name and numerical index. This index appears after the instance name, represented by a pound sign (#) and a number. This index makes it easier to monitor multiple instances, such as when you are monitoring threads of a process. To turn off the index display, click Properties and clear the Allow Duplicate Counter Instances check box.

You can sort entries in ascending or descending order by object, counter, instance, or computer by clicking the appropriate column name in the counter legend.

Tip   To match a line in a graph with the counter for which it is charting values, double-click a position in the graph line to highlight the corresponding counter in the legend. If the chart lines are close together, try to find a point in the graph where they diverge. Otherwise, System Monitor might not be able to pinpoint the value you are interested in viewing.

The value bar is located beneath the graph area and above the legend. The value bar contains the Last, Average, Minimum, and Maximum values for the counter currently selected. The values are calculated over the time period and number of samples displayed in the graph, not over the time that has elapsed since monitoring was started. The Duration value in the value bar indicates the total elapsed time displayed in the graph (based on the update interval).

Monitoring System and Network Performance

Although network administrators tend to be concerned primarily with the network performance characteristics that are trackable by System Monitor, network activity can also influence the performance of the computer as a whole. You should monitor other resources along with network activity, such as disk, memory, and processor activity. System Monitor enables you to track network and system activity using a single tool.

The use of the following counters is suggested as part of your normal monitoring configuration:

■ Cache\Data Map Hits %

■ Cache\Fast Reads/sec

■ Cache\Lazy Write Pages/sec

■ Logical Disk\% Disk Space

■ Memory\Pages/sec

■ Memory\Available Bytes

■ Memory\Nonpaged Pool Allocs

■ Memory\Nonpaged Pool Bytes

- Memory\Paged Pool Allocs
- Memory\Paged Pool Bytes
- PhysicalDisk\% Disk Time
- Processor(_Total)\% Processor Time
- System\Context Switches/sec
- System\Processor Queue Length
- Processor(_Total)\Interrupts/sec

Monitoring network activity with System Monitor involves examining performance data at each network layer, as defined in the Open Systems Interconnection (OSI) reference model. System Monitor provides performance objects for collection of data that reflects transmission rates, packet queue lengths, and other network performance data.

Note Because of the overhead of the protocol headers, actual transmission rates might differ from the rates specified for the network connection.

When monitoring performance data for your network, begin with the lowest level components and work your way up. Monitor the objects over periods ranging from days to weeks to a month. Using this data, determine a *performance baseline,* the level of performance you expect under a typical workload. A performance baseline gives you a reference point that you can use to compare performance over time, to identify growth trends, changing demands, or the emergence of a bottleneck. If performance within the baseline range becomes unsatisfactory, tune the network.

When performance data is incompatible with your baseline values, investigate the cause. Abnormal network counter values on a server sometimes indicate problems with the computer's memory, processor, or disks. For that reason, the best approach to monitoring a server is to watch the network counters in conjunction with the Processor(_Total)\% Processor Time, PhysicalDisk\% Disk Time, and Memory\Pages/sec statistics.

For example, if a dramatic increase in Pages/sec is accompanied by a decrease in Bytes Total/sec handled by a server, the computer is probably running short of physical memory for network operations. Most network resources, including network adapters and protocol software, use unpaged memory. If a computer is paging excessively, it could be because most of its physical memory has been allocated to network activities, leaving a small amount of memory for processes that use paged memory. To verify this situation, check the computer system event log for entries indicating that it has run out of paged or unpaged memory. Also monitor the unpaged pool memory and overall memory counters.

Using the Performance Logs and Alerts Snap-In

With Performance Logs and Alerts, you can collect performance data automatically from local or remote computers. You can view logged counter data by using System Monitor, or you can export the data to spreadsheet programs or databases for analysis and report generation. Note that, because logging runs as a service, data collection can occur regardless of whether any user is logged on to the computer being monitored. The Performance Logs and Alerts snap-in enables you to perform the following tasks:

- Collect data in a comma-delimited or tab-separated format for easy import to spreadsheet programs. A binary log-file format is also provided for circular logging or for logging instances such as threads or processes that might begin after the log starts collecting data. (*Circular logging* is the process of continuously logging data to a single file, overwriting previous data with new data.)

- View counter data during collection and after collection has stopped.

- Define start and stop times, filenames, file sizes, and other parameters for automatic log generation.

- Manage multiple logging sessions from a single console window.

- Set an alert on a counter, thereby stipulating that a message be sent, a program be run, or a log be started when the selected counter has a value that exceeds or falls below a specified setting.

Similar to System Monitor, Performance Logs and Alerts supports the definition of performance objects, performance counters, and object instances; furthermore, it supports the setting of sampling intervals for monitoring data about hardware resources and system services. Performance Logs and Alerts also offers the following additional options related to recording performance data:

- Starting and stopping logging. Either manually, on demand, or automatically start and stop logging based on a user-defined schedule.

- Creating trace logs. Using the default system data provider or another provider, trace logs record data when certain activities occur, such as disk input/output (I/O) operations or page faults. When the event occurs, the provider sends the data to the Performance Logs and Alerts snap-in. This recording and sending of data differs from the operation of counter logs; when counter logs are in use, the service obtains data from the system when the update interval has elapsed, rather than waiting for a specific event. A parsing tool is required to interpret the trace log output. Developers can create such a tool by using application programming interfaces (APIs) provided on the Microsoft Web site, *http://msdn.microsoft.com.*

- Defining a program that runs when a log is stopped.

- Configuring additional settings for automatic logging, such as automatic file renaming, and setting parameters for stopping and starting a log based on the elapsed time or the file size.

Note You can work with data from a log file while the service is collecting data and has the log file locked. For example, Microsoft Excel can import an active log file, but it opens a read-only version of the locked log.

In Performance Logs and Alerts, you can define settings for counter logs, trace logs, and alerts. The details pane of the console window shows logs and alerts that you have created, as shown in Figure 14.8.

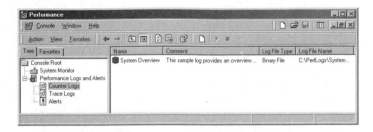

Figure 14.8 Logs and alerts in the Performance Logs and Alerts snap-in

You can define multiple logs or alerts to run simultaneously. Each log or alert is a saved configuration that you define. If you have configured the log for automatic starting and stopping, a single log can generate many individual log data files. For example, if you were generating a log file for each day's activity, one file would close at 11:59 P.M. today, and a new file would open at midnight tomorrow.

Table 14.3 explains the query summary information provided by the columns in the details pane.

Table 14.3 The Columns in the Details Pane

Column	Description
Name	This column provides the name of the log or alert. Think of it as a "friendly name" describing the type of data you are collecting or the condition you are monitoring. One log can generate multiple log files. A sample log file, named System Overview, has been pre-defined for counter logging. You can start logging by using this file or by defining your own settings as appropriate.
Comment	This column includes any descriptive information about the log or alert.
Log File Type	This column contains the log-file format you define. For alert, the type is always alerts; for trace logs, it is always sequential. For logs, this type can be binary, binary circular, text-CSV (for comma-delimited text), or text-TSV (for tab-delimited text).
Log File Name	This column lists the path and base filename you defined for the files generated by this log. The base filename is used for automatically naming new files.

To see the parameters defined for each log, select the log name in the details pane and, from the Action menu, choose Properties. In the Properties dialog box that appears, choose how to name your log files, determine when logging is scheduled to occur, and decide which performance objects and counters you want to monitor in your log.

If a log is currently running and collecting data (based on the schedule you defined for the log or alert), a green data icon appears next to the log or alert. If a red icon appears, the log or alert has been defined but is not currently running.

Note You can configure more than one type of log to run at a time. One log can generate multiple log files if the Restart option is selected or if you start and stop the log multiple times. However, these individual log files do not appear in the console window. Use Windows Explorer to view a listing of these files.

Using the Shared Folders Snap-In

Windows 2000 includes the Shared Folders snap-in so that you can easily monitor access to network resources, view sessions and open files, disconnect users from shared folders, and send administrative messages to users. You monitor access to network resources to assess and manage the current use of your network servers. The three primary reasons why it is important to assess and manage network resources are as follows:

- **Maintenance.**   To perform maintenance tasks on network resources, you might need to periodically make certain resources unavailable to users. To do this, you first have to determine which users are currently accessing a resource so that you can notify them before taking the resource offline.

- **Security.**   To maintain network security, you might want to monitor user access to resources that are confidential to verify that only authorized users are accessing them.

- **Planning.**   Meeting the expanding needs of the network's users requires that you determine which resources are being used and how much they are being used, so that you can plan for future system growth.

The Shared Folders snap-in is included as part of the Computer Management console, which you can access from the Administrative Tools program group. As with any MMC snap-in, you can also add the Shared Folders snap-in to a custom console, specifying whether you want to monitor the resources on the local computer or on a remote computer.

Not all users are permitted to use the Shared Folders snap-in to monitor access to network resources, however. In a domain, a user must be a member of the Administrators, Server Operators, or local Power Users group; in a workgroup, a user must be a member of the Administrators group or the Power Users group.

The Shared Folders snap-in appears in MMC with three folders, called Shares, Sessions, and Open Files, as shown in Figure 14.9. The Shares folder contains a list of all the shares on the computer. The Sessions folder lists the users who are currently connected to the computer shares, and the Open Files folder lists the files that the connected users are accessing. The following sections examine the functions you can perform by using these three folders.

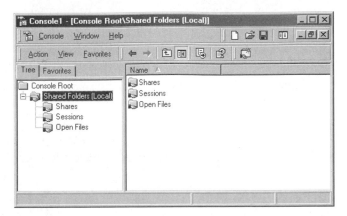

Figure 14.9   The Shared Folders MMC snap-in

Monitoring Shared Folders

You monitor access to shared folders to determine how many users are currently connected to each shared folder on a computer running Windows 2000. You can also monitor open files to determine which users are gaining access to the files, and you can disconnect users from one open file or from all open files. You use the Shares folder in the Shared Folders snap-in to view a list of all shared folders on the computer and to determine how many users have a connection to each folder. In Figure 14.10, the Shares folder is selected in the Computer Management scope pane, and all the shared folders on the computer are listed in the details pane.

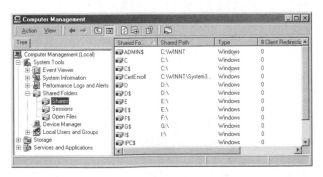

Figure 14.10   The Shares folder in the Computer Management console

The columns in the details pane provide the following information about each share on the computer:

- **Shared Folder.** The shared folders on the computer, using the names assigned to the folders when the shares were created
- **Shared Path.** The paths to the shared folders on the host computer
- **Type.** The operating system that must be running on a computer so that it can gain access to the shared folders
- **# Client Redirections.** The number of clients who have made a remote connection to the shared folders
- **Comment.** Descriptive text about the shared folders, using the information provided when the shares were created

---

Note   Windows 2000 does not automatically update the list of shared folders, open files, and user sessions. To update these lists, select Refresh from the Action menu.

Determining How Many Users Can Access a Shared Folder Concurrently

You can use the Shared Folders snap-in to view and modify the maximum number of users who are permitted to access a folder. With the Shares folder selected in the scope pane, select the shared folder for which you want to determine the maximum number of concurrent users who can access the folder in the details pane. Then, select Properties in the Action menu to display the Properties dialog box for the shared folder (see Figure 14.11). The General tab contains a User Limit box in which you can impose a limit by selecting the Allow option button and specifying a number of users in the Users selector.

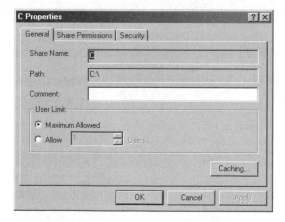

Figure 14.11   The Properties dialog box for a shared folder

In this same dialog box, you can manage the permissions for the share by clicking the Security tab.

Sharing a Folder

In addition to monitoring shares, you can use the Shared Folders snap-in to share an existing folder or to create a new folder and share it. You can also modify the share permissions and NTFS permissions when you share the folder. The biggest advantage of this capability is that you can use it to create and share folders on other computers on the network. The Shared Folders snap-in is the only graphical tool that can create a new shared folder on a remote computer using Windows 2000.

To create a new shared folder using the Shared Folders snap-in, you select the Shares folder in the scope pane and then select New File Share from the Action menu to launch the Create Shared Folder Wizard, as shown in Figure 14.12. In this wizard, you supply the path to the folder you want to share, the name you want to give the share, and then the permissions you want to assign to it. When you use the Shared Folders snap-in to share an existing folder or to create a new shared folder, Windows 2000 assigns the shared folder Full Control permission to the Everyone group by default. You can also assign NTFS permissions when you share the folder.

Figure 14.12   The Create Shared Folder Wizard

Monitoring User Sessions

You can also use the Shared Folders snap-in to monitor which users are currently accessing the shared folders on a server from a remote computer, and you can view the resources to which the users have connections. You can disconnect users and send administrative messages to computers and users, including computers and users who aren't currently accessing network resources. This information enables you to determine which users you should contact when you need to stop sharing a folder or shut down the server on which the shared folder resides. You can disconnect one or more users in order to free idle connections to the shared folder, to prepare for a backup or restore operation, to shut down a server, or to change group membership and permissions for the shared folder.

Use the Sessions folder in the Shared Folders snap-in to view a list of the users with a current network connection to the computer that you are monitoring, as shown in Figure 14.13.

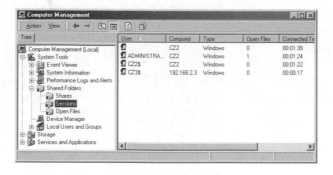

Figure 14.13   The Sessions folder in the Shared Folders snap-in

The columns in the details pane of the Sessions folder provide the following information about each of the computer connections:

- **User.**   The users with a current network connection to the computer being monitored
- **Computer.**   The name of the user's computer
- **Type.**   The operating system running on the user's computer
- **Open Files.**   The number of files that the user has open on the computer being monitored
- **Connected Time.**   The time that has elapsed since the user established the current session
- **Idle Time.**   The time that has elapsed since the user last gained access to a resource on the computer being monitored
- **Guest.**   Whether this computer authenticated the user as a member of the built-in Guest account

Disconnecting Users

From the Sessions folder, you can disconnect one or all of the currently connected users. You might have to disconnect users so that you can do any of the following:

- Cause changes to shared folder and NTFS permissions to take effect immediately. A connected user retains all permissions for a shared resource that Windows 2000 assigned when the user connected to it. Windows 2000 evaluates the permissions again the next time the user establishes a connection.
- Free idle connections on a busy computer so that other users can access the shared resources. User connections to resources might remain active for several

minutes after a user finishes accessing the resource. Disconnecting user connections frees up the connection immediately.

- Shut down a server.

Note After you disconnect a user, the user can immediately establish a new connection. If you disconnect a user who is currently accessing a shared folder from a Windows-based client computer, the client automatically reestablishes the connection with the shared folder. This connection is reestablished without user intervention unless you change the permissions to prevent the user from accessing the shared folder or you stop sharing the folder.

To disconnect a specific user, follow this procedure:

1. In the Shared Folders snap-in, select the Sessions folder in the scope pane.
2. Select the user you want to disconnect in the details pane and select Close Session from the Action menu.

Caution Disconnecting a user session immediately severs all access to the files on the connected share, including files that the user currently has open. This can result in data loss. Therefore, you should always give fair warning to users to save their work before severing connections. One way to perform this task is to send them an administrative message, as explained in the next section.

You can also disconnect all the current sessions at one time. To do this, select the Sessions folder in the scope pane and select Disconnect All Sessions from the Action menu.

Sending Administrative Messages to Users

Using the Shared Folders snap-in, you can send administrative messages to one or more users or computers on the network. For example, you might want to send administrative messages to users connected to a computer when a disruption to the computer or to its resource availability occurs. Some of the most common reasons for sending administrative messages are to notify users when you intend to do any of the following:

- Perform a backup or restore operation
- Disconnect users from a resource
- Upgrade software or hardware
- Shut down the computer

To send an administrative message, select the Shared Folders icon in the scope pane and in the Action menu, point to All Tasks and choose Send Console Message to open the Send Console Message dialog box. By default, all currently connected computers to which you can send a message appear in the list of recipients. You can add other users or computers to this list by clicking Add, even if they don't have a current connection to resources on the computer.

Monitoring Open Files

You can use the Open Files folder in the Shared Folders snap-in to view a list of the files in the computer's shared folders that are currently open and to find out which users are connected to each file, as shown in Figure 14.14. You can use this information when you need to contact users to notify them that you are shutting down the system. Additionally, when a user is attempting to access a file in a shared folder and cannot do so because it is locked open, you can use the Open Files list to determine who is using it.

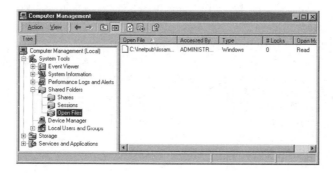

Figure 14.14   The Open Files folder in the Shared Folders snap-in

When you select the Open Files folder in the scope pane of the snap-in, the columns in the details pane provide the following information about each of the files currently in use:

- **Open File.**   The name of the open file on the computer.
- **Accessed By.**   The logon name of the user who has the file open.
- **Type.**   The operating system running on the computer where the user is logged on.
- **# Locks.**   The number of locks on the file. Programs can request the operating system to lock a file to gain exclusive access and prevent other programs from making changes to the file.
- **Open Mode.**   The type of access that the user's application requested when it opened the file, such as Read or Write.

You can use the Open Files folder to disconnect users from one open file or from all open files. For example, if you make changes to the NTFS permissions for a file that is currently opened by a user, the new permissions won't affect that user until the file is closed and reopened. You can force these changes to take place immediately by doing either of the following:

- Disconnect all users from all open files. Select the Open Files folder and choose Disconnect All Open Files from the Action menu.

- Disconnect all users from one open file. Select a file in the details pane and choose Close Open File from the Action menu.

Caution   You can force the user to reopen the file by forcibly disconnecting the user from it. As with disconnecting a session, however, this type of disconnection can cause data loss if you do not warn the user beforehand to save any changes made to the file.

Exercise 1: Monitoring System Performance Parameters

In this exercise you create a System Monitor graph containing a number of counters that provide information on vital system functions.

1. Click Start and from the Programs/Administrative Tools group, open the Performance console.

2. Right-click anywhere in the field of the (empty) graph and, from the pop-up menu, choose Add Counters to display the Add Counters dialog box.

3. From the Performance Object drop-down list, select Processor.

4. Click the Select Counters From List option and, in the list of counters, select %Processor Time.

5. Click the Select Instances From List option and, from the list of instances, select Total.

6. Click Add to add the counter to the graph.

7. From the Performance Object drop-down list, select Memory.

8. From the Counters list, select Available MBytes.

9. Click Add.

10. Click Close. What do you see?

11. Click View Histogram and then View Report. What do you see when you click these buttons?

Lesson Review

1. What is the danger inherent in disconnecting a user from a share without prior notification?

2. Which of the following tasks cannot be performed by the Shared Folders snap-in?

    a. Send an administrative message to another user on the network

    b. Share an existing printer on the local computer

    c. Share an existing folder on the local computer

    d. Create a new shared folder on a remote computer

3. What must you do before modifications you have made to the NTFS permissions for a shared folder have their full effect?

Lesson Summary

- Event Viewer enables you to view and search through the various log files maintained by Windows 2000.

- The System Monitor snap-in enables you to display continually updated system performance statistics in a variety of formats.

- The Performance Logs and Alerts snap-in collects performance data from computers all over the network and set alerts to inform you of unusual system activity.

- The Shared Folders MMC snap-in enables you to monitor the shared folders on a computer running Windows 2000, the users connected to the shares, and the files that the users have open.

- From the Shares folder, you can create new shares on the local computer or a remote computer and monitor the number of connections to each share.

- From the Sessions folder, you can monitor each user connection to the computer and forcibly disconnect a user or all users.

- From the Open Files folder, you can monitor the files that a network user is accessing and disconnect the user from a specific file or from all shared files.

Lesson 2: Monitoring Network Services

All the Windows 2000 services that you have learned about in the previous chapters, including the Dynamic Host Configuration Protocol (DHCP), the Windows Internet Name Service (WINS), the Domain Name System (DNS), and the Routing and Remote Access Service (RRAS), have some means of monitoring their activities. This enables the Windows 2000 network administrator to ensure that the services are operating as needed.

After this lesson, you will be able to

- Monitor the activity of the DHCP, WINS, DNS, and RRAS services
- Monitor IPsec activity

Estimated lesson time: 20 minutes

Monitoring DHCP Activity

The primary reason for monitoring DHCP activity is to ensure that the Internet Protocol (IP) address scopes you have created are not being depleted. If clients fail to obtain Transmission Control Protocol/Internet Protocol (TCP/IP) configuration settings from your DHCP server, the first thing you should do is check to see that the clients are properly configured to use DHCP. After that, you should check the DHCP server itself to make sure that IP addresses are available for allocation.

Viewing DHCP Statistics

To view statistics for your DHCP server, open the DHCP console from the Start menu's Administrative Tools program group, select the icon for your server in the scope pane, and then select Display Statistics from the Action menu to open a Server Statistics dialog box like the one shown in Figure 14.15.

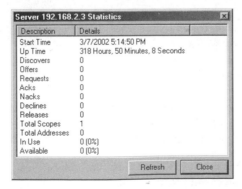

Figure 14.15   The DHCP console's Server Statistics dialog box

This dialog box displays the following information:

- **Start Time.**   Specifies the date and time that the DHCP service was last started
- **Up Time.**   Specifies the amount of time that the DHCP service has been running since it was last started
- **Discovers.**   Specifies the number of DHCPDISCOVER messages that the server has received from clients
- **Offers.**   Specifies the number of DHCPOFFER messages that the server has transmitted to clients
- **Requests.**   Specifies the number of DHCPREQUEST messages that the server has received from clients
- **Acks.**   Specifies the number of DHCPACK messages that the server has transmitted to clients
- **Nacks.**   Specifies the number of DHCPNAK messages that the server has transmitted to clients
- **Declines.**   Specifies the number of DHCPDECLINE messages that the server has received from clients
- **Releases.**   Specifies the number of DHCPRELEASE messages that the server has received from clients
- **Total Scopes.**   Specifies the number of operational scopes (IP address pools) on the DHCP server
- **Total Addresses.**   Specifies the total number of IP addresses available in all the server's scopes
- **In Use.**   Specifies the number of IP addresses that are currently assigned by the DHCP server, in both numerical and percentage forms
- **Available.**   Specifies the number of IP addresses that are currently available for allocation by the DHCP server, in both numeric and percentage form

By default, the information in the Server Statistics dialog box is static; to update the display, you must click the Refresh button. However, you can configure the DHCP console to automatically update the statistics at an interval you select. To do this select the DHCP server's icon in the console's scope pane and select Properties from the Action menu to open the server's Properties dialog box (see Figure 14.16). Select the Automatically Update Statistics Every check box and specify a time interval using the Hours and Minutes selectors. Click OK to close the Properties dialog box, and then open the Server Statistics dialog box again. The information displayed will now be automatically updated when the time interval you specified lapses.

Just because the Server Statistics dialog box indicates that IP addresses are available for allocation does not mean that the server is capable of assigning an address to any DHCP client on your network. The In Use and Available statistics refer to all the DHCP server's allocatable addresses, in all its scopes. If all the available addresses are located in one scope, clients on subnets serviced by the other scopes cannot obtain addresses.

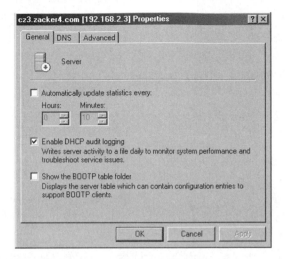

Figure 14.16 A DHCP server's Properties dialog box

DHCP Logging

Every DHCP server's Properties dialog box also contains an Enable DHCP Audit Logging check box; selecting this check box causes the server to maintain a daily log of DHCP activities. The log files are located in the *%systemroot%*\System32\dhcp folder and are named DhcpSrvLog with an extension consisting of the three-letter abbreviation for the day of the week, as follows:

- DhcpSrvLog.Sun
- DhcpSrvLog.Mon
- DhcpSrvLog.Tue
- DhcpSrvLog.Wed
- DhcpSrvLog.Thu
- DhcpSrvLog.Fri
- DhcpSrvLog.Sat

As each day begins, the DHCP server overwrites the log file created on the same day the previous week. The logs are comma-delimited text files in which each line is an entry denoting an event. The fields on each line are as follows:

- **ID.** Contains a numerical code that identifies the reason for the log entry. Windows 2000 DHCP Server uses a list of codes that represent common DHCP activities (such as the starting and stopping of the DHCP service) and common error conditions. The code values are accessible from the DHCP console's online help system.

- **Date.** Specifies the date on which the log entry was created
- **Time.** Specifies the time at which the log entry was created
- **Description.**   Contains a description of the event that triggered the log entry
- **IP Address.**   Contains the IP address of the DHCP client (if any) involved in the event that triggered the log entry
- **Host Name.**   Contains the host name of the DHCP client involved in the event that triggered the log entry
- **MAC Address.**   Contains the hardware address of the network interface adapter in the DHCP client involved in the event that triggered the log entry

Using DHCP Performance Counters

In addition to the Server Statistics dialog box and the logs, installing DHCP on a Windows 2000 Server computer also adds a series of specialized DHCP counters to the System Monitor snap-in, which is accessible from the Performance console. These counters are as follows:

- **Acks/sec.**   Specifies the number of DHCPACK messages being transmitted by the DHCP server each second
- **Active Queue Length.**   Specifies the number of incoming packets waiting to be processed by the DHCP server
- **Conflict Check Queue Length.**   Specifies the number of outgoing conflict detection (ping) packets waiting to be transmitted by the DHCP server
- **Declines/sec.**   Specifies the number of DHCPDECLINE messages being received by the DHCP server each second
- **Discovers/sec.**   Specifies the number of DHCPDISCOVER messages being received by the DHCP server each second
- **Duplicates Dropped/sec.**   Specifies the number of duplicate packets being received by the DHCP server each second
- **Informs/sec.**   Specifies the number of DHCPINFORM messages being received by the DHCP server each second
- **Milliseconds Per Packet (Avg).**   Specifies the amount of time (in milliseconds) that the server is taking to respond to an incoming message
- **Nacks/sec.**   Specifies the number of DHCPNAK messages being transmitted by the DHCP server each second
- **Offers/sec.**   Specifies the number of DHCPOFFER messages being transmitted by the DHCP server each second
- **Packets Expired/sec.**   Specifies the number of packets in the DHCP server's message queue that are expiring each second
- **Packets Received/sec.**   Specifies the number of packets received by the DHCP server each second

- **Releases/sec.**   Specifies the number of DHCPRELEASE messages being received by the DHCP server each second

- **Requests/sec.**   Specifies the number of DHCPREQUEST messages being received by the DHCP server each second

You can add these counters to the System Monitor display just as you would any of the default counters supplied with Windows 2000. For more information about using System Monitor, see Lesson 1 of this chapter.

Monitoring WINS Activity

WINS is a service that is largely self-sufficient; its core functions rarely need monitoring. However, in an environment where multiple WINS servers coexist on the same network, it is important to make sure that the replication between the servers proceeds as intended. To view information about the ongoing operation of a WINS server, you open the WINS console from the Administrative Tools program group in the Start menu, select the icon for your WINS server in the scope pane, and choose Display Server Statistics from the Action menu to open a WINS Server Statistics dialog box, as shown in Figure 14.17.

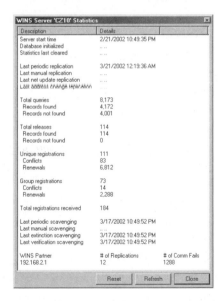

Figure 14.17   A WINS Server Statistics dialog box

The information supplied in the dialog box is as follows:

- **Server Start Time.**   Specifies the date and time that the WINS service was last started

- **Database Initialized.**   Specifies the date and time when static mappings were last imported into the WINS database

- **Statistics Last Cleared.**   Specifies the date and time when an administrator last reset the WINS server statistics counters
- **Last Periodic Replication.**   Specifies the date and time that the last automated WINS database replication occurred
- **Last Manual Replication.**   Specifies the date and time that an administrator last triggered a WINS database replication manually
- **Last Net Update Replication.**   Specifies the date and time that the last WINS database replication occurred as the result of a push notification message
- **Last Address Change Replication.**   Specifies the date and time that the last change to the WINS database was replicated
- **Total Queries.**   Specifies the total number of name query request messages received by the WINS server
  - **Records Found.**   Specifies the number of requested names successfully resolved by the WINS database
  - **Records Not Found.**   Specifies the number of requested names that could not be resolved by the WINS database
- **Total Releases.**   Specifies the number of name release request messages received by the WINS server
  - **Records Found.**   Specifies the number of names successfully released from the WINS database
  - **Records Not Found.**   Specifies the number of names that could not be released from the WINS database
- **Unique Registrations.**   Specifies the number of name registration request messages containing unique Network Basic Input/Output System (NetBIOS) names received by the WINS server
  - **Conflicts.**   Specifies the number of unique names that the WINS server could not register because they already existed in the database
  - **Renewals.**   Specifies the number of unique name registrations processed by the WINS server that were renewals of names already in the database
- **Group Registrations.**   Specifies the number of name registration request messages containing group NetBIOS names received by the WINS server
  - **Conflicts.**   Specifies the number of group names that the WINS server could not register because they already existed in the database
  - **Renewals.**   Specifies the number of group name registrations processed by the WINS server that were renewals of names already in the database
- **Total Registrations Received.**   Specifies the total number of name registration request messages received by the WINS server

- **Last Periodic Scavenging.**   Specifies the date and time that the last automated scavenging of the WINS database occurred

- **Last Manual Scavenging.**   Specifies the date and time that an administrator last triggered a manual scavenging of the WINS database

- **Last Extinction Scavenging.**   Specifies the date and time that names were last scavenged from the WINS database based on the extinction interval

- **Last Verification Scavenging.**   Specifies the date and time that names were last scavenged from the WINS database based on the verification interval

- **WINS Partner.**   Lists the IP addresses of the WINS server's replication partners and specifies the number of replications and the number of communications failures that have occurred for each

By clicking Reset in the WINS Server Statistics dialog box, you can set all the counters back to zero and blank out all the time references except for the Server Start Time. As with the Server Statistics dialog box in the DHCP console, the information in the WINS Server Statistics dialog box does not change unless you click Refresh to update it or configure the WINS console to update it automatically. Here also, you configure the refresh rate by opening the server's Properties dialog box, selecting the Automatically Update Statistics Every check box, and specifying an interval in the selectors provided.

You can also track WINS activities by configuring the server to log the events that occur. Unlike DHCP, WINS can save its log information to the Windows 2000 system log, viewable in the Event Viewer console. Logging to the system log is optional; you activate this feature by clicking the Advanced tab in the WINS server's Properties dialog box and selecting the Log Detailed Events To Windows Event Log check box. When you enable this logging feature, WINS creates an event for every change to the WINS database and every WINS server activity. On a busy network, this can fill the system log with a lot of entries very quickly and consume a significant amount of system resources while doing so.

Monitoring DNS Activity

The Microsoft DNS Server included with Windows 2000 differs from the DHCP and WINS servers in that it has its own separate log that appears in the Event Viewer console. Any errors that occur are easily visible from that console, along with informational messages about the service's ongoing activities. In addition to this primary log, DNS Server also has the capability to maintain an additional log that you can use for debugging purposes, as shown in Figure 14.18. This alternate log is a simple text file stored in the *%systemroot%*\System32\dns folder with the name Dns.log. The service does not maintain this log by default because it slows down the operation of the DNS server.

Figure 14.18   The Logging tab of a DNS server's Properties dialog box

There might also be times when you want to view the information about previously resolved names that the DNS Server service has stored in its cache. By default, the DNS console displays only two folders subordinate to each server icon, the Forward Lookup Zones folder and the Reverse Lookup Zones folder. Neither of these contains the cached information. To display the DNS name cache, select Advanced from the View menu to display a third folder, called Cached Lookups. By expanding this folder (see Figure 14.19), you can view the cached information for any of the top-level domains processed by the server.

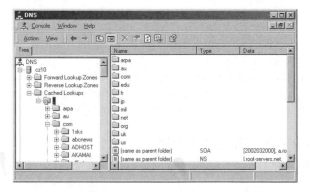

Figure 14.19   The cached information stored in Microsoft DNS Server

Monitoring RRAS Activity

Throughout this book you have learned about the many functions of the Windows 2000 RRAS service, including local area network router, dynamic router, remote access server, virtual private network (VPN) server, and network address translation (NAT) server. The Routing and Remote Access console has a variety of screens that display information about the service's ongoing activities.

As with most MMC snap-ins, you can use the Routing and Remote Access console to manage the RRAS service on multiple servers. When you do this, you can select the Server Status icon in the console's scope pane to display a list of the servers you have added to the console (see Figure 14.20), along with the current state of each one, the number of ports on the server, and the number of ports that are currently in use. This is a quick way to check on port availability on all your servers.

Figure 14.20   The RRAS console's Server Status display

To display information about the individual ports on a RRAS server, you can select the Ports icon in the scope pane, which causes a list of the ports on the computer to appear in the details pane. Selecting a port and choosing Status from the Action menu opens a Port Status dialog box (see Figure 14.21) that contains statistics about the port's current status, the number of bytes that have passed through it, and any transmission errors that have occurred. The information in this dialog box is not dynamic, so you must click Refresh to update it. You can also click Reset to return all the counters to zero.

Figure 14.21   A RRAS Port Status dialog box

To display information about the RRAS service's routing activities, you can expand a server icon to display the IP Routing icon. Select General under IP Routing and choose Show TCP/IP Information from the Action menu to display the TCP/IP Information window shown in Figure 14.22. This window contains a variety of TCP/IP statistics, including the number of routes in the routing table and the number of packets processed by the various TCP/IP network and transport layer protocols.

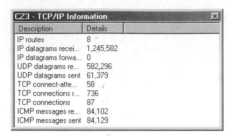

Figure 14.22   The RRAS TCP/IP Information Window

Monitoring Routing Protocols

If you elect to run dynamic routing protocols such as the Routing Information Protocol (RIP) and Open Shortest Path First (OSPF) on your RRAS server, you can use additional information windows to monitor the activities of the protocols. To view these windows, expand the server icon in the scope pane of the Routing and Remote Access console and then perform one of the following procedures:

- **Select RIP and choose Show Neighbors from the Action menu.**   Displays a list of the other RIP routers exchanging messages with RRAS, along with the number of bad packets and bad routes attributable to each one

- **Select OSPF and choose Show Areas from the Action menu.**   Displays a list of the OSPF areas configured on the server, whether they are operational or not, and how many link state calculations have been performed on the interface

- **Select OSPF and choose Show Link-State Database from the Action menu.**   Displays the entire OSPF link state database

- **Select OSPF and choose Show Neighbors from the Action menu.** Displays a list of the other OSPF routers exchanging messages with RRAS, along with information about them

- **Select OSPF and choose Show Virtual Interfaces from the Action menu.** Displays a list of the OSPF virtual interfaces you have configured in RRAS

RRAS Logging

Like many other Windows 2000 services, RRAS maintains its own logs, and you can configure the amount of information that the service stores in the logs. Every server listed in the Routing and Remote Access console has a folder called Remote Access Logging beneath it, with one Local File entry. If you are using a RADIUS server to manage your RRAS authentication and accounting, you might have other logs listed in the folder. The Local File entry specifies the location of the log, which by default is in the *%systemroot%*\System32\Log Files folder.

To configure logging for the entire RRAS server, you open the Properties dialog box for the server and click the Event Logging tab (see Figure 14.23). Here, you can specify whether you want to disable server logging, log only errors, log errors and warnings, or log the maximum amount of information. You can also enable logging of all Point-to-Point Protocol (PPP) information, including negotiations between your clients and the server. As is usually the case, increasing the detail of the log provides more information but also makes the logs more difficult to examine and slows down the server.

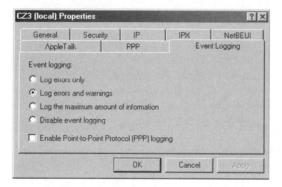

Figure 14.23   The Event Logging tab of a RRAS server's Properties dialog box

In addition to these global logging options, you can also configure each individual log by selecting it in the Remote Access Logging folder and choosing Properties from the Action menu to display the Properties dialog box shown in Figure 14.24. In the Settings tab, you can specify whether to log accounting or authentication requests, or both, and periodic status messages. In the Local File tab, you specify the format of the log file, its location, and how often it should be overwritten.

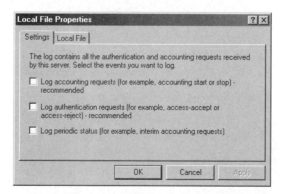

Figure 14.24   The Local File Properties dialog box

Monitoring IPsec Activity

To monitor the activities of the Internet Protocol security (IPsec) extensions on a Windows 2000 computer, you can check the system log in Event Viewer for IPsec-related events, but there is also an IP Security Monitor tool included with Windows 2000 that displays more detailed information, as shown in Figure 14.25. The program is called Ipsecmon.exe and is located in the *%systemroot%*\System32 folder. Ipsecmon.exe enables you to view information about the IPsec connections currently active on the computer, plus statistics specifying the number of bytes and packets of various types transmitted and received.

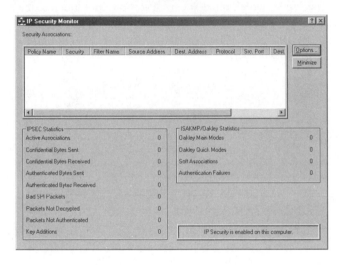

Figure 14.25   The Ipsecmon.exe utility

Ipsecmon.exe has only a single control setting. You can click Options to specify a refresh interval for the display.

Lesson Review

1. Which of the following services has its own log in the Event Viewer console?

   a. WINS

   b. DNS

   c. RRAS

   d. DHCP

2. Which tool do you use to monitor IPsec activity in real time?

   a. IP Security Monitor

   b. System Monitor

   c. Event Viewer

   d. Network Monitor

3. In which of the following logs can you specify which activities are to be monitored?

   a. DHCP

   b. DNS

   c. WINS

   d. DNS debug

Lesson Summary

- You can monitor DHCP activity from the DHCP console by examining the DHCP log files or by using the DHCP counters provided with the Performance console.

- You can monitor WINS activity from the WINS console or by examining the logs maintained by the service.

- Microsoft DNS Server has its own log in the Event Viewer console, and it can also maintain a debugging log containing only information about the activities you specify.

- The Routing and Remote Access console includes a variety of statistics display functions that enable you to monitor the many activities performed by the service.

- Windows 2000 includes a separate program called Ipsecmon.exe that displays information about ongoing IPsec activities.

Lesson 3: Using Network Monitor

Unlike System Monitor, which is used to monitor anything from hardware to software, Network Monitor focuses exclusively on network activity. Network Monitor enables you to view network activity by capturing actual packets and, through analysis of the packets, detect problems on a network. For example, when two or more computers cannot communicate, you can use Network Monitor to diagnose hardware and software problems. You can also copy a log of network activity into a file and send the file to a professional network analyst or technical support organization. Network application developers can use Network Monitor to monitor and debug network applications as they develop them.

After this lesson, you will be able to

- Understand the workings of Network Monitor
- Capture packets with Network Monitor
- Enable capture and display filters

Estimated lesson time: 20 minutes

Overview of Network Monitor

Network Monitor tracks network activity by capturing network traffic. The version of Network Monitor included with Windows 2000 Server can monitor traffic transmitted only to or from the computer on which it is running. To monitor traffic passing between other computers on the network or on remote networks, you must use the version of Network Monitor that ships with Microsoft Systems Management Server (SMS) version 1.2 or 2.0. Network Monitor monitors the network data stream, which consists of all information transferred over a network at any given time. Prior to transmission, this information is divided by the network software into smaller pieces, called frames or packets. Each frame contains the following information:

- The source address of the computer that sent the message
- The destination address of the computer that received the frame
- Headers from each protocol used in the construction of the frame
- The application data or a portion of the information being carried inside the frame
- A footer that usually contains a cyclical redundancy check (CRC) value to verify the integrity of the frame after transmission

The process by which Network Monitor copies frames is called *capturing*. You can use Network Monitor to capture all local network traffic or you can single out a subset of frames to be captured. You can also make a capture respond to events on your network. For example, you can make the network start an executable file when Network Monitor detects a particular set of conditions on the network. This capability is similar to the system alerts feature of the Performance Logs and Alerts snap-in.

After you have captured data, you can view it in the Network Monitor user interface. Network Monitor does much of the data analysis for you by translating the raw captured data into its logical frame structure. Network Monitor also displays overall network segment statistics for broadcast frames, multicast frames, network use, total bytes received per second, and total frames received per second.

Network Monitor Security

One of the reasons Windows 2000 Network Monitor captures only those frames—including broadcast and multicast frames—sent to or from the local computer, is security. The ability to capture and analyze the packets on the network means that the program can read the data carried within the packets, which contains passwords and other sensitive information. To help protect your network from unauthorized use of Network Monitor installations, Network Monitor can detect other installations of Network Monitor that are running on the local segment of your network. Network Monitor can also detect all instances of the Network Monitor driver being used remotely (by either the SMS Network Monitor version or the network segment object in System Monitor) to capture data on your network.

When Network Monitor detects other Network Monitor installations running on the network, it displays the following information:

- The name of the computer
- The name of the user logged on the computer
- The state of Network Monitor on the remote computer (running, capturing, or transmitting)
- The hardware address of the network interface adapter on the remote computer
- The version number of Network Monitor on the remote computer

In some instances, your network architecture might prevent one installation of Network Monitor from detecting another. For example, if an installation is separated from yours by a router that does not forward multicasts, your copy of Network Monitor cannot detect that installation.

Network Monitor uses a Network Device Interface Specification (NDIS) feature to copy all the frames leaving and arriving at the network interface adapter to its *capture buffer,* a resizable storage area in memory. The default size of the capture buffer is 1 megabyte (MB); however, you can adjust the size manually as needed. The buffer is a memory-mapped file and occupies disk space.

Note Because Network Monitor uses the Local-Only mode of NDIS instead of Promiscuous mode (in which the network adapter processes all frames sent on the network by any node), you can use Network Monitor even if your network adapter does not support Promiscuous mode. Networking performance is not affected when you use an NDIS driver to capture frames. (Putting the network adapter in Promiscuous mode can add 30 percent or more to the load on the CPU.)

Installing Network Monitor Tools

The Windows 2000 Network Monitor tools include both the Network Monitor console and the Network Monitor driver. These tools are not installed by default on Windows 2000 Server. You can install them from Control Panel using the following procedure:

1. Click Start, point to Settings, and select Control Panel.

2. Double-click the Add/Remove Programs icon.

3. Click Add/Remove Windows Components to launch the Windows Components Wizard.

4. In the Components list, select Management And Monitoring Tools, and then click Details.

5. Select Network Monitor Tools and click OK.

6. Click Next to perform the installation. You might be prompted to insert your Windows 2000 distribution CD into the CD-ROM drive.

7. Click Finish to close the wizard and complete the installation.

After it is installed, the Network Monitor console appears in the Administrative Tools program group and Network Monitor Driver is listed in the Local Area Connection Properties dialog box.

Capturing Frame Data

To capture frame data, Network Monitor and the Network Monitor driver must be installed on the computer running Windows 2000. The Network Monitor driver (also called the Network Monitor agent) enables Network Monitor to receive frames from a network interface adapter. When using the SMS version of Network Monitor, the agent enables the application to capture packets from a remote computer, including those accessed with a dial-up network connection. When the user of a computer running SMS Network Monitor connects remotely to a computer on which the Network Monitor agent has been installed and that user initiates a capture, the computer running the agent captures the network packets and transmits them to the computer running Network Monitor, which stores and displays them.

Note Network Monitor drivers for Windows operating systems other than Windows 2000 are provided with SMS. When you install Network Monitor on a computer running Windows 2000, the Network Monitor driver is automatically installed as well.

To capture data, open Network Monitor and, from the Capture menu, select Start. As frames are captured from the network, statistics about the frames are displayed in the Network Monitor Capture window, as shown in Figure 14.26.

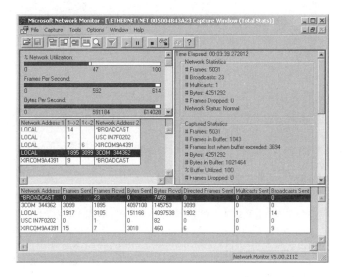

Figure 14.26 The Network Monitor Capture window

Network Monitor displays session statistics from the first 100 unique network sessions it detects. To reset statistics and see information about the next 100 network sessions, select Clear Statistics from the Capture menu.

Using Capture Filters

Network Monitor can often provide an embarrassment of riches. A capture of only a few minutes can consist of thousands of packets, and sometimes the most difficult part of analyzing network traffic is locating the packets that are significant to your task. For this reason, Network Monitor includes an extensive system of capture filters that enable you to specify the types of network information you want to monitor. For example, to see only a specific subset of computers or protocols, you can create an address database, use the database to add addresses to your filter, and then save the filter to a file. By filtering frames, you save both buffer resources and time. Later, if necessary, you can load the capture filter file and use the filter again.

To design a capture filter, you specify decision statements in the Capture Filter dialog box, as shown in Figure 14.27.

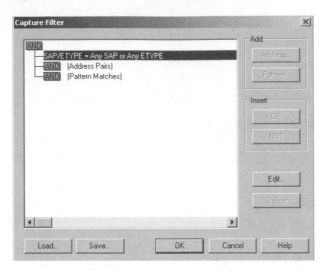

Figure 14.27   The Capture Filter dialog box

To open the Capture Filter dialog box, from the Capture menu, choose Filter, click the funnel toolbar icon, or press F8. The dialog box displays the decision tree of a filter, which is a graphical representation of the filter's logic. When you include or exclude information from your capture specifications, the decision tree reflects these specifications.

Filtering by Protocol

To capture frames that use a specific protocol, specify the protocol on the SAP/ETYPE = line of the capture filter. By default, all the protocols that Network Monitor supports are enabled. For example, to capture only IP frames, disable all protocols and then enable IP ETYPE 0×800 and IP SAP 0×6.

Filtering by Address

To capture frames from specific computers on your network, specify one or more address pairs in a capture filter. You can monitor up to four specific address pairs simultaneously. An address pair consists of the following:

- The addresses of the two computers between which you want to monitor traffic
- Arrows that specify the traffic direction you want to monitor
- The *Include* or *Exclude* statement, indicating how Network Monitor should respond to a frame that meets the specifications of a filter.

Regardless of the sequence in which statements appear in the Capture Filter dialog box, *Exclude* statements are evaluated first. Therefore, if a frame meets the criteria specified in an *Exclude* statement in a filter containing both an *Exclude* and *Include* statement, that frame is discarded. Network Monitor does not test the excluded frame with *Include* statements to see whether it also meets those criteria.

Filtering by Data Pattern

By specifying a pattern match in a capture filter, you can do the following:

- Limit a capture to only those frames containing a specific pattern of ASCII or hexadecimal data

- Specify how many bytes (offsets) into the frame the pattern must occur

When you filter based on a pattern match at a specific point in the data, you must specify where the pattern occurs in the frame (how many bytes from the beginning or end). If your network medium uses variable-sized frames, specify a place to begin counting in for a pattern match from the end of the topology header.

Displaying Captured Data

To simplify the packet analysis process, Network Monitor interprets the raw data collected during the capture and displays it in the Capture Summary window. To display captured information in the Capture Summary window, while the capture is running, choose Stop And View from the Capture menu. You can also display the Capture Summary window by opening a captured data file with the .cap extension. If you have stopped a capture, you can view the data in the Capture Summary window by choosing Display Captured Data from the Capture menu, by clicking the glasses toolbar icon, or by pressing F12. Figure 14.28 shows the key elements in the Capture Summary window.

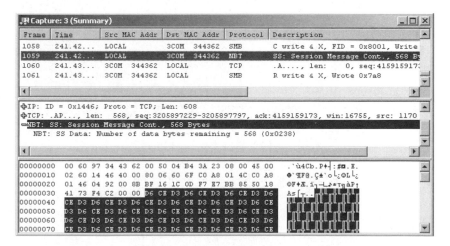

Figure 14.28   The Network Monitor Capture Summary window

Using Display Filters

You can use a display filter to specify which frames in a captured sample of network traffic you want to display. Like a capture filter, a display filter enables you to single out specific types of information. But because a display filter operates on data that has already been captured, it does not affect the contents of the Network Monitor capture buffer.

You can filter the display of captured data using the following criteria:

- The source or destination address of the frame
- The protocols used to construct the frame
- The contents of the protocol header and footer fields in the frame

The Capture Summary window must be active in Network Monitor for the Display Filter dialog box to appear. Figure 14.29 shows the Display Filter dialog box, which you access from the Display menu by pressing F8 or by clicking the funnel toolbar icon.

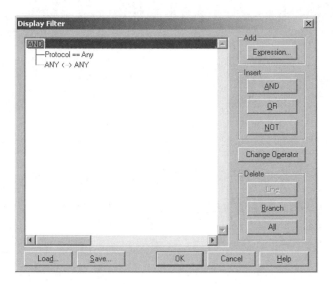

Figure 14.29   The Display Filter dialog box

To create a display filter, specify *Decision* statements in the Display Filter dialog box. Information in the Display Filter dialog box is in the form of a decision tree, which is a graphical representation of a filter's logic. When you modify display filter specifications, the decision tree reflects these modifications. You must click OK to save the specified *Decision* statement and add it to the decision tree before adding another *Decision* statement.

Although capture filters are limited to four address filter expressions, display filters are not. With display filters, you can also use AND, OR, and NOT logic. When you display captured data, all available information about the captured frames appears in the Frame Viewer window. To display only those frames generated by a specific protocol, edit the Protocol line in the Display Filter dialog box.

The values in protocol header and footer fields define the purpose of the protocol. Because the purpose of protocols varies, the fields and their functions differ from one protocol to another. Suppose, for example, that you have captured a large number of frames that use the Server Message Block (SMB) protocol but you want to examine only those frames in which the SMB protocol was used to create a directory on your computer. In this instance, you can single out frames in which the SMB command field contains the value that is equivalent to the Make Directory command.

When you display captured data, all addresses from which information was captured appear in the Frame Viewer window. To display only those frames originating from a specific computer, edit the ANY < – > ANY line in the Display Filter dialog box.

Network Monitor Performance Issues

Network Monitor creates a memory-mapped file for its capture buffer. For best results, make sure you create a capture buffer large enough to accommodate the traffic you need.

In addition, although you cannot adjust the frame size, you can configure Network Monitor to store only part of the frame, thereby reducing the amount of wasted capture buffer space. For example, if you are interested in the data only in the frame headers, you can set the frame size (in bytes) to the size of only the headers. Network Monitor then discards the frame data as it stores the frames in the capture buffer.

Running Network Monitor in the background is a way to reduce the amount of system resources necessary to operate the program. To run Network Monitor in the background, from the Capture menu, choose Dedicated Capture Mode. You can use this strategy to reduce resource use if network packets are being dropped rather than captured.

Exercise 1: Capturing Frames with Network Monitor

In this exercise you use Network Monitor to capture a series of frames generated by a file copy procedure and create a display filter to limit the display to the Transmission Control Protocol (TCP) protocol frames.

1. From the Administrative Tools program group on the Start menu, choose Network Monitor to launch Network Monitor.

2. From the Capture menu, choose Start to begin the process of capturing frames.

3. In Windows Explorer, copy a series of files from a drive on the computer running Network Monitor to a shared folder on another Windows computer on the network.

4. From the Capture menu, choose Stop And View to display the Capture Summary window. Notice that the window contains a list of frames using various protocols, including TCP and NetBEUI Frame (NBF).

5. From the Display menu, choose Options to open the Display Options dialog box.

6. Select Auto (Based On Protocols In Display Filter).

7. Click OK.

8. From the Display menu, choose Filter to open the Display Filter dialog box.

9. Double-click Protocol == Any to open the Expression window.

10. Click the Protocol tab and then click Disable All.

11. In the Disabled Protocols list box, select TCP and click Enable.

12. Click OK to close the Expression dialog box.

13. Click OK to close the Display Filter dialog box. What happens to the display in the Capture Summary window?

Lesson Review

1. What kind of data does a frame contain?

2. What is a capture filter, and what is it used for?

3. Which Network Monitor filter features should you specify to filter out all network traffic except for traffic between two computers and to locate specific data within the packets?

Lesson Summary

- The Network Monitor program included with Windows 2000 Server enables you to capture network traffic and display the contents of individual frames for analysis.

- The Windows 2000 Network Monitor application only captures packets sent to or transmitted by the computer on which it is running. The version of Network Monitor included with Microsoft SMS can capture all the traffic on a network.

- Capture filters enable you to specify the types of frames you want to capture, based on addresses, protocols, and other criteria.

- Display filters enable you to select packets in a captured sample for analysis, based on the same criteria as capture filters.

- Network Monitor decodes the frames it captures based on established protocol standards and displays the contents of the frames in an easily understandable format.

Questions and Answers

Chapter 1

Lesson 1: The OSI Reference Model

Page 16

Lesson Review

1. Which layer of the OSI reference model is responsible for controlling access to the network medium?

   The data-link layer

2. Which layer of the OSI model is responsible for translating different syntaxes?

   The presentation layer

3. Which layer of the OSI model identifies a packet's final destination?

   The network layer

4. UDP and IP are both what kind of protocols?

   a. Connection-oriented

   b. Transport layer

   c. Network layer

   d. Connectionless

   d

5. What is the name of the process by which a receiving system instructs a sending system to slow down its transmission rate?

   Flow control

Lesson 2: Installing and Binding Windows 2000 Network Components

Page 24

Exercise 1: Installing and Binding Protocols

▶ **Procedure 1: Installing the NetBEUI protocol**

2. Right-click the Local Area Connection icon and select Properties from the pop-up menu to display the Local Area Connection Properties dialog box. What networking components do you see listed in the dialog box?

In a default Windows 2000 installation, the components list should contain the Client for Microsoft Networks, Internet Protocol (TCP/IP), and File and Printer Sharing for Microsoft Networks modules.

7. Return to the Network And Dial-Up Connections window and open the Properties dialog box for the modem connection you created. What components do you see listed? Why do you see the components you do?

The components list in the Properties dialog box contains the three default components plus the NetBEUI Protocol module, just like the Local Area Connection Properties dialog box. This is because installing a component in one connection binds it automatically to all the connections.

▶ **Procedure 2: Unbinding protocols**

3. Clear the check box next to the Internet Protocol (TCP/IP) module and click Close. What does this do, and why would you want to do it?

Clearing the check box unbinds the TCP/IP protocol from the NIC installed in the computer. Because the LAN uses only NetBEUI, the connection has no need for the TCP/IP protocol module.

5. Clear the check box next to the NetBEUI Protocol module and click Close. Why would you want to do this?

The modem connection is used to connect to the Internet, which uses the TCP/IP protocols exclusively. Therefore, the connection has no need for the NetBEUI protocol.

Page 25

Lesson Review

1. What is the protocol traditionally associated with NetWare networking?

   a. NetBEUI

   b. IPX

   c. TCP/IP

   d. Ethernet

   b

2. What is the Windows component that enables an application to access a network resource in the same way as a local one?

   a. Redirector

   b. Protocol

   c. Client

   d. Service

   a

3. Which of the following Windows network components is not required for client functionality?

   a. Redirector

   b. Service

   c. Protocol

   d. Network interface adapter driver

   b

4. Which of the following Windows 2000 networking modules do you not install from the Network And Dial-Up Connections dialog box?

   a. Services

   b. Clients

   c. Protocols

   d. Network interface adapter drivers

   d

Chapter 2

Lesson 1: TCP/IP Overview

Page 42

Exercise 1: Examining ARP Traffic with Network Monitor

4. Type the name of another Windows computer on your network in the Open box using Universal Naming Convention (UNC) notation, such as \\server. Click OK. What happens? What is the purpose of this step?

   When you click OK, Windows opens an Explorer window containing the shares on the computer you specified. The purpose of this step is to force the computer to perform an ARP address resolution sequence so that Network Monitor can capture its messages.

10. Click OK to close the Expression dialog box and click OK again to close the Display Filter dialog box. What happens to the Capture window display (see Figure 2.6)?

    Applying the display filter causes the display to show only the ARP and RARP packets in the sample capture, as shown in the figure.

11. In the Capture window, locate a frame entry in which Local appears in the Src MAC Addr column and double-click it to display the contents of the frame, as shown in Figure 2.7.

    What type of ARP message is encapsulated in the frame?

    The frame contains an ARP Request message.

    What is the destination MAC address for the frame? Why is this?

    The destination is the broadcast address. All ARP Request messages are broadcasts because the object is to discover the MAC address of the target system needed to send unicasts.

    Notice that the frame contains four address fields, two for the sender's hardware (MAC) and protocol (IP) addresses and two for the target system's hardware and protocol addresses. Which of the four does not contain a value in this packet?

    The target's Hardware Address field does not contain a value because this address is yet to be discovered.

12. Locate a frame farther down in the Capture window with Local in the Dst MAC Addr column. The Src MAC Addr column should contain the name of the computer you typed earlier in the Run dialog box. Click the frame to display its contents, as shown in Figure 2.8.

    What type of ARP message is encapsulated in the frame?

    The frame contains an ARP Reply message.

    Which of the four address fields in the frame contains the hardware address for the computer whose name you typed earlier in the Run dialog box? Why is this so?

    The sender's Hardware Address field contains the newly discovered hardware address. This is because the computer that was the target of the ARP Request message is now the sender of the ARP Reply message, so the computer reverses the sender and target value fields when formulating the reply. You can tell this by examining the IP addresses in the fields.

Page 45

Exercise 2: TCP/IP Protocols

Match the protocols in the left column with the appropriate descriptions in the right column.

1. DHCP		a.	Transmits e-mail messages between servers
2. ARP		b.	Routes datagrams to their final destination
3. IP		c.	Provides transport layer services
4. POP3		d.	Resolves host names into IP addresses
5. SNMP		e.	Connects two systems at the link layer
6. ICMP		f.	Converts IP addresses into hardware addresses
7. TCP		g.	Automatically configures TCP/IP clients
8. DNS		h.	Enables e-mail clients to retrieve messages from servers
9. PPP		i.	Carries network management data to a central console
10. SMTP		j.	Carries error messages from routers to end systems

1. **g**
2. **f**
3. **b**
4. **h**
5. **i**
6. **j**
7. **c**
8. **d**
9. **e**
10. **a**

Page 45

Lesson Review

1. How does ARP minimize the number of broadcasts it generates?

   It does so by caching resolved hardware addresses.

2. Which of the following fields is blank in an ARP Request message?

   a. Sender Hardware Address

   b. Sender Protocol Address

   c. Target Hardware Address

   d. Target Protocol Address

   c

3. Why are ARP Request messages transmitted as broadcasts?

   They are transmitted as broadcasts because the system doesn't have the destination hardware address needed to send it as a unicast.

4. Which of the following fields in an ARP Reply message contains a value supplied by the system transmitting the message?

   a. Sender Hardware Address

   b. Sender Protocol Address

   c. Target Hardware Address

   d. Target Protocol Address

   a

5. Which application layer protocol uses two port numbers at the server?

   a. SMTP

   b. HTTP

   c. DHCP

   d. FTP

   d

Lesson 2: IP Addressing and Subnetting

Page 60

Exercise 1: Subnetting a Class B Address

1. How many bits do you need for the subnet identifier?

   6

2. What subnet mask will you use for the computers?

   255.255.252.0

3. How many hosts will each of your subnets support?

   1022

4. Specify the range of IP addresses you can use for your first subnet.

   172.28.4.1 through 172.28.7.254

5. Specify the range of IP addresses you can use for your fiftieth subnet.

   172.28.200.1 through 172.28.203.254

Lesson Review

1. Which of the following is the proper notation for an unregistered Class C network address?

   a. 192.168.72.0/24

   b. 192.168.0.0/24

   c. 192.24.0.0/16

   d. 192.16.223.0/8.223.0/8

   a

2. You are constructing a new 100-node TCP/IP network that you plan to connect to the Internet. Your ISP has assigned you the network address 192.168.224.0/24. What subnet mask would you use to create four subnets of 25 hosts each?

   a. 255.255.255.0

   b. 255.255.224.0

   c. 255.255.255.224

   d. 255.255.224.255

   c

3. You are the new administrator of a 2000 node network. There is only one router on the entire network, which provides all the computers with Internet access. The company's ISP has assigned the following eight network addresses to them:

   10.24.32.0/24

   10.24.33.0/24

   10.24.34.0/24

   10.30.35.0/24

   10.30.36.0/24

   10.30.37.0/24

   10.30.38.0/24

   10.30.39.0/24

What subnet mask could you use to minimize the complexity of the routing tables while maintaining the existing Internet connectivity?

a. 255.255.252.0

b. 255.255.255.252

c. 255.255.255.248

d. 255.255.248.0

d

4. How many host identifier bits do you have left after subnetting a Class A network address using the subnet mask 255.252.0.0?

a. 2

b. 10

c. 18

d. 22

c

5. Which of the following formulas do you use to determine how many subnets you can create with a given number of bits?

a. $256 - 2^x$

b. $2^x - 256$

c. $2^x - 2$

d. $x^2 - 2$

c

Lesson 3: Understanding TCP and UDP

Page 74

Exercise 1: TCP Header Fields

Match the TCP header field in the left column with the correct description in the right column.

1. Source Port   a. Specifies how many bytes the sender can transmit

2. Sequence Number   b. Specifies the number of bytes in the sequence that have been successfully transmitted

3. Checksum   c. Specifies the functions of messages used to initiate and terminate connections

4. Window   d. Contains information for the application layer

5. Urgent Pointer   e. Specifies which of the bytes in the message should receive special treatment from the receiving system

6. Data Offset   f. Identifies the application or protocol that generated the data carried in the TCP message

7. Destination Port   g. Used to reassemble segments that arrive at the destination out of order

8. Acknowledgment Number   h. Specifies the length of the TCP header

9. Control Bits   i. Contains error detection information

10. Data   j. Specifies the application that will make use of the data in the message

1. f

2. g

3. i

4. a

5. e

6. h

7. j

8. b

9. c

10. d

Page 75

Exercise 2: TCP and UDP Functions

Specify whether each of the following statements describes TCP, UDP, or both.

1. It provides flow control.

2. It is used for DNS communications.

3. It detects transmission errors.

4. It is used to carry DHCP messages.

5. It divides data to be transmitted into segments.

6. It acknowledges transmitted messages.

7. It is used for Web client/server communications.

8. It requires a connection establishment procedure.

9. It contains a Length field.

10. It uses a pseudo-header in its checksums.

1. TCP

2. Both

3. Both

4. Both

5. TCP

6. Both

7. TCP

8. TCP

9. UDP

10. Both

Page 75

Lesson Review

1. In TCP, what does "delayed acknowledgment" mean?

   a. A predetermined time interval must pass before the receiving system can acknowledge a data packet.

   b. Data segments are not acknowledged until the entire sequence has been transmitted.

   c. The receiving system doesn't have to generate a separate acknowledgment message for every segment.

   d. A data segment must be acknowledged before the next segment is transmitted.

   c

2. What does the Data Offset field in the TCP header specify?

   a. The length of the TCP header

   b. The location of the current segment in the sequence

   c. The length of the Data field

   d. The checksum value used for error detection

   a

3. What is the combination of an IP address and a port number called?

   a. A sequence number

   b. A checksum

   c. A data offset

   d. A socket

   d

4. Which of the following TCP/IP systems uses an ephemeral port number?

    a. The client

    b. The server

    c. The system initiating the TCP connection

    d. The system terminating the TCP connection

    a

5. What flag does the first message transmitted in any TCP connection contain?

    a. ACK

    b. SYN

    c. FIN

    d. PSH

    b

6. What TCP header field provides flow control?

    a. Window

    b. Data Offset

    c. Acknowledgment

    d. Sequence Number

    a

7. Which of the following services does the UDP protocol provide?

    a. Flow control

    b. Guaranteed delivery

    c. Error detection

    d. None of the above

    c

Chapter 3

Lesson 1: Installing and Configuring TCP/IP

Page 90

Exercise 1: TCP/IP Configuration Requirements

For each of the network scenarios listed, specify which of the following TCP/IP parameters (a, b, c, d, e, or a combination of these) you must configure to provide a computer running Windows 2000 with full communications capabilities.

1. A private internetwork using Windows NT domains
2. A single peer-to-peer LAN
3. A corporate internetwork using Active Directory
4. A peer-to-peer LAN using a shared Internet connection
5. A Windows NT internetwork with a router connected to the Internet

a. IP address
b. Subnet mask
c. Default gateway
d. DNS server address
e. WINS server address

1. A private internetwork using Windows NT domains

   a, b, c, e

2. A single peer-to-peer LAN

   a, b

3. A corporate internetwork using Active Directory

   a, b, c, d

4. A peer-to-peer LAN using a shared Internet connection

   a, b, d

5. A Windows NT internetwork with a router connected to the Internet

   a, b, c, d, e

Page 91

Lesson Review

1. Which of the Windows 2000 Control Panel tools do you use to install the Microsoft TCP/IP client?

   Network And Dial-Up Connections

2. When performing the TCP/IP installation procedure, what does the lack of a Local Area Connection icon indicate? (Choose all that apply.)

   a. No network interface adapter is installed in the computer.

   b. No network interface adapter driver is installed in the computer.

   c. The network to which the computer is connected does not support TCP/IP.

   d. No DHCP server is on the network.

   a, b

3. Which of the following components is not installed by default during the Windows 2000 setup process when a Plug and Play network interface adapter is present in the computer?

   a. The NetBIOS Extended User Interface (NetBEUI) Protocol

   b. The Internet Protocol (TCP/IP) module

   c. Client for Microsoft Networks

   d. File and Printer Sharing for Microsoft Networks

   a

4. Which of the following services is not used on a Windows 2000 Active Directory network?

   a. DHCP

   b. WINS

   c. DNS

   d. IPsec

   b

5. What is the function of a DNS suffix?

   The function of a DNS suffix is to complete unqualified DNS names so that a DNS server can resolve them.

6. Which of the following is a valid reason for assigning more than one IP address to a single network interface adapter?

   a. To balance the network traffic load between the addresses

   b. To support multiple subnets on one network

   c. To provide fault tolerance

   d. To support both TCP and UDP traffic

   b

7. How many default gateway addresses does a computer need to function on a LAN?

    a. 0

    b. 1

    c. 2

    d. 3

    a

8. How does Windows 2000 supply a subnet mask for the IP address you specify?

    a. By performing a reverse DNS name resolution on the address

    b. By checking the values of the first three address bits

    c. By checking the Hosts file

    d. By querying the directory service

    b

9. What is the function of an Lmhosts file?

    The function of an Lmhosts file is to resolve NetBIOS names into IP addresses.

Lesson 2: Using the Windows 2000 TCP/IP Tools

Page 106

Exercise 1: TCP/IP Utilities

Match the utilities in the left column with their functions in the right column.

1. FTP	a. Provides remote control access to server
2. Ipconfig.exe	b. Displays TCP/IP configuration on a Windows 98 system
3. Tracert.exe	c. Creates cache entries containing IP and hardware addresses
4. Ping.exe	d. Displays NetBIOS connection information
5. Telnet	e. Tests communications between two computers
6. Netstat	f. Transfers files between two computers
7. Winipcfg.exe	g. Displays network traffic statistics
8. Nbtstat.exe	h. Lists the routers forwarding packets to a particular destination
9. Arp.exe	i. Releases and renews IP address assignments on Windows 2000

1. **f**

2. **i**

3. **h**

4. **e**

5. **a**

6. **g**

7. **b**

8. **d**

9. **c**

Page 107

Lesson Review

1. Which TCP/IP utility should you use to most easily identify which router on your internetwork is malfunctioning?

   a. Ipconfig.exe

   b. Ping

   c. Tracert.exe

   d. Netstat

   c

2. Which of the following protocols does the Ping.exe program never use to carry its messages?

   a. Ethernet

   b. ICMP

   c. IP

   d. UDP

   d

3. Which of the following commands displays the routing table on the local computer?

   a. Arp –r

   b. Netstat –r

   c. Nbtstat –r

   d. Telnet –r

   b

4. Which command would you use to purge the local computer's NetBIOS name cache?

   a. Nbtstat –p

   b. Nbtstat –P

   c. Nbtstat –r

   d. Nbtstat –R

   d

Chapter 4

Lesson 1: Introducing IPX and NWLink

Page 119

Exercise 1: IPX Properties

1. Transport Control	a. Contains a value assigned by the network administrator or the NetWare installation program
2. Source Socket	b. Is not used in the current IPX protocol implementation
3. Destination Network Address	c. Has a maximum value of 16.
4. Checksum	d. Contains a 6-byte value.
5. Source Hardware Address	e. Identifies the application that generated the packet.

1. c

2. e

3. a

4. b

5. d

Page 120

Lesson Review

1. What is the IPX header's equivalent to the TTL field in the IP header?

   a. Packet Type

   b. Transport Control

   c. Checksum

   d. Source Socket

   b

2. Which of the following statements about IPX is untrue?

   a. IPX routes datagrams between different types of networks.

   b. IPX has its own network addressing system.

   c. IPX uses a checksum to verify the proper transmission of data.

   d. The IPX header is larger than the IP header.

   c

3. How many bytes long is the information that IPX uses to identify the datagram's destination computer on a particular network?

   a. 2

   b. 4

   c. 6

   d. 10

   d

4. What is the maximum number of routers that an IPX datagram can pass through on the way to its destination?

   a. 0

   b. 16

   c. 128

   d. 256

   b

Lesson 2: Using the Windows 2000 NetWare Clients

Page 132

Exercise 1: Installing and Configuring NWLink

2. Right-click the Local Area Connection icon and select Properties from the shortcut menu to open the Local Area Connection Properties dialog box. What networking components are currently installed on the computer?

   The default networking configuration for a computer with a network interface adapter present when Windows 2000 is installed consists of the Client for Microsoft Networking, Internet Protocol (TCP/IP), and File and Printer Sharing for Microsoft Networks modules.

5. Select NWLink IPX/SPX/NetBIOS Compatible Transport Protocol, and then click OK to return to the Local Area Connection Properties dialog box. What networking components have been added to the components list?

   The NWLink NetBIOS and NWLink IPX/SPX/NetBIOS Compatible Transport Protocol modules have been added to the components list.

8. Select Local Area Connection in the Connections list. What is the binding order for the File and Printer Sharing for Microsoft Networks module?

   When you install the NWLink protocol, Windows 2000 automatically places it at the top of the binding order. This means that when the computer connects to another Windows system with both NWLink and TCP/IP installed, it will use NWLink. TCP/IP connections are used only when NWLink is not supported by both computers.

9. In the bindings for Local Area Connection list, select NWLink IPX/SPX/ NetBIOS Compatible Transport Protocol and click the down arrow to move it below Internet Protocol (TCP/IP). How does this modify the networking behavior of the computer?

   By moving the Internet Protocol (TCP/IP) module above the NWLink IPX/SPX/NetBIOS Compatible Transport Protocol module, you cause the computer to use TCP/IP as its default networking protocol, using NWLink only when one of the two computers does not support TCP/IP.

Page 134

Lesson Review

1. What is NWLink and how does it relate to Windows 2000?

   NWLink is the Microsoft implementation of IPX/SPX. You must use this protocol if you want to use Gateway Service for NetWare or Client Service for NetWare to connect to NetWare servers.

2. What is SPX?

   SPX, or Sequenced Packet Exchange, is a transport protocol that offers connection-oriented services over IPX. SPX is used by applications that require a continuous connection, and it provides reliable delivery using sequencing and acknowledgments and verifies successful packet delivery to any network destination by requesting verification from the destination on receipt of the data. SPX also provides a packet burst mechanism that enables the transfer of multiple data packets without requiring that each packet be sequenced and acknowledged individually.

3. What is Gateway Service for NetWare?

   Gateway Service for NetWare enables you to create a gateway through which Microsoft client computers without Novell NetWare client software can access NetWare file and print resources.

4. When choosing between using Client Service for NetWare and Gateway Service for NetWare, what should you consider?

   If you intend to create or indefinitely maintain a heterogeneous environment composed of both servers running Windows 2000 and servers running NetWare, consider using Client Service for NetWare. If you intend to migrate gradually from NetWare to Windows 2000 or if you want to reduce administration, consider using Gateway Service for NetWare.

5. What is the NWLink autodetection mechanism?

The Windows 2000 NWLink autodetection mechanism detects the frame type and network number that are configured on NetWare servers on the same network. NWLink autodetection is the recommended option for configuring both the network number and the frame type. If the autodetection mechanism selects an inappropriate frame type and network number for a particular adapter, you can manually specify an NWLink frame type or network number for that given adapter.

6. Which of the following is not true of the SPX protocol?

   a. It is connection-oriented.

   b. It operates at the transport layer only.

   c. Clients use it to access server files.

   d. It provides flow control.

   c

7. At which layers of the OSI reference model does the NCP provide functions?

   The transport, session, presentation, and application layers

Chapter 5

Lesson 1: Introducing DHCP

Page 150

Exercise 1: DHCP Message Types

1. Place the following DHCP message types in the order in which a successful IP address assignment procedure uses them.

   a. DHCPACK

   b. DHCPOFFER

   c. DHCPREQUEST

   d. DHCPDISCOVER

   d, b, c, a

2. Place the following DHCP message types in the proper order for an unsuccessful attempt to renew an IP address lease.

   a. DHCPDISCOVER

   b. DHCPREQUEST (broadcast)

   c. DHCPREQUEST (unicast)

   d. DHCPNAK

   c, b, d, a

Page 150   **Lesson Review**

1. What happens to a DHCP client when its attempts to renew its IP address lease fail and the lease expires?

   TCP/IP communication stops and the computer begins the process of negotiating a new lease.

2. Which of the following message types is not used during the DHCP lease assignment process?

   a. DHCPDISCOVER

   b. DHCPRELEASE

   c. DHCPOFFER

   d. DHCPREQUEST

   b

3. What is the name of the time during the lease renewal process when a DHCP client begins broadcasting DHCPREQUEST messages?

   a. Lease identification cookie

   b. Rebinding time

   c. Renewal time

   d. Init value

   b

Lesson 2: Using the DHCP Server

Page 169   ## Exercise 1: Examining DHCP Traffic

11. Click OK to close the Expression dialog box and click OK again to close the Display Filter dialog box. What happens to the Capture window display (see Figure 5.27)?

    Applying the display filter causes the display to show only the DHCP packets in the sample capture.

12. Double-click the first packet you see with Release in the Description column. In the bottom pane of the Capture window, expand the DHCP portion of the packet to display the message fields, as shown in Figure 5.28.

    What caused the DHCPRELEASE message to be generated?

    The ipconfig /release command caused the DHCP client to generate a DHCPRELEASE message and transmit it to the server as a unicast.

14. Click the Discover message that follows the Release message and expand the DHCP message section (see Figure 5.30).

What initiated the creation of the DHCPDISCOVER message?

The message was generated when you executed the ipconfig /renew command on the client workstation.

Why do the four IP address fields (Ciaddr, Yiaddr, Siaddr, and Giaddr) all contain values of 0.0.0.0?

The IP address fields have no values because the client is not currently configured with an IP address.

16. Click the Offer message that follows the Discover message. Expand the message and its Option field (see Figure 5.31).

What IP address has the server offered the client?

You can tell from the Yiaddr field that the server has offered the client the same IP address that the client requested in the DHCPDISCOVER message, 192.168.2.70.

What are the functions of the options listed in the Option field?

The Option field contains the subnet mask to be used with the IP address, as well as lease definition options (Renewal Time Value, Rebinding Time Value, and IP Address Lease Time) and the DHCP options configured by the administrator (Router and Domain Name Server). The field also contains a Server Identifier option, which specifies the IP address of the DHCP server offering the lease.

17. Click the Request message that follows the Offer message. Expand the message and its Option field (see Figure 5.32).

What is the function of the Client-Identifier option in the Option field?

This option specified the media access control (MAC) address of the network interface adapter in the client computer. The DHCP server uses this value, plus the IP address it has leased to the client, to form the lease identification cookie, which it will use to uniquely identify this lease in its database.

Page 174

Exercise 2: Configuring Scopes

1. What value should you assign to the Router option for the scope?

    a. 192.168.6.32

    b. 192.168.7.32

    c. 192.168.6.33

    d. 192.168.6.34

    c

2. What IP addresses should you use when creating the reservations for the two Internet servers?

   a. 192.168.6.44 and 192.168.6.45

   b. 192.168.6.45 and 192.168.6.46

   c. 192.168.6.46 and 192.168.6.47

   d. 192.168.6.47 and 192.168.6.48

   b

3. What IP address range should you use when creating the scope for the subnet?

   a. 192.168.6.33–192.168.6.46

   b. 192.168.6.33–192.168.6.44

   c. 192.168.6.34–192.168.6.44

   d. 192.168.6.34–192.168.6.46

   d

Page 174

Lesson Review

1. What is the function of a user class ID?

   A user class ID enables you to identify specific DHCP clients on a subnet to assign them options that are different from those assigned to the other clients.

2. What type of DHCP messages do servers use to compile a list of the other DHCP servers on the network?

   DHCPINFORM

3. For a network with 9000 client workstations on 10 subnets at 6 locations, what is the minimum number of DHCP servers needed to service the entire network?

   a. 1

   b. 6

   c. 9

   d. 10

   a

4. When you create a reservation, how does the DHCP server know which computer should be assigned the IP address you specify?

   The server assigns the address based on the MAC address of the network interface adapter in the client computer. You specify this address when creating the reservation.

5. What program do you use to assign a user class to a specific DHCP client interface?

   Ipconfig.exe

Lesson 3: Administering DHCP

Page 185   **Lesson Review**

1. You are the administrator of a network that has a Windows 2000 Server computer with RRAS configured to function as the router between Network A and Network B. There is another Windows 2000 server on Network A that is running the Windows 2000 DHCP Server service. As the network is currently configured, the workstations on Network A—all of which are DHCP clients—can access the network. The DHCP clients on Network B cannot. How should you modify the configuration of the router computer to enable the computers on Network B to access the network? (Choose all that apply.)

   a. Configure a DHCP relay agent to run on the interface to Network A.

   b. Configure a DHCP relay agent to run on the interface to Network B.

   c. Create a static route to the IP address of the interface to Network A.

   d. Create a static route to the IP address of the interface to Network B.

   e. Configure the DHCP relay agent in the router with the IP address of the interface to Network B.

   f. Configure the DHCP relay agent in the router with the IP address of the DHCP server on Network A.

   b, f

2. Describe the integration of DHCP with DNS.

   A DHCP server can enable dynamic updates in the DNS name space for any DHCP clients that support these updates. Scope clients can then use DNS with dynamic updates to update their computer name–to–IP-address mapping information whenever changes occur to their DHCP-assigned address.

3. What program do you use to compact the DHCP database?

   You use the Jetpack.exe program.

Lesson 4: Troubleshooting DHCP

Page 192   **Lesson Review**

1. How can you force a DHCP server to assign new IP addresses with a different network identifier to all the clients on the network?

   You do this by creating a new scope with a range of new addresses and then modifying the IP address of the server itself to one that uses the same network identifier as the new scope.

2. What type of messages, broadcast or unicast, do Windows 2000 DHCP servers use to send DHCPOFFER messages in response to DHCPDISCOVER messages, by default?

   Windows 2000 DHCP servers use broadcast messages, unless you modify the default behavior.

3. What is the most common symptom of DHCP-related problems?

   The most common symptom is the failure of clients to obtain IP addresses and other TCP/IP configuration parameters from DHCP servers.

Chapter 6

Lesson 1: Understanding IP Routing

Page 205   **Exercise 1: Routing Tables**

Place the following steps of the routing table search process in the proper order.

1. Default gateway search
2. Host address search
3. Network address search

   2, 3, 1

Page 205   **Lesson Review**

1. What type of route does a packet use if its Destination IP Address and data-link layer Destination Address values refer to different computers?

   a. The default gateway

   b. A direct route

   c. The default route

   d. An indirect route

   d

2. What is a TCP/IP system with interfaces to two different networks called?

   a. A bridge

   b. Multihomed

   c. A switch

   d. All of the above

   b

3. In a Windows routing table, what column contains the address of the router that should be used to reach a particular network or host?

   a. Network Address

   b. Netmask

   c. Gateway Address

   d. Interface

   c

4. What does a router do when it fails to find a routing table entry for a particular network or host?

   The router uses the default gateway entry.

5. In a Windows routing table, what is the Network Destination value for the default gateway entry?

   a. 0.0.0.0

   b. The address of the network to which the router is connected

   c. 255.255.255.255

   d. The address of the router's network interface

   a

Lesson 2: Routing with RRAS

Page 221

Exercise 1: Configuring RRAS

1. You are the network administrator of a corporate network that consists of three subnets connected by a single router. The router has three network interface adapters installed, which are configured as follows:

   ▪ Subnet A: IP address 10.60.4.1, subnet mask 255.255.255.0

   ▪ Subnet B: IP address 10.60.5.1, subnet mask 255.255.255.0

   ▪ Subnet C: IP address 10.60.6.2, subnet mask 255.255.255.0

   Subnet B and Subnet C both contain client computers. Subnet A does not. Subnet B and Subnet C each contain a Windows 2000 DHCP server that is responsible for assigning IP addresses to client computers on the local subnet only. The scope properties on the two DHCP servers are as follows:

- Subnet B scope: Start IP Address 10.60.5.100, End IP Address 10.60.5.254, Subnet Mask 255.255.255.0
- Subnet C scope, Start IP Address 10.60.6.100, End IP Address 10.60.6.254, Subnet Mask 255.255.0.0

Subnet A contains a Web server and provides the entire internetwork with Internet connectivity. However, the network is experiencing connectivity problems. Clients on Subnet B can communicate with any host on their own subnet, but they cannot communicate with hosts on Subnet C. Clients on Subnet C cannot communicate with hosts on Subnet B, but they can successfully connect to Subnet A. What should you do to correct this problem?

a. Delete and re-create the scope on the Subnet B DHCP server to reflect the correct subnet mask

b. Modify the routing table on the router to enable routing from Subnet B to Subnet A and Subnet C

c. Delete and re-create the scope on the Subnet C DHCP server to reflect the correct subnet mask

d. Modify the routing table on each Subnet B host computer to enable direct connectivity to hosts on Subnet A and Subnet C

e. Delete and re-create the scopes on both the Subnet B and Subnet C DHCP servers to reflect the same configuration information for both subnets

c

2. Your Windows 2000 network has three subnets, A, B, and C. Subnet A is located at the corporate headquarters, and Subnet C is located at a remote office. Subnet B is a WAN link that connects a router on Subnet A to a router at Subnet C. Both routers are Windows 2000 Servers using demand-dial connections for the WAN link. Router AB connects Subnet A to Subnet B, and Router BC connects Subnet B to Subnet C. What two steps must you take to allow a client on Subnet C to access a share on Subnet A? (Choose two.)

a. Configure a static route for Subnet A on the demand-dial interface of Router AB

b. Configure a static route for Subnet B on the demand-dial interface of Router BC

c. Configure a static route for Subnet C on the demand-dial interface of Router BC

  d. Configure a static route for Subnet A on the demand-dial interface of Router BC

  e. Configure a static route for Subnet B on the demand-dial interface of Router AB

  f. Configure a static route for Subnet C on the demand-dial interface of Router AB

  d, f

Page 222

Lesson Review

1. Which of the configuration tasks must you perform after creating a demand-dial interface in RRAS?

  a. Specify an IP address for the interface

  b. Create a static routing table entry for the interface

  c. Select an authentication protocol for the interface connection

  d. Specify the number of redial attempts the interface should perform

  b

2. A demand-dial interface enables RRAS to route traffic between which types of network interfaces? (Choose all that apply.)

  a. Two LANs

  b. A LAN and a modem connection

  c. Two modem connections

  d. A LAN and a VPN

  b, c, d

3. Which of the following statements regarding this Route.exe command is not true?

```
ROUTE ADD 171.29.0.0 MASK 255.255.0.0 171.29.32.19 IF
171.29.32.19 METRIC 1
```

  a. The destination is a network to which the computer is directly connected.

  b. The command is using an incorrect subnet mask.

  c. The gateway used by the route is on the same network as the computer whose routing table this is.

  d. It should not be necessary to run this command on the computer.

  b

Lesson 3: Using Dynamic Routing Protocols

Page 233

Exercise 1: Configuring RRAS

You are the network administrator of a branch office for a large corporation. Your network is connected to the corporate headquarters using a Windows 2000 RRAS server at each site configured with a demand-dial interface using ISDN. Your network regularly exchanges sensitive company data, e-mail, and application traffic with computers at the corporate headquarters. Your goals when configuring the RRAS server are as follows:

- All data transmitted over the ISDN link should be secure.
- Rogue routers should be prevented from exchanging router information with either router.
- Both routers should be able to validate each other.
- Both routers should automatically maintain up-to-date routing tables.
- Traffic over the ISDN link during peak business hours should be minimized.

In attempting to achieve these goals, you take the following actions:

- Enable MS-CHAP as the authentication protocol on both RRAS servers.
- Enable OSPF on the demand-dial interfaces.
- Set the Require Encryption option on both RRAS servers.

Which results do these actions produce? (Choose all that apply.)

a. All data transmitted over the connection is secure.

b. Prevent rogue routers from exchanging router information with either router.

c. Both routers will be able to validate each other.

d. Both routers maintain up-to-date routing tables.

e. Traffic over the link during peak business hours will be minimized.

a, d

Page 234

Exercise 2: Static and Dynamic Routing

Specify whether each of the following terms is associated with static routing, dynamic routing, both, or neither.

1. Routed

2. Default gateway

3. Convergence

4. Route.exe

5. Link-state routing

6. Routing and Remote Access

7. Distance vector routing

8. Route Add

9. Autonomous system

10. Metric

1. Dynamic

2. Both

3. Dynamic

4. Static

5. Dynamic

6. Both

7. Dynamic

8. Static

9. Dynamic

10. Dynamic

Page 234

Lesson Review

1. Which of the following is not a dynamic routing protocol?

   a. OSPF

   b. RIP

   c. ICMP

   d. EGP

   c

2. What is the name for the use of metrics based on the number of hops between a source and a destination?

   a. Distance vector routing

   b. Loose source routing

   c. Link-state routing

   d. OSPF routing

   a

3. What is the primary difference between OSPF and RIP?

   OSPF uses link-state routing, and RIP uses distance vector routing.

4. Which of the following fields is not included in a RIP version 1 route?

   a. Metric

   b. Subnet Mask

   c. IP Address

   d. Address Family Identifier

   b

5. What is the primary criticism leveled at RIP?

   RIP generates an excessive amount of broadcast traffic that consumes network bandwidth.

6. What is the name of the process of updating routing tables to reflect changes in the network?

   a. Divergence

   b. Link-state routing

   c. Minimal routing

   d. Convergence

   d

7. On a Windows 2000 Professional computer, what command do you use to display the contents of the routing table?

   Route Print

8. The Next Hop IP Address in a RIP version 2 route ends up in which column of a Windows routing table?

   a. Network Destination

   b. Netmask

   c. Gateway

   d. Interface

   c

Chapter 7

Lesson 1: IP Host Naming and DNS

Page 249

Exercise 1: Understanding DNS Terminology

Match the terms in the left column with the definitions in the right column.

1. Zone transfer	a. Is not the authority for a zone
2. Caching-only server	b. Contains both subdomains and hosts
3. Primary zone database file	c. Provides redundancy
4. Second-level domain	d. Is used for reverse name resolution
5. in-addr.arpa	e. Contains changes made to the zone database

1. c

2. a

3. e

4. b

5. d

Page 250

Lesson Review

1. Name the three components of the DNS.

   Resolver, name servers, and domain name space

2. List three reasons to have a secondary name server.

   It operates as a redundant name server (you should have at least one redundant name server for each zone).

   If you have clients in remote locations, you should have a secondary name server to avoid communicating across slow links.

   A secondary name server reduces the load on the primary name server.

3. What does the first word in a full DNS name identify?

   a. The top-level domain

   b. The second-level domain

   c. The DNS server

   d. The host

   d

4. Describe the difference between a domain and a zone.

   A domain is a branch of the DNS name space. A zone is a portion of a domain that exists as a separate file on the disk storing resource records.

5. What is the portion of the DNS name space that is stored in a DNS name server?

   a. A host

   b. A domain

   c. A zone

   d. A root name

   c

Lesson 2: Resolving Host Names with DNS

Page 260

Exercise 1: Understanding DNS Communications

1. Which of the following sequences of DNS name servers are involved when a user in the New York office attempts to connect to the New York Web server?

   a. ns3

   b. ns3, root name server, ns1, ns3

   c. ns3, root name server, ns1

   d. ns3, ns1, ns3

   a

2. Which of the following sequences of DNS name servers are involved when a user in the New York office attempts to connect to the Los Angeles Web server?

   a. ns3, ns2

   b. ns3, root name server, ns1, ns2

   c. ns3, root name server, ns1

   d. ns3, root name server, ns2

   c

3. Which of the following sequences of DNS name servers are involved when a user in the Los Angeles office attempts to connect to the New York Web server?

   a. ns2, root name server, ns3

   b. ns2, ns3

   c. ns2, root name server, ns1, ns3

   d. ns2, ns1, ns3

   b

Page 261

Lesson Review

1. What is the name of the DNS domain that contains address-to-name mappings?

   in-addr.arpa

2. Describe the difference between a primary master name server, a secondary master name server, and a master name server.

   A primary master name server has zone information in locally maintained zone files. A secondary master name server downloads zone information from another name server. A master name server is the source of the downloads for a secondary master name server (which could be a primary master or secondary master name server).

3. What is the host name of a DNS FQDN formed by the reverse name mapping of the IP address 10.56.128.65?

   a. 65

   b. in-addr

   c. 10

   d. arpa

   a

Lesson 3: Planning a DNS Implementation

Page 264

Exercise 1: Implementing DNS

Scenario 1: Designing DNS for a Small Network

1. How many DNS domains will you need to configure?

   One (or zero, if the company has an ISP to manage the name server)

2. How many subdomains will you need to configure?

   Zero

3. How many zones will you need to configure?

   One (or zero, if the company has an ISP to manage the name server)

4. How many primary name servers will you need to configure?

   One (or zero, if the company has an ISP to manage the name server)

5. How many secondary name servers will you need to configure?

   One (or zero, if the company has an ISP to manage the name server)

6. How many DNS cache-only servers will you need to configure?

   Zero

Scenario 2: Designing DNS for a Medium-Size Network

1. How many DNS domains must you create?

   You need at least one DNS domain in which you can create both hosts (computers or services) and subdomains.

2. How many subdomains do you need?

   Three. Your DNS domain includes multiple sites, so you should create three subdomains that reflect these groupings.

3. How many zones should you create?

   Four. You can distribute administrative tasks to different groups in the primary sites by configuring four zones. This also provides more efficient data distribution.

4. How many primary master name servers do you need?

   Four. The primary sites can maintain their own equipment and that of the branch offices connected to them. Therefore, you must configure four primary master name servers.

5. How many secondary master name servers do you need?

   The branch offices have between 25 and 250 users needing access to all four of the primary sites. When you create a secondary master server for a zone, clients can still resolve names for that zone even if the primary master server for the zone goes down; therefore, you should configure four secondary master name servers.

6. How many caching-only servers do you need?

   You should create 10 caching-only servers (1 per branch office). This will speed up the DNS name resolution process, reduce DNS-related query traffic, and improve reliability.

7. Use the following mileage chart to design a zone/branch office configuration based on the geographical proximity between each primary site and branch office. Branch offices should be in the same zone as the nearest primary site.

Mileage Chart	Atlanta	Boston	Chicago	Portland, OR
Dallas	807	1817	934	2110
Denver	1400	1987	1014	1300
Kansas City	809	1454	497	1800
Los Angeles	2195	3050	2093	1143
Miami	665	1540	1358	3300
Montreal	1232	322	846	2695

New Orleans	494	1534	927	2508
Salt Lake City	1902	2403	1429	800
San Francisco	2525	3162	2187	700
Washington, DC	632	435	685	2700

Answers: Zones for each branch office (based on geographical proximity):

Portland, OR	Boston	Chicago	Atlanta
Los Angeles	Montreal	Denver	Dallas
Salt Lake City	Washington, DC	Kansas City	Miami
San Francisco			New Orleans

Scenario 3: Designing DNS for a Large Network

1. How many new DNS domains do you need?

   Zero (the domain for this company is provided by the corporate headquarters in Geneva).

2. How many subdomains must you create?

   Eleven. Remember that you want to give control of the equipment to each subsidiary and to have a resource domain in each subsidiary.

3. How many zones must you create?

   Each of the regional headquarters' subsidiaries will maintain total control of users within their areas. Therefore, you should create 11 zones.

4. How many primary master name servers do you need?

   One of the requirements defined in this scenario is that the line-of-business applications running on the computers must be configured as servers within the domains. Therefore, you should create 11 primary master name servers.

5. How many secondary master name servers do you need?

   You can configure servers to host as many different primary or secondary zones as is practical. In this case, line-of-business applications must be available to all sites within their areas as well as to the other regional headquarters. Therefore, you should create 11 secondary master name servers for redundancy. When you create a secondary master name server for a zone, clients can still resolve names for that zone even if the primary server for the zone goes down.

6. How many DNS caching-only servers should you create?

   Three or more, at least one per regional headquarters.

Page 270

Lesson Review

1. What is the primary reason for creating a secondary master name server?

   A secondary master name server provides redundancy for the zone in case the primary master name server fails.

2. What are the primary reasons for creating caching-only DNS servers?

   Caching-only servers provide faster name resolution services for the clients on the local network and reduce the amount of internetwork DNS traffic.

3. What is the primary factor of an internetwork's design that makes the deployment of additional DNS name servers necessary?

   The division of the network among different sites connected by relatively slow WAN links.

Chapter 8

Page 279

Lesson 1: Installing and Configuring Windows 2000 DNS

Lesson Review

1. Which of the following active files is created by default during the installation of Windows 2000 DNS Server?

   a. BOOT

   b. Boot.dns

   c. CACHE

   d. Cache.dns

   d

2. Which of the following best describes the function of a caching-only server?

   a. A caching-only server is one that uses a Cache.dns file to configure itself.

   b. A caching-only server is the authority for only a single zone.

   c. A caching-only server is not the authority for any domain or zone.

   d. A caching-only server maintains a zone database but does not service client name resolution requests.

   c

3. What is BIND?

   BIND is the Berkeley Internet Name Domain, one of the earliest DNS server implementations currently in use.

Lesson 2: Working with Zones

Page 290

Exercise 1: Configuring Zones

► **Procedure 2: Creating a reverse lookup zone**

5. Ensure that Network ID is selected, and type the network identifier for your network's IP addresses in the Network ID text box. For example, if the IP address of your server is 192.168.18.43, with a subnet mask of 255.255.255.0, type **192.168.18** in the Network ID text box. What happens when you enter the network identifier?

   In the Reverse Lookup Zone Name box, the in-addr.arpa name is appended to the Network ID value, with the bytes reversed. For example, the network identifier 192.168.18 appears as 18.168.192.in-addr.arpa.

7. Ensure that Create A New File With This File Name is selected. What value appears in the box provided?

   The name that appears in the box by default is the Reverse Lookup Zone Name value from the previous page, with a .dns extension. In the previous example, the filename is 18.168.192.in-addr.arpa.dns.

Page 292

Lesson Review

1. What are the advantages of using the Active Directory–integrated zone type?

   - **Active Directory–integrated zones use multiple-master updates and have enhanced security based on the capabilities of Active Directory service.**

   - **Zones are replicated and synchronized to new domain controllers automatically whenever a new zone is added to an Active Directory domain.**

   - **By integrating storage of your DNS namespace in Active Directory service, you simplify the planning and administration for both DNS and Active Directory service.**

   - **Directory replication is faster and more efficient than standard DNS replication.**

2. What must be done when you delegate zones within a namespace?

   When you delegate zones within a namespace, you must also create NS resource records to point to the authoritative DNS server for the new zone. This is necessary both to transfer authority and to provide correct referral to other DNS servers and clients of the new servers being made authoritative for the new zone.

3. How do dynamic updates improve the efficiency of Windows 2000 DNS Server?

Dynamic updates enable computers to automatically update their resource records in the DNS database. Before dynamic updates, administrators had to make all DNS additions and modifications manually. Dynamic updates enable DNS Server to support computers with IP addresses that change because of DHCP address assignments.

Lesson 3: Working with Resource Records

Page 300

Exercise 1: Adding Resource Records

▶ **Procedure 1: Creating a host record**

4. Right-click the zone you created in Exercise 1, Procedure 1 of Lesson 2, and from the pop-up menu, choose New Host. What happens?

The New Host dialog box appears.

▶ **Procedure 2: Viewing resource records**

2. Click the icon for the forward lookup zone in which you created the Host (A) resource records. What do you see in the zone?

The zone contains the SOA and NS resource records that the server creates automatically, plus the server1 and server2 host records you created manually.

3. Click the icon for the reverse lookup zone corresponding to the forward lookup zone you created. What do you see and why?

The reverse lookup zone contains a PTR record named with the IP address of the server2 resource record. This record is the result of selecting the Create Associated Pointer (PTR) Record check box when you created the server2 record.

Page 302

Lesson Review

1. What type of resource record do you create to represent a domain controller on a Windows 2000 network?

A Service (SRV) record

2. Which two types of resource records can contain the same IP address and host name?

   a. SOA and A

   b. PTR and A

   c. A and CNAME

   d. PTR and CNAME

   b

3. Which resource records does the DNS console create automatically when you create a forward lookup zone?

An SOA record and an NS record

Lesson 4: Configuring Zone Transfers

Page 308

Lesson Review

1. What is the purpose of the SOA resource record?

The SOA resource record identifies which name server is the authoritative source of information for data within this domain. The first record in the zone database file must be the SOA record. The SOA resource record also stores properties such as version information and timings that affect zone renewal or expiration. These properties affect how often transfers of the zone are performed between servers authoritative for the zone.

2. Why is an IXFR query more efficient than an AFXR query?

An IFXR query enables the secondary server to pull only those zone changes it needs to synchronize its copy of the zone with its source, either a primary master or secondary master name server for the zone. An AXFR query provides a full transfer of the entire zone database.

3. What is the purpose of DNS notification?

DNS notification enables master DNS servers to notify secondary master name servers when changes to the zone database have occurred. This enables the secondary master server to issue a zone transfer request as soon as it is needed.

Lesson 5: Monitoring and Troubleshooting DNS

Page 316

Lesson Review

1. What is the difference between a simple query and a recursive query?

A simple query is one that can be satisfied by the server to which it is sent, whereas a recursive query requires the server to forward the request to other DNS servers.

2. Give three reasons why a zone transfer might fail to occur.

Network connectivity problems, one of the servers or zones is shut down or paused, the SOA serial numbers are the same on both DNS servers, the zone database contains nonstandard or unsupported data, or the servers are running incompatible DNS server implementations.

3. What is the first thing to check if dynamic updates fail to occur?

The first thing you should check is whether both of the DNS implementations involved support the dynamic update standard.

Chapter 9

Lesson 1: Introducing NetBIOS

Page 333

Exercise 1: NetBIOS Name Resolution Concepts

Match the terms in the left column with the appropriate descriptions in the right column.

1. M node

   a. Default name resolution mechanism for computers running the Windows operating system that are not configured to use WINS

2. NetBIOS name cache

   b. Uses broadcast name resolution, with WINS as a fallback

3. Broadcast name resolution

   c. Fallback name resolution mechanism for a modified b node computer

4. H node

   d. First non-DNS name resolution mechanism used by all computers running the Windows operating system

5. Lmhosts

   e. Uses WINS name resolution, with broadcasts as a fallback

1. b

2. d

3. a

4. e

5. c

Page 333

Lesson Review

1. What is the function of a WINS server?

   a. To convert IP addresses into hardware addresses

   b. To convert host names into IP addresses

   c. To convert IP addresses into host names

   d. To convert NetBIOS names into IP addresses

   d

2. You are the administrator of a Windows NT network that uses the broadcast method for NetBIOS name resolution, with a centrally located Lmhosts file as a fallback, for the resolution of server names on other networks. When the primary domain controller (Server1) for the Sales domain on your network malfunctions, you decide to promote one of your backup domain controllers (Server3) to primary domain controller (PDC) status. In addition to removing the entry for Server1 from the Lmhosts file, which of the following other entries should you add?

    a. 192.168.43.56 Server3 #DOM:Sales

    b. 192.168.43.56 Server3 #PRE #DOM:Sales

    c. 192.168.43.56 Server3 #DOMAIN:Sales

    d. 192.168.43.56 #PRE Server3 #DOM:Sales

    b

3. Which of the following name resolution mechanisms can resolve only the names of computers on the local network?

    a. NetBIOS name cache

    b. Lmhosts

    c. Broadcast name resolution

    d. WINS

    c

4. Which of the following is the fastest NetBIOS name resolution mechanism?

    a. NetBIOS name cache

    b. Lmhosts

    c. Broadcast name resolution

    d. WINS

    a

5. Which of the following node types can use an Lmhosts file for NetBIOS name resolution?

    a. B node

    b. Modified b node

    c. M node

    d. H node

    b

Lesson 2: WINS Name Registration and Resolution

Page 344

Lesson Review

1. List two reasons why WINS is an improvement over the broadcast name resolution method.

   WINS is an improvement because it uses unicasts instead of broadcasts and because it can service clients anywhere on an internetwork, not just on the local network.

2. What is the name of the property that determines when a WINS client should renew its name registration?

   The Time to Live (TTL) value

3. When does a WINS name release occur?

   When a WINS client shuts down

Lesson 3: Implementing WINS

Page 352

Exercise 1: Installing and Configuring WINS

▶ **Procedure 2: Configuring DHCP to support WINS**

4. In the Server Name text box, type the name of your WINS server, and then click Resolve. What happens?

   The IP address assigned to the WINS server appears in the IP Address text box.

7. In the Byte text box, type **8** so that the text box entry reads 0x8. The value 0x8 sets the node type to h node. What does this mean?

   The node type specifies what NetBIOS name resolution mechanisms the client computer should use. An h node Windows client uses WINS to resolve NetBIOS names by default and switches to broadcast name resolution if the WINS server fails or is unavailable.

8. Click OK. What happens?

   The two server options appear in the details pane.

▶ **Procedure 3: Testing WINS settings (optional)**

2. Type **ipconfig /release**, and then press ENTER. What happens?

   A message appears stating that the IP address has been successfully released for the adapter Local Area Connection.

3. Type **ipconfig /renew**, and then press ENTER. What happens?

The computer displays the IP configuration as it renews its lease with the DHCP server.

Page 354

Lesson Review

1. You are the administrator of a network that consists of computers running a variety of operating systems, including Windows 2000 Server, Windows 2000 Professional, Windows 95, Windows 98, and OS/2 with Microsoft LAN Manager version 2.2c, all on the same subnet with a single WINS server. The OS/2 computers are running a NetBIOS application, and you want them to be able to use NetBIOS names to access the computers running Windows operating systems on the network, but OS/2 does not include a WINS client. What should you do to enable the applications on the OS/2 computers to resolve NetBIOS names using the WINS database?

   a. Install a DHCP relay agent on the network.

   b. Configure one of the other computers running Windows on the network to function as a proxy agent.

   c. Configure the OS/2 computer to function as a WINS proxy agent.

   d. Add static mappings for the OS/2 computers to the WINS database.

   b

2. You are the administrator of a routed network with 6 Windows 2000 computers and 250 Window workstations on various subnets. After installing the WINS service on one of the Windows 2000 servers and configuring your DHCP server to supply the WINS server address to all your clients, you discover that the computers on the same subnet as the WINS server all function normally, but that the computers on the other subnets cannot access file and print services running on the computer running the WINS server. All other TCP/IP connectivity, such as Internet access, is not affected. What should you do?

   a. Install WINS proxy agents on the remote subnets.

   b. Configure the computers on the remote subnets to use DNS for name resolution instead of WINS.

   c. Enable dynamic updates on the WINS server.

   d. Configure the WINS server to use its own IP address as its WINS client address.

   d

3. How do you manually compact the database on a Windows 2000 WINS server?

   a. Use the Compact command and specify the *systemroot*\System32\wins folder.

   b. Stop the WINS server. Run the Jetpack.exe utility with the name of the database file. Restart the WINS server.

   c. Back up the WINS database. Use Jetpack.exe to compact the copy of the database. Perform an authoritative restore of the backup.

   d. Stop the WINS server. Use the Compact command to compress the database. Restart the WINS server.

   b

4. On a mixed Windows and UNIX network, you deploy a WINS server to provide NetBIOS name resolution services and configure the WINS clients accordingly. Later, you discover that the computers running Windows operating systems on the network cannot access UNIX resources by using their NetBIOS names. What should you do to resolve the problem?

   a. Install a WINS proxy agent on one of the other computers running Windows.

   b. Install a WINS proxy agent on one of the UNIX computers.

   c. Create static mappings for the UNIX computers on the WINS server.

   d. Create static mappings for the WINS server on the UNIX computers.

   c

5. How do you configure a Windows 2000 WINS server to back up its database automatically?

   a. Use the Jetpack.exe utility from the command line.

   b. Specify a backup folder in the WINS server's Properties dialog box.

   c. Use a third-party backup utility to back up the Sysvol folder.

   d. Use the file replication service to replicate the WINS database to a different location.

   b

Lesson 4: Configuring WINS Replication

Page 362   ### Lesson Review

1. What is the difference between the replication configuration parameters of push and pull partners?

   Push partners initiate replication based on the number of changes that have been made to the WINS database, whereas pull partners initiate replication at timed intervals.

2. Which type of replication partnership is preferable when traversing a slow WAN link?

   A pull partnership is preferable, because you can configure replication to occur when traffic is lightest.

3. What is the minimum number of WINS servers required to support a 5000 node routed network in a single location?

   Only one WINS server is required, because a single server can service up to 10,000 clients. However, for fault tolerance reasons, more WINS servers are recommended.

Chapter 10

Lesson 1: Using Packet Filters

Page 375

Lesson Review

1. Which of the following criteria are used to filter packets in service dependent filtering?

   a. Hardware addresses

   b. IP addresses

   c. Protocol identifiers

   d. Port numbers

   d

2. Under what conditions can packet filtering slow down network performance?

   When a router is configured with a large number of packet filters, it must compare each packet it processes with every filter in the list. This can slow down the routing process, affecting the overall performance of the network.

3. Which of the following can you do with RRAS packet filters that you can't do with Windows TCP/IP client packet filters? (Choose all that apply.)

   a. Create separate filters for each of the computer's network interfaces

   b. Apply one set of filters to all the computer's network interfaces

   c. Apply filters to traffic routed by the computer

   d. Filter ICMP traffic

   c, d

Lesson 2: Using IPsec

Page 388

Exercise 1: Understanding IPsec Terminology

Match the terms in the left column with the definitions in the right column.

1. ESP	a. Protects the IP header against modification
2. Security association	b. Requires end system support for IPsec
3. AH	c. Provides tunneling without encryption
4. L2TP	d. Uses a header and a footer to encapsulate the datagram's payload
5. Transport mode	e. Specifies the security mechanisms used by two connected computers

1. d

2. e

3. a

4. c

5. b

Page 389

Lesson Review

1. Which of the following protocols do not provide encryption services? (Choose all that apply.)

    a. AH

    b. ESP

    c. L2TP

    d. ICMP

    a, c, d

2. Which of the following statements are true about IPsec's tunnel mode?

    a. Tunnel mode requires all end systems and intermediate systems to support IPsec.

    b. ESP in tunnel mode encapsulates the datagram's original IP header.

    c. The two IP headers in a tunnel mode IPsec packet have the same source IP address and destination IP address values.

    d. Tunnel mode requires a separate protocol, such as L2TP, to provide encryption services.

    b

3. How does IPsec provide protection against denial of service attacks?

By providing a packet filtering mechanism that enables an administrator to block unauthorized traffic.

Lesson 3: Deploying IPsec

Page 406

Exercise 1: Using IPsec

▶ **Procedure 1: Testing communications**

2. At the command prompt, type **ping** *ipaddress*, where *ipaddress* is the address of the other computer, and then press ENTER. What happens?

The computer successfully pings the other system, producing a display like the following:

```
C:\>ping 192.168.2.3
Pinging 192.168.2.3 with 32 bytes of data:
Reply from 192.168.2.3: bytes=32 time<10ms TTL=128
Reply from 192.168.2.3: bytes=32 time<10ms TTL=128
Reply from 192.168.2.3: bytes=32 time<10ms TTL=128
Reply from 192.168.2.3: bytes=32 time<10ms TTL=128
Ping statistics for 192.168.2.3:
   Packets: Sent = 4, Received = 4, Lost = 0 (0% loss),
Approximate round trip times in milli-seconds:
   Minimum = 0ms, Maximum =  0ms, Average =  0ms
```

▶ **Procedure 3: Testing IPsec**

1. Test the network connection by repeating Procedure 1. What happens? Why?

The attempt to ping the other computer is now unsuccessful because you have configured your computer to require secured communications, and the other computer is not configured to use IPsec.

2. Now, repeat Procedure 2 on the second computer and test the network connection again. What happens now? Why?

The ping test is now successful because both computers are configured to use IPsec.

Page 408

Lesson Review

1. What is the function of an IPsec filter list?

IP filter lists check datagrams for a match against each filter specification. This permits filtering based on the source and destination addresses, DNS names, protocols, or port numbers.

2. Which of the following IPsec components must be assigned before secured communications can take place?

   a. Policies
   b. Rules
   c. Filter lists
   d. Filter actions

   a

3. Which of the following actions is the best way to create an IPsec rule that will secure all Internet e-mail traffic to your external mail servers?

   a. Enable the Secure Server (Require Security) policy.
   b. Create a new IPsec policy that uses the addresses of the external servers as destinations with the All IP traffic filter list and the Require Security action.
   c. Create a new IPsec policy that uses the addresses of the external servers as destinations and uses a filter list that specifies TCP ports 25 and 110.
   d. Modify the All IP Traffic filter list to specify the addresses of the external mail servers as the only destinations.

   c

Chapter 11

Lesson 1: Introducing the Remote Access Service

Page 420

Exercise 1: RAS Authentication Protocols

Match the protocols in the left column with the descriptions in the right column.

1. CHAP	a. Included with Windows 2000 RAS to support non-Windows RAS clients
2. EAP	b. Transmits passwords in clear text
3. SPAP	c. Enables users to change passwords during logon
4. MS-CHAP	d. Enables the RAS client and server to have an open conversation
5. PAP	e. Designed for use with Shiva products

1. a

2. d

3. e

4. c

5. b

Page 420

Lesson Review

1. You are the network administrator for a financial firm that is deploying a Windows 2000 RAS server. To provide the greatest possible security, the company has issued smart cards to all the remote users. Which of the following authentication protocols should you use on the RAS server?

   a. MS-CHAP v2

   b. EAP-TLS

   c. CHAP

   d. EAP-MD5 CHAP

   b

2. In a RAS installation that provides point-to-LAN remote access connectivity, which of the following functions does the RAS server perform? (Choose all that apply.)

   a. Bridge

   b. File server

   c. Router

   d. Authentication server

   c, d

3. How does the RAS callback feature provide additional security?

   By configuring the RAS server to always call back to a specific number, you can prevent users from connecting to the server using other numbers.

4. Which of the following is the primary protocol that Windows 2000 RAS uses for its WAN connections?

   a. VPN

   b. SLIP

   c. Asynchronous NetBEUI

   d. PPP

   d

Lesson 2: Configuring a Remote Access Server

Page 430

Exercise 1: Configuring a RAS Server

10. Select the Ports icon in the RRAS console. What do you see in the details pane?

    The details pane should contain 11 entries, 10 VPN devices (5 each for PPTP and L2TP) and one modem of the type installed in the computer.

12. Click the IP tab. Is remote network access using IP enabled? How can you tell?

Yes, IP is enabled, because the Enable IP Routing and Allow IP-based Remote Access And Demand-Dial Connections check boxes are selected.

13. Click the IPX tab. Is remote access using IPX enabled? How can you tell?

Yes, IPX is enabled, because the Allow IPX-Based Remote Access And Demand-Dial Connections check box is selected.

Page 431

Lesson Review

1. How do you configure RAS to permit only inbound connections on a specific modem?

   You open the Ports Properties dialog box, select the modem, click Configure, and make sure the Demand-Dial Routing Connections (Inbound And Outbound) check box is cleared.

2. Which of the following RAS parameters enables the callback feature?

   a. LCP Extensions

   b. Software compression

   c. Multilink

   d. MPPC

   a

3. Which of the following protocols require RAS clients to have addresses? (Choose all that apply.)

   a. IP

   b. IPX

   c. NetBEUI

   d. AppleTalk

   a, b

Lesson 3: Managing Remote Access Security

Page 447

Exercise 1: Creating a Remote Access Policy

▶ **Procedure 1: Creating a new user and group**

11. Click the Dial-In tab and click the Control Access Through Remote Access Policy option button. Why is this step essential to this exercise?

   This step is essential because without it the user will not be granted access to the RAS server based on its group membership, which is controlled by a remote access policy.

▶ **Procedure 2: Creating a remote access policy**

8. Click Grant Remote Access Permission, and then click Next to proceed to the User Profile page. What would happen when Katie Jordan tried to connect to the RAS server if you selected the Deny Remote Access Permission option?

Katie's connection would be rejected because she is a member of the Remote Users group.

What would happen if you selected the Deny Remote Access Permission option in the new policy and then reversed the order of the two policies in the list?

The Remote Users Group Membership policy would still reject Katie's connection, no matter where it appears in the list. A connection must meet the criteria of all the policies before being granted server access.

Page 448

Lesson Review

1. You are the new administrator of a network that is setting up a RAS server to provide remote access to a large number of home users with various types of computers. When some of the users report being unable to connect to the RAS server, you discover that the only authentication protocol their RAS clients support that uses encrypted passwords is CHAP. To accommodate these users, you enable the use of CHAP in the RAS server's Properties dialog box. However, the users are still unable to connect to the server. Which of the following steps should you take to provide these users with RAS access? (Choose all that apply.)

   a. Add support for MS-CHAP in the server's Properties dialog box.

   b. Disable the Link Control Protocol (LCP) Extensions option in the server's Properties dialog box.

   c. Modify the users' accounts by enabling the Store Passwords Using Reversible Encryption option.

   d. Modify the users' accounts by enabling the User Must Change Password At Next Logon option.

   c, d

2. You are creating new remote access policies on a RAS server to restrict server access to specific groups at specific times of the day. What should you do to the default Allow Access If Dial-In Permission Is Enabled policy to prevent it from interfering with your new policies?

   a. Delete the default policy.

   b. After creating your new policies, move the default policy to the bottom of the list.

   c. After creating your new policies, make sure that the default policy remains at the top of the list.

   d. Nothing. The default policy will not interfere with your new policies.

   d

3. You are the administrator of a RAS installation that must service two groups of users: a crew of traveling salespeople who dial in from various locations at any time of the day or night and a group of customers who dial in from their offices during business hours to check the status of their orders. To ensure the security of the network, you have been instructed to use callbacks and access time restrictions wherever possible. Which of the following settings should you configure to increase network security? (Choose three.)

a. Enable the Always Callback To option for all dial-in users.

b. Create a separate user group for the customers.

c. Create a remote access policy granting server access to users that meet Windows-Groups and Day-And-Time-Restrictions conditions.

d. Enable the Set By Caller callback option for the salespeople.

e. Enable the Always Callback To option for customers only.

b, c, and e

Lesson 4: Virtual Private Networking

Page 459

Exercise 1: Creating a VPN Connection

▶   **Procedure 3: Establishing a VPN connection**

3. Type **shoepf** in the User Name text box and click Connect. What happens? Why?

An Error Connecting To VPN Connection message box appears, stating that the account does not have permission to dial in. This is because the Sharon Hoepf account, as configured in Procedure 1, has the Deny Access option selected in the Dial-In tab of the user object's Properties dialog box.

6. Type **mlee** in the User Name text box and click Connect. What happens? Why?

A Connection Complete message box appears, indicating that the client has successfully connected to the VPN server. This is because the Mark Lee user object has the Allow Access option selected in the Dial-In tab of the user object's Properties dialog box.

8. Expand the Remote Access Clients node in the scope pane. What do you see?

You see an entry in the details pane for the mlee user object, which is currently connected to the server using a tunneled VPN connection.

12. Type **kjordan** in the User Name text box and click Connect. What happens? Why?

A Connection Complete message box appears, indicating that the client has successfully connected to the VPN server. This is because the Katie Jordan object is configured to use remote access policies when connecting to

the server and has satisfied the policy's conditions by belonging to the Remote Access Users group.

Page 462   ## Lesson Review

1. How is the Deny Access remote access permission (in mixed mode or native mode) similar in function to the native-mode domain default remote access policy?

   The Deny Access remote access permission does not allow a user with this setting to use remote access to connect to the server. The native-mode domain remote access policy is Allow Access If Dial-In Permission Is Enabled. The default policy's properties, however, are Deny Remote Access Permission At All Times.

2. List the four tunneling protocols that VPNs can use.

   The four tunneling protocols are PPTP, L2TP, IPsec, and IP-IP.

3. How does virtual private networking reduce the cost of supporting remote access clients?

   VPNs reduce remote access networking costs by eliminating the need for remote users at distant locations to dial long distance directly into a RAS server. By connecting to the Internet using local ISPs, both the client and the server minimize telephone charges.

Chapter 12

Lesson 1: Introducing NAT

Page 470   ### Exercise 1: Understanding NAT Communications

Put the following steps of the NAT communication process into the correct order.

1. The NAT router transmits the packet to the Internet server.
2. The Internet server transmits a reply message.
3. The client receives a message from the NAT router.
4. The NAT router creates a NAT table entry.
5. The NAT router puts an unregistered address into the packet's Destination IP Address field.
6. The client transmits a request to its default gateway.
7. The NAT router puts a registered IP address into the packet's Source IP Address field.

   6, 4, 7, 1, 2, 5, 3

Page 471   **Lesson Review**

1. Which of the following best describes the function of a NAT editor?

   a. A NAT editor enables you to manually configure static address mappings.

   b. A NAT editor modifies the IP addresses and port numbers in TCP, UDP, and IP headers.

   c. A NAT editor modifies IP addresses and port numbers outside of TCP, UDP, and IP headers.

   d. A NAT editor assigns unregistered IP addresses to client computers.

   c

2. Which of the following elements is not stored in a NAT table entry?

   a. The ephemeral port number selected by the client

   b. The client computer's unregistered IP address

   c. The ephemeral port number selected by the NAT router

   d. The IP address of the destination Internet server

   d

3. What is the function of a static address mapping?

   A static address mapping enables a computer with an unregistered IP address to be always available from the Internet, using the same registered address.

Lesson 2: Installing and Configuring NAT

Page 489   **Exercise 1: Configuring a NAT Installation**

1. What IP addresses will the RRAS server assign to the client computers on the local network?

   a. 192.168.10.1 through 192.168.10.10

   b. 192.168.10.11 through 192.168.10.255

   c. 207.209.68.45 through 207.209.68.54

   d. 207.209.68.1 through 207.209.68.44 and 207.209.68.55 through 207.209.68.255

   b

2. When you enable NAT's name resolution component, what DNS server address will be supplied to the client computers?

   a. 192.168.10.1

   b. 192.168.6.2

c. x.y.z.45

d. A DNS server address supplied by the ISP when the demand-dial interface connects.

a

3. What parameters should you use when creating the static route to the Internet?

a. Interface: Local Area Connection
Destination: 192.168.10.0
Network Mask: 255.255.255.0
Gateway: 192.168.10.1

b. Interface: Remote Router
Destination: 0.0.0.0
Network Mask: 255.255.255.0
Gateway: x.y.z.45

c. Interface: Local Area Connection
Destination: 192.168.10.1
Network Mask: 255.255.255.0
Gateway: None

d. Interface: Remote Router
Destination: 0.0.0.0
Network Mask: 0.0.0.0
Gateway: None

d

Page 490

Lesson Review

1. You are the administrator of an unregistered network that uses NAT to access the Internet. You are deploying a Web server hosting a company home page on the local network, and you want users on the Internet to be able to access it. Which of the following tasks must you perform to make this possible? (Choose all that apply.)

a. Create an address pool containing two or more registered IP addresses assigned by your ISP.

b. Create a static route for the interface providing Internet access in which the value of the Destination field is the registered IP address you want Internet clients to use to access the Web server, and the Gateway value is the RRAS server's registered IP address.

c. Create a reservation using one of the registered IP addresses assigned by your ISP and the Web server's unregistered IP address.

d. Configure the Web server to use multiple IP addresses, one of which is unregistered and one of which is a registered address assigned by your ISP.

a, c

2. On an unregistered network using NAT and a cable modem to access the Internet, users on the client computers cannot access Internet servers using fully qualified domain names (FQDNs). However, they can access the same servers using IP addresses. When you investigate the problem, you discover that the Windows 2000 Server computer functioning as the NAT router can access Internet servers using both IP addresses and FQDNs. Which of the following could be the cause of the problem? (Choose all that apply.)

   a. The RRAS computer does not have a DNS server address specified in its TCP/IP configuration.

   b. The name resolution component of the NAT protocol is disabled.

   c. There is no RRAS filter in place allowing DNS packets to pass to the Internet.

   d. The Connect To The Public Network When A Name Needs To Be Resolved check box in the Name Resolution tab of the Network Address Translation (NAT) Properties dialog box is not selected.

   b

3. You are deploying NAT on a Windows 2000 Server computer with a NIC connection to the local network and a demand-dial connection to an ISP. The IP address of the local network connection is 10.5.87.2. The registered IP address assigned by your ISP is x.y.z.172. When you open the Network Address Translation (NAT) Properties dialog box and click the Address Assignment tab, what value do you see in the IP Address box?

   a. 0.0.0.0

   b. 10.0.0.0

   c. x.y.z.0

   d. 192.168.0.0

   d

Lesson 3: Installing Internet Connection Sharing

Page 497

Lesson Review

1. Which of the following configuration tasks are not automatically performed when you activate ICS on a Windows 2000 computer? (Choose all that apply.)

   a. The IP address of the Local Area Connection on the ISC computer is configured as 192.168.0.1.

   b. The client computers on the local network are configured to obtain TCP/IP settings using DHCP.

   c. The ICS computer is configured to process client name resolution requests.

   d. The ICS computer is configured to satisfy FTP requests generated by Internet users.

   b, d

2. How does the address assignment component in ICS differ from the one in NAT?

The ICS address assignment component is automatically enabled with the ICS service and is permanently configured with preselected IP addresses and other settings. The NAT address assignment component is more configurable, enabling you to specify the addresses you want to assign.

3. Which of the following tasks must you perform before enabling ICS on a Windows 2000 computer?

   a. Start the DHCP service.

   b. Create a connection providing Internet access.

   c. Configure the Local Area Connection with the IP address 192.168.0.1.

   d. Obtain a registered IP address from your ISP.

   b

Chapter 13

Lesson 1: Introducing Certificates

Page 507

Exercise 1: Understanding Certificates and Encryption

Match the terms in the left column with the definitions in the right column.

1. Policy module   a. Encrypts or decrypts data, but not both

2. Private key   b. Issues certificates to users outside the organization

3. Certificate template c. Specifies where to store newly created certificates

4. Exit module   d. Determines whether a certificate request should be approved or denied

5. Stand-alone CA   e. Specifies the attributes to be included in new certificates

1. d

2. a

3. e

4. c

5. b

Page 507

Lesson Review

1. What are certificates and what is their purpose?

   A certificate (digital certificate, public key certificate) is a digital document that attests to the binding of a public key to an entity. The main purpose of a certificate is to generate confidence that the public key contained in the certificate actually belongs to the entity named in the certificate.

2. What is a certificate authority (CA) and what does it do?

   Certificates are issued by a CA, which can be any trusted service or entity willing to vouch for the identities of those to whom it issues certificates and their association with specific keys.

3. What are the four types of Microsoft certificate authorities?

   Enterprise root CA, enterprise subordinate CA, stand-alone root CA, and stand-alone subordinate CA.

Lesson 2: Installing and Configuring Microsoft Certificate Services

Page 523

Lesson Review

1. A Java software development company sells its products over the Web using credit cards and allows clients to download Web browser applications immediately after completing the e-commerce transaction. The company has an enterprise root CA, which has issued a certificate for their enterprise subordinate CA, which the company uses to secure the credit card transactions. However, some of the customers are complaining that they cannot run the Web applications because they are not digitally signed. What should the company do to add digital signing capabilities to its Web site?

   a. Request a Code Signing certificate from the enterprise root CA.

   b. Request a User Signature Only certificate from the enterprise subordinate CA.

   c. Request a Code Signing certificate from a commercial CA.

   d. Request a User Signature Only certificate from the enterprise root CA.

   c

2. A network administrator running Windows 2000 servers without Active Directory installs a stand-alone root CA on one of the network's computers. Some weeks later, she is instructed to deploy Active Directory on the same computer. What must she do to the CA to make this possible?

   a. Revoke all the certificates issued by the CA and then reissue them after installing Active Directory.

   b. Select the Active Directory check box in the Storage tab of the CA's Properties dialog box.

    c. Obtain a new certificate for the CA.

    d. Uninstall the CA and reinstall it.

d

3. After installing a stand-alone root CA on a Windows 2000 Server computer, the network administrator is dismayed to find that users have been requesting certificates, but no one has been receiving them. What is the most likely cause of the problem?

    a. The exit module is improperly configured and is publishing the certificates in the wrong place.

    b. The CA's own certificate is invalid; one must be obtained from a commercial CA.

    c. The certificate requests are being held in the "pending" queue until an administrator manually approves them.

    d. The users have been sending their requests to the wrong CA.

c

Lesson 3: Managing Certificates

Page 536 ### Exercise 1: Requesting a Certificate Using the CA Web Interface

▶ **Procedure 1: Requesting a certificate**

4. On the Web Browser Certificate–Identifying Information page, type your name and your e-mail address in the boxes provided. Click Submit. What happens?

A Certificate Pending page appears, informing you that the CA has received the certificate request but that you must wait for an administrator to issue the certificate.

▶ **Procedure 2: Approving a certificate request**

4. In the Action menu, point to All Tasks and select Issue. What happens?

The certificate request is moved from the Pending Requests folder to the Issues Certificates folder, indicating that the certificate has been issued.

▶ **Procedure 3: Checking the status of a certificate request**

3. On the Check On A Pending Certificate Request page, verify that a Web Browser Certificate entry with today's date is selected in the Please Select The Certificate Request You Want To Check box. Click Next. What happens?

A Certificate Issued page appears, stating that the certificate has been issued.

Page 537   **Lesson Review**

1. You are the administrator of a Windows 2000 network using certificates to secure e-mail communications. One of your users believes that his private key has been compromised. Which of the following steps should you take to address the situation? (Choose all that apply.)

   a. Revoke the user's existing certificate.

   b. Issue a new certificate to the user.

   c. Publish the CRL for the CA that issued the user's certificate.

   d. Uninstall and reinstall the CA.

   a, b, and c

2. How do you prevent specific users from requesting certain types of certificates from a CA?

   You prevent users from requesting specific types of certificates by denying them the Enroll permission in the Certificate Templates folder of the Active Directory Sites and Services console.

3. As the administrator responsible for managing your company's CA, you immediately revoke the certificates of users who leave the company and regularly publish the CRL. A month after leaving, however, one of the former employees has decided to come back to the company. What do you do to reinstate the user's credentials?

   a. Move the user's certificate from the Revoked Certificates folder to the Issued Certificates folder in the Certification Authority console.

   b. Issue the user a new certificate.

   c. Restore the user's certificate from a backup.

   d. Delete the user's certificate listing from the CRL.

   b

Chapter 14

Lesson 1: Monitoring Windows 2000 Activity

Page 559   **Exercise 1: Monitoring System Performance Parameters**

10. Click Close. What do you see?

    You see two lines in the graph, representing the two counters. To make the counter values easier to read, you might have to click Properties and adjust the Vertical Scale parameters in the Graph tab.

11. Click View Histogram and then View Report. What do you see when you click these buttons?

You see the same counter information expressed in different formats, a histogram-style bar graph and a report with numerical indicators.

Page 560

Lesson Review

1. What is the danger inherent in disconnecting a user from a share without prior notification?

If the user is currently working on a shared file and has not saved changes, those changes will be lost when the connection is severed.

2. Which of the following tasks cannot be performed by the Shared Folders snap-in?

   a. Send an administrative message to another user on the network

   b. Share an existing printer on the local computer

   c. Share an existing folder on the local computer

   d. Create a new shared folder on a remote computer

   b

3. What must you do before modifications you have made to the NTFS permissions for a shared folder have their full effect?

Disconnect all users currently connected to the share, forcing them to reconnect using the new permissions.

Lesson 2: Monitoring Network Services

Page 573

Lesson Review

1. Which of the following services has its own log in the Event Viewer console?

   a. WINS

   b. DNS

   c. RRAS

   d. DHCP

   b

2. Which tool do you use to monitor IPsec activity in real time?

   a. IP Security Monitor

   b. System Monitor

   c. Event Viewer

   d. Network Monitor

   a

3. In which of the following logs can you specify which activities are to be monitored?

   a. DHCP

   b. DNS

   c. WINS

   d. DNS debug

   d

Lesson 3: Using Network Monitor

Page 582

Exercise 1: Capturing Frames with Network Monitor

13. Click OK to close the Display Filter dialog box. What happens to the display in the Capture Summary window?

    The Capture Summary window now contains only the TCP frames.

Page 582

Lesson Review

1. What kind of data does a frame contain?

   A frame contains the source address of the computer that sent the message, the destination address of the computer that the frame was sent to, headers from each protocol used within the frame, and the payload being sent.

2. What is a capture filter, and what is it used for?

   A capture filter enables you to specify the types of network information you want to monitor. For example, to see only a specific subset of computers or protocols, you can create an address database, use the database to add addresses to your filter, and then save the filter to a file. By filtering frames, you save both buffer resources and analysis time. Later, if necessary, you can load the capture filter file and use the filter again.

3. Which Network Monitor filter features should you specify to filter out all network traffic except for traffic between two computers and to locate specific data within the packets?

   First, filter for address pairs where you specify the hardware address of each computer, and then specify pattern matches where you filter for specific patterns in hex or ASCII contained in the frames.

Glossary

A

abstract syntax The native format used by a computer to encode information generated by an application or process. The presentation layer of the Open System Interconnection (OSI) reference model receives data from the application in the system's abstract syntax and is responsible for converting it to a common transfer syntax understood by both communicating systems. *See also* transfer syntax.

access control list (ACL) The mechanism for limiting access to certain items of information or certain controls based on users' identity and their membership in various predefined groups. Access control is typically used by system administrators to control user access to network resources such as servers, directories, and files and is typically implemented by granting permissions to users and groups for access to specific objects.

access permissions Features that control access to Microsoft Windows 2000 shares. Permissions can be set for the following access levels: No Access—prevents access to the shared directory, its subdirectories, and its files; Read—allows viewing of file and subdirectory names, changing to a shared directory's subdirectory, viewing data in files, and running applications; Change—allows viewing of file and subdirectory names, changing to a shared directory's subdirectories, viewing data in files and running application files, adding files and subdirectories to a shared directory, changing data in files, and deleting subdirectories and files; Full Control—includes the same permissions as Change, plus changing permissions and taking ownership of the NTFS files and directories only.

account *See* user account.

account lockout A Windows 2000 security feature that locks a user account if a number of failed logon attempts occur within a specified amount of time, based on security policy lockout settings. After an account is locked, users cannot use it to log on.

ACL *See* access control list (ACL).

Active Directory The enterprise directory service included with the Microsoft Windows 2000 Server, Advanced Server, and Datacenter Server operating systems. Active Directory service is a hierarchical directory service that consists of objects that represent users, computers, groups, and other network resources. The objects are arranged in a tree display that consists of hierarchical layers ranging upward from organizational units, to domains, to trees, and to forests. Objects are composed of attributes that contain information about the resource the object represents. When users log on to the network, their user names and passwords are authenticated against the Active Directory database by a computer that has been designated as a domain controller. This one single logon can grant them access to resources anywhere on the network. *See also* directory service.

Active Directory Domains and Trusts console An administrative tool that enables you to manage trust relationships between domains. These domains can be Microsoft Windows 2000 domains in the same forest, Windows 2000 domains in different forests, pre–Windows 2000 domains, and even Kerberos v5 realms.

Active Directory Sites and Services console An administrative tool that contains information about the physical structure of your network. Active Directory uses this information to determine how to replicate directory information and handle service requests.

Active Directory Users and Computers console An administrative tool designed to perform day-to-day Active Directory administration tasks.

These tasks include creating, deleting, modifying, moving, and setting permissions on objects stored in the directory. These objects include organizational units, users, contacts, groups, and computers.

Address Resolution Protocol (ARP) A Transmission Control Procotol/Internet Protocol (TCP/IP) protocol used to resolve the IP addresses of computers on a local area network (LAN) into the hardware (or media access control [MAC]) addresses needed to transmit data-link layer frames to them. Before transmitting an IP datagram, TCP/IP clients broadcast an ARP request message containing the IP address of the destination computer to the local network. The computer using that IP address must then respond with an ARP reply message containing its hardware address. With the information in the reply message, the computer can encapsulate the IP datagram in the appropriate data-link layer frame and transmit it to the destination system.

administrator A person responsible for setting up and managing domain controllers, servers, and local computers, their services, user and group accounts, and password and permission assignments, and for helping users with networking issues.

agent A program that performs a background task for a user and reports to the user when the task is done or when some expected event has taken place.

analog Related to a continuously variable physical property, such as voltage, pressure, or rotation. An analog device can represent an infinite number of values within the range the device can handle. *See also* analog line, digital.

analog line A communications line, such as a telephone line, that carries information in analog (continuously variable) form. To minimize distortion and noise interference, an analog line uses amplifiers to strengthen the signal periodically during transmission.

API *See* application programming interface (API).

AppleTalk A proprietary suite of networking protocols developed by Apple for use by its Macintosh computers. AppleTalk includes AppleShare, a file and printer-sharing solution that enables a Macintosh computer to function as a network server. AppleTalk is rarely used today, as Macintosh computers now communicate using the industry standard Transmission Control Protocol/Internet Protocol (TCP/IP) protocols.

application A complete, self-contained set of computer instructions that you use to perform a specific task, such as word processing, accounting, or data management. An application is also called a *program.*

application layer The top layer of the Open Systems Interconnection (OSI) reference model, which provides the entrance point used by applications to access the networking protocol stack. Some of the protocols operating at the application layer include the Hypertext Transfer Protocol (HTTP), the Simple Mail Transfer Protocol (SMTP), the Dynamic Host Configuration Protocol (DHCP), the File Transfer Protocol (FTP), and the Simple Network Management Protocol (SNMP).

application programming interface (API) A set of routines that an application program uses to request and carry out lower level services performed by the operating system.

ARP *See* Address Resolution Protocol (ARP).

ARPANET (Advanced Research Projects Agency Network) A pioneering wide area network (WAN) commissioned by the Department of Defense, ARPANET was designed to facilitate the exchange of information between universities and other research organizations. ARPANET, which became operational in the 1960s, is the network from which the Internet evolved.

Arp.exe A command-line utility provided by the TCP/IP client included with the Microsoft Windows operating systems, which enables you to display and manipulate the information stored in the cache created by the Address Resolution Protocol (ARP). By preloading the ARP cache, you can save time and network traffic by eliminating the ARP transaction that the TCP/IP client uses to resolve the IP address of each system it transmits to into a hardware address. *See also* Address Resolution Protocol (ARP).

ASCII (American Standard Code for Information Interchange) A coding scheme that assigns numeric values to letters, numbers, punctuation marks, and certain other characters. By standardizing the values used for these characters, ASCII enables computers and computer programs to exchange information.

asynchronous transmission A form of data transmission in which information is sent one character at a time, with variable time intervals between characters. Asynchronous transmission does not rely on a shared timer that allows the sending and receiving units to separate characters by specific time periods. Therefore, each transmitted character consists of a number of data bits (that compose the character itself), preceded by a start bit and ending in an optional parity bit followed by a 1-, 1.5-, or 2-stop bit.

attribute A unit of information that makes up an object in a directory service, such as Active Directory.

auditing A process that tracks network activities by user accounts and a routine element of network security. Auditing can produce records of list users who have accessed—or attempted to access—specific resources; help administrators identify unauthorized activity; and track activities such as logon attempts, connection and disconnection from designated resources, changes made to files and directories, server events and modifications, password changes, and logon parameter changes.

authentication Verification typically based on user name, password, and time and account restrictions.

authoritative server A Domain Name System (DNS) server that has been designated as the definitive source of information about the computers in a particular domain. When resolving a computer's DNS name into its IP address, DNS servers consult the authoritative server for the domain in which that computer is located. Whatever information the authoritative server provides about that domain is understood by all DNS servers to be correct. *See also* Domain Name System (DNS).

authorization A process that verifies that the user has the correct rights or permissions to access a resource.

automatic allocation An operational mode of Dynamic Host Configuration Protocol (DHCP) servers in which the server permanently assigns an IP address and other Transmission Control Protocol/Internet Protocol (TCP/IP) configuration settings to a client from a pool of addresses. *Compare with* dynamic allocation, which assigns addresses in the same way but reclaims them when a lease of a given duration expires, and manual allocation, which permanently assigns specific addresses to clients. *See also* Dynamic Host Configuration Protocol (DHCP).

AXFR *See* full zone transfer (AXFR).

B

bandwidth In communications, the difference between the highest and lowest frequencies in a given range. For example, a telephone accommodates a bandwidth of 3000 Hz, or the difference between the lowest (300 Hz) and highest (3300 Hz) frequencies it can carry. In computer networks, greater bandwidth indicates faster or greater data-transfer capability.

baseband network A network that uses a medium that can carry only one signal at a particular time. *Compare with* broadband network, which is a network that carries multiple signals at once, using a technique called multiplexing. Most local area networks (LANs) are baseband networks; your local cable television system is an example of a broadband network.

bind To associate two pieces of information with one another.

binding A process that establishes the communication channel between a protocol driver and a network interface card (NIC) driver.

bit Short for binary digit: either 1 or 0 in the binary number system. In processing and storage, a bit is the smallest unit of information handled by a computer. It is represented physically by an element such as a single pulse sent through a circuit or small spot on a magnetic disk capable of storing either a 1 or 0. Eight bits make a byte.

bits per second (bps) A measure of the speed at which a device can transfer data.

BOOTP *See* Bootstrap Protocol (BOOTP).

Bootstrap Protocol (BOOTP) A server application that can supply client computers with IP addresses, other Transmission Control Protocol/Internet Protocol (TCP/IP) configuration parameters, and executable boot files. As the progenitor to the Dynamic Host Configuration Protocol (DHCP), BOOTP provides the same basic functions, except that it does not allocate IP addresses from a pool and reclaim them after a specified length of time. Administrators must supply the IP address and other settings for each computer to be configured by the BOOTP server. *See also* Dynamic Host Configuration Protocol (DHCP), Reverse Address Resolution Protocol (RARP).

bottleneck The limiting factor when analyzing performance of a system or network. Poor performance results when a device uses noticeably more CPU time than it should, consumes too much of a resource, or lacks the capacity to handle the load. Potential bottlenecks can be found in the CPU, memory, network interface card (NIC), and other components.

bps *See* bits per second (bps).

broadband network A network that uses a medium that can carry multiple signals simultaneously, using a technique called multiplexing. The most common example of broadband communications is the typical cable television network, which transmits the signals corresponding to dozens of TV channels over one cable. *Compare with* a baseband network, which can carry only one signal on its medium.

broadcast A message transmitted to all the other computers on the local network. Data-link layer protocols have special addresses designated as broadcast addresses, which means that every computer that receives the message will read it into memory and process it. Local area networks (LANs) use broadcasts for a variety of tasks, such as to discover information about other computers on the network.

byte A unit of information consisting of eight bits. In computer processing or storage, a byte is equivalent to a single character, such as a letter, numeral, or punctuation mark. Because a byte represents only a small amount of information, amounts of computer memory are usually given in kilobytes (1,024 bytes or 2 raised to the 10th power), megabytes (1,048,576 bytes or 2 raised to the 20th power), gigabytes (1,024 megabytes), terabytes (1,024 gigabytes), petabytes (1,024 terabytes), or exabytes (1,024 petabytes).

C

CA *See* certificate authority (CA).

cache For Domain Name System (DNS) and Windows Internet Name Service (WINS), a local information store of resource records for recently resolved names of remote hosts. Typically, the cache is built dynamically as the computer queries and resolves names. It also helps optimize the time required to resolve queried names.

Carrier Sense Multiple Access with Collision Detection (CSMA/CD) The Media Access Control (MAC) mechanism used by Ethernet networks to regulate access to the network. Before they can transmit data, CSMA/CD systems listen to the network to determine if it is in use. If the network is free, the system transmits its data. Sometimes, another computer transmits at precisely the same time, however, causing a signal quality error or collision. Collisions are normal occurrences on Ethernet networks, and network interface adapters are capable of detecting them and compensating for them by discarding the collided packets and retransmitting them in a controlled manner.

CCITT *See* Comité Consultatif International Téléphonique et Télégraphique (CCITT).

certificate A collection of data used for authentication and secure exchange of information on nonsecured networks, such as the Internet. A certificate securely binds a public key to the entity that holds the corresponding private key. Certificates are digitally signed by the issuing CA and can be managed for a user, computer, or service. The most widely accepted format for certificates is defined by the ITU-T X.509 international standard.

certificate authority (CA) An entity responsible for establishing the authenticity of public keys belonging to users or other CAs. Activities of a CA can include binding public keys to distinguished names through signed certificates, managing certificate serial numbers, and revoking certificates.

certificate services Software services that enable a computer to act as a certificate authority which issues, renews, manages, and revokes digital certificates for an organization. Digital certificates have many uses including secure e-mail, Web-based authentication, and smart card authentication.

child domain For Domain Name System (DNS), a domain located in the name space tree directly beneath another directory name (the parent domain). For example, sales.microsoft.com would be a child domain of the microsoft.com parent domain. A child domain is also called a subdomain.

client A program designed to communicate with a server program on another computer, usually to request and receive information. The client provides the interface with which the user can view and manipulate the server data. A client can be a module in an operating system, such as the Client for Microsoft Networks in Windows 2000, which enables the user to access resources on the network's other computers, or a separate application, such as a Web browser or e-mail reader.

client/server networking A computing model in which data processing tasks are distributed between clients, which request, display, and manipulate information, and servers, which supply and store information. By having each individual client be responsible for displaying and manipulating its own data, the server is relieved of a large part of the processing burden. The alternative is a mainframe or minicomputer system in which one computer performs all the processing for all the users, who work with terminals that do not have processors (dumb terminals).

collision In local area networking, a condition that occurs when two computers transmit data at precisely the same time, and their signals both occupy the same cable, causing data loss. On some types of networks, such as Ethernet, collisions are a normal occurrence, whereas on Token Ring networks, they are an indication of a serious problem. Also called a signal quality error.

Comité Consultatif International Téléphonique et Télégraphique (CCITT) An organization (in English, the International Telegraph and Telephone Consultative Committee) that, until 1992, developed and published international communications standards, such as those that govern modem signaling, compression, and error correction protocols. The organization is now known as the Telecommunication Standardization Sector of the International Telecommunication Union (ITU-T). The CCITT also published the document that defined the Open Systems Interconnection (OSI) reference model, called "The Basic Reference Model for Open Systems Interconnection."

command A word or phrase, usually found on a menu, that you click to carry out an action. You click a command on a menu or type a command at the command prompt. You can also type a command in the Run dialog box, which you open in the Start menu by clicking Run.

command prompt window A window displayed on the desktop used to interface with the operating system's command line.

Commercial COMSEC Endorsement Program (CCEP) A data-encryption standard introduced by the National Security Agency. Vendors who have the proper security clearance can join CCEP and be authorized to incorporate classified algorithms into communications systems. *See also* encryption.

computer account An account that is created by a domain administrator and that uniquely identifies the computer on the domain. The Microsoft Windows 2000 computer account matches the name of the computer joining the domain.

connectionless A type of protocol that transmits messages to a destination without first establishing a connection with the destination system. Connectionless protocols have very little overhead and are used primarily for transactions that consist of a single request and reply. Both the Internet Protocol (IP) and the User Datagram Protocol (UDP) are connectionless protocols.

connection-oriented A type of protocol that transmits a series of messages to a destination to establish a connection before sending any application data. Establishing the connection ensures that the destination system is active and ready to receive data. Connection-oriented protocols are typically used to send large amounts of data, such as entire files, which must be split into multiple packets and which are useless unless every packet arrives at the destination without error. The Transmission Control Protocol (TCP) is a connection-oriented protocol.

console A collection of administrative tools.

console tree The left pane in a Microsoft Management Console (MMC) display, which lists the items contained in the console. By default, the console tree appears in the left pane of a console window, but it can be hidden. The items in the console tree and their hierarchical organization determine the capabilities of a console.

contention Competition among stations on a network for the opportunity to use a communication line or network resource. Two or more computers attempt to transmit over the same cable at the same time, thus causing a collision on the cable. Such a system needs regulation to eliminate data collisions on the cable that can destroy data and bring network traffic to a halt. *See also* Carrier-Sense Multiple Access with Collision Detection (CSMA/CD).

convergence The process by which dynamic routers update their routing tables to reflect the current state of the internetwork. The primary advantage of dynamic routing is that it enables routers to modify their routing information automatically as the configuration of the network changes. For example, should a router malfunction, the other nearby routers, after failing to receive regular updates from it, will eventually remove it from their routing tables, thus preventing computers on the network from using that router. The elapsed time between the failure of the router and its removal from the routing tables of the other routers is the convergence period.

counter log Collects performance counter data in a comma-separated or tab-separated format for easy import to spreadsheet programs. You can view logged counter data using System Monitor or by exporting the data to spreadsheet programs or databases for analysis and report generation.

counters The individual system attributes or processes monitored by the Performance console in Microsoft Windows 2000.

CRC *See* cyclical redundancy check (CRC).

cryptography The processes, art, and science of keeping messages and data secure. Cryptography is used to enable and ensure confidentiality, data integrity, authentication (entity and data origin), and nonrepudiation.

CSMA/CD *See* Carrier Sense Multiple Access with Collision Detection (CSMA/CD).

cyclical redundancy check (CRC) An error detection mechanism in which a computer performs a calculation on a data sample with a specific algorithm and then transmits the data and the results of the calculation to another computer. The receiving computer then performs the same calculation and compares its results to those supplied by the sender. If the results match, the data has been transmitted successfully. If the results do not match, the data has been damaged in transit.

D

daemon UNIX term for a computer program or process that runs continuously in the background and performs tasks at predetermined intervals or in response to specific events. Called a service by Microsoft Windows operating systems, a daemon typically performs server tasks, such as spooling print jobs, handling e-mail, and transmitting Web files.

data encapsulation The process by which information generated by an application is packaged for transmission over a network by successive protocols operating at the various layers of the Open Systems Interconnection (OSI) reference model. A protocol packages the data it receives from the layer above by adding a header (and sometimes a footer) containing protocol-specific information used to ensure that the data arrives at its destination intact.

data encryption *See* encryption.

Data Encryption Standard (DES) A commonly used, highly sophisticated algorithm developed by the U.S. National Bureau of Standards for encrypting and decoding data. *See also* encryption.

datagram A term for the unit of data used by the Internet Protocol (IP) and other network layer protocols. Network layer protocols accept data from transport layer protocols and package it into datagrams by adding their own protocol headers. The protocol then passes the datagrams down to a data-link layer protocol for further packaging before they are transmitted over the network.

data-link layer The second layer from the bottom of the Open Systems Interconnection (OSI) reference model. Protocols operating at the data-link layer are responsible for packaging network layer data, addressing it to its next destination, and transmitting it over the network. Some of the local area network (LAN) protocols operating at the data-link layer are Ethernet, Token Ring, and the Fiber Distributed Data Interface (FDDI). Wide area network (WAN) protocols operating at the data-link layer include the Point-to-Point Protocol (PPP) and the Serial Line Internet Protocol (SLIP).

default gateway The router on the local network used by a Transmission Control Protocol/Internet Protocol (TCP/IP) client computer to transmit messages to computers on other networks. To communicate with other networks, TCP/IP computers consult their routing tables for the address of the destination network. If they locate the address, they send their packets to the router specified in the table entry, which relays them to the desired network. If no specific entry for the network exists, the computer sends the packets to the router specified in the default gateway entry, which the user (or a Dynamic Host Configuration Protocol [DHCP] server) supplies as one of the basic configuration parameters of the TCP/IP client.

DES *See* Data Encryption Standard (DES).

Destination Address A 48-bit field in data-link layer protocol headers that contains a hexadecimal sequence used to identify the network interface to which a frame will be transmitted.

Destination IP Address A 32-bit field in the Internet Protocol (IP) header that contains a value used to identify the network interface to which a packet will be transmitted.

details pane The pane on the right side of the Microsoft Management Console (MMC) that displays the details for the selected item in the scope pane. The details can be a list of items or they can be administrative properties, services, and events that are acted on by a console or snap-in.

device driver A program that enables a specific device, such as a modem, network card, or printer, to communicate with an operating system, such as Microsoft Windows 2000. For example, without a device driver, a network interface adapter cannot communicate with the computer's operating system. Although a device might be installed on your system, Windows 2000 cannot use the device until you have installed and configured the appropriate driver. If a device is listed in the Hardware Compatibility List (HCL), a driver is usually included with Windows 2000. Device drivers load automatically (for all enabled devices) when a computer is started, and thereafter run invisibly.

DHCP *See* Dynamic Host Configuration Protocol (DHCP).

DHCP client Any network-enabled device that supports the ability to communicate with a DHCP server for the purpose of obtaining a dynamically leased Internet Protocol (IP) address and other Transmission Control Protocol/Internet Protocol (TCP/IP) configuration settings.

DHCP scope A range of Internet Protocol (IP) addresses that are available to be leased or assigned to Dynamic Host Configuration Protocol (DHCP) clients by the DHCP service.

DHCP server In Microsoft Windows 2000 Server, a computer running the Microsoft DHCP Server service that offers dynamic configuration of Internet Protocol (IP) addresses and related information to Dynamic Host Configuration Protocol (DHCP)–enabled clients.

dial-up connection A communications link to a remote system or network that is created by a device that uses the Public Switched Telephone Network (PSTN). This includes modems with a standard phone line, ISDN cards with high-speed ISDN lines, or X.25 networks. If you are a typical user, you might have one or two dial-up connections, perhaps to the Internet and to your corporate network. In a more complex server situation, multiple network modem connections might be used to implement an advanced routing configuration.

digital A system that encodes information numerically, such as 0 and 1, in a binary context. Computers use digital encoding to process data. A digital signal is a discrete binary state, either on or off. *See also* analog.

digital line A communication line that carries information only in binary-encoded (digital) form. To minimize distortion and noise interference, a digital line uses repeaters to regenerate the signal periodically during transmission. *See also* analog line.

digital signature A means for originators of a message, file, or other digitally encoded information to bind their identity to the information. The process of signing information entails transforming the information, as well as some secret information held by the sender, into a tag called a signature. Digital signatures are used in public key environments and they provide nonrepudiation and integrity services.

Digital Subscriber Line (DSL) A type of point-to-point, digital wide area network (WAN) connection that uses standard telephone lines to provide high-speed communications. DSL is available in many different forms, including Asymmetrical Digital Subscriber Line (ADSL) and High-bit-rate Digital Subscriber Line (HDSL). The various DSL technologies differ greatly in their speeds and in the maximum possible distance between the installation site and the telephone company's nearest central office. DSL connections are used for many applications, ranging from local area network (LAN) and Private Branch Exchange (PBX) interconnections to consumer Internet access.

direct route An Internet Protocol (IP) transmission to a destination on the local network, in which the Destination IP Address and the data-link layer protocol's Destination Address identify the same computer. *Compare with* indirect route, in which the IP destination is on another network and the data-link layer Destination Address identifies a router on the local network used to access the destination network.

directory An information source (for example, a telephone directory) that contains information about people, computer files, or other objects. In a file system, a directory stores information about files. In a distributed computing environment (such as a Microsoft Windows 2000 domain), the directory stores information about objects such as printers, fax servers, applications, databases, and other users.

directory database The physical storage for each replica of the Active Directory service. The directory database is also called the *data store*.

directory service A database containing information about network entities and resources, used as a guide to the network and an authentication resource by multiple users. Early network operating systems included basic flat file directory services, such as Windows NT domains and the Novell NetWare bindery. Today's directory services, such as Microsoft's Active Directory and Novell Directory Services (NDS) tend to be hierarchical and designed to support large enterprise networks. *See also* Active Directory, Novell Directory Services (NDS).

distance vector protocol A dynamic routing protocol that rates the relative efficiency of network routes by the number of hops to the destination. This is not necessarily an efficient method because having networks of different speeds can cause a route with fewer hops to take longer to transmit data than one requiring more hops. The most common distance vector routing protocol is the Routing Information Protocol (RIP). *Compare with* link state protocol.

DIX An acronym for Digital Equipment Corporation (DEC), Intel, and Xerox, the three corporations responsible for developing and publishing the original Ethernet standard.

DNS *See* Domain Name System (DNS).

DNS name server In the DNS client/server model, the server containing information about a portion of the Domain Name System (DNS) database that makes computer names available to client resolvers querying for name resolution across the Internet.

domain A group of computers and other devices on a network that are administered as a single unit. On the Internet, domain names are hierarchical constructions (such as *microsoft.com*) that form the basis for the Domain Name System (DNS). On a Microsoft Windows 2000 network, a domain is a group of users, computers, and other resources for which information is stored in a directory service on a server called a domain controller.

domain controller A computer running Microsoft Windows 2000 or Windows NT that has been designated for storing and processing directory service information. Windows NT domains and the Windows 2000 Active Directory service store their directory service databases on domain controllers, which also authenticate users accessing network resources.

domain model A grouping of one or more domains with administration and communication links between them that is arranged for the purpose of user and resource management.

domain name space The database structure used by the Domain Name System (DNS).

Domain Name System (DNS) A distributed, hierarchical name space designed to provide Transmission Control Protocol/Internet Protocol (TCP/IP) networks (such as the Internet) with friendly names for computers and users. Although TCP/IP computers use IP addresses to identify each other, people work better with names. DNS provides a naming system for network resources and a service for resolving those names into IP addresses. TCP/IP computers frequently access DNS servers to send them the names of the computers they want to access. The DNS server communicates with other DNS servers on the network to find out the IP address associated with the requested name and then sends it back to the client computer, which initiates communications with the destination system using its IP address.

driver *See* device driver.

DSL *See* Digital Subscriber Line (DSL).

dynamic allocation An operational mode of Dynamic Host Configuration Protocol (DHCP) servers in which the server assigns an IP address and other Transmission Control Protocol/Internet Protocol (TCP/IP) configuration settings to a client from a pool of addresses and then reclaims them when a lease of a given duration expires. This enables you to move computers to different subnets without having to manually release the previously allocated IP addresses from the other subnets. *Compare with* automatic allocation, manual allocation. *See also* Dynamic Host Configuration Protocol (DHCP).

Dynamic Host Configuration Protocol (DHCP) A service that automatically configures the Transmission Control Protocol/Internet Protocol (TCP/IP) client computers on a network by assigning them unique IP addresses and other configuration parameters. DHCP servers can assign IP addresses to clients from a pool and reclaim them when a lease of a set duration expires. Virtually all operating systems include a DHCP client, and most of the major server operating systems, such as Microsoft Windows 2000 Server, Windows NT Server, Novell NetWare, and many forms of UNIX, include DHCP server software. DHCP is a cross-platform service that can support various operating systems with a single server. *See also* automatic allocation, dynamic allocation, manual allocation.

dynamic routing A system in which routers automatically build their own routing tables using specialized protocols to communicate with other nearby routers. By sharing information in this way, a router builds up a composite picture of the internetwork on which it resides, enabling it to route traffic more efficiently. The two basic types of routing protocols are distance vector routing protocols, like the Routing Information Protocol (RIP), and link state routing protocols, like the Open Shortest Path First (OSPF) protocol.

dynamic update Enables clients with dynamically assigned Internet Protocol (IP) addresses to register directly with a server running the Domain Name System (DNS) service and update their DNS resource records automatically. Dynamic updates eliminate the need for other Internet naming services, such as Windows Internet Name Service (WINS), in a homogeneous environment.

E

e-mail A service that transmits messages in electronic form to specific users on a network.

EFS *See* encrypting file system (EFS).

encrypting file system (EFS) A Microsoft Windows 2000 feature that enables users to encrypt files and folders on an NTFS volume to keep them safe from intruders who have physical access to the disk.

encryption The process of making information indecipherable in order to protect it from unauthorized viewing or use, especially during transmission or when the data is stored on a transportable magnetic medium. A key is required to decode the information. *See also* Commercial COMSEC Endorsement Program (CCEP), data encryption standard (DES).

end system On a Transmission Control Protocol/Internet Protocol (TCP/IP) network, a computer or other device that is the original sender or ultimate recipient of a transmission. The end systems in a TCP/IP transmission are identified by the Source IP Address and Destination IP Address fields in the IP header. All the other systems (that is, routers) involved in the transmission are known as intermediate systems.

ephemeral port A Transmission Control Protocol (TCP) or User Datagram Protocol (UDP) port number of 1024 or higher, chosen at random by a Transmission Control Protocol/Internet Protocol (TCP/IP) client computer during the initiation of a transaction with a server. Because the client initiates the communication with the server, it can use any port number beyond the range of the well-known port numbers (which run up to 1023). The server reads the ephemeral port number from the transport layer protocol header's Source Port field and uses it to address its replies to the client. *Compare with* well-known port.

Ethernet Common term used to describe IEEE 802.3, a data-link layer local area network (LAN) protocol developed in the 1970s, which is now the most popular protocol of its kind in the world. Ethernet runs at 10 megabits per second (Mbps), is based on the Carrier Sense Multiple Access with Collision Detection (CSMA/CD) Media Access Control (MAC) mechanism, and supports a variety of physical layer options, including coaxial, unshielded twisted pair (UTP), and fiberoptic cables. More recent revisions of the protocol support speeds of 100 Mbps (Fast Ethernet) and 1,000 Mbps (Gigabit Ethernet). *See also* Carrier Sense Multiple Access with Collision Detection (CSMA/CD).

event An action or occurrence to which a program might respond. Examples of events are mouse clicks, key presses, and mouse movements. Also, any significant occurrence in the system or in a program that requires users to be notified or an entry to be added to a log.

event logging The Microsoft Windows 2000 process of recording an audit entry in the audit trail whenever certain events occur, such as services starting and stopping or users logging on and off and accessing resources. You can use Event Viewer to review Windows 2000 events.

Event Viewer A Microsoft Management Console (MMC) snap-in that maintains and displays logs about application, security, and system events on your computer.

expand To show hidden directory levels in a directory or console tree.

F

fast link pulse (FLP) A variation on the normal link pulse signal that enables dual-speed Fast Ethernet devices to negotiate the fastest transmission speed they have in common. *See also* normal link pulse.

fault tolerance The ability of a computer or an operating system to respond to an event such as a power outage or a hardware failure in such a way that no data is lost and any work in progress is not interrupted.

FDDI *See* Fiber Distributed Data Interface (FDDI).

Fiber Distributed Data Interface (FDDI) A data-link layer local area network (LAN) protocol running at 100 megabits per second (Mbps) and designed for use with fiber-optic cable. Typically used for backbone networks, FDDI uses the token-passing Media Access Control (MAC) mechanism and supports a double ring topology that provides fault tolerance in the event of a system disconnection or cable failure. Originally the principal 100-Mbps LAN protocol, FDDI has since largely been replaced by the Fast Ethernet and Gigabit Ethernet fiber-optic options.

File Transfer Protocol (FTP) An application layer Transmission Control Protocol/Internet Protocol (TCP/IP) protocol designed to perform file transfers and basic file management tasks on remote computers. FTP is a mainstay of Internet communications. FTP client support is integrated into most Web browsers and FTP server support is integrated into many Web server products. FTP is also an important UNIX tool; all UNIX systems support both FTP client and server functions. FTP is unique among TCP/IP protocols in that it uses two simultaneous TCP connections. One, a control connection, remains open during the entire life of the session between the FTP client and the FTP server. When the client initiates a file transfer, a second connection is opened between the two computers to carry the transferred data. This connection closes at the conclusion of the data transfer.

firewall A hardware or software product designed to isolate part of an internetwork to protect it against intrusion by outside processes. Typically used to protect a private network from intrusion from the Internet, firewalls use a number of techniques to provide this protection, while still allowing certain types of traffic through. Some of these techniques include packet filtering and network address translation (NAT). Once intended only for large network installations, there are now smaller firewall products designed to protect small networks and individual computers from Internet intruders.

flow control A function of certain data transfer protocols that enables a system receiving data to transmit signals to the sender instructing it to slow down or speed up its transmissions. This prevents the receiving system from overflowing its buffers and being forced to discard incoming data. For example, the Transmission Control Protocol (TCP) implements its flow control mechanism by using a Microsoft Windows field to specify the number of bytes that it is capable of receiving from the sender.

FLP *See* fast link pulse (FLP).

folder A grouping of files or other folders, graphically represented by a folder icon, in both Microsoft Windows 2000 and Macintosh environments. Also called a directory.

forward lookup In Domain Name System (DNS), a query process in which the friendly DNS domain name of a host computer is searched to find its Internet Protocol (IP) address.

FQDN *See* fully qualified domain name (FQDN).

frame Unit of data constructed, transmitted, and received by data-link layer protocols such as Ethernet and Token Ring. Data-link layer protocols create frames by packaging the data they receive from network layer protocols inside a header and footer. Frames can be different sizes, depending on the protocol used to create them.

FTP *See* File Transfer Protocol (FTP).

full zone transfer (AXFR) The standard query type supported by all Domain Name System (DNS) servers to update and synchronize zone data when the zone has been changed. When a DNS query is made using AXFR as the specified query type, the entire zone is transferred as the response.

fully qualified domain name (FQDN) A DNS domain name that has been stated unambiguously so as to indicate with absolute certainty its location in the domain name space. Fully qualified domain names differ from relative names in that they can be stated with a trailing period (.)—for example, host.example.microsoft.com.—to qualify their position to the root of the name space.

G

gateway On a Transmission Control Protocol/ Internet Protocol (TCP/IP) network, the term gateway is often used synonymously with the term router, referring to a network layer device that connects two networks and relays traffic between them as needed, such as the default gateway specified in a TCP/IP client configuration. However, the term gateway is also used to refer to an application layer device that relays data between two different services, such as an e-mail gateway that enables two separate e-mail services to communicate with each other.

GB Gigabyte, equal to 1000 megabytes, 1,000,000 kilobytes, or 1,000,000,000 bytes.

GBps Gigabytes per second, a unit of measurement typically used to measure the speed of data storage devices.

Gbps Gigabits per second, a unit of measurement typically used to measure network transmission speed.

group In networking, an account containing other accounts that are called members. The permissions and rights granted to a group are also provided to its members; thus, groups offer a convenient way to grant common capabilities to collections of user accounts.

group account A collection of user accounts. By making a user account a member of a group, you give the related user all the rights and permissions granted to the group.

group memberships The groups to which a user account belongs. Permissions and rights granted to a group are also provided to its members. In most cases, the actions a user can perform in Microsoft Windows 2000 are determined by the group memberships of the account with which the user is logged on to the network.

group policy The Microsoft Windows 2000 Microsoft Management Console (MMC) snap-in used to specify the behavior of users' desktops. A group policy object (GPO), which an administrator creates using the Group Policy snap-in, is the mechanism for configuring desktop settings.

group policy object (GPO) A collection of group policy settings. GPOs are essentially the documents created by the Group Policy snap-in. GPOs are stored at the domain level and they affect users and computers contained in sites, domains, and organizational units. In addition, each Microsoft Windows 2000 computer has exactly one group of settings stored locally, called the *local GPO*.

H

handshaking A term applied to network communications. Refers to the process by which information is transmitted between the sending and receiving devices to maintain and coordinate data flow between them. Proper handshaking ensures that the receiving device will be ready to accept data before the sending device transmits.

hierarchical name space A name space, such as the Domain Name System (DNS) and Active Directory service, that has a tiered structure that allows names and objects to be nested within each other.

histogram A chart consisting of horizontal or vertical bars, the widths or heights of which represent the values of certain data.

hop A unit of measurement used to quantify the length of a route between two computers on an internetwork, as indicated by the number of routers that packets must pass through to reach the destination end system. For example, if packets must be forwarded by four routers in the course of their journey from end system to end system, the destination is said to be four hops away from the source. Distance vector routing protocols like the Routing Information Protocol (RIP) use the number of hops as a means to compare the relative efficiency of routes.

host name The name of a device on a network. For a device on a Microsoft Windows 2000 network, this can be the same as the computer name.

Hosts An ASCII text file used by Transmission Control Protocol/Internet Protocol (TCP/IP) computers to resolve host names into IP addresses. The Hosts file is a simple list of the host names used by TCP/IP computers and their equivalent IP addresses. When a user or an application refers to a computer using a host name, the TCP/IP client looks it up in the Hosts file to determine its IP address. The Hosts file was the original name resolution method for what later became the Internet until the number of computers on the network grew too large to manage using this technique. Eventually, the Domain Name System (DNS) was created to perform the same function in a more efficient and manageable way. TCP/IP computers still have the ability to use a Hosts file for name resolution, but because the names and addresses of each computer must be added manually, this method is rarely used today.

HTTP *See* Hypertext Transfer Protocol (HTTP).

hub A hardware component to which cables running from computers and other devices are connected, joining all the devices into a network. In most cases, the term hub refers to an Ethernet multiport repeater, a device that amplifies the signals received from each connected device and forwards them to all the other devices simultaneously. *See also* multiport repeater.

Hypertext Transfer Protocol (HTTP) Application layer protocol that is the basis for World Wide Web communications. Web browsers generate HTTP GET request messages containing Uniform Resource Locators (URLs) and transmit them to Web servers, which reply with one or more HTTP Response messages containing the requested files. HTTP traffic is encapsulated using the Transmission Control Protocol (TCP) at the transport layer and the Internet Protocol (IP) at the network layer. Each HTTP transaction requires a separate TCP connection.

I

IANA *See* Internet Assigned Numbers Authority (IANA).

ICMP *See* Internet Control Message Protocol (ICMP).

IEEE *See* Institute of Electrical and Electronic Engineers (IEEE).

IEEE 802.2 Standard document published by the Institute of Electrical and Electronic Engineers (IEEE) defining the Logical Link Control (LLC) sublayer used by the IEEE 802.3, IEEE 802.5, and other protocols.

IEEE 802.3 Standard document published by the Institute of Electrical and Electronic Engineers (IEEE) defining what is commonly referred to as the Ethernet protocol. Although there are slight differences from the original DIX Ethernet standards, such as the omission of the Ethertype field and the separation of the data-link layer into two sublayers, the Media Access Control (MAC) sublayer and the Logical Link Control (LLC) sublayer, IEEE 802.3 retains the defining characteristics of Ethernet, including the Carrier Sense Multiple Access with Collision Detection (CSMA/CD) MAC mechanism. IEEE 802.3 also adds to the physical layer options defined in the DIX Ethernet standards by including support for unshielded twisted pair (UTP) cable.

IETF *See* Internet Engineering Task Force (IETF).

IIS *See* Internet Information Services (IIS).

IMAP *See* Internet Mail Access Protocol (IMAP).

in-addr.arpa domain A special top-level Domain Name System (DNS) domain reserved for reverse mapping of Internet Protocol (IP) addresses to DNS host names.

incremental zone transfer (IXFR) An alternate query type that some Domain Name System (DNS) servers can use to update and synchronize zone data when a zone is changed. When IXFR is supported between DNS servers, servers can keep track of and transfer only those incremental resource record changes between each version of the zone.

indirect route An Internet Protocol (IP) transmission to a destination on a different network, in which the Destination IP Address and the data-link layer protocol's Destination Address identify different computers. *Compare with* direct route, in which the IP destination is on the same network and the data-link layer Destination Address identifies the same computer as the Destination IP Address.

Institute of Electrical and Electronic Engineers (IEEE) An organization, founded in 1963, dedicated to the development and publication of standards for the computer and electronics industries. Best known in computer networking for the IEEE 802 series of documents defining the data-link layer local area network (LAN) protocols commonly known as Ethernet and Token Ring.

Integrated Services Digital Network (ISDN) A dial-up communications service that uses standard telephone lines to provide high-speed digital communications. Originally conceived as a replacement for the existing analog telephone service, it never achieved its anticipated popularity, Today, ISDN is used in the United States primarily as an Internet access technology, although it is more commonly used for wide area network (WAN) connections in Europe and Japan. The two most common ISDN services are the Basic Rate Interface (BRI), which provides two 64-kilobytes per second (Kbps) B channels and one 16-Kbps D (control) channel, and the Primary Rate Interface (PRI), which provides 23 64-Kbps B channels and one 64-Kbps D channel.

intermediate system On a Transmission Control Protocol/Internet Protocol (TCP/IP) network, a router that relays traffic generated by an end system from one network to another. The end systems in a TCP/IP transmission are identified by the Source IP Address and Destination IP Address fields in the IP header. All the other systems (that is, routers) involved in the transmission are known as intermediate systems.

International Organization for Standardization (ISO) An organization, founded in 1946, that consists of standards bodies from over 75 countries, such as the American National Standards Institute (ANSI) from the United States. The ISO is responsible for the publication of many computer-related standards, the best known of which is "The Basic Reference Model for Open Systems Interconnection," commonly known as the OSI reference model. (ISO is not an acronym; it's a name derived from the Greek word *isos,* meaning "equal.")

International Telecommunications Union (ITU) An organization, founded in 1865, devoted to the development of treaties, regulations, and standards governing telecommunications. Since 1992 it has included the standards development organization formerly known as the Comité Consultatif International Téléphonique et Télégraphique (CCITT), which was responsible for the creation of modem communication, compression, and error correction standards.

International Telecommunications Union-Telecommunication (ITU-T) The sector of the International Telecommunications Union (ITU) responsible for telecommunication standards. Its responsibilities include standardizing modem design and operations and standardizing protocols for networks and facsimile transmission. ITU is an international organization within which governments and the private sector coordinate global telecom networks and services.

internet *See* internetwork.

Internet A packet-switching internetwork that consists of thousands of individual networks and millions of computers around the world. No central managing body owns or administers the Internet; all administration chores are distributed among users all over the network.

Internet Assigned Numbers Authority (IANA) The organization responsible for the assignment of unique parameter values for the Transmission Control Protocol/Internet Protocol (TCP/IP) protocols, including IP address assignments for networks and protocol number assignments. The "Assigned Numbers" Requests for Comments (RFC) document (currently RFC 1700) lists all the protocol number assignments and many other unique parameters regulated by the IANA.

Internet Control Message Protocol (ICMP) A network layer Transmission Control Protocol/Internet Protocol (TCP/IP) protocol that carries administrative messages, particularly error messages and informational queries. ICMP error messages are primarily generated by intermediate systems that, because the packets they route travel no higher than the network layer, have no other means of signaling errors to the end system that transmitted the packet. Typical ICMP error messages inform the sender that the network or host to which a packet is addressed could not be found, or that the Time to Live value for a packet has expired. ICMP query messages request information (or simply a response) from other computers, and are the basis for TCP/IP utilities like Ping, which is used to test the ability of one computer on a network to communicate with another.

Internet Engineering Task Force (IETF) The primary standards ratification body for the Transmission Control Protocol/Internet Protocol (TCP/IP) protocol and the Internet. The IETF publishes Requests for Comments (RFCs), which are the working documents for what eventually become Internet standards. The IETF is an international body of network designers, operators, software programmers, and other technicians, all of whom devote part of their time to the development of Internet protocols and technologies.

Internet Information Services (IIS) Software services that support Web site creation, configuration, and management, along with other Internet functions. Microsoft Internet Information Services include Network News Transfer Protocol (NNTP), File Transfer Protocol (FTP), and Simple Mail Transfer Protocol (SMTP).

Internet Mail Access Protocol (IMAP) An application layer Transmission Control Protocol/Internet Protocol (TCP/IP) protocol used by e-mail clients to download mail messages from a server. E-mail traffic between servers and outgoing e-mail traffic from clients to servers use the Simple Mail Transfer Protocol (SMTP). *See also* Post Office Protocol 3 (POP3).

Internet Protocol (IP) The primary network layer protocol in the Transmission Control Protocol/Internet Protocol (TCP/IP) suite. IP is the protocol that is ultimately responsible for end-to-end communications on a TCP/IP internetwork, and it includes functions such as addressing, routing, and fragmentation. IP packages data that it receives from transport layer protocols into data units called datagrams by applying a header containing the information needed to transmit the data to its destination. The IP addressing system uses 32-bit addresses to uniquely identify the computers on a network and specifies the address of the destination system as part of the IP header. IP is also responsible for routing packets to their destinations on other networks by forwarding them to other routers on the network. When a datagram is too large to be transmitted over a particular network, IP breaks it into fragments and transmits each in a separate packet.

Internet service provider (ISP) A type of company whose business is supplying consumers or businesses with Internet access. At the consumer level, an ISP provides users with dial-up access to the ISP's networks, which are connected to the Internet, as well as other end-user services, such

as access to Domain Name System (DNS), e-mail, and news servers. At the business level, ISPs provide high-bandwidth Internet connections using leased telephone lines or other technologies and sometimes provide other services, such as registered IP addresses, Web site hosting, and DNS domain hosting.

internetwork A group of interconnected local area networks (LANs) or wide area networks (WANs), or both, that are connected so that any computer can transmit data to any other computer. The networks are connected by routers, which are responsible for relaying packets from one network to another. The largest example of an internetwork is the Internet, which is composed of thousands of networks around the world. Private internetworks consist of a smaller number of LANs, often at various locations and connected by WAN links.

Internetwork Packet Exchange (IPX) A network layer protocol used by Novell NetWare networks. IPX performs many of the same functions as the Internet Protocol (IP), but instead of being a self-contained addressing system like IP, IPX is designed for use on local area networks (LANs) only and uses a network identifier assigned by the network administrator plus the network interface adapter's hardware address to identify the individual computers on the network. Unlike IP, IPX is not based on an open standard. Novell owns all rights to the protocols of the IPX protocol suite, although Microsoft has developed its own IPX-compatible protocol for inclusion in the Microsoft Windows operating systems.

Intranet A Transmission Control Protocol/Internet Protocol (TCP/IP) network owned by a private organization that provides services such as Web sites only to that organization's users.

IP *See* Internet Protocol (IP).

IP address A 32-bit address assigned to Transmission Control Protocol/Internet Protocol (TCP/IP) client computers and other network equipment that uniquely identifies that device on the network. The IP uses IP addresses to transmit packets to the destinations. Expressed as four 8-bit decimal values separated by periods (for example, 192.168.71.19), the IP address consists of a network identifier (which specifies the network that the device is located on) and a host identifier (which identifies the particular device on that network). The sizes of the network and host identifiers can vary depending on the address class. For a computer to be accessible from the Internet, it must have an IP address containing a network identifier registered with the Internet Assigned Numbers Authority (IANA).

Ipconfig.exe A Microsoft Windows 2000 command-line utility used to view the Transmission Control Protocol/Internet Protocol (TCP/IP) configuration parameters for a particular computer. A graphical version of the tool, called Winipcfg.exe, is included with Windows 95, Windows 98, and Windows Me. Ipconfig.exe is most useful on computers with TCP/IP clients configured automatically by a Dynamic Host Configuration (DHCP) server because it is the easiest way to view the assigned settings for the client system. You can also use Ipconfig.exe to release and renew DHCP-assigned TCP/IP configuration parameters.

IPsec *See* IP Security protocol (IPsec).

IP Security protocol (IPsec) A set of Transmission Control Protocol/Internet Protocol (TCP/IP) protocol extensions designed to provide encrypted network layer communications. For computers to communicate using IPsec, they must share a public key.

IPv6 New version of the Internet Protocol (IP) that expands the IP address space from 32 to 128 bits. *See also* Internet Protocol (IP).

IPX *See* Internetwork Packet Exchange (IPX).

ISDN *See* Integrated Services Digital Network (ISDN).

ISO *See* International Organization for Standardization (ISO).

ISP *See* Internet service provider (ISP).

ITU *See* International Telecommunications Union (ITU).

ITU-T *See* International Telecommunications Union-Telecommunication (ITU-T).

IXFR *See* incremental zone transfer (IXFR).

K

Kbps Kilobits per second, a unit of measurement typically used to measure network transmission speed.

Kerberos V5 An Internet standard security protocol for handling authentication of user or system identity. With Kerberos V5, passwords that are sent across network lines are encrypted, not sent as plain text. Kerberos V5 also includes other security features.

L

LAN *See* local area network (LAN).

Layer 2 Tunneling Protocol (L2TP) A protocol used to establish virtual private network connections across the Internet. *See also* virtual private network (VPN).

layering The coordination of various protocols in a specific architecture that enables the protocols to work together to ensure that the data is prepared, transferred, received, and acted on as intended.

LDAP *See* Lightweight Directory Access Protocol (LDAP).

lease identification cookie A string that consists of a computer's Internet Protocol (IP) address and its hardware address, which a Dynamic Host Configuration Protocol (DHCP) server uses to uniquely identify a client in its database. *See also* Dynamic Host Configuration Protocol (DHCP).

Lightweight Directory Access Protocol (LDAP) The primary access protocol for the Active Directory service. LDAP version 3 is defined by a set of proposed standard documents published by the Internet Engineering Task Force (IETF), including RFC 2251.

link state protocol A dynamic routing protocol that rates the relative efficiency of network routes by the properties of the connections providing access to the destination. *Compare with* distance vector protocols, which use the number of hops to rate the efficiency of a network. The most common of the link state protocols is the Open Shortest Path First (OSPF) protocol.

local computer A computer that you can access directly without using a communications line or a communications device, such as a network card or a modem.

local group For computers running Microsoft Windows 2000 Professional and member servers, a group that can be granted permissions and rights from its own computer and (if the computer participates in a domain) user accounts and global groups both from its own domain and from trusted domains.

local user account For Microsoft Windows 2000 Server, a user account provided in a domain for a user whose global account is not in a trusted domain. A local account is not required where trust relationships exist between domains.

log file A file that stores messages generated by an application, service, or operating system. These messages are used to track the operations performed. Log files are usually plain text (ASCII) files and often have a .log extension.

LLC *See* Logical Link Control sublayer (LLC).

Lmhosts An ASCII text file used by Windows Transmission Control Protocol/Internet Protocol (TCP/IP) computers to resolve Network Basic Input/Output System (NetBIOS) names into IP addresses. Like the Hosts file used to resolve host names into IP addresses, an Lmhosts file is a list of the NetBIOS names assigned to computers on the network and their corresponding IP addresses. Lmhosts files can also contain special entries used to preload the computer's NetBIOS name cache or to identify the domain controllers on the network. Windows systems can use individual Lmhosts files for NetBIOS name resolution, but they more commonly use either network broadcast transmissions or the Windows Internet Name Service (WINS).

load balancing A technique used to scale the performance of a server-based program (such as a Web server) by distributing its client requests across multiple servers within the cluster. Typically, each host can specify the load percentage that it will handle, or the load can be equally distributed across all the hosts. If a host fails, the load is dynamically redistributed among the remaining hosts.

local area network (LAN) A collection of computers that are connected to each other using a shared medium. The computers communicate with each other using a common set of protocols. *Compare with* wide area network (WAN), metropolitan area network (MAN).

Logical Link Control (LLC) sublayer One of the two sublayers of the data-link layer defined by the Institute of Electrical and Electronic Engineers (IEEE) 802 standards. The LLC standard (IEEE 802.2) defines additional fields carried within the data field of data-link layer protocol headers. *See also* Media Access Control (MAC) sublayer.

M

MAC *See* Media Access Control (MAC).

management information base (MIB) The object-oriented database in which a network management agent stores the information that it will eventually transmit to a network management console using a protocol like the Simple Network Management Protocol (SNMP). Agents are built into network hardware and software products to enable them to report the status of the product to a central console monitored by a network administrator.

manual allocation An operational mode of Dynamic Host Configuration Protocol (DHCP) servers in which the server assigns clients IP addresses and other Transmission Control Protocol/Internet Protocol (TCP/IP) configuration settings specified by the server administrator for each computer. The IP addresses are not assigned randomly from a pool, as in the automatic and dynamic allocation modes. The result is no different from configuring the TCP/IP clients by hand, but using the manual allocation mode of a DHCP server prevents the administrator from having to travel to the client computer and prevents other computers on the network from being assigned duplicate addresses. Manual allocation is typically used for clients that must have a specific IP address, such as a Web server that must be accessible from the Internet using a DNS name. *See also* Dynamic Host Configuration Protocol (DHCP).

master server An authoritative Domain Name System (DNS) server for a zone. Master servers can vary and will be one of two types (either primary or secondary masters), depending on how the server obtains its zone data.

maximum transmission unit (MTU) The largest physical packet size that a system can transmit over a network. As packets are routed through an internetwork, they might have to pass through individual networks with different MTUs. When a packet exceeds the MTU for a particular network, the network layer protocol (Internet Protocol [IP],

in most cases) divides the packet into fragments smaller than the MTU for the outgoing network. The protocol then repackages each fragment into a separate packet and transmits them. If necessary, fragments can be split into still smaller fragments by other routers along the way to the destination. Packets remain fragmented for the rest of their journey and are not reassembled until they reach the end system that is the packet's ultimate destination.

MB Megabyte, equal to 1000 kilobytes or 1,000,000 bytes.

MBps Megabytes per second, a unit of measurement typically used to measure the speed of data storage devices.

Mbps Megabits per second, a unit of measurement typically used to measure network transmission speed.

media In networking, a term used to describe the data-carrying hardware mechanism that computers and other network devices use to send information to each other. In computers, a term used to describe a means of storing data in a permanent fashion, such as a hard or floppy disk.

Media Access Control (MAC) A method by which computers determine when they can transmit data over a shared network medium. When multiple computers are connected to a single network segment, two computers transmitting data at the same time cause a collision, which destroys the data. The MAC mechanism implemented in the data-link layer protocol prevents these collisions from occurring or permits them to occur in a controlled manner. The MAC mechanism is the defining characteristic of a data-link layer local area network (LAN) protocol. The two most common MAC mechanisms in use today are Carrier Sense Multiple Access with Collision Detection (CSMA/CD), which is used by Ethernet networks, and token passing, which is used by Token Ring and Fiber Distributed Data Interface (FDDI) networks, among others.

Media Access Control (MAC) sublayer One of the two sublayers of the data-link layer defined by the Institute of Electrical and Electronic Engineers (IEEE) 802 standards. The MAC sublayer defines the mechanism used to regulate access to the network medium. *See also* Logical Link Control (LLC) sublayer.

member server A computer that runs Microsoft Windows 2000 Server but is not a domain controller of a Windows 2000 domain. Member servers participate in a domain but do not store a copy of the directory database. For a member server, permissions can be set on resources that allow users to connect to the server and use its resources. Resource permissions can be granted for domain global groups and users as well as for local groups and users.

Metric A field in a Transmission Control Protocol/Internet Protocol (TCP/IP) computer's routing table that contains a value rating the relative efficiency of a particular route. When routing packets, a router scans its routing table for the desired destination, and if there are two possible routes to that destination listed in the table, the router chooses the one with the lowest metric value. Depending on how the routing information is inserted into the table, the metric can represent the number of hops needed to reach the destination network, or it can contain a value that reflects the actual time needed to reach the destination.

MIB *See* management information base (MIB).

Microsoft Management Console (MMC) A framework for hosting administrative tools, called consoles. A console may contain tools, folders, or other containers, World Wide Web pages, and other administrative items. These items are displayed in the left pane of the console, called a console tree. A console has one or more windows that can provide views of the console tree. The main MMC window provides commands and tools for authoring consoles. The authoring features of MMC and the console tree itself may be hidden when a console is in User Mode.

minimal routing The process of routing Internet Protocol (IP) using only the default routing table entries created by the operating system. *Compare with* static routing, dynamic routing.

mixed mode The default domain mode setting on Microsoft Windows 2000 domain controllers. Mixed mode enables Windows NT backup domain controllers and Windows 2000 domain controllers to coexist in a domain. Mixed mode does not support the universal and nested group enhancements of Windows 2000. The domain mode setting can be changed to Windows 2000 native mode when all Windows NT domain controllers are removed from a domain.

MMC *See* Microsoft Management Console (MMC).

modem Short for modulator/demodulator, a hardware device that converts the digital signals generated by computers into analog signals suitable for transmission over a telephone line, and back again. A dial-up connection between two computers requires a modem at each end, both of which support the same communication protocols. Modems take the form of internal devices that plug into one of a computer's expansion slots or external devices that connect to one of the computer's serial ports. The term modem is also used incorrectly, in many cases, to describe any device that provides a connection to a wide area communications service, such as a cable television or Digital Subscriber Line (DSL) connection. These devices are not actually modems because the service is digital, and no analog/ digital conversion takes place.

MTU *See* maximum transmission unit (MTU).

multicast A network transmission with a destination address that represents a group of computers on the network. Transmission Control Protocol/Internet Protocol (TCP/IP) multicast addresses are defined by the Internet Assigned Numbers Authority (IANA) and represent groups of computers with similar functions, such as all the routers on a network. *Compare with* broadcast and unicast.

multihomed A computer with two or more network interfaces, whether they take the form of network interface adapters, dial-up connections using modems, or other technologies. On a Transmission Control Protocol/Internet Protocol (TCP/IP) network, each of the network interfaces in a multihomed computer must have its own IP address.

multiple master replication A technique usually associated with a directory service, in which identical copies of a database are maintained on various computers scattered throughout a network. In multiple master replication, users can make changes to any copy of the database, and the changes to that copy are replicated to all the other copies. This is a complex technique because it is possible for different users to make changes to the same record on different masters. The system must therefore have a mechanism for reconciling data conflicts in the various masters, such as using time stamps or version numbers to assign priorities to data modifications. Microsoft's Active Directory service uses multiple master replication. *Compare with* single master replication.

multiplexing Any one of several techniques used to transmit multiple signals over a single cable or other network medium simultaneously. Multiplexing works by separating the available bandwidth of the network medium into separate bands, by frequency, wavelength, time, or other criteria, and transmitting a different signal in each band. Local area network (LAN) media carry only one signal and therefore do not use multiplexing, but some networks, such as cable television and telephone networks, do.

multiport repeater A network connection device used primarily on Ethernet networks that propagates signals received through any of its ports out through all its other ports and also amplifies the signals so they can travel longer distances. Also called a hub.

N

name resolution The process of converting a computer or other device's name into an address. Computers communicate using numeric addresses, but humans work better with names. To be able to send data to a particular destination identified by name in the user interface, the computer must first resolve that name into an address. On Transmission Control Protocol/Internet Protocol (TCP/IP) networks, for example, Domain Name System (DNS) names and Network Basic Input/Output System (NetBIOS) names must be resolved into IP addresses. Computers can use several name resolution methods, depending on the type of name and type of address involved, including table lookups using text files such as Hosts and Lmhosts; independent processes, such as broadcast message generation; and network services, such as DNS and the Windows Internet Name Service (WINS). *Compare with* Address Resolution Protocol (ARP).

name space A set of unique names for resources or items used in a shared computing environment. For MMC, the name space is represented by the console tree, which displays all the snap-ins and resources that are accessible to a console. For DNS, name space is the vertical or hierarchical structure of the domain name tree. For example, each domain label, such as host1, used in a fully qualified domain name, such as host1.example.microsoft.com, indicates a branch in the domain name space tree.

NAT *See* network address translation (NAT).

native mode The condition in which all domain controllers in the domain have been upgraded to Microsoft Windows 2000 and an administrator has enabled native mode operation (through the Active Directory Domains and Trusts console).

Nbtstat.exe A Windows command-line utility that displays information about the Network Basic Input/Output System (NetBIOS) over Transmission Control Protocol/Internet Protocol (TCP/IP) connections that the system uses when communicating with other Windows computers on a TCP/IP network.

NDIS *See* Network Driver Interface Specification (NDIS).

NDS *See* Novell Directory Services (NDS).

NetBEUI *See* NetBIOS Extended User Interface (NetBEUI).

NetBIOS An application programming interface (API) that provides computers with a name space and other local area networking functions.

NetBIOS Extended User Interface (NetBEUI) Transport protocol sometimes used by the Microsoft Windows operating systems for local area networking. NetBEUI was the default protocol in the first version of Windows NT and in Windows for Workgroups; it has since been replaced as the default Windows protocol by Transmission Control Protocol/Internet Protocol (TCP/IP). NetBEUI is a simplified networking protocol that requires no configuration and is self-adjusting. However, the protocol is suitable only for small networks because it is not routable. NetBEUI identifies computers by the Network Basic Input/Output System (NetBIOS) names (or computer names) assigned during the Windows installation. Because NetBIOS uses no network identifier, there is no way for the protocol to route traffic to systems on another network.

Netstat.exe A command-line utility supplied with Windows operating systems, which displays information about a Transmission Control Protocol/Internet Protocol (TCP/IP) computer's current network connections and about the traffic generated by the various TCP/IP protocols.

network address translation (NAT) A firewall technique that enables Transmission Control Protocol/Internet Protocol (TCP/IP) client computers using unregistered IP addresses to access the Internet. Client computers send their Internet service requests to a NAT-equipped router, which substitutes its own registered IP address for the client's unregistered address and forwards the request on to the specified server. The server sends its reply to the NAT router, which then relays it back to the original client. This renders the unregistered clients invisible to the Internet, preventing direct access to them. *See also* firewall.

network analyzers Network troubleshooting tools, sometimes called *protocol analyzers*. They perform real-time network traffic analysis and capture packets for decoding and analysis. They can also generate statistics based on the network traffic to help create a picture of the network's cabling, software, file server, clients, and network interface cards (NICs).

Network Driver Interface Specification (NDIS) A multiprotocol device driver interface used by the Microsoft Windows operating system for its network interface adapter drivers. The NDIS driver enables a single adapter and its data-link layer protocol to support traffic generated by the Transmission Control Protocol/Internet Protocol (TCP/IP), Internetwork Packet Exchange (IPX), and NetBEUI protocols, in any combination.

network interface adapter A hardware device that provides a computer with access to a local area network (LAN). Network interface adapters can be integrated into a computer's motherboard or take the form of an expansion card, in which case they are called network interface cards (NICs). The adapter, along with its driver, implements the data-link layer protocol on the computer. The adapter has one or more connectors for network cables or some other interface to the network medium. The network interface adapter and its driver are responsible for functions such as the encapsulation of network layer protocol data into data-link layer protocol frames, the encoding and decoding of data into the signals used by the network medium, and the implementation of the protocol's Media Access Control (MAC) mechanism.

network layer The third layer from the bottom of the Open Systems Interconnection (OSI) reference model. Protocols operating at the network layer are responsible for packaging transport layer data into datagrams, addressing them to its final destination, routing them across the internetwork, and fragmenting the datagrams as needed. The Internet Protocol (IP) is the most common protocol operating at the network layer, although Novell NetWare networks use a proprietary network layer protocol called Internetwork Packet Exchange (IPX).

Network Time Protocol (NTP) An application layer Transmission Control Protocol/Internet Protocol (TCP/IP) protocol used to synchronize the clocks in network computers.

NIC *See* network interface adapter.

NLP *See* normal link pulse (NLP).

node Any uniquely addressable device on a network, such as a computer, router, or printer.

normal link pulse (NLP) The signal generated by standard Ethernet network interface adapters and hubs, which the devices use to signal that they have been cabled together properly. When an adapter or hub receives the NLP signal from the device to which it's connected, it lights up a light-emitting diode (LED), which indicates that communication is taking place. *Compare with* the fast link pulse (FLP) signals used by Fast Ethernet devices.

notify list A list maintained by the primary master for a zone of other Domain Name System (DNS) servers that should be notified when zone changes occur. The notify list is made up of Internet Protocol (IP) addresses for DNS servers configured as secondary masters for the zone. When the listed servers are notified of a change to the zone, they initiate a zone transfer with another DNS server and update the zone.

Novell Directory Services (NDS) Formerly known as NetWare Directory Services, the first hierarchical, object-oriented directory service to achieve commercial success. NDS was first released as part of NetWare 4.0 in 1993 and has matured into a robust product that now supports other platforms in addition to NetWare, such as UNIX, Microsoft Windows NT, and Windows 2000. NDS provides networks with single logon capabilities and the ability to support third-party applications through the use of schema extensions. *See also* directory service.

Novell NetWare One of the leading network operating systems.

Nslookup.exe A command-line utility that enables you to generate Domain Name System (DNS) queries and send them to specific name servers for testing and troubleshooting your DNS installation.

NTFS NTFS file system is one of the file systems included with the Microsoft Windows 2000 and Windows NT operating systems. Compared to the file allocation table (FAT) file system also supported by Windows, NTFS supports larger volumes, includes transaction logs to aid in recovery from disk failures, and enables network administrators to control access to specific directories and files. The main drawback to NTFS is that the drives are not accessible by any operating systems other than Windows 2000 and Windows NT. If you boot the computer with an MS-DOS disk, for example, the NTFS drives are invisible.

O

object An entity such as a file, folder, shared folder, printer, or Active Directory object described by a distinct, named set of attributes. For example, the attributes of a file object include its name, location, and size; the attributes of an Active Directory user object might include the user's first name, last name, and e-mail address.

Open Shortest Path First (OSPF) A dynamic routing protocol that exchanges information with other routers on the network to update the system's routing table with current information about the configuration of the internetwork. OSPF is a link state protocol that evaluates routes based on their actual performance, rather than using a less accurate measurement like the number of hops needed to reach a particular destination. *Compare with* distance vector protocol, in general, and the Routing Information Protocol (RIP), in particular.

Open Systems Interconnection (OSI) reference model A theoretical model defined in documents published by the International Organization for Standardization (ISO) and the Telecommunication Standards Section of the International Telecommunication Union (ITU-T) used for reference and teaching purposes that divides the computer networking functions into seven layers: application, presentation, session, transport, network, datalink, and physical (from top to bottom). However, the layers do not correspond exactly to any of the currently used networking protocol stacks.

operating system The primary program running on a computer, which processes input and output, runs other programs, and provides access to the computer's hardware.

organizational unit (OU) A type of Active Directory container object used within domains. OUs are logical containers into which you can place users, groups, computers, and other OUs. An OU can contain objects only from its parent domain. An OU is the smallest scope to which you can apply a group policy or delegate authority.

organizationally unique identifier (OUI) The three-byte hexadecimal value assigned by the Institute of Electrical and Electronic Engineers (IEEE) identifying the manufacturer of a network interface adapter, which is used as the first three bytes of the adapter's hardware address.

OSI *See* Open Systems Interconnection (OSI) reference model.

OSPF *See* Open Shortest Path First (OSPF).

OU *See* organizational unit (OU).

OUI *See* organizationally unique identifier (OUI).

owner In Microsoft Windows 2000, the person who controls how permissions are set on objects and grants permissions to others.

P

packet The largest unit of data that can be transmitted over a data network at any one time. Messages generated by applications are split into pieces and packaged into individual packets for transmission over the network. Each packet is transmitted separately and can take a different route to the destination. When all the packets arrive at the destination, the receiving computer reassembles them into the original message. This is the basic functionality of a packet-switching network.

packet filtering A firewall technique in which a router is configured to prevent certain packets from entering a network. Packet filters can be created based on hardware addresses, Internet Protocol (IP) addresses, port numbers, or other criteria. For example, you can configure a router to allow only certain computers to access the network from the Internet or allow your network users access to Internet e-mail but deny them access to Internet Web servers. Although typically used to prevent intrusion into a private network from the Internet, you can also use packet filtering to limit access to one of the local area networks (LANs) on a private internetwork.

parent domain In the Domain Name System (DNS), a domain that is located in the name space tree directly above other derivative domain names (child domains). For example, microsoft.com would be the parent domain of example.microsoft.com, a child domain.

password A security measure used to restrict logon names to user accounts and access to computer systems and resources. A password is a unique string of characters that must be provided before a logon name or an access is authorized. For Microsoft Windows 2000, a password for a user account can be up to 14 characters long and is case-sensitive.

path A sequence of directory (or folder) names that specifies the location of a directory, file, or folder within the directory tree. Each directory name and filename within the path (except for the first) must be preceded by a backslash (\).

PDC *See* primary domain controller (PDC).

PDU *See* protocol data unit (PDU).

performance alert A Microsoft Windows 2000 feature that detects when a predefined counter value rises above or falls below the configured threshold and notifies a user by means of the Messenger service.

performance counter In System Monitor, a data item associated with a performance object. For each counter selected, System Monitor presents a value corresponding to a particular aspect of the performance defined for the performance object.

Performance Logs and Alerts A tool that provides you with the ability to create counter logs, trace logs, and system alerts automatically from local or remote computers.

performance monitor A tool for monitoring network performance that can display statistics, such as the number of packets sent and received, server-processor utilization, and the amount of data going into and out of the server.

performance object In System Monitor, a logical collection of counters that is associated with a resource or service that can be monitored.

performance object instance In System Monitor, a term used to distinguish between multiple performance objects of the same type on a computer.

physical layer The bottom layer of the Open Systems Interconnection (OSI) reference model, which defines the nature of the network medium itself, how it should be installed, and what types of signals it should carry. In the case of local area networking, the physical layer is closely related to the data-link layer immediately above it because the data-link layer protocol includes the physical layer specifications.

Ping A Transmission Control Protocol/Internet Protocol (TCP/IP) command-line utility used to test whether a computer can communicate with another computer on the network. Ping generates Internet Control Message Protocol (ICMP) Echo Request messages and transmits them to the computer specified on the command line. The target computer, on receiving the messages, transmits them back to the sender as ICMP Echo Replies. The system running Ping then displays the elapsed times between the transmission of the requests and the receipt of the replies. Virtually every TCP/IP client implementation includes a version of Ping.

PKI *See* public key infrastructure (PKI).

Plain Old Telephone Service (POTS) Common phrase referring to the Public Switched Telephone Network (PSTN), the standard copper-cable telephone network used for analog voice communications around the world. *See* Public Switched Telephone Network.

Plug and Play A set of specifications that enables a computer to automatically detect and configure a hardware device and install the appropriate device drivers.

pointer (PTR) resource record A resource record used in a reverse lookup zone created within the in-addr.arpa domain to designate a reverse mapping of a host Internet Protocol (IP) address to a host Domain Name System (DNS) domain name.

Point-to-Point Protocol (PPP) A data-link layer Transmission Control Protocol/Internet Protocol (TCP/IP) protocol used for wide area network (WAN) connections, especially dial-up connections to the Internet and other service providers. Unlike its progenitor, the Serial Line Internet Protocol (SLIP), PPP includes support for multiple network layer protocols, link quality monitoring protocols, and authentication protocols. PPP is used for connections between two computers only, and therefore does not need many of the features found in local area network (LAN) protocols, such as address fields for each packet and a Media Access Control (MAC) mechanism.

Point-to-Point Tunneling Protocol (PPTP) A data-link layer protocol used to provide secured communications for virtual private network (VPN) connections. VPNs are private network connections that use the Internet as a network medium. To secure the data as it is transmitted across the Internet, the computers use a process called tunneling, in which the entire data-link layer frame generated by an application process is encapsulated within an Internet Protocol (IP) datagram. This arrangement violates the rules of the Open Systems Interconnection (OSI) reference model, but it enables the entire PPP frame generated by the user application to be encrypted inside an IP datagram.

policy The mechanism by which computer settings are configured automatically, as defined by the administrator. Depending on context, this can refer to Microsoft Windows 2000 group policy, a remote access server (RAS) policy, a Windows NT 4 system policy, or a specific setting in a group policy object (GPO).

POP3 *See* Post Office Protocol 3 (POP3).

port A code number identifying a process running on a Transmission Control Protocol/Internet Protocol (TCP/IP) computer. Transport layer protocols, such as the Transmission Control Protocol (TCP) and the User Datagram Protocol (UDP), specify the port number of the source and destination application processes in the header of each message they create. The combination of an IP address and a port number is called a socket; it identifies a specific application on a specific computer on a specific network. Port numbers lower than 1024 are called well-known port numbers, which the Internet Assigned Numbers Authority (IANA) assigns to common applications. The TCP port number 80, for example, is the well-known port number for Web servers. Port numbers 1024 and above are ephemeral port numbers, which are selected at random by clients for each transaction they initiate with a server. Because of tremendous growth in network applications many of these high ports have been put to use. For example, Microsoft Terminal Services uses TCP port 3389. Alternatively, a port is a hardware connector in a computer or other network device that is used to attach cables that run to other devices.

Post Office Protocol 3 (POP3) An application layer Transmission Control Protocol/Internet Protocol (TCP/IP) protocol used by e-mail clients to download messages from an e-mail server. E-mail traffic between servers and outgoing e-mail traffic from clients to servers uses the Simple Mail Transfer Protocol (SMTP). *See also* Internet Mail Access Protocol (IMAP).

POTS *See* Plain Old Telephone Service (POTS).

PPP *See* Point-to-Point Protocol (PPP).

PPTP *See* Point-to-Point Tunneling Protocol (PPTP).

presentation layer The second layer from the top of the Open Systems Interconnection (OSI) reference model, which is responsible for translating the syntaxes used by different types of computers on a network. A computer translates the data generated by its applications from its own abstract syntax to a common transport syntax suitable for transmission over the network. When the data arrives at its destination, the presentation layer on the receiving system translates the transfer syntax into the computer's own native abstract syntax.

primary domain controller (PDC) On a Microsoft Windows NT network, the server that maintains the master copy of the domain's user-accounts database and validates logon requests. Every NT domain is required to have one, and only one, PDC. *See also* domain, domain controller.

primary master An authoritative Domain Name System (DNS) server for a zone that can be used as a point of update for the zone. Only primary masters have the ability to be updated directly to process zone updates, which include adding, removing, or modifying resource records that are stored as zone data. Primary masters are also used as the first sources for replicating the zone to other DNS servers.

primary zone database file The master zone database file. Changes to a zone, such as adding domains or hosts, are performed on the server that contains the primary zone database file.

private key The secret half of a cryptographic key pair that is used with a public key algorithm. Private keys are typically used to decrypt a symmetric session key, digitally sign data, or decrypt data that has been encrypted with the corresponding public key.

promiscuous mode Operational mode available in some network interface adapters that causes the adapter to read and process all the packets transmitted over the local area network (LAN), and not just the packets addressed to it. Protocol analyzers use promiscuous mode to capture comprehensive samples of network traffic for later analysis.

protocol A documented format for the transmission of data between two networked devices. A protocol is essentially a "language" that a computer uses to communicate, and the other computer to which it is connected must use the same language for communication to take place. In most cases, network communication protocols are defined by open standards created by bipartisan committees. However, there are still a few proprietary protocols in use. Computers use many different protocols to communicate, which has given rise to the Open Systems Interconnection (OSI) reference model, which defines the layers at which different protocols operate.

Protocol An ASCII text file found on Transmission Control Protocol/Internet Protocol (TCP/IP) systems that lists the codes used in the Protocol field of the Internet Protocol (IP) header. This field identifies the transport layer protocol that generated the data carried within the datagram, ensuring that the data reaches the appropriate process on the receiving computer. The protocol numbers are registered by the Internet Assigned Numbers Authority (IANA) and are derived from the "Assigned Numbers" Request for Comments document.

protocol analyzers *See* network analyzers.

protocol data unit (PDU) A generic term for the data constructions created by the protocols operating at the various layers of the Open Systems Interconnection (OSI) reference model. For example, the PDU created by data-link layer protocols are called frames, and network layer PDUs are called datagrams.

protocol driver The driver responsible for offering four or five basic services to other layers in the network, while "hiding" the details of how the services are actually implemented. Services performed include session management, datagram service, data segmentation and sequencing, acknowledgment, and possibly routing across a wide area network (WAN).

protocol stack The multilayered arrangement of communications protocols that provides a data path ranging from the user application to the network medium. Although based on the Open Systems Interconnection (OSI) reference model, not every layer in the model is represented by a separate protocol. On a computer connected to a local area network (LAN), for example, the protocol stack generally consists of protocols at the application, transport, network, and data-link layers, the latter of which includes a physical layer specification.

proxy server An application layer firewall technique that enables Transmission Control Protocol/Internet Protocol (TCP/IP) client systems to access Internet resources without being susceptible to intrusion from outside the network. A proxy server is an application that runs on a computer with a registered IP address, whereas the clients use unregistered IP addresses, causing them to remain invisible from the Internet. Client applications are configured to send their Internet service requests to the proxy server instead of directly to the Internet, and the proxy server relays the requests to the appropriate Internet server, using its own registered address. On receiving a response from the Internet server, the proxy server relays it back to the original client. Proxy servers are designed for specific applications, and the client must be configured with the address of the proxy server. Administrators can also configure the proxy server to cache Internet information for later use and to restrict access to particular Internet sites. *See also* firewall. *Compare with* network address translation (NAT).

PSTN *See* Public Switched Telephone Network (PSTN).

public key The nonsecret half of a cryptographic key pair that is used with a public key algorithm. Public keys are typically used when encrypting a session key, verifying a digital signature, or encrypting data that can be decrypted with the corresponding private key.

public key cryptography A method of cryptography in which two different keys are used: a public key for encrypting data and a private key for decrypting data.

public key infrastructure (PKI) The term generally used to describe the laws, policies, standards, and software that regulate or manipulate certificates and public and private keys. In practice, it is a system of digital certificates, certification authorities, and other registration authorities that verify and authenticate the validity of each party involved in an electronic transaction. Standards for PKI are still evolving, even though they are being widely implemented as a necessary element of electronic commerce.

Public Switched Telephone Network (PSTN) The standard copper-cable telephone network used for analog voice communications around the world. Also known as Plain Old Telephone Service (POTS).

Q

query A specific request for data retrieval, modification, or deletion.

R

RADIUS *See* Remote Authentication Dial-In User Service (RADIUS).

RARP *See* Reverse Address Resolution Protocol (RARP).

RAS *See* Remote Access Server (RAS).

redirector A network client component that determines whether a resource requested by an application is located on the network or on the local system and sends the request either to the local input/output system or to the networking protocol stack. A computer can have multiple redirectors to support different networks, such as a Microsoft Windows network and a Novell NetWare network.

refresh To update displayed information with current data.

refresh interval A period of time used by secondary masters of a zone to determine how often to check if their zone data needs to be refreshed. When the refresh interval expires, the secondary master checks with its source for the zone to see if its zone data is still current or if it needs to be updated using a zone transfer. This interval is set in the SOA (start-of-authority) resource record for each zone.

remote access Part of the integrated Microsoft Windows 2000 Routing and Remote Access service that provides remote networking for telecommuters, mobile workers, and system administrators who monitor and manage servers at multiple branch offices. Users with a computer running Windows 2000 and Network and Dial-Up Connections can dial in to remotely access their networks for services such as file and printer sharing, electronic mail, scheduling, and SQL database access.

Remote Access Server (RAS) Any Microsoft Windows 2000–based computer configured to accept remote access connections.

Remote Authentication Dial-In User Service (RADIUS) A security authentication protocol based on clients and servers and widely used by Internet service providers (ISPs) on non-Microsoft remote servers. RADIUS is the most popular means of authenticating and authorizing dial-up and tunneled network users today.

remote computer A computer that can be accessed only by using a communications line or a communications device, such as a network card or a modem.

remote user A user who dials in to the server over modems and telephone lines from a remote location.

replication The process of copying data from a data store or file system to multiple computers to synchronize the data. The Active Directory service provides multiple-master replication of the directory between domain controllers within a given domain. The replicas of the directory on each domain controller are writeable, enabling administrators to apply updates to any replica of a given domain. The replication service automatically copies the changes from a given replica to all other replicas.

Request for Comments (RFC) A document published by the Internet Engineering Task Force (IETF) that contains information about a topic related to the Internet or to the Transmission Control Protocol/Internet Protocol (TCP/IP) suite. For example, all the TCP/IP protocols have been documented and published as RFCs and eventually might be ratified as Internet standards. Some RFCs are only informational or historical, however, and are not submitted for ratification as a standard. After they are published and assigned numbers, RFCs are never changed. If a new version of an RFC document is published, it is assigned a new number and cross-indexed to indicate that it renders the old version obsolete.

requester (LAN requester) Software that resides in a computer and forwards requests for network services from the computer's application programs to the appropriate server. *See also* redirector.

resolver Another name for the Domain Name System (DNS) client found on every Transmission Control Protocol/Internet Protocol (TCP/IP) computer. Whenever the computer attempts to access a TCP/IP system using a DNS name, the resolver generates a DNS Request message and sends it to the DNS server specified in the computer's TCP/IP client configuration. The DNS server then takes the necessary steps to resolve the requested name into an IP address and returns the address to the resolver in the client computer. The resolver can then furnish the IP address to the TCP/IP client, which uses it to transmit a message to the desired destination. *See also* Domain Name System (DNS).

resource Any part of a computer system. Users on a network can share computer resources, such as hard disks, printers, modems, CD-ROM drives, and even the processor.

resource record The unit in which a Domain Name System (DNS) server stores information about a particular computer. The information stored in a resource record depends on the type of record it is, but typically a resource record includes the host name of a computer and its equivalent IP address. In most cases, administrators must manually create the resource records on a DNS server, but recent additions to the DNS standards define a method for dynamically updating the information in resource records as needed. This capability is central to the DNS functionality required by the Active Directory service. *See also* Domain Name System (DNS).

Reverse Address Resolution Protocol (RARP) Progenitor of the Bootstrap Protocol (BOOTP) and the Dynamic Host Configuration Protocol (DHCP), an alternative mode of the Address Resolution Protocol (ARP) that enables a computer to retrieve an Internet Protocol (IP) address from an RARP server by broadcasting its hardware address. Designed for use on diskless workstations, RARP is limited in that it can receive only an IP address from the server and not other Transmission Control Protocol/Internet Protocol (TCP/IP) configuration parameters,

and also in that an administrator must manually configure the RARP server with a specific IP address for every RARP client.

reverse lookup In Domain Name System (DNS), a query process by which the Internet Protocol (IP) address of a host computer is searched to find its friendly DNS domain name.

reverse name resolution The process of resolving an Internet Protocol (IP) address into a Domain Name System (DNS) name, which is the opposite of the normal name-to-address resolution performed by DNS servers. Reverse DNS name resolution is accomplished using an extension to the DNS name space consisting of a domain called in-addr.arpa, which contains four levels of subdomains named using the numbers 0 through 255. These subdomains contain resource records called pointers; each pointer contains an IP address and its equivalent DNS name. A DNS server looks up an IP address by locating the domain name equivalent to the address. For example, the IP address 192.168.1.15 becomes the domain name 15.1.168.192.in-addr-arpa.

RFC *See* Request for Comments (RFC).

RIP *See* Routing Information Protocol (RIP).

root domain The domain at the top of the DNS name space hierarchy, represented as a period (.).

root name server One of a handful of servers that represent the top of the Domain Name System (DNS) name space by supplying other DNS servers with the Internet Protocol (IP) addresses of the authoritative servers for all the top-level domains in the DNS. When resolving a DNS name into an IP address, a DNS server that is unable to resolve the name itself sends a DNS request to one of the root name servers identified in the server's configuration. The root name server reads the top-level domain (that is, the last word, such as *com* in *www.microsoft.com*) from the requested name and supplies the requesting server with the IP address for that top-level domain. The requesting server then transmits the same request to the top-level domain server that the root name server supplied. The root name servers are also the authoritative servers for some of the top-level domains, so they can eliminate a step from the process and supply the address of the second-level domain's authoritative server. *See also* Domain Name System (DNS), authoritative server.

routed A UNIX daemon, pronounced "route-dee," that was the original implementation of the Routing Information Protocol (RIP), the most popular of the distance vector routing protocols. *See also* distance vector protocol, dynamic routing.

router A network layer hardware or software device that connects two networks and relays traffic between them as needed. Using a table containing information about the other routers on the network, a router examines the destination address of each packet it receives, selects the most efficient route to that destination, and forwards the packet to the router or computer that is the next step in its path. Routers can connect two local area networks (LANs) or provide access to remote resources by connecting a LAN to a distant network using a wide area network (WAN) link. One of the most common scenarios involves using routers to connect a LAN to the network of an Internet service provider (ISP), thus providing Internet access to all the LAN's users.

Routing Information Protocol (RIP) A dynamic routing protocol that enables routers to receive information about the other routers on the network, which enables them to keep their routing tables updated with the latest information. RIP works by generating at frequent intervals broadcast messages that contain the contents of the router's routing table. Other routers use this information to update their own tables, thus spreading the routing information all over the network. Routers also take the absence of RIP messages from a particular router to be a sign that it's not functioning and then remove that router from their tables after a given interval. RIP is frequently criticized for the large amount of broadcast traffic that it generates on the network and for the limitations of its distance vector routing method, which evaluates routes based solely on the number of hops between the source and the destination. *See also* distance vector protocol, dynamic routing.

routing table A list maintained in every Transmission Control Protocol/Internet Protocol (TCP/IP) computer of network destinations and the routers and interfaces that the computer should use to transmit to them. In a computer that is not a router, the routing table contains only a few entries, the most frequently used of which is the default gateway entry. On a router, the routing table can contain a great many entries that are either manually added by a network administrator or automatically created by a dynamic routing protocol. When there is more than one routing table entry for a specific destination, the computer selects the best route based on a metric, which is a rating of the route's relative efficiency.

S

scope The pool of Internet Protocol (IP) addresses on a given subnet that a Dynamic Host Configuration Protocol (DHCP) server is configured to assign to clients when using the automatic or dynamic allocation method. *See also* Dynamic Host Configuration Protocol (DHCP), automatic allocation, dynamic allocation.

secondary master An authoritative Domain Name System (DNS) server for a zone that is used as a source for replication of the zone to other servers. Secondary masters update their zone data only by transferring zone data from other DNS servers. They do not have the ability to perform zone updates.

second-level domains Domain names that are rooted hierarchically at the second tier of the domain name space directly beneath the top-level domain names such as .com and .org. When Domain Name System (DNS) is used on the Internet, second-level domains are names, such as microsoft.com, that are registered and delegated to individual organizations and businesses according to their top-level classification. The organization then assumes further responsibility for parenting management and growth of its name into additional subdomains.

Secure Hypertext Transfer Protocol (S-HTTP or HTTPS) A security protocol that provides authentication and encryption services to Web client/server transactions. *See also* Hypertext Transfer Protocol (HTTP).

Secure Sockets Layer (SSL) A security protocol that provides authentication and encryption services to Web client/server transactions. *See also* Hypertext Transfer Protocol (HTTP).

security Making computers and data stored on them safe from harm or unauthorized access.

security log An event log containing information about security events that are specified in the audit policy.

segment A section of a network that is bounded by hubs, bridges, routers, or switches. Depending on the data-link layer protocol and type of cable being used, a segment may consist of more than one length of cable. For example, a thin Ethernet network uses separate pieces of coaxial cable to connect each computer to the next one on the bus, but all those pieces of cable together are called a segment.

Sequenced Packet Exchange (SPX) A connection-oriented transport-layer protocol that is part of Novell's IPX protocol suite. *See also* Internetwork Packet Exchange (IPX).

Serial Line Internet Protocol (SLIP) A data-link layer Transmission Control Protocol/Internet Protocol (TCP/IP) protocol used for wide area network (WAN) connections, especially dial-up connections to the Internet and other service providers. Because it is used for connections between two computers only, SLIP does not need many of the features found in local area network (LAN) protocols, such as address fields for each packet and a Media Access Control (MAC) mechanism. SLIP is the simplest of protocols, consisting only of a single End Delimiter byte that is transmitted after each IP datagram. Unlike its successor, the Point-to-Point Protocol (PPP), SLIP has no inherent security capabilities or any other additional services. For this reason, it is rarely used today.

server A computer that provides shared resources to network users.

server message block (SMB) The protocol developed by Microsoft, Intel, and IBM that defines a series of commands used to pass information between network computers. The redirector packages SMB requests into a network control block (NCB) structure that can be sent over the network to a remote device. The network provider listens for SMB messages destined for it and removes the data portion of the SMB request so that it can be processed by a local device.

service Microsoft Windows term for a computer program or process that runs continuously in the background and performs tasks at predetermined intervals or in response to specific events. Called daemons by UNIX operating systems, services typically perform server tasks, such as sharing files and printers, handling e-mail, and transmitting Web files.

service-dependent filtering A type of packet filtering used in firewalls that limits access to a network based on the port numbers specified in packets' transport layer protocol headers. The port number identifies the application that generated the packet or that is destined to receive it. With this technique, network administrators can limit access to a network to specific applications or prevent users from accessing specific applications outside the network. *See also* firewall, port, packet filtering.

Service Pack (SP) A software update package provided by Microsoft for one of its products. A Service Pack contains a collection of fixes and enhancements packaged into a single self-installing archive file.

service (SRV) resource record A resource record used in a zone to register and locate well-known Transmission Control Protocol/Internet Protocol (TCP/IP) services. The SRV resource record is specified in RFC 2052 and is used in Microsoft Windows 2000 or later to locate domain controllers for Active Directory service.

Services An ASCII text file found on Transmission Control Protocol/Internet Protocol (TCP/IP) systems that lists the codes used in the Source Port and Destination Port fields of the TCP and User Datagram Protocol (UDP) headers. These fields identify the application process that generated the data carried within the packet, or for which it is destined. The port numbers are registered by the Internet Assigned Numbers Authority (IANA) and derived from the "Assigned Numbers" Request for Comments document.

session layer The third layer from the top of the Open Systems Interconnection (OSI) reference model. There are no specific session layer protocols, but there are 22 services that the session layer performs, which are incorporated into various application layer protocols. The most important of these functions are dialog control and dialog separation. Dialog control provides two modes for communicating systems—two-way alternate (TWA) mode or two-way simultaneous (TWS) mode—and dialog separation controls the

process of inserting checkpoints in the data stream to synchronize functions on the two computers.

share To make resources, such as folders and printers, available to other users on the network.

shared folder A folder on a computer that has been made available to other users on the network.

shared folder permissions Permissions that restrict a shared resource's availability over the network to specific users.

shared resource Any device, data, or program that is used by more than one other device or program. For Microsoft Windows 2000, shared resources refer to any resource that is made available to network users, such as folders, files, and printers. A shared resource can also refer to a resource on a server that is available to network users.

Simple Mail Transfer Protocol (SMTP) An application layer Transmission Control Protocol/Internet Protocol (TCP/IP) protocol used to carry e-mail messages between servers and from clients to servers. To retrieve e-mail from mail servers, clients typically use the Post Office Protocol (POP3) or the Internet Mail Access Protocol (IMAP).

Simple Network Management Protocol (SNMP) An application layer Transmission Control Protocol/Internet Protocol (TCP/IP) protocol and query language used to transmit information about the status of network components to a central network management console. Components embedded into network hardware and software products called SNMP agents are responsible for collecting data about the activities of the products they service, storing the data in a management information base (MIB), and transmitting that data to the console at regular intervals using SNMP messages.

single master replication A technique usually associated with a directory service in which identical copies of a database are maintained on various computers scattered throughout a network. In single master replication, users can make changes on only one copy of the database (the master), and the master replicates those changes to all the other copies. This is a relatively simple technique compared to multiple master replication because data only travels in one direction. However, the system is limited in that users might have to connect to a master located at another site to make changes to the database.

sliding window A technique used to implement flow control in a network communications protocol. By acknowledging the number of bytes that have been successfully transmitted and specifying the number of bytes that it is capable of receiving, a computer on the receiving end of a data connection creates a "window" that consists of the bytes the sender is authorized to transmit. As the transmission progresses, the window slides along the byte stream, and might change its size, until all data has been transmitted and received successfully.

SLIP *See* Serial Line Internet Protocol (SLIP).

smart card A credit card-sized device used to securely store public and private keys, passwords, and other types of personal information. To use a smart card, you need a smart card reader attached to the computer and a personal identification number for the smart card. In Microsoft Windows 2000, smart cards can be used to enable certificate-based authentication and single sign-on to the enterprise.

SMB *See* server message block (SMB).

SMTP *See* Simple Mail Transfer Protocol (SMTP).

snap-in A type of tool you can add to a console supported by Microsoft Management Console (MMC). A stand-alone snap-in can be added by itself; an extension snap-in can only be added to extend the function of another snap-in.

SNMP *See* Simple Network Management Protocol (SNMP).

SNMP agent A software component integrated into a network hardware or software product that is designed to gather ongoing status information about the product, store it in a management information base (MIB), and transmit it to a central network management console at regular intervals using Simple Network Management Protocol (SNMP) messages.

socket On a Transmission Control Protocol/Internet Protocol (TCP/IP) network, the combination of an IP address and a port number, which together identify a specific application process running on a specific computer. The Uniform Resource Locators (URLs) used in Internet client applications express a socket as the IP address followed by the port number, separated by a colon, as in 192.168.1.17:80.

Source IP Address A 32-bit field in the Internet Protocol (IP) header that contains a value used to identify the particular network interface from which a packet originated.

SP *See* Service Pack (SP).

SPX *See* Sequenced Packet Exchange (SPX).

stand-alone server A computer that runs Microsoft Windows 2000 Server but does not participate in a domain. A stand-alone server has only its own database of users, and it processes logon requests by itself. It does not share account information with any other computer and cannot provide access to domain accounts.

start-of-authority (SOA) resource record A record that indicates the starting point or original point of authority for information stored in a zone. The SOA resource record is the first resource record created when adding a new zone. It also contains several parameters used by other computers that use Domain Name System (DNS) to determine how long they will use information for the zone and how often updates are required.

static routing A method for creating a Transmission Control Protocol/Internet Protocol (TCP/IP) router's routing table, in which a network administrator manually creates the table entries. *Compare with* dynamic routing, in which routing table entries are automatically created by specialized routing protocols that exchange information with the other routers on the network.

subdirectory A directory within a directory. Also called a *folder within a folder.*

subnet A group of computers on a Transmission Control Protocol/Internet Protocol (TCP/IP) network that share a common network identifier. In some cases, a TCP/IP network is divided into multiple subnets by modifying the subnet mask and designating some of the host identifier bits as subnet identifier bits. This enables the administrator to divide a network address of a particular class into multiple subnets, each of which contains a group of the hosts supported by the class.

subnet mask A Transmission Control Protocol/Internet Protocol (TCP/IP) configuration parameter that specifies which bits of the IP address identify the host and which bits identify the network on which the host resides. When the subnet mask is viewed in binary form, the bits with a value of 1 are the network identifier and the bits with a value of 0 are the host identifier.

synchronous A form of communication that relies on a timing scheme coordinated between two devices to separate groups of bits and transmit them in blocks called frames. Special characters are used to begin the synchronization and periodically check its accuracy. Because the bits are sent and received in a timed, controlled (synchronized) fashion, start and stop bits are not required. Transmission stops at the end of one transmission and starts again with a new one. It is a start/stop approach and is more efficient than asynchronous transmission. If an error occurs, the synchronous error detection and correction scheme implements a retransmission. However, because

more sophisticated technology and equipment are required to transmit synchronously, it is more expensive than asynchronous transmission.

syntax The order in which you must type a command and the elements that follow the command.

System Monitor A tool that enables you to collect and view extensive data about the usage of hardware resources and the activity of system services on computers you administer.

systemroot The path and folder name where the Microsoft Windows 2000 system files are located. Typically, this is C:\Winnt, although you can designate a different drive or folder when you install Windows 2000. You can use the value %systemroot% to replace the actual location of the folder that contains the Windows 2000 system files. To identify your systemroot folder, click Start, select Run, and then type **%systemroot%**.

T

TCP *See* Transmission Control Protocol (TCP).

TDI *See* transport driver interface (TDI).

Telecommunications Network Protocol (Telnet) An application layer Transmission Control Protocol/Internet Protocol (TCP/IP) client/server protocol used to remotely control a computer at another location. A mainstay of UNIX networking, Telnet is a true remote control application. When you access another computer and run a program, it is the processor in the remote computer that executes that program. The Telnet service is command-line-based, making it relatively useless on Microsoft Windows computers, which rely on a graphical interface. However, all versions of Windows include a Telnet client. Windows 2000 also includes a Telnet server, but compared to a UNIX Telnet implementation, you can do relatively few things with it. This is because the primary user interface in a UNIX operating system is character-based, whereas the Windows interface is primarily graphical.

Telnet *See* Telecommunications Network Protocol (Telnet).

Time to Live (TTL) A timer value included in packets sent over Transmission Control Protocol/ Internet Protocol (TCP/IP)–based networks that tells routers when a packet has been forwarded too many times. For Domain Name System (DNS), TTL values are used in resource records within a zone to determine how long requesting clients should cache and use this information when it appears in a query response answered by a DNS server for the zone.

token passing A Media Access Control (MAC) mechanism used on ring topology networks that uses a separate frame type called a token, which circulates around the network from computer to computer. Only the computer in possession of the token is permitted to transmit its data, which prevents computers from transmitting at the same time, causing collisions. On receipt of the token, a computer transmits a packet and either regenerates a new token immediately or waits for the packet to circulate around the network and return to its source, at which time the computer removes the packet and transmits the token frame. Unlike the Carrier Sense Multiple Access with Collision Detection (CSMA/CD) MAC mechanism, no collisions occur on a properly functioning token passing network. Token passing is used by several different data-link layer protocols, including Token Ring and Fiber Distributed Data Interface (FDDI).

Token Ring A data-link layer protocol originally developed by IBM that is used on local area networks (LANs) with a ring topology. Running at 4 megabits per second (Mbps) or 16 Mbps, Token Ring networks use the token passing Media Access Control (MAC) mechanism. Although they use a logical ring topology, Token Ring networks are physically cabled like a star, using a hub called a multistation access unit (MAU) that transmits incoming packets out through each successive port in turn. Early Token Ring networks used a shielded twisted pair (STP) cable known as IBM Type 1, but today most Token Ring networks use unshielded twisted pair (UTP) cable.

top-level domain The highest level in the Domain Name System (DNS) name space and the rightmost word in a DNS name. For example, in the DNS name *www.microsoft.com*, *com* is the top-level domain. Domain names that are rooted hierarchically at the first tier of the domain name space directly beneath the root (.) of the Domain Name System (DNS) name space. On the Internet, top-level domain names such as .com and .org are used to classify and assign second-level domain names (such as microsoft.com) to individual organizations and businesses according to their organizational purpose.

Tracert.exe A Transmission Control Protocol/ Internet Protocol (TCP/IP) command-line utility that displays the path that packets are taking to a specific destination. Tracert.exe uses Internet Control Message Protocol (ICMP) Echo Request and Echo Reply messages with varying Time to Live (TTL) values in the IP header. This causes packets to time out at each successive router on the way to the destination, and the error messages generated by the timeouts enable the Tracert.exe program to display a list of the routers forming the path to the destination.

transfer syntax A format used to encode application information for transmission over a network. The presentation layer of the Open Systems Interconnection (OSI) reference model is responsible for converting application data from its native abstract syntax to a common transfer syntax understood by both communicating systems. *See also* abstract syntax.

Transmission Control Protocol (TCP) A Transmission Control Protocol/Internet Protocol (TCP/IP) transport layer protocol used to transmit large amounts of data generated by applications, such as entire files. TCP is a connection-oriented protocol that provides guaranteed delivery service, packet acknowledgment, flow control, and error detection. The two computers involved in the TCP transaction must exchange a specific series of messages called a three-way handshake to establish a connection before any application is transmitted. The receiving computer also transmits periodic acknowledgment messages to verify the receipt of the data packets, and the two computers also perform a connection termination procedure after the data is transmitted. These additional messages, plus the large 20-byte TCP header in every packet, greatly increase the protocol's control overhead.

Transmission Control Protocol/Internet Protocol (TCP/IP) A set of networking protocols used on the Internet that provides communications across interconnected networks made up of computers with diverse hardware architectures and various operating systems. TCP/IP includes standards for how computers communicate and conventions for connecting networks and routing traffic.

transport driver interface (TDI) An interface in the Microsoft Windows networking stack that is located between the file system driver and the transport protocols, enabling any protocol written to TDI to communicate with the file system drivers.

transport layer The middle (fourth) layer of the Open Systems Interconnection (OSI) reference model that contains protocols providing services that are complementary to the network layer protocol. A protocol suite typically has both connection-oriented and connectionless protocols at the transport layer, providing different types of service to suit the needs of different applications. In the Transmission Control Protocol/Internet Protocol (TCP/IP) suite, the transport layer protocols are the TCP and the User Datagram Protocol (UDP).

trap A message generated by a Simple Network Management Protocol (SNMP) agent and transmitted immediately to the network management console, indicating that an event requiring immediate attention has taken place.

Trivial File Transfer Protocol (TFTP) A connectionless application layer Transmission Control Protocol/Internet Protocol (TCP/IP) protocol that transmits data files in User Datagram Protocol (UDP) packets with no authentication and no interactive interface.

TTL *See* Time to Live (TTL).

tunnel A logical connection over which data is encapsulated. Typically, both encapsulation and encryption are performed and the tunnel is a private, secure link between a remote user or host and a private network.

tunneling A technique for transmitting data over a network by encapsulating it within another protocol. For example, Novell NetWare networks at one time supported Transmission Control Protocol/Internet Protocol (TCP/IP) only by encapsulating IP datagrams within NetWare's native Internetwork Packet Exchange (IPX) protocol. The Point-to-Point Tunneling Protocol (PPTP) also uses tunneling to carry PPP frames inside IP datagrams.

U

UDP *See* User Datagram Protocol (UDP).

UNC *See* Universal Naming Convention (UNC).

unicast A network transmission addressed to a single computer only. *Compare with* broadcast, multicast.

Uniform Resource Locator (URL) Provides the hypertext links between documents on the World Wide Web (WWW). Every resource on the Internet has its own location identifier, or URL, that specifies the server to access as well as the access method and the location. URLs can use various protocols, including File Transfer Protocol (FTP) and Hypertext Transfer Protocol (HTTP).

Universal Naming Convention (UNC) The standard used for a full Microsoft Windows 2000 name of a resource on a network. It conforms to the *server**share* syntax, where servername is the name of the server and sharename is the name of the shared resource. UNC names of directories or files can also include the directory path under the share name, with the following syntax: *server**share*\ *directory**filename*.

unqualified name An incomplete Domain Name System (DNS) name that identifies only the host and not the domain in which the host resides. Some Transmission Control Protocol/Internet Protocol (TCP/IP) clients can handle unqualified names by automatically appending to them the name of the domain in which the computer is located or by appending user-specified domain names.

user account A record that consists of all the information that defines a user to Microsoft Windows 2000. This includes the user name and password required for the user to log on, the groups in which the user account has membership, and the rights and permissions the user has for using the computer and network and accessing their resources. For Windows 2000 Professional and member servers, user accounts are managed with the Local Users and Groups console. For Windows 2000 Server domain controllers, user accounts are managed with the Active Directory Users and Computers console.

User Datagram Protocol (UDP) A connectionless Transmission Control Protocol/Internet Protocol (TCP/IP) transport layer protocol used for short transactions, usually consisting of a single request and reply. UDP keeps overhead low by supplying almost none of the services provided by its connection-oriented transport layer counterpart, the TCP, such as packet acknowledgment and flow control. UDP does offer an error detection service, however. Because it is connectionless, UDP generates no additional handshake messages, and its header is only eight bytes long.

user name A unique name identifying a user account to Microsoft Windows 2000. An account's user name must be unique among the other group names and user names within its own domain or workgroup.

V

virtual private network (VPN) A technique for connecting to a network at a remote location using the Internet as a network medium. A user can dial in to a local Internet service provider (ISP) and connect through the Internet to a private network at a distant location, using a protocol like the Point-to-Point Tunneling Protocol (PPTP) to secure the private traffic.

VPN *See* virtual private network (VPN).

W

WAN *See* wide area network (WAN).

Web server A computer that is maintained by a system administrator or Internet service provider (ISP) and that responds to requests from a user's Web browser.

well-known port Transmission Control Protocol/Internet Protocol (TCP/IP) port numbers that have been permanently assigned to specific applications and services by the Internet Assigned Numbers Authority (IANA). Well-known ports make it possible for client programs to access services without having to specify a port number. For example, when you type a Uniform Resource Locator (URL) into a Web browser, the port number 80 is assumed because this is the port associated with Web servers.

wide area network (WAN) A network that spans a large geographical area using long-distance point-to-point connections, rather than shared network media as with a local area network (LAN). WANs can use a variety of communication technologies for their connections, such as leased telephone lines, dial-up telephone lines, and Integrated Services Digital Network (ISDN) or Digital Subscriber Line (DSL) connections. The Internet is the ultimate example of a WAN. *Compare with* local area network (LAN).

Windows 2000 Professional A high-performance, secure network client computer and corporate desktop operating system that includes the best features of Microsoft Windows 98, significantly extending the manageability, reliability, security, and performance of Windows NT Workstation 4.0. Windows 2000 Professional can be used as a desktop operating system, networked in a peer-to-peer workgroup environment, or used as a workstation in a Windows 2000 Server domain environment.

Windows 2000 Server A file, print, and applications server, as well as a Web server platform that contains all the features of Microsoft Windows 2000 Professional plus many new server-specific functions. This product is ideal for small- to medium-sized enterprise application deployments, Web servers, workgroups, and branch offices.

Windows Internet Name Service (WINS) A service supplied with the Microsoft Windows NT and Windows 2000 operating systems that registers the Network Basic Input/Output System (NetBIOS) names and Internet Protocol (IP) addresses of the computers on a local area network (LAN) and resolves NetBIOS names into IP addresses for its clients as needed. WINS is the most efficient name resolution method for NetBIOS-based networks because it uses only unicast transmissions. Other methods rely on the repeated transmission of broadcast messages, which can generate large amounts of network traffic.

Winipcfg.exe A graphical utility included with Microsoft Windows 95, Windows 98, and Windows Me that you can use to view the Transmission Control Protocol/Internet Protocol (TCP/IP) configuration parameters for a particular computer. A command-line version of the tool—called Ipconfig.exe—is included with Windows 2000 and Windows NT. Winipcfg.exe is most useful on computers with TCP/IP clients configured automatically by a Dynamic Host Configuration Protocol (DHCP) server because it is the easiest way to view the assigned settings for the client system. You can also use Winipcfg.exe to release and renew DHCP-assigned TCP/IP configuration parameters.

WINS *See* Windows Internet Name Service (WINS).

X

X.500 A standard published by the International Telecommunications Union (ITU) and the International Organization for Standardization (ISO) that defines the structure of a global directory service. Microsoft's Active Directory service and NetWare's Novell Directory Services are both based on the X.500 design.

X.509 A document published by the International Telecommunications Union (ITU) that defines the structure of digital certificates.

Z

zone In a Domain Name System (DNS) database, a zone is a subtree of the DNS database that is administered as a single, separate entity. This administrative unit can consist of a single domain or a domain with subdomains. A DNS zone administrator sets up one or more name servers for the zone.

zone database file The file where name–to–IP-address mappings for a zone are stored.

zone transfer The process by which Domain Name System (DNS) servers interact to maintain and synchronize authoritative name data. When a DNS server is configured as a secondary master for a zone, it periodically queries another DNS server configured as its source for the zone. If the version of the zone kept by the source is different, the secondary master server will pull zone data from its source DNS server to synchronize zone data.

Index

Symbols and Numbers

(pound) sign, 239, 326–27
3DES (Triple Data Encryption), 380

A

A (Host)
    creating, 299
    dynamic updates and, 182, 184
    exercise, 300–301
    overview of, 295
abstract syntax, 14
access control
    remote access and, 416
    VPNs and, 459
accreditation, domain name
        registrars, 245
ACK flags, TCP, 72–73
ACK messages, TCP, 66, 68–70
Acknowledgement Number field
    SPX, 115
    TCP, 65
Acks/sec, performance counter, 564
Active Directory domain controller,
        155–56
Active Directory Installation Wizard,
        274, 281
Active Directory–integrated zones,
        282–83, 285–86
Active Directory Sites and Services
        console, 527
Active Directory User Object
        folder, 530
Active Directory Users and Computers
        console, 396, 437–38
Active Queue Length, performance
        counter, 564
Add Address Pool dialog box, NAT, 483
Add Counters dialog box, System
        Monitor, 547
Add Exclusions dialog box, New
        Scope Wizard, 158
Add Filter dialog box, packet filters, 370

Add IP Filter dialog box, packet
        filters, 373
Add Remote Access Policy Wizard,
        440–44
Add Reservation dialog box, 484
Add Server dialog box, DHCP, 176–77
Add Special Port dialog box, NAT,
        484–85
Add Standalone Snap-In dialog box,
        certificates, 527–29
Add/Remove Programs dialog box,
        153–54, 510–14
Add/Remove Snap-In dialog box,
        Certificates console, 527–29
address allocation component, ICS, 494
Address Assignment function, NAT,
        486–87
Address Family Identifier field, RIP
        version 2, 227
Address Leases list, DHCP, 177
address pools, creating, 482–84
Address Pool tab, NAT properties,
        482–83
Address Range Assignment page,
        RRAS Setup Wizard, 418–19
Address Resolution Protocol. See ARP
        (Address Resolution Protocol)
addresses, filtering by, 578
addresses, hardware. See hardware
        addresses
administrators
    CSNW and, 121
    EFS recovery keys, removing, 535–36
    GSNW and, 128, 132
    OSI model and, 7
    Shared Folders snap-in and, 552–59
Advanced tab
    Edit Dial-In Profile dialog box, 447
    RIP properties, 231
    WINS replication partner
        properties, 360
Advanced TCP/IP Settings dialog box,
        86–90
    DNS tab, 87–89
    IP Settings tab, 86–87
    Lmhosts, 325–26
    Options tab, 90, 368
    WINS tab, 89–90, 347–48

AH (Authentication Header), IPsec,
        382–84
alerts. See Performance Logs and
        Alerts snap-in
Alias (CNAME), 295
Allocation Number field, SPX, 115
American Standard Code for Informa-
        tion Interchange (ASCII), 14
ANCOUNT field
    DNS, 253–54
    NeBT (NetBIOS over TCP/IP), 341
Answer section, NeBT, 342–44
antireplay, IPsec, 381
application layer
    attacks directed at, 379
    OSI model, 5, 14–15
    TCP/IP model, 31, 41–42
Application log, Event Viewer, 540–41
Applications tab, ICS settings, 495–96
Apply Static Routes, Dial-In tab, 438
Applying Changes page, RRAS, 474
ARCOUNT field, DNS, 253–54
areas, defined, 232
Areas tab, OSPF properties, 232
ARP (Address Resolution Protocol)
    Arp.exe and, 100–101
    DHCP communications with, 148
    exercise with, 42–45
    overview of, 38–39
    RARP vs., 138
    as TCP/IP link layer protocol, 31
ARPANET, 28, 239
Arp.exe, 100–101
AS (autonomous systems), 225, 232
ASCII (American Standard Code for
        Information Interchange), 14
Assign A Static IP Address, Dial-In
        tab, 438
audit logging, 178, 187
authentication
    Internet Key Exchange protocol
        and, 390
    IPsec and, 380
    PKI and, 502
    PPP connection phase and, 35
    remote access security and, 413–15,
        433–36

Authentication Data and Padding field, AH, 384

Authentication Data field, ESP, 386

Authentication Header (AH), IPsec, 382–84

Authentication Method page, IP security rules, 398

Authentication Methods dialog box, RAS, 435–36

Authentication tab, dial-in profiles, 446

authorization, DHCP Server, 154–56

autodetection mechanism, NWLink, 125–26

automated enrollment, certificates, 526–27

automatic allocation, DHCP, 141

Automatic Certificate Request Setup Wizard, 526–27

automatic replication partners, WINS, 360

autonomous systems (AS), 225, 232

Auto-Static Update Mode, RIP installation, 230

B

B (broadcast) node, NetBIOS, 330

backbones, defined, 232

backups, CA, 519–21

BACP (Bandwidth Allocation Control Protocol), 429

bandwidth
OSPF and, 232
SPXII and, 114

Bandwidth Allocation Control Protocol (BACP), 429

Bandwidth Allocation Protocol (BAP), 429

baseband medium, 8

Berkeley Internet Name Domain (BIND), 276

binary method, subnetting, 54–56

BIND (Berkeley Internet Name Domain), 276

binding
CSNW and, 123
exercise in, 25
Windows 2000 networking and, 23–24

BOOT file, 276

BOOTP (Bootstrap Protocol), 139, 145

border routing, OSPF, 226

broadband medium, 8

broadcast (B) node, 330

broadcasts
DHCP servers and, 146–48
NetBIOS name resolution and, 327–29
troubleshooting, 190–91

browser, defined, 21

burst mode, SPX, 114

byte, IP address structure, 47

C

CA (certificate authority). *See also* MCS (Microsoft Certificate Services)
backing up and restoring, 519–22
certificate creation, 504–05
certificate templates and, 505–07
configuring, 514–18
MCS as, 509
overview of, 503
properties, 515–18
protecting, 510
types of, 503–04

CA Identifying page, 513

cables, 7

Cache Lookups folder, DNS, 568

caching
DNS names, 257–58
NetBIOS names, 322

caching-only DNS name server
defined, 249
DNS proxy vs., 469
implementing, 277–78

calculators, 53

callback
Dial-In tab options, 438
remote access security and, 415

caller ID, 416

capture buffer, 575

Capture Filter dialog box, 578

capture filters, Network Monitor, 577–79

capturing, Network Monitor
exercise, 582
frame data, 576–77
frames, 574–75

Carrier Sense Multiple Access with Collision Detection (CSMA/CD), 8

CBC (Cipher Block Chaining), IPsec, 381

CCITT (Comité Consultatif International Téléphonique et Télégraphique), 4

certificate authority. *See* CA (certificate authority)

Certificate dialog box, 530–31

Certificate Request Wizard, 532–34

Certificate Revocation dialog box, 534–35

Certificate Services. *See* MCS (Microsoft Certificate Services)

Certificate Services Web Enrollment Support module, 526

certificate store, 529

certificates, 502–07
CAs and, 503–04
contents of, 503
digital, 502–03
enrollment of, 525–27
generating, 505
requesting, 532–34
revoking, 534–35
templates for, 505–06
viewing, 530–31

Certificates console, 527–34

Certificates Snap-In dialog box, 528–29, 532–34

Certification Authority Backup Wizard, 519–21

Certification Authority console
backing up CAs, 519–21
configuring CAs, 514–18
restoring CAs, 521–22
revoking certificates, 534–35

Certification Authority page, 533

Certification Authority Restore Wizard, 521–22

Certification Authority Type page, 511

Certification Path tab, 531
Chaddr field, DHCP, 143, 147
CHAP (Challenge Handshake
    Authentication Protocol),
    414, 436
Checksum field
    IPX, 113
    TCP, 65, 70–71
    UDP, 74
Ciaddr field, DHCP, 143
Cipher Block Chaining (CBC), 381
circuit switching, 28
CLASS field, resource records, 254, 296
classes
    IP addresses, 50, 57–59
    user, 164–67
Client for Microsoft Networks, 21
Client FQDN, 182
Client (Respond Only), IPsec, 393
Client Service for NetWare. *See* CSNW
    (Client Service for NetWare)
clients
    DHCP, 188–89
    Windows 2000, 21
CNAME (Alias), 295
.com domain, 244–45
Comité Consultatif International
    Téléphonique et Télégraphique
    (CCITT), 4
Common Configurations page, RRAS,
    208, 417, 473
Completing The IP Security Filter
    Action Wizard page, 405
Completing The New Zone Wizard
    page, 284
Completing The Routing and Remote
    Access Server Setup Wizard
    page, 419–20
Completion Code field, NCP, 117
Conditions page, Add Remote Access
    Policy Wizard, 440–41
configuration settings, DHCP, 188–89
Configure Device dialog box, RAS
    server, 427–28
Configure DHCP Options page, 159
Configure Gateway dialog box, 130–32

Conflict Detection Attempts
    selector, 179
Conflict Queue Length, performance
    counter, 564
Connection Control field, SPX, 115
Connection Number High field, NCP,
    116, 117
Connection Number Low field, NCP,
    116, 117
Connection Status field, NCP, 117
Connection Type page, demand dial
    interface, 212, 475
connectionless protocols, 12–13, 110
connection-oriented protocols
    overview of, 11–13
    SPX, 114
    TCP, 63, 65–66
Control Access Through Remote
    Access Policy, VPNs, 459
Control Bits field, TCP, 65, 72–73
counters
    DHCP performance, 564–65
    System Monitor, 546–49
CRC (cyclical redundancy check),
    9, 574
Create IP Security Rule Wizard, 397–99
CryptoAPI programming interface, 509
Cryptographic Service Provider page,
    532–33
cryptographic service provider (CSP),
    509–10, 512
CSMA/CD (Carrier Sense Multiple
    Access with Collision
    Detection), 8
CSNW (Client Service for NetWare)
    configuring, 126–27
    installing, 121–24
    Windows 2000 and, 21
    Windows 2000/NetWare
        compatibility, 118–19
CSP (cryptographic service provider),
    509–10, 512
Custom Security Method Settings
    dialog box, IPsec, 405
cyclical redundancy check (CRC), 9, 574

D

Data, NCP, 117
data encapsulation, OSI model, 5–7
Data Encryption Algorithm (DES), 380
Data field
    IP, 37
    IPX, 113
    NCP, 117
    SPX, 115
    TCP, 65
    UDP, 74
data modification, IPsec, 378, 379
Data Offset field, TCP, 65
data pattern, filtering by, 579
Data Storage Location page, Windows
    Components Wizard, 513
data transfer, VPN, 453–54
databases
    compacting, 180, 350–51
    replicating, 359–62
    restoring, 521–22
datagram formats, 35–36, 112
data-link layer, OSI model
    IPX and, 111–12
    network interface adapters, 19
    overview of, 8–9
    protocol stack and, 5
    transmission process, 9–10
Datastream Type field, SPX, 115
Date field, DHCP logging, 564
debugging, DNS server, 312–13,
    567–68
Decision statements, display filters,
    580–81
Declines/sec, performance counter,
    564
Default Action tab, CA (certificate
    authority), 516–17
default gateways, 198–99, 201
Default Gateway text box, TCP/IP,
    85–86
Default Response Rule Authentication
    Method page, IPsec, 395
delayed acknowledgements, TCP, 69
Delegated Domain Name page, New
    Delegation Wizard, 287

Demand Dial Interface Wizard, 211–14, 475–76

Demand-Dial Connections page, RRAS, 208

demand-dial interfaces, 210–16
  configuring, 214–16
  implementing, 210–14
  installing RIP on, 230

denial of service (DOS) attacks, 378–79

DES (Data Encryption Algorithm), 380

Description field, DHCP logging, 564

Destination Connection ID field, SPX, 115

Destination IP address field, IP, 37–38

Destination Network Address field, IPX, 113

Destination Node Address field, IPX, 113

Destination Port field, TCP, 65

Destination Port field, UDP message, 74

Destination Socket field, IPX, 113

destination variable, 219

Details tab, Certificate dialog box, 530–31

device drivers, 19

DHCP console
  configuration options, 161–64
  DHCP Server authorization, 155
  monitoring activity, 176–79
  reservations, 167–68
  scopes, 156–60
  Server Statistics dialog box, 561–63
  superscopes, 161

DHCP (Dynamic Host Configuration Protocol)
  as application layer protocol, 14, 42
  communications with, 146–50
  conflict detection, 179
  as connectionless protocol, 12
  database compaction, 180
  DNS integration, 182–85
  exercise, 150
  IP address assignments, 140–41
  IP address leases, 149–50
  messaging, 141–46
  monitoring, 176–79, 561–65

DHCP (Dynamic Host Configuration Protocol) *(continued)*
  origins of, 138–41
  relay agents, 180–81
  troubleshooting, 187–92
  UDP and, 73–74
  Windows 2000 and, 21
  WINS support, 352–53

DHCP relay agents, 180–81

DHCP Server, 152–75
  authorizing, 154–56
  configuration options, 161–64
  conflict detection and, 179
  DHCP database and, 180
  DNS server integration, 182–85
  exercise, 169–74
  monitoring, 176–79
  overview of, 152–53
  reservations and, 167–68
  scopes and, 156–60
  Server Statistics dialog box, 561–63
  superscopes and, 161
  troubleshooting, 187, 189–92
  user classes and, 164–67
  Windows 2000 installation and, 153–54

DHCPACK message type, 144, 148–50, 184

DHCPDECLINE message type, 144, 148

DHCPDISCOVER message type
  communications and, 146–48
  defined, 144
  leasing and, 150
  relay agents and, 180–81
  troubleshooting DHCP servers, 191

DHCPINFORM message type, 144, 148

DHCPNACK message type, 144, 148–50

DHCPOFFER message type
  communications and, 146–48
  defined, 144
  relay agents and, 181
  troubleshooting DHCP servers, 191

DHCPRELEASE message type, 144

DHCPREQUEST message type
  communications and, 147–48
  defined, 144
  dynamic DNS updates, 184
  leasing and, 149–50

Dial Out Credentials page, 213–14, 476

Dial-In Constraints tab, dial-in profiles, 446

dial-in properties, 437–38

dial-in remote access, 410–12, 436

Dial-In tab, Active Directory, 437–38, 439–45

Dial-In tab, user accounts, 459

dialing properties, configuring, 215

dialog, separation/control, 13

digital certificates, 502–03

Dijkstra algorithm, 232

direct route, IP routing, 196

Directory service log, Event Viewer, 541

Discovers/sec, performance counter, 564

Display Filter dialog box, 580–81

display filters, Network Monitor, 580–81

distance vector routing, 226

DNS console
  DNS server installation, 276
  monitoring, 567–68
  resource records, 297–300
  zones, 280–84

DNS (Domain Name System), 238–50. *See also* Windows 2000 DNS Server
  as application layer protocol, 14, 42
  as connectionless protocol, 12
  DHCP integration with, 182–85
  DNS caching-only servers vs. DNS proxy, 469
  implementing, 263–71
  monitoring activity, 310–13, 567–68
  UDP and, 73–74

DNS host names, 238–50
  designing, 240–41
  exercise, 249
  host names, 238, 246
  host tables and, 238–40
  name guidelines, 246
  name servers, 247–49

DNS host names *(continued)*
  name space, 241–47
  resolvers, 249
  root domain, 243–44
  second-level domains, 245–46
  top-level domains, 244–45
  zones, 246–47
DNS name resolution, 251–62
  DNS messaging, 251–55
  exercise, 260–61
  name server caching, 257–58
  resolving names, 255–57
  reverse name lookups, 258–60
DNS proxy, 469
DNS server log, Event Viewer, 541
DNS servers. *See also* Windows 2000
    DNS Server
  caching, 257–58
  defined, 241
  DHCP and, 163–64
  exercise, 260–61
  overview of, 247–49
  planning implementation of, 263–71
  TCP/IP configuration, 86
  VPN management, 459
  WINS name servers vs., 336
DNS tab, advanced TCP/IP settings,
    87–89
domain name servers, 247–49
domain name space, DNS, 241–47
  defined, 241
  hierarchical structure of, 241–43
  host names, 246
  naming guidelines, 246
  root domain, 243–44
  second-level domains, 245–46
  top-level domains, 244–45
  zones, 246–47
Domain Name System. *See* DNS
    (Domain Name System)
domain speculators, 245
domains
  defined, 241
  root domains, 243–44
  second-level domains, 245–46
  top-level domains, 244–45
  Windows 2000 vs. DNS, 243

DOS (denial of service) attacks, 378–79
dotted decimal notation,
    IP addressing, 47
Duplicates Dropped/sec, performance
    counter, 564
dynamic allocation, DHCP, 141
dynamic DNS updates, 182–85
Dynamic Host Configuration Protocol.
    See DHCP (Dynamic Host
    Configuration Protocol)
dynamic mappings, NAT, 469
dynamic routing protocols, 224–36
  exercise, 234
  OSPF, 231–33
  overview of, 224–26
  RIP, 226–31
  routing tables and, 202–03
  RRAS, 570
dynamic updates
  exercise, 292
  troubleshooting, 315
  zone configuration and, 289–90

E

EAP (Extensible Authentication
    Protocol), 414–15, 435
EBCDIC (Extended Binary Coded
    Decimal Interchange Code), 14
Echo Reply, ICMP
  defining, 40
  Ping.exe and, 94–95
  Tracert.exe and, 95
Echo Request, ICMP
  defining, 40
  DHCP communications and, 147
  Ping.exe and, 94–95
  Tracert.exe and, 95–96
Edit Dial-In Profile dialog box, 429,
    445–47
editors, NAT, 469–70
.edu domain, 244–45
EFS (Encrypting File System), 535
Encapsulating Security Payload (ESP),
    384–86

encapsulation
  IP, 36
  IPX, 112–13
  overview of, 452–53
  TCP, 64–65
Encrypting File System (EFS), 535
encryption
  deployment, 392
  Internet Key Exchange protocol
    and, 390
  keys, 500–502
  at network layer of OSI model,
    379–80
  PKI and, 501
Encryption tab, dial-in profiles, 446–47
End option, DHCP messages, 144
end systems, TCP/IP, 40, 194
end-to-end protocols, 32
enrollment, certificates, 525–27
enterprise CA, 503–04
Enterprise Policy module, 527
enterprise root CA, 504, 509, 514
enterprise subordinate CA, 504, 509, 514
Enterprise Trust folder, certificates, 530
ephemeral port numbers, 68, 466
error correction, 13, 70–71
error detection, 9, 13
error messages, ICMP, 40
ESP (Encapsulating Security Payload),
    384–86
Ethernet frame types, 111–12, 125–26
event logs
  accessing remote, 544
  DNS server, 311–13
  RAS server, 426
  RRAS server, 571
  viewing, 541–42
Event Properties dialog box, 542
Event Viewer, 540–44
Event Viewer console, 541–42
events, locating, 542–44
Exclude statements, 578–79
exclusive mode, DNS servers, 255
exit module, 505
Exit Module tab, CA properties, 517

EXPIRE (Expires After) subfield, SOA, 295

Extended Binary Coded Decimal Interchange Code (EBCDIC), 14

Extensible Authentication Protocol (EAP), 414–15, 435

External Routing tab, OSPF, 233

F

Failed Requests folder, CA console, 515

FCS (Frame Check Sequence) field, 9

File field, DHCP message, 143

File replication service log, Event Viewer, 541

File Transfer Protocol (FTP), 14, 31, 41

Filter Action General Options page, IPsec, 403–04

Filter Action Name page, IPsec, 403

Filter Action page, IPsec, 398–99, 402

filter actions, 396, 402–05

Filter command, Event Viewer, 543–44

filter list, 396, 399–402

Filter Properties dialog box, 401–02

filters, display, 580–81

FIN flag, TCP, 72–73

Find dialog box, Event Viewer, 543–44

firewalls, 366–67

Flags field

   DHCP, 143

   DNS, 252–53

   IP, 37

flow control, 12, 71–72

forward lookup queries, 255–57

forward lookup zones, 281, 290–91

forwarders, 255

FQDN (fully qualified domain name)

   Client FQDN, 182

   overview of, 242

   reverse name lookups and, 259–60

Fragment Offset field, IP, 37

fragmentation

   IP, 38

   network layer protocols and, 10

   segmentation vs., 11–12

Frame Check Sequence (FCS) field, 9

frame types, 111–12, 125–26

Framed-Protocol dialog box, remote access policies, 442

frames

   capture filters and, 577–79

   capturing, 574–77

   data-link layer protocols and, 8

   PPP, 33–34

   SLIP, 32–33

FTP (File Transfer Protocol), 14, 31, 41

Ftp.exe, 106

fully qualified domain name. *See* FQDN (fully qualified domain name)

Function field, NCP, 116

G

Gateway Address column, routing tables, 198–201

Gateway Service for Netware. *See* GSNW (Gateway Service for Netware)

Gateway Service for Netware dialog box, 129–30

gateways

   activating, 131–32

   creating, 130

   default, 201

   defining, 199

   enabling, 130–31

   security, 132

General tab

   CA properties, 515, 530

   NAT properties, 486–87

   OSPF properties, 232

   RIP properties, 231

Giaddr field, DHCP, 143

.gov domain, 244–45

group membership, access control and, 438–45

GSNW (Gateway Service for Netware), 127–32

   configuring, 129–30

   enabling, 21, 118–19, 130–31

   gateways, 130–32

   installing, 128–29

   overview of, 127–28

guaranteed delivery, connection-oriented protocols, 11

H

H node (hybrid node) type, 330–31

half close connection, TCP, 73

hardware, IP routing, 203–05

hardware addresses

   converting IP to, 100–101

   data-link layer and, 8

   IPX and data-link layer and, 110

   packet filtering on, 365

Header Checksum field, IP, 37

Header section, NeBT, 340–41

HINFO (Host Information), 296

Hlen field, DHCP, 143

Hops field, DHCP, 143

Host (A). *See* A (Host)

host identifiers, 47, 49, 51

Host Information (HINFO), 296

Host Name field, DHCP logging, 564

host names. *See* DNS host names

host tables, 238–39

Hosts file, 238–39

HTTP (Hypertext Transfer Protocol), 14, 31, 41

HTTPS (Secure Hypertext Transfer Protocol), 41

Htype field, DHCP message, 142

hybrid node (H node) type, 330–31

Hypertext Transfer Protocol (HTTP), 14, 31, 41

I

IANA (Internet Assigned Numbers Authority)

   Internet routing and, 464–65

   IP address classes, 50

   overview of, 48

   private network addresses, 51–52

   unregistered addresses and, 465

IAS (Internet Authentication Service), 433

ICANN (Internet Corporation for Assigned Names and Numbers), 245

ICMP (Internet Control Message Protocol)
overview of, 39–40
packet filter configuration, 374–75
as TCP/IP internet layer protocol, 31
type and code values for, 374–75
ICS (Internet Connection Sharing), 492–98
configuring, 494–97
installing, 493–94
NAT vs., 492
routing software and, 205
ICV (integrity check value), 381
ID field
DHCP logging, 563
DNS, 252
IETF (Internet Engineering Task Force)
DNS standards, 240
RARP standards, 138
TCP/IP standards, 28–29
IGMP (Internet Group Management Protocol), 31, 230
IHL (Internet Header Length) field, IP, 37
IIS (Internet Information Services), 21
IKE (Internet Key Exchange) protocol, 390
IMAP4 (Internet Mail Access Protocol), 41
in-addr.arpa domain, 259–60
inbound connections, 427–28
Include statements, 578–79
Informs/sec, performance counter, 564
init state, defined, 146
initial sequence number (ISN), 66
Instance, System Monitor snap-in, 548
.int domain, 244–45
Integrated Services Digital Network (ISDN), 412
integrity, IPsec, 381
integrity check value (ICV), 381
Interface column, routing tables, 198–200
Interface Name page, demand dial interface, 211, 475
Interface Selector, static routes, 218

interfaces, NAT
creating, 481–82
properties, 482–86
interior routing protocols, 224
Intermediate Certification Authorities folder, certificates, 530
intermediate systems, TCP/IP, 40, 194–95
International Organization for Standardization (ISO), 4
Internet
autonomous systems of, 225
domain speculators and, 245
host tables as insufficient for, 239
IPX's incompatibility with, 110–11
as largest TCP/IP network, 48
NAT configuration for access to, 478–79
routing to, 464–65
VPN servers, integrating with, 457–58
Internet Assigned Numbers Authority. *See* IANA (Internet Assigned Numbers Authority)
Internet Authentication Service (IAS), 433
Internet Connection Server page, RRAS, 473–74
Internet Connection Server Setup page, RRAS, 473
Internet Connection Sharing. *See* ICS (Internet Connection Sharing)
Internet Connection Sharing Application dialog box, 495–96
Internet Connection Sharing Settings dialog box, 495–96
Internet Control Message Protocol. *See* ICMP (Internet Control Message Protocol)
Internet Corporation for Assigned Names and Numbers (ICANN), 245
Internet Engineering Task Force. *See* IETF (Internet Engineering Task Force)
Internet Group Management Protocol (IGMP), 31, 230
Internet Header Length (IHL) field, IP, 37

Internet Information Services (IIS), 21
Internet Key Exchange (IKE), 390
internet layer, TCP/IP, 31, 35
Internet Mail Access Protocol (IMAP4), 41
Internet Network Information Center (InterNIC), 245
Internet Protocol (TCP/IP) Properties dialog box
Lmhosts implementation, 324
packet filter configuration, 368
TCP/IP configuration, 83–84, 86
WINS client configuration, 347–48
Internet routers, 204
Internet Service Provider (ISP), 464–65
Internetwork Packet Exchange. *See* IPX (Internetwork Packet Exchange)
internetworks
defining, 194
IP routing and, 195–97
routing tables and, 202–03
transit, 451
InterNIC (Internet Network Information Center), 245
IP Address Assignment page, RRAS, 418
IP Address field
DHCP, 564
RIP, 227
IP addressing, 47–62. *See also* NAT (network address translation)
ARP and, 38–39
classes, 50
exercise, 60
NAT and, 468
overview of, 10
packet filtering and, 365
private networks and, 51–52
rules, 51
scopes, 156–60
structure of, 47–48
subnet masks, 49–52
subnetting, 52–59
TCP/IP configuration, 84–86
VPN and, 459

IP addressing, DHCP
  assigning, 140–41
  communications and, 148
  troubleshooting clients, 188
  troubleshooting servers, 191–92
IP Address Range, scopes, 157
IP Filter List dialog box, 400
IP Filter List page, 398
IP Filter Wizard, 400
IP host naming. *See* DNS host names
IP (Internet Protocol)
  as connectionless protocol, 12
  as internet layer protocol, 31
  overview of, 35–38
  RAS server options, 424–25
IP routing. *See* dynamic routing
  protocols; routing IP
IP security. *See* IPsec (IP security)
IP Security Filter Action Wizard, 403–05
IP Security Policies on Local Machine
  snap-in, 392
IP Security Policies snap-in, 392–93
IP Security Policy Management
  snap-in, 392
IP Security Policy Name Page, 394
IP Security Policy Wizard, 394–95, 396
IP Settings tab, advanced TCP/IP
  setting, 86–87
IP tab, Edit Dial-In Profile dialog
  box, 446
IP Traffic Security page, IP Security
  Filter Action Wizard, 404–05
Ipconfig.exe, 99–100
IP-IP network layer tunneling
  technique, 456
IPsec driver, 391
IPsec (IP security), 377–89
  advantages of, 379–80
  exercise, 388
  functions, 380–81
  L2TP tunneling and, 388
  monitoring activity, 572
  overview of, 377–81
  protocols, 382–86
  standards, 382
  transport mode/tunnel mode and,
    386–87
  tunneling protocols and, 456

IPsec (IP security), deploying, 390–408
  components, 390–91
  exercises, 406–07
  filter actions, 402–05
  overview of, 391
  policies, 393–96
  policy filter list, 399–402
  Policy Management, 392–93
  policy rules, 396–99
  tunnel mode configuration, 406
IPsec Policy Agent service, 390
IPsec Policy Management, 392–93
Ipsecmon.exe utility, 572
IPX (Internetwork Packet Exchange),
    109–20
  addressing, 10
  datagram format, 112–14
  data-link layer, 111–12
  exercise, 119
  NetWare Core Protocol and, 116–18
  overview of, 20, 110–11
  RAS server options, 425–26
  Sequenced Packet Exchange and,
    114–16
  Windows 2000/NetWare
    compatibility and, 118–19
ISDN (Integrated Services Digital
  Network), 412
ISN (initial sequence number), 66
ISO (International Organization for
  Standardization), 4
ISP (Internet Service Provider), 464–65
Issued Certificates folder, CA
  console, 515
Items To Back Up page, Certification
  Authority Backup Wizard, 519
Items To Restore page, Certification
  Authority Restore Wizard,
    521–22
iterative query, 255
ITU-T (Telecommunications
  Standardization Sector of
  the International Tele-
  communication Union),
  4, 503

J
Jetpack.exe program, 180, 350–51

K
Kerberos V5, 395
keys
  CA management of, 510
  compromised, 379
  encryption, 500–502
  Internet Key Exchange protocol, 390

L
L2TP tunneling protocol
  defining, 388
  overview of, 454–55
  PPTP vs., 455–56
  VPN and, 453–54
LAN (local area network)
  IPX and, 110
  RIP and, 230
  VPNs and, 457
LCP (Link Control Protocol), 424,
    428–29
Lease Duration page, New Scope
  Wizard, 159
lease identification cookie, DHCP, 148
leases, DHCP
  monitoring DHCP activity, 177
  overview of, 149–50
  scopes and, 159–60
  troubleshooting DHCP servers,
    190–91
Length field
  IPX, 113
  UDP, 74
letter transposition code, encryption, 500
Link Control Protocol (LCP), 424,
    428–29
link dead, PPP, 35
link establishment, PPP, 35
link layer protocols, TCP/IP, 30–31, 32
link open, PPP connection phase, 35
link quality monitoring, PPP, 35
link termination, PPP, 35

link-state routing, 231–32
litigation, domain names and, 245
Lmhosts file
    implementing, 323–26
    overview of, 90
    tags, 326–27
Local Area Connection properties
    CSNW and, 122, 123–24
    GSNW, 129
    ICS installation, 494
    Lmhosts implementation, 323–24
    NAT configuration, 478–79
    NWLink configuration, 124
    packet filters configuration, 367
    TCP/IP configuration, 83
    TCP/IP installation, 80–82
    WINS client configuration, 347–48
local area networks. *See* LANs (local
    area networks)
Local File Properties dialog box,
    RRAS logging, 571
Local Security Settings console, 393–95
Local Users and Groups, dial-in
    properties, 437
Local-Only mode, NDIS, 576
logging
    DHCP, 563–64
    DNS server, 567–68
    RRAS, 570–71
    WINS, 567
Logging tab, DNS server properties,
    312–13
logs. *See* Event Viewer; Performance
    Logs and Alerts snap-in

M

M (mixed mode) node, 330
MAC Address field, DHCP, 564
MAC (media access control)
    addresses. *See* hardware
    addresses
Mail Exchanger (MX), 296
Managing Multiple Remote Access
    Servers page, 418–19
manual allocation, DHCP
    configuration, 141

master servers, 248, 314
maximum segment size (MSS), 66
maximum transmission unit (MTU), 38
MCS (Microsoft Certificate Services),
    499–538
    backing up/restoring CAs, 519–22
    certificate enrollment, 525–27
    certificate revocation, 534–35
    certificates, 502–07
    Certificates console, 527–34
    configuring CAs, 514–18
    EFS recovery keys, 535
    encryption keys and, 500–502
    exercises, 507, 522–23
    installation, 509–14
    overview of, 500
    Windows 2000 and, 21
media access control (MAC)
    addresses. *See* hardware
    addresses
message digest, 381
message header, DNS, 252–53
Message Type, DHCP, 144, 150
messaging, DHCP, 141–46
    End option, 144
    Message Type option, 144, 150
    Option Overload option, 141–45
    other options, 145–46
    overview of, 141–44
    Pad option, 144
    Vendor-Specific Information
        option, 145
messaging, DNS, 251–55
    message header, 252–53
    overview of, 251
    Question section, 253
    request types, 254–55
    response sections, 253–54
messaging, WINS, 335–39
    name registration, 335–37
    name release, 338
    name renewal, 337–38
    name resolution, 338–39
    NeBT formats, 339–44
Metric column, routing tables, 198–200

Metric field, RIP version 2, 228
Microsoft Certificate Services. *See* MCS
    (Microsoft Certificate Services)
Microsoft Challenge Handshake
    Authentication Protocol
    (MS-CHAP), 414, 436
Microsoft node types, 330–32
Microsoft Windows 2000. *See*
    Windows 2000
Microsoft Windows 2000 DNS Server.
    See Windows 2000 DNS Server
Microsoft Windows 2000 network
    components. *See* Windows
    2000 network components
Microsoft Windows 2000 Server, 205
Microsoft Windows Authentication
    option, 435
Microsoft Windows Calculator, 53
Microsoft Windows Components
    Wizard. *See* Windows
    Components Wizard
Microsoft Windows Internet Name
    Service. *See* WINS (Windows
    Internet Name Service)
Microsoft-enhanced h mode type,
    331–32
.mil domain, 244–45
Milliseconds Per Packet (Avg),
    performance counter, 564
Minimum (default) TTL (MINIMUM)
    subfield, SOA, 295
mixed mode, Active Directory, 439
mixed mode (M) node, NetBIOS, 330
MNAME (Primary Server) subfield,
    SOA, 295
Modified b node type, 330
modular routers, 203–04
monitoring, Network Monitor, 574–83
    capture filters, 577–79
    display filters, 580–81
    displaying captured data, 579–80
    exercise, 582
    frame data, 576–77
    installing tools, 576
    overview of, 574–75
    performance issues, 581
    security, 575–76

monitoring, network services, 561–73
    DHCP activity, 176–79, 561–65
    DNS activity, 310–13, 567–68
    IPsec activity, 572
    RRAS activity, 568–71
    WINS activity, 565–67
monitoring, Windows 2000, 540–60
    Event Viewer, 540–44
    exercises, 559
    Performance console, 544–52
    Shared Folders snap-in, 552–59
MS-CHAP (Microsoft Challenge
    Handshake Authentication
    Protocol), 414, 436
MSS (maximum segment size), 66
MTU (maximum transmission unit), 38
multicast transmissions, RIP, 228, 230
multihomed computers, 205
Multilink connections, 424, 428–29
Multilink tab, dial-in profiles, 429, 446
multiplexing, 19
mutual authentication, remote access
    security, 415
MX (Mail Exchanger), 296

N

Nacks/sec, performance counter, 564
NAME field, resource records, 254, 296
name overwrite demand messages,
    NetBIOS, 328–29
name query request messages
    NetBIOS, 327–29
    WINS, 336, 338–39
name refresh request messages, WINS,
    337–38
name registration request messages,
    328–29, 336
name resolution
    defined, 238
    ICS, 494
    NAT, 469, 488–89
    WINS, 89–90, 338–39
Name Resolution tab, NAT properties,
    488–89
name servers. *See also* DNS servers
    NetBIOS, 330
    WINS, 459

Name Servers page, New Delegation
    Wizard, 287
names
    NetBIOS caching, 322
    WINS registration, 335–37
    WINS release, 338
    WINS renewal, 337–38
NAME-TRN_ID field, NeBT, 340
NAT (network address translation),
    463–98
    components, 468–79
    exercises, 470, 489–90
    ICS installation and configuration,
        492–98
    implementing, 472
    interface properties, 482–86
    Internet routing and, 204, 464–65
    NAT editors, 469–70
    node, 481–82, 486–88
    overview of, 465–70
    private network addresses and, 51–52
    properties, 486–88
    RRAS configuration, 478–82
    RRAS installation, 472–77
NAT routing protocol, 480–81
NBNS (NetBIOS name servers), 330
Nbstat.exe, 103–04
NCP (NetWare Core Protocol), 116–18
NDIS boundary layer, defined, 20
NDIS (Network Device Interface
    Specification), 20
NDS (Novell Directory Services),
    126–27, 130
NeBT formats, 339–44
    Answer section, 342–44
    Header section, 340–41
    Question section, 342
negative acknowledgement, TCP, 70
negative caching, DNS name
    servers, 258
negative name query response
    messages, 336, 338–39
negative name refresh response
    messages, 337
negative name registration response
    messages, 328–29, 336
negative name release response
    messages, 338

Neighbors tab, RIP properties, 231
.net domain, 244–45
NetBEUI (NetBIOS Enhanced User
    Interface)
    DHCP clients, troubleshooting, 188
    installation exercise, 24
    NetBIOS and, 318
    overview of, 20
    RAS connections, 412
    RAS server options, 426
NetBIOS name servers (NBNS), 330
NetBIOS (Network Basic Input/Output
    System), 318–34
    broadcast transmissions and, 327–29
    exercise, 333
    Lmhosts file and, 322–27
    name caching, 322
    name registration/resolution, 321
    name servers, 330
    naming, 318–21
    node types, 330–32
Netlogon, defined, 21
Netmask column, routing tables,
    198–200
Netstat.exe, 101–03
NetWare, 109–35
    Client Service configuration, 126–27
    Client Service installation, 121–24
    exercises, 119, 132–34
    Gateway Service installation and
        configuration, 127–32
    IPX overview, 110–11
    IPX protocols, 111–17
    NWLink configuration, 124–26
    Windows 2000 compatibility with,
        21, 118–19
NetWare Core Protocol (NCP), 116–18
network adapter drivers, 20, 119
Network Address column, routing
    tables, 198–201
network address translation. *See* NAT
    (network address translation)
Network Address Translation (NAT)
    Properties dialog box, 481,
    486–88

Network and Dial-Up Connections
window
CSNW installation, 121–24
GSNW installation, 128–29
ICS installation, 493–94
Lmhosts implementation, 323–24
NWLink configuration, 124–26
packet filter configuration, 367
TCP/IP configuration, 83
TCP/IP installation, 81
WINS client configuration, 347–48
Network Basic Input/Output System.
See NetBIOS (Network Basic
Input/Output System)
network components. *See* Windows
2000 network components
Network Device Interface
Specification (NDIS), 20
network identifiers
IP address structure and, 47
IP addressing rules for, 51
overview of, 48–49
Network Information Center (NIC), 239
network interface adapters, 19
network interface card. *See* NIC
(network interface card)
network interface layer, TCP/IP, 30–31
network layer, OSI model
encrypting transmissions, 379–80
internet layer of TCP/IP vs., 31
overview of, 9–11
PPP connection phase, 35
protocol stack, 5
RAS server configuration, 424
routing, 194
Network Monitor, 574–83
capture filters and, 577–79
capturing frame data, 576–77
display filters and, 580–81
displaying captured data, 579–80
exercise, 582
installing tools, 576
IP security and, 377–78
overview of, 574–75
performance issues, 581
security, 575–76

Network Monitor Capture window, 577
Network Monitor console, installing, 576
Network Monitor driver, installing, 576
network protocols, securing. *See* IPsec
(IP security); packet filters
Network Solutions, Inc., 245
Network Time Protocol (NTP), 42
Network Type page, IP security
rules, 398
Networking Services dialog box
DHCP Server, 154
WINS Server, 345–46
Networking tab, demand-dial interface
properties, 215–16
New Class dialog box, DHCP, 165
New Delegation Wizard, 287–89
New Interface For Network Address
Translation Properties dialog
box, 481
New Interface For RIP Version 2 For
Internet Protocol dialog box, 229
New Replication Partner dialog box, 360
New Reservation dialog box, 168
New Resource Record dialog box,
287, 300
New Routing Protocol dialog box, 228,
480–81
New Scope Wizard, 156–60
New Share dialog box, 131–32
New Static Mapping dialog box, 348–49
New Zone Wizard, 281–84
Next Header field
AH, 384
ESP, 386
Next Hop IP Address field, RIP
version 2, 228
NIC (Network Information Center), 239
NIC (network interface card)
adapters and, 19
NAT configuration and, 478
Windows 2000 and, 22–23
NM-FLAGS field, NeBT, 340
node addresses, IPX, 110
node types, NetBIOS, 330–32
nonexclusive mode, DNS servers, 255
nonrepudiation
IPsec, 380
PKI and, 502

Northwind Traders, DNS design
large networks, 268–70
medium-size networks, 265–68
small networks, 264–65
Novell Client for
Windows NT/2000, 119
Novell Directory Services (NDS),
126–27, 130
NRCOUNT field, NeBT message
header, 341
NS (Name Server), 285–86, 295
NSCOUNT field
DNS, 253–54
NeBT, 341
Nslookup.exe, 104–05, 258
NTGATEWAY group, 130
NTP (Network Time Protocol), 42
NWLink
configuring, 124–26
CSNW and, 123
exercise, 132–34
overview of, 20
Windows 2000/NetWare
compatibility, 118–19
NWLink IPX/SPX/NetBIOS
Compatible Transport Protocol
Properties dialog box, 124–26

O

octet, IP addresses, 47
ODI (Open Data-Link Interface), 119
offered window, TCP, 72
Offers/sec, performance counter, 564
one-way transform, 381
Op field, DHCP message, 142
OPCODE field, NeBT message
header, 340
Open Data-Link Interface (ODI), 119
Open Files folder, sharing folders and,
553, 558–59
Open Shortest Path First. *See* OSPF
(Open Shortest Path First)
Open Systems Interconnection. *See*
OSI (Open Systems
Interconnection) reference
model

Options field
  DHCP, 143–46
  IP, 37
  TCP, 65
Options tab, advanced TCP/IP
    settings, 90
.org domain, 244–45
organizationally unique identifier
    (OUI), 8
OSI (Open Systems Interconnection)
    reference model, 4–17
  application layer, 14–15
  applying in real world, 15–16
  data encapsulation, 5–7
  data-link layer, 8–9
  network layer, 9–11
  overview of, 4–5
  packet filtering and, 365–66
  physical layer, 7
  presentation layer, 14
  session layer, 13
  TCP/IP architecture vs., 29–30
  transport layer, 11–13
OSPF (Open Shortest Path First)
  border routing and, 226
  defined, 224
  installing, 232–33
  as interior routing protocols, 224–25
  monitoring, 570
  understanding, 231–32
OSPF Properties dialog box, 232–33
OUI (organizationally unique
    identifier), 8
Overload option, DHCP messages,
    144–45

P

P (point-to-point) node, 330
packet filters, 364–76
  IPsec and, 381
  overview of, 364–67
  RRAS configuration, 371–75
  TCP/IP client configuration, 367–71
Packet Type field, IPX, 113

packets
  burst, 114
  capturing, 377–78
  switching, 28
  TCP acknowledgement, 68–70
Packets Expired/sec, performance
    counter, 564
Packets Received/sec, performance
    counter, 564
Pad Length field, ESP, 386
Pad option, DHCP, 144
PAP (Password Authentication
    Protocol), 413, 436
password compromise, IPsec, 378
Pathping.exe, 97–99
Payload Data and Padding field,
    ESP, 386
Payload length field, AH, 384
Pending Request folder, CA
    console, 515
performance baselines, 549
Performance console, 544–52
  overview of, 544–45
  Performance Logs and Alerts snap-in,
    550–52
  system and network performance,
    548–49
  System Monitor snap-in, 545–48
Performance Logs and Alerts snap-in,
    544, 550–52
Periodic Update Mode, RIP, 230
Permissions page, Add Remote Access
    Policy Wizard, 443
Personal folder, Certificates
    console, 529
Phone Number page, Demand Dial
    Interface Wizard, 212–13, 476
physical layer, OSI model
  network interface adapters at, 19
  overview of, 7
  protocol stack, 5
Ping, 93–95
PKI (public key infrastructure), 501
Pointer (PTR), 296, 301
point-to-point (P) node, 330
Point-to-Point Protocol. See PPP
    (Point-to-Point Protocol)

Point-to-Point Tunneling Protocol
    (PPTP), 454–56
policies, IPsec
  creating in Active Directory, 393–95
  filter actions, 402–05
  filter lists, 399–402
  Policy Management and, 396
  remote access policies, 438–45
  rules, 396–99
  for tunnel mode, 406
policy module, defined, 505
Policy Module tab, CA properties, 516
Policy Name page, Add Remote
    Access Policy Wizard, 440
Policy Settings folder, CA console, 515
POP3 (Post Office Protocol), 41
PORT field, SRV, 296
port numbers
  DHCP client/server, 142
  DNS name server, 251
  ephemeral, 466
  NAT interface and, 484–85
  packet filtering and, 365–66, 369–70
  TCP well-known, 67–68
Port Status dialog box, RRAS, 569
ports, RAS server, 427
Ports Properties dialog box, RAS
    server, 427
positive acknowledgement with
    retransmission, TCP, 70
positive name query response
    messages, 328–29, 336, 338–39
positive name refresh response
    messages, 337
positive name registration response
    messages, 336
positive name release response
    messages, 338
Post Office Protocol (POP3), 41
pound (#) sign, 239, 326–27
PPP (Point-to-Point Protocol)
  L2TP tunneling and, 388
  overview of, 33–35
  RAS connections, 412
  RAS multilink connections, 428–29
  RAS server options, 423–24
  as TCP/IP link layer protocol, 31, 32

PPTP (Point-to-Point Tunneling Protocol), 454, 455–56
presentation layer, OSI model, 5, 14
primary master servers, 263
primary master zone database file, 248
Primary Server (MNAME) subfield, SOA, 295
primary zone database file, 248
PRIORITY field, SRV, 296
private keys, 501, 512
private network addresses, 51–52
profiles, remote access, 445–47
promiscuous mode
    defined, 377–78
    NDIS, 576
properties
    certificates, 531
    Certification Authority console, 515–18
    demand-dial interface, 214–16
    DHCP server, 179, 563–64
    DNS server, 568
    filter actions, 402–05
    filter lists, 399–401
    NAT configuration, 486–88
    NAT interface, 482–86
    RRAS interface, 372
    RRAS logging, 571–72
    rules, 397
    shared folders, 554–55
    Windows 2000 networking components, 23–24
properties, RAS server, 422–26
    authentication options, 433–36
    event logging options, 426
    general options, 422–23
    IP options, 424–25
    IPX options, 425–26
    NetBEUI options, 426
    network layer protocol options, 424
    PPP options, 423–24
    security options, 423
PROTO field, SRV, 296
Protocol field, IP, 37

protocol identification
    data-link layer protocols and, 9
    network layer protocols and, 11
    packet filtering on, 365
protocol stacks
    OSI, 4–5, 15–16
    TCP/IP, 30–31
    Windows 2000, 18
protocols. See also by individual type
    data encapsulation and, 5–6
    filtering by, 578
    overview of, 4
    suites, 19
    Windows 2000 network, 20
Protocols and Security page, demand dial interface, 213, 476
Provide Password page, Certification Authority Restore Wizard, 522
proxy agents, WINS, 350
pseudo-header, TCP, 71
PSTN (Public Switched Telephone Network), 411
PTR (Pointer), 182, 296, 301
Public and Private Key Pair page, 512
public key infrastructure (PKI), 501
public keys, 501
Public Switched Telephone Network (PSTN), 411
pull partner, WINS, 356–58
push partner, WINS, 356–58

Q

QCLASS field, DNS, 253
QDCOUNT field, DNS, 253
QDCOUNT field, NeBT, 341
QNAME field, DNS, 253
QTYPE field, DNS, 253
quad, IP address, 47
queries
    forward lookup, 255–57
    iterative, 255
    name query request, 327–29, 336, 338–39
    negative name query response, 336, 338–39

queries (continued)
    positive name query response, 328–29, 336, 338–39
    recursive, 254–55, 310–11, 469
    Simple Query, 310–11
Question section, DNS, 253
Question section, NeBT, 342

R

RADIUS (Remote Authentication Dial-In User Service), 433–34
RADIUS Authentication dialog box, 434
RARP (Reverse Address Resolution Protocol), 39, 138
RAS (Remote Access Service)
    authentication, 433–36
    dial-in, 410–12
    exercise, 420, 447–48
    installing, 416–20
    overview of, 413–16
    policies, 438–45
    profiles, 445–47
    protocols, 412–13
    user account dial-in properties, 437–38
RAS (Remote Access Service), VPN support, 451–62
    exercises, 458–59
    implementing, 451–56
    Internet and, 457–58
    managing, 458–59
    routed environments and, 457
RAS server configuration, 422–32
    event logging options, 426
    exercise in, 431–32
    general options, 422–23
    inbound connections, 427–28
    IP options, 424–25
    IPX options, 425–26
    multilink options, 428–29
    NetBEUI options, 426
    network layer options, 424
    PPP options, 423–24
    security options, 423
    using RRAS with DHCP, 430

raw Ethernet, 111
RCODE field, NeBT, 341
RDATA field, DNS, 254
RDATA field, NeBT, 343
RDLENGTH field, DNS, 254
RDLENGTH field, NeBT, 343
rebinding time value, DHCP leasing, 149–50
recursive query, DNS
 defined, 469
 monitoring servers, 310–11
 overview of, 254–55
Refresh Interval (REFRESH) subfield, SOA, 295
Relay Agent Service, DHCP, 146
relay agents, DHCP, 180–81
Releases sec, performance counter, 565
remote access account lockout, 416
Remote Access Logging folder, RRAS, 571–72
Remote Access Permission, Dial-In tab, 438
remote access policies, 438–45, 447–48
Remote Access Policies list, 444–45, 445–47
Remote Access Policies node, 439–40
remote access profile, 445–47
Remote Access Service. See RAS (Remote Access Service)
Remote Authentication Dial-In User Service (RADIUS), 433–34
Remote Client Protocols page, RRAS, 417
remote control access, Telnet, 106
renewal time value, DHCP leasing, 149
renewing state, DHCP leasing, 149
replay, SPAP, 413
replication, WINS, 356–62
 automatic partners, 360
 databases, 359–62
 number of servers, 359
 overview of, 356
 push/pull partners and, 356–58
Replication Partners list, WINS database, 360
Reply message format, NCP, 117
reply messages, RIP, 226

Reply/Response Type field, NCP, 117
REQUEST folder, Certificates console, 530
Request for Secure Communication page, IPsec, 394–95
Request message format, NCP, 116–17
request messages, RIP, 226
Request Security (Server) policy, IPsec, 393, 396–97
Request Type field, NCP, 116
request types, DNS, 254–55
Request for Comments. See RFC (Request for Comments)
Requests sec, performance counter, 565
reservations, DHCP
 creating, 167–68
 scopes and, 156
 troubleshooting, 187
Reserve Addresses dialog box, address pools, 483–84
Reserved field
 AH, 384
 TCP, 65
resolvers, DNS
 defined, 241
 name resolution, 255–57
 overview of, 249
resource identifier codes, NetBIOS, 319–20
Resource Record Type dialog box, 299
resource records, 294–302
 creating, 298–300
 exercises, 300–302
 types of, 294–97
 viewing, 297–98, 301
response sections, DNS, 253–54
Responsible Person (RNAME) subfield, SOA, 295
restoration, CA management, 510
RETRY (Retry Interval) subfield, SOA, 295
Reverse Address Resolution Protocol (RARP), 39, 138
Reverse Lookup Zone page, New Zone Wizard, 284
reverse lookup zones
 creating, 281, 284
 exercise, 291–92

reverse name lookups
 domain for, 244
 overview of, 256
 performing, 258–60
Revoked Certificates dialog box, 535
Revoked Certificates folder, CA console, 514
RFC (Request for Comments)
 DNS standards, 240
 PPP standards, 34
 RARP standards, 138
 TCP/IP standards, 28–29
RIP (Routing Information Protocol)
 defined, 224
 installing, 228–31
 as interior routing protocol, 224–25
 monitoring, 570
 overview of, 226–28
 version 1 vs. 2, 227–28
RIP Properties dialog box, 229, 231
RNAME (Responsible Person) subfield, SOA, 295
rogue DHCP server, 154–56
root domain, DNS, 243–44
Root Hints tab, DNS server properties, 277–78
Route Add command, 219
Route Change command, 219
Route Delete command, 219
Route Print command, 198, 219
Route Tag field, RIP version 2, 227
routed environments, VPN, 457
Routed Protocols page, RRAS, 208
Route.exe, 218–21
routers
 configuring, 161–64
 IP and, 38
 network layer protocols and, 10
 packet filtering and, 366
 Pathping.exe and, 97–99
 Tracert.exe and, 95–97
 types of, 203–04
Routing and Remote Access console. See RRAS console

Routing and Remote Access Server Setup Wizard
  NAT installation, 472–75
  RRAS configuration, 207–09, 416–20
  RRAS demand-dial interface, 210
Routing and Remote Access Service. *See* RRAS (Routing and Remote Access Service)
Routing Information Protocol. *See* RIP (Routing Information Protocol)
routing IP, 193–236
  exercise, 205
  hardware for, 203–05
  principles of, 194–97
  routing tables, 197–203, 205
  software for, 205
routing tables, 197–203
  creating, 202–03
  exercise, 205
  overview of, 197–98
  route selection, 201–02
  router routing and, 200
  static routes, 217–18
  workstation routing and, 198–200
RR_CLASS field, NeBT, 343
RR_NAME field, NeBT, 343
RR_TYPE field, NeBT, 343
RRAS (Routing and Remote Access Service), 207–23
  configuration exercises, 221–22, 233–34
  configuring, 207–10
  demand-dial interfaces, 214–16
  demand-dial routing, 210–14
  DHCP and, 430
  DHCP relay agents and, 181
  monitoring, 568–71
  NAT configuration, 478–82
  NAT installation, 472–77
  packet filters and, 371–75
  RIP installation, 228–31
  routing software and, 205
  static routes, 217–21
  Windows 2000 and, 21

RRAS console
  demand-dial interface, 210–14
  logging, 570–71
  monitoring, 568–70
  NAT installation, 472–77
  NAT interface creation, 481–82
  NAT interface properties, 482–86
  packet filters, 371
  Remote Access Policies node, 439–40
  RIP installation, 228
  RRAS, as remote access server, 416–20
  RRAS configuration, 207, 209
  Server Status display, 569
  static routes, 217–18, 479–80
RRAS Input Filters dialog box, 372–74
RRAS Output Filters dialog box, 372–74
rules, IPsec
  creating, 396–99
  defined, 396
  new filter list for, 399–400

S

Scope Name dialog box, 157
Scope Options dialog box, 161–64, 166–67
scopes, DHCP
  activating, 160
  creating, 156–60
  exercise, 174
  overview of, 140
  superscopes, 161
  troubleshooting, 187, 191–92
secondary master name servers
  defined, 248
  DNS implementation and, 263
  troubleshooting, 314
secondary zone database files, 248
second-level domains, DNS, 245–46
secret key encryption, 500–501
Secs field, DHCP, 143
Secure Hypertext Transfer Protocol (S-HTTP), 41
Secure Server (Require Security), IPsec, 393

Secure Sockets Layer (SSL), 380
security. *See also* certificates; IPsec (IP security); MCS (Microsoft Certificate Services)
  demand-dial interface, 216
  gateway resources and, 132
  Network Monitor and, 575–76
  RAS server, 423
  remote access, 413–16
  Telnet and, 105
security, RAS, 433–50
  authentication, 433–36
  exercise, 447–48
  overview of, 413–16
  policies, 438–45
  profiles, 445–47
  user account dial-in properties, 437–38
Security log, Event Viewer, 540
Security Parameters Index, AH, 384
Security Parameters Index field, ESP, 386
Security tab
  CA properties, 518
  RIP properties, 231
segmentation, 11–12
segments, TCP, 64
Select A Device page, demand dial interface, 476
Select A Password page, CA backup, 520
Select Attribute dialog box, Add Remote Access Policy Wizard, 441–43
Select NetWare Logon dialog box, CSNW, 126–27
Select Network Client dialog box, CSNW, 122–23
Select Network Component Type dialog box
  CSNW installation, 122
  GSNW installation, 129
  TCP/IP installation, 81
Select Network Protocol dialog box, TCP/IP, 81–82
Send Console message dialog box, session monitoring, 558

Sequence Number field
AH, 384
ESP, 386
NCP, 116, 117
SPX, 115
TCP, 65
sequence, TCP, 64
Sequenced Packet Exchange (SPX, SPXII), 114–16
Serial Line Internet Protocol. *See* SLIP (Serial Line Internet Protocol)
Serial Number (SERIAL) subfield, SOA, 294
Server Options dialog box, 161–64, 166–67
Server (Request Security) policy, IPsec, 393, 396–97
Server Statistics dialog box
DHCP, 177–78, 561–63
WINS, 565–66
servers, 21. *See also* DHCP server; DNS server
SERVICE field, SRV, 296
Service (SRV), 274, 296
service-dependent filtering, 365–66
Services tab, ICS, 496
session layer, OSI model, 5, 13
Sessions folder, Shared Folders
defined, 553
disconnecting users, 556–57
monitoring user sessions, 555–56
Shared Folders snap-in, 552–59
disconnecting users, 556–57
monitoring open files, 558–59
monitoring shared folders, 553–54
monitoring user sessions, 555–56
overview of, 552–53
sending administrative messages, 557–58
shared folder access, 554
sharing folders, 555
Shares folder, 553–55
Sharing tab, connection properties, 493–94
Sharing tab, Internet connection properties, 494–95

Shiva Password Authentication Protocol (SPAP), 413, 436
S-HTTP (Secure Hypertext Transfer Protocol), 41
Siaddr field, DHCP, 143
signaled errors, 13
signaling scheme, 5–6
signatures, IPsec, 381
signing, Windows 2000 PKI, 501
Simple Mail Transfer Protocol (SMTP), 14, 41
Simple Network Management Protocol (SNMP), 14, 42
Simple Query, 310–11
slaves, 255
sliding windows, TCP, 72
SLIP (Serial Line Internet Protocol)
OSI data-link layer and, 9
overview of, 32–33
RAS connections and, 412
TCP/IP link layer and, 31, 32
SMTP (Simple Mail Transfer Protocol), 14, 41
Sname field, DHCP, 143
SNAP (Subnetwork Access Protocol), 112
SNMP (Simple Network Management Protocol), 14, 42
SOA (Start of Authority), 294
sockets, TCP, 67–68
Software Compression, 424
Source Connection ID field, SPX, 115
Source IP address field, IP, 37–38
Source Network Address field, IPX, 113
Source Node Address field, IPX, 113
Source Port field, TCP, 65
Source Port field, UDP, 74
Source Socket field, IPX, 113
SPAP (Shiva Password Authentication Protocol), 413, 436
Special Ports tab, NAT interface properties, 484–85
spoofing, 378
SPX (Sequenced Packet Exchange), 114–16
SPXII (Sequenced Packet Exchange), 114

SRI (Stanford Research Center), 239
SRV (Service), 274, 296
SSL (Secure Sockets Layer), 380
stand-alone CA, 504, 509, 522–23
stand-alone servers, 437
stand-alone subordinate CA, 504, 509, 514
standard primary zones, 282–83
standard secondary zones, 282–83
standards
certificate, 503
DHCP, 180
DNS, 240
Ethernet, 111–12
IPsec, 382
multilink connections, 428–29
NetWare, 110
PPP, 34
RIP, 226
TCP/IP, 28–29
Stanford Research Center (SRI), 239
Start of Authority (SOA), 294
static mappings, 348–50, 469
Static Route dialog box, 217–18, 480
static routes
creating, 217–21
exercise, 234
NAT configuration and, 479–80
routing tables and, 202–03
RRAS console and, 217–18
Storage tab, CA properties, 518
Subcomponents Of Networking Services list, Windows 2000 DHCP Server, 275–76
subdomains, 287
Subfunction field, NCP, 117
Subfunction Length field, NCP, 117
subnet identifiers, 52–53
Subnet Mask field, RIP, 227
subnet masks, 49–52
calculating, 52–53
IP address classes, 50
IP address rules, 51
overview of, 49–50
private network addresses, 51–52
RRAS and, 479

Subnet Mask text box, TCP/IP, 85
subnetting, 52–59
  binary method calculation, 54–56
  Class B network calculation, 57–59
  exercise, 60
  overview of, 52
  scopes, creating, 156–60
  subnet mask calculation, 52–53
  subtraction method calculation, 56–57
Subnetwork Access Protocol
    (SNAP), 112
subtraction method, subnetting, 56–57
superscopes, 161
switches, 204
symmetric encryption algorithms, 380
SYN messages, TCP, 66, 68–70
syntax
  Arp.exe, 101
  converting, 14
  NBstat.exe, 103–04
  Netstat.exe, 101–03
  Nslookup.exe, 104–05
  Pathping.exe, 97–98
  Ping.exe, 93–94
  Route.exe, 218–19
  Telnet.exe, 105
  Tracert.exe, 96–97
System log, Event Viewer, 540
System Monitor snap-in, 544, 545–48
system performance. See monitoring

T

T1 value, DHCP, 149
T2 value, DHCP, 149–50
tags, Lmhosts, 326–27
TARGET field, SRV, 296
Task Number field, NCP, 116, 117
TCP (Transmission Control Protocol),
    63–73
  as connection-oriented protocol, 11,
    65–66
  encapsulation, 64–65
  error correction, 70–71
  exercises, 74–75
  flow control, 12, 71–72

TCP (Transmission Control Protocol)
    (continued)
  overview of, 63–64
  packet acknowledgement, 68–70
  ports and sockets, 67–68
  as TCP/IP transport layer protocol, 31
  terminating connections, 72–73
TCP/IP (Transmission Control
    Protocol/Internet Protocol)
  advanced properties, 86–90
  application layer protocols, 41–42
  architecture, 29–31
  ARP and, 38–39
  basic properties, 83–86
  demand-dial interface, 215–16
  DHCP parameters for, 141
  exercise, 90
  exercises, 42–45
  ICMP and, 39–40
  installing, 80–83
  IP and, 35–38
  link layer protocols, 32
  NetBIOS names, 321
  overview of, 20
  PPP and, 33–35
  SLIP and, 32–33
  standards, 28–29
  UDP and, 72–73, 75–76
TCP/IP client, 367–71
TCP/IP Filtering dialog box, 368–69
TCP/IP Information window,
    RRAS, 570
TCP/IP utilities, 93–108
  Arp.exe, 100–101
  Ftp.exe, 106
  Ipconfig.exe, 99–100
  Nbstat.exe, 103–04
  Netstat.exe, 101–03
  Nslookup.exe, 104–05
  Pathping.exe, 97–99
  Ping, 93–95
  Telnet.exe, 105
  Tracert.exe, 95–97
TCP/IP WINS Server dialog box,
    89, 348
TDI (transport driver interface), 21

Telecommunications Standardization
    Sector of the International
    Telecommunication Union
    (ITU-T), 4, 503
Telnet (Telecommunications Network
    Protocol), 42
Telnet.exe, 105
TFTP (Trivial File Transfer Protocol),
    41, 139
three-way handshakes, TCP, 65–66
Time field, DHCP logging, 564
Time to Live. See TTL (Time to Live)
token passing, 8
tools, Windows 2000 TCP/IP. See
    TCP/IP utilities
top-level domains, DNS, 244–45
TOS (Type of Service) field, IP, 37
Total Length field, IP, 37
trace logs, 550
Tracert.exe, 95–97
transfer syntax, 14
transit internetworks, 451
translation component, NAT, 468
Transmission Control Protocol. See
    TCP (Transmission Control
    Protocol)
Transmission Control Protocol/Internet
    Protocol. See TCP/IP (Trans-
    mission Control Protocol/
    Internet Protocol)
Transport Control field, IPX, 113
transport driver interface (TDI), 21
transport layer, OSI model, 5, 11–13
transport layer protocols, TCP/IP, 31
transport mode, 386–87
Triple Data Encryption (3DES), 380
Trivial File Transfer Protocol (TFTP),
    41, 139
troubleshooting
  DHCP clients, 188–89
  DHCP, preventing problems, 187
  DHCP servers, 190–92
  networking problems, 7
  Windows 2000 DNS Server, 313–17
Trusted Root Certification Authorities
    folder, 529–30

TTL (Time to Live)
  DNS field for, 254
  IP field for, 37
  name server caching and, 257–58
  NeBT and, 343
  SRV field for, 296
  Tracert.exe field for, 95–96
  WINS and, 337–38
Tunnel Endpoint page, IPsec, 397–98
tunnel maintenance, VPN, 453–54
tunnel mode
  IPsec, 406
  L2TP tunneling, 388
  overview of, 386–87
tunneling protocols, 452–54
Two-Way Alternate (TWA) model, 13
Two-Way Simultaneous (TWS)
    model, 13
TYPE field, DNS, 254
Type of Service (TOS) field, IP, 37

U

UDP (User Datagram Protocol)
  as connectionless protocol, 12
  DNS using, 251
  exercise, 75
  overview of, 72–73
  ports, 67
  as TCP/IP transport layer protocol, 31
UNIX, Telnet for, 105
unqualified names, TCP/IP, 88
unregistered IP addresses. *See* NAT
    (network address translation)
unshielded twisted pair (UTP) cables, 7
unsignaled errors, 13
Urgent Pointer field, TCP, 65
user account dial-in properties, RAS,
    437–38
user classes, DHCP, 164–67

User Datagram Protocol. *See* UDP
    (User Datagram Protocol)
User Profile page, Add Remote Access
    Policy Wizard, 443
users
  RAS authentication, 413–15
  VPN and, 458–60
users, shared folders and
  determining access, 554
  disconnecting, 556–57
  monitoring sessions, 555–56
  overview of, 552–53
  sending administrative messages,
    557–58
utilities, TCP/IP. *See* TCP/IP utilities
UTP (unshielded twisted pair) cables, 7

V

Vendor-Specific Information
    option, 145
verification, Windows 2000 PKI, 502
Verify Caller ID, Dial-In tab, 438
VeriSign, 245
Version field, IP, 37
views, certificate, 530–31
Virtual Interfaces tab, OSPF
    properties, 233
VPN (virtual private network), 451–62
  exercises, 458–59, 461
  implementing, 451–56
  Internet and, 457–58
  IPsec connection to, 387
  managing, 458–59
  overview of, 410
  routed environments and, 457

W

WACK (wait for acknowledgement
    response), 338–39
WANs (wide area networks)
  as network interface adapters, 19
  PPP and, 33–35
  WINS Server replication and, 358
Web-based enrollment, 525–26
WEIGHT field, SRV, 296
wide area networks. *See* WANs (wide
    area networks)
Window field, TCP, 65
Windows 2000
  DCHP Relay Agent, 181
  gateways, 130–31
  NetWare compatibility, 118–19
  PKI features, 501–02
  WINS clients, 347–48
Windows 2000 DNS Server, 273–316
  Active-Directory integrated zones,
    285–86
  caching-only server, 277–78
  installing, 274–79
  monitoring, 310–13
  resource records, 298–302
  resource records types, 294–97
  resource records, viewing, 297–98
  troubleshooting, 313–17
  zone delegation, 286–89
  zone exercises, 290–92
  zone transfers, 303–09
  zones, 280–85
  zones, dynamic updates and, 289–90
Windows 2000, monitoring, 540–60
  Event Viewer, 540–44
  exercises, 559
  Performance console, 544–52
  Shared Folders snap-in, 552–59

Windows 2000 network components,
18–46
  binding, 23–24
  clients, 21
  exercise, 24–25
  installing, 22–23
  network interface adapters, 19
  protocol stack, 18
  protocols, 20
  services, 21–22
Windows 2000 Server, 205
Windows Authentication option, 435
Windows Calculator, 53
Windows Components Wizard
  Certificate Services, 510–14
  Windows 2000 DHCP Server
    installation, 153–54, 275–76
  WINS Server installation, 345–47
Winipcfg.exe, 99–100
WINS (Windows Internet Name
Service), 345–54
  exercises, 352–54
  installing, 352
  messaging, 335–39
  monitoring activity, 565–67
  NetBT formats and, 339–44
  non-WINS clients, 348–50
  replication, 356–62
  Server Statistics dialog box, 565–66
  Windows 2000 and, 21
  WINS client configuration, 347–48
  WINS database, 350–51
  WINS Server installation, 345–47
WINS (Windows Internet Name
Service), NetBIOS and, 318–34
  broadcast transmissions and, 327–29
  exercise, 333
  Lmhosts file, 322–27
  name caching, 322
  name servers, 330
  naming, 318–21

WINS (Windows Internet Name
Service), NetBIOS and
(continued)
  node types, 330–32
  registering/resolving names, 321
  resource identifier codes, 319–20
WINS client, 347–48
WINS console
  database replication and, 359–60
  static mappings, 348–50
WINS database, 350–51
WINS double ring replication
topology, 358
WINS proxy agent, 350
WINS Server
  configuring, 347–48
  database backups with, 351
  installing, 345–47
WINS Server, replication
  automatic partners and, 360
  databases and, 359
  how many to use, 359
  push/pull partners and, 356–58
WINS Server dialog box, TCP/IP, 89
WINS snap-in, 347
WINS tab, advanced TCP/IP settings
  Lmhosts implementation, 325–26
  overview, 89–90
  WINS client configuration, 347–48
workstations, 21, 198–200

X

X.509 Extensions tab, 516–17
Xid field, DHCP, 143

Y

Yiaddr field, DHCP, 143, 147

Z

Zone File page, New Zone Wizard, 283
Zone Name page, New Zone Wizard,
281–82
zone transfers, 303–09
  DNS notification and, 307–08
  example of, 304–06
  incremental, 304
  overview of, 248
  security of, 306–07
  troubleshooting, 314
Zone Type page, New Zone Wizard,
281–82
zones, 280–92
  Active-Directory integrated, 285–86
  creating, 280–85
  delegating, 286–89, 314
  dynamic updates and, 289–90
  exercises, 290–92
  overview of, 246–47
  troubleshooting, 314

Get a **Free**
e-mail newsletter, updates,
special offers, links to related books,
and more when you

register on line!

Register your Microsoft Press® title on our Web site and you'll get a FREE subscription to our e-mail newsletter, *Microsoft Press Book Connections.* You'll find out about newly released and upcoming books and learning tools, online events, software downloads, special offers and coupons for Microsoft Press customers, and information about major Microsoft® product releases. You can also read useful additional information about all the titles we publish, such as detailed book descriptions, tables of contents and indexes, sample chapters, links to related books and book series, author biographies, and reviews by other customers.

Registration is easy. Just visit this Web page and fill in your information:

http://www.microsoft.com/mspress/register

Microsoft®

- -

Proof of Purchase

Use this page as proof of purchase if participating in a promotion or rebate offer on this title. Proof of purchase must be used in conjunction with other proof(s) of payment such as your dated sales receipt—see offer details.

ALS: Microsoft® Windows® 2000 Network Infrastructure Administration, Second Edition

0-7356-1870-4

CUSTOMER NAME

Microsoft Press, PO Box 97017, Redmond, WA 98073-9830

MICROSOFT LICENSE AGREEMENT

Book Companion CD

IMPORTANT—READ CAREFULLY: This Microsoft End-User License Agreement ("EULA") is a legal agreement between you (either an individual or an entity) and Microsoft Corporation for the Microsoft product identified above, which includes computer software and may include associated media, printed materials, and "online" or electronic documentation ("SOFTWARE PRODUCT"). Any component included within the SOFTWARE PRODUCT that is accompanied by a separate End-User License Agreement shall be governed by such agreement and not the terms set forth below. By installing, copying, or otherwise using the SOFTWARE PRODUCT, you agree to be bound by the terms of this EULA. If you do not agree to the terms of this EULA, you are not authorized to install, copy, or otherwise use the SOFTWARE PRODUCT; you may, however, return the SOFTWARE PRODUCT, along with all printed materials and other items that form a part of the Microsoft product that includes the SOFTWARE PRODUCT, to the place you obtained them for a full refund.

SOFTWARE PRODUCT LICENSE

The SOFTWARE PRODUCT is protected by United States copyright laws and international copyright treaties, as well as other intellectual property laws and treaties. The SOFTWARE PRODUCT is licensed, not sold.

1. **GRANT OF LICENSE.** This EULA grants you the following rights:

   a. **Software Product.** You may install and use one copy of the SOFTWARE PRODUCT on a single computer. The primary user of the computer on which the SOFTWARE PRODUCT is installed may make a second copy for his or her exclusive use on a portable computer.

   b. **Storage/Network Use.** You may also store or install a copy of the SOFTWARE PRODUCT on a storage device, such as a network server, used only to install or run the SOFTWARE PRODUCT on your other computers over an internal network; however, you must acquire and dedicate a license for each separate computer on which the SOFTWARE PRODUCT is installed or run from the storage device. A license for the SOFTWARE PRODUCT may not be shared or used concurrently on different computers.

   c. **License Pak.** If you have acquired this EULA in a Microsoft License Pak, you may make the number of additional copies of the computer software portion of the SOFTWARE PRODUCT authorized on the printed copy of this EULA, and you may use each copy in the manner specified above. You are also entitled to make a corresponding number of secondary copies for portable computer use as specified above.

   d. **Sample Code.** Solely with respect to portions, if any, of the SOFTWARE PRODUCT that are identified within the SOFTWARE PRODUCT as sample code (the "SAMPLE CODE"):

      i. **Use and Modification.** Microsoft grants you the right to use and modify the source code version of the SAMPLE CODE, *provided* you comply with subsection (d)(iii) below. You may not distribute the SAMPLE CODE, or any modified version of the SAMPLE CODE, in source code form.

      ii. **Redistributable Files.** Provided you comply with subsection (d)(iii) below, Microsoft grants you a nonexclusive, royalty-free right to reproduce and distribute the object code version of the SAMPLE CODE and of any modified SAMPLE CODE, other than SAMPLE CODE, or any modified version thereof, designated as not redistributable in the Readme file that forms a part of the SOFTWARE PRODUCT (the "Non-Redistributable Sample Code"). All SAMPLE CODE other than the Non-Redistributable Sample Code is collectively referred to as the "REDISTRIBUTABLES."

      iii. **Redistribution Requirements.** If you redistribute the REDISTRIBUTABLES, you agree to: (i) distribute the REDISTRIBUTABLES in object code form only in conjunction with and as a part of your software application product; (ii) not use Microsoft's name, logo, or trademarks to market your software application product; (iii) include a valid copyright notice on your software application product; (iv) indemnify, hold harmless, and defend Microsoft from and against any claims or lawsuits, including attorney's fees, that arise or result from the use or distribution of your software application product; and (v) not permit further distribution of the REDISTRIBUTABLES by your end user. Contact Microsoft for the applicable royalties due and other licensing terms for all other uses and/or distribution of the REDISTRIBUTABLES.

2. **DESCRIPTION OF OTHER RIGHTS AND LIMITATIONS.**

   - **Limitations on Reverse Engineering, Decompilation, and Disassembly.** You may not reverse engineer, decompile, or disassemble the SOFTWARE PRODUCT, except and only to the extent that such activity is expressly permitted by applicable law notwithstanding this limitation.

   - **Separation of Components.** The SOFTWARE PRODUCT is licensed as a single product. Its component parts may not be separated for use on more than one computer.

   - **Rental.** You may not rent, lease, or lend the SOFTWARE PRODUCT.

- **Support Services.** Microsoft may, but is not obligated to, provide you with support services related to the SOFTWARE PRODUCT ("Support Services"). Use of Support Services is governed by the Microsoft policies and programs described in the user manual, in "online" documentation, and/or in other Microsoft-provided materials. Any supplemental software code provided to you as part of the Support Services shall be considered part of the SOFTWARE PRODUCT and subject to the terms and conditions of this EULA. With respect to technical information you provide to Microsoft as part of the Support Services, Microsoft may use such information for its business purposes, including for product support and development. Microsoft will not utilize such technical information in a form that personally identifies you.

- **Software Transfer.** You may permanently transfer all of your rights under this EULA, provided you retain no copies, you transfer all of the SOFTWARE PRODUCT (including all component parts, the media and printed materials, any upgrades, this EULA, and, if applicable, the Certificate of Authenticity), **and** the recipient agrees to the terms of this EULA.

- **Termination.** Without prejudice to any other rights, Microsoft may terminate this EULA if you fail to comply with the terms and conditions of this EULA. In such event, you must destroy all copies of the SOFTWARE PRODUCT and all of its component parts.

3. **COPYRIGHT.** All title and copyrights in and to the SOFTWARE PRODUCT (including but not limited to any images, photographs, animations, video, audio, music, text, SAMPLE CODE, REDISTRIBUTABLES, and "applets" incorporated into the SOFTWARE PRODUCT) and any copies of the SOFTWARE PRODUCT are owned by Microsoft or its suppliers. The SOFT-WARE PRODUCT is protected by copyright laws and international treaty provisions. Therefore, you must treat the SOFTWARE PRODUCT like any other copyrighted material **except** that you may install the SOFTWARE PRODUCT on a single computer provided you keep the original solely for backup or archival purposes. You may not copy the printed materials accompanying the SOFTWARE PRODUCT.

4. **U.S. GOVERNMENT RESTRICTED RIGHTS.** The SOFTWARE PRODUCT and documentation are provided with RESTRICTED RIGHTS. Use, duplication, or disclosure by the Government is subject to restrictions as set forth in subparagraph (c)(1)(ii) of the Rights in Technical Data and Computer Software clause at DFARS 252.227-7013 or subparagraphs (c)(1) and (2) of the Commercial Computer Software—Restricted Rights at 48 CFR 52.227-19, as applicable. Manufacturer is Microsoft Corporation/One Microsoft Way/Redmond, WA 98052-6399.

5. **EXPORT RESTRICTIONS.** You agree that you will not export or re-export the SOFTWARE PRODUCT, any part thereof, or any process or service that is the direct product of the SOFTWARE PRODUCT (the foregoing collectively referred to as the "Restricted Components"), to any country, person, entity, or end user subject to U.S. export restrictions. You specifically agree not to export or re-export any of the Restricted Components (i) to any country to which the U.S. has embargoed or restricted the export of goods or services, which currently include, but are not necessarily limited to, Cuba, Iran, Iraq, Libya, North Korea, Sudan, and Syria, or to any national of any such country, wherever located, who intends to transmit or transport the Restricted Components back to such country; (ii) to any end user who you know or have reason to know will utilize the Restricted Components in the design, development, or production of nuclear, chemical, or biological weapons; or (iii) to any end user who has been prohibited from participating in U.S. export transactions by any federal agency of the U.S. government. You warrant and represent that neither the BXA nor any other U.S. federal agency has suspended, revoked, or denied your export privileges.

DISCLAIMER OF WARRANTY

NO WARRANTIES OR CONDITIONS. MICROSOFT EXPRESSLY DISCLAIMS ANY WARRANTY OR CONDITION FOR THE SOFTWARE PRODUCT. THE SOFTWARE PRODUCT AND ANY RELATED DOCUMENTATION ARE PROVIDED "AS IS" WITHOUT WARRANTY OR CONDITION OF ANY KIND, EITHER EXPRESS OR IMPLIED, INCLUDING, WITHOUT LIMITA-TION, THE IMPLIED WARRANTIES OF MERCHANTABILITY, FITNESS FOR A PARTICULAR PURPOSE, OR NONINFRINGEMENT. THE ENTIRE RISK ARISING OUT OF USE OR PERFORMANCE OF THE SOFTWARE PRODUCT REMAINS WITH YOU.

LIMITATION OF LIABILITY. TO THE MAXIMUM EXTENT PERMITTED BY APPLICABLE LAW, IN NO EVENT SHALL MICROSOFT OR ITS SUPPLIERS BE LIABLE FOR ANY SPECIAL, INCIDENTAL, INDIRECT, OR CONSEQUENTIAL DAM-AGES WHATSOEVER (INCLUDING, WITHOUT LIMITATION, DAMAGES FOR LOSS OF BUSINESS PROFITS, BUSINESS INTERRUPTION, LOSS OF BUSINESS INFORMATION, OR ANY OTHER PECUNIARY LOSS) ARISING OUT OF THE USE OF OR INABILITY TO USE THE SOFTWARE PRODUCT OR THE PROVISION OF OR FAILURE TO PROVIDE SUPPORT SERVICES, EVEN IF MICROSOFT HAS BEEN ADVISED OF THE POSSIBILITY OF SUCH DAMAGES. IN ANY CASE, MICROSOFT'S ENTIRE LIABILITY UNDER ANY PROVISION OF THIS EULA SHALL BE LIMITED TO THE GREATER OF THE AMOUNT ACTUALLY PAID BY YOU FOR THE SOFTWARE PRODUCT OR US$5.00; PROVIDED, HOWEVER, IF YOU HAVE ENTERED INTO A MICROSOFT SUPPORT SERVICES AGREEMENT, MICROSOFT'S ENTIRE LIABILITY REGARDING SUPPORT SERVICES SHALL BE GOVERNED BY THE TERMS OF THAT AGREEMENT. BECAUSE SOME STATES AND JURISDICTIONS DO NOT ALLOW THE EXCLUSION OR LIMITATION OF LIABILITY, THE ABOVE LIMITATION MAY NOT APPLY TO YOU.

MISCELLANEOUS

This EULA is governed by the laws of the State of Washington USA, except and only to the extent that applicable law mandates governing law of a different jurisdiction.

Should you have any questions concerning this EULA, or if you desire to contact Microsoft for any reason, please contact the Microsoft subsidiary serving your country, or write: Microsoft Sales Information Center/One Microsoft Way/Redmond, WA 98052-6399.

System Requirements

To get the most out of *ALS: Microsoft Windows 2000 Network Infrastructure Administration, Second Edition*, you will need a computer equipped with the following minimum configuration:

- Microsoft Windows 2000 Server or Microsoft Windows 2000 Advanced Server (A 120-day evaluation edition of Windows 2000 Server is included with this textbook.)

- Microsoft PowerPoint or Microsoft PowerPoint Viewer (PowerPoint Viewer is included on the Supplemental Course Material Student CD-ROM.)

- Microsoft Word or Microsoft Word Viewer (Word Viewer is included on the Supplemental Course Material Student CD-ROM.)

- Microsoft Internet Explorer 5.01 or later (Microsoft Internet Explorer 6 is included on the Supplemental Course Material Student CD-ROM.)

- 32-bit 166-MHz Intel Pentium-compatible processor

- 128 MB RAM minimum, 256 MB RAM recommended

- 2-GB hard disk with a minimum of 1 GB free space (Additional free hard disk space is required if you are installing over a network.)

- 12X or faster CD-ROM drive

- Super Video Graphics Array (SVGA) monitor capable of 800 x 600 resolution (1024 x 768 is recommended)

- High-density 3.5-inch disk drive, unless your CD-ROM drive is bootable and supports starting the setup program from a CD-ROM

- Microsoft Mouse or compatible pointing device